Brief Contents

W9-BXN-041

WRITING PARAGRAPHS AND ESSAYS 1

UNIT 1 WRITING PARAGRAPHS 1

Chapter 1 Understanding the Writing Process 2
Chapter 2 **TEST**ing Your Paragraphs 28

UNIT 2 PATTERNS OF PARAGRAPH DEVELOPMENT 49

Chapter 3 Using Exemplification 50
Chapter 4 Using Narration 62
Chapter 5 Using Description 72
Chapter 6 Using Process 82
Chapter 7 Using Cause and Effect 94
Chapter 8 Using Comparison and Contrast 106
Chapter 9 Using Classification 122
Chapter 10 Using Definition 132
Chapter 11 Using Argument 144

UNIT 3 WRITING ESSAYS 159

Chapter 12 Writing an Essay 160
Chapter 13 Writing Introductions and Conclusions 194
Chapter 14 Patterns of Essay Development 206

REVISING AND EDITING YOUR WRITING 261

UNIT 4 WRITING SENTENCES 261

Chapter 15 Writing Simple Sentences 262
Chapter 16 Writing Compound Sentences 276
Chapter 17 Writing Complex Sentences 294
Chapter 18 Writing Varied Sentences 308
Chapter 19 Using Parallelism 326
Chapter 20 Using Words Effectively 334

UNIT 5 SOLVING COMMON SENTENCE PROBLEMS

Chapter 21 Run-Ons 354
Chapter 22 Sentence Fragments 370
Chapter 23 Subject-Verb Agreement 394
Chapter 24 Illogical Shifts 410
Chapter 25 Dangling and Misplaced Modifiers 420

UNIT 6 UNDERSTANDING BASIC GRAMMAR 433

Chapter 26 Verbs: Past Tense 434
Chapter 27 Verbs: Past Participles 446
Chapter 28 Nouns and Pronouns...................... 462
Chapter 29 Adjectives and Adverbs.................. 488
Chapter 30 Grammar and Usage for ESL Writers 500

UNIT 7 UNDERSTANDING PUNCTUATION, MECHANICS, AND SPELLING 541

Chapter 31 Using Commas 542
Chapter 32 Using Apostrophes........................ 560
Chapter 33 Using Other Punctuation Marks.... 570
Chapter 34 Understanding Mechanics 578
Chapter 35 Understanding Spelling 596

BECOMING A CRITICAL READER 621

UNIT 8 READING ESSAYS 621

Chapter 36 Reading Critically 622
Chapter 37 Readings for Writers 634

APPENDIXES

A. Strategies for College Success 712
B. Using Research in Your Writing.................. 725

Focus on Writing

Paragraphs and Essays

Second Edition

Laurie G. Kirszner
University of the Sciences in Philadelphia

Stephen R. Mandell
Drexel University

Bedford/St. Martin's   Boston ◆ New York

For Bedford/St. Martin's

Senior Developmental Editor: Ellen Darion
Senior Production Editor: Harold Chester
Senior Production Supervisor: Dennis J. Conroy
Marketing Manager: Casey Carroll
Art Director: Lucy Krikorian
Text Design: Claire Seng-Niemoeller
Copy Editor: Diana P. George
Photo Research: Melissa Cliver Photography; Rachel Youdelman
Cover Design: Marine Bouvier Miller
Composition: Graphic World Inc.
Printing and Binding: RR Donnelley and Sons

President: Joan E. Feinberg
Editorial Director: Denise B. Wydra
Editor in Chief: Karen S. Henry
Director of Development: Erica T. Appel
Director of Marketing: Karen R. Soeltz
Director of Production: Susan W. Brown
Associate Director, Editorial Production: Elise Kaiser
Managing Editor: Shuli Traub

Manufactured in the United States of America.

5   4   3   2   1
f   e   d   c

For information, write: Bedford/St. Martin's, 75 Arlington Street, Boston, MA 02116
(617-399-4000)

ISBN-10: 0-312-60345-2   ISBN-13: 978-0-312-60345-8   (Instructor's Annotated Edition)
ISBN-10: 0-312-60341-X   ISBN-13: 978-0-312-60341-0   (Student Edition)

Acknowledgments

Acknowledgments and copyrights appear at the back of the book on page 759, which constitutes an extension of the copyright page.

Preface for Instructors

When we set out to write a new paragraph-to-essay developmental text, we knew what we wanted to accomplish. We wanted *Focus on Writing: Paragraphs and Essays* to reflect two of our central beliefs: first, that in college, writing comes first and second, that students learn writing and grammar skills best in the context of their own writing. We also knew that we had an opportunity to bring developmental textbooks to another level—to recognize the students taking basic writing classes today and to engage them in a new and different way. Our students may be basic writers, but they live in a sophisticated world of images. We wanted to engage our students with a highly visual book and a contemporary design that reflected the most recent pedagogy about reaching basic writers. Consequently, the pages of *Focus on Writing* have clean, open margins, with the most important information moved directly into the body of the text, and an up-to-date look that takes the needs of today's basic writing students seriously. Because we also wanted this book to be accessible, the text explanations and instructions are clear and streamlined throughout to make them as transparent as possible. When teachers and students who used the first edition of *Focus on Writing* responded enthusiastically to the book's approach and design, we saw that our beliefs about what basic writing students would respond to were right on target. In this second edition, then, we retained the major elements of the book's design as well as our focus on presenting grammar in the context of the students' own writing.

Focus on Writing begins with thorough coverage of the writing process and includes extensive writing practice throughout the text. Most chapters open with a writing prompt that asks students to respond to an evocative and contemporary visual. Students practice not only by working through effective exercises but also by applying each chapter's concepts to their own original writing, giving them a sense of ownership of their work. We included lots of grammar support to help basic writers understand and apply the fundamentals of good writing, and our up-to-date exercise topics relate to students as citizens of the world beyond the college campus.

Further, because we know that the issues of the developmental classroom are not limited to writing, *Focus on Writing* offers other resources such as help with college study skills, ESL usage, research skills, and critical reading in a format that is flexible enough to support a variety of teaching styles and to meet the needs of individual students.

We wrote this book for our own interested, concerned, and hardworking students, and we tailored the book's approach and content to them. Instead of exercises that reinforce the idea that writing is a dull, pointless, and artificial activity, we chose fresh, contemporary examples (both student and professional) and worked hard to develop interesting exercises and writing assignments. Throughout this second edition of *Focus on Writing*, we try to talk *to* students, not *at* or *down* to them. We try to be concise without being abrupt, thorough without being repetitive, direct without being rigid, specific without being prescriptive, and flexible without being inconsistent. Our most important goal remains a simple one: to create an engaging text that motivates students to improve their writing and that gives them the tools to do so.

Organization

Focus on Writing: Paragraphs and Essays is divided into three general sections: "Writing Paragraphs and Essays," "Revising and Editing Your Writing," and "Becoming a Critical Reader." The first section is a comprehensive discussion of the writing process. The second section presents thorough coverage of sentence skills, grammar, punctuation, mechanics, and spelling. The third section introduces students to critical reading skills and includes nineteen professional essays, each illustrating a particular pattern of development. Finally, two appendixes—Appendix A, "Strategies for College Success," and Appendix B, "Using Research in Your Writing"—provide help with skills that students will need in other courses.

Features

With *Focus on Writing* we aimed to create a complete and contemporary paragraph-to-essay text for developmental writers in a format that students could relate to. Guided by our "student writing first" philosophy, we created the following innovative features designed to make students' writing practice meaningful, productive, and enjoyable.

TEST *is a powerful tool that helps students understand how paragraphs and essays work and how to revise their own writing.* Introduced early in the book, the easy-to-remember **TEST** acronym helps students self-check their paragraphs for unity, support, and coherence: students test paragraphs for **t**opic sentence, **e**vidence, **s**ummary statement, and **t**ransitions; they test essays for **t**hesis statement, **e**vidence, **s**ummary statement, and **t**ransitions. Clear and practical **TEST** Checklists allow students to quickly see where their drafts need more work before they revise toward a final draft.

TESTing an Argument Paragraph

Topic Sentence Unifies Your Paragraph

☐ Do you have a clearly worded topic sentence that states your paragraph's main idea?

☐ Does your topic sentence state your position on a debatable issue?

Evidence Supports Your Paragraph's Topic Sentence

☐ Does all your evidence support your paragraph's main idea?

☐ Have you included enough evidence to support your points, or do you need to add more?

Summary Statement Reinforces Your Paragraph's Unity

☐ Does your paragraph end with a strong statement that reinforces your main idea?

Transitions Add Coherence to Your Paragraph

☐ Do you use transitional words and phrases to let readers know when you are moving from one point to another?

☐ Do you use transitional words and phrases to indicate when you are addressing opposing arguments?

☐ Do you need to add transitions to make your paragraph more coherent?

The book's striking design is uncluttered and clear while the visual presentation of material helps students stay on track. Lively, eye-catching photographs in every chapter get students writing immediately. The open design uses color, call-out boxes, and highlighting to emphasize important information and new concepts with a minimum of distractions, keeping basic writing students focused.

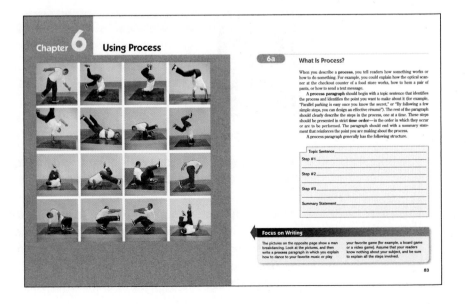

Clear, step-by-step coverage of every stage of the writing process helps students master drafting, revising, and editing. Nine chapters on paragraph writing cover the patterns of development, supported by plenty of student-friendly examples and exercises. Models of student writing, one for each pattern of development, show every stage of the writing process, with a final, finished student paragraph annotated to show how it has been improved. Two more chapters on the writing process and three on essay writing cover the rhetorical skills students need to master.

"Writing-in-context" activities, a hallmark of our developmental books, get students writing immediately and help them practice rhetorical skills while revising and editing their own writing. In each chapter, students respond in writing to a full-page photo or other visual. Then, a series of *Flashback* and *Revising and Editing* activities throughout the chapters ask students to return to their initial writing, apply new skills they are learning, and create a polished draft.

Focus on Writing: *Flashback*

Look back at your response to the Focus on Writing activity on page 463. Have you used any reflexive pronouns? If so, label each one. If not, write a new sentence that includes a reflexive pronoun.

Focus on Writing: *Revising and Editing*

Look back at your response to the Focus on Writing activity on page 463. **TEST** what you have written. Then, revise and edit your work, incorporating the corrections you made for this chapter's Flashback activities.

Thorough grammar coverage with clear explanations gives students lots of practice and lots of support.

- **Uncomplicated explanations of grammar topics help students master the essentials.** Clear instructions, basic definitions, and well-illustrated examples make fundamental grammar issues easy to grasp. *Grammar in Context* boxes in the paragraph chapters highlight issues particularly relevant to each rhetorical mode.

Grammar in Context: Definition	A definition paragraph often includes a formal definition of the term or idea you are going to discuss. When you write a formal definition, be careful not to use the phrase *is where* or *is when*.
	Happiness is ~~when you have~~ a feeling of contentment or joy.

- **Hundreds of exercises offer abundant practice.** Exercises range from very basic to more challenging, with topics that developmental students find engaging. Additional practice is available at the nearly 9,000-item online database, *Exercise Central*.

- **Checklists and mastery tests help reinforce new skills.** Review Checklists in the grammar chapters ask students to review key concepts before they move on. Chapter Reviews, and the five-paragraph, multi-error Unit Reviews, give students hands-on practice editing paragraphs and essays.

Self-Assessment Checklist: Writing a Comparison-and-Contrast Essay	☐ Does your introduction identify the two subjects you will compare and contrast and indicate whether you will discuss similarities or differences?
	☐ Does your thesis statement indicate why you are comparing your two subjects and what point you will make about them?
	☐ Do you discuss all significant points of comparison or contrast that apply to your two subjects?
	☐ Do you treat similar points for both of your subjects?
	☐ Is your essay's organization consistent with either a point-by-point comparison or a subject-by-subject comparison?
	☐ Does each topic sentence clearly identify the subject and the point of comparison or contrast being discussed?
	☐ Do you include enough transitional words and phrases to move readers from one subject or point to another?
	☐ Does your conclusion remind readers what your two subjects are and whether you have focused on similarities or differences?
	☐ What problems did you experience during the process of writing your essay? What would you do differently next time?

- **A full chapter on grammar and usage for ESL students addresses the concerns of nonnative speakers.** Chapter 30 addresses issues of special interest to nonnative speakers while marginal ESL tips throughout the Instructor's Annotated Edition help teachers support these students. The packageable ancillary, *The Bedford/St. Martin's ESL Workbook*, offers even more practice.

Focus on Writing *helps students make the connection between reading and writing.* Chapter 36, "Reading Critically," guides students through the process of critical reading and includes a sample annotated reading. Chapter 37, "Readings for Writers," contains nineteen professional and student essays that illustrate the major rhetorical patterns. End-of-reading questions focus on meaning, strategy, structure, style, and topics for writing, helping students develop critical reading and thinking skills.

Two appendixes help students with research and vocabulary development. Appendix A, "Strategies for College Success," introduces students to practical strategies that they can use throughout their college careers. Appendix B, "Using Research in Your Writing," introduces students to the process of doing research for college, including finding print and Internet sources, and documenting sources using MLA style. The marginal *Word Power* boxes throughout the book expand students' vocabularies as they work on their own writing.

What's New in This Edition

More support for moving from paragraph to essay: A new chapter, "Patterns of Essay Development," provides nine complete model student essays, one for each rhetorical mode, and one professional essay that combines several different patterns of development. Now students have more support for moving from paragraphs to essays, with thorough instruction and examples for every stage of both the paragraph and essay writing processes.

Expanded use of **TEST** *for essays:* The very popular and successful tool students applied to their paragraphs in the first edition now works for essays as well as paragraphs. All grammar chapters now end with a *Revising and Editing* activity asking students to test their essays for thesis statement, evidence, summary statement, and transitions; the final practice in each section of the new "Patterns of Essay Development" chapter also asks students to apply **TEST** to their essays.

● **Practice 14-18**

Following the guidelines in 12H, **TEST** your comparison-and-contrast essay to make sure it includes a thesis statement, sufficient supporting evidence, a summary statement that reinforces the essay's main idea, and all the transitions readers need to follow your discussion. Then, revise and edit your essay.

New contemporary readings ranging from simple to more challenging include "My Two Lives" by Jhumpa Lahiri; "But What Do You Mean?" by Deborah Tannen; and "Impounded Fathers" by Edwidge Danticat.

New strategy questions focusing on mode, structure, and style now follow the readings, emphasizing the reading-writing connection and helping students develop critical reading and thinking skills.

Ancillaries

Focus on Writing does not stop with a book. Online and in print, you will find both free and affordable premium resources to help students get even more out of the book and your course. We also offer convenient instructor resources, such as downloadable sample syllabi, classroom activities, transparency masters, and more. To order any of the products below, or to learn more about them, contact your Bedford/St. Martin's sales representative by emailing Sales Support at sales_support@bfwpub.com, or visit the Web site at **bedfordstmartins.com/focusonwriting/catalog**.

Companion Web site for *Focus on Writing* at bedfordstmartins.com/ focusonwriting   Send students to free and open resources, or upgrade to an expanding collection of innovative digital content—all in one place. The companion Web site for *Focus on Writing* provides access to *Exercise Central*, the largest free online database of editing exercises (see p. x). Additional free resources include help with taking standardized tests, building vocabulary, and conducting a job search; annotated student paragraphs and essays; *Grammar Girl* podcasts; and useful forms mentioned in the book. Premium resources available through the companion Web site for *Focus on Writing* site include *WritingClass* and *Re:Writing Plus*.

- *WritingClass* **at yourwritingclass.com**   Students are online all the time. *WritingClass* keeps them on target. At one easy-to-use site, students can see if there is a new assignment, click through and complete the activity, and check back to find out how they did. *WritingClass* makes it easy for you to set assignments—and see when students have done them. There are options for building online discussions, adding multimedia tutorials, and more—but you choose how much or how little you want to do online.
- *Re:Writing Plus,* **now with** *VideoCentral,* **at bedfordstmartins .com/rewritingbasics**   This impressive resource gathers all of our premium digital content for the writing class into one online collection. It includes innovative and interactive help with writing a paragraph; tutorials and practices that show how writing works in students' real-world experience; *VideoCentral*, with over fifty brief videos for the

writing classroom; the first-ever peer review game; *i•cite: visualizing sources*; plus hundreds of models of writing and hundreds of readings. *Re:Writing Plus* can be purchased separately or packaged with *Focus on Writing* at a significant discount.

Exercise Central 3.0 **at bedfordstmartins.com/exercisecentral**   Completely free, *Exercise Central 3.0* is the largest database of editing exercises on the Internet and a comprehensive resource for skill development as well as skill assessment. In addition to providing over 9,000 exercises offering immediate feedback and reporting to an instructor grade book, *Exercise Central 3.0* can help identify students' strengths and weaknesses, recommend personalized study plans, and provide tutorials for common problems.

Supplemental Exercises to Accompany Focus on Writing, **Second Edition (ISBN-10: 0-312-60342-8 / ISBN-13: 978-0-312-60342-7)** This print ancillary provides students with even more practice on essential skills and can be packaged at a discount. Perforated pages are easy to copy and distribute.

Make-a-Paragraph Kit with Exercise Central to Go **(ISBN-10: 0-312-45332-9 / ISBN-13: 978-0-312-45332-9)** This fun, interactive CD-ROM includes "Extreme Paragraph Makeover," a brief animation teaching students about paragraph development. It also contains exercises to help students build their own paragraphs, audiovisual tutorials on four of the most common errors for basic writers, and the content from *Exercise Central to Go: Writing and Grammar Practices for Basic Writers.*

The Bedford/St. Martin's ESL Workbook, **Second Edition (ISBN-10: 0-312-54034-5 / ISBN-13: 978-0-312-54034-0)** This comprehensive collection of exercises covers grammatical issues for multilingual students with varying English-language skills and cultural backgrounds. Instructional introductions precede exercises in a broad range of topic areas.

The Bedford/St. Martin's Planner with Grammar Girl's Quick and Dirty Tips **(ISBN-10: 0-312-48023-7 / ISBN-13: 978-0-312-48023-3)** This appealing resource includes everything that students need to plan and use their time effectively, with advice on preparing schedules and to-do lists, and with blank schedules and calendars (monthly and weekly) for planning. Integrated into the planner are pointers on fixing common grammar errors, with tips from Mignon Fogarty, host of the popular *Grammar Girl's Quick and Dirty Tips for Better Writing* podcast, and from other podcast hosts. Also included are advice on note taking and succeeding on tests, an address book, and an annotated list of useful Web sites.

Exercise Central to Go: Writing and Grammar Practices for Basic Writers **CD-ROM (ISBN-10: 0-312-44652-7 / ISBN-13: 978-0-312-44652-9)** provides hundreds of practice items to help students build their writing and editing skills. No Internet connection necessary.

Journal Writing: A Beginning **(ISBN-10: 0-312-59027-X / ISBN-13: 978-0-312-59027-7)** Designed to give students an opportunity to use writing as a way to explore their thoughts and feelings, this writing journal includes a generous supply of inspirational quotations placed throughout the pages, tips for journaling, and suggested journal topics.

From Practice to Mastery **(for the Florida College Basic Skills Exit Tests) (ISBN-10: 0-312-41908-2 / ISBN-13: 978-0-312-41908-0)** Full of practical instruction and plenty of examples, this handy book gives students all the resources they need to practice for—and pass—the Florida College Basic Skills Exit Tests on reading and writing.

For Instructors

Instructor's Annotated Edition of *Focus on Writing*, **Second Edition (ISBN-10: 0-312-60345-2 / ISBN-13: 978-0-312-60345-8)** Contains answers to all of the practice exercises, plus numerous ESL and teaching tips that offer ideas, reminders, and cross-references that are immediately helpful to teachers at any level.

Classroom Resources for Instructors Using Focus on Writing, **Second Edition (ISBN-10: 0-312-60343-6 / ISBN-13: 978-0-312-60343-4)** Offers advice for teaching developmental writing as well as chapter-by-chapter pointers for using *Focus on Writing* in the classroom. It contains answers to all of the book's practice exercises, sample syllabi, additional teaching materials, and full chapters on collaborative learning.

Diagnostic and Mastery Tests to Accompany Focus on Writing, **Second Edition (ISBN-10: 0-312-60344-4 / ISBN-13: 978-0-312-60344-1)** Offers diagnostic and mastery tests that complement the topics covered in *Focus on Writing*.

Transparency Masters to Accompany Focus on Writing, **Second Edition (ISBN-10: 0-312-66756-6 / ISBN-13: 978-0-312-66756-6)** Includes numerous models of student writing and is downloadable from the *Focus on Writing* Web site at **bedfordstmartins.com/focusonwriting**.

Testing Tool Kit: A Writing and Grammar Test Bank (ISBN-10: 0-312-43032-9 / ISBN-13: 978-0-312-43032-0)   This test bank CD-ROM allows instructors to create secure, customized tests and quizzes from a pool of nearly 2,000 questions covering forty-seven topics. It also includes ten pre-built diagnostic tests.

Teaching Developmental Writing: Background Readings, **Third Edition (ISBN-10: 0-312-43283-6 / ISBN-13: 978-0-312-43283-6)** Edited by Susan Naomi Bernstein, this professional resource is a print volume offering a collection of essays on topics of interest to basic writing instructors, along with editorial apparatus pointing out practical classroom applications. The new edition includes revised chapters on technology and the writing process and focuses on topics relevant to instructors who work with multilingual students in the developmental writing course.

The Bedford Bibliography for Teachers of Basic Writing, **Third Edition (ISBN-10: 0-312-58154-8 / ISBN-13: 978-0-312-58154-1)** (also available online at **bedfordstmartins.com/basicbib**)   Compiled by members of the Conference on Basic Writing under the general editorship of Gregory R. Glau and Chitralekha Duttagupta, this annotated list of books, articles, and periodicals was created specifically to help teachers of basic writing find valuable resources.

TeachingCentral at **bedfordstmartins.com/teachingcentral**   Offers the entire list of Bedford/St. Martin's print and online professional resources in one place. You will find landmark reference works, source-books on pedagogical issues, award-winning collections, and practical advice for the classroom—all free for instructors.

Content cartridges   These are available for the most common course management systems—Blackboard, WebCT, Angel, and Desire2Learn—and allow you to easily download Bedford/St. Martin's digital materials for your course. For more information about our course management offerings, visit **bedfordstmartins.com/cms**.

CourseSmart e-Book for Focus on Writing (ISBN-10: 0-312-60358-4 / ISBN-13: 978-0-312-60358-8)   We have partnered with CourseSmart to offer a downloadable version of *Focus on Writing*, Second Edition, at about half the price of the print book. To learn more about this low-cost alternative visit **www.coursesmart.com**.

Ordering Information

Use these ISBNs to order the following supplements packaged with your students' books:

Focus on Writing, Second Edition, with:

- *The Bedford/St. Martin's ESL Workbook*, Second Edition
  ISBN-10: 0-312-54034-5 / ISBN-13: 978-0-312-54034-0
- *The Bedford/St. Martin's Planner*
  ISBN-10: 0-312-48023-7 / ISBN-13: 978-0-312-48023-3
- *Exercise Central to Go* CD-ROM
  ISBN-10: 0-312-44652-7 / ISBN-13: 978-0-312-44652-9
- *From Practice to Mastery* (for Florida)
  ISBN-10: 0-312-41908-2 / ISBN-13: 978-0-312-41908-0
- *Journal Writing: A Beginning*
  ISBN-10: 0-312-59027-X / ISBN-13: 978-0-312-59027-7
- *Make-a-Paragraph Kit* CD-ROM
  ISBN-10: 0-312-45332-9 / ISBN-13: 978-0-312-45332-9
- *Re:Writing Plus* Access Card
  ISBN-10: 0-312-56366-3 / ISBN-13: 978-0-312-56366-0
- *Supplemental Exercises*
  ISBN-10: 0-312-60342-8 / ISBN-13: 978-0-312-60342-7
- *WritingClass*
  ISBN-10: 0-312-56367-1 / ISBN-13: 978-0-312-56367-7

Acknowledgments

In our work on *Focus on Writing*, we have benefited from the help of a great many people.

Franklin E. Horowitz of Teachers College, Columbia University, drafted an early version of Chapter 30, "Grammar and Usage for ESL Writers," and his linguist's insight continues to inform that chapter. Linda Stine and Linda Stengle of Lincoln University devoted energy and vision to the preparation of the helpful ancillary *Classroom Resources for Instructors Using Focus on Writing*. Linda Mason Austin of McLennan Community College drew on her extensive experience to contribute Teaching Tips and ESL Tips to the *Instructor's Annotated Edition*. Susan Naomi Bernstein's work on the compilation and annotation of *Teaching Developmental Writing: Background Readings* reflects her deep commitment to scholarship and teaching. We are very grateful to all of these contributors.

We thank Laura King, Michelle McSweeney, Jessica Carroll, Beth Castrodale, Kristen Blanco, Stephanie Hopkins, Judith Lechner, Carolyn Lengel, Carol Sullivan, Charlotte Gale, and Pamela Gerth for their contributions to the exercises and writing activities in the text, and Linda Stine for developing the PowerPoint presentation featured on the *Focus on Writing* Web site. Laura King, Weena McKenzie, Kelly Lockmer, Lynette Ledoux, and Michelle McSweeney's work on the ancillary booklets was invaluable. Michael Dockray reviewed the ESL chapter and made helpful suggestions.

It almost goes without saying that *Focus on Writing* could not exist without our students, whose words appear on almost every page of the book, in sample sentences, paragraphs, and essays. We thank all of them, past and present, who allowed us to use their work.

Instructors throughout the country have contributed suggestions and encouragement at various stages of the book's development. For their collegial support we thank Sandra Albers, Leeward Community College; Elizabeth Altruda, Middlesex County College; Sheilagh Badanic, Douglas College; Laura Barlond-Maas, Olivet College; Craig Barto, Charleston Southern University; Kristina Beckman, University of Arizona; Michael Berndt, Normandale Community College; Jan S. Bishop, Greenville Technical College; Lawrence Blasco, Wor-Wic Community College; Janet Brennar, Community College of Philadelphia; Julie Brevig, Santa Rosa Junior College; Jan Bromley, Douglas College; Alan Brownlie, Anne Arundel Community College; Elizabeth Butts, Delaware County Community College; Nancy Canavera, Charleston Southern University; Janet Carmichael, Wayne Community College; Rita Coronado, Riverside Community College; Judy D. Covington, Trident Technical College; Tom Hong Do, Golden West College; Jennifer Ferguson, Cazenovia College; Adam Fischer, Bowie State University; Audrey Forrest-Carter, Winston-Salem State University; Christopher Gilliard, Macomb College; Tracy Gorrell, Robert Morris University; Gwen Graham, Holmes Community College; Jessica Grecco, Urban College of Boston; Beth Heelander, Lexington Community College; Elaine S. Herrick, Temple College; Linda Lora Hulbert, Wayne State University; Maria Jacketti, Pennsylvania State University, Hazelton; Lonny Kaneko, Highline Community College; Cynthia Krause, Wilbur Wright College; Patsy Krech, University of Memphis; Jennifer Leamy, Wake Technical Community College; Kathy Leland, Folsom Lake College; Mimi Leonard, Wytheville Community College; Marci MacGregor, Broward Community College; Eric Mecklenburg, Hawaii Community College; Elzbieta Newman, University of Texas at Brownsville; Laura Novak, Bismarck State College; Kelley Paystrup, Snow College; Suzan Phillips, Charleston Southern University; Tom Pierce, Central New Mexico Community College; Janet Kay Porter, Leeward Community College; Melissa Rayborn, Valencia Community College;

Melissa Renfrow, Maple Woods Community College; Sharisse Turner, Tallahassee Community College; Tondalaya W. VanLear, Dabney S. Lancaster Community College; Rhonda Wallace, Cuyahoga Community College; Michael T. Warren, Maple Woods Community College; Kim Watkins, Mount San Antonio College; George Wheelock, Anne Arundel Community College; Julie Yankanich, Camden County College.

At Bedford/St. Martin's, we thank founder and former president Chuck Christensen along with president Joan Feinberg, who believed in this project and gave us support and encouragement from the outset. We thank Karen Henry, editor in chief, and Erica Appel, director of development, for overseeing this edition, and Nancy Perry, our longtime friend and former editor in chief, for helping us to conceptualize the book. We are also grateful to Shannon Walsh and Melissa Cook, editorial assistants, for helping with numerous tasks, big and small, as well as to Dennis Conroy, senior production supervisor; Harold Chester, senior project editor; and Shuli Traub, managing editor, for guiding the book ably through production. Anna Palchik, senior art director, offered invaluable help at the initial stages of design, and Claire Seng-Niemoeller, book designer, created an extraordinary look for *Focus on Writing*, one that brings an entirely fresh perspective to the developmental writing text. Melissa Cliver and Rachel Youdelman provided the engaging photos in our text. Lucy Krikorian, art director, oversaw the finalized design and art program. Thanks also go to Casey Carroll, marketing manager, and his team; to our outstanding copyeditor, Diana Puglisi George; and to our terrific proofreaders, Roberta Sobotka and Julie Nemer. And finally, we thank our editor, Ellen Darion, whose hard work and dedication kept the project moving along.

We are grateful for the continued support of our families—Mark, Adam, and Rebecca Kirszner; and Demi, David, and Sarah Mandell. Finally, we are grateful for the survival and growth of the writing partnership we entered into when we were graduate students. We had no idea then of the wonderful places our collaborative efforts would take us. Now, we know.

Laurie G. Kirszner
Stephen R. Mandell

Contents

Preface for Instructors   iii

A Note to Students   xxxi

Checklists for Writing Paragraphs and Essays   xxxii

Writing Paragraphs and Essays

Unit One

Writing Paragraphs   1

1 Understanding the Writing Process   2

STEP 1: Planning   4

a   Understanding Paragraph Structure   4

b   Focusing on Your Assignment, Purpose, and Audience   5

c   Finding Ideas   6

    Freewriting 7 • Brainstorming 8 • Clustering 10 • Journal Writing 12

d   Identifying Your Main Idea and Writing a Topic Sentence   14

STEP 2: Organizing   17

e   Choosing Supporting Points   17

f   Arranging Your Supporting Points   18

STEP 3: Drafting   19

g   Drafting Your Paragraph   19

h   TESTing Your Paragraph   21

STEP 4: Revising and Editing   22

i   Revising Your Paragraph   22

    SELF-ASSESSMENT CHECKLIST: REVISING YOUR PARAGRAPH   22

j   Editing Your Paragraph   24

    SELF-ASSESSMENT CHECKLIST: EDITING YOUR PARAGRAPH   24

    REVIEW CHECKLIST: WRITING A PARAGRAPH   27

2 TESTing Your Paragraphs   28

a   Using a Topic Sentence to Unify Your Paragraph   30
b   Using Evidence to Support Your Paragraph's Main Idea   35
c   Using a Summary Statement to Reinforce Your Paragraph's Unity   38
d   Using Transitions to Add Coherence to Your Paragraph   40
    CHAPTER REVIEW   45
    REVIEW CHECKLIST: TESTING YOUR PARAGRAPHS   48

Unit Two   **Patterns of Paragraph Development**   49

3 Using Exemplification   50

a   What Is Exemplification?   51
b   Writing an Exemplification Paragraph   55
    CHAPTER REVIEW   60
    Checklist: TESTing an Exemplification Paragraph   61

4 Using Narration   62

a   What Is Narration?   63
b   Writing a Narrative Paragraph   66
    CHAPTER REVIEW   70
    Checklist: TESTing a Narrative Paragraph   71

5 Using Description   72

a   What Is Description?   73
b   Writing a Descriptive Paragraph   77
    CHAPTER REVIEW   80
    Checklist: TESTing a Descriptive Paragraph   81

6 Using Process   82

a   What Is Process?   83
    Process Explanations 84 • Instructions 84

b   Writing a Process Paragraph   88
CHAPTER REVIEW   92
Checklist: TESTing a Process Paragraph   93

7   Using Cause and Effect   94

a   What Is Cause and Effect?   95
Causes 96 • Effects 97
b   Writing a Cause-and-Effect Paragraph   100
CHAPTER REVIEW   104
Checklist: TESTing a Cause-and-Effect Paragraph   105

8   Using Comparison and Contrast   106

a   What Is Comparison and Contrast?   107
Subject-by-Subject Comparisons 108 • Point-by-Point Comparisons 109
b   Writing a Comparison-and-Contrast Paragraph   113
CHAPTER REVIEW   120
Checklist: TESTing a Comparison-and-Contrast Paragraph   121

9   Using Classification   122

a   What Is Classification?   123
b   Writing a Classification Paragraph   127
CHAPTER REVIEW   130
Checklist: TESTing a Classification Paragraph   131

10   Using Definition   132

a   What Is Definition?   133
b   Writing a Definition Paragraph   138
CHAPTER REVIEW   142
Checklist: TESTing a Definition Paragraph   143

11   Using Argument   144

a   What Is Argument?   145
b   Writing an Argument Paragraph   151

CHAPTER REVIEW   157

Checklist: TESTing an Argument Paragraph   158

Unit Three

Writing Essays   159

12 Writing an Essay   160

STEP 1: Planning   161

a   Understanding Essay Structure   161
b   Focusing on Your Assignment, Purpose, and Audience   167
c   Finding Ideas   169
    Freewriting 169 • Brainstorming 170
d   Identifying Your Main Idea and Stating Your Thesis   171

STEP 2: Organizing   176

e   Choosing Supporting Points   176
f   Arranging Your Supporting Points   177

STEP 3: Drafting   179

g   Drafting Your Essay   179

STEP 4: TESTing   181

h   TESTing Your Essay   181

STEP 5: Revising and Editing   182

i   Revising Your Essay   182
    SELF-ASSESSMENT CHECKLIST: REVISING YOUR ESSAY   182
j   Editing Your Essay   183
    SELF-ASSESSMENT CHECKLIST: EDITING YOUR ESSAY   183
k   Checking Your Essay's Format   187
    CHAPTER REVIEW   189
    REVIEW CHECKLIST: WRITING AN ESSAY   193

13 Writing Introductions and Conclusions   194

a   Introductions   195
    *Beginning with a Narrative 196 • Beginning with a Question
    (or a Series of Questions) 196 • Beginning with a Definition 196 •
    Beginning with a Quotation 197 • Beginning with an Unexpected
    Statement 197*

b　Conclusions　199

*Concluding with a Narrative 200 • Concluding with a
Recommendation 200 • Concluding with a Quotation 200 •
Concluding with a Prediction 201*

CHAPTER REVIEW　202
REVIEW CHECKLIST: INTRODUCTIONS AND CONCLUSIONS　205

14　**Patterns of Essay Development**　206

a　Exemplification　207

Model Exemplification Essay 209

SELF-ASSESSMENT CHECKLIST: WRITING AN EXEMPLIFICATION
ESSAY　212

b　Narration　212

Model Narrative Essay 214

SELF-ASSESSMENT CHECKLIST: WRITING A NARRATIVE ESSAY　217

c　Description　217

Model Descriptive Essay 220

SELF-ASSESSMENT CHECKLIST: WRITING A DESCRIPTIVE ESSAY　223

d　Process　224

Model Process Essay 226

SELF-ASSESSMENT CHECKLIST: WRITING A PROCESS ESSAY　229

e　Cause and Effect　229

Model Cause-and-Effect Essay 232

SELF-ASSESSMENT CHECKLIST: WRITING A CAUSE-AND-EFFECT
ESSAY　235

f　Comparison and Contrast　235

Model Comparison-and-Contrast Essay 238

SELF-ASSESSMENT CHECKLIST: WRITING A COMPARISON-AND-CONTRAST
ESSAY　241

g　Classification　241

Model Classification Essay 243

SELF-ASSESSMENT CHECKLIST: WRITING A CLASSIFICATION ESSAY　246

h　Definition　246

Model Definition Essay 248

SELF-ASSESSMENT CHECKLIST: WRITING A DEFINITION ESSAY　251

i　Argument　251

Model Argument Essay 254

SELF-ASSESSMENT CHECKLIST: WRITING AN ARGUMENT ESSAY　257

CHAPTER REVIEW   258
REVIEW CHECKLIST: PATTERNS OF ESSAY DEVELOPMENT   260

Revising and Editing Your Writing

Unit Four   ## Writing Sentences   261

15 Writing Simple Sentences   262

a   Subjects   263
b   Prepositional Phrases   266
c   Verbs   268
     Action Verbs 268 • Linking Verbs 269 • Helping Verbs 270
     CHAPTER REVIEW   273
     REVIEW CHECKLIST: WRITING SIMPLE SENTENCES   275

16 Writing Compound Sentences   276

a   Using Coordinating Conjunctions   277
b   Using Semicolons   282
c   Using Transitional Words and Phrases   283
     CHAPTER REVIEW   290
     REVIEW CHECKLIST: WRITING COMPOUND SENTENCES   293

17 Writing Complex Sentences   294

a   Identifying Complex Sentences   295
b   Using Subordinating Conjunctions   297
c   Using Relative Pronouns   301
     CHAPTER REVIEW   305
     REVIEW CHECKLIST: WRITING COMPLEX SENTENCES   307

18 Writing Varied Sentences   308

a   Varying Sentence Types   309
b   Varying Sentence Openings   311
     Beginning with Adverbs 311 • Beginning with Prepositional Phrases 312

c   Combining Sentences   315

Using -ing Modifiers 315 • *Using -ed Modifiers 316* • *Using a Series of Words 317* • *Using Appositives 320*

d   Varying Sentence Length   321

CHAPTER REVIEW   323
REVIEW CHECKLIST: ACHIEVING SENTENCE VARIETY   325

19   Using Parallelism   326

a   Recognizing Parallel Structure   327
b   Using Parallel Structure   329

Paired Items 329 • *Items in a Series 329* • *Items in a List or in an Outline 330*

CHAPTER REVIEW   331
REVIEW CHECKLIST: USING PARALLELISM   333

20   Using Words Effectively   334

a   Using Specific Words   335
b   Using Concise Language   337
c   Avoiding Slang   340
d   Avoiding Clichés   341
e   Using Similes and Metaphors   343
f   Avoiding Sexist Language   344

CHAPTER REVIEW   346
REVIEW CHECKLIST: USING WORDS EFFECTIVELY   348

Unit Review   349

Unit Five   Solving Common Sentence Problems   353

21   Run-Ons   354

a   Recognizing Run-Ons   355
b   Correcting Run-Ons   358

CHAPTER REVIEW   367
REVIEW CHECKLIST: RUN-ONS   369

22 Sentence Fragments   370

a   Recognizing Fragments   371
b   Missing-Subject Fragments   373
c   Phrase Fragments   375
    Appositive Fragments 375 • *Prepositional Phrase Fragments 377*
d   Incomplete-Verb Fragments   379
    -ing Fragments 379 • *Infinitive Fragments 382*
e   Dependent Clause Fragments   384
    CHAPTER REVIEW   390
    REVIEW CHECKLIST: SENTENCE FRAGMENTS   393

23 Subject-Verb Agreement   394

a   Understanding Subject-Verb Agreement   395
b   Compound Subjects   397
c   *Be, Have,* and *Do*   399
d   Words between Subject and Verb   400
e   Collective Noun Subjects   402
f   Indefinite Pronoun Subjects   403
g   Verbs before Subjects   405
    CHAPTER REVIEW   407
    REVIEW CHECKLIST: SUBJECT-VERB AGREEMENT   409

24 Illogical Shifts   410

a   Shifts in Tense   411
b   Shifts in Person   413
c   Shifts in Voice   415
    CHAPTER REVIEW   417
    REVIEW CHECKLIST: ILLOGICAL SHIFTS   419

25 Dangling and Misplaced Modifiers   420

a   Correcting Dangling Modifiers   421
b   Correcting Misplaced Modifiers   423

CHAPTER REVIEW   426
REVIEW CHECKLIST: DANGLING AND MISPLACED MODIFIERS   428

Unit Review   429

Unit Six — Understanding Basic Grammar   433

26 Verbs: Past Tense   434

a   Regular Verbs   435
b   Irregular Verbs   436
c   Problem Verbs: *Be*   439
d   Problem Verbs: *Can/Could* and *Will/Would*   440
     Can/Could 440 • *Will/Would 441*
     CHAPTER REVIEW   443
     REVIEW CHECKLIST: VERBS: PAST TENSE   445

27 Verbs: Past Participles   446

a   Regular Past Participles   447
b   Irregular Past Participles   448
c   The Present Perfect Tense   453
d   The Past Perfect Tense   455
e   Past Participles as Adjectives   457
     CHAPTER REVIEW   459
     REVIEW CHECKLIST: VERBS: PAST PARTICIPLES   461

28 Nouns and Pronouns   462

a   Identifying Nouns   463
b   Forming Plural Nouns   463
c   Identifying Pronouns   467
d   Pronoun-Antecedent Agreement   468
e   Special Problems with Agreement   470
     Compound Antecedents 470 • *Indefinite Pronoun Antecedents 471* •
     Collective Noun Antecedents 474

f   Pronoun Case   476

Subjective Case 476 • Objective Case 477 • Possessive Case 477

g   Special Problems with Case   478

Pronouns in Compounds 478 • Pronouns in Comparisons 480 •
Who *and* Whom *481*

h   Reflexive Pronouns   482

CHAPTER REVIEW   484

REVIEW CHECKLIST: NOUNS AND PRONOUNS   487

29   **Adjectives and Adverbs**   488

a   Identifying Adjectives and Adverbs   489

b   Comparatives and Superlatives   492

*Forming Comparatives and Superlatives 493 • Solving Special Problems
with Comparatives and Superlatives 493*

CHAPTER REVIEW   497

REVIEW CHECKLIST: ADJECTIVES AND ADVERBS   499

30   **Grammar and Usage for ESL Writers**   500

a   Subjects in Sentences   501

b   Plural Nouns   504

c   Count and Noncount Nouns   505

d   Determiners with Count and Noncount Nouns   507

e   Articles   510

*The Definite Article 510 • Indefinite Articles 511 • No Article 512 •
Articles with Proper Nouns 512*

f   Negative Statements and Questions   514

Negative Statements 514 • Questions 514

g   Verb Tense   517

h   Stative Verbs   518

i   Modal Auxiliaries   520

j   Gerunds   522

k   Placing Modifiers in Order   523

Required Order 523 • Preferred Order 523

l   Choosing Prepositions   525

m   Prepositions in Familiar Expressions   526

n   Prepositions in Phrasal Verbs   530

Separable Phrasal Verbs 530 • *Inseparable Phrasal Verbs 531*

CHAPTER REVIEW   534

REVIEW CHECKLIST: GRAMMAR AND USAGE FOR ESL WRITERS   536

Unit Review   **538**

Unit Seven

Understanding Punctuation, Mechanics, and Spelling   541

31 Using Commas   542

a   Commas in a Series   543

b   Commas with Introductory Phrases and Transitional Words and Phrases   545

Introductory Phrases 545 • *Transitional Words and Phrases 546*

c   Commas with Appositives   548

d   Commas with Nonrestrictive Clauses   550

e   Commas in Dates and Addresses   552

Dates 552 • *Addresses 552*

f   Unnecessary Commas   554

CHAPTER REVIEW   557

REVIEW CHECKLIST: USING COMMAS   559

32 Using Apostrophes   560

a   Apostrophes in Contractions   561

b   Apostrophes in Possessives   563

Singular Nouns and Indefinite Pronouns 563 • *Plural Nouns 563*

c   Incorrect Use of Apostrophes   564

CHAPTER REVIEW   567

REVIEW CHECKLIST: USING APOSTROPHES   569

33 Using Other Punctuation Marks   570

a   Semicolons   571

b   Colons   573

c   Dashes and Parentheses   574
     CHAPTER REVIEW   576
     REVIEW CHECKLIST: USING OTHER PUNCTUATION MARKS   577

34 Understanding Mechanics   578

a   Capitalizing Proper Nouns   579
b   Punctuating Quotations   582
c   Setting Off Titles   586
d   Hyphens   589
e   Abbreviations   589
f   Numbers   590
     CHAPTER REVIEW   592
     REVIEW CHECKLIST: UNDERSTANDING MECHANICS   595

35 Understanding Spelling   596

a   Becoming a Better Speller   597
b   *ie* and *ei*   599
c   Prefixes   600
d   Suffixes   601
     Words Ending in Silent e *601* • *Words Ending in* -y *602* • *Doubling the Final Consonant 603*
e   Commonly Confused Words   605
     CHAPTER REVIEW   614
     REVIEW CHECKLIST: UNDERSTANDING SPELLING   616

Unit Review   617

Becoming a Critical Reader

Unit Eight   Reading Essays   621

36 Reading Critically   622

a   Previewing   623
b   Highlighting   626
c   Annotating   628
d   Outlining   630

e Summarizing 632

f Writing a Response Paragraph 633

REVIEW CHECKLIST: READING CRITICALLY 633

37 Readings for Writers 634

a Exemplification 635

Judith Ortiz Cofer, *Don't Call Me a Hot Tamale* 636

Nicols Fox, *Volunteer Workers of the World, Unite* 640

b Narration 643

Yiyun Li, *Orange Crush* 643

David Matthews, *Pick One* 646

c Description 650

Alex Espinoza, *An American in Mexico* 650

Rachel Carson, *A Fable for Tomorrow* 653

d Process 656

Adam Goodheart, *Mummy Arts* 656

Amy Ma, *My Grandmother's Dumpling* 659

e Cause and Effect 666

John Schwartz, *The Poncho Bearer* 667

John Hartmire, *At the Heart of a Historic Movement* 670

f Comparison and Contrast 674

Jhumpa Lahiri, *My Two Lives* 674

William Zinsser, *The Transaction* 678

g Classification 681

Deborah Tannen, *But What Do You Mean?* 681

Carolyn Foster Segal, *The Dog Ate My Disk, and Other Tales of Woe* 689

h Definition 693

Gayle Rosenwald Smith, *The Wife-Beater* 693

Paul Hoffman, *Triskaidekaphobia* 696

i Argument 701

Bobbi Buchanan, *Don't Hang Up, That's My Mom Calling* 702

Charles Murray, *For Most People, College Is a Waste of Time* 704

Edwidge Danticat, *Impounded Fathers* 708

APPENDIX A. Strategies for College Success   712

1   Orientation Strategies   712
2   First-Week Strategies   712
3   Day-to-Day Strategies   714
4   Time-Management Strategies   716
5   Note-Taking Strategies   718
    During Class 719 • *After Class 720* • *Before the Next Class 720*
6   Homework Strategies   720
7   Exam-Taking Strategies   721
    Before the Exam 721 • *During the Exam 722*

APPENDIX B. Using Research in Your Writing   725

1   Choosing a Topic   725
2   Doing Research   726
    Finding Information in the Library 726 • *Finding Information on the Internet 727*
3   Taking Notes   728
    Paraphrasing 728 • *Summarizing 729* • *Quoting 730*
4   Watching Out for Plagiarism   731
    Rule 1. Document Ideas from Your Sources 732 • *Rule 2. Place Borrowed Words in Quotation Marks 732* • *Rule 3. Use Your Own Phrasing 732* • *Rule 4. Distinguish Your Ideas from the Source's Ideas 733*
5   Developing a Thesis   734
6   Making an Outline   734
7   Writing Your Paper   735
8   Documenting Your Sources   736
    Parenthetical References in the Text 736 • *The Works-Cited List 738* • *Sample MLA-Style Paper 742*

Answers to Odd-Numbered Exercise Items   748
Index   761
Index of Rhetorical Patterns   779
Correction Symbols   782

A Note to Students

It's no secret that writing will be very important in most of the courses you take in college. Whether you write lab reports or English papers, midterms or final exams, your ability to organize your thoughts and express them in writing will help to determine how well you do. In other words, succeeding at writing is the first step toward succeeding in college. Perhaps even more important, writing is a key to success outside the classroom. On the job and in everyday life, if you can express yourself clearly and effectively, you will stand a better chance of achieving your goals and making a difference in the world.

Whether you write as a student, as an employee, as a parent, or as a concerned citizen, your writing almost always has a specific purpose. For example, when you write an essay, a memo, a letter, or a research paper, you are writing not just to complete an exercise but to give other people information or to tell them your ideas or opinions. That is why, in this book, we don't just ask you to do grammar exercises and fill in blanks; in each chapter, we also ask you to apply the skills you are learning to a writing assignment of your own.

As teachers—and as former students—we know how demanding college can be and how hard it is to juggle assignments with work and family responsibilities. We also know that you don't want to waste your time. That's why in *Focus on Writing* we make information easy to find and use and include many different features to help you become a better writer.

Laurie G. Kirszner
Stephen R. Mandell

Checklists for Writing Paragraphs and Essays

Units 1–3 of *Focus on Writing* include a number of checklists designed to help you check, revise, and fine-tune your paragraphs and essays. You can use these checklists both in your writing course and in other courses that include written assignments. The following list shows the page number for each checklist.

Self-Assessment Checklist: Revising Your Paragraph	22
Self-Assessment Checklist: Editing Your Paragraph	24
TESTing an Exemplification Paragraph	61
TESTing a Narrative Paragraph	71
TESTing a Descriptive Paragraph	81
TESTing a Process Paragraph	93
TESTing a Cause-and-Effect Paragraph	105
TESTing a Comparison-and-Contrast Paragraph	121
TESTing a Classification Paragraph	131
TESTing a Definition Paragraph	143
TESTing an Argument Paragraph	158
Self-Assessment Checklist: Revising Your Essay	182
Self-Assessment Checklist: Editing Your Essay	183
Self-Assessment Checklist: Writing an Exemplification Essay	212
Self-Assessment Checklist: Writing a Narrative Essay	217
Self-Assessment Checklist: Writing a Descriptive Essay	223
Self-Assessment Checklist: Writing a Process Essay	229
Self-Assessment Checklist: Writing a Cause-and-Effect Essay	235
Self-Assessment Checklist: Writing a Comparison-and-Contrast Essay	241
Self-Assessment Checklist: Writing a Classification Essay	246
Self-Assessment Checklist: Writing a Definition Essay	251
Self-Assessment Checklist: Writing an Argument Essay	257

Unit One
Writing Paragraphs

1 Understanding the Writing Process 2
2 TESTing Your Paragraphs 28

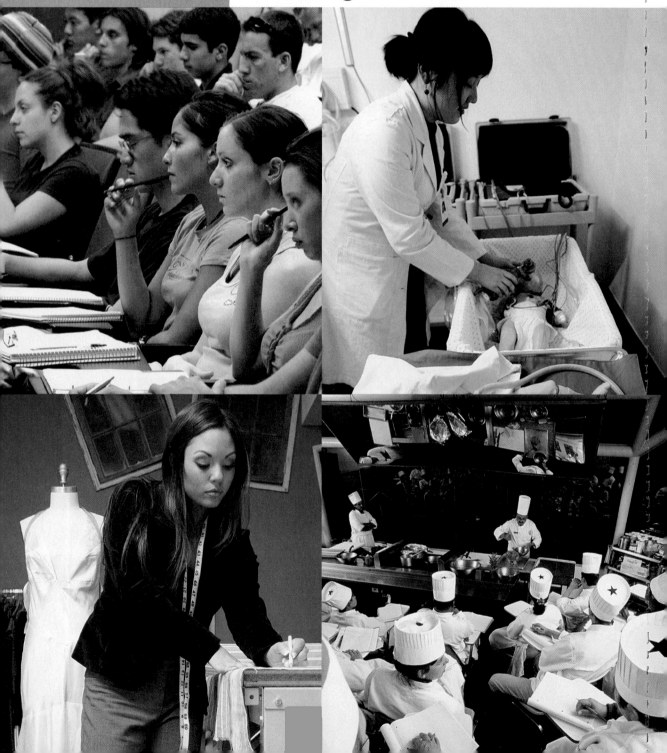

Writing is not just something you do in school; writing is a life skill. If you can write clearly, you can express your ideas convincingly to others—in school, on the job, and in your personal life.

Writing takes many different forms. In college, you might write a single paragraph, an essay exam, a short paper, or a long research paper, or you might post comments on a class discussion board. At work, you might write a memo, a proposal, or a report. In your personal life, you might write a letter or an email asking for information or pointing out a problem that needs to be solved, or you might post comments on a blog.

Writing is important. If you can write, you can communicate; if you can communicate effectively, you can succeed in school and beyond.

This chapter takes you through the process of writing a paragraph.

Highlight: The Writing Process

Writing is a **process**, a series of steps that begins in your college classes when you get an assignment.

Step 1: Planning   You start by thinking about what you want to say and finding ideas to write about. Then, you identify the main idea you want to get across.

Step 2: Organizing   Once you have material to write about, you arrange the points that support your main idea in an order that makes sense to you.

Step 3: Drafting   When you have decided on an arrangement for your ideas, you write a draft.

Step 4: Revising and Editing   Finally, you revise and edit your draft until you are satisfied with it.

Focus on Writing

As the pictures on the opposite page show, students in college today may find themselves either in a traditional classroom or in a more career-oriented setting. What do you think is the primary purpose of college—to give students a general education or to prepare them for specific careers? Look at the pictures, and think about this question carefully as you read the pages that follow. This is the topic you will be writing about as you move through this chapter.

STEP 1: PLANNING

1a Understanding Paragraph Structure

Before you can begin the process of writing a paragraph, you need to have a basic understanding of paragraph structure. Because paragraphs are central to almost every form of writing, learning how to write one is an important step in becoming a competent writer. Although a paragraph can be a complete piece of writing in itself—as it is in a short classroom exercise or an exam answer—most of the time, a paragraph is part of a longer piece of writing.

A **paragraph** is a group of sentences that is unified by a single main idea. The **topic sentence** states the main idea, and the rest of the sentences in the paragraph provide **evidence** (details and examples) to support the main idea. The sentences in a paragraph are linked by **transitions,** words and phrases (such as *also* and *for example*) that show how ideas are related. At the end of the paragraph, a **summary statement** reinforces the main idea.

Paragraph Structure

Topic sentence —
Evidence (details and examples) —
Summary statement —

    To write a paragraph, you need a main idea, supporting evidence, transitions, and a summary statement. First, state the main idea of the paragraph in a topic sentence. This idea unifies the paragraph. Then, add sentences to provide support. In these sentences, you present evidence (details and examples) to help readers understand your main idea. Next, check to make sure you have linked these sentences with transitions. Finally, write a summary statement, a sentence that sums up the paragraph's main idea. If you follow this general structure, you are on your way to writing an effective paragraph.

Transitions (boxed) —

Note that the first sentence of a paragraph is **indented**, starting about half an inch from the left-hand margin. Every sentence begins with a capital letter and, in most cases, ends with a period. (Sometimes a sentence ends with a question mark or an exclamation point.)

● Practice 1-1

Bring two paragraphs to class—one from a newspaper or magazine article and one from a textbook. Compare your paragraphs with those brought in by other students. What features do all your paragraphs share? How are the journalistic paragraphs different from the ones from textbooks?

1b Focusing on Your Assignment, Purpose, and Audience

In college, the writing process usually begins with an assignment that tells you what to write about. Instead of jumping in headfirst and starting to write, take time to consider some questions about your **assignment** (*what* you are expected to write about), your **purpose** (*why* you are writing), and your **audience** (*for whom* you are writing). Finding out the answers to these questions at this point will save you time in the long run.

Questions about Assignment, Purpose, and Audience

Assignment

- What is your assignment? Is the assignment included on your course syllabus or posted on the class Web site?
- Do you have a word or page limit?
- When is your assignment due?
- Will you be expected to work on your assignment only at home, or will you be doing some work in class?
- Will you be expected to work on your own or with others?
- Will you be allowed to revise your work?

Purpose

- Are you expected to express your personal reactions—for example, to tell how you feel about a piece of music or a news event?
- Are you expected to present information—for example, to describe a scientific process or to summarize a story or essay you have read?
- Are you expected to evaluate a reading, experience, or performance or to take a position on a controversial issue?

Audience

- Who will read your paper—just your instructor or other students in your class? Will other members of your college community read your work?
- How much are your readers likely to know about your topic?
- Will your readers expect you to use formal or informal language?

● Practice 1-2

Each of the following writing tasks has a different audience and purpose. Think about how you would approach each task. (Use the Questions about Assignment, Purpose, and Audience on p. 5 and above to help you decide on the best strategy.) Discuss your ideas with your class or in a small group.

1. For the other students in your writing class, describe your best or worst educational experience.

2. For the instructor of an introductory psychology course, discuss how early educational experiences can affect a student's performance throughout his or her schooling.

3. Write some comments that you could post on your local school board's Web site in which you try to convince members to make two or three specific changes that you believe would improve the schools you attended or those your children might attend.

4. Write an email to a past or current work supervisor telling what you appreciate about his or her guidance and how it has helped you develop and grow as an employee.

1c   Finding Ideas

Once you know what, why, and for whom you are writing, you can begin to find ideas to write about. This process can be challenging, and it is different for every writer.

Stella Drew, a student in an introductory writing course, was given the following assignment.

Should community service—unpaid work in the community—be a required part of the college curriculum? Write a paragraph in which you answer this question.

Before she drafted her paragraph, Stella used a variety of strategies to help her find ideas to write about. The pages that follow illustrate the four strategies her instructor asked the class to try: *freewriting, brainstorming, clustering,* and *journal writing.*

Freewriting

When you **freewrite,** you write for a set period of time—perhaps five minutes—without stopping, and you keep writing even if what you are writing doesn't seem to have a point or a direction. Your goal is to relax and let ideas flow without worrying about whether or not they are related (or even make sense). Sometimes you can freewrite without a topic in mind, but at other times you will focus your attention on a particular topic. This strategy is called **focused freewriting.**

When you finish freewriting, read what you have written. Then, underline any ideas you think you might be able to use. If you find an idea you want to explore further, freewrite again, using that idea as a starting point.

Here is Stella's focused freewriting on the topic of whether or not community service should be a required part of the college curriculum.

Community service. Community service. Sounds like what you do
instead of going to jail. Service to the community — service in the
community. Community center. College community — community college.
Community service — I guess it's a good idea to do it — but when?
In my spare time — spare time — that's pretty funny. So after school
and work and all the reading and studying I also have to do <u>service</u>?
Right. And what could I do anyway? Work with kids. Or homeless
people. Old people? Sick people? Or not people — maybe animals.
Or work for a political candidate. Does that count? But when would
I do it? Maybe other people have time, but I don't. OK idea, could
work — but not for me.

Freewriting

● Practice 1-3

Reread Stella's freewriting on the topic of community service for college students. If you were advising her, which of her ideas would you suggest she explore further? Underline these ideas in her freewriting.

● Practice 1-4

Now, it is time for you to begin the work that will result in a finished paragraph. (You already have your assignment from the Focus on Writing box on p. 3: to write about whether the primary purpose of college is to give students a general education or to prepare them for specific careers.)

Your first step is to freewrite about this assignment. On a sheet of lined paper (or on your computer), write for at least five minutes without stopping. If you have trouble thinking of something to write, keep recopying the last word you have written until something else comes to mind.

● Practice 1-5

Reread the freewriting you did for Practice 1-4. Underline any ideas you think you might use in your paragraph. Then, choose one of these ideas, and use it as a starting point for another five-minute focused freewriting exercise.

Brainstorming

When you **brainstorm**, you type or write down all the ideas about your topic that you can think of. Unlike freewriting, brainstorming is often scattered all over the page. You don't have to use complete sentences; single words or phrases are fine. You can underline, star, or box important points.

| Highlight: Collaborative Brainstorming | Usually, you brainstorm on your own. At times, however, you may find it helpful to do **collaborative brainstorming**, working with other students to find ideas. Sometimes your instructor may ask you and another student to brainstorm together. At other times, the class might brainstorm as a group while your instructor writes the ideas you think of on the board or displays them on a screen. Whichever method you use, your goal is the same: to come up with as much material about your topic as you can. |

You can also ask questions, make lists, draw arrows to connect ideas, and even draw pictures or diagrams.

Stella's brainstorming on the topic of community service appears below.

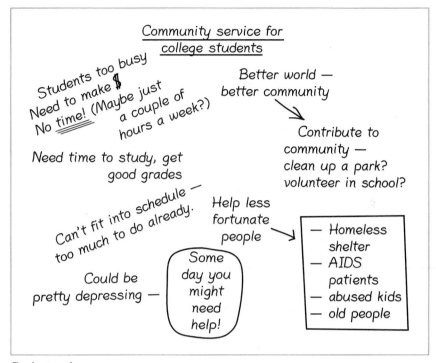

Brainstorming

● Practice 1-6

Reread Stella's brainstorming notes on community service (above). How is her brainstorming similar to her freewriting on the same subject (p. 7)? How is it different? If you were advising Stella, which ideas would you suggest she write more about? Which ideas should she cross out?

● Practice 1-7

On a sheet of *unlined* paper, brainstorm about your assignment: What do you think is the primary purpose of college — to give students a general education or to prepare them for specific careers?

Begin by writing your topic, "The purpose of college," at the top of the page. Write quickly, without worrying about using complete sentences. Try writing on different parts of the page, making lists, and drawing arrows to connect related ideas.

When you have finished, look over what you have written. Which ideas are the most interesting? Did you come up with any new ideas as you brainstormed that you did not discover while freewriting?

● **Practice 1-8**

Working as a class or in a group of three or four students, practice collaborative brainstorming:

- First, decide as a group on a topic for brainstorming. (Your instructor may assign a topic.)
- Next, choose one person to write down ideas on a blank sheet of paper or on the board. (If your group is large enough, you might choose two people to write down ideas and have them compare notes at the end of the brainstorming session.)
- Then, discuss the topic informally, with each person contributing at least one idea.
- Finally, review the ideas that have been written down. As a group, try to identify interesting connections among ideas and suggest ideas that might be explored further.

Clustering

Clustering, sometimes called *mapping*, is another strategy that can help you find ideas to write about. When you cluster, you begin by writing your topic in the center of a sheet of paper. Then, you branch out, writing related ideas on the page in groups, or clusters, around the topic. As you add new ideas, you circle them and draw lines to connect the ideas to one another and to the topic at the center. (These lines will look like spokes of a wheel or branches of a tree.) As you move from the center to the corners of the page, your ideas will get more and more specific.

Sometimes one branch of your cluster exercise will give you all the material you need. At other times, you may decide to write about the ideas from several branches—or to choose one or two ideas from each branch. If you find you need additional material after you finish your first cluster exercise, you can cluster again on a new sheet of paper, this time beginning with a topic from one of the branches.

Stella's clustering on the topic of community service for college students appears on the next page.

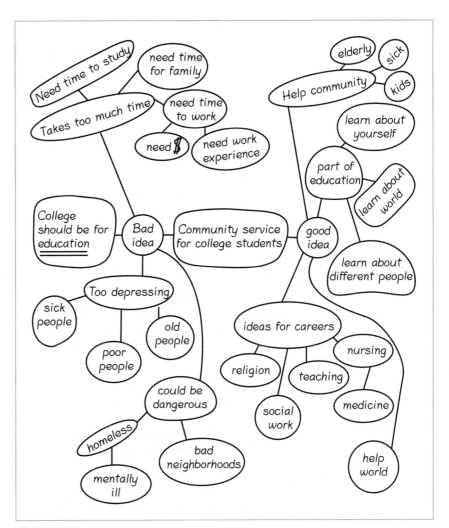

Clustering

● Practice 1-9

Reread Stella's clustering on community service (above). How is it similar to her brainstorming on the same subject (p. 9)? How is it different? If you were advising Stella, which branches of the cluster diagram would you say seem most promising? Why? Can you add any branches? Can you extend any of her branches further? Write in your additions on Stella's cluster diagram. Then, discuss your suggestions with your class or in a small group of students.

● Practice 1-10

Try clustering on your Focus on Writing activity:

> What do you think is the primary purpose of college—to give students a general education or to prepare them for specific careers?

Begin by writing your topic, "The Purpose of College," in the center of a blank sheet of unlined paper. Circle the topic, and then branch out with specific ideas and examples, continuing to the edge of the page if you can. When you have finished, look over what you have written. What are the most interesting ideas in your cluster diagram? Which branches seem most promising as the basis for further writing? What new ideas have you come up with that you did not discover during your freewriting or brainstorming?

Journal Writing

A **journal** is a notebook or a computer file in which you keep an informal record of your thoughts and ideas. In a journal, you can reflect, question, summarize, or even complain. Your journal is also a place where you can record your thoughts about your assignments and note possible ideas to write about. Here, you can try to resolve a problem, restart a stalled project, argue with yourself about your topic, or comment on a draft of your paper. You can also try out different versions of sentences, keep track of details or examples, or keep a record of interesting things you read, see, or hear.

Journal writing works best when you write regularly, preferably at the same time each day, so that it becomes a habit. Once you have started making regular entries in your journal, take the time every week or so to go back and reread what you have written. You may find material you want to explore in further journal entries—or even an idea for a paper.

Here is Stella's journal entry on the topic of community service for college students.

I'm not really sure what I think about community service. I guess I think it sounds like a good idea, but I still don't see why we should have to do it. I can't fit anything else into my life. I guess it would be possible if it was just an hour or two a week. And maybe we could get credit and a grade for it, like a course. Or maybe it should just be for people who have the time and want to do it. But if it's not required, will anyone do it?

Journal entry

Highlight: Journals	Here are some subjects you can write about in your journal.

- **Your school work** In your journal, you can explore ideas for writing assignments. Your journal can also be a place where you think about what you have learned, ask questions about concepts you are having trouble understanding, and examine new ideas and new ways of seeing the world. Writing regularly in a journal about what you are studying in school can even help you become a better student.

- **Your job** In your journal, you can record job-related successes and frustrations, examine conflicts with coworkers, or analyze how you handled problems on the job. Reading over these entries can help you understand your strengths and weaknesses and become a more effective employee.

- **Your ideas about current events** Expressing your opinions in your journal is a good way to explore your reactions to social or political issues in the news. Your entries may encourage you to write to your local or school newspaper or to public officials—and even to become involved in community service or political activities.

- **Your impressions of what you see around you** Many writers carry their journals with them everywhere so they can record interesting or unusual things they observe. If you get into the habit of recording what you see, you can later incorporate your observations into essays or other pieces of writing.

- **Your personal life** Although you may not want to record the intimate details of your life if your instructor plans to read your journal, such entries are very common in private journals. Writing about relationships with family and friends, personal problems, hopes and dreams—all the details of your life—can help you develop a better understanding of yourself and others.

● Practice 1-11

Buy a notebook to use as a journal. (Your instructor may require a specific size and format, particularly if journals are going to be collected at some point, or he or she may ask you to keep your journal in a computer file.) Find a regular time when you can write for fifteen minutes or so in your journal—during your lunch break, for example, or when you check your email. Make entries daily or several times a week, depending on your schedule and your instructor's requirements. For your first journal entry, write down your thoughts about the topic you have been working on in this chapter: the purpose of college.

Identifying Your Main Idea and Writing a Topic Sentence

When you think you have enough material to write about, it is time for you to identify your **main idea**—the idea you will develop in your paragraph.

To find a main idea for your paragraph, begin by looking over what you have already written. As you read through your freewriting, brainstorming, clustering, or journal entries, look for the central idea that your material seems to support. The sentence that states this main idea will be your paragraph's **topic sentence**.

The topic sentence is usually the first sentence of your paragraph. The topic sentence of your paragraph is important because it tells both you and your readers what the focus of your paragraph will be. An effective topic sentence has three characteristics.

1. **A topic sentence is a complete sentence.** There is a difference between a *topic* and a *topic sentence*. The **topic** is what the paragraph is about. A **topic sentence**, however, is a complete sentence that includes a subject and a verb and expresses a complete thought.

Topic	Community service
Topic sentence	Community service should be required for college students.

2. **A topic sentence is more than just an announcement of what you plan to write about.** A topic sentence makes a point about the topic the paragraph discusses.

Announcement	In this paragraph, I will explain my ideas about community service.
Topic sentence	My ideas about community service changed after I started to volunteer at a homeless shelter.

3. **A topic sentence presents an idea that can be discussed in a single paragraph.** If your topic sentence is too broad, you will not be able to discuss it in just one paragraph. If your topic sentence is too narrow, you will not be able to say much about it.

Topic sentence too broad	Students all over the country participate in community service, making important contributions to their communities.

| **Topic sentence too narrow** | Our school has a community service requirement for graduation. |
| **Effective topic sentence** | Requiring community service for college students will accomplish three goals. |

When Stella Drew reviewed her notes, she saw that they focused on both the value of doing community service and the problems it presents. She thought her paragraph could include both these ideas if she wrote about how community service requires time and commitment but is still worthwhile. She made this point in a topic sentence.

Community service takes time, but it is so important that college students should be required to do it.

When Stella thought about how to express her topic sentence, she knew it had to be a complete sentence, not just a topic, and that it would have to make a point, not just announce what she planned to write about. When she reread the topic sentence she had written, she felt confident that it did these things. Her topic sentence was neither too broad nor too narrow, and it made a statement she could support in a paragraph.

● Practice 1-12

Read the following items. Put a check mark next to each one that has all three characteristics of an effective topic sentence.

Examples:

The common cold. ____

Many people are convinced that large doses of vitamin C will prevent the common cold. ___✔___

1. Climate change, a crisis for our cities. ____

2. High school science courses should teach students about climate change. ____

3. In this paragraph, I will discuss global warming. ____

4. Buying books online. ____

5. College students can save money by buying their textbooks online. ____

● Practice 1-13

Decide whether each of the following statements could be an effective topic sentence for a paragraph. If a sentence is too broad, write "too broad" in the blank following the sentence. If the sentence is too narrow, write "too narrow" in the blank. If the sentence is an effective topic sentence, write "OK" in the blank.

> **Example:** Thanksgiving always falls on the fourth Thursday in
> November. _too narrow_

1. Wireless computer networks are changing the world. _____

2. There are five computer terminals in the campus library. _____

3. Our school should set up a campus-wide wireless network. _____

4. Soccer is not as popular in the United States as it is in Europe. _____

5. Americans enjoy watching many types of sporting events on television. _____

6. One quality distinguishes a good coach from a bad one. _____

7. Vegetarianism is a healthy way of life. _____

8. Uncooked spinach has fourteen times as much iron as steak does. _____

9. Fast-food restaurants are finally meeting the needs of vegetarians. _____

10. Medical schools in this country have high standards. _____

● Practice 1-14

In Practices 1-4, 1-7, and 1-10, you practiced freewriting, brainstorming, and clustering. Now, you are ready to write a paragraph in response to your Focus on Writing activity.

> What do you think is the primary purpose of college—to give students a general education or to prepare them for specific careers?

Your first step is to find a main idea for your paragraph. Look over the work you have done so far, and try to decide what central idea your material can best support. On the lines below, write a topic sentence that expresses this idea.

Your topic sentence: _____

_____

STEP 2: ORGANIZING

1e

Choosing Supporting Points

After you have stated your paragraph's main idea in a topic sentence, review your notes again. This time, look for specific **evidence** (details and examples) to support your main idea. Write or type your topic sentence at the top of a blank page. Then, as you review your notes, list all the points you think you might be able to use to support this topic sentence.

Stella chose several points from her notes to write about. After she read through her list of points, she crossed out three that she thought would not support her topic sentence.

Main idea: Community service takes time, but it is so important that college students should be required to do it.

- ~~Community service helps people.~~
- ~~Some community service activities could be boring.~~
- Community service can help the world.
- Community service helps the community.
- College students are busy.
- Community service takes a lot of time.
- ~~Community service might not relate to students' majors.~~
- Community service can be upsetting or depressing.
- Community service can be part of a student's education.

● Practice 1-15

Now, continue your work on your own paragraph about the purpose of a college education. Reread your freewriting, brainstorming, and clustering, and list the points you believe can best support your topic sentence.

Your topic sentence:

_____

_____

_____

Your supporting points:

● _____

● _____

● _____

● _____

● _____

Check carefully to make sure each point on your list supports your topic sentence. Cross out any points that do not.

1f   Arranging Your Supporting Points

Your next step is to arrange your supporting points in the order in which you plan to discuss them in your paragraph.

When she read over her list of supporting points, Stella saw that she had two different kinds of points: some points dealt with the *problems* of doing community service, and other points dealt with the *advantages* of doing community service. When she arranged her points, she decided to group them into two categories under the headings "problems" and "advantages," rearranging the points within the two categories in the order in which she planned to discuss them.

Topic sentence: Community service takes time, but it is so important that college students should be required to do it.

Problems
- Community service takes a lot of time.
- College students are busy.
- Community service can be upsetting or depressing.

Advantages
- Community service helps the community.
- Community service can be part of a student's education.
- Community service can help the world.

● **Practice 1-16.**

Look over the supporting points you listed in Practice 1-15. Decide which of your points are about going to college to get an education and which are about going to college to prepare for a career. Then, arrange your supporting points under the two headings below in the order in which you plan to write about them.

Getting a general education:

● _____

● _____

● _____

● _____

Preparing for a career:

● _____

● _____

● _____

● _____

STEP 3: DRAFTING

1g

Drafting Your Paragraph

Once you have written a topic sentence for your paragraph, selected the points you will discuss, and arranged them in the order in which you plan to write about them, you are ready to write a first draft.

In a **first draft**, your goal is to get your ideas down in writing. Begin your paragraph with a topic sentence that states the paragraph's main idea. Then, following the list of points you plan to discuss, write or type without worrying about correct wording, spelling, or punctuation. If a new idea—one that is not on your list—occurs to you, write it down. Don't worry about whether it fits with your other ideas. Your goal is not to produce a perfect piece of writing but simply to create a draft. (Later on, when you revise, you will have a chance to rethink ideas and rework sentences.)

Because you will be making changes to this draft—adding or crossing out words and phrases, reordering ideas and details, clarifying connections between ideas, and so on—you should leave wide margins, skip lines, and leave extra blank lines in places where you might need to add material. Feel free to be messy and to cross out; remember, the only person who will see this draft is you. (If you are typing, you can use large type or leave extra space between lines to make the draft easier to revise.)

When you have finished your draft, don't make any changes right away. Take a break (overnight if possible), and think about something—anything—else. Then, return to your draft, and read it with a fresh eye.

Here is the first draft of Stella's paragraph on the topic of community service for college students.

Why Community Service Should Be Required

Community service takes time, but it is so important that college students should be required to do it. When college students do community service, they volunteer their time to do good for someone or for the community. Working in a soup kitchen, raking leaves for senior citizens, and reading to children are all examples of community service. Community service can require long hours and take time away from studying and jobs. It can force students to deal with unpleasant situations, but overall it is rewarding and helpful to others. Community service is good for the community and can be more fulfilling than playing sports or participating in clubs. Community service can be an important part of a college education. Students can even discover what they want to do with their lives. Community service can make the world a better place.

First draft

● Practice 1-17

Reread Stella's draft paragraph. If you were advising her, what would you suggest that she change in her draft? What would you tell her to add? What do you think she should cross out? Discuss your ideas with your class or in a small group.

● **Practice 1-18**

Write a draft of your paragraph about the purpose of a college education, using the material you came up with for Practices 1-14 and 1-15. Be sure your paragraph states your main idea and supports it with specific examples and details. If you handwrite your draft, leave wide margins and skip lines; if you type your draft, leave extra space between lines. When you are finished, give your paragraph a title.

STEP 4: TESTING

1h   TESTing Your Paragraph

When you have finished your draft, the first thing you should do is "test" what you have written to make sure it includes all the elements of an effective paragraph. You do this by asking yourself the following four **TEST** questions.

Highlight: TESTing Your Paragraph

▧ **Topic sentence**—Does your paragraph have a topic sentence that states its main idea?

▧ **Evidence**—Does your paragraph include examples and details that support your topic sentence?

▧ **Summary statement**—Does your paragraph end with a statement that reinforces its main idea?

▧ **Transitions**—Does your paragraph include transitional words and phrases that show readers how your ideas are related?

As you reread your paragraph, **TEST** it to identify the four elements of an effective paragraph. If your paragraph includes these four basic elements, you are off to a very good start. If it does not, you will need to add whatever is missing.

When Stella reread her draft, she used the **TEST** strategy to help her take a quick inventory of her paragraph.

- She decided that her topic sentence clearly stated her main idea.
- She thought she had enough evidence to support her topic sentence.
- She noticed that her paragraph had no summary statement.
- She realized she needed to add transitions to connect her ideas.

● **Practice 1-19**

TEST your draft paragraph for the four elements of an effective paragraph: **T**opic sentence, **E**vidence, **S**ummary statement, and **T**ransitions. (If any elements are missing, you will have to add them.)

STEP 5: REVISING AND EDITING

1i   Revising Your Paragraph

Once you have **TEST**ed your paragraph to see if it is complete, you are ready to revise it.

Revision is the process of reseeing, rethinking, reevaluating, and rewriting your work. Revision usually involves more than substituting one word for another or correcting a comma here and there. Often, it means moving sentences, adding words and phrases, or even changing the direction or emphasis of your ideas. To get the most out of the revision process, begin by carefully rereading your draft. Then, use the checklist below to guide your revision.

Self-Assessment Checklist: Revising Your Paragraph	☐ Is your topic sentence clearly worded?
	☐ Do you have enough evidence (details and examples) to support your paragraph's main idea, or do you need to look back at your notes or try to think of additional supporting evidence?
	☐ Should you cross out any examples or details?
	☐ Do you need to explain anything more fully or more clearly?
	☐ Do your transitional words and phrases show readers how your ideas are connected?

Self-Assessment Checklist: Revising Your Paragraph continued	☐ Does every sentence say what you mean? ☐ Can you combine any sentences to make your writing flow more smoothly? ☐ Should you move any sentences? ☐ Are all your words necessary, or can you cut some? ☐ Should you change any words to make them more specific? ☐ Does your summary statement clearly reinforce the main idea of your paragraph?

Guided by the Self-Assessment Checklist above, Stella revised her paragraph, writing her changes in by hand on her typed draft.

Why Community Service Should Be Required

Community service takes time, but it is so important that college students should be required to do it. When college students do community service, they ~~volunteer their time to~~ do good for someone or for the community. ~~Working~~ *For example, they work* in a soup kitchen, ~~raking~~ *rake* leaves for senior citizens, ~~and reading~~ *or read* to children ~~are all examples of community service. Community service~~ *These activities* can require long hours and take time away from studying and jobs. ~~It can force students~~ *important things like* *However, community service is worth the time it takes.* ~~to deal with unpleasant situations, but overall it is rewarding and helpful to others.~~ Community service ~~is good for the community and~~ can be more fulfilling than playing sports or participating in clubs. *for students* *other college activities, such as* Community service can *also* be an important part of a college education. Students can even discover what they want to do with their lives. *learn about themselves, about their communities, and about their world, and* *they can* *Finally,* ~~C~~ommunity service can make the world a better place. *For all these reasons, community service should be a required part of the college curriculum.*

Revised draft

When she revised, Stella did not worry about being neat. She crossed out material, added ideas, and made changes in her words and sentences. When she felt her revision was complete, she was ready to move on to edit her paragraph.

1j

Editing Your Paragraph

When you **edit**, you check for correct grammar, punctuation, mechanics, and spelling. You also proofread carefully for errors that your computer spell checker may not identify. In addition, you check to make sure that you have indented the first sentence of your paragraph and that every sentence begins with a capital letter and ends with a period.

Remember, editing is a vital last step in the writing process. Many readers will not take your ideas seriously if your paragraph contains grammatical or mechanical errors. You can use the checklist below to guide your editing.

Self-Assessment Checklist: Editing Your Paragraph	
☐	Are all your sentences complete and grammatically correct?
☐	Do all your subjects and verbs agree?
☐	Have you used correct verb tenses?
☐	Are commas used where they are required?
☐	Have you used apostrophes correctly?
☐	Have you used other punctuation marks correctly?
☐	Have you used capital letters where they are required?
☐	Are all words spelled correctly?

For help with grammar, punctuation, mechanics, and spelling, see Units 6–7 of this text.

When Stella edited her paragraph, she checked her grammar, punctuation, mechanics, and spelling and looked carefully for typos. The final typed version of her paragraph appears on the next page.

Why Community Service Should Be Required

Topic sentence ———

    Community service takes time, but it is so important that college students should be required to do it. When college students do community service, they do good for someone or for the community. For example, they work in a soup kitchen, rake leaves for senior citizens, or read to children. These activities can require long hours and take time away from

Evidence (details and examples) ———

important things like studying and jobs. However, community service is worth the time it takes. Community service can be more fulfilling for students than other college activities, such as playing sports or participating in clubs. Community service can also be an important part of a college education. Students can learn about themselves, about their communities, and about their world, and they can even discover what they want to do with their lives. Finally, community service can make the

Summary statement ———

world a better place. For all these reasons, community service should be a required part of the college curriculum.

Transitions (boxed) ———

● **Practice 1-20**

Reread the final draft of Stella's paragraph about community service for college students (above), and compare it with her first draft (p. 20). Then, answer the following questions about her revision.

1. Did Stella revise her paragraph's topic sentence? If so, why? If not, why not? Do you agree with her decision?

2. Did Stella add any new material to her paragraph? Can you think of any new points she *should* have added?

3. What did Stella cross out? Why do you think she deleted this material? Do you think she should cross out any additional material?

4. Why do you think Stella added "For example" (line 3), "However" (line 6), and "also" (line 9) to her final draft?

5. Why do you think Stella added the word "Finally" in her next-to-last sentence?

6. In her revision, Stella added a sentence at the end of the paragraph. Do you think this sentence is necessary? Why or why not?

● Practice 1-21

Generally speaking, what kinds of changes did Stella make as she revised her paragraph? Which do you think are her most effective changes? Why? Do you think she needs to make any additional changes? Discuss your reactions to Stella's revised paragraph with your class or in a small group of students.

● Practice 1-22

Use the Self-Assessment Checklist on pages 22–23 to evaluate the paragraph you drafted for Practice 1-18. What additions can you make to support your topic sentence more fully? Should anything be crossed out because it does not support your main idea? Can anything be stated more clearly?

Now, revise your draft. Cross out unnecessary material and material you want to rewrite, and add new and rewritten material between the lines and in the margins. After you finish your revision, edit your paragraph, checking grammar, punctuation, mechanics, and spelling—and look carefully for typos. As you edit, use the Self-Assessment Checklist on page 24 as a guide.

Review Checklist: Writing a Paragraph

- ☐ Learning to write a paragraph is an important step in becoming a competent writer. (See 1A.)
- ☐ Before you start to write, consider your assignment, purpose, and audience. (See 1B.)
- ☐ Use freewriting, brainstorming, clustering, and journal writing to help you find ideas. (See 1C.)
- ☐ Identify your main idea and write a topic sentence. (See 1D.)
- ☐ Choose points to support your topic sentence. (See 1E.)
- ☐ Arrange your supporting points in a logical order. (See 1F.)
- ☐ Write a first draft of your paragraph. (See 1G.)
- ☐ **TEST** your paragraph (See 1H.)
- ☐ Revise your paragraph. (See 1I.)
- ☐ Edit your paragraph. (See 1J.)

Chapter 2

TESTing Your Paragraphs

As you learned in Chapter 1, it is a good idea to **TEST** every paragraph as soon as you finish drafting. Testing will tell you whether or not your paragraph includes all the elements of an effective paragraph.

- **T**opic sentence
- **E**vidence
- **S**ummary statement
- **T**ransitions

If you **TEST** the following paragraph, you will see that it contains all four elements of an effective paragraph.

WORD POWER
innovation something newly invented; a new way of doing something

Although most people do not know it, the modern roller coaster got its start in Coney Island in Brooklyn, New York. First, in 1888, the Flip Flap Railway, which featured a circular loop, was built. The coaster was the first to go upside down, but it frequently injured riders' necks. Next, in 1901, the Loop-the-Loop, which was safer than the Flip Flap Railway, was built. Then, from 1884 through the 1930s, over thirty roller coasters were constructed in Coney Island. Finally, in 1927, the most famous roller coaster in history, the Cyclone, was built at a cost of over $100,000. Although it began operating over eighty years ago, it is still the standard by which all roller coasters are measured. It has steep drops, a lot of momentum, and only lap belts to hold riders in their seats. Still in operation, the Cyclone is the most successful ride in Coney Island history. It is the last survivor of the wooden roller coasters that once drew crowds to Coney Island. With their many innovations, Coney Island's roller coasters paved the way for the high-tech roller coasters in amusement parks today.

Focus on Writing

The picture on the opposite page shows rows of wooden mail boxes, one kind of filing system. How do you organize the papers (schoolwork, bills, important records, notes and reminders, and so on) in your life? Does everything have its place, or do you arrange papers more randomly? Look at the picture, and write about how you organize the papers that are part of your life.

Using a Topic Sentence to Unify Your Paragraph

The first thing you do when you **TEST** a paragraph is look at the **topic sentence (T)**. An effective paragraph focuses on a single main idea, and the topic sentence states that main idea.

A paragraph is **unified** when all the paragraph's sentences support the main idea stated in the topic sentence. A paragraph is not unified when its sentences wander from the main idea stated in the topic sentence. When you revise, you can make your paragraphs unified by crossing out sentences that do not support your topic sentence.

The following paragraph is not unified because it contains sentences that do not support the paragraph's topic sentence. (These sentences have been crossed out.)

> The weak economy has led many people to move away from the rural Ohio community where I was raised. Over the years, farmland has become more and more expensive. Years ago, a family could buy each of its children twenty-five acres on which they could start farming. Today, the price of land is so high that the average farmer cannot afford to buy this amount of land, and those who choose not to farm have few alternatives. ~~After I graduate, I intend to return to my town and get a job there. Even though many factories have moved out of the area, I think I will be able to get a job. My uncle owns a hardware store, and he told me that after I graduate, he will teach me the business. I think I can contribute something to both the business and the community.~~ Young people just cannot get good jobs anymore. Factories have moved out of the area and taken with them the jobs that many young people used to get after high school. As a result, many eighteen-year-olds have no choice but to move away to find employment.

The following revised paragraph is unified. It discusses only the idea that is stated in the topic sentence.

> <mark>The weak economy has led many people to move away from the rural Ohio community where I was raised.</mark> Over the years, farmland has become more and more expensive. Years ago, a family could buy each of its children twenty-five acres on which they could start farming. Today, the price of land is so high that the average farmer cannot afford to buy this amount of land, and those who choose not to farm have few alternatives. Young people just cannot get good jobs

T E S T

Topic Sentence
Evidence
Summary Statement
Transitions

anymore. Factories have moved out of the area and taken with them the jobs that many young people used to get after high school. As a result, many eighteen-year-olds have no choice but to move away to find employment.

● **Practice 2-1**

The following paragraphs are not unified because some sentences do not support the topic sentence. First, underline the topic sentence in each paragraph. Then, cross out any sentences in each paragraph that do not support the topic sentence.

1. The one thing I could not live without is my car. In addition to attending school full time, I hold down two part-time jobs that are many miles from each other, from where I live, and from school. Even though my car is almost twelve years old and has close to 120,000 miles on it, I couldn't manage without it. I'm thinking about buying a new car, and I always check the ads online, but I haven't found anything I want that I can afford. If my old car breaks down, I guess I'll have to, though. I couldn't live without my digital voice recorder because I use it to record all the class lectures I attend. Then I can play them back while I'm driving or during my breaks at work. Three nights a week and on weekends, I work as a counselor at a home for teenagers with problems, and my other job is in the tire department at Sears. Without my car, I'd be lost.

2. Studies conducted by Dr. Leonard Eron over a period of thirty years suggest that the more television violence young boys are exposed to, the more aggressive they are as teenagers and adults. In 1960, Eron questioned parents about how they treated their sons at home as well as about how much television they watched. There is more violence on television today than there was then. Ten years later, he interviewed these families again and discovered that whether or not teenage sons were aggressive depended less on how they had been treated by their parents than on how much violent television programming they had watched as children. Returning in 1990, he found that these same young men, now in their thirties, were still more likely to be aggressive and to commit crimes. Researchers estimate that a child today is likely to watch 100,000 violent acts on television before finishing elementary school.

3. Libraries today hold a lot more than just books. Of course, books still outnumber anything else on the shelves, but more and more libraries

are expanding to include other specialized services. For example, many libraries now offer extensive collections of CDs, ranging from classical music to jazz to country to rock. In addition, many have large collections of vintage movies on videotape. Some libraries even stock the most recent DVDs. However, most people probably get more movies from Netflix or pay-per-view than from libraries. In addition, the children's section often has games and toys that young patrons can play with in the library or even check out. Most important, libraries offer free access to computerized databases, which provide much more detailed and up-to-date information than print sources. These databases enable even the smallest libraries to access as much information as large libraries do. People who don't know how to use a computer are going to be out of luck.

● Practice 2-2

The following paragraph has no topic sentence. Read it carefully, and then choose the most appropriate topic sentence from the list that follows the paragraph.

Some people keep all the books they have ever read. They stack old paperbacks on tables, on the floor, and on their nightstands. Other people save magazines or newspapers. Still others save movie-ticket stubs or postcards. Serious collectors save all sorts of things—including old toys, guns, knives, plates, figurines, maps, stamps, baseball cards, comic books, beer bottles, playbills, movie posters, dolls, clocks, old televisions, political campaign buttons, and even coffee mugs. Some things—such as matchbook covers or restaurant menus—may have value only to the people who collect them. Other items—such as stamps or coins—may be worth a lot of money. A very few collectors concentrate on items that are so large that housing a collection can present some real challenges. For example, people who collect automobiles or antique furniture may have to rent a garage or even a warehouse in which to store their possessions.

Put a check mark next to the topic sentence that best expresses the main idea of the paragraph above.

1. Everyone, regardless of age or occupation, seems to have the urge to collect. ____

2. Collecting things like matchbooks and restaurant menus can be fun, but collecting jewelry or coins can be very profitable. ____

3. The things people collect are as different as the people who collect them. ____

4. In spite of the time and expense, collecting can be an interesting and fulfilling hobby. ____

5. Before you begin to collect things as a hobby, you should know what you are getting into. ____

● Practice 2-3

The following paragraphs do not have topic sentences. Think of a topic sentence that expresses each paragraph's main idea, and write it on the lines above the paragraphs.

Example: *Possible answer: Rock and roll originated in African-American*
music but was reinterpreted by white performers.

Early 1950s African-American musicians included performers such as Johnny Ace, Big Joe Turner, and Ruth Brown. Groups like the Drifters and the Clovers were also popular. By the mid-1950s, white performers such as Bill Haley and the Comets, Jerry Lee Lewis, and Elvis Presley were imitating African-American music. Their songs had a beat and lyrics that appealed to a white audience. Eventually, this combination of black and white musical styles became known as rock and roll.

1. _____

The Japanese word *manga* was first used in the 1700s to describe illustrated books. Early manga comics first started appearing in the late 1800s, when artists working in Europe began to influence those working in Japan. These early manga were similar to French and British political cartoons of the day. Modern-style manga, which were first produced in Japan during the U.S. occupation in the late 1940s, looked like American comic books. The first post–World War II manga focused on stereotypically male topics, such as space travel and sports. Today, there are many types of manga, including romance, horror, mystery, and comedy, and they appeal to both adults and children around the world.

2. _____

_____

_____

First, you have to find a suitable job to apply for. Once you decide to apply, you have to put together your résumé and send it to your potential employer. Then, when you are invited in for an interview, you need to decide what you are going to wear. At the interview, you need to speak slowly and clearly and answer all questions directly and honestly. After the interview, you need to send a note to the person who interviewed you, thanking him or her. Finally, if everything goes well, you will get an email or a phone call offering you the job.

3. _____

_____

_____

There are no written records left by the Native Americans themselves. Most of the early European settlers in North America were more interested in staying alive than in writing about the Native Americans. In addition, as the westward expansion took place, the Europeans encountered the Native Americans in stages, not all at once. Also, the Native Americans spoke at least fifty-eight different languages, which made it difficult for the Europeans to speak with them. Most important, by the time scholars decided to study Native American culture, many of the tribes no longer existed. Disease and war had wiped them out.

● **Practice 2-4**

Read the following topic sentences. Then, write a paragraph that develops the main idea that is stated in each topic sentence. After you finish, check to make sure that all the sentences in your paragraph support your topic sentence.

1. On my first day as president, I would do three things.

2. My parents prepared me for life by teaching me a few important lessons.

3. Planning a successful party is easy if you follow a few simple steps.

2b Using Evidence to Support Your Paragraph's Main Idea

The next thing you do when you **TEST** a paragraph is to make sure you have enough **evidence (E)**—specific examples and details—to support the main idea stated in your topic sentence.

The following paragraph does not include enough evidence to support the paragraph's main idea.

> Although pit bulls have a bad reputation, they actually make good pets. Part of their problem is that they can look frightening. Actually, however, pit bulls are no worse than other breeds of dogs. Even so, the bad publicity they get has given them a bad reputation. Pit bulls really do not deserve their bad reputation, though. Contrary to popular opinion, pit bulls can (and do) make friendly, affectionate, and loyal pets.

The following revised paragraph includes plenty of evidence (details and examples) to support the topic sentence.

TEST
- Topic Sentence
- Evidence
- Summary Statement
- Transitions

> Although pit bulls have a bad reputation, they actually make good pets. Part of their problem is that they can look frightening. Their wide, powerful jaws, short muscular legs, and large teeth are ideally suited for fighting, and they were bred for this purpose. In addition, some pit bulls—especially males—can be very aggressive toward both people and other dogs. Actually, however, pit bulls are no worse than other breeds of dogs. As several recent newspaper articles have pointed out, the number of reported bites by pit bulls is no greater than the number of bites by other breeds. In fact, some breeds, such as cocker spaniels, bite more frequently than pit bulls. Even so, the bad publicity they get has given them a bad reputation. The problem is that whenever a pit bull attacks someone, the incident is reported on the evening news. Contrary to popular opinion, pit bulls can (and do) make friendly, affectionate, and loyal pets.

Note: Length alone is no guarantee that a paragraph includes enough supporting evidence. A long paragraph that consists of one generalization after another will still not include enough support for the topic sentence.

● Practice 2-5

Underline the specific supporting evidence in each of the following paragraphs.

1. Hearing people have some mistaken ideas about the deaf community. First, some hearing adults think that all deaf people consider themselves disabled and would trade anything not to be "handicapped." Hearing people do not realize that many deaf people do not consider themselves handicapped and are proud to be part of the deaf community, which has its own language, customs, and culture. Second, many hearing people think that all deaf people read lips, so there is no need to learn sign language to communicate with them. However, lip reading—or speech reading, as deaf people call the practice—is difficult. Not all hearing people say the same words in the same way, and facial expressions can also change the meaning of the words. If hearing people make more of an attempt to understand the deaf culture, communication between them will improve.

2. In 1996, the National Basketball Association (NBA) approved a women's professional basketball league. Within fifteen months, eight teams had been formed, four in the Eastern Conference and four in the Western Conference. Next, the teams began to draft players for these teams and to select a logo and uniforms. The final logo selected, a red, white, and blue shield, showed the silhouette of a woman player dribbling the ball, with the letters "WNBA" above her. The uniforms consisted of shorts and jerseys in the colors of the different teams. That first season, games were played in the summer when the television sports schedule was lighter so they could be televised during prime time. At the end of that season, the Houston Comets became the first WNBA champions. Today, the WNBA consists of thirteen teams that each play thirty-four regular-season games televised to audiences worldwide.

3. One of the largest celebrations of the passage of young girls into womanhood occurs in Latin American and Hispanic cultures. This event is called La Quinceañera, or the fifteenth year. It acknowledges that a young woman is now of marriageable age. The day usually begins with a Mass of Thanksgiving. The young woman wears a full-length white or pastel-colored dress and is attended by fourteen friends and relatives who serve as maids of honor and escorts. Her parents and godparents surround her at the foot of the altar. When the Mass ends, other young relatives give small gifts to those who attended, while the young woman places a bouquet of flowers on the altar of the Virgin. Following the Mass is an elaborate party, with dancing, cake, and toasts. Finally, to end the evening, the young woman dances a waltz with her favorite escort. For young Hispanic women, the Quinceañera is an important milestone.

● Practice 2-6

Provide two or three specific examples or details to support each of the following topic sentences.

1. When it comes to feeding a family, there are several alternatives to fast food.

    ● _____

    ● _____

    ● _____

2. A romantic relationship with a coworker can create some serious problems.

    ● _____

    ● _____

    ● _____

3. When scheduling classes, you need to keep several things in mind.

    ● _____

    ● _____

    ● _____

4. Consumers should take the following steps to protect themselves from identity theft.

    ● _____

    ● _____

    ● _____

5. Choosing the right cell phone was harder than I thought it would be.

    ● _____

    ● _____

    ● _____

● Practice 2-7

The two paragraphs that follow do not include enough supporting evidence. Suggest some examples and details that might help each writer develop his or her ideas more fully.

1. Anyone in a supermarket checkout line can get the latest news on celebrities' misbehavior, which is typically given a lot more attention than their good deeds. Cheating, drug addiction, and crime among the rich and famous are all on display. Supermarket tabloids report rumors as if they were confirmed facts. Celebrities' bad deeds get the most press because they sell the most papers.

2. The Latina cartoon character Dora the Explorer has been a favorite of preschoolers and their parents since 1999. She has many traits that make her appealing. Even though she was already incredibly popular, Dora's creators decided to change her appearance in 2009. Image makeovers such as this are not always successful. Time will tell if the creators made the right choice in changing Dora's looks.

2c   Using a Summary Statement to Reinforce Your Paragraph's Unity

The third thing you do when you **TEST** a paragraph is to make sure it ends with a **summary statement (S)** — a sentence that reinforces your main idea. By reminding readers what your paragraph is about, a summary statement helps to further **unify** your paragraph.

The following paragraph has no summary statement.

> Overpopulation is one of the biggest concerns for scientists. In 1900, there were 1.6 billion people on Earth, a quarter of today's population. At that time, life expectancy was also much shorter than it is now. By 2000, the world's population had grown to over 6 billion, and today, the average life expectancy worldwide is almost sixty-five years. The low death rate, combined with a high birth rate, is adding the equivalent of one new Germany to the world's population each year. According to a United Nations study, if present trends continue, by 2050 the world's population will be between 7.3 and 10.5 billion—so large that much of the world may be either malnourished or starving.

The summary statement in the following revised paragraph reinforces the paragraph's main idea—and brings the paragraph to a close.

T E S T

Topic Sentence

Evidence

Summary
Statement

Transitions

Overpopulation is one of the biggest concerns for scientists. In 1900, there were 1.6 million people on Earth, a quarter of today's population. At that time, life expectancy was also much shorter than it is now. By 2000, the world's population had grown to over 6 billion, and today, the average life expectancy worldwide is almost sixty-five years. The low death rate, combined with a high birth rate, is adding the equivalent of one new Germany to the world's population each year. According to a United Nations study, if present trends continue, by 2050 the world's population will be between 7.3 and 10.5 billion—so large that much of the world may be either malnourished or starving. Given these increases, it is no wonder that scientists who study population are worried.

● Practice 2-8

Read the following two paragraphs, which do not include summary statements. Then, on the lines below each paragraph, write a summary statement that adds unity to the paragraph by reinforcing the main idea stated in the topic sentence. Be careful not to use the same wording as the topic sentence.

1. Founded more than fifty years ago, NASCAR has become one of the most successful spectator sports in the world. In December 1947, Bill France formed the National Association for Stock Car Auto Racing (NASCAR). The first NASCAR race was held at Daytona Beach's auto racecourse in 1948. From this modest start, France turned NASCAR into a highly successful business. Attendance grew 8.2 percent during 1997, and 2,102,000 fans attended the thirty-one NASCAR events in 1998. This was the first time that NASCAR attendance topped the two million mark. Then, in 2007, NASCAR negotiated a new multimillion-dollar television deal with Fox Sports / Speed, TNT, and ABC / ESPN. As a result, these networks now televise NASCAR's most popular events.

_____

_____

2. The best way to deal with scrap tires that are worn out is to recycle them. Since the early 1990s, there has been an enormous growth in the demand for recycled tire rubber—"crumb rubber"—particularly in North America. The new products made from this material are often better than similar products made of conventional materials. For example, recycled tires are used to make mulch that serves as ground

cover in playgrounds. This material is safer because it cushions falls, and it is cheaper than gravel or wood chips. Material from recycled tires can also be mixed with asphalt to pave roads. The new surface is less expensive and more durable than surfaces made from conventional asphalt. Finally, recycled tires can be used to produce high-volume, low-tech products, such as livestock mats, railroad crossings, removable speed bumps, and athletic mats.

2d Using Transitions to Add Coherence to Your Paragraph

The final thing you do when you **TEST** a paragraph is make sure the paragraph includes **transitions (T)** that connect ideas in a clear, logical order.

Transitional words and phrases create **coherence** by indicating how ideas are connected in a paragraph—for example, in *time order*, *spatial order*, or *logical order*. By signaling the order of ideas in a paragraph, these words and phrases make it easier for readers to follow your discussion.

- You use **time** signals to show readers the order in which events occurred.

   In 1883, my great-grandfather came to this country from Russia.

- You use **spatial** signals to show readers how people, places, and things stand in relation to one another. For example, you can move from top to bottom, from near to far, from right to left, and so on.

   Next to my bed is a bookcase that also serves as a room divider.

- You use **logical** signals to show readers how your ideas are connected. For example, you can move from the least important idea to the most important idea or from the least familiar idea to the most familiar idea.

   Certain strategies can help you do well in college. First, you should learn to manage your time effectively.

Because transitional words and phrases create coherence, a paragraph without them is difficult to understand. You can avoid this problem by checking to make sure you have included all the words and phrases that you need to link the ideas in your paragraph.

Frequently Used Transitional Words and Phrases

Some Words and Phrases That Signal Time Order

after	finally	phrases that
afterward	later	include dates
at first	next	(for example,
before	now	"In June,"
during	soon	"In 1904")
earlier	then	
eventually	today	

Some Words and Phrases That Signal Spatial Order

above	in front	on the left
behind	inside	on the right
below	in the center	on top
beside	near	over
in back	next to	under
in between	on the bottom	

Some Words and Phrases That Signal Logical Order

also	in fact
although	last
as a result	moreover
consequently	next
first . . . second . . . third	not only . . . but also
for example	one . . . another
for instance	similarly
furthermore	the least important
however	the most important
in addition	therefore

The following paragraph has no transitional words and phrases to link ideas.

During his lifetime, Jim Thorpe faced many obstacles. Thorpe was born in 1888, the son of an Irish father and a Native American mother. He was sent to the Carlisle Indian School in Pennsylvania. "Pop" Warner, the legendary coach at Carlisle, discovered Thorpe. Thorpe left Carlisle to play baseball for two seasons in the newly formed East Carolina minor league. He returned to Carlisle, played football, and was named to the All-American team. Thorpe went to the Olympic games in Stockholm, where he won two gold medals. Thorpe's career took a dramatic turn for the worse when a sportswriter who had seen him play baseball in North Carolina exposed him as a professional. The Amateur Athletic Union stripped him of his records and medals. Thorpe died in 1953. The International Olympic Committee returned Thorpe's Olympic medals to his family in 1982. Ironically, only in death was Thorpe able to overcome the difficulties that had frustrated him while he was alive.

The following revised paragraph is coherent because it includes transitional words and phrases that connect its ideas.

During his lifetime, Jim Thorpe faced many obstacles. Thorpe was born in 1888, the son of an Irish father and a Native American mother. In 1904, he was sent to the Carlisle Indian School in Pennsylvania. The next year, "Pop" Warner, the legendary coach at Carlisle, discovered Thorpe. Thorpe left Carlisle in 1909 to play baseball for two seasons in the newly formed East Carolina minor league. In 1912, he returned to Carlisle, played football, and was named to the All-American team. Thorpe then went to the Olympic games in Stockholm, where he won two gold medals. The next year, however, Thorpe's career took a dramatic turn for the worse when a sportswriter who had seen him play baseball in North Carolina exposed him as a professional. As a result, the Amateur Athletic Union stripped him of his records and medals. Thorpe died in 1953. After years of appeals, the International Olympic Committee returned Thorpe's Olympic medals to his family in 1982. Ironically, only in death was Thorpe able to overcome the difficulties that had frustrated him while he was alive.

TEST

▨ Topic Sentence
▨ Evidence
▨ Summary Statement
▨ Transitions

● **Practice 2-9**

Read the following paragraph carefully. Then, select transitional words and phrases from the alphabetized list below, and write them in the appropriate blanks. When you have finished, reread your paragraph to make sure that it is coherent.

Transitions

afterward	last month
before	soon
in front	then
inside	

Spelling bees cans be stressful, but they can also be fun. _____, my sister Elizabeth competed in a televised regional spelling bee. _____ the competition, she and I tried to think of ways to make her less nervous. We decided to arrive early to relax and play games. On the grass _____ of the auditorium, we played leapfrog and read to each other from her favorite book of jokes. _____, I squeezed her hand and reminded her that I would be just a wink or a smile away. She _____ took her place on the stage. _____, she was talking and laughing with the kids around her. As the competition began, she grinned at me across the rows of seats. On each of her turns, she sounded confident as she spelled the words *triumvirate*, *caboose*, and *stethoscope*. _____, she gave me a hug, chattered about the new friends she had met, and said she couldn't wait to do the spelling bee again next year.

● Practice 2-10

The following paragraph includes no transitions. Read the paragraph carefully. Then, after consulting the list of transitional words and phrases on page 41, add appropriate transitional words and phrases to connect the paragraph's ideas in **time order**.

In 1856, my great-great-great-grandparents, Anne and Charles McGinley, faced many hardships to come to the United States. _____ they left Ireland, their landlords, who lived in England, raised the rent on their land so much that my ancestors could not afford to pay it. _____ it took them three years to save the money for passage. _____ they had saved the money, they had to look for a ship that was willing to take them. _____, my great-great-great-grandparents were able to leave. They and their ten children spent four long months on a small ship. Storms, strong tides, and damaged sails made the trip longer than it should have been. _____, in November 1856, they saw land, and two days later they sailed into New York Harbor. _____ they took a train to Baltimore, Maryland, where their cousins lived and where we live today. At that time, they couldn't have known how thankful their descendants would be for their sacrifice.

● **Practice 2-11**

The following paragraph includes no transitions. Read the paragraph carefully. Then, after consulting the list of transitional words and phrases on page 41, add appropriate transitional words and phrases to connect the paragraph's ideas in **spatial order**.

The casinos in Atlantic City are designed to make sure you don't pay attention to anything except gambling. As soon as you walk in the door, you are steered toward the gaming room. _____ of you are the slot machines, blinking and making lots of noise. _____ of the slot machines are the table games — blackjack, roulette, and craps. _____ the gambling area, the ceiling is painted a dull, neutral color. _____ the floor is a carpet that has a complicated pattern that is hard to look at. Both the ceiling and the carpet are designed to make sure that gamblers look just at the games they are playing. _____ of the casino are the bathrooms, and you have to walk through the entire slot machine area if you want to use one. The casino designers are betting that you will not be able to resist stopping to play. As you can see, the design of the casinos makes it difficult for the average person to resist the lure of gambling.

● **Practice 2-12**

The following paragraph includes no transitions. Read the paragraph carefully. Then, after consulting the list of transitional words and phrases on page 41, add appropriate transitional words and phrases to connect the paragraph's ideas in **logical order**.

My high school had three silly rules. The _____ silly rule was that only seniors could go outside the school building for lunch. In spite of this rule, many students went outside to eat because the cafeteria was not big enough to hold everyone. Understanding the problem, the teachers just looked the other way as long as we came back to school on time. The _____ silly rule was that we had to attend

95 percent of all the classes for each course. If we did not, we were supposed to fail. Of course, that rule was never enforced, because if it were, almost every student in the school would have failed everything. The _____ silly rule was that students were not supposed to throw their hats into the air at graduation. At one point in the past, a parent—no one can remember who—complained that a falling hat could poke someone in the eye. _____, graduating classes were told that under no circumstances could they throw their hats into the air. _____, on graduation day, we did what every graduating class has always done—ignored the silly rule and threw our hats into the air.

Focus on Writing: *Revising and Editing*

Review the work you did for the Focus on Writing activity on page 29. Next, **TEST** your paragraph for unity, support, and coherence. Make sure your paragraph includes a topic sentence, evidence (supporting examples and details), a summary statement, and clear transitions between sentences. Then, prepare a final revised and edited draft of your paragraph.

Chapter Review

Editing Practice

TEST each of the following paragraphs for unity, support, and coherence. Begin by underlining the topic sentence. Then, cross out any sentences that do not support the topic sentence. If necessary, add evidence (details and examples) to support the topic sentence. Next, decide whether you need to make any changes to the paragraph's summary statement. (If the paragraph includes no summary statement, write one.) Finally, add transitional words and phrases where they are needed.

1.　　In 1979, a series of mechanical and human errors in Unit 2 of the nuclear generating plant at Three Mile Island, near Harrisburg, Pennsylvania, caused an accident that changed the nuclear power industry. A combination of stuck valves, human error, and poor decisions caused a partial meltdown of the reactor core. Large amounts of radioactive gases were released into the atmosphere. The governor of Pennsylvania evacuated pregnant women from the area. Other residents panicked and left their homes. The nuclear regulatory agency claimed that the situation was not really dangerous and that the released gases were not a health threat. Activists and local residents disagreed with this. The reactor itself remained unusable for more than ten years. Large demonstrations followed the accident, including a rally of more than 200,000 people in New York City. Some people came just because the day was nice. By the mid-1980s, as a result of the accident at Three Mile Island, new construction of nuclear power plants in the United States had stopped.

2.   A survey of cigarette advertisements shows how tobacco companies have consistently encouraged people to smoke. One of the earliest television ads showed two boxes of cigarettes dancing to an advertising jingle. Many people liked these ads. Other advertisements were more subtle. Some were aimed at specific audiences. Marlboro commercials, with the rugged Marlboro man, targeted men. Virginia Slims made an obvious pitch to women by saying, "You've come a long way, baby!" Salem, a mentholated cigarette, showed rural scenes and targeted people who liked the freshness of the outdoors. Kent, with its "micronite filter," appealed to those who were health conscious by claiming that Kent contained less tar and nicotine than any other brand. This claim was not entirely true. Other brands had less tar and nicotine. Merit and other high-tar and high-nicotine cigarettes began to use advertisements that were aimed at minorities. Cigarette companies responded to the national decline in smoking by directing advertising at young people. Camel introduced the cartoon character Joe Camel, which was aimed at teenagers and young adults.

3.   Cities created police forces for a number of reasons. The first reason was status: after the Civil War, it became a status symbol for cities to have a uniformed police force. A police force provided jobs. This meant that politicians were able to reward people who had worked to support them. Police forces made people feel safe. Police officers helped visitors find their way. They took in lost children and sometimes fed the homeless. They directed traffic, enforced health regulations, and provided other services. Police officers kept order. Without a police force, criminals would have made life in nineteenth-century cities unbearable.

Collaborative Activities

1. Working in a group, list the reasons why you think students decide to attend your school. After working together to arrange these reasons in logical order—for example, from least to most important—write a topic sentence that states the main idea these reasons suggest. Finally, on your own, draft a paragraph in which you discuss why students attend your school.

2. In a newspaper or magazine, find an illustration or photograph that includes a lot of details. Then, write a paragraph describing what you see. (Include enough supporting examples so that readers will be able to "see" it almost as clearly as you can.) Decide on a specific spatial order—from top to bottom or from left to right, for example—that makes sense to you, and follow this order as you organize the details in your paragraph. Finally, trade paragraphs with another student, and offer suggestions that could improve his or her paragraph.

3. Bring to class a paragraph from a newspaper or a magazine article or from one of your textbooks. Working in a group, **TEST** each paragraph to see if it includes all the elements of an effective paragraph. If any paragraph does not follow the guidelines outlined in this chapter, work as a group to revise it.

Review Checklist: TESTing Your Paragraphs

☐ A topic sentence states a paragraph's main idea. (See 2A.)

☐ A paragraph should be unified, with all its sentences supporting the paragraph's main idea. (See 2A.)

☐ A paragraph should include enough evidence—details and examples—to support its main idea. (See 2B.)

☐ A paragraph should end with a summary statement that reinforces its main idea and helps to unify the paragraph. (See 2C.)

☐ A paragraph should be coherent, with its sentences arranged in time order, spatial order, or logical order. (See 2D.)

☐ A paragraph should include transitional words and phrases that indicate how ideas are connected. (See 2D.)

Unit Two

Patterns of Paragraph Development

3 Using Exemplification   50
4 Using Narration   62
5 Using Description   72
6 Using Process   82
7 Using Cause and Effect   94
8 Using Comparison and Contrast   106
9 Using Classification   122
10 Using Definition   132
11 Using Argument   144

Chapter 3

Using Exemplification

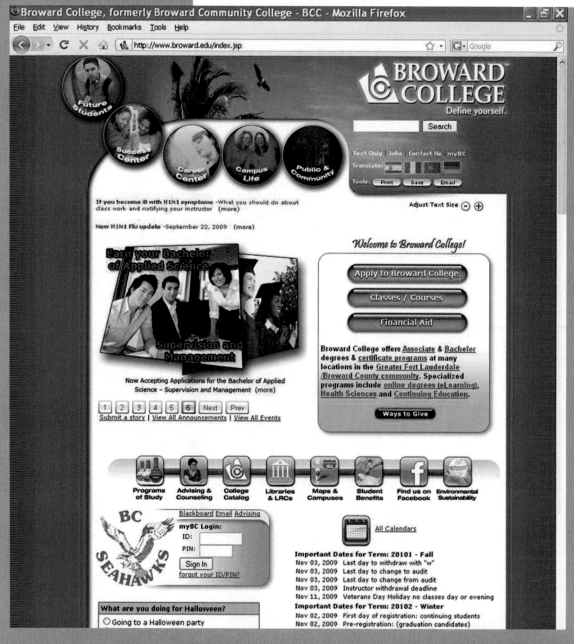

In Chapters 1 and 2, you learned how to write effective paragraphs. In Chapters 3 through 11, you will learn different ways of organizing your ideas within paragraphs. Understanding these patterns of paragraph development can help you organize ideas and become a more effective, more confident writer.

3a   What Is Exemplification?

What do we mean when we tell a friend that an instructor is *good* or that a football team is *bad*? What do we mean when we say that a movie is *boring* or that a particular war was *wrong*? To clarify general statements like these, we use **exemplification**—that is, we give **examples** to illustrate a general idea. In daily conversation and in school, you use specific examples to help explain your ideas.

General Statement	*Specific Examples*
Today is going to be a hard day.	Today is going to be a hard day because I have a history test in the morning and a lab quiz in the afternoon. I also have to go to work an hour earlier than usual.

Focus on Writing

The picture on the opposite page shows the home page of the Broward College Web site. Many Broward students go to this site for information about the school and the support services offered there. Look at the image of the home page, and then write an **exemplification** paragraph listing the programs and services your school offers (or should offer) to help students adjust to college.

General Statement	Specific Examples
My car is giving me problems.	My car is burning oil and won't start on cold mornings. In addition, I need a new set of tires.

An **exemplification paragraph** explains or clarifies a general idea with specific examples. Personal experiences, class discussions, observations, conversations, and reading can all be good sources of examples.

An exemplification paragraph begins with a topic sentence that states the paragraph's main idea. The topic sentence is followed by examples supporting the general statement made in the topic sentence. Examples should be arranged in **logical order**—for example, from least important to most important or from general to specific. How many examples you need depends on your topic sentence. A complicated statement might require many examples to support it. A simple, straightforward statement might require fewer examples. The paragraph ends with a summary statement that sums up its main idea.

An exemplification paragraph generally has the following structure.

Topic Sentence _____

Example #1 _____

_____

Example #2 _____

_____

Example #3 _____

_____

Summary Statement _____

_____

The following paragraph uses examples to support the idea that Philadelphia is an exciting city to visit.

Visiting Philadelphia

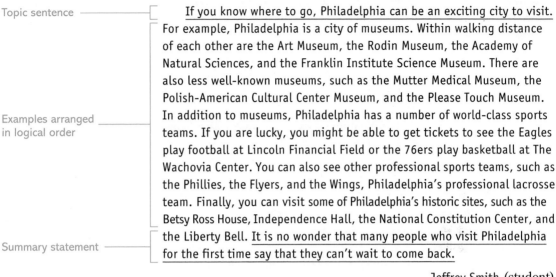

Topic sentence —— If you know where to go, Philadelphia can be an exciting city to visit. For example, Philadelphia is a city of museums. Within walking distance of each other are the Art Museum, the Rodin Museum, the Academy of Natural Sciences, and the Franklin Institute Science Museum. There are also less well-known museums, such as the Mutter Medical Museum, the Polish-American Cultural Center Museum, and the Please Touch Museum. In addition to museums, Philadelphia has a number of world-class sports teams. If you are lucky, you might be able to get tickets to see the Eagles play football at Lincoln Financial Field or the 76ers play basketball at The Wachovia Center. You can also see other professional sports teams, such as the Phillies, the Flyers, and the Wings, Philadelphia's professional lacrosse team. Finally, you can visit some of Philadelphia's historic sites, such as the Betsy Ross House, Independence Hall, the National Constitution Center, and the Liberty Bell. It is no wonder that many people who visit Philadelphia for the first time say that they can't wait to come back.

Examples arranged in logical order

Summary statement

Jeffrey Smith (student)

When you write an exemplification paragraph, be sure to include appropriate transitional words and phrases. These transitions will help readers follow your discussion by indicating how your examples are related and how each example supports the topic sentence.

Some Transitional Words and Phrases for Exemplification

also	furthermore	the most important
finally,	in addition	example
first . . . second . . .	moreover	the next example
(and so on)	one example . . .	
for example	another example . . .	
for instance	specifically	

Grammar in Context: Exemplification

When you write an exemplification paragraph, always use a comma after the introductory transitional word or phrase that introduces an example.

> For example, Philadelphia is a city of museums.
>
> In addition to museums, Philadelphia has a number of world-class sports teams.
>
> Finally, you can visit some of Philadelphia's historic sites. . . .

For information on using commas with introductory transitional words and phrases, see 31B.

● Practice 3-1

Read this exemplification paragraph; then, follow the instructions on page 55.

Jobs of the Future

College students should take courses that prepare them for the careers that will be in demand over the next ten years. For example, the health-care field will have tremendous growth. Hundreds of thousands of medical workers—such as home-care aides, dental hygienists, and registered nurses—will be needed. Also, there will be an ongoing demand for workers who can operate and repair the specialized machines used in hospitals, labs, and other medical settings. In addition, a wide range of "green" jobs will become available as many industries work to improve their environmental practices. For example, construction workers, architects, and landscapers will be needed to create eco-friendly living and working spaces. Finally, education will be an attractive area for job seekers in the coming years. Many new teachers, especially ones who are experienced with computers, will be needed to replace the teachers who retire during the next ten years. Students who know what jobs will be available can prepare themselves for the future.

Bill Broderick (student)

1. Underline the topic sentence of the paragraph.

2. List the specific examples the writer uses to support his topic sentence. The first example has been listed for you.

   health-care jobs
   _____

   _____

   _____

3. Circle the transitions that the writer uses to connect ideas in the paragraph.

4. Underline the paragraph's summary statement.

● **Practice 3-2**

Following are four possible topic sentences for exemplification paragraphs. Copy the topic sentences on a separate sheet of paper. Then, list three or four examples you could use to support each topic sentence. For example, if you were writing a paragraph about how difficult the first week of your new job was, you could mention waking up early, getting to know your coworkers, and learning new routines.

1. Getting a student loan can be challenging.

2. Internships give students valuable opportunities to develop job skills.

3. Good health care is sometimes difficult to get.

4. Some reality television shows insult the intelligence of their viewers.

3b   # Writing an Exemplification Paragraph

When Sarah Herman was asked to write a paragraph about work, she had little difficulty deciding on a topic. She had just finished a summer job waiting on tables in Sea Isle City, a beach community in New Jersey. She knew, without a doubt, that this was the worst job she had ever had.

Once she had decided on her topic, Sarah brainstormed to find ideas to write about. After reviewing her brainstorming notes, she listed several examples that could support her topic sentence.

Restaurant too big

Boss disrespectful

No experience

Kitchen chaotic

Customers rude

Tips bad

After reading her list, Sarah wrote the following topic sentence to express the main idea of her paragraph.

Topic Sentence: Waiting on tables was the worst job I ever had.

After Sarah identified her main idea, she eliminated examples that she thought did not support her topic sentence. Then, she arranged the remaining examples in an order in which she could discuss them most effectively—in this case, from least important to most important example.

Topic Sentence: Waiting on tables was the worst job I ever had.

1. No experience
2. Customers rude
3. Tips bad
4. Boss disrespectful

Using her list of points as a guide, Sarah wrote the following draft of her paragraph.

Waiting on tables was the worst job I ever had. I had little experience as a food server. The first day of work was so bad that I almost quit. The customers were rude. All they wanted was to get their food as fast as possible so they could get back to the beach or the boardwalk. They were often impolite and demanding. The tips were bad. It was hard to be pleasant when you knew that the people you were waiting on were probably going to leave you a bad tip. Finally, the owner of the restaurant did not show us any respect. He often yelled at us, saying that if we didn't work harder, he would fire us. He never did, but his constant threats didn't do much to help our morale.

When she finished her draft, Sarah met with her instructor, who suggested that her paragraph would be stronger if she made some of her examples more specific. For example, what experience did she have that made her want to quit? Exactly how were customers rude? Her instructor also reminded her that she needed to **TEST** her paragraph. As she applied the **TEST** strategy, Sarah assessed her paragraph and made some changes.

- She checked her **topic sentence** and decided that it was effective.
- She evaluated her **evidence**. Then, she added more examples and details and deleted irrelevant details.
- She noticed that she did not have a **summary statement**, so she added one at the end of her paragraph.
- She added more **transitions** to make it easier for readers to follow her discussion.

After making these changes, she went on to revise and edit her draft. The final draft below includes all the elements that Sarah looked for when she applied the **TEST** strategy.

My Worst Job

Waiting on tables was the worst job I ever had. First, I had never worked in a restaurant before, so I made a lot of mistakes. Once, I forgot to bring salads to a table I waited on. A person at the table complained so loudly that the owner had to calm him down. I was so frustrated and upset that I almost quit. Second, the customers at the restaurant were often rude. All they wanted was to get their food as fast as possible so they could get back to the beach or the boardwalk. They were on vacation, and they wanted to be treated well. As a result, they were frequently very demanding. No one ever said, "excuse me," "please," or "thank you," no matter what I did for them. Third, the tips were usually bad. It was hard to be pleasant when you knew that the people you were waiting on were probably going to leave you a bad tip. Finally, the owner of the restaurant never showed his workers any respect. He would yell at us, saying that if we didn't work harder, he would fire us. He never did, but his constant threats didn't do much to help our morale. Even though I survived the summer, I promised myself that I would never wait on tables again.

T E S T

Topic Sentence

Evidence

Summary Statement

Transitions

● Practice 3-3

Now, you are ready to write a draft of an exemplification paragraph. Choose one of the topics below (or choose your own topic) for an exemplification paragraph. Then, use one or more of the strategies described in 1C to help you think of as many examples as you can for the topic you have chosen.

Effective (or ineffective) teachers	Things you can't do without
Qualities that make a great athlete	Terrible dates
Successful movies	Extreme sports
Challenges that older students face	Role models
Traditions your family follows	Rude behavior
Unattractive clothing styles	Politicians
Peer pressure	Acts of courage
The benefits of iPods	Credit-card debt

● Practice 3-4

Review your notes from Practice 3-3, and list the examples that can best help you develop a paragraph on the topic you have chosen.

_____

_____

_____

_____

● Practice 3-5

Reread your list of examples from Practice 3-4. Then, draft a topic sentence that introduces your topic and communicates the main idea your paragraph will discuss.

_____

_____

_____

_____

● Practice 3-6

Arrange the examples you listed in Practice 3-4 in a logical order—for example, from least important to most important.

1. _____

2. _____

3. _____

4. _____

● Practice 3-7

Draft your exemplification paragraph. Then, using the **TEST** checklist on page 61, check your paragraph for unity, support, and coherence.

● Practice 3-8

Now, revise your exemplification paragraph.

● Practice 3-9

Prepare a final edited draft of your exemplification paragraph.

Focus on Writing: *Revising and Editing*

Look back at your response to the Focus on Writing activity on page 51. Using the **TEST** checklist on page 61, evaluate the paragraph you wrote for unity, support, and coherence. Then, prepare a final revised and edited draft of your paragraph.

Chapter Review

Focus on Writing

The billboard pictured below shows a public service advertisement promoting HIV/AIDS awareness. Study the picture carefully, and then write an exemplification paragraph explaining what is effective (or ineffective) about this ad. Begin with a topic sentence that states your opinion of the ad's strengths or weaknesses. Then, after briefly describing the ad, give specific examples to support the opinion you state in your topic sentence.

Real-World Writing

Write a one-paragraph memo to your employer suggesting improvements in your workplace environment. Or, write an email to your school's dean of students suggesting improvements to a campus service (the writing center, the student health office, or the financial aid office, for example).

TESTing an Exemplification Paragraph

Topic Sentence Unifies Your Paragraph

☐ Do you have a clearly worded topic sentence that states your paragraph's main idea?

☐ Does your topic sentence state an idea that can be supported by examples?

Evidence Supports Your Paragraph's Topic Sentence

☐ Do all your examples support your main idea?

☐ Do you need to add more examples?

Summary Statement Reinforces Your Paragraph's Unity

☐ Does your paragraph end with a statement that reinforces your main idea?

Transitions Add Coherence to Your Paragraph

☐ Do you use a transitional word or phrase to introduce each example your paragraph discusses?

☐ Do you need to add any transitions to make your paragraph more coherent?

Chapter 4 Using Narration

What Is Narration?

Narration is writing that tells a story. A **narrative paragraph** begins with a topic sentence that tells readers why you are telling a particular story—for example, to explain how an experience you had as a child changed you or to show that the Battle of Gettysburg was the turning point in the Civil War.

Effective narrative paragraphs include only those events that tell the story and avoid irrelevant information. The more specific the details you include, the better your narrative paragraph will be. Narrative paragraphs present events in **time order**, the order in which events actually occurred. A summary statement reinforces the paragraph's main idea.

A narrative paragraph generally has the following structure.

Topic Sentence _____

Event #1 _____

_____

Event #2 _____

_____

Event #3 _____

_____

Summary Statement _____

_____

Focus on Writing

The picture on the opposite page shows a scene from the movie *The Princess Bride*, a fairy tale that includes giants, an evil prince, and a beautiful princess. Look at the picture, and then write a **narrative** paragraph in which you retell a fairy tale, folk tale, or children's story that you know well. Make sure your topic sentence states the point of the story.

The student writer of the following paragraph presents a series of events to support the idea that the fashion designer Chloe Dao had a difficult life.

Overnight Success

Topic sentence —

Chloe Dao had to overcome a lot of difficulties to become a successful fashion designer. When Dao was a baby, her parents decided to leave her native country, Laos, and come to the United States. Unfortunately, the Viet Cong captured her and her family as they tried to cross the border. They were sent to a refugee camp, where they stayed for four years. In 1979, when she was eight, Dao and her family were allowed to come to the United States. Once they arrived, they had to earn enough money to live on. Dao's mother worked three jobs. On the weekends, the entire family ran the snack bar at a flea market. Finally, they saved enough money to open a dry cleaning business. When she was twenty, Dao moved to New York to attend school. After she graduated, she got a job as production manager for designer Melinda Eng. Eventually, she opened a boutique, where she featured clothes that she designed. Her big break came in 2006 when she was chosen as a finalist on the reality show *Project Runway*. Although Chloe Dao may appear to be an "overnight success," she had to struggle to get where she is today.

Events arranged in time order —

Summary statement —

Christine Clark (student)

As you arrange your ideas in your narrative paragraphs, be sure to use clear transitional words and phrases, as the student writer does in the paragraph above. These signals help readers follow your narrative by indicating the order of the events you discuss.

Some Transitional Words and Phrases for Narration

after	later	phrases including
as	later on	specific dates
as soon as	meanwhile	(for example,
before	next	"in 2006")
by this time	now	phrases including
earlier	soon	specific times (for
eventually	suddenly	example, "after
finally	then	two days," "the
first . . . second . . .	when	following year,"
third . . .	while	"at 3 o'clock,"
immediately		and "five minutes
in time		later")

Grammar in Context: Narration	When you write a narrative paragraph, you tell a story. As you become involved in your story, you might begin to string events together without proper punctuation. If you do, you will create a **run-on**.

Incorrect (run-on)	Dao's mother worked three jobs on the weekends, the entire family ran a snack bar at a flea market.
Correct	Dao's mother worked three jobs. On the weekends, the entire family ran the snack bar at a flea market.

For information on how to identify and correct run-ons, see Chapter 21.

● Practice 4-1

Read this narrative paragraph; then, follow the instructions on page 66.

Two men who risked their lives in the 1904 Harwick mine disaster were the inspiration for the Hero Fund, a charity that awards money to heroes and their families. The Harwick mine disaster began with a small explosion near the entry to the Harwick mine in Pennsylvania. Within seconds, this small explosion caused a chain reaction in which more and more explosive coal dust was stirred up and ignited. Then, a strong blast sent materials and even a mule flying out of the mine shaft. Ten hours later, a rescue party led by Selwyn Taylor went down into the mine. The rescue party found only one survivor, but Taylor believed more men might still be alive deep within the mine. As he advanced, however, Taylor was himself overcome by fumes. The following day, another rescue worker, Daniel Lyle, was also overcome by fumes while searching for survivors. Neither Taylor nor Lyle found any survivors, and both men died as a result of their efforts. Three months after the mine disaster, Pittsburgh steelmaker Andrew Carnegie founded the Hero Fund to give financial assistance to the families of those injured or killed while performing heroic acts. The Hero Fund continues to honor people like Selwyn Taylor and Daniel Lyle, ordinary people who take extraordinary risks to save others' lives.

Kevin Smiley (student)

1. Underline the topic sentence of the paragraph.

2. List the major events of the narrative. The first event has been listed for you.

   A small explosion occurred near the entry to the mine. _____

   _____

   _____

   _____

   _____

   _____

   _____

3. Circle the transitional words and phrases that the writer uses to link events in time.

4. Underline the paragraph's summary statement.

● **Practice 4-2**

Below are four possible topic sentences for narrative paragraphs. Copy each topic sentence on a separate sheet of paper, and then list three or four events that could support each topic sentence. For example, if you were recalling a barbecue that turned into a disaster, you could tell about burning the hamburgers, spilling the soda, and forgetting to buy paper plates.

1. A recent experience made me realize that I was no longer as young as I thought.

2. The first time I _____, I got more than I bargained for.

3. I did not think I had the courage to _____, but when I did, I felt proud of myself.

4. I remember my reaction to one news event very clearly.

4b   Writing a Narrative Paragraph

Todd Kinzer's instructor asked the class to write a paragraph about an experience that had a great impact on them. Todd tried to narrow this topic by listing some experiences that he could possibly write about.

> Accident at camp—Realized I wasn't as strong as I thought I was
>
> Breaking up with Lindsay—That hurt .
>
> Shooting the winning basket in my last high school game—Sweet
>
> The last Thanksgiving at my grandparents' house—Happy and sad

As Todd looked over the experiences on his list, he realized that he could write about any of them. He decided, however, to focus on the last Thanksgiving he spent at his grandparents' house. This occasion was especially meaningful to him because his grandfather died shortly after that Thanksgiving.

Todd began his writing process by freewriting on his topic. He wrote down whatever came into his mind about the dinner, without worrying about spelling, punctuation, or grammar. Here is Todd's freewriting paragraph.

> Thanksgiving. Who knew? I remember the smells when I woke up. I can see Granddad at the stove. We were all happy. He told us stories about when he was a kid. I had heard some of them before, but so what? I loved to hear them. We ate so much I could hardly move. Turkey has something in it that puts you to sleep. We watched football all afternoon and evening. Too bad Granddad died. I still can't believe it. I guess I have my topic.

When he looked over his freewriting, Todd thought he had enough ideas for a first draft of his paragraph. His draft appears below.

> Last Thanksgiving, my grandparents were up early. My grandfather stuffed the turkey, and my grandmother started cooking the other dishes. When I got up, I could smell the turkey in the oven. The table was already set for dinner, so we ate breakfast in the kitchen. My grandfather told us about the Thanksgivings he remembered from when he was a boy. When we sat down for dinner, a fire was burning in the fireplace. My grandmother said grace. My grandfather carved the turkey, and we all passed around dishes of food. For dessert, we had pecan pie and ice cream. After dinner, we watched football on TV. When I went to bed, I felt happy. This was my grandfather's last Thanksgiving.

Todd realized that his first draft needed work. Before he wrote his next draft, he tried to remember what other things had happened that Thanksgiving; he also tried to decide which idea was most important and what additional details could make his narrative more complete.

To help him plan his revision, he applied the **TEST** strategy to his paragraph; then, he made some changes.

- He added a **topic sentence** that stated his paragraph's main idea.
- He added some more details and examples and crossed out sentences that did not belong in his paragraph; now, all his **evidence** supported his main idea.
- He wrote a stronger **summary statement**.
- He added **transitional words and phrases** to indicate the time order of the events in his paragraph.

After making these changes, Todd made some additional revisions; then, he edited his paragraph, checking his grammar, punctuation, mechanics, and spelling and looking carefully for typos. The final draft below includes all the elements Todd looked for when he applied the **TEST** strategy.

Thanksgiving Memories

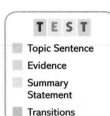

T E S T

Topic Sentence

Evidence

Summary Statement

Transitions

This past Thanksgiving was happy and sad because it was the last one I would spend with both my grandparents. The holiday began early. At 5 o'clock in the morning, my grandfather woke up and began to stuff the turkey. About an hour later, my grandmother began cooking corn pie and pineapple casserole. At 8 o'clock, when I got up, I could smell the turkey cooking. While we ate breakfast, my grandfather told us about Thanksgivings he remembered when he was a boy. Later, my grandfather made a fire in the fireplace, and we sat down for dinner. After my grandmother said grace, my grandfather carved and served the turkey. The rest of us passed around dishes of sweet potatoes, mashed potatoes, green beans, asparagus, cucumber salad, relish, cranberry sauce, apple butter, cabbage salad, stuffing, and, of course, corn pie and pineapple casserole. For dessert, my grandmother served pecan pie with scoops of ice cream. After dinner, we turned on the TV and the whole family watched football all evening. That night, I remember thinking that life couldn't get much better. Four months later, my grandfather died in his sleep. For my family and me, Thanksgiving would never be the same.

● Practice 4-3

Now, you are ready to write a draft of your narrative paragraph. Choose one of the topics below (or choose your own topic) for a narrative paragraph. Then, use one or more of the strategies described in 1C to help you recall events and details about the topic you have chosen.

A difficult choice	An embarrassing situation
A frightening situation	A surprise

A time of self-doubt	A sudden understanding or insight
A success	Something funny a friend did
An act of violence	Unexpected good luck
A lesson you learned	A conflict with authority
A happy moment	An event that changed your life
An instance of injustice	An important decision

● Practice 4-4

Review your notes from Practice 4-3, and list the events that can best help you develop a narrative paragraph on the topic you have chosen.

_____

_____

_____

_____

_____

_____

● Practice 4-5

Reread your list of events from Practice 4-4. Then, draft a topic sentence that introduces your topic and communicates the main idea your paragraph will discuss.

_____

_____

_____

● Practice 4-6

Write down the events you listed in Practice 4-4 in the order in which they occurred.

1. _____

2. _____

3. _____

4. _____

5. _____

● **Practice 4-7**

Draft your narrative paragraph. Then, using the **TEST** checklist on page 71, check your paragraph for unity, support, and coherence.

● **Practice 4-8**

Now, revise your narrative paragraph.

● **Practice 4-9**

Prepare a final edited draft of your narrative paragraph.

Focus on Writing: *Revising and Editing*

Look back at your response to the Focus on Writing activity on page 63. Using the **TEST** checklist on page 71, evaluate the paragraph you wrote for unity, support, and coherence. Then, prepare a final revised and edited draft of your paragraph.

Chapter Review

Focus on Writing

The picture below shows a bride and groom at the drive-through window of a Las Vegas wedding chapel. Study the picture carefully, and then write a narrative paragraph that tells the story behind it.

Real-World Writing

Assume that you are filling out a personality profile for an online dating service. One of the questions asks you to tell a story about yourself that illustrates your best character trait. Write a narrrative paragraph that tells this story.

TESTing a Narrative Paragraph

Topic Sentence Unifies Your Paragraph

☐ Do you have a clearly worded topic sentence that states your paragraph's main idea?

☐ Does your topic sentence give readers an idea why you are telling the story?

Evidence Supports Your Paragraph's Topic Sentence

☐ Do you include enough information about the events you discuss?

☐ Do all your examples and details support your paragraph's main idea?

☐ Do you need to include more specific details to add interest to your narrative?

Summary Statement Reinforces Your Paragraph's Unity

☐ Does your paragraph end with a statement that reinforces your main idea?

Transitions Add Coherence to Your Paragraph

☐ Do your transitions indicate the time order of events in your paragraph?

☐ Do you need to add transitions to make your paragraph more coherent?

What Is Description?

In a personal email, you may describe a new boyfriend or girlfriend. In a biology lab paper, you may describe the structure of a cell. In a report for a nursing class, you may describe a patient you observed.

When you write a **description**, you choose words that paint a picture for your readers. You use language that creates a vivid impression of what you have seen, heard, smelled, tasted, or touched. The more details you include, the better your description will be.

The following description is flat because it includes no specific details.

Flat description   I saw a beautiful sunrise.

In contrast, the description below is full of details that convey the writer's experience to readers.

Rich description   Early this morning, as I walked along the sandy beach, I saw the sun rise slowly out of the ocean. At first, the ocean looked red. Then, it turned slowly to pink, to aqua, and finally to blue. As I stood watching the sun, I heard the waves hit the shore, and I felt the cold water swirl around my toes. For a moment, even the small grey and white birds that ran along the shore seemed to stop and watch the dazzling sight.

The revised description relies on sight (*looked red*; *turned slowly to pink, to aqua, and finally to blue*), touch (*the sandy beach*; *felt the cold water*), and sound (*heard the waves hit the shore*).

Focus on Writing

The picture on the opposite page shows two college maintenance workers. Look at the picture, and then write a paragraph in which you **describe** a person you encounter every day—for example, a street vendor, a bus driver, or a worker in your school cafeteria.

A **descriptive paragraph** should have a topic sentence that states the paragraph's main idea. (*My sister's room is a pigpen.*) This topic sentence should be followed by the details that support it. These details should be arranged in a definite **spatial order**, the order in which you observed the scene you are describing—for example, from near to far or from top to bottom. The paragraph ends with a summary statement that reinforces the main idea stated in the topic sentence.

A descriptive paragraph generally has the following structure.

Topic Sentence _____

Detail #1 _____

_____

Detail #2 _____

_____

Detail #3 _____

_____

Summary Statement _____

_____

Highlight: Description

Vague, overused words—such as *good*, *nice*, *bad*, and *beautiful*—do not help readers see what you are describing. When you write a descriptive paragraph, use specific words and phrases that make your writing come alive.

The student writer of the following paragraph uses descriptive details to support the idea that the Lincoln Memorial is a monument to American democracy.

The Lincoln Memorial

Topic sentence ——————

Descriptive details arranged in spatial —— order

The Lincoln Memorial was built to celebrate American democracy. In front of the monument is a long marble staircase that leads from a reflecting pool to the memorial's entrance. Thirty-six columns—which symbolize the thirty-six states reunited after the Civil War—surround the building. Inside the building are three rooms. The first room contains the nineteen-foot statue of Lincoln. Seated in a chair, Lincoln looks exhausted after the long Civil War. One of Lincoln's hands is a fist, showing his strength, and the other is open, showing his kindness. On either side of the first room are the two other rooms. Carved on the wall of the second room is the Gettysburg Address. On the wall of the third room is the Second Inaugural Address. Above the Gettysburg Address is a mural showing an angel freeing the slaves. Above the Second Inaugural Address is another mural, which depicts the people of the North and the South coming back together. As its design shows, the Lincoln Memorial was built to celebrate both the sixteenth president and the nation's struggle for democracy.

Descriptive details arranged in spatial order

Summary statement

Nicole Lentz (student)

As you arrange your ideas in a descriptive paragraph, be sure to use appropriate transitional words and phrases. These signals will lead readers from one detail to another.

Some Transitional Words and Phrases for Description

above	in front of	on top of
behind	inside	outside
below	nearby	the first . . . the
between	next to	second . . .
beyond	on	the next
in	on one side . . .	under
in back of	on the other side . . .	

Grammar in Context: Description

When you write a descriptive paragraph, you sometimes use **modifiers**— words and phrases that describe other words in the sentence. A modifier should be placed as close as possible to the word it is supposed to modify. If you place a modifying word or phrase too far from the word it modifies, you create a **misplaced modifier** that will confuse readers.

Confusing Seated in a chair, the long Civil War has clearly exhausted Lincoln. (Was the Civil War seated in a chair?)

Clear Seated in a chair, Lincoln looks exhausted after the long Civil War.

For information on how to identify and correct misplaced modifiers, see Chapter 25.

● Practice 5-1

Read this descriptive paragraph; then, follow the instructions below it.

Red Rocks

In a national park near Denver, Colorado, the outdoor amphitheater known as Red Rocks is a unique setting for concerts. On either side of the theater are two giant rocks—each three hundred feet high—that keep the sound inside the seating area. Behind the stage is an enormous rock wall, which forces sound from the stage outward toward the audience. In front of the stage, the seating area is sloped, allowing everyone to see the performance. Built into the rocks below the stage is a restaurant that is open before, during, and after the shows. Because Red Rocks is an outdoor theater, it has no roof, so the audience can look up during nighttime concerts and see the moon and stars. In the distance, the Denver skyline is a dramatic backdrop. There is no other theater in the world quite like Red Rocks.

Alyssa Yoonas (student)

1. Underline the topic sentence of the paragraph.

2. In a few words, summarize the main idea of the paragraph.

_____

3. What are some of the details the writer uses to support this main idea? The first detail has been listed for you.

Two giant rocks keep the sound within the seating area.

_____

_____

_____

_____

_____

4. Underline the paragraph's summary statement.

● Practice 5-2

Each of the four topic sentences below states a main idea for a descriptive paragraph. Copy the topic sentences on a separate sheet of paper, and then list three or four details that could support each one. For example, to support the idea that sitting in front of a fireplace is relaxing, you could describe the crackling of the fire, the pine scent of the smoke, and the changing colors of the flames.

1. One look at the face of the traffic-court judge convinced me that I was in trouble.

2. The dog looked as if it had been living on the streets for a long time.

3. The woman behind the makeup counter was a walking advertisement for every product she sold.

4. One of the most interesting stores I know sells vintage clothing.

5b   Writing a Descriptive Paragraph

When Jared Lopez was asked to write a descriptive paragraph about someone he admired, he decided to write about his uncle Manuel, who had been a father figure for him.

Because he was familiar with his topic, Jared did not have to brainstorm or freewrite to find ideas. He decided to begin his paragraph with a general description of his uncle and then concentrate on his uncle's most noticeable feature: his hands. Here is the first draft of Jared's paragraph.

> My uncle's name is Manuel, but his friends call him Manny. He is over six feet tall, and he has long arms and legs. Although he is over fifty, he keeps in shape. Before he started his construction company, he used to be a stonemason. Uncle Manny's eyes are dark brown, almost black. They make him look very serious. When he laughs, however, he looks friendly. His nose is long and straight, and it makes Uncle Manny look very distinguished. Most interesting to me are Uncle Manny's hands. Even though he hasn't worked as a stonemason for years, his hands are still rough and scarred. They are large and strong, but they can be gentle too.

When Jared reread his draft, he felt it did not really focus on his uncle's most important qualities—strength and gentleness. In addition, his sentences seemed choppy. To help him assess his paragraph's strengths and weaknesses, he applied the **TEST** strategy and then made some changes.

- He added a **topic sentence** that stated the main idea of his description.
- He added more details in his description to give readers more **evidence** of his uncle's strength and gentleness.
- He wrote a stronger **summary statement** to unify his paragraph.
- He included more **transitions** to move readers from one part of his description to the next.

After making these changes, Jared revised and edited his draft. The final draft below includes all the elements Jared looked for when he applied the **TEST** strategy.

T E S T
Topic Sentence
Evidence
Summary Statement
Transitions

My Uncle Manny

My uncle Manuel is a strong but gentle person who took care of my mother and me when my father died. Manuel, or "Manny" as his friends and family call him, is over six feet tall. This is unusual for a Mexican of his generation. The first thing most people notice about my uncle Manny is his eyes. They are large and dark brown, almost black. They make him look very serious. When he laughs, however, the sides of his eyes crinkle up and he looks warm and friendly. Another thing that stands out is his nose, which is long and straight. My mother says it makes Uncle Manny look strong and distinguished. The most striking thing about Uncle Manny is his hands. Even though he hasn't worked as a stonemason since he opened his own construction company ten years ago, his hands are still rough and scarred from carrying stones. No matter how much he tries, he can't get rid of the dirt under the skin of his fingers. Uncle Manny's hands are big and rough, but they are also gentle and comforting. To me, they show what he really is: a strong and gentle man.

● Practice 5-3

Now, you are ready to write a draft of a descriptive paragraph. Choose one of the topics below (or choose your own topic) for a descriptive paragraph. Then, use one or more of the strategies described in 1C to help you come up with specific details about the topic you have chosen. If you can, observe your subject directly and write down your observations.

A favorite place	A favorite article of clothing
A place you felt trapped in	A useful object
A quiet place on campus	A pet
An unusual person	A building you think is ugly
Your dream house	Your car or truck

A family member or friend　　The car you would like to have
A work of art　　　　　　　　A statue or monument
Your most treasured possession　Someone you admire
Your workplace　　　　　　　A cooking disaster

● **Practice 5-4**

List the details you came up with in Practice 5-3 that can best help you
develop a descriptive paragraph on the topic you have chosen.

_____

_____

_____

_____

_____

● **Practice 5-5**

Reread your list of details from Practice 5-4. Then, draft a topic sentence that
summarizes the idea you want to convey in your paragraph.

_____

_____

● **Practice 5-6**

Arrange the details you listed in Practice 5-4. You might arrange them in
the order in which you are looking at them—for example, from left to right,
near to far, or top to bottom.

1. _____

2. _____

3. _____

4. _____

5. _____

6. _____

7. _____

● **Practice 5-7**

Draft your descriptive paragraph. Then, using the **TEST** checklist on page 81,
check your paragraph for unity, support, and coherence.

● **Practice 5-8**

Now, revise your descriptive paragraph.

● **Practice 5-9**

Prepare a final edited draft of your descriptive paragraph.

Focus on Writing: *Revising and Editing*

Look back at your response to the Focus on Writing activity on page 73. Using the **TEST** checklist on page 81, evaluate your paragraph for unity, support, and coherence. Then, prepare a final revised and edited draft of your paragraph.

Chapter Review

Focus on Writing

The picture below shows a house surrounded by lush landscaping. Write a paragraph describing the house for a real estate brochure. Use your imagination to invent details that describe its setting, exterior, and interior. Your goal in this descriptive paragraph is to persuade a prospective buyer to purchase the house.

Real-World Writing

Imagine that you have volunteered to read to a blind person. At one point, the book you are reading mentions something that your listener has never seen—for example, a particular apparatus, work of art, or item of clothing. Write a one-paragraph description of this item that will help the sightless person "see" it.

TESTing a Descriptive Paragraph

Topic Sentence Unifies Your Paragraph

☐ Do you have a clearly stated topic sentence that states your paragraph's main idea?

☐ Does your topic sentence identify the person, place, or thing you will describe in your paragraph?

Evidence Supports Your Paragraph's Topic Sentence

☐ Do all your examples and details help to support your paragraph's main idea?

☐ Do you have enough descriptive details, or do you need to include more?

Summary Statement Reinforces Your Paragraph's Unity

☐ Does your paragraph end with a statement that reinforces your main idea?

Transitions Add Coherence to Your Paragraph

☐ Do your transitions lead readers from one detail to the next?

☐ Do you need to add transitions to make your paragraph more coherent?

What Is Process?

When you describe a **process**, you tell readers how something works or how to do something. For example, you could explain how the optical scanner at the checkout counter of a food store works, how to hem a pair of pants, or how to send a text message.

A **process paragraph** should begin with a topic sentence that identifies the process and identifies the point you want to make about it (for example, "Parallel parking is easy once you know the secret," or "By following a few simple steps, you can design an effective résumé"). The rest of the paragraph should clearly describe the steps in the process, one at a time. These steps should be presented in strict **time order**—in the order in which they occur or are to be performed. The paragraph should end with a summary statement that reinforces the point you are making about the process.

A process paragraph generally has the following structure.

Topic Sentence _____

Step #1 _____

_____

Step #2 _____

_____

Step #3 _____

_____

Summary Statement _____

_____

Focus on Writing

The pictures on the opposite page show a man breakdancing. Look at the pictures, and then write a **process** paragraph in which you explain how to dance to your favorite music or play your favorite game (for example, a board game or a video game). Assume that your readers know nothing about your subject, and be sure to explain all the steps involved.

There are two types of process paragraphs: **process explanations** and **instructions**.

Process Explanations

In a **process explanation**, your purpose is to help readers understand how something works or how something happens—for example, how a cell phone operates or how a computer functions. In this case, you do not expect readers to perform the process. The student writer of the following paragraph, a volunteer firefighter, explains how a fire extinguisher works.

How a Fire Extinguisher Works

Topic sentence — Even though many people have fire extinguishers in their homes, most people do not know how they work. A fire extinguisher is a metal cylinder filled with a material that will put out a fire. All extinguishers operate the same way. First, the material inside the cylinder is put under pressure. When an operating lever on top of the metal

Step-by-step explanation presented in time order — cylinder is squeezed, a valve opens. Then, the pressure inside the fire extinguisher is released. As the compressed gas in the cylinder rushes out, it carries the material in the fire extinguisher along with it. Next, a nozzle at the top of the cylinder concentrates the stream of liquid, gas, or powder coming from the fire extinguisher so it can be aimed at a fire. Finally, the material comes in contact with the fire and puts it

Summary statement — out. A fire extinguisher is a well-designed piece of equipment that should be in every home, located where it can be easily reached when it is needed.

David Turner (student)

Instructions

When you write instructions, your purpose is to give readers the information they need to actually perform a task or activity—for example, to fill out an application, to operate a piece of machinery, or to change a tire. Because you expect readers to follow your instructions, you address them directly, using **commands** to tell them what to do ("check the gauge" . . . "pull the valve"). In the following paragraph, the writer provides a humorous set of instructions on how to get food out of a vending machine.

Man vs. Machine

Topic sentence —————— <u>There is a foolproof method of outsmarting a vending machine that refuses to give up its food.</u> First, approach the vending machine coolly. Make sure that you don't seem frightened or angry. The machine will sense these emotions and steal your money. Second, be polite. Say hello, compliment the machine on its selection of goodies, and smile. Be careful. If the machine thinks you are trying to take advantage of it, it will steal your money. Third, if the machine steals your money, remain calm. Ask nicely to get the food you paid for. Finally, it is time to get serious. Hit the side of the vending machine with your fist. If this doesn't work, lower your shoulder and throw yourself at the machine. (A good kick or two might also help.) When the machine has had enough, it will drop your snack, and you can grab it. <u>If you follow these few simple steps, you should have no trouble walking away from vending machines with the food you paid for.</u>

Step-by-step instructions presented in time order

Summary statement

Adam Cooper (student)

Transitions are very important in process paragraphs like the two you have just read. Words like *first*, *second*, *third*, and so on enable readers to clearly identify each step. In addition, they establish a sequence that lets readers move easily though the process you are describing.

Some Transitional Words and Phrases for Process

after that	immediately	the first (second, third) step
as	later	
as soon as	meanwhile	the next step
at the same time	next	the last step
at this point	now	then
before	once	when
finally	soon	while
first (second, third)		

Grammar in Context: Process

When you write a process paragraph, you may find yourself making illogical shifts in tense, person, and voice. If you shift from one tense, person, or voice to another without good reason, you may confuse readers.

Confusing　First, the vending machine should be approached coolly. Make sure that you don't seem frightened or angry. (illogical shift from passive to active voice)

Clear　First, approach the vending machine coolly. Make sure that you don't seem frightened or angry. (consistent use of active voice)

For information on how to avoid illogical shifts in tense, person, and voice, see Chapter 24.

● Practice 6-1

Read this process paragraph; then, follow the instructions on page 87.

An Order of Fries

I never realized how much work goes into making French fries until I worked at a potato processing plant in Hermiston, Oregon. The process begins with freshly dug potatoes being shoveled from trucks onto conveyor belts leading into the plant. During this stage, workers must pick out any rocks that may have been dug up with the potatoes because these could damage the automated peelers. After the potatoes have gone through the peelers, they travel on a conveyor belt through the "trim line." Here, workers cut out any bad spots, being careful not to waste potatoes by trimming too much. Next, the potatoes are sliced in automated cutters and then fried for about a minute. After this, they continue along a conveyor belt to the "wet line." Here, workers again look for bad spots, and they throw away any rotten pieces. At this point, the potatoes go to a second set of fryers for three minutes before being moved to subzero freezers for ten minutes. Then, it's on to the "frozen line" for a final inspection. The inspected fries are weighed by machines and then sealed into five-pound plastic packages, which are weighed again by workers who also check that the packages are properly sealed. The bags are then packed into boxes and made ready for shipment to various restaurants across the western United States. This complicated process goes on twenty-four hours a day to bring consumers the fries they enjoy so much.

Cheri Rodriguez (student)

1. Underline the topic sentence of the paragraph.
2. Is this a process explanation or instructions? _____
   How do you know? _____
3. List the steps in the process. The first step has been listed for you.
   The potatoes are unloaded, and the rocks are sorted out.
   _____
   _____
   _____
   _____
   _____
   _____
4. Underline the paragraph's summary statement.

● **Practice 6-2**

Following are four possible topic sentences for process paragraphs. Copy the topic sentences on a separate sheet of paper. Then, list three or four steps that explain the process each topic sentence identifies. For example, if you were explaining the process of getting a job, you could list preparing a résumé, looking at ads in newspapers or online, writing a job application letter, and going on an interview. Make sure each step follows logically from the one that precedes it.

1. Downloading music from the Internet is a simple process.
2. Getting the most out of a student-teacher conference requires preparation.
3. Breaking up with someone you are dating can be a tricky process.
4. Choosing the perfect outfit for a job interview is challenging.

6b Writing a Process Paragraph

When Manasvi Bari was assigned to write a paragraph in which she explained a process she performed every day, she decided to write about how to get a seat on a crowded subway car. To make sure she had enough to write about, she made the following list of possible steps she could include.

Get into the train

Get the first seat

Look as if you need help

Get to a pole

Don't travel during rush hour

Choose your time

Be alert

Squeeze in

After looking over her list, Manasvi crossed out steps that she didn't think were essential to the process she wanted to describe.

Get into the train

Get the first seat

Look as if you need help

~~Get to a pole~~

~~Don't travel during rush hour~~

~~Choose your time~~

Be alert

Squeeze in

Once she had decided on her list of steps, she rearranged them in the order in which they should be performed.

Get into the train

Be alert

Get the first seat

Squeeze in

Look as if you need help

At this point, Manasvi thought that she was ready to begin writing her paragraph. Here is her first draft.

> When the train arrives, get into the car as fast as possible. If you see an empty seat, grab it, and sit down immediately. If there is no seat, ask people to move down, or squeeze into a space that seems too small. If none of this works, you'll have to use some imagination. Look helpless. Drop your books, and look as if the day can't get any worse. Sometimes a person will get up and give you a seat. If this strategy doesn't work, stand near someone who looks as if he or she is going to get up. When the person gets up, jump into the seat as fast as you can. Don't let the people who are getting on the train get the seat before you do.

Manasvi showed the draft of her paragraph to a writing center tutor. Together, they applied the **TEST** strategy and made the following decisions.

- They decided that she needed to add a **topic sentence** that identified the process and stated the point she wanted to make about it.
- They decided that her **evidence**—the details and examples that described the steps in her process—was clear and complete.
- They decided that she needed to add a **summary statement** that reinforced the point of the process.
- They decided that she needed to add **transitions** that helped readers follow the steps in the process.

After she made her changes, Manasvi revised and edited her paragraph. The final draft below includes all the elements Manasvi looked for when she applied the **TEST** strategy.

Surviving Rush Hour

Anyone who takes the subway to school in the morning knows how hard it is to find a seat, but by following a few simple steps, you should be able to get a seat almost every day. First, when the train arrives, get into the car as fast as possible. Be alert. As soon as you see an empty seat, grab it, and sit down immediately. Meanwhile, if there is no seat, ask people to move down, or try to squeeze into a space that seems too small. If none of this works, the next step is to use some imagination. Look helpless. Drop your books, and look as if the day can't get any worse. Sometimes a person will get up and give you a seat. Don't be shy. Take it, and remember to say thank you. Finally, if this strategy doesn't work, stand near someone who looks as if he or she is going to get up. When the person gets up, jump into the seat as fast as you can. By following these steps, you should be able to get a seat on the subway and arrive at school rested and relaxed.

T E S T
- Topic Sentence
- Evidence
- Summary Statement
- Transitions

● **Practice 6-3**

Now, you are ready to write a draft of a process paragraph. Choose one of the topics below (or choose your own topic) for a process paragraph. Use one or more of the strategies described in 1C to help you come up with as many steps as you can for the topic you have chosen.

Making a major purchase	Buying a book or CD online
Strategies for winning arguments	Your typical work or school day
How to save money	How to discourage telemarketers
Your morning routine	A process involved in a hobby
How to use a digital camera	Painting a room
How to perform a particular household repair	How to make your favorite dish
How to apply for financial aid	How to prepare for a storm

● Practice 6-4

Review your notes on the topic you chose in Practice 6-3, and decide whether to write a process explanation or a set of instructions. Then, on the lines below, choose the steps from the list you wrote in Practice 6-3 that can best help you develop a process paragraph on your topic.

_____   _____

_____   _____

_____   _____

_____   _____

● Practice 6-5

Reread your list of steps from Practice 6-4. Then, draft a topic sentence that identifies the process you will discuss and communicates the point you will make about it.

_____

_____

_____

● Practice 6-6

Review the steps you listed in Practice 6-4. Then, write them down in time order, moving from the first step to the last.

1. _____   4. _____

2. _____   5. _____

3. _____   6. _____

● Practice 6-7

Draft your process paragraph. Then, using the **TEST** checklist on page 93, check your paragraph for unity, support, and coherence.

● **Practice 6-8**

Now, revise your process paragraph.

● **Practice 6-9**

Prepare a final edited draft of your process paragraph.

Focus on Writing: *Revising and Editing*

Look back at your response to the Focus on Writing activity on page 83. Using the **TEST** checklist on page 93, evaluate your paragraph for unity, support, and coherence. Then, prepare a final revised and edited draft of your paragraph.

Chapter Review

Focus on Writing

The picture below shows a scene of people in the process of moving. Study the picture carefully, and then list the steps involved in planning a move. Use this list to help you write a process paragraph that gives readers step-by-step instructions in the order in which the steps need to be done.

Real-World Writing

Imagine that you will have to miss a day of work. Write a one-paragraph memo explaining your typical workday to the employee who will substitute for you. Your goal is to help that employee understand exactly how to do your job and in what order to perform various tasks.

TESTing a Process Paragraph

Topic Sentence Unifies Your Paragraph

☐ Do you have a clearly worded topic sentence that states your paragraph's main idea?

☐ Does your topic sentence identify the process you will discuss?

☐ Does your topic sentence indicate whether you will be explaining a process or giving instructions?

Evidence Supports Your Paragraph's Topic Sentence

☐ Have you included all the steps in the process?

☐ If your paragraph is a set of instructions, have you included all the information readers need to perform the process?

Summary Statement Reinforces Your Paragraph's Unity

☐ Does your paragraph end with a statement that reinforces your main idea?

Transitions Add Coherence to Your Paragraph

☐ Do your transitions move readers from one step in the process to the next?

☐ Do you need to add transitions to make your paragraph more coherent?

What Is Cause and Effect?

Why is the cost of college so high? How does smoking affect a person's health? What would happen if the city increased its sales tax? How dangerous is swine flu? All these questions have one thing in common: they try to determine the causes or effects of an action, event, or situation. A **cause** is something or someone that makes something happen. An **effect** is a result of a particular cause.

Cause	Effect
Increased airport security ⟶	Long lines at airports
Weight gain ⟶	Health risks
Seatbelt laws passed ⟶	Increased use of seatbelts

A **cause-and-effect paragraph** helps readers understand why something happened or is happening or shows readers how one thing affects something else. A cause-and-effect paragraph begins with a topic sentence that tells readers whether the paragraph is focusing on causes or on effects (for example, "There are several reasons why the cost of gas is so high" or "Going to the writing center has given me confidence as well as skills"). The rest of the paragraph should discuss the causes or the effects, one at a time. The causes or effects are arranged in **logical order**—for example, from least important to most important. The paragraph ends with a summary statement that reinforces the main idea.

Focus on Writing

The picture on the opposite page shows someone talking on a cell phone while working on a laptop. Look at the picture, and then write a **cause-and-effect** paragraph in which you describe the impact of a particular electronic appliance or gadget on your life or on the life of your family—for example, the cell phone, the iPod, or the TV remote. Be sure that your topic sentence identifies the item that has an impact on you and your family and that the rest of the paragraph discusses how it affects you.

A cause-and-effect paragraph generally has the following structure.

Topic Sentence
Cause (or effect) #1
Cause (or effect) #2
Cause (or effect) #3
Summary Statement

Causes

The following paragraph focuses on **causes**.

Health Alert

Topic sentence — For a number of reasons, Americans are gaining weight at an alarming rate. First, many Americans do not eat healthy food. They eat a lot of food that is high in salt and contains a good deal of saturated fat. Also, many Americans eat on the run, grabbing a doughnut or muffin on the way to work and eating fast food for lunch or dinner. Another reason Americans are gaining weight is that they eat too much. They take too much food and think they must eat everything on their plates. They do not stop eating when they are full, and they often have second helpings and dessert. But the most important cause for this alarming weight gain is that many Americans do not exercise. They sit on the couch and watch hours of television or play video games and get up only to have a snack or a soda. The result of this unhealthy lifestyle is easy to predict—significant weight gain. Unless Americans begin eating better, many will develop severe health problems in the future.

Causes of weight gain arranged in logical order

Summary statement

Jen Toll (student)

Effects

The paragraph below focuses on **effects**.

Second Thoughts

Topic sentence ——————

When I dropped out of high school before my senior year, I had no idea how this action would affect my life. The first effect was that I became a social outcast. At the beginning, my friends called and asked me to go out with them. Gradually, however, school activities took up more and more of their time. Eventually, they had no time for me. Another effect was that I found myself stuck in a dead-end job. When I was in school, working part-time at a bookstore didn't seem so bad, but once it became my full-time job, I knew that I was going nowhere. Without a diploma or some college education, I could not get a better job. The most important effect was that my girlfriend broke up with me. One day, she told me that she didn't like dating a drop-out. She said I had no goals and no future. I had to agree with her. When I heard that she had started dating a college student, something clicked. I went to school at night and got my GED and then applied to community college. Now, I realize how wrong I was to drop out of high school and how lucky I am to have a second chance.

Effects of dropping out arranged in logical order ——————

Summary statement ——————

Dan Tarr (student)

Transitions in cause-and-effect paragraphs, as illustrated in the two paragraphs above, introduce causes or effects. They may also show the connections between a cause and its effects or between an effect and its causes. In addition, they may indicate which cause or effect is more important than another.

Some Transitional Words and Phrases for Cause and Effect

another cause	moreover	the most important
another effect	since	cause
as a result	so	the most important
because	the first (second,	effect
consequently	third, final) cause	the most important
finally	the first (second,	reason
for (meaning	third, final) effect	therefore
"because")	the first (second,	
for this reason	third, final) reason	

Grammar in Context: Cause and Effect

When you write a cause-and-effect paragraph, be careful not to confuse the words *affect* and *effect*. *Affect* is a verb meaning "to influence." *Effect* is a noun meaning "result."

When I dropped out of high school before my senior year, I had no idea how this action would ~~effect~~ *affect* my life. (*affect* is a verb.)

The first ~~affect~~ *effect* was that I became a social outcast. (*effect* is a noun.)

For more information on *effect* and *affect*, see Chapter 35.

● **Practice 7-1**

Read this cause-and-effect paragraph; then, follow the instructions on page 99.

Several reasons may lead employees to become "whistleblowers," people in an organization who report misconduct. First, whistleblowers may act because of training they received at professional school or on the job. Lawyers, doctors, and journalists all take classes that focus on professional ethics. Most companies also publish standards that they expect employees to read and follow. Second, whistleblowers may be guided by their own values. Their sense of right and wrong may have been shaped by their religious upbringing, or they may have learned a clear sense of right and wrong at home or at school. Third, some employees may become whistleblowers to avoid being blamed for the wrongdoing of others. They may believe that if someone they are working with (or for) is doing something unethical, people will think that they are doing the same thing. So, to protect themselves, they report the misconduct. Whatever their reason for speaking up, employees are more likely to do so if their company has a complaint procedure that offers confidentiality. Even without confidentiality, however, some courageous employees are willing to risk losing their jobs to reveal a practice that may harm the public.

Sean Burrell (student)

1. Underline the topic sentence of the paragraph.

2. Does this paragraph deal mainly with the causes or the effects of whistle-blowing? _____ How do you know?

   _____

   _____

3. List some of the causes the writer describes. The first cause has been listed for you.

   They may act because of training they received at professional school

   or on the job.

   _____

   _____

   _____

4. Underline the paragraph's summary statement.

● Practice 7-2

Following are four possible topic sentences for cause-and-effect paragraphs. List the effects that could result from the cause identified in each topic sentence. For example, if you were writing a paragraph about the effects of excessive drinking on campus, you could list low grades, health problems, and excessive absences from classes.

1. Having a baby can change your life.

2. Learning a second language has many advantages.

3. The iPhone was a huge success for a number of reasons.

4. Impulse buying can have negative effects on a person's finances.

● Practice 7-3

List three causes that could support each of the following topic sentences.

1. The causes of binge drinking are easy to identify.

2. Chronic unemployment can have many causes.

3. The benefits of college are not hard to explain.

4. There are several reasons why professional athletes' salaries are so high.

5. Eighteen- to twenty-nine-year-olds tend not to vote in national elections for a number of reasons.

7b

Writing a Cause-and-Effect Paragraph

When Sean Jin was asked to write a cause-and-effect essay for his composition class, he had no trouble thinking of a topic because he was following a debate in his hometown about building a Wal-Mart superstore there. He decided to write a paragraph that discussed the effects that such a store would have on the local economy.

His instructor told the class that the main challenge in planning a cause-and-effect essay is making sure that a **causal relationship** exists—that one event actually causes another. In other words, just because one event follows another closely in time, students should not assume that the first event caused the second.

With this advice in mind, Sean listed the effects a Wal-Mart would have on his small town.

Provide new jobs

Offer low-cost items

Pay low wages

Push out small businesses

After reviewing his list of effects, Sean wrote the following first draft of his paragraph.

Wal-Mart can have good and bad effects on a small town. First, it provides jobs. A large store needs a lot of employees. So, many people from the area will be able to work. Also, Wal-Mart's prices are low. Families on tight budgets may be able to buy things they can't afford to buy at other stores. Not all of Wal-Mart's effects are positive. Wal-Mart pays employees less than other stores. Wal-Mart provides jobs, but those jobs don't pay very much. Also, when Wal-Mart comes into an area, many small businesses are forced to close. They just can't match Wal-Mart's prices or stock as much merchandise as Wal-Mart can.

When he finished his draft, Sean went to the writing center and met with a tutor. After going over his paragraph with the tutor and applying the **TEST** strategy, Sean decided to make several changes.

- He decided that he needed to sharpen his **topic sentence** to tie his discussion of Wal-Mart to the small town in which he lived.
- He decided to provide more **evidence** to support his topic sentence — for example, what exactly does Wal-Mart pay its salespeople?
- He decided to add a **summary statement** to reinforce his main idea.
- He decided to add **transitions** to identify positive and negative effects.

After making these changes, Sean revised and edited his paragraph. The final draft below includes all the elements Sean looked for when he applied the **TEST** strategy.

Wal-Mart Comes to Town

When Wal-Mart comes to a small town like mine, it can have good and bad effects. The first and most positive effect is that it provides jobs. A large Wal-Mart Superstore needs a lot of employees, so many people will be able to find work. In my rural town, over 15 percent of the people are out of work. Wal-Mart could give these people a chance to improve their lives. Another positive effect that Wal-Mart can have is to keep prices low so families on tight budgets will be able to buy things they cannot afford to buy at other stores. My own observations show that many items at a local Wal-Mart are cheaper than those at other stores. Not all of Wal-Mart's effects are positive, however. One negative effect Wal-Mart can have is that it can actually lower wages in an area. My aunt, a longtime employee, says that Wal-Mart pays beginning workers between $8 and $10 an hour. This is less than they would get in stores that pay union wages. Another negative effect Wal-Mart can have is to drive other smaller businesses out. When Wal-Mart comes into an area, many small businesses are forced to close. They just cannot match Wal-Mart's prices or selection of merchandise. It is clear that although Wal-Mart can have a number of positive effects, it can also have some negative ones.

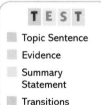

T E S T

Topic Sentence

Evidence

Summary Statement

Transitions

● Practice 7-4

Now, you are ready to write a draft of a cause-and-effect paragraph. Choose one of the following topics (or choose your own topic) for a paragraph that examines causes or effects. Then, use one or more of the strategies described in 1C to help you think of as many causes or effects as you can for the topic you have chosen.

Why reality shows are popular

Some causes (or effects) of stress

The negative effects of credit cards

Why college students should learn time-management skills

The reasons you decided to attend college

The impact of a particular government policy

How becoming a vegetarian might change (or has changed) your life

The benefits of home cooking

Why a particular sport is popular

How an important event in your life influenced you

The effects of violent song lyrics on teenagers

Why some people find writing difficult

The major reasons that high school or college students drop out of school

How managers can get the best (or the worst) from their employees

● Practice 7-5

Review your notes on the topic you chose in Practice 7-4, and create a cluster diagram. Write the topic you have chosen in the center of a sheet of paper, and draw arrows branching out to specific causes or effects.

● Practice 7-6

Choose a few of the most important causes or effects from the cluster diagram you made in Practice 7-5, and list them here.

_____

_____

_____

_____

_____

_____

_____

● Practice 7-7

Reread your list of causes or effects from Practice 7-6. Then, draft a topic sentence that introduces your topic and communicates the point you will make about it.

_____

_____

_____

● Practice 7-8

List the causes or effects you will discuss in your paragraph, arranging them in an effective order—for example, from least to most important.

1. _____

2. _____

3. _____

4. _____

● Practice 7-9

Draft your cause-and-effect paragraph. Then, using the **TEST** checklist on page 105, check your paragraph for unity, support, and coherence.

● Practice 7-10

Now, revise your cause-and-effect paragraph.

● Practice 7-11

Prepare a final edited draft of your cause-and-effect paragraph.

Focus on Writing: *Revising and Editing*

Look back at your response to the Focus on Writing activity on page 95. Using the **TEST** checklist on page 105, evaluate the paragraph you wrote for unity, support, and coherence. Then, prepare a final revised and edited draft of your paragraph.

Chapter Review

Focus on Writing

The picture below shows a happy couple, recent lottery winners, with a sign announcing their prize. Imagine you have won a multimillion-dollar lottery. How would your life change? Write a cause-and-effect paragraph that discusses specific ways in which your life would be different.

Real-World Writing

Imagine you have attended a community meeting. Some of your neighbors object to a proposal to build a new minimum-security prison nearby, and they appoint you to write a paragraph (to be sent to your city council representative) summarizing their objections. Write a paragraph outlining the negative effects you believe this new facility will have on your neighborhood.

TESTing a Cause-and-Effect Paragraph

Topic Sentence Unifies Your Paragraph

☐ Do you have a clearly worded topic sentence that states your paragraph's main idea?

☐ Does your topic sentence identify the cause or effect on which your paragraph will focus?

Evidence Supports Your Paragraph's Topic Sentence

☐ Do you need to add any important causes or effects?

☐ Do you need to explain your causes or effects in more detail?

☐ Do all your details and examples support your paragraph's main idea?

Summary Statement Reinforces Your Paragraph's Unity

☐ Does your paragraph end with a statement that reinforces your main idea?

Transitions Add Coherence to Your Paragraph

☐ Do your transitions show how your ideas are related?

☐ Do your transitions clearly introduce each cause or effect?

☐ Do you need to add transitions to make your paragraph more coherent?

What Is Comparison and Contrast?

When you buy something—for example, an air conditioner, a camera, a hair dryer, or a computer—you often comparison-shop. You look at various models to determine how they are alike and how they are different. Eventually, you decide which one you want to buy. In other words, you *compare and contrast*. When you **compare**, you look at how two things are similar. When you **contrast**, you look at how they are different.

Comparison-and-contrast paragraphs can examine just similarities or just differences, or they can examine both. A comparison-and-contrast paragraph begins with a topic sentence that tells readers whether the paragraph is going to discuss similarities or differences. The topic sentence should also make clear the focus of the comparison (for example, "Toni Morrison and Maya Angelou have similar ideas about the effects of discrimination" or "My parents and I have different definitions of success"). The rest of the paragraph should discuss the same or similar points for both subjects. Points should be arranged in **logical order**—for example, from least important to most important. A comparison-and-contrast paragraph ends with a summary statement that reinforces the main point of the comparison.

There are two kinds of comparison-and-contrast paragraphs: *subject-by-subject comparisons* and *point-by-point comparisons*.

Focus on Writing

The picture on the opposite page shows a family at home. Look at the picture, and then write a **comparison-and-contrast** paragraph in which you explain how your family life is different from (or similar to) the life of the family shown here.

Subject-by-Subject Comparisons

In a **subject-by-subject comparison**, you divide your comparison into two parts and discuss one subject at a time. In the first part of the paragraph, you discuss all your points about one subject. Then, in the second part, you discuss all your points about the other subject. (In each part of the paragraph, you discuss the points in the same order.)

A subject-by-subject comparison is best for paragraphs in which you do not discuss too many complicated points. Readers will have little difficulty remembering the points you discuss for the first subject when you move on to discuss the second subject.

A subject-by-subject comparison generally has the following structure.

Topic Sentence_____

_____

*Subject A*_____

Point #1_____

_____

Point #2_____

_____

Point #3_____

_____

*Subject B*_____

Point #1_____

_____

Point #2_____

_____

Point #3_____

_____

Summary Statement_____

_____

The writer of the following paragraph uses a subject-by-subject comparison to compare two ways of traveling to Boston.

Getting to Boston

Topic sentence ──────

Subject A: Going to
Boston by car ──────

Subject B: Going to
Boston by train ──────

Summary
statement ──────

When I visited my sister in Boston last year, taking the train was better than traveling by car. Driving to Boston from Philadelphia takes about six-and-a-half hours. I often drive alone with only my car radio or iPod for company. By the third hour, I am bored and tired. Traffic is also a problem. The interstate roads are crowded and dangerous. Trucks often drive well above the speed limit, and cars weave in and out of lanes. If there is an accident, I might have to wait for over an hour until the police clear the highway. Going by train, however, is much better. When I went last year, I met other students and had some interesting conversations. In contrast to when I drove, on the train I was able to take a nap when I got tired and snack when I got hungry. I was even able to plug my laptop into an outlet on the train and work on some assignments. Best of all, I never got stuck in traffic. As a result, when I finally got to Boston, I was rested and ready for a visit with my sister. This experience showed me that going to Boston by train is much better than driving.

Tad Curen (student)

Point-by-Point Comparisons

When you write a **point-by-point comparison**, you discuss a point about one subject and then discuss the same point for the second subject. You use this alternating pattern throughout the paragraph.

A point-by-point comparison is a better strategy for paragraphs in which you discuss many points. It is also a better choice if the points you are discussing are technical or complicated. Because you compare the two subjects one point at a time, readers will be able to see each point of comparison before moving on to the next point.

A point-by-point comparison generally has the following structure.

Topic Sentence _____

_____

Point 1 _____

Subject A _____

_____

Subject B _____

_____

Point 2 _____

Subject A _____

_____

Subject B _____

_____

Point 3 _____

Subject A _____

_____

Subject B _____

_____

Summary Statement _____

_____

In the following paragraph, the writer uses a point-by-point-comparison to compare two characters in a short story.

Two Sisters

Topic sentence ——————

Point 1: Different personalities ——————

Point 2: Different attitudes toward life ——————

Although they grew up together, Maggie and Dee, the two sisters in Alice Walker's short story "Everyday Use," are very different. Maggie, who was burned in a fire, is shy and has low self-esteem. When she walks, she shuffles her feet and looks down at the ground. Her sister Dee, however, is confident and outgoing. She looks people in the eye when she talks to them and is very opinionated. Maggie and Dee also have different attitudes toward life. Maggie never complains or asks for anything more than she has. She has remained at home with her mother in rural Georgia. In contrast, Dee has always wanted nicer things. She has gone away

Point 3: Different
attitudes toward
tradition

to school and hardly ever visits her mother and Maggie. The biggest difference between Maggie and Dee is their attitude toward tradition. Although Maggie values her family's rural American traditions, Dee values her African heritage. Maggie cherishes her family's handmade quilts and furniture, hoping to use them with her own family. In contrast, Dee sees the handmade objects as things to be displayed and shown off, not used every day. The many differences between

Summary statement

Maggie and Dee add conflict and tension to the story.

Margaret Caracappa (student)

Transitions are important in a comparison-and-contrast paragraph. Transitions tell readers when you are moving from one point (or one subject) to another. Transitions also make your paragraph more coherent by showing readers whether you are focusing on similarities (for example, *likewise* or *similarly*) or on differences (for example, *although* or *in contrast*).

Some Transitional Words and Phrases for Comparison and Contrast

although	one difference . . . another difference . . .
but	one similarity . . . another similarity . . .
even though	on the contrary
however	on the one hand . . . on the other hand . . .
in comparison	similarly
in contrast	though
like	unlike
likewise	whereas
nevertheless	

Grammar in Context: Comparison and Contrast

When you write a comparison-and-contrast paragraph, you should express the points you are comparing in **parallel** terms to highlight their similarities or differences.

Not parallel   Although Maggie values her family's traditions, the African heritage of her family is the thing that Dee values.

Parallel   Although Maggie values her family's traditions, Dee values her African heritage.

For more information on revising to make ideas parallel, see Chapter 19.

● **Practice 8-1**

Read this comparison-and-contrast paragraph; then, follow the instructions below.

Virtual and Traditional Classrooms

Taking a course online is very different from taking a course in a traditional classroom. One difference is that students in an online course have more flexibility than students in a traditional course. They can do their schoolwork at any time, scheduling it around other commitments, such as jobs and childcare. Students in a traditional course, however, must go to class at a specific time and place. Another difference is that students in an online course can feel isolated from the teacher and other students because they never actually come into physical contact with them. Students in a traditional classroom, however, are able to connect with the teacher and their classmates because they interact with them in person. A final difference is that in an online course, students use email or a discussion board to discuss course material. A student who is a slow typist or whose Internet connection is unreliable is clearly at a disadvantage. In a traditional course, most of the discussion takes place in the classroom, so technology is not an issue. Because online and traditional courses are so different, students must think carefully about which type of course best fits their needs.

William Hernandez (student)

1. Underline the topic sentence of the paragraph.
2. Does this paragraph deal mainly with similarities or differences? _____ How do you know? _____

_____

3. Is this paragraph a subject-by-subject or point-by-point comparison? _____ How do you know? _____

_____

4. List some of the contrasts the writer describes. The first contrast has been listed for you.

When it comes to their schedules, students in an online course have

more flexibility than students in a traditional course do.

_____

_____

_____

_____

_____

5. Underline the paragraph's summary statement.

● **Practice 8-2**

Following are three topic sentences. Copy the topic sentences on a separate sheet of paper. Then, list three or four similarities or differences between the two subjects in each topic sentence. For example, if you were writing a paragraph comparing health care provided by a local clinic with health care provided by a private doctor, you could discuss the cost, the length of waiting time, the quality of care, and the frequency of follow-up visits.

1. My mother (or father) and I are very much alike.

2. My friends and I have different views on _____.

3. Two of my college instructors have very different teaching styles.

Writing a Comparison-and-Contrast Paragraph

When Jermond Love was asked to write a comparison-and-contrast paragraph for his composition class, he began by brainstorming to find a topic that he could write about. When he reviewed his brainstorming notes, he came up with the following topics.

Football and soccer

Fast food and home cooking

The difference between my brother and me

Life in Saint Croix versus life in the United States

Jermond decided that he would write about the differences between life in New York City and life in Saint Croix, the Caribbean island on which he was raised. He listed a few subjects that he thought he could compare and contrast. Then, he crossed out the ones he didn't want to write about.

Size

Population

~~Economy~~

Friendliness

~~Businesses~~

Lifestyle

After brainstorming some more, Jermond listed the points he could discuss for each of his four subjects. He began with basic information and then moved on to the idea he wanted to emphasize: the different lifestyles.

Size

    Saint Croix

        Small size

        Small population

        Christiansted and Frederiksted

    New York

        Large size

        Large population

        Five boroughs

Lifestyle

    Saint Croix

        Laid-back

        Friendly

    New York

        In a hurry

        Not always friendly

Because he would not discuss many points in this paragraph and because the points were not very complicated, Jermond decided to use a point-by-point organization. He thought his readers would have an easier time following his paragraph if he discussed his points of contrast one at a time instead of grouping them.

Here is the first draft of Jermond's paragraph.

Life in Saint Croix is very different from life in New York City. Saint Croix is much smaller than New York City. Saint Croix has a total population of about 60,000 people. The two main towns are Christiansted and Frederiksted. New York City is very large. Its residents are crowded into five boroughs. The lifestyle in Saint Croix is different from the lifestyle of New York City. In Saint Croix, people operate on "island time." Everyone is friendly. People don't see any point in getting anyone upset. In New York City, people are always in a hurry. They don't take the time to slow down and enjoy life. As a result, people can seem unfriendly. They don't take the time to get to know anyone. I hope when I graduate I can stay in New York City but visit my home in Saint Croix whenever I can.

Jermond put his paragraph aside for a day and then reread it. Although he was generally satisfied with what he had written, he thought that it could be better. To help students revise their paragraphs, his instructor paired students and asked them to read and discuss each other's paragraphs. After working with a classmate on his draft and applying the **TEST** strategy, Jermond made the following decisions.

- He decided that his **topic sentence** was clear and specific.
- He saw that he needed more **evidence**—details to help readers understand the differences between his two subjects. Would readers know the location of Saint Croix? Would they know the population of Christiansted and Frederiksted? Would they know what he meant by "island time"?
- He decided to change his **summary statement** because it didn't really reinforce the idea in his topic sentence.
- Finally, he decided that he needed to add **transitional words and phrases** that would show when he was moving from one subject to another.

After making these changes, Jermond revised and edited his paragraph, adding background about Saint Croix. (The classmate who read his draft had pointed out that many people in the class would not know anything about it.)

The final draft below includes all the elements Jermond looked for when he applied the **TEST** strategy.

Saint Croix versus the United States

Life in Saint Croix is very different from life in New York City. One difference between Saint Croix and New York is that Saint Croix is much smaller than New York. Saint Croix, the largest of the United States Virgin Islands, has a population of about 60,000. The two main towns on the island are Christiansted, with a population of about 3,000, and Frederiksted, with a population of only about 830. Unlike Saint Croix, New York City is large. It has a population of over 8 million crowded into the five boroughs of Manhattan, Brooklyn, the Bronx, Queens, and Staten Island. My neighborhood in Brooklyn is more than twice the size of Christiansted and Frederiksted combined. Another difference between Saint Croix and New York City is their lifestyles. Life in Saint Croix is slower than life in New York. In Saint Croix, people operate on "island time." Things get done, but people don't rush to do them. When workers say "later," they can mean "this afternoon," "tomorrow," or even "next week." No one seems to mind, as long as the job gets done. People don't see any point in getting anyone upset. In New York, however, people are always in a hurry. They don't take the time to slow down and enjoy life. Everything is fast—fast food, fast cars, fast Internet access. As a result, people can seem unfriendly. Although Saint Croix and New York City are so different, life is interesting in both places.

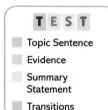

T E S T

▨ Topic Sentence
▨ Evidence
▨ Summary
    Statement
▨ Transitions

● Practice 8-3

Now, you are ready to write a draft of a comparison-and-contrast paragraph. Choose one of the topics below (or choose your own topic) for a paragraph exploring similarities or differences. Then, use one or more of the strategies described in 1C to help you think of as many similarities and differences as you can for the topic you have chosen. (If you use clustering, create a separate cluster diagram for each of the two subjects you are comparing.)

Two popular television personalities or radio talk-show hosts

Dog owners versus cat owners

Two laptops you would consider buying

How you act in two different situations (home and work, for example) or with two different sets of people (such as your family and your friends)

A vacation you took versus your ideal vacation

Men's and women's attitudes toward dating, shopping, or conversation

Your goals when you were in high school versus your goals today

A movie compared to its sequel

Two competing consumer items, such as two car models, two computer systems, or two cell phones

Two cultures' attitudes toward dating and marriage

Two generations' attitudes toward a particular subject (for example, how people in their forties and people in their teens view a political issue)

● **Practice 8-4**

Review your notes on the topic you chose in Practice 8-3, and decide whether to focus on similarities or differences. On the following lines, list the similarities or differences that can best help you develop a comparison-and-contrast paragraph on the topic you have selected.

_____

_____

_____

_____

_____

● **Practice 8-5**

Reread your list of similarities or differences from Practice 8-4. Then, draft a topic sentence that introduces your two subjects and indicates whether your paragraph will focus on similarities or on differences.

_____

_____

_____

● Practice 8-6

Decide whether you will write a subject-by-subject or a point-by-point comparison. Then, use the appropriate outline below to help you plan your paragraph. Before you begin, decide on the order in which you will present your points—for example, from least important to most important. (For a subject-by-subject comparison, begin by deciding which subject you will discuss first.)

Subject-by-Subject Comparison

Subject A _____

    Point 1 _____

    Point 2 _____

    Point 3 _____

    Point 4 _____

Subject B _____

    Point 1 _____

    Point 2 _____

    Point 3 _____

    Point 4 _____

Point-by-Point Comparison

Point 1 _____

    Subject A _____

    Subject B _____

Point 2 _____

    Subject A _____

    Subject B _____

Point 3 _____

    Subject A _____

    Subject B _____

Point 4 _____

    Subject A _____

    Subject B _____

● Practice 8-7

Draft your comparison-and-contrast paragraph. Then, using the **TEST** checklist on page 121, check your paragraph for unity, support, and coherence.

● Practice 8-8

Now, revise your comparison-and-contrast paragraph.

● Practice 8-9

Prepare a final edited draft of your comparison-and-contrast paragraph.

Focus on Writing: *Revising and Editing*

Look back at your response to the Focus on Writing activity on page 107. Using the **TEST** checklist on page 121, evaluate your paragraph for unity, support, and coherence. Then, prepare a final revised and edited draft of your paragraph.

Chapter Review

Focus on Writing

The pictures below show two famous war memorials. Study the two photographs carefully, and then write a paragraph in which you compare them, considering both what the monuments look like and their emotional impact on you.

Iwo Jima memorial statue near Arlington National Cemetery

Vietnam Veterans Memorial in Washington, D.C.

Real-World Writing

Assume you ordered a product advertised in a TV infomercial. When it arrives, you are disappointed to discover that what you see is not exactly what you expected. Write a one-paragraph email to the manufacturer in which you compare the way the product was supposed to perform to the way it actually performed. (If you like, you may use information from an actual infomercial in your paragraph.)

TESTing a Comparison-and-Contrast Paragraph

Topic Sentence Unifies Your Paragraph

☐ Do you have a clearly worded topic sentence that states your paragraph's main idea?

☐ Does your topic sentence indicate whether you are focusing on similarities or on differences?

Evidence Supports Your Paragraph's Topic Sentence

☐ Do all your examples and details support your main idea?

☐ Do your examples and details show how your two subjects are alike or different?

☐ Do you need to discuss additional similarities or differences?

Summary Statement Reinforces Your Paragraph's Unity

☐ Does your paragraph end with a statement that reinforces your main idea?

Transitions Add Coherence to Your Paragraph

☐ Do your transitions indicate whether you are focusing on similarities or on differences?

☐ Do transitional words and phrases lead readers from one subject or point to the next?

☐ Do you need to add transitions to make your paragraph more coherent?

What Is Classification?

Classification is the act of sorting items (people, things, or ideas) into categories or groups. You classify when you organize your bills into those you have to pay now and those you can pay later or when you sort the clothes in a dresser drawer into piles of socks, T-shirts, and underwear. College assignments also require you to classify. For example, a question on a history exam may ask you to discuss the different groups who fought in the American Revolution: colonists, British soldiers, and British sympathizers (Tories).

In a **classification paragraph**, you tell readers how items can be sorted into categories or groups. The topic sentence introduces the subject of the paragraph and sometimes also identifies the categories you will discuss. (For example, "Animals can be classified as vertebrates or invertebrates" or "Before you go camping, you should sort the items you are thinking of packing into three categories: those that are absolutely necessary, those that could be helpful, and those that are not really necessary.")

The rest of the paragraph discusses each of the categories, one at a time. Your discussion of each category should include enough details and examples to show how it is different from the other categories. You should also treat all categories in the same way. In other words, you should not discuss features of one category that you do not discuss for the others. In addition, the categories should be arranged in **logical order**—for example, from most important to least important or from smallest to largest. Finally, each category should be **distinct**—that is, none of the items in one category should also fit into another category. For example, you would not classify novels into mysteries, romances, and paperbacks, because both mystery novels and romance novels could also be paperbacks.

Focus on Writing

The picture on the opposite page shows boxers being classified according to their weight categories (heavyweight, middleweight, lightweight, featherweight, and so on). Look at the picture, and then write a **classification** paragraph that discusses the types of players in a sport that you follow. Why is each player placed within a particular category?

A classification paragraph should end with a summary statement that reinforces the main point stated in the topic sentence.

A classification paragraph generally has the following structure.

| Topic Sentence _____ |
| _____ |
| Category #1 _____ |
| _____ |
| Category #2 _____ |
| _____ |
| Category #3 _____ |
| _____ |
| Summary Statement _____ |
| _____ |

The writer of the following paragraph classifies items into three distinct groups.

Types of Bosses

Topic sentence — **Basically, I've had three kinds of bosses in my life: the uninterested boss, the supervisor, and the micromanager.** The first type is an uninterested boss. This boss doesn't care what workers do as long as they do the job. When I was a counselor at summer camp, my boss fell into this *First type of boss* — category. As long as no campers (or worse yet, parents) complained, he left you alone. He never cared if you followed the activity plan for the day or gave the kids an extra snack to keep them quiet. The second type of boss is the supervisor. This kind of boss will check you once in a while and give you helpful advice. You'll have a certain amount of freedom but not too much. When I was a salesperson at the Gap, my boss fell into *Second type of boss* — this category. She helped me through the first few weeks of the job and encouraged me to do my best. At the end of the summer, I had learned a lot about retail business and had good feelings about the job. The last, and worst, type of boss is the micromanager. This kind of boss gets *Last type of boss* — involved in everything. My boss at Taco Bell was this kind of person. No one could do anything right. There was always a better way to do anything

Last type of boss ———

you tried to do. If you rolled a burrito one way, he would tell you to do it another way. If you did it the other way, he would tell you to do it the first way. This boss never seemed to understand that people need praise every once in a while. <u>Even though the supervisor expects a lot and makes

Summary statement ———

you work, it is clear to me that this boss is better than the other types.</u>

Melissa Burrell (student)

Transitions are important in a classification paragraph. They introduce each new category and tell readers when you are moving from one category to another (for example, *the first type, the second type*). Transitions can also indicate which categories you think are more important than others (for example, *the most important, the least important*).

Some Transitional Phrases for Classification

one kind . . . another kind	the first type . . . the second type
one way . . . another way	the most (or least) important group
the first (second, third) category	the next part
the first group . . . the last group	

Grammar in Context: Classification

When you write a classification paragraph, you may list the categories you are going to discuss. If you use a colon to introduce your list, make sure that a complete sentence comes before the colon.

Incorrect   Basically, bosses can be divided into: the uninterested boss, the supervisor, and the micromanager.

Correct   <u>Basically, I've had three kinds of bosses in my life:</u> the uninterested boss, the supervisor, and the micromanager.

For more information on how to use a colon to introduce a list, see 33B.

● **Practice 9-1**

Read this classification paragraph; then, follow the instructions on page 126.

Three Kinds of Shoppers

Shoppers can be sorted into three categories: practical, recreational, and professional. The first category is made up of practical shoppers, those who shop because they need something. You can recognize them because they go right to the item they are looking for in the store and then leave. They do not waste time browsing or walking aimlessly from store to store. For them, shopping is a means to an end. The next category is made up of recreational shoppers, those who shop for entertainment. For them, shopping is like going to the movies or out to dinner. They do it because it is fun. They will spend hours walking through stores looking at merchandise. More often than not, they will not buy anything. For recreational shoppers, it is the activity of shopping that counts, not the purchase itself. The third category is made up of "professional shoppers," those who shop because they feel they have to. For them, shopping is a serious business. You can see them in any mall, carrying four, five, or even six shopping bags. Whenever you walk through a mall, you will see all three types of shoppers.

Kimberly Toomer (student)

1. Underline the topic sentence of the paragraph.

2. What is the subject of the paragraph? _____

3. What three categories does the writer describe?

   _____

   _____

   _____

4. Circle the transitional phrases the writer uses to introduce the three categories.

5. Underline the paragraph's summary statement.

● **Practice 9-2**

Classify the following groups of items into categories.

1. All the items in your backpack

2. Buildings on your college campus

3. Magazines or newspapers you read (or Web sites you visit regularly)

9b   Writing a Classification Paragraph

In a college composition course, Corey Levin participated in a service-learning experience at a local Ronald McDonald House, which housed families of seriously ill children receiving treatment at nearby hospitals. While there, he met several professional athletes, and he was surprised to learn that they regularly donated their time and money to charity.

After he finished his service-learning project, Corey was asked by his composition instructor to write a paragraph about something he had learned from his experience. Corey decided to write a paragraph that classified the ways in which professional athletes give back to their communities. To help him find ideas to write about, he jotted down the following list of categories.

> Starting foundations
>
> Guidance
>
> Responding to emergencies

Corey then listed examples under each of the three categories.

> Starting foundations
>> Michael Jordan
>>
>> Troy Aikman
>
> Guidance
>> Shaquille O'Neal
>>
>> The Philadelphia 76ers
>
> Responding to emergencies
>> Ike Reese
>>
>> Vince Carter

After completing this informal outline, Corey drafted a topic sentence for his paragraph: *High-profile athletes find many ways to give back to their communities.* Then, using his informal outline as a guide, Corey wrote the following draft of his paragraph.

> High-profile athletes find many ways to give back to their communities. Many athletes as well as teams do a lot to help people. For example, Michael Jordan built a Boys' & Girls' Club. Troy Aikman builds playgrounds for kids in hospitals. Shaquille O'Neal's Shaq's Paq helps

inner-city children. The Philadelphia 76ers visit schools. They have donated over five thousand books. Ike Reese collects clothing and food for families that need help. Vince Carter founded the Embassy of Hope Foundation. It distributes food to needy families at Thanksgiving and throws a Christmas party for disadvantaged families.

Following his instructor's suggestion, Corey emailed his draft to a classmate for feedback. In her email reply to Corey, she made the following suggestions based on the **TEST** strategy.

- Keep the **topic sentence** the way it is. "Many ways" shows you're writing a classification paragraph.
- Add more specific **evidence**. Give examples of each category of "giving back" to support the topic sentence. You also need to explain the athletes' contributions in more detail.
- Add a **summary statement** to sum up the paragraph's main idea.
- Add **transitions** to introduce the three specific categories you're discussing.

With these comments in mind, Corey revised and edited his paragraph. The final draft below includes all the elements Corey looked for when he applied the **TEST** strategy.

T E S T
- Topic Sentence
- Evidence
- Summary Statement
- Transitions

Giving Back

High-profile athletes find many ways to give back to their communities. One way to give back is to start a charitable foundation to help young fans. For example, Michael Jordan and the Chicago Bulls built a Boys' & Girls' Club on Chicago's West side. In addition, Troy Aikman set up a foundation that builds playgrounds for children's hospitals. Another way athletes give back to their communities is by mentoring, or giving guidance to young people. Many athletes work to encourage young people to stay in school. Shaquille O'Neal's Shaq's Paq, for example, provides guidance for inner-city children. The Philadelphia 76ers visit schools and have donated over five thousand books to local libraries. One more way athletes can contribute to their communities is to respond to emergencies. Football player Ike Reese collects clothing and food for families that need help. Basketball player Vince Carter founded the Embassy of Hope Foundation. It distributes food to needy families at Thanksgiving and hosts a Christmas party for disadvantaged families. These are just some of the ways that high-profile athletes give back to their communities.

● **Practice 9-3**

Now, you are ready to write a draft of a classification paragraph. Choose one of the topics below (or choose your own topic) for a classification paragraph. Then, use one or more of the strategies described in 1C to help you classify the members of the group you have chosen into as many categories as necessary.

Your friends	Popular music
Drivers	Fitness routines
Commuters on public transportation	Popular Web sites
Television shows	Part-time jobs
Clothing styles	Teachers
Parents or children	Popular movies
Types of success	T-shirt slogans
Radio stations	Stores in a shopping mall

● **Practice 9-4**

Review the information you came up with for the topic you chose in Practice 9-3. On the following lines, list three or four categories you can develop in your paragraph.

Category 1: _____

Category 2: _____

Category 3: _____

Category 4: _____

● **Practice 9-5**

Reread the list you made in Practice 9-4. Then, draft a topic sentence that introduces your subject.

_____

_____

● **Practice 9-6**

List below the categories you will discuss in your classification paragraph in the order in which you will discuss them.

1. _____

2. _____

3. _____

4. _____

● Practice 9-7

Draft your classification paragraph. Then, using the **TEST** checklist on page 131, check your paragraph for unity, support, and coherence.

● Practice 9-8

Now, revise your classification paragraph.

● Practice 9-9

Prepare a final edited draft of your classification paragraph.

Focus on Writing: *Revising and Editing*

Look back at your response to the Focus on Writing activity on page 123. Using the **TEST** checklist on page 131, evaluate the paragraph you wrote for unity, support, and coherence. Then, prepare a final revised and edited draft of your paragraph.

Chapter Review

Focus on Writing

The picture below shows a cafeteria foodline. Look at the photo, and think about all the kinds of foods you eat in a typical week. Then, write a paragraph in which you classify the foods you eat.

Real-World Writing

Assume that you spend several hours each week helping elementary-school children improve their reading skills. As the school year goes along, you find yourself using a variety of materials—everything from comic books to Web sites—with your students. To guide future tutors, write a classification paragraph discussing the kinds of reading material—besides books—that can be used to help your students become better readers.

TESTing a Classification Paragraph

Topic Sentence Unifies Your Paragraph

☐ Do you have a clearly worded topic sentence that states your paragraph's main idea?

☐ Does your topic sentence identify the categories you will discuss?

Evidence Supports Your Paragraph's Topic Sentence

☐ Do all your examples and details support your paragraph's main idea?

☐ Do your examples and details indicate how each category is distinct from the others?

☐ Do you need to include more examples or details?

Summary Statement Reinforces Your Paragraph's Unity

☐ Does your paragraph end with a statement that reinforces your main idea?

Transitions Add Coherence to Your Paragraph

☐ Do your transitions clearly indicate which categories are more important than others?

☐ Do your transitions tell readers when you are moving from one category to another?

☐ Do you need to add transitions to make your paragraph more coherent?

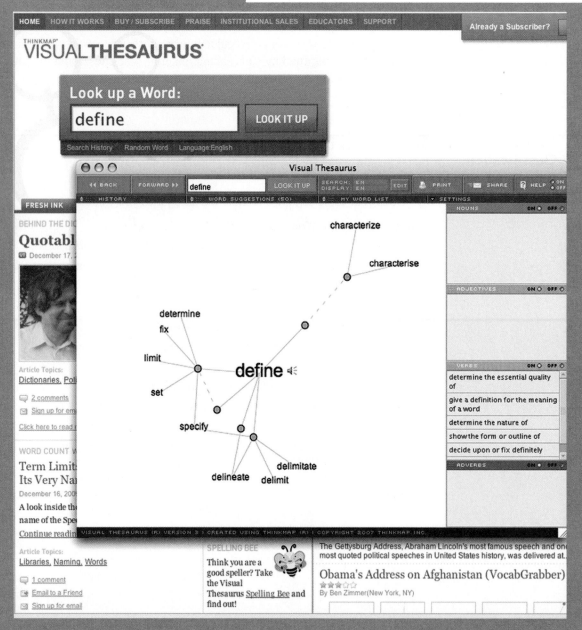

What Is Definition?

During a conversation, you might say that a friend is *stubborn*, that a stream is *polluted*, or that a neighborhood is *dangerous*. Without some explanation, however, these terms mean very little. In order to make yourself clear, you have to define what you mean by *stubborn, polluted,* or *dangerous*. Academic assignments also may involve definition. In a history paper, for example, you might have to define *imperialism*; on a biology exam, you might be asked to define *mitosis*.

A **definition** tells what a word means. When you want your readers to know exactly how you are using a specific term, you define it.

When most people think of definitions, they think of the **formal definitions** in a dictionary. Formal definitions have a three-part structure that includes the following components.

- The term to be defined
- The general class to which the term belongs
- The things that make the term different from all other items in the general class to which the term belongs

Term	Class	Differentiation
Ice hockey	is a game	played on ice by two teams on skates who use curved sticks to try to hit a puck into an opponent's goal.
Spaghetti	is a pasta	made in the shape of long, thin strings, usually served with a sauce.

Focus on Writing

The picture on the opposite page shows the home page of an online dictionary. Look at the picture, and then write a **definition** paragraph about a new word you learned in one of your college courses. Assume that your readers are not familiar with the word you are defining.

A single-sentence formal definition is often not enough to define a specialized term (*point of view* or *premeditation*, for example), an abstract concept (*happiness* or *success*, for example), or a complicated subject (*climate change* or *autism*, for example). In such cases, you need to expand the basic formal definition by writing a definition paragraph.

A **definition paragraph** is an expanded formal definition. Definition paragraphs do not follow any one particular pattern of development. In fact, a definition paragraph may define a term by using any of the patterns discussed in this text. For example, a definition paragraph may explain a concept by *comparing* it to something else or by giving *examples*. Like other kinds of paragraphs, a definition paragraph ends with a summary statement that reinforces the main point of the paragraph.

Here is one possible structure for a definition paragraph. Notice that it uses a combination of **narration** and **exemplification** to make its point.

Topic Sentence _____

_____

Point #1 _____

    Narration _____

_____

Point #2 _____

      Example _____

      Example _____

Point #3 _____

      Example _____

      Example _____

Summary Statement _____

_____

The writer of the following paragraph uses several patterns of development—including classification, cause and effect, and exemplification—to define the term *happiness*.

Happiness

Topic sentence ——— Although people disagree about what brings happiness (a feeling of contentment or joy), I know exactly what happiness means to me. The

First kind of happiness ——— first kind of happiness is the result of money. It comes from unexpectedly finding a twenty-dollar bill in my pocket. It comes from hitting the jackpot on a slot machine after putting in just one quarter. The second

Second kind of happiness ——— kind of happiness is about success. It comes from getting an A on a test or being told that my financial aid has been renewed for another year.

Third kind of happiness ——— The most valuable kind of happiness comes from the small things in life that make me feel good. This kind of happiness is taking time to have a cup of coffee before class or eating lunch at an old-fashioned diner. It is watching kids play Little League ball in the summer or playing pick-up basketball with my friends. It is finding out that I can still run a couple of miles even though I haven't exercised in a while or that I can remember all the state capitals that I had to memorize in school. For me, happiness

Summary statement ——— is more than just money or success; it is the little things that bring joy to my life.

Edward Fernandez (student)

Transitions are important for definition paragraphs. In the paragraph above, the transitional words and phrases *The first kind*, *The second kind*, and *The most valuable kind* introduce the categories the writer uses to define *happiness* and tell readers when they are moving from one category to the next.

The following box lists some of the transitional words and phrases that are used in definition paragraphs. In addition to these transitions, you can use the transitional words and phrases for the specific pattern (or patterns) that you use to develop your paragraph.

Some Transitional Words and Phrases for Definition

also	like
first (second, third)	one characteristic . . . another characteristic
for example	one way . . . another way
in addition	specifically
in particular	the first kind . . . the second kind
	unlike

Grammar in Context: Definition

A definition paragraph often includes a formal definition of the term or idea you are going to discuss. When you write a formal definition, be careful not to use the phrase *is where* or *is when*.

Happiness is when you have a feeling of contentment or joy.

● Practice 10-1

Read this definition paragraph; then, follow the instructions below.

Writer's Block

Writer's block is the inability to start writing. For college students, writer's block almost always involves assigned writing, such as a research paper or an essay exam. Sometimes writer's block is caused by poor preparation: the writer has not allowed enough time to think and make notes. In this case, the writer simply begins writing and finds that he or she has nothing to say. However, even prepared writers with many ideas already on paper can experience writer's block. It is like being tongue-tied, only writer's block is more like being "brain-tied." All the ideas keep bouncing around but will not settle into any order, and the writer cannot decide what to say first. Often, the only cure for writer's block is to give up for a while, find something else to do, and try again later. By doing this, the writer can give the mind a chance to clear so ideas have a chance to regroup and, eventually, to begin flowing.

Thaddeus Eddy (student)

1. Underline the topic sentence of the paragraph.
2. What is the subject of this definition? _____
3. What is the writer's one-sentence definition of the subject?

   _____

   _____

4. List some of the specific information the writer uses to define his sub-ject. The first piece of information has been listed for you.

For college students, it almost always involves assigned writing.

_____

_____

5. What patterns of development does the writer use in his definition? List them here.

_____

_____

_____

6. Underline the paragraph's summary statement.

● **Practice 10-2**

Following are four possible topic sentences for definition paragraphs. Each topic sentence includes an underlined word. In the space provided, list two possible patterns of development that you could use to expand a definition of the underlined word. For example, you could define the word *discrimination* by giving examples (exemplification) and by telling a story (narration).

1. During the interview, the job candidate made a <u>sexist</u> comment.

   Possible strategy: _____

   Possible strategy: _____

2. <u>Loyalty</u> is one of the chief characteristics of golden retrievers.

   Possible strategy: _____

   Possible strategy: _____

3. More than forty years after President Johnson's Great Society initiative, we have yet to eliminate <u>poverty</u> in the United States.

   Possible strategy: _____

   Possible strategy: _____

4. The problem with movies today is that they are just too <u>violent</u>.

   Possible strategy: _____

   Possible strategy: _____

10b   Writing a Definition Paragraph

On a history exam, Lorraine Scipio was asked to write a one-paragraph definition of the term *imperialism*. Lorraine had studied for the exam, so she
knew what *imperialism* was. Because she wanted to make sure that she did
not leave anything out of her definition (and because she had a time limit),
she quickly listed her points on the inside cover of her exam book. Then,
she crossed out two items that did not seem relevant.

A policy of control

Military

~~Lenin~~

Establish empires

Cultural superiority

Raw materials and cheap labor

Africa, etc.

~~Cultural imperialism~~

Nineteenth-century term

Next, Lorraine reorganized her points in the order in which she planned to
write about them.

Establish empires

Nineteenth-century term

Cultural superiority

Africa, etc.

Raw materials and cheap labor

A policy of control

Military

Consulting the points on her list, Lorraine wrote the following draft of
her definition paragraph. Notice that she uses several patterns to develop
her definition.

> The goal of imperialism was to set up an empire. The imperialist country
> thought that it was better than the country it took over. It said that it
> was helping the other country. But it wasn't. Countries such as Germany,
> Belgium, Spain, and England did this in Africa when they stole large areas

of land. It happened in North and South America when Spain, Portugal, England, and France took territory there. The imperialist countries did not help these countries. The point of imperialism was to take as much out of the other countries as possible. In South America and Mexico, Spain stole tons of gold. It made slaves of the natives and forced them to work in mines. Then they sent troops to protect their interests. Imperialism kept the people in occupied countries in poverty. It broke down local governments and local traditions. Many people thought it was wrong.

After she finished writing her paragraph, Lorraine reread it quickly, using the **TEST** strategy to help her to make sure her paragraph answered the exam question. Then, she made the following changes.

- Because the question asked for a definition, she added a **topic sentence** that included a formal definition.
- She strengthened her **evidence**, explaining her supporting details more fully. She also deleted some vague statements that did not support her topic sentence.
- She added **transitional words and phrases** to make the connections between her ideas clearer.
- She added a **summary statement** to reinforce the negative effects of imperialism.

Lorraine made her changes directly on the draft she had written, crossing out unnecessary information and adding missing information. She also edited her paragraph for grammar, punctuation, and mechanical errors. Then, because she had some extra time, she neatly copied over her revised and edited draft.

The final draft of Lorraine's exam answer appears below. (Because this is an exam answer, she does not include a title.) Notice that the final draft includes all the elements Lorraine looked for when she applied the **TEST** strategy.

TEST

Topic Sentence
Evidence
Summary Statement
Transitions

Imperialism was a nineteenth-century term that referred to the policy by which one country took over the land or the government of another country. The object of imperialism was to establish an empire. The imperialist country thought that it was superior to the country it took over. It justified its actions by saying that it was helping the other country. For instance, countries such as Germany, Belgium, Spain, and England followed their imperialist ambitions in Africa when they claimed large areas of land. The point of imperialism was to take as much out of the occupied countries as possible. For example, in South America and Mexico,

Spain removed tons of gold from the areas it occupied. It made the natives slaves and forced them to work in mines. In order to protect their interests, imperialist countries sent troops to occupy the country and to keep order. As a result, imperialism kept the people in occupied countries in poverty and often broke down local governments and local traditions. Although European imperialism occasionally had benefits, at its worst it brought slavery, disease, and death.

| Highlight: Writing Paragraph Answers on Exams | When you write paragraph answers on exams, you have limited time, so you need to be well prepared. Know your subject well, and memorize important definitions. You may have time to write an outline, a rough draft, and a final draft, but you will have to work quickly. In all cases, though, you should take the time to apply the **TEST** strategy to be sure you have included all the elements of a good paragraph: a topic sentence, evidence, a summary statement, and transitions. |

● **Practice 10-3**

Now, you are ready to write a draft of a definition paragraph. Choose one of the topics below (or choose your own topic) for a definition paragraph. Then, use one or more of the strategies described in 1C to help you define the term you have chosen to discuss. Name the term, and then describe it, give examples of it, tell how it works, explain its purpose, consider its history or future, or compare it with other similar things. In short, do whatever works best for defining your specific subject.

A negative quality, such as envy, dishonesty, or jealousy

An ideal, such as the ideal friend or neighborhood

A type of person, such as a worrier or a show-off

A social concept, such as equality, opportunity, or discrimination

An important play or strategy in a particular sport or game

A hobby you pursue or an activity associated with that hobby

A technical term or specific piece of equipment that you use in your job

An object (such as an article of clothing) that is important to your culture or religion

A basic concept in a course you are taking

A particular style of music or dancing

A controversial term whose definition not all people agree on, such as *affirmative action*, *right to life*, or *gun control*

A goal in life, such as success or happiness

● Practice 10-4

Review your notes for the topic you chose in Practice 10-3. List the details that can best help you to develop a definition paragraph.

● Practice 10-5

Reread your notes from Practice 10-4. Then, draft a topic sentence that summarizes the main point you want to make about the term you are going to define.

● Practice 10-6

List the ideas you will discuss in your paragraph, arranging them in an effective order.

1. _____
2. _____
3. _____
4. _____
5. _____

● Practice 10-7

Draft your definition paragraph. Then, using the **TEST** checklist on page 143, check your paragraph for unity, support, and coherence.

● Practice 10-8

Now, revise your definition paragraph.

● Practice 10-9

Prepare a final edited draft of your definition paragraph.

Focus on Writing: *Revising and Editing*

Look back at your response to the Focus on Writing activity on page 133. Using the **TEST** checklist on page 143, evaluate the paragraph you wrote for unity, support, and coherence. Then, prepare a final revised and edited draft of your paragraph.

Chapter Review

Focus on Writing

The pictures below show Americans from several different backgrounds. Look at the pictures carefully, and then write a paragraph that defines the term *American*. In what way do the people in the pictures fit (or not fit) your definition? Begin your paragraph with a topic sentence that identifies the term you will define. Then, in the rest of the paragraph, use any of the patterns of development discussed in this text to help you define the term.

Real-World Writing

For a brochure designed to encourage people to buy homes in your neighborhood, write a one-paragraph definition of the word *community*. Develop your definition with examples that demonstrate that your neighborhood has the people, resources, and qualities that make up a community.

TESTing a Definition Paragraph	**T**opic Sentence Unifies Your Paragraph

Topic Sentence Unifies Your Paragraph

☐ Do you have a clearly worded topic sentence that states your paragraph's main idea?

☐ Does your topic sentence identify the term you are defining?

Evidence Supports Your Paragraph's Topic Sentence

☐ Do all your examples and details support your paragraph's main idea?

☐ Do you need to add more examples or details to help you define your term?

Summary Statement Reinforces Your Paragraph's Unity

☐ Does your paragraph end with a statement that reinforces your main idea?

Transitions Add Coherence to Your Paragraph

☐ Are your transitions appropriate for the pattern (or patterns) of development you use?

☐ Do you need to add transitions to make your paragraph more coherent?

What Is Argument?

When most people hear the word *argument*, they think of heated exchanges on television interview programs. These discussions, however, are more like shouting matches than arguments. True **argument** involves taking a well-thought-out position on a **debatable issue**—an issue about which reasonable people may disagree (for example, "Should intelligent design be taught in high school classrooms?" or "Should teenagers who commit felonies be tried as adults?"). In an argument, you attempt to convince people of the strength of your ideas not by shouting but by presenting **evidence**. In the process, you also address opposing ideas. If they are strong, you acknowledge their strengths and try to **refute** (argue against) them. If your evidence is solid and your logic is sound, you will present a convincing argument.

When you write an **argument paragraph**, your purpose is to persuade readers that your position has merit. To write an effective argument paragraph, follow these guidelines:

- *Begin with a clear topic sentence that states your position.* Use words like *should*, *should not*, or *ought to* in your topic sentence to make your position clear to readers.

    The federal government should lower the tax on gasoline.

    The city should not build a new sports stadium.

Focus on Writing

The picture on the opposite page shows a person placing a vote in a ballot box. Look at the picture, and then write an **argument** paragraph that takes a stand for or against one of the following policies:

- Requiring paper ballots that can be hand-counted.

- Requiring electronic ballots that can be registered in computer databases.
- Permitting people to vote from their home computers.

Include examples from your own experience or from your reading to support your position.

- *Present points that support your topic sentence.* For example, if your purpose is to argue for placing warning labels on unhealthy snack foods, you should give several reasons why this would be a good idea.
- *Support your points with convincing evidence.* Supporting each of your points with specific evidence will strengthen your position.

Highlight: Evidence for an Argument Paragraph

Two kinds of **evidence** can be used to support the points you make in your arguments: *facts* and *examples.*

1. A **fact** is a piece of information that can be verified. If you make a point, you should be prepared to support it with facts—for example, statistics, observations, or statements that are widely accepted as true.
2. An **example** is a specific illustration of a general statement. To be convincing, an example should be clearly related to the point you are making.

- *Identify and refute opposing arguments.* Try to imagine what your opponent's arguments might be, and refute them by showing how they are inaccurate or weak. By addressing these objections in your paragraph, you strengthen your position.
- *End with a strong summary statement.* A summary statement reinforces the main idea of your paragraph. In an argument paragraph, it is especially important to summarize the position you introduced in your topic sentence.

An argument paragraph generally has the following structure.

Topic Sentence _____

_____

Point #1 _____

_____

Point #2 _____

_____

Point #3 _____

_____

Opposing Argument #1 (plus refutation) _____

_____

Opposing Argument #2 (plus refutation) _____

_____

Summary Statement _____

_____

The writer of the following paragraph argues against placing a tax on soda.

Taxing Soda

Topic sentence ——

        The proposed tax on soda is a bad idea because it is unfair, unnec-
essary, and unworkable. The first reason a soda tax is a bad idea is that
it is not fair. The American Medical Association (AMA) says that the tax
will fight obesity in the United States. However, people should be
allowed to decide for themselves whether they should drink soda. It
is not fair for a group of doctors or politicians to decide what is best
for everybody. Another reason a soda tax is a bad idea is that it is

Arguments in support
of the topic sentence ——

unnecessary. It would be better to set up educational programs to
help children make decisions about what they eat. In addition, the AMA
should educate parents so they will stop buying soda for their children.
Finally, a soda tax is a bad idea because it will not work. As long as
soda is for sale, children will drink it. The only thing that will work
is outlawing soda completely, and no one is suggesting this. Of course,

Opposing arguments
plus refutations ——

some people think that soda should be taxed because it has no nutritional
value. This is true, but many snack foods have little or no nutritional

Opposing arguments
plus refutations

Summary
statement

value, and no one is proposing that we tax them. In addition, not everyone who drinks soda is overweight, let alone obese, but a tax on soda would hurt everyone, including healthy adults. The key to helping young people develop good eating habits is not to tax them but to teach them what a healthy diet is.

Ashley Hale (student)

Transitions are important for argument paragraphs. In the paragraph above, the transitional words and phrases *The first reason, Another reason,* and *Finally* tell readers they are moving from one point to another. Later in the paragraph, the transitional phrases *Of course* and *In addition* introduce two opposing arguments that the writer goes on to refute.

Some Transitional Words and Phrases for Argument

accordingly	first . . . second . . .	on the one hand . . .
admittedly	however	on the other hand
although	in addition	since
because	in conclusion	the first reason . . .
but	in fact	another reason
certainly	in summary	therefore
consequently	meanwhile	thus
despite	moreover	to be sure
even so	nevertheless	truly
even though	nonetheless	
finally	of course	

Grammar in Context: Argument

When you write an argument paragraph, you need to show the relationships among your ideas. You do this by creating compound and complex sentences.

Compound Sentence
The only thing that will work is outlawing soda completely. No one is suggesting this.
, and no

Complex Sentence
Recently, some people have suggested taxing soda. They think it is not healthy for young people.
because they

● **Practice 11-1**

Read this argument paragraph; then, follow the instructions on page 150.

In Support of a Guest-Worker Program

America should create a guest-worker program that allows immigrants to work legally in the United States. First, a guest-worker program would fill gaps in the American workforce. These gaps occur because American citizens are unwilling to do certain kinds of work—for example, the hot, difficult work of planting, harvesting, and picking crops. Many illegal immigrants are willing to be migrant farm workers, but the law does not permit this. As a result, in places where such laws are strictly enforced, crops have been left to rot because farmers could not find American citizens willing to pick them. A guest-worker program would prevent situations like this from occurring. In addition, a guest-worker program would allow workers who are currently here illegally to apply for guest-worker status and thus lead more normal lives. Guest workers who needed help could call the police without worrying about being arrested and deported. They would also feel free to visit relatives in their home countries, knowing that they could legally return to America. Finally, under a guest-worker program, workers would have to pay taxes, but they would also be guaranteed access to health care and education. This arrangement is much better than the current situation, in which the government does not collect taxes from all illegal immigrants, and many illegal immigrants go without social services. Some people argue that instead of making it easier for illegal immigrants to work in America, we should make it harder. They say that America should build more walls and place armed guards at the Mexican-American border. However, walls and guards are expensive, and immigrants always find a way around them. Since immigrants are necessary for our economy, we should establish a guest-worker program that will enable them to work and live peacefully.

Scott Rathmill (student)

1. Underline the topic sentence of the paragraph.

2. What issue is the subject of the paragraph?

   _____

3. What is the writer's position?

   _____

   _____

4. What points does the writer use to support his topic sentence?

   _____

   _____

   _____

   _____

5. List some of the evidence that the writer uses to support his points. The first piece of evidence has been listed for you.

   Guest workers could fill in for American citizens, who are unwilling to

   do farm work.

   _____

   _____

   _____

   _____

   _____

6. What other evidence could the writer have used?

   _____

   _____

7. What opposing argument does the writer address?

   _____

   _____

8. How does the writer refute this argument?

_____

_____

9. Underline the paragraph's summary statement.

● **Practice 11-2**

Following are four topic sentences for argument paragraphs. List two or three points that could support each topic sentence. For example, if you were arguing in support of laws requiring motorcycle riders to wear safety helmets, you could say helmets cut down on medical costs and save lives.

1. Marijuana use for certain medical conditions should be legalized.

2. All student athletes should be paid a salary by their college or university.

3. College students caught cheating should be expelled.

4. The U.S. government should provide free health care for all.

● **Practice 11-3**

Choose one of the topic sentences from Practice 11-2. Then, list two pieces of evidence that could support each point you listed. For example, if you were arguing that wearing safety helmets saves lives, you could list "accident statistics" and "statements by emergency room physicians."

_____

_____

11b

Writing an Argument Paragraph

Phillip Zhu was asked to write an argument paragraph on a topic that interested him. Because he was taking a course in computer ethics, he was able to write about an issue that had been discussed in class: the way employers have recently begun searching social networking sites, such as Facebook, to find information about job applicants.

Phillip had already formed an opinion about this issue, and he knew he had the information he needed to support his position. For this reason, he was able to write a topic sentence right away.

Employers should not use social networking sites to find information about job applicants.

Phillip then listed the following ideas that he could use to support his topic sentence.

Social networking sites should be private

People exaggerate on social networking sites

Stuff meant to be funny

No one warns applicant

Need email address to register

Expect limited audience

Employers can misinterpret what they find

Employers going where they don't belong

Not an accurate picture

Not fair

Not meant to be seen by job recruiters

Phillip then arranged his ideas into an informal outline.

Social networking sites should be private
    Need email address to register
    Expect limited audience
    Employers going where they don't belong
People exaggerate on social networking sites
    Stuff meant to be funny
    Not meant to be seen by job recruiters
    No one warns applicant
Employers can misinterpret what they find
    Not an accurate picture
    Not fair

Once Phillip finished his informal outline, he tried to think of possible arguments against his position because he knew he would have to consider and refute opposing arguments in his paragraph. He came up with two possible arguments against his position:

1. Employers should be able to find out as much as they can.
2. Applicants have only themselves to blame.

Phillip then wrote the following draft of his paragraph.

> Employers should not use social networking sites to find information about job applicants. For one thing, social networking sites should be private. By going on these sites, employers are going where they do not belong. People also exaggerate on social networking sites. They say things that are not true, and they put things on the sites they would not want job recruiters to see. No one ever tells applicants that recruiters search these sites, so they feel safe posting all kinds of material. Employers can misinterpret what they read. Employers and recruiters need to get as much information as they can. They should not use unfair ways to get this information. Applicants have only themselves to blame for their problems. They need to be more careful about what they put up online. This is true, but most applicants don't know that employers will search social networking sites.

After finishing his draft, Phillip scheduled a conference with his instructor. Together, they went over his paragraph and applied the **TEST** strategy. They agreed that Phillip needed to make the following changes.

- They decided he needed to make his **topic sentence** more specific and more forceful.
- They decided he should add more **evidence** (details and examples) to his discussion. For example, what social networking sites is he talking about? Which are restricted? How do employers gain access to these sites?
- They decided he needed to delete irrelevant discussion blaming job applicants for the problems.
- They decided he should add **transitional words and phrases** to clearly identify the points he is making in support of his argument and also to identify the two opposing arguments he discusses.
- They decided he needed to add a strong **summary statement** to reinforce his position.

After making these changes, Phillip revised and edited his paragraph. The final draft below includes all the elements Phillip looked for when he applied the **TEST** strategy.

Unfair Searching

Employers should not use social networking sites, such as MySpace and Facebook, to find information about job applicants. First, social networking sites should be private. People who use these sites do not expect employers to access them. However, some employers routinely search social networking sites to find information about job applicants. Doing this is not right, and it is not fair. By visiting these sites, employers are going where they do not belong. Another reason employers should not use information from social networking sites is that people frequently exaggerate on them or say things that are not true. They may also put statements and pictures on the sites that they would not want job recruiters to see. Because no one ever tells applicants that recruiters search these sites, they feel safe posting embarrassing pictures or making exaggerated claims about drinking or sex. Finally, employers can misinterpret the material they see. As a result, they may reject a good applicant because they take seriously what is meant to be a joke. Of course, employers need to get as much information about a candidate as they can. They should not, however, use unfair tactics to get this information. In addition, prospective employers should realize that the profile they see on a social networking site does not accurately represent the job applicant. For these reasons, employers should not use social networking sites to do background checks.

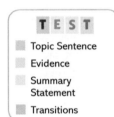

T E S T
- Topic Sentence
- Evidence
- Summary Statement
- Transitions

● **Practice 11-4**

Now, you are ready to write a draft of an argument paragraph. Choose one of the topics below (or choose your own topic) for an argument paragraph. Then, use one or more of the strategies described in 1C to help you focus on a specific issue to discuss in an argument paragraph.

An Issue at Your School

Grading policies	Financial aid
Required courses	Student activity fees
Attendance policies	Childcare facilities
Course offerings	Sexual harassment policies
Dining facilities	The physical condition of classrooms

An Issue in Your Community

The need for a traffic signal, a youth center, or something else you think would benefit your community

An action you think local officials should take, such as changing school hours, cleaning up a public space, or improving a specific service

A new law you would like to see enacted

A current law you would like to see repealed

A controversy you have been following in the news

● Practice 11-5

Once you have focused on an issue in Practice 11-4, write a journal entry about your position on the issue. Consider the following questions: Why do you feel the way you do? Do you think many people share your views, or do you think you are in the minority? What specific actions do you think should be taken? What objections are likely to be raised against your position? How might you respond to these objections?

● Practice 11-6

Review your notes for the topic you chose in Practice 11-4, and select the points that best support your position. List these points below. Then, list the strongest arguments against your position.

Supporting points: _____

_____

Opposing arguments: _____

_____

● Practice 11-7

Draft a topic sentence that clearly expresses the position you will take in your paragraph.

_____

_____

● Practice 11-8

In the space provided, arrange the points that support your position in an order that you think will be convincing to your audience.

1. _____

2. _____

3. _____

4. _____

5. _____

● Practice 11-9

In the space provided, list the evidence (facts and examples) that you could use to support each of your points.

Evidence for point 1: _____

_____

Evidence for point 2: _____

_____

Evidence for point 3: _____

_____

● Practice 11-10

Draft your argument paragraph. Then, using the **TEST** checklist on page 158, check your paragraph for unity, support, and coherence.

● Practice 11-11

Now, revise your argument paragraph.

● Practice 11-12

Prepare a final edited draft of your argument paragraph.

Focus on Writing: *Revising and Editing*

Look back at your response to the Focus on Writing activity on page 145. Using the **TEST** checklist on page 158, evaluate the paragraph you wrote for unity, support, and coherence. Then, prepare a final revised and edited draft of your paragraph.

Chapter Review

Focus on Writing

The picture below shows a driver sending a text message. Many states are considering (or have already adopted) a ban on texting by drivers in moving vehicles. Look at the picture, and then write an argument paragraph in which you argue either that this ban is a good idea or that the convenience of texting outweighs the possible risk of accidents.

Real-World Writing

Your school has proposed banning trans fats at all food outlets on campus—including independently owned food stands and trucks that serve students. Write a one-paragraph editorial for your school newspaper in which you argue either for or against this idea.

TESTing an Argument Paragraph

Topic Sentence Unifies Your Paragraph

☐ Do you have a clearly worded topic sentence that states your paragraph's main idea?

☐ Does your topic sentence state your position on a debatable issue?

Evidence Supports Your Paragraph's Topic Sentence

☐ Does all your evidence support your paragraph's main idea?

☐ Have you included enough evidence to support your points, or do you need to add more?

Summary Statement Reinforces Your Paragraph's Unity

☐ Does your paragraph end with a strong statement that reinforces your main idea?

Transitions Add Coherence to Your Paragraph

☐ Do you use transitional words and phrases to let readers know when you are moving from one point to another?

☐ Do you use transitional words and phrases to indicate when you are addressing opposing arguments?

☐ Do you need to add transitions to make your paragraph more coherent?

Unit Three

Writing Essays

12 Writing an Essay   160

13 Writing Introductions and Conclusions   194

14 Patterns of Essay Development   206

Much of the writing you do in school will be more than just one paragraph. Often, you will be asked to write an **essay**—a group of paragraphs on a single subject. When you write an essay, you follow the same process you follow when you write a paragraph: you begin by planning and then move on to organizing your ideas, drafting, **TEST**ing, and revising and editing.

In this chapter, you will see how the strategies you learned for writing paragraphs can help you write essays.

STEP 1: PLANNING

<table>
<tr><td>12a</td><td>

Understanding Essay Structure

</td></tr>
</table>

An **essay** is a group of paragraphs on a single subject.

Understanding the structure of a paragraph can help you understand the structure of an essay. In a paragraph, the main idea is stated in a **topic sentence**, and the rest of the paragraph supports this main idea with **evidence** (details and examples). **Transitional words and phrases** help readers follow the discussion. The paragraph ends with a **summary statement** that reinforces the main idea.

Paragraph

The **topic sentence** states the main idea of the paragraph.

Evidence (details and examples) supports the main idea.

Transitional words and phrases show the connections between ideas.

A **summary statement** ends the paragraph.

Focus on Writing

The picture on the opposite page shows a window washer working on a skyscraper. Look at the picture, and then think of the hardest job you ever had. This is the topic you will be writing about as you go through this chapter. (If you have never had a job, you may write about a specific task that you disliked or about a hard job that a friend or relative has had.)

The structure of an essay is similar to the structure of a paragraph:

- The essay's first paragraph—the **introduction**—begins with opening **remarks** and closes with a **thesis statement**. This thesis statement, like a paragraph's topic sentence, presents the main idea.
- The **body** of the essay contains several paragraphs that support the thesis statement. Each body paragraph begins with a **topic sentence** that states the main idea of the paragraph. The other sentences in the paragraph support the topic sentence with **evidence** (details and examples).
- **Transitional words and phrases** lead readers from sentence to sentence and from paragraph to paragraph.
- The last paragraph—the **conclusion**—ends the essay. The conclusion includes a **summary statement** that sums up the essay's main idea and reinforces the thesis. It ends with concluding remarks.

Many of the essays you will write in college will have a **thesis-and-support** structure.

Essay

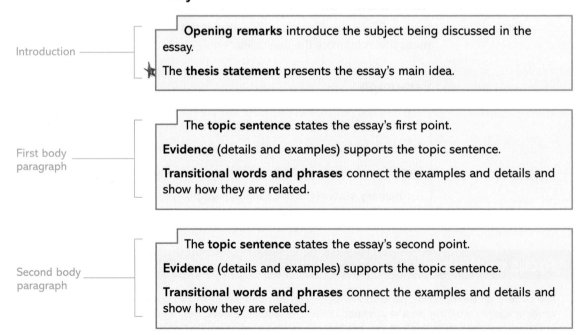

Introduction

    Opening remarks introduce the subject being discussed in the essay.

The **thesis statement** presents the essay's main idea.

First body paragraph

    The **topic sentence** states the essay's first point.

Evidence (details and examples) supports the topic sentence.

Transitional words and phrases connect the examples and details and show how they are related.

Second body paragraph

    The **topic sentence** states the essay's second point.

Evidence (details and examples) supports the topic sentence.

Transitional words and phrases connect the examples and details and show how they are related.

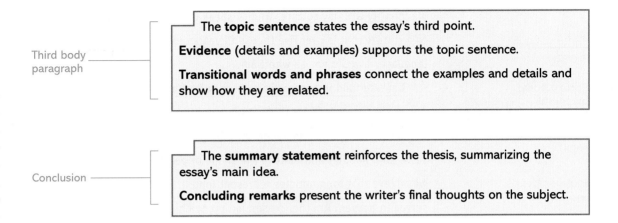

Third body paragraph

> The **topic sentence** states the essay's third point.
>
> **Evidence** (details and examples) supports the topic sentence.
>
> **Transitional words and phrases** connect the examples and details and show how they are related.

Conclusion

> The **summary statement** reinforces the thesis, summarizing the essay's main idea.
>
> **Concluding remarks** present the writer's final thoughts on the subject.

The following student essay illustrates this thesis-and-support structure (note that transitional words and phrases are shaded).

Becoming Chinese American

Introduction

Although I was born in Hong Kong, I have spent most of my life in the United States. However, my parents have always made sure that I did not forget my roots. They always tell stories of what it was like to live in Hong Kong. To make sure my brothers and sisters and I know what is happening in China, my parents subscribe to Chinese cable TV. When we were growing up, we would watch the celebration of the Chinese New Year,

Thesis statement

the news from Asia, and Chinese movies and music videos. As a result, I value Chinese culture even though I am an American.

First body paragraph

(Topic sentence states essay's first main point)

The Chinese language is an important part of my life as a Chinese American. Unlike some of my Chinese friends, I do not think the Chinese language is unimportant or embarrassing. First, I feel that it is my duty as a Chinese American to learn Chinese so that I can pass it on to my children. In addition, knowing Chinese enables me to communicate with

Evidence (details and examples)

my relatives. Because my parents and grandparents do not speak English well, Chinese is our main form of communication. Finally, Chinese helps me identify with my culture. When I speak Chinese, I feel connected to a culture that is over five thousand years old. Without the Chinese language, I would not be who I am.

Second body paragraph

(Topic sentence states essay's second main point)

Evidence (details and examples)

Chinese food is another important part of my life as a Chinese American. One reason for this is that everything we Chinese people eat has a history and a meaning. At a birthday meal, for example, we serve long noodles and buns in the shape of peaches. This is because we believe that long noodles represent long life and that peaches are served in heaven. Another reason is that to Chinese people, food is a way of reinforcing ties between family and friends. For instance, during a traditional Chinese wedding ceremony, the bride and the groom eat nine of everything. This is because the number nine stands for the Chinese words "together forever." By taking part in this ritual, the bride and groom start their marriage by making Chinese customs a part of their life together.

Third body paragraph

(Topic sentence states essay's third main point)

Evidence (details and examples)

Religion is the most important part of my life as a Chinese American. At various times during the year, Chinese religious festivals bring together the people I care about the most. During Chinese New Year, my whole family goes to the temple. Along with hundreds of other families, we say prayers and welcome each other with traditional New Year's greetings. After leaving the temple, we all go to Chinatown and eat dim sum until the lion dance starts. As the colorful lion dances its way down the street, people beat drums and throw firecrackers to drive off any evil spirits that may be around. Later that night, parents give children gifts of money in red envelopes that symbolize joy and happiness in the coming year.

(Summary statement reinforces essay's main idea)

My family has taught me how important it is to hold on to my Chinese culture. When I was six, my parents sent me to a Chinese-American grade school. My teachers thrilled me with stories of Fa Mulan, the Shang Dynasty, and the Moon God. I will never forget how happy I was when I realized how special it is to be Chinese. This is how I want my own

Conclusion

children to feel. I want them to be proud of who they are and to pass
their language, history, and culture on to the next generation.

● **Practice 12-1**

Following is an essay organized according to the diagram on pages 162–63.
Read the essay, and then answer the questions that follow it.

Enhanced Water

Flavored or "enhanced" water has grown in popularity since it was
introduced in the late 1990s. Most enhanced waters are owned by soft
drink companies like Coca-Cola and Pepsi. These companies have spent
millions of dollars trying to convince consumers that enhanced water is
better than ordinary water. However, this is not necessarily the case.

There is no question that our bodies need fluid to stay hydrated. In
fact, most experts say that people should drink about 64 ounces (eight
cups) of water per day. Only athletes and people who are involved in
strenuous activities, such as hiking, need to drink significantly more
water. These individuals may benefit from the salt and carbohydrates
found in sports drinks like Gatorade, but they are the exception. People
who exercise at a normal rate, for about an hour a day, usually need
only a few additional cups of plain water to restore lost fluids.

Despite marketing claims, it is not clear that enhanced water is
more healthful than regular water. The labels on most enhanced water
drinks, such as VitaminWater and SoBe Lifewater, make health claims
that have not been scientifically proven. For instance, the label on
VitaminWater's drink "Defense" implies that its vitamins and minerals will
prevent a person from getting sick. Scientists generally agree, however,
that there is no magic formula for preventing illness. Another example
of a misleading claim appears on the label on SoBe's strawberry-kiwi-
flavored "Calm-o-mile" drink, which lists herbs that are supposed to
relieve stress. However, the amount of herbs found in this drink is too
small to provide any health benefits. Moreover, many enhanced water
drinks actually contain ingredients that the body does not need—for
example, caffeine, artificial flavors and colors, and sugar or artificial
sweeteners.

In addition to making questionable marketing claims, manufacturers of enhanced waters present nutritional information in a confusing
way. For example, just a quick glance at the label for a SoBe Lifewater
drink would lead someone to believe that a serving has 40 calories,

16 grams of carbohydrates, and 10 grams of sugar. These amounts may sound reasonable, but a closer look at the label reveals that each 20-ounce bottle actually contains two and a half servings. In other words, a person who drinks the whole bottle is actually consuming 100 calories, 40 grams of carbohydrates, and 25 grams of sugar—more carbohydrates and sugar than in a glazed doughnut.

In most cases, regular tap water is all people need to stay healthy and hydrated. The drink manufacturers ignore this fact, saying that enhanced water is lower in calories and sugar than non-diet soft drinks. They also say that, although the herbs and vitamins in their drinks may not have proven health benefits, at least they are not harmful. Finally, the drink manufacturers claim that their products get people to drink more fluids. Although all these claims are largely true, consumers do not need the extra ingredients in enhanced water or its extra cost.

1. Underline the essay's thesis statement.

2. Underline the topic sentence of each body paragraph.

3. What point does the first body paragraph make? What evidence supports this point?

_____

_____

_____

_____

_____

4. What point does the second paragraph make? What evidence supports this point?

_____

_____

_____

_____

_____

5. What point does the third body paragraph make? What evidence supports this point?

_____

_____

6. What transitions does the essay include? How do they connect the essay's ideas?

_____

_____

_____

_____

_____

7. Where in the conclusion does the writer restate the essay's thesis? Underline this statement.

12b Focusing on Your Assignment, Purpose, and Audience

An essay usually begins with an assignment given to you by your instructor. Before you focus on your assignment, however, you should think about your essay's **audience** and **purpose**. In other words, take the time to think about who will be reading your essay and what you hope to accomplish by writing it. After doing this, you will be ready to consider your assignment.

The following assignments are typical of those you might be given in your composition class:

● Discuss some things you would like to change about your school.
● What can college students do to improve the environment?
● Discuss an important decision you made during the past three years.

Because these assignments are so general, they would be difficult to write about. What specific things would you change? Exactly what could you do to improve the environment? Which decision should you write about? Answering these questions will help you find a **topic** that you can write about.

Assignment	_Topic_
Discuss some things you would change about your school.	Three things I would change about Jackson County Community College

What can college students do to improve the environment?

A campus recycling project

Discuss an important decision you made during the past three years.

Deciding to go back to school

● Practice 12-2

Decide whether you could discuss the following topics in a short essay. If a topic is suitable, write *OK* in the blank. If it is not, write in the blank a revised version of the same topic that is narrow enough for a brief essay.

Examples: Successful strategies for quitting smoking _____*OK*_____

Horror movies _____*1950s Japanese monster movies*_____

1. Violence in American public schools _____

   _____

2. Ways to improve your study skills _____

   _____

3. Using pets as therapy for nursing-home patients _____

   _____

4. Teachers _____

   _____

5. Reasons children lie to their parents _____

   _____

Focus on Writing: *Flashback*

Look back at the Focus on Writing activity on page 161. To narrow the topic to one you can write about, you need to decide which job to focus on. List a few jobs you could discuss.

12c   Finding Ideas

Before you start writing about a topic, you need to find out what you have to say about it. Sometimes ideas will come to you easily. More often, you will have to use a strategy like *freewriting* or *brainstorming*, to help you come up with ideas about your topic.

Freewriting

When you **freewrite**, you write about anything that enters your mind for a fixed period of time without stopping. When you do **focused freewriting**, you freewrite with a specific topic in mind. Then, you read what you have written and choose the ideas you think you can use.

The following focused freewriting was written by a student, Jared White, on the topic "Deciding to go back to school."

> Deciding to go back to school. When I graduated high school, I swore I'd never go back to school. Hated it. Couldn't wait to get out. What was I thinking? How was I supposed to support myself? My dad's friend needed help. He taught me how to paint houses. I made good money, but it was boring. I couldn't picture myself doing it forever. Even though I knew I was going to have to go back to school, I kept putting off the decision. Maybe I was lazy. Maybe I was scared—probably both. I had this fear of being turned down. How could someone who had mostly bad grades all through high school go to college? Also, I'd been out of school for six years. And even if I did get in (a miracle!), how would I pay for it? How would I live? I met a guy while I was painting who told me that I could get into community college. Tuition was a lot lower than I thought. Then, I just had to push myself to go. Well, here I am—the first one in my family to go to college.

● Practice 12-3

Reread Jared White's focused freewriting. If you were advising Jared, which ideas would you suggest that he explore further? Why?

Focus on Writing: *Flashback*

Choose two of the jobs you listed for the Flashback activity on page 168. Freewrite about each of them. Then, choose the job that suggested the most interesting material. Circle the ideas that you would like to develop further in an essay.

Brainstorming

When you **brainstorm** (either individually or in collaboration with others), you write down (or type) all the ideas you can think of about a particular topic. You can make a list or you can make notes scattered all over a sheet of paper. After you have recorded as much material as you can, you look over your notes to decide which ideas are useful and which are not.

Here is Jared White's brainstorming list about his decision to go back to school.

Deciding to Go Back to School

Money a problem

No confidence

Other students a lot younger

Paying tuition—how?

No one in family went to college

Friends not in college

Couldn't picture myself in college

Relationship with Beth

Considered going to trade school

Computer programmer?

Grades bad in high school

Time for me to grow up

Wondered if I would get in

Found out about community college

Went to Web site

Admission requirements not bad

Afraid—too old, failing out, looking silly

Took time to get used to routine

Found other students like me

Liked studying

● Practice 12-4

Reread Jared White's brainstorming. Which ideas would you advise him to explore further?

Focus on Writing: *Flashback*

Review the freewriting you did for the Flashback activity on page 170. Brainstorm about the job for which you have the most interesting ideas. What ideas about the job did you get from brainstorming that you did not get from freewriting?

12d   Identifying Your Main Idea and Stating Your Thesis

After you have gathered information about your topic, you need to decide what point you want to make about it. You will then express this point in a **thesis statement**: a single sentence that clearly expresses the main idea that you will discuss in the rest of your essay.

Topic	*Thesis Statement*
Three things I would change about Jackson County Community College	If I could change three things about Jackson County Community College, I would expand the food choices, decrease class size in first-year courses, and ship some of my classmates to the North Pole.
A campus recycling project	The recycling project recently begun on our campus should be promoted more actively.

> Deciding to go back to school   I decided that if I really wanted to attend college full time, I could.

Like a paragraph's topic sentence, an essay's thesis statement tells readers what to expect. An effective thesis statement has two important characteristics.

1. An effective thesis statement makes a point about a topic. For this reason, it must do more than state a fact or announce what you plan to write about.

Statement of fact	Many older students are returning to college.
Announcement	In this essay, I would like to discuss the difficulties many older students have going back to college.
Effective thesis statement	I decided that if I really wanted to attend college full time, I could.

A statement of fact is not an effective thesis statement because it takes no position and gives you nothing to develop in your essay. After all, how much can you say about the *fact* that many older students are returning to college? Likewise, an announcement of what you plan to discuss gives readers no idea what position you will take on your topic. Remember, an effective thesis statement makes a point.

2. An effective thesis statement is clearly worded and specific.

Vague thesis statement	Television commercials are not like real life.
Effective thesis statement	Television commercials do not accurately portray women or minorities.

The vague thesis statement above gives little indication of the ideas that the essay will discuss. It does not say, for example, *why* television commercials are not realistic. The effective thesis statement is more focused. It signals that the essay will probably give examples of television commercials that present unrealistic portrayals of women and minorities.

> **Highlight: Stating Your Thesis**
>
> You can sometimes revise a vague thesis statement by including in it a list of the specific points that you will discuss. Revised in this way, the thesis acts as a road map, telling readers what to expect as they read.
>
> | | |
> |---|---|
> | **Vague thesis statement** | Raising tropical fish is a good hobby. |
> | **Effective thesis statement** | Raising tropical fish is a good hobby because it is inexpensive, interesting, and educational. |

When Jared White looked over his notes, he saw that they included ideas about how difficult it would be to return to school. They also included information about how to overcome these difficulties. Jared decided that his essay could discuss the challenges he faced when he decided to return to college as an older student. He presented this idea in a thesis statement.

> I decided that if I really wanted to attend college full time, I could.

Jared knew that his thesis statement had to be a complete sentence. He also knew that it had to make a point about his topic. Finally, he knew that it had to be both clearly worded and specific. When Jared reviewed his thesis statement, he felt sure that it did these things and that it expressed an idea he could develop in his essay.

● **Practice 12-5**

In the space provided, indicate whether each of the following items is a statement of fact (*F*), an announcement (*A*), a vague statement (*VS*), or an effective thesis (*ET*).

Examples:

My drive to school takes more than an hour. __*F*__

I hate my commute between home and school. __*VS*__

1. Students who must commute a long distance to school are at a disadvantage compared to students who live close to campus. __*ET*__

2. In this paper, I will discuss cheating and why students shouldn't cheat. __*A*__

3. Schools should establish specific policies that will discourage students from cheating. ES

4. Cheating is a problem. VS

5. Television infomercials are designed to sell products. F

6. I would like to explain why some television infomercials are funny. A

7. Single parents have a rough time. VS

x 8. An article in the newspaper says that young people are starting to abuse alcohol and drugs at earlier ages than in the past. ES

9. Alcohol and drug abuse are major problems in our society. VS

10. Families can use several strategies to help children avoid alcohol and drugs. ES

● **Practice 12-6**

Label each of the following thesis statements *F* if it is a statement of fact, *A* if it is an announcement, *VS* if it is a vague statement, or *ET* if it is an effective thesis. Revise those that are not effective thesis statements.

1. Different types of amusement parks appeal to different types of people.

   ⎯⎯

2. There are three reasons why Election Day should be a national holiday.

   ⎯⎯

3. Every four years, the United States elects a new president. ⎯⎯

4. My paper will prove that CDs are better than MP3 downloads. ⎯⎯

5. The largest fish in the sea is the whale shark. ⎯⎯

6. Scientists once believed that the dinosaurs were killed off by the arrival of a new Ice Age. ⎯⎯

7. NASCAR could take several steps to make their sport safer. ⎯⎯

8. This paper will discuss the increase in the number of women in the military since the 1970s. ⎯⎯

9. Movies provide great entertainment. ⎯⎯

10. Computers have enabled instructors to develop new teaching techniques. _____

● Practice 12-7

Rewrite the following vague thesis statements.

> **Example:** My relatives are funny.
>
> **Rewrite:** *My relatives think they are funny, but sometimes their humor can be offensive.*

1. Texting can save time.
2. Airport security could be better.
3. Athletes are paid too much.
4. Some people get their identities from their clothes.
5. Being single has advantages.

● Practice 12-8

A list of broad topics for essays follows. Select five of these topics, and draft a thesis statement for each.

Terrorism	Required courses
Reality television	Computer games
✓U.S. immigration policies	✓Disciplining children
✓Music	Street sense
✓Dieting	National ID cards

Focus on Writing: *Flashback*

Review your freewriting and brainstorming from the Flashback activities on page 170 and page 171. Then, draft a thesis statement for your essay.

STEP 2: ORGANIZING

Choosing Supporting Points

Once you have developed a thesis statement, look over your freewriting and brainstorming again. Identify the points that best support your thesis, and cross out those that do not.

Jared White made the following list of supporting points about his decision to go back to school. After he reviewed his list, he crossed out several points he thought would not support his thesis.

Thesis statement: I decided that if I really wanted to attend college full time, I could.

Deciding to Go Back to School

Money a problem

~~No confidence~~

Other students a lot younger

Paying tuition—how?

No one in family went to college

Friends not in college

Couldn't picture myself in college

~~Relationship with Beth~~

~~Considered going to trade school~~

~~Computer programmer?~~

Grades bad in high school

~~Time for me to grow up~~

Wondered if I would get in

Found out about community college

Admission requirements not bad

Afraid—too old, failing out, looking silly

~~Took time to get used to routine~~

Found other students like me

Liked studying

● **Practice 12-9**

Look at Jared's list of supporting points on page 176. Are there any points he crossed out that you think he should have kept? Are there any other points he should have crossed out?

12f ## Arranging Your Supporting Points

After you have selected the points you think will best support your thesis, arrange them into groups. For example, after reviewing his list of points, Jared White saw that they could be arranged in three groups of excuses for not going back to school: not being able to pay tuition, not being a good student in high school, and not being able to picture himself in college.

After you have come up with your own groups, arrange them in the order in which you will discuss them (for example, from general to specific, or from least important to most important). Then, arrange the supporting points for each group in the same way. This list can serve as an **informal outline** to guide you as you write.

Jared arranged his points in the following informal outline.

Excuse 1: Not being able to pay tuition

    Money a problem

    Found out about community college

Excuse 2: Not being a good student in high school

    Grades bad in high school

    Wondered if I would get in

    Admission requirements not bad

Excuse 3: Not being able to picture myself in college

    No one in family went to college

    Friends not in college

    Afraid—too old, failing out, looking silly

    Found other students like me

    Liked studying

● **Practice 12-10**

Look over Jared's list of points above. Do you think his arrangement is effective? Can you suggest any other ways he might have arranged his material?

**Highlight:
Preparing
a Formal
Outline**

Formal outlines contain a combination of numbered and lettered head-ings and use Roman numerals, capital letters, and Arabic numerals (and sometimes lowercase letters) to show the relationships among ideas. For example, the most important (and most general) ideas are assigned a Roman numeral; the next most important ideas are assigned capital letters. Each level develops the idea above it, and each new level is indented.

Here is a formal outline of the points that Jared White planned to discuss in his essay.

Thesis statement: I decided that if I really wanted to attend college full time, I could.

I.   Not being able to pay tuition
    A.   Money a problem
    B.   Community college
        1.   Tuition low
        2.   Expenses reasonable
II.   Not being a good student in high school
    A.   Grades bad
        1.   Didn't care about high school
        2.   Didn't do homework
    B.   Anxiety about getting in
    C.   Admissions requirements
        1.   High school diploma
        2.   County residence
        3.   Placement tests
III.   Not being able to picture myself in college
    A.   Family no help
    B.   Friends not in college
    C.   Fear of going
        1.   Too old
        2.   Couldn't keep up
    D.   Fears disappeared
        1.   Found other students like me
        2.   Liked studying

Focus on Writing: *Flashback*

Review your freewriting and brainstorming from the Flashback activities on pages 170 and 171. List the points you plan to use to support your thesis statement. Then, cross out any points that do not support your thesis statement. Finally, group the remaining points, and arrange them in an order in which you could write about them.

STEP 3: DRAFTING

12g ## Drafting Your Essay

After you have decided on a thesis for your essay and arranged your points in the order in which you will discuss them, you are ready to draft your essay.

At this stage of the writing process, you should not worry about spelling or grammar or about composing a perfect introduction or conclusion. Your main goal is to get your ideas down so you can react to them. Remember that the draft you are writing will be revised, so leave room for your changes: write on every other line, and leave extra space between lines if you are typing. Follow your informal outline, but don't hesitate to depart from it if you think of new points.

As you draft your essay, be sure that it has a **thesis-and-support** structure—that is, it should state a thesis and support it with evidence (details and examples).

Jared White used a thesis-and-support structure in the first draft of his essay.

Going Back to School

I was out of school for six years after I graduated from high school. The decision to return to school was one I had a lot of difficulty making. I had been around enough to know that without more education, I'd never get anywhere in life, but I always found reasons for not taking the plunge. However, after a lot of thinking, I realized that my reasons for not going to college were just excuses. I decided that if I really wanted to attend college full time, I could.

My first excuse for not going to college was that I couldn't afford to go to school full time. I had worked since I finished high school, but I hadn't put much money away. I kept wondering how I would pay for books and tuition. I needed to support myself and pay for rent, food, and car expenses. I was working as a house painter, and a house I was painting belonged to a college instructor. Painting wasn't hard work, but it was boring. I'd start in the morning and work without a break until lunch. We began talking. When I told him about my situation, he told me I should look at our local community college. I went online and looked at the college's Web site. I found out that tuition was forty dollars a credit, much less than I thought it would be.

Now that I had taken care of my first excuse, I had to deal with my second—that I hadn't been a good student in high school. When I was a teenager, I didn't care much about school. School bored me to death. Now that I was considering going back to school, though, I wondered what price I would have to pay for my laziness and immaturity. The answer to this question was not as bad as I thought it would be. According to the community college's Web site, all I needed to be admitted was a high school diploma and county residence. I would have to take some placement tests, but I would be judged on my ability, not my high school grades. The Web site was easy to navigate, and I had no problem finding information.

I had a hard time picturing myself in college. No one in my family had ever gone to college. My friends were just like me; they all went to work right after high school. I had no role model or mentor who could give me advice. I thought I was just too old for college. After all, I was probably at least six years older than most of the students. How would I be able to keep up with the younger students in the class? I hadn't opened a textbook for years, and I'd never really learned how to study. Most of my fears disappeared during my first few weeks of classes. I saw a lot of students who were as old as I was, and some were even older. Studying didn't seem to be a problem either. I actually enjoyed learning. History, which had put me to sleep in high school, suddenly became interesting. So did math and English. It soon became clear to me that I was going to like being in college.

Going to college as a full-time student has changed my life, both personally and financially. I am no longer the same person I was in high school. I allowed laziness and insecurity to hold me back. Now, I have options that I didn't have before. When I graduate from community college, I plan to transfer to the state university and get a four-year degree.

● Practice 12-11

Reread Jared White's first draft. What changes would you suggest he make? What might he add? What might he delete?

Focus on Writing: *Flashback*

Draft an essay about the job you chose in the Flashback activity on page 170. Be sure to include the thesis statement you developed in the Flashback activity on page 175 as well as the points you listed in the Flashback activity on page 178.

STEP 4: TESTING

12h

TESTing Your Essay

Before you begin to revise the first draft of your essay, you should **TEST** it to make sure it contains the four elements that make it clear and effective.

As you reread your essay, use the **TEST** strategy to identify the four elements of an effective essay. If your essay includes these four elements, you can move on to revise and edit it. If not, you should supply whatever is missing.

When Jared reread the draft of his essay, he used the **TEST** strategy to help him quickly survey his essay.

- He decided that his thesis statement clearly stated his main idea.
- He thought he could add some more evidence in his body paragraphs and delete some irrelevant details.
- He thought his summary statement summed up the idea expressed in his thesis statement.
- He realized he needed to add more transitions to connect ideas.

Focus on Writing: *Flashback*

Using the Highlight box above as a guide, evaluate the essay you drafted for the Flashback activity on page 180. (You may want to get feedback on your draft from another student.)

STEP 5: REVISING AND EDITING

12i Revising Your Essay

When you **revise** your essay, you resee, rethink, reevaluate, and rewrite your work. Some of the changes you make—such as adding, deleting, or rearranging sentences or even whole paragraphs—will be major. Other changes will be small—for example, adding or deleting words or phrases.

Before you begin revising, put your essay aside for a while. This "cooling-off" period allows you to see your draft more objectively when you return to it. (Keep in mind that revision is usually not a neat process. When you revise, feel free to write directly on your draft: draw arrows, underline, cross out, and write above lines and in the margins.)

Even when you write on a computer, it is a good idea to print out a hard copy and revise by hand on the page. With a hard copy, you are able to see a full page—or even two pages next to each other—as you revise. When you have finished, you can type your changes into your document. Do not delete sentences or paragraphs until you are certain you do not need them; instead, temporarily move unwanted material to the end of your draft.

To get the most out of revision, read your essay carefully, and use the following checklist as your guide.

Self-Assessment Checklist: Revising Your Essay	☐ Does your essay have an introduction, a body, and a conclusion?
	☐ Is your thesis statement clearly worded?
	☐ Does each body paragraph have a topic sentence?
	☐ Does each topic sentence introduce a point that supports the thesis?
	☐ Does each body paragraph include enough details and examples to support the topic sentence?
	☐ Are the body paragraphs unified, well developed, and coherent?

12j   Editing Your Essay

When you **edit** your essay, you check grammar and sentence structure. Then, you look at punctuation, mechanics, and spelling.

As you edit, think carefully about the questions in the Self-Assessment Checklist below.

Self-Assessment Checklist: Editing Your Essay	**Editing for Common Sentence Problems** ☐ Have you avoided run-ons? (See Chapter 21.) ☐ Have you avoided sentence fragments? (See Chapter 22.) ☐ Do your subjects and verbs agree? (See Chapter 23.) ☐ Have you avoided illogical shifts? (See Chapter 24.) ☐ Have you avoided dangling and misplaced modifiers? (See Chapter 25.) **Editing for Grammar** ☐ Are your verb forms and verb tenses correct? (See Chapters 26 and 27.) ☐ Have you used nouns and pronouns correctly? (See Chapter 28.) ☐ Have you used adjectives and adverbs correctly? (See Chapter 29.) **Editing for Punctuation, Mechanics, and Spelling** ☐ Have you used commas correctly? (See Chapter 31.) ☐ Have you used apostrophes correctly? (See Chapter 32.) ☐ Have you used capital letters where they are required? (See 34A.) ☐ Have you used quotation marks correctly where they are needed? (See 34B.) ☐ Have you spelled every word correctly? (See Chapter 35.)

When Jared White typed the first draft of his essay about deciding to return to college, he left extra space so he could write more easily in the space between the lines. His draft, with his handwritten revision and editing changes as well as the transitions he added after he finished **TEST**ing his essay appears on the following page.

The other day, my sociology instructor mentioned that half the students enrolled in college programs across the country are twenty-five or older. His remarks caught my attention because I am one of those students.

~~Going Back to School~~ *Starting Over*

I was out of school for six years after I graduated from high school. The decision to return to school was one I had a lot of difficulty making. I had been around enough to know that without more education, I'd never get anywhere in life, but I always found reasons for not taking the plunge. However, after a lot of thinking, I realized that my reasons for not going to college were just excuses. I decided that if I really wanted to attend college full time, I could.

My first excuse for not going to college was that I couldn't afford to go to school full time. I had worked since I finished high school, but I hadn't put much money away. I kept wondering how I would pay for books and tuition. I *also* needed to support myself and pay for rent, food, and car expenses. *The solution to my problem came unexpectedly.* I was working as a house painter, and a house I was painting belonged to a college instructor. ~~Painting wasn't hard work, but it was boring. I'd start in the morning and work without a break until lunch.~~ *During my lunch break, we* ~~We~~ began talking. When I told him about my situation, he told me I should look at our local community college. *Later,* I went online and looked at the college's Web site. I found out that tuition was forty dollars a credit, much less than I thought it would be.

The money I'd saved, along with what I could make painting houses on the weekends, could get me through.

Now that I had taken care of my first excuse, I had to deal with my second—that I hadn't been a good student in high school. When I was a teenager, I didn't care much about school. *In fact, school* ~~School~~ bored me ~~to death~~. Now that I was considering going back to school, though, I wondered what price I would have to pay for my laziness and immaturity. The answer to this question was not as bad as I thought it would be. According to the community college's Web site, all I needed to be admitted was a high school diploma and county residence. I would have to take some placement tests, but I would be judged on my ability, not my high school grades. ~~The Web site was easy to navigate, and I had no problem finding information.~~

In class, I would stare out the window or watch the second hand of the clock move slowly around. I never bothered with homework. School just didn't interest me.

My biggest problem still bothered me:
I had a hard time picturing myself in college. No one in my family
had ever gone to college. My friends were just like me; they all went to
work right after high school. I had no role model or mentor who could
Besides,
give me advice. I thought I was just too old for college. After all, I was
probably at least six years older than most of the students. How would
I be able to keep up with the younger students in the class? I hadn't
opened a textbook for years, and I'd never really learned how to study.
However, most
Most of my fears disappeared during my first few weeks of classes. I saw
a lot of students who were as old as I was, and some were even older.
Studying didn't seem to be a problem either. I actually enjoyed learning.
History, which had put me to sleep in high school, suddenly became
interesting. So did math and English. It soon became clear to me that I
was going to like being in college.

Going to college as a full-time student has changed my life, both
personally and financially. I am no longer the same person I was in high
In the past,
school. I allowed laziness and insecurity to hold me back. Now, I have
options that I didn't have before. When I graduate from community
college, I plan to transfer to the state university and get a four-year
degree. *The other day, one of my instructors asked me if I had ever
considered becoming a teacher. The truth is, I never had, but now
I might. I'd like to be able to give kids like me the tough, realistic
advice I wish someone had given me.*

● Practice 12-12

What kind of material did Jared White add to his draft? What did he delete?
Why do you think he made these changes? Write your answers on a separate
sheet of paper.

When his revisions and edits were complete, Jared proofread his essay
to make sure he had not missed any errors. The final revised and edited
version of his essay appears on pages 186–87. (Marginal annotations have
been added to highlight key features of his paper; transitional words and
phrases are shaded.) Notice that the final draft includes all the elements
Jared looked for when he applied the **TEST** strategy.

Jared White
Professor Wilkinson
English 120
7 Oct. 2009

Starting Over

Introduction

The other day, my sociology instructor mentioned that half the students enrolled in college programs across the country are twenty-five or older. His remarks caught my attention because I am one of those students. I was out of school for six years after I graduated from high school. The decision to return to school was one I had a lot of difficulty making. I had been around enough to know that without more education, I would never get anywhere in life, but I always found reasons for not taking the plunge. However, after a lot of thinking, I realized that my reasons for not going to college were just excuses. I decided that if I really wanted to attend college full time, I could.

Thesis statement

Topic sentence (first main point)

My first excuse for not going to college was that I couldn't afford to go to school full time. I had worked since I finished high school, but I hadn't put much money away. I kept wondering how I would pay for books and tuition. I also needed to support myself and pay for rent, food, and car expenses. The solution to my problem came unexpectedly. I was working as a house painter, and a house I was painting belonged to a college instructor. During my lunch break, we began talking. When I told him about my situation, he told me I should look at our local community college. Later, I went online and looked at the college's Web site. I found out that tuition was forty dollars a credit, much less than I thought it would be. The money I'd saved, along with what I could make painting houses on the weekends, could get me through.

Evidence (details and examples)

Body paragraphs

Now that I had taken care of my first excuse, I had to deal with my second—that I hadn't been a good student in high school. When I was a teenager, I didn't care much about school. In fact, school bored me. In class, I would stare out the window or watch the second hand on the clock move slowly around. I never bothered with homework. School just didn't interest me. Now that I was considering going back to school, though, I wondered what price I would have to pay for my laziness and immaturity. The answer to this question was not as bad as I thought it would be. According to the community college's Web site, all I needed to be admitted was a high school diploma and county residence. I would have to take some placement tests, but I would be judged on my ability, not my high school grades.

Topic sentence (second main point)

Evidence (details and examples)

Topic sentence
(third main point)

Evidence (details
and examples)

Body paragraphs —————

Summary statement

Conclusion

My biggest problem still bothered me: I had a hard time picturing myself in college. No one in my family had ever gone to college. My friends were just like me; they all went to work right after high school. I had no role model or mentor who could give me advice. Besides, I thought I was just too old for college. After all, I was probably at least six years older than most of the students. How would I be able to keep up with the younger students in the class? I hadn't opened a textbook for years, and I'd never really learned how to study. However, most of my fears disappeared during my first few weeks of classes. I saw a lot of students who were as old as I was, and some were even older. Studying didn't seem to be a problem either. I actually enjoyed learning. For example, history, which had put me to sleep in high school, suddenly became interesting. So did math and English. It soon became clear to me that I was going to like being in college.

Going to college as a full-time student has changed my life, both personally and financially. I am no longer the same person I was in high school. In the past, I allowed laziness and insecurity to hold me back. Now, I have options that I didn't have before. When I graduate from community college, I plan to transfer to the state university and get a four-year degree. The other day, one of my instructors asked me if I had ever considered becoming a teacher. The truth is, I never had, but now I might. I'd like to be able to give kids like me the tough, realistic advice that I wish someone had given me.

● Practice 12-13

Reread the final draft of Jared White's essay. Do you think this draft is better than his first draft (pp. 179–80)? What other changes could Jared have made?

12k ## Checking Your Essay's Format

The **format** of an essay is the way it looks on a page—for example, the size of the margins, the placement of page numbers, and the amount of space between lines. Most instructors expect you to follow a certain format when you type an essay. The model essay format illustrated on the following page is commonly used in composition classes. Before you hand in an essay, you should make sure that it follows this model (or the guidelines your instructor gives you).

Essay Format: Sample First Page

8½"

1"

½"

White 1

Jared White

Double-space

Professor Wilkinson

English 120

7 Oct. 2009

Title (centered)

Starting Over

Double-space

The other day, my sociology instructor mentioned that half

the students enrolled in college programs across the country are

twenty-five or older. His remarks caught my attention because I

am one of those students. I was out of school for six years after I

graduated from high school. The decision to return to school was

one I had a lot of difficulty making. I had been around enough to

know that without more education, I would never get anywhere in

life, but I always found reasons for not taking the plunge. However,

after a lot of thinking, I realized that my reasons for not going

to college were just excuses. I decided that if I really wanted to

attend college full time, I could.

←1"→

←1"→

Indent ½ inch

My first excuse for not going to college was that I couldn't

afford to go to school full time. I had worked since I finished high

school, but I hadn't put much money away. I kept wondering how

I would pay for books and tuition. I also needed to support myself

and pay for rent, food, and car expenses. The solution to my prob-

lem came unexpectedly. I was working as a house painter, and a

house I was painting belonged to a college instructor. During my

lunch break, we began talking. When I told him about my situation,

he told me I should look at our local community college. Later, . . .

1"

Focus on Writing: *Revising and Editing*

Now, revise and edit your draft, using the Self-Assessment Checklists on pages 182 and 183 to guide you. When you have finished, make sure the format of your essay follows your instructor's guidelines. Then, prepare a final revised and edited draft of your essay.

Chapter Review

Editing Practice

1. The following student essay is missing its thesis statement and topic sentences and has no summary statement. First, write an appropriate thesis statement on the lines provided. (Make sure your thesis statement clearly communicates the essay's main idea.) Then, fill in the topic sentences for the second, third, and fourth paragraphs. Finally, add a summary statement in the conclusion.

Preparing for a Job Interview

I have looked at a lot of books and many Web sites that give advice on how to do well on a job interview. Some recommend practicing your handshake, and others suggest making eye contact. This advice is useful, but not many books tell how to get mentally prepared for an interview. [Thesis statement:] _____

_____

_____

[Topic sentence for the second paragraph:] _____

_____

_____

Feeling good about how I look is important, so I usually wear a jacket and tie to an interview. Even if you will not be dressing this formally on the job, try to make a good first impression. For this reason, you should never come to an interview dressed in jeans or shorts. Still, you should be careful not to overdress. For example, wearing a suit or a dressy dress to an interview at a fast-food restaurant might make you feel good, but it could also make you look as if you do not really want to work there.

    [Topic sentence for the third paragraph:] _____

_____

_____

Going on an interview is a little like getting ready to compete in a sporting event. You have to go in with the right attitude. If you think you are not going to be successful, chances are that you will not be. So, before I go on any interview, I spend some time building my confidence. I tell myself that I can do the job and that I will do well in the interview. By the time I get to the interview, I have convinced myself that I am the right person for the job.

    [Topic sentence for the fourth paragraph:] _____

_____

_____

Most people go to an interview knowing little or nothing about the job. They expect the interviewer to tell them what they will have to do. Once, an interviewer told me that he likes a person who has taken the time to do his or her homework. Since that time, I have always done some research before I go on an interview—even for a part-time job. Most of the time, my research is nothing more than a quick look at the company Web site, but this kind of research really pays off. At my last interview, for example, I was able to talk in detail about the job I would do. The interviewer must have been impressed because she offered me the job on the spot.

    [Summary statement:] _____

_____

_____

Of course, following my suggestions will not guarantee that you get a job. You still have to do well at the interview itself. Even so, getting mentally prepared for the interview will give you an advantage over people who do almost nothing before they walk in the door.

2. Now, using the topic sentence below, write another body paragraph that you could add to the essay above. (This new paragraph will go right before the essay's conclusion.)

    Another way to prepare yourself mentally is to anticipate and answer some typical questions interviewers ask. [New body paragraph:]

_____

_____

_____

_____

Collaborative Activities

1. On your own, find a paragraph in a magazine or a newspaper about an issue that interests you. Working in a group of three students, select one of the paragraphs. Choose three points about the issue discussed that you could develop in a short essay, and then brainstorm about these points. Finally, write a sentence that could serve as the thesis statement for an essay.

2. Working in a group, come up with thesis statements suitable for essays on three of the following topics.

Living on a budget	Gun safety
Social-networking sites	Online dating
Safe driving	Patriotism
Parenthood	Bad habits
Honesty	Preparing for a test

3. Exchange your group's three thesis statements with those of another group. Choose the best one of the other group's thesis statements. A member of each group can then read the thesis statement to the class and explain why the group chose the thesis statement it did.

Review Checklist: Writing an Essay

☐ Most essays have a thesis-and-support structure. The thesis statement presents the main idea, and the body paragraphs support the thesis. (See 12A.)

☐ Begin by focusing on your assignment, audience, and purpose to help you find a topic. (See 12B.)

☐ Find ideas to write about. (See 12C.)

☐ Identify your main idea, and develop an effective thesis statement. (See 12D.)

☐ List the points that best support your thesis, and arrange them in the order in which you plan to discuss them. (See 12E, 12F.)

☐ Write your first draft, making sure your essay has a thesis-and-support structure. (See 12G.)

☐ **TEST** your essay. (See 12H.)

☐ Revise your essay. (See 12I.)

☐ Edit your essay. (See 12J.)

☐ Make sure your essay's format is correct. (See 12K.)

Chapter 13

Writing Introductions and Conclusions

When you draft an essay, you usually focus on the **body** because it is the section in which you develop your ideas. A well-constructed essay, however, is more than a series of body paragraphs. It also includes an **introduction** and a **conclusion**, both of which contribute to the overall effectiveness of your writing.

13a   Introductions

An **introduction** is the first thing people see when they read your essay. If your introduction is interesting, it will make readers want to read further. If it is not, they may get bored and stop reading.

Your introduction should be a full paragraph that moves from general to specific ideas. It should begin with some general **opening remarks** that will draw readers into your essay. The **thesis statement**, a specific sentence that presents the main idea of your essay, usually comes at the end of the introduction. The following diagram illustrates the general shape of your introduction.

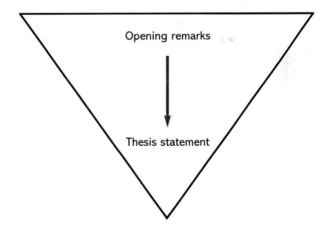

Opening remarks

Thesis statement

Focus on Writing

The picture on the opposite page shows firefighters on their way to a job. Look at the picture, and then print out a copy of the essay about your hardest job that you wrote for

Chapter 12. As you go through this chapter, you will be working on the introduction and conclusion of that essay.

Here are some options you can experiment with when you write your introductions. (In each of the sample introductory paragraphs that follow, the thesis statement is underlined and labeled.)

Beginning with a Narrative

You can begin an essay with a **narrative** drawn from your own experience or from a current news event.

Thesis statement

On September 11, 2001, terrorists crashed two airplanes into the twin towers at the World Trade Center. Ignoring the danger to themselves, hundreds of firefighters rushed inside the buildings to try to save as many lives as possible. Their actions enabled thousands of people to get out, but half the firefighters—over three hundred—died when the twin towers collapsed. The sad fact is that until a tragedy occurs, most people never think about how difficult a firefighter's job really is.

Richard Pogue (student)

Beginning with a Question (or a Series of Questions)

Asking one or more **questions** at the beginning of your essay is an effective strategy. Because readers expect you to answer the questions, they will want to read further.

Thesis statement

What's wrong with this picture? A teenage girl sits under a Christmas tree, opening her presents. She is excited when she gets a new sweater and the running shoes she has been wanting. On the surface, everything seems fine. However, the girl's parents are uncomfortable because they know that children from developing countries probably worked long hours in sweatshops to make the American teenager's Christmas presents. Instead of feeling guilty, people like this girl's parents should take steps to end child labor and help poor children live better lives.

Megan Davia (student)

Beginning with a Definition

A **definition** at the beginning of your essay can give readers important information. As the following introduction shows, a definition can help explain a complicated idea or a confusing concept.

The term *good parent* is not easy to define. Some things about being a good parent are obvious—keeping children safe, taking them to the doctor for checkups, helping them with their homework, and staying up with them when they are sick. Other things are not so obvious, however. I found this out last year when I became a volunteer at my daughter's middle school. Until that time, I never would have believed that one morning a week could do so much to improve my daughter's attitude toward school.

Thesis statement

Russ Hightower (student)

Beginning with a Quotation

A **quotation**—for example, an appropriate saying or some interesting dialogue—can draw readers into your essay.

According to the comedian Jerry Seinfeld, "When you're single, you are the dictator of your own life. . . . When you're married, you are part of a vast decision-making body." In other words, before you can do anything when you are married, you have to talk it over with someone else. These words kept going through my mind as I thought about asking my girlfriend to marry me. The more I thought about Seinfeld's words, the more I put off asking. I never thought about the huge price that I would pay for this delay.

Thesis statement

Dan Brody (student)

Beginning with an Unexpected Statement

You can begin your essay with a surprising or **unexpected statement**. Because your statement takes readers by surprise, it catches their attention.

Some of the smartest people I know never went to college. In fact, some of them never finished high school. They still know how to save 20 percent on the price of a dinner, fix their own faucets when they leak, get discounted prescriptions, get free rides on a bus to Atlantic City, use public transportation to get anywhere in the city, and live on about twenty-two dollars a day. These are my grandparents' friends. Some people would call them old and poor. I would call them survivors who have learned to make it through life on nothing but a Social Security check.

Thesis statement

Sean Ragas (student)

**Highlight:
What to
Avoid in
Introductions**

- Do not begin your essay by announcing what you plan to write about.

  Phrases to Avoid

  This essay is about . . .

  In my essay, I will discuss . . .

- Do not apologize for your ideas.

  Phrases to Avoid

  Although I don't know much about this subject . . .

  I might not be an expert, but . . .

● **Practice 13-1**

Look through the essays in Chapter 37, locating one introduction you think is particularly effective. What are the strengths of the introduction you chose?

**Highlight:
Choosing
a Title**

Every essay should have a **title** that suggests the subject of the essay and makes people want to read it.

- Capitalize all words in your title except for articles (*a*, *an*, *the*), prepositions (*at, to, of, around*, and so on), and coordinating conjunctions (*and, but*, and so on), unless a word is the first or last word of the title.
- Do not underline your title or enclose it in quotation marks.
- Center the title at the top of the first page. Double-space between the title and the first line of your essay.

As you consider a title for your paper, think about the following options.

A title can highlight a key word or term.

  The Wife-Beater

  Orange Crush

A title can be a straightforward announcement.

  For Most People, College Is a Waste of Time

  Don't Hang Up, That's My Mom Calling

A title can establish a personal connection with readers.

  My Grandmother's Dumpling

  Volunteer Workers of the World, Unite

A title can be a familiar saying or a quotation from your essay.

  The Dog Ate My Disk, and Other Tales of Woe

  Don't Call Me a Hot Tamale

Focus on Writing: *Flashback*

Look back at the essay you reprinted for the Focus on Writing activity on page 195. Evaluate your introduction. Does it prepare readers for the essay to follow? Does it include a thesis statement? Is it likely to interest readers? Draft a different opening paragraph using one of the options presented in 13A. Be sure to include a clear thesis statement.

After you have finished drafting a new introduction, think of a new title that will attract your readers' attention. (Use one of the options listed in the second Highlight box on p. 198.)

13b Conclusions

Because your **conclusion** is the last thing readers see, they often judge your entire essay by its effectiveness. For this reason, conclusions should be planned, drafted, and revised carefully.

Like an introduction, a conclusion should be a full paragraph. It should begin with a specific **summary statement** that reinforces the essay's main idea, and it should end with some general **concluding remarks**. The following diagram illustrates the general shape of a conclusion.

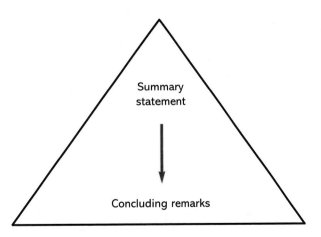

Summary statement

Concluding remarks

Here are some options you can experiment with when you write your conclusions. (In each of the sample concluding paragraphs that follow, the summary statement is underlined and labeled.)

Concluding with a Narrative

A **narrative** conclusion can bring an event discussed in the essay to a logical, satisfying close.

Summary statement

> Being a firefighter is a challenging and often dangerous job. The firefighters who died on September 11, 2001, show how true this fact is. They rushed into the two burning World Trade Center towers without thinking about what could happen to them. Even as the buildings were falling down, they continued to help people escape. At the end of the day, they did the job they had been trained to do, and they did it well. These brave people are role models for me and for other volunteer firefighters around the country. They remind all of us of how important the job we do really is.
>
> Richard Pogue (student)

Concluding with a Recommendation

Once you think you have convinced readers that a problem exists, you can make a **recommendation** in your conclusion about how the problem should be solved.

Summary statement

> Several steps can be taken to deal with the problem of child labor. First, people should educate themselves about the problem. They can begin by going to Web sites that give information about child labor. Then, they can join an organization such as Human Rights Watch or the Global Fund for Children. These groups sponsor programs that help child laborers in their own countries. Finally, people can stop supporting businesses that benefit either directly or indirectly from child labor. If all of us are committed to change, we can do a lot to reduce this problem worldwide.
>
> Megan Davia (student)

Concluding with a Quotation

A well-chosen **quotation**—even a brief one—can be an effective concluding strategy. In the following paragraph, the quotation reinforces the main idea of the essay.

Summary statement

> Volunteering at my daughter's middle school has done a lot to help both her and me. She now likes to go to school, and her grades have improved. I now understand how much effort it takes to be a good parent. What I am most proud of is that no one told me what to

do. I just figured it out for myself. I guess Dr. Spock was right when he said to parents in his book *Baby and Child Care,* "Trust yourself. You know more than you think you do."

Russ Hightower (student)

Concluding with a Prediction

This type of conclusion includes a **prediction** that looks to the future.

Summary statement

My hesitation cost me more than I ever could have dreamed. When she thought that I didn't want to marry her, Jen broke up with me. For the past three months, I have been trying to get back together with her. We have gone out a few times, and I am trying to convince her to trust me again. I hope that sometime soon we will look back at this situation and laugh. Meanwhile, all I can do is tell Jen that I am sorry and keep hoping.

Dan Brody (student)

● **Practice 13-2**

Look through the essays in Chapter 37, locating one conclusion you think is particularly effective. Be prepared to explain the strengths of the conclusion you chose.

Highlight: What to Avoid in Conclusions

- Do not introduce any new ideas. Your conclusion should sum up the ideas you discuss in your essay, not open up new lines of thought.

- Do not apologize for your opinions, ideas, or conclusions. Apologies will undercut your readers' confidence in you.

Phrases to Avoid

I may not be an expert . . .

At least that's my opinion . . .

I could be wrong, but . . .

- Do not use overused phrases to announce your essay is coming to a close.

Phrases to Avoid

In summary, . . .

In conclusion, . . .

Focus on Writing: *Flashback*

Look again at the essay you reprinted for the Focus on Writing activity on page 195. Evaluate your conclusion. Is it suitable for your topic? Does it reinforce your essay's thesis? Does it bring your essay to a clear and satisfying close that will leave a strong impression on readers? Try drafting a different concluding paragraph using one of the options presented in 13B.

Focus on Writing: *Revising and Editing*

Reread your responses to the Flashback activity above and the one on page 199. Are the new paragraphs you wrote more effective than the introduction and conclusion of the essay you wrote in Chapter 12? If so, substitute them for the opening and closing paragraphs of that essay.

Chapter Review

Editing Practice

The following student essay has an undeveloped introduction and conclusion. Decide what introductory and concluding strategies would be most appropriate for the essay. Then, rewrite both the introduction and the conclusion to make them more effective. Finally, suggest an interesting title for the essay.

Careers in sports medicine can provide good pay and satisfying work environments.

There are many jobs within the field of sports medicine, but most jobs fall into one of two categories. The first category involves sports injuries. Jobs in this area focus on helping people prevent or recover from sports-related injuries. Careers in this category, which range from occupational therapy to orthopedic surgery, often require advanced degrees or medical training. The second category involves helping people to achieve healthy lives or to improve their athletic performance. Jobs in this category include sports nutrition and physical training, and they typically require a certificate in the field as well as an undergraduate degree.

Jobs in sports medicine are much more exciting than the average office job. For those who enjoy physical activity, sports medicine is just right because jobs in this field often require people to be in constant motion most of the day. These jobs also require strong communication and people skills because they involve working with a variety of people with different needs. In addition, no two days in sports medicine are ever quite the same. Clients continually come and go as their needs change or their injuries heal.

As with most health-care fields, sports medicine is growing, and the demand for people to fill jobs is always increasing. Jobs for physical therapists and physical therapist assistants will be among the fastest growing over the next decade. The pay is good, and layoffs are rare—even in a weak economy.

For people with the right interests and skills, a career in sports medicine may be an excellent choice.

Collaborative Activities

1. Bring to class several copies of an essay you wrote for another class. Have each person in your group comment on your essay's introduction and conclusion. Revise the introduction and conclusion in response to your classmates' suggestions.

2. Find a magazine or newspaper article that interests you. Make a copy of the article, cutting off the introduction and conclusion, and bring

the body of the article to class. Ask your group to decide on the best strategy for introducing and concluding the article. Then, collaborate on writing new opening and closing paragraphs and an interesting title.

3. Working in a group, think of interesting and appropriate titles for essays on each of the topics listed below. Try to use as many of the different options outlined in the second Highlight box on page 198 as you can.

> The difficulty of living with a roommate
> The joys of living in the city (or in the country)
> The responsibilities of having a pet
> The stress of job interviews
> The obligation to vote
> The many uses of texting
> The problems of being in a long-term relationship
> The need for religious tolerance

Review Checklist: Introductions and Conclusions

☐ The introduction of your essay should prepare readers for the ideas to follow and should include a thesis statement. It should also create interest. (See 13A.) You can begin an essay with any of the following strategies.

A narrative	A quotation
A question	An unexpected statement
A definition	

☐ Your title should suggest the subject of your essay and make people want to read further. (See 13A.)

☐ The conclusion of your essay should include a summary statement and make some general concluding remarks. (See 13B.) You can conclude an essay with any of the following strategies.

A narrative	A quotation
A recommendation	A prediction

As you learned in Chapters 3 through 11, writers have a variety of options for developing ideas within a paragraph. These options include *exemplification*, *narration*, *description*, *process*, *cause and effect*, *comparison and contrast*, *classification*, *definition*, and *argument*. When you write an **essay**, you can use these same patterns of development to help you organize your material.

In your college courses, different assignments and writing situations call for different patterns of essay development.

- If an essay exam question asked you to compare two systems of government, you would use *comparison and contrast.*
- If an English composition assignment asked you to tell about a childhood experience, you would use *narration.*
- If a section of an environmental science research paper called for examples of dangerous waste-disposal practices, you would use *exemplification.*

In this chapter, you will learn how to use different options for arranging material in an essay.

14a   Exemplification

Exemplification illustrates a general statement with specific examples. An **exemplification essay** uses examples to support a thesis.

> ### Writing an Exemplification Essay
> - Make sure your topic calls for exemplification.
> - Find ideas to write about.
> - Identify your main idea, and write a thesis statement.
> - Choose examples and details to support your thesis.
> - Arrange your supporting examples in a logical order.
> - Draft your essay.
> - **TEST** your essay.
> - Revise your essay.
> - Edit your essay.
>
> (For detailed information on the process of writing an essay, see Chapter 12.)

Highlight: Topics for Exemplification

The wording of your assignment may suggest exemplification. For example, you may be asked to *illustrate* or to *give examples*. In an exemplification essay, the thesis statement states the main idea that the examples support.

Assignment	*Thesis Statement*
Education: Should children be taught only in their native languages or in English as well? Support your answer with specific examples of students' experiences.	The success of students in a bilingual third-grade class suggests the value of teaching elementary school students in English as well as in their native languages.
Literature: Does William Shakespeare's *Othello* have to end tragically? Support your position with references to specific characters.	Each of the three major characters in *Othello* contributes to the play's tragic ending.
Composition: Discuss the worst job you ever had, including plenty of specific examples to support your thesis.	My summer job at a fast-food restaurant was my all-time worst job because of the endless stream of rude customers, the many boring and repetitive tasks I had to perform, and my manager's insensitive treatment of employees.

In an exemplification essay, each body paragraph can develop a single example or discuss several related examples. The topic sentence should introduce the example (or group of related examples) that each paragraph will discuss.

Highlight: Options for Organizing Exemplification Essays

One Example per Paragraph	*Several Related Examples per Paragraph*
¶1 Introduction	¶1 Introduction
¶2 First example	¶2 First group of examples
¶3 Second example	¶3 Second group of examples
¶4 Third example	¶4 Third group of examples
¶5 Conclusion	¶5 Conclusion

Transitional words and phrases should introduce your examples and indicate how one example is related to another.

Highlight: Transitions for Exemplification	also	furthermore	the most important example
	besides	in addition	the next example
	finally	moreover	
	first	one example . . . another example	
	for example		
	for instance	specifically	

Model Exemplification Essay

The following student essay, "Going to Extremes" by Kyle Sims, uses examples to illustrate the characteristics of extreme sports. Two of the body paragraphs group several brief examples together; one paragraph focuses on a single example. Notice how Kyle uses clear topic sentences and helpful transitions to introduce his examples and link them to one another.

Going to Extremes

For years, sports like football, baseball, and basketball have been popular in cities, suburbs, and small rural towns. For some young people, however, these sports no longer seem exciting, especially when compared to "extreme sports," such as snowboarding and BMX racing. Extreme sports are different from more familiar sports because they are dangerous, they are physically challenging, and they require specialized equipment.

First, extreme sports are dangerous. For example, snowboarders take chances with snowy hills and unpredictable bumps. They zoom down mountains at high speed, which is typical of extreme sports. In addition, snowboarders and skateboarders risk painful falls as they do their tricks. Also, many extreme sports, like rock climbing, bungee jumping, and skydiving, are performed at very high altitudes. Moreover, the bungee jumper has to jump from a very high place, and there is always a danger of getting tangled with the bungee cord. People who participate in extreme sports accept—and even enjoy—these dangers.

In addition, extreme sports are very difficult. For instance, surfers have to learn to balance surfboards while dealing with wind and waves. Bungee jumpers may have to learn how to do difficult stunts while jumping off a high bridge or a dam. Another example of the physical challenge of extreme sports can be found in BMX racing. BMX racers have to learn to steer a lightweight bike on a dirt track that has jumps and banked corners. These extreme sports require skills that most people do not naturally have. Special skills like these have to be learned, and participants in extreme sports enjoy this challenge.

Finally, almost all extreme sports require specialized equipment. For example, surfers need surfboards that are light but strong. They can choose epoxy boards, which are stronger, or fiberglass boards, which are lighter. They can choose shortboards, which are shorter than seven feet and are easier to maneuver. Or, they can use longboards, which are harder and slower to turn in the water but are easier to learn on. Also, surfers have to use special wax on their boards to keep from slipping as they are paddling out into the water. For surfing in cold water, they need wet suits that trap their own body heat. Other extreme sports require different kinds of specialized equipment, but those who participate in them are willing to buy whatever they need.

Extreme sports have become increasingly popular in recent years, and television has helped to increase their popularity. For example, in 2010, snowboarding and other extreme sports were prominently featured in the Winter Olympics. In the future, the Olympics will include skateboarding and BMX racing. Already, the Summer and Winter X Games are televised on ESPN and ABC. Sports like BMX racing, snowboarding, surfing, and snowmobiling get national attention on these programs. With all this publicity, extreme sports are likely to become even more popular.

● **Practice 14-1**

1. Underline the thesis statement of "Going to Extremes." Then, restate the thesis in your own words.

2. List the examples of extreme sports that Kyle gives in paragraph 2. What examples of dangers does he give in paragraph 3? In paragraph 4, Kyle discusses surfing, giving examples of the equipment surfers need. List this equipment.

3. How does Kyle introduce his examples? Underline some of the transitional words and phrases that serve this purpose.

4. Is the introduction effective? How else might Kyle have opened his essay?

5. Is Kyle's conclusion effective? How else could he have ended his essay?

6. What is this essay's greatest strength? What is its greatest weakness?

Grammar in Context: Exemplification

When you write an exemplification essay, you may introduce your examples with transitional words and phrases like *First* or *In addition*. If you do, be sure to use a comma after the introductory word or phrase.

First, extreme sports are dangerous.

In addition, extreme sports are very difficult.

Finally, almost all extreme sports require specialized equipment.

For information on using commas with introductory transitional words and phrases, see 31B.

● **Practice 14-2**

Following the writing process outlined in Chapter 12, draft an exemplification essay on one of the following topics.

Reasons to start (or not to start) college right after high school

The three best products ever invented

What kinds of people or images should appear on U.S. postage stamps?

Advantages (or disadvantages) of being a young parent

Athletes who really are role models

Four items students need to survive in college

What messages do various hip-hop artists send to listeners?

Study strategies that work

Traits of a good employee

Three or four recent national or world news events that gave you hope— or events that upset or shocked you

● **Practice 14-3**

Following the guidelines in 12H, **TEST** your exemplification essay to make sure it includes a thesis statement, sufficient supporting evidence, a summary statement that reinforces the essay's main idea, and all the transitions readers need to follow your discussion. Then, revise and edit your essay.

☐ Does your introduction give readers a clear idea of what to expect?

☐ Does your essay include a thesis that clearly states the main idea your examples support?

☐ Do all your examples support your thesis, or should some be deleted?

☐ Do you have enough examples to support your thesis, or do you need more examples?

☐ Do you have enough transitional words and phrases to introduce your examples and to show how they are related?

☐ Does your conclusion bring your essay to a satisfying close?

☐ What problems did you experience in writing your essay? What would you do differently next time?

14b   Narration

Narration tells a story, presenting events in chronological (time) order, moving from beginning to end. A **narrative essay** can tell a personal story, or it can recount a recent or historical event or a fictional story.

Writing a Narrative Essay

- Make sure your topic calls for narration.
- Find ideas to write about.
- Identify your main idea, and write a thesis statement.
- Choose events and details to support your thesis.
- Arrange events in clear chronological order.
- Draft your essay.
- **TEST** your essay.
- Revise your essay.
- Edit your essay.

(For detailed information on the process of writing an essay, see Chapter 12.)

Highlight: Topics for Narration

The wording of your assignment may suggest narration. For example, you may be asked to tell, trace, summarize events, or recount. In a narrative essay, the thesis statement expresses the point your narrative will make.

Assignment	Thesis Statement
Composition: Tell about a time when you had to show courage even though you were afraid.	In extraordinary circumstances, a person can exhibit great courage and overcome fear.
American history: Summarize the events that occurred during President Franklin Delano Roosevelt's first one hundred days in office.	Although many thought they were extreme, the measures enacted by Roosevelt during his first one hundred days in office were necessary to fight the nation's economic depression.
Political science: Trace the development of the Mississippi Freedom Democratic Party.	As the Mississippi Freedom Democratic Party developed, it found a voice that spoke for equality and justice.

In a narrative essay, each paragraph can discuss one event or several related events.

Highlight: Options for Organizing Narrative Essays

One Event per Paragraph	Several Events per Paragraph
¶1 Introduction	¶1 Introduction
¶2 First event	¶2 First group of events
¶3 Second event	¶3 Second group of events
¶4 Third event	¶4 Third group of events
¶5 Conclusion	¶5 Conclusion

Note: Sometimes, to add interest to your narrative, you may decide not to use exact chronological order. For example, you might begin with the end of your story and then move back to the beginning to trace the events that led to this outcome. However you arrange the events, carefully worded topic sentences and clear transitional words and phrases will help readers follow your narrative.

Highlight: Transitions for Narration	after	eventually	next
	as	finally	now
	as soon as	first ... second ... third	soon
	at first		then
	at the same time	immediately	two hours (days, months, years) later
	before	later	
	by this time	later on	when
	earlier	meanwhile	

Model Narrative Essay

The following student essay, "Reflections" by Elaina Corrato, is a narrative that relates the events of the day of the writer's thirtieth birthday. Transitional words and phrases link events in chronological order and help keep readers on track.

Reflections

WORD POWER

milestone an important event; a turning point

Turning thirty did not bother me at all. My list of "Things to Do before I Die" was far from complete, but I knew I had plenty of time to do them. In fact, turning thirty seemed like no big deal to me. If anything, it was a milestone I was happy to be approaching. Unfortunately, other people had different ideas about this milestone, and eventually their ideas made me rethink my own.

As the big day approached, my family kept teasing me about it. My sister kept asking me if I felt different. She couldn't believe I wasn't upset, but I didn't pay any attention to her. I was looking forward to a new chapter in my life. I liked my job, I was making good progress toward my college degree, and I was healthy and happy. Why should turning thirty be a problem? So, I made no special plans for my birthday, and I decided to treat it as just another day.

My birthday was on a Saturday that year, and I enjoyed the chance to sleep in. After I got up and had breakfast, I did my laundry and then set out for the supermarket. I rarely put on makeup or fixed my hair on Saturdays. After all, I didn't have to go to work or to school. I was only running errands in the neighborhood. Later on, though, as I waited in line at the deli counter, I caught sight of my reflection in the mirrored meat case. At first, I thought it wasn't really me. The woman staring back at me looked so old! She had bags under her eyes, and she even had a few gray hairs. I was so upset by my reflection that on my way home I stopped and bought a mud mask—guaranteed to make me look younger.

As I walked up the street toward my house, I saw something attached to the front railing. When I got closer, I realized that it was a bunch of balloons, and they were black balloons. There was also a big sign that said "Over the Hill" in big black letters. I'd been trying to think about my birthday in positive terms, but my family seemed to have other ideas. Obviously, it was time for the mud mask.

After quickly unloading my groceries, I ran upstairs to apply the mask. The box promised a "rejuvenating look," and that was exactly what I wanted. I spread the sticky brown mixture on my face, and it hardened instantly. As I sat on my bed, waiting for the mask to work its magic, I heard the doorbell ring. Then, I heard familiar voices and my husband calling me to come down, saying that I had company. I couldn't answer him. I couldn't talk (or even smile) without cracking the mask. At this point, I retreated to the bathroom to make myself presentable for my friends and family. This task was not easy.

When I managed to scrub off the mud mask, my face was covered with little red pimples. Apparently, my sensitive skin couldn't take the harsh chemicals. At first, I didn't think the promise of "rejuvenated" skin was what I got. I had to admit, though, that my skin did look a lot younger. In fact, when I finally went downstairs to celebrate my birthday, I looked as young as a teenager—a teenager with acne.

WORD POWER
rejuvenate to make young again; to restore to a youthful appearance

● Practice 14-4

1. Underline the thesis statement of "Reflections." Then, restate it in your own words.

2. Underline the transitional words and phrases Elaina uses to link the day's events in chronological order.

3. What specific events and situations support Elaina's thesis? List as many as you can.

4. Do you think paragraph 2 is necessary? How would Elaina's essay be different without it?

5. Do you think Elaina's conclusion should restate her thesis and summarize all the events her essay discusses, or is her conclusion effective? Explain your answer.

6. What is this essay's greatest strength? What is its greatest weakness?

Grammar in Context: Narration

When you write a narrative essay, you tell a story. When you get caught up in your story, you might sometimes find yourself stringing a list of incidents together without proper punctuation, creating a **run-on**.

Incorrect   As the big day approached, my family kept teasing me about it, my sister kept asking me if I felt any different.

Correct   As the big day approached, my family kept teasing me about it. My sister kept asking me if I felt any different.

For information on how to identify and correct run-ons, see Chapter 21.

● **Practice 14-5**

Following the writing process outlined in Chapter 12, draft a narrative essay on one of the following topics.

The story of your education

Your idea of a perfect day

The plot summary of a terrible book or movie

A time when you had to make a split-second decision

Your first confrontation with authority

An important historical event

A day everything went wrong

A story from your family's history

Your employment history, from first to most recent job

A biography of your pet

● **Practice 14-6**

Following the guidelines in 12H, **TEST** your narrative essay to make sure it includes a thesis statement, sufficient supporting evidence, a summary statement that reinforces the essay's main idea, and all the transitions readers need to follow your discussion. Then, revise and edit your essay.

Self-Assessment Checklist: Writing a Narrative Essay	☐ Does your introduction set the scene and introduce important people and places?
	☐ Does your essay include a thesis that makes a point about your narrative?
	☐ Are the events you discuss arranged in clear chronological (time) order?
	☐ Do you include enough examples and details to make your narrative interesting? Are all your examples and details relevant?
	☐ Do topic sentences and transitional words and phrases make the sequence of events clear?
	☐ Does your conclusion remind readers why you have told them your story?
	☐ What problems did you experience in writing your essay? What would you do differently next time?

14c   Description

Description tells what something looks, sounds, smells, tastes, or feels like. A **descriptive essay** uses details to give readers a clear, vivid picture of a person, place, or object.

Writing a Descriptive Essay
- Make sure your topic calls for description.
- Find ideas to write about.
- Decide what dominant impression you want to convey.
- Choose details that help to convey your dominant impression.
- If possible, write a thesis statement that your details will support.
- Arrange your details in an effective order.
- Draft your essay.
- **TEST** your essay.
- Revise your essay.
- Edit your essay.

(For detailed information on the process of writing an essay, see Chapter 12.)

Highlight:
Topics for
Description

The wording of your assignment may suggest description. For example, it may ask you to *describe* or to *tell what an object looks like*. In a descriptive essay, the thesis statement makes a point about the subject you will describe.

Assignment	Thesis Statement
Composition: Describe a room that was important to you when you were a child.	Pink-and-white striped wallpaper, tall shelves of cuddly stuffed animals, and the smell of Oreos dominated the bedroom I shared with my sister.
Scientific writing: Describe a piece of scientific equipment.	The mass spectrometer is a complex instrument, but every part is ideally suited to its function.
Art history: Choose one modern painting and describe its visual elements.	The disturbing images crowded together in Pablo Picasso's *Guernica* suggest the brutality of war.

When you plan a descriptive essay, your goal is to create a single **dominant impression**, a central idea that all the details convey—for example, the liveliness of a street scene or the quiet of a summer night. This dominant impression unifies the description and gives readers an overall sense of what the person, place, object, or scene looks like (and perhaps what it sounds, smells, tastes, or feels like). Often—although not always—your details will make a point about the subject you are describing.

Highlight: Options for Organizing Descriptive Essays

Least to Most Important	Top to Bottom	Far to Near
¶1 Introduction	¶1 Introduction	¶1 Introduction
¶2 Least important details	¶2 Details at top	¶2 Distant details
¶3 More important details	¶3 Details in middle	¶3 Closer details
¶4 Most important details	¶4 Details on bottom	¶4 Closest details
¶5 Conclusion	¶5 Conclusion	¶5 Conclusion

As the second Highlight box on page 218 illustrates, you can arrange details in a descriptive essay in a variety of different ways. For example, you can move from least to most important details, from the top of an object to the bottom (or from bottom to top or side to side), or from far from a scene to near it (or from near to far). Each body paragraph may focus on one key characteristic of the subject you are describing or on several related descriptive details.

When you describe a person, place, object, or scene, you can use **objective description**, reporting only what your senses of sight, sound, smell, taste, and touch tell you: *The columns were two feet tall and made of white marble.* Or, you can use **subjective description**, conveying your attitude or your feelings about what you observe: *The columns were tall and powerful looking, and their marble surface seemed as smooth as ice.* Many essays combine these two kinds of description.

Descriptive writing is frequently enriched by **figures of speech**—expressions that use language to create special or unusual effects.

- A **simile** uses *like* or *as* to compare two unlike things.

    Her smile was like sunshine.

- A **metaphor** compares two unlike things without using *like* or *as*.

    Her smile was a light that lit up the room.

- **Personification** suggests a comparison between a nonliving thing and a person by giving the nonliving thing human traits.

    The sun smiled down on the crowd.

As you write, use transitional words and expressions to guide readers through your description. (Many of these useful transitions are prepositions or other words and phrases that indicate location or distance.)

Highlight: Transitions for Description			
	above	in front of	outside
	behind	inside	over
	below	nearby	the least important
	between	next to	
	beyond	on	the most important
	in	on one side . . . on the other side	
	in back of		under

Model Descriptive Essay

The following student essay, "My Grandfather's Globe" by Mallory Cogan, uses description to create a picture of an object that is important to her. Using specific details and figures of speech to describe the shapes and colors on the surface of an old globe, Mallory conveys a vivid impression of this object.

My Grandfather's Globe

Each afternoon, sunlight slants through the windows of my grandfather's room. Slowly, slowly, it sweeps over the bookshelves, as if browsing through the books. Late in the day, just before the light disappears altogether, it rests on a globe in the corner. My grandfather bought this globe in 1939, just before World War II. The world has changed since then, but the globe reminds me what the world used to look like.

Turning the globe left, I begin my world tour. The blue of the Pacific Ocean gives way to the faded pinks, browns, and oranges of North and South America. What catches my attention first is a large area dotted with lakes and bays in the north. This is the Dominion of Canada, now simply Canada. In the far north, the Canadian mainland breaks into islands that reach into the Arctic Ocean. Looking down, I locate the multicolored United States. To the north, Canada sprawls and breaks apart; to the south Mexico narrows, then curves east like a scorpion's tail, extended by the uneven strip of land that is Central America. This strip of land is connected to the northernmost part of South America. South America, in the same colors as the United States, looks like a face in profile looking east, with a nose extending into the Atlantic Ocean and a long neck that narrows as it reaches toward Antarctica at the South Pole.

As I trace the equator east across the Atlantic Ocean, my finger lands in French Equatorial Africa. The huge African continent, shaped like a fat boomerang, is labeled with names of European countries. A large, kidney-shaped purple area to the northwest is called French West Africa. To the east, about halfway down the continent, is the Belgian Congo, a substantial orange splotch that straddles the equator. On the eastern coast just above the equator is a somewhat smaller, almost heart-shaped yellow area called Italian East Africa. These regions, once European colonies, are now divided into dozens of independent countries.

Moving north, I follow the thick blue ribbon of the Mediterranean Sea until I reach Western Europe. I pause on yellow, boot-shaped Italy and glance to the west and southwest at purple France and orange Spain. The northwestern coasts of both countries extend slightly into the Atlantic, as if tipping their hats. To the northwest of France, the pink clusters of the British Isles droop like bunches of grapes.

Looking eastward, I am distracted by a water stain in Germany. I trace it as it drips down Italy and across the Mediterranean, landing in the Sahara Desert on the African continent. Following the stain back into Europe, I look north, where Norway, Sweden, and Finland look like a three-headed beast reaching their long necks toward the rest of Europe. Returning to Germany, I move east, through Poland. On a modern globe, I would find Belarus and the Ukraine on Poland's eastern border. On this globe, however, my finger passes directly into a vast area called the Union of Soviet Socialist Republics, today called Russia. The U.S.S.R. looks like a wide scarf across the northern part of the Asian continent; there is plenty of room for its long name to be displayed horizontally across the country's light-brown surface. Still in the southern half of the country, I travel east, crossing the landlocked Caspian Sea into a region of the U.S.S.R. called Turkistan, now the country of Turkmenistan. Here I pause to scan the countries to the southeast. Afghanistan, in green, looks as if it is being held in a sling between light purple Iran to the west and pink India to the east. India looks like an ice-cream cone with a melting scoop, and green Nepal to the northwest could be a sliver of mint chocolate tilting on the top of that melting scoop.

Looking north again, I continue moving east. In Tibet, I carefully touch a small tear in the globe and then continue into China's vast interior. Just as the U.S.S.R. blankets the northern part of the Asian continent, China spreads over much of the southeast. I notice that China's borders on this globe are different from what they are today. On my grandfather's globe, China includes Mongolia but not a purple region to the northwest labeled Manchoukuo, also known as Manchuria. Today, it is just the opposite. Following Manchoukuo to its southern border, I notice a strip of land that extends into the sea, surrounded by water on three sides. The area is small, so its name—Chosen—has been printed in the Sea of Japan to the east. Today, it is called Korea.

Backtracking west and dropping south, past China's southern border, I see Siam, now called Thailand. Siam is shaped like a three-leaf clover with a stem that hangs down. Wrapped along its eastern border, bordering two of its "leaves," is a purple country called French Indo-China. Today, this region is divided into the countries of Cambodia, Laos, and Vietnam. Bordering Siam on the west is the larger country of Burma, in pink. Like Siam, Burma is top-heavy, like a flower or a clover with a thin stem. Tracing that stem south, I come to the numerous islands of Indonesia, which look like splashes of yellow paint spreading east-west along, above, and below the equator. I do not need to travel much farther before I arrive at an island bigger than any other on this globe: Australia. This country is pink and shaped like half of a very thick doughnut. On Australia's eastern coast is the Pacific; on its western coast is the Indian Ocean.

Having completed my tour, I give the globe a spin, closing my eyes and running my finger along it until the spinning stops. When I open my eyes, I find I am back in the Pacific. Of course, it is not surprising that I would land in the ocean, since water covers seventy percent of the Earth. Still, countries—not oceans—are what interest me most about this globe. The shifting names and borders of countries remind me that although the world seems fixed, just as it did to the people of 1939, it is always changing. The change simply happens very slowly, like the sun crossing the room. Caught at any single moment, the world, like the light, appears still.

● Practice 14-7

1. Underline Mallory's thesis statement. Then, restate it in your own words.

2. What dominant impression of the globe does Mallory convey to readers? List some of the specific details she uses to convey this dominant impression.

3. What determines the order in which details are presented in this essay?

4. What trasitional words and phrases does Mallory use to move her readers from one part of the globe to another? Do you think any transitions need to be added? If so, where?

5. Is this essay primarily a subjective or an objective description?

6. What is this essay's greatest strength? What is its greatest weakness?

Grammar in Context: Description	When you write a descriptive essay, you may use **modifiers** to describe your subject. Be very careful to avoid creating **dangling modifiers**, phrases that modify a word that does not appear in the sentence.

                            ┌─── MODIFIER ───→

Confusing   Turning the globe left, my world tour begins.
                     (Is the world tour turning the globe?)

                            ┌─── MODIFIER ───→

Clear   Turning the globe left, I begin my world tour.

For information on how to identify and correct dangling modifiers, see 25B.

● **Practice 14-8**

Following the writing process outlined in Chapter 12, draft a descriptive essay on one of the following topics.

An abandoned building
A person or fictional
  character who makes you
  laugh (or frightens you)
Your room (or your closet
  or desk)
A family photograph

A historical site or monument
An advertisement
An object you cherish
Someone whom everyone notices
Someone whom no one notices
The home page of a Web site you
  visit often

● **Practice 14-9**

Following the guidelines in 12H, **TEST** your descriptive essay to make sure it includes a thesis statement, sufficient supporting evidence, a summary statement that reinforces your dominant impression, and all the transitions readers need to follow your discussion. Then, revise and edit your essay.

Self-Assessment Checklist: Writing a Descriptive Essay	☐ Does your introduction identify the subject of your description and convey your essay's dominant impression?
	☐ Does your essay include a thesis statement that expresses the dominant impression you want to convey and makes a point about your subject?
	☐ Do you describe your subject in enough detail, or do you need to add more details to create a more vivid picture?
	☐ Do all the details in your essay help to convey your dominant impression, or should some be deleted?
	☐ Are your details arranged in an effective order within your essay and within paragraphs?
	☐ Do your topic sentences and transitional words and phrases move readers smoothly from one part of your description to another?
	☐ Does your conclusion reinforce your dominant impression and leave readers with a clear sense of your essay's purpose?
	☐ What problems did you experience in writing your essay? What would you do differently next time?

14d   Process

A **process** is a series of chronological steps that produces a particular result. **Process essays** explain the steps in a procedure, telling how something is (or was) done. A process essay can be organized as either a *process explanation* or a set of *instructions*.

Writing a Process Essay

- Make sure your topic calls for process.
- Decide whether you want to explain a process or write instructions.
- Find ideas to write about.
- Identify your main idea, and write a thesis statement.
- Identify the most important steps in the process.
- List the steps in the process in chronological order.
- Draft your essay.
- **TEST** your essay.
- Revise your essay.
- Edit your essay.

(For detailed information on the process of writing an essay, see Chapter 12.)

Highlight: Topics for Process

The wording of your assignment may suggest process. For example, you may be asked to *explain a process*, *give instructions*, *give directions*, or *give a step-by-step account*. In a process essay, the thesis statement identifies the process and indicates why you are writing about it.

Assignment	Thesis Statement
American government: Explain the process by which a bill becomes a law.	The process by which a bill becomes a law is complex, involving numerous revisions and a great deal of compromise.
Pharmacy practice: Summarize the procedure for conducting a clinical trial of a new drug.	To ensure that drugs are safe and effective, scientists follow strict procedural guidelines for testing and evaluating them.
Technical writing: Write a set of instructions for applying for a student internship in a government agency.	If you want to apply for a government internship, you need to follow several important steps.

If your purpose is simply to help readers understand a process, not actually perform it, you will write a process explanation. **Process explanations**, like the first two examples in the Highlight box on page 224, often use present tense verbs ("Once a bill *is* introduced in Congress" or "A scientist first *submits* a funding application") to explain how a procedure is generally carried out. However, when a process explanation describes a specific procedure that was completed in the past, it uses past tense verbs ("The next thing I *did*").

If your purpose is to enable readers to actually perform the steps in a process, you will write instructions. **Instructions**, like the last example in the Highlight box on page 224, always use present tense verbs in the form of commands to tell readers what to do ("First, *meet* with your adviser").

Whether your essay is a process explanation or a set of instructions, you can either devote a full paragraph to each step of the process or group a series of minor steps together in a single paragraph.

Highlight: Options for Organizing Process Essays	*One Step per Paragraph*	*Several Steps per Paragraph*
	¶1 Introduction	¶1 Introduction
	¶2 First step in process	¶2 First group of steps
	¶3 Second step in process	¶3 Second group of steps
	¶4 Third step in process	¶4 Third group of steps
	¶5 Conclusion	¶5 Conclusion

As you write your process essay, discuss each step in the order in which it is performed, making sure your topic sentences clearly identify the function of each step or group of steps. (If you are writing instructions, you may also include reminders or warnings that readers might need to know when performing the process.)

Transitions are extremely important in process essays because they enable readers to follow the sequence of steps in the process and, in the case of instructions, to perform the process themselves.

Highlight: Transitions for Process	after that	immediately	the final step
	as	later	the first (second, third) step
	as soon as	meanwhile	
	at the end	next	then
	at the same time	now	the next step
	before	once	when
	finally	soon	while
	first	subsequently	

Model Process Essay

The following student essay, Jen Rossi's "For Fun and Profit," explains the process of selling at a flea market. Because Jen assumed her readers would be unlikely to perform this process, she did not write her essay in the form of instructions. Instead, she wrote a process explanation, using present tense verbs to explain how she generally proceeds. Notice how clear transitions move readers smoothly through the steps of the process.

For Fun and Profit

My first experience selling items at a flea market was both fun and profitable. In fact, it led to a hobby that is also a continuing source of extra money. That first time took a lot of work, but the routine I established then has made each flea market easier.

The first step in the process is to call to reserve a spot at the flea market. Then, I recruit a helper—usually my brother or one of my roommates—and we get to work.

The next step is sorting through all the items I managed to accumulate since the last flea market. My helper comes in handy here, encouraging me to sell ugly or useless things I may want to hold on to. We make three piles—keep, sell, and trash—and one by one, we place every item in a pile. (Before we decide to sell or throw out an item, I check with all my roommates to make sure I'm not accidentally throwing out one of their prized possessions.)

Next comes pricing the items for sale, which is actually the hardest step for me. It's always difficult to accept the fact that I might have to set a low price for something that has sentimental value for me (a giant stuffed animal, for example). It's just as hard to set a high price on the ugly lamp or old record album that might turn out to be someone's treasure. At my first flea market, I returned with a lot of unsold items, and I later realized I had sold other items too cheaply. I never made these mistakes again.

The next step is my least favorite: packing up items to be sold. I usually borrow my friend's van for the heavy items (boxes of books or dishes, for example). The small items (knickknacks, artificial flowers, stray teaspoons) can be transported in my brother's car.

The final steps in my preparation take place on the day before the event. I borrow a couple of card tables from friends of my parents. Then, I go to the bank and get lots of dollar bills and quarters, and I collect piles of newspaper and plastic supermarket bags. Now, my planning is complete.

On the day of the flea market, I get up early, and my helper and I load the two vehicles. When we arrive at the site where the event is to be held, one of us unloads the cars. The other person sets things up, placing small items (such as dishes and DVDs) on the card tables and large items (such as my parents' old lawnmower) on the ground near the tables.

Then, the actual selling begins. Before I can even set up our tables, people start picking through my things, offering me cash for picture frames, pots and pans, and video games. We develop a system as the day goes on: one of us persuades buyers that that old meat grinder or vase is just what they've been looking for, and the other person negotiates the price with prospective buyers. Then, while one of us wraps small items in the newspapers or bags we brought (and helps carry large items to people's cars), the other person takes the money and makes change.

Finally, at the end of the day, I count my money and give a share to my helper. We then load all the unsold items into the car and van and bring them back to my apartment. We store them in the back of my closet so it will be easy to pack them up again for the next flea market.

● Practice 14-10

1. List the major steps in the process of selling at a flea market. Does Jen present these steps in strict chronological order?

2. What identifies Jen's essay as a process explanation rather than a set of instructions?

3. Underline some of the transitional words and phrases that introduce the steps in the process. Are any other transitions needed?

4. Underline Jen's thesis statement. Then, restate it in your own words.

5. Do you think this essay needs a stronger summary statement? If so, suggest some alternatives.

6. What is the essay's greatest strength? What is its greatest weakness?

Grammar in Context: Process

When you write a process essay, you may have problems keeping tense, person, and voice consistent throughout. If you shift from one tense, person, or voice to another without good reason, you will confuse your readers.

Confusing	We make three piles—keep, sell, and trash—and one by one, every item was placed in a pile. (shift from active to passive voice and from present to past tense)
Clear	We make three piles—keep, sell, and trash—and one by one, we place every item in a pile. (consistent voice and tense)

For information on how to avoid illogical shifts in tense, person, and voice, see Chapter 24.

● **Practice 14-11**

Following the writing process outlined in Chapter 12, draft a process essay on one of the following topics. (Note: Before you begin, decide whether a process explanation or a set of instructions will be more appropriate for your purpose.)

An unusual recipe

Finding an apartment

Applying for a job

Getting dressed for a party or concert

A religious ceremony

A task you often perform at work

A do-it-yourself project that didn't get done

Your own writing process

A self-improvement program (past, present, or future)

● **Practice 14-12**

Following the guidelines in 12H, **TEST** your process essay to make sure it includes a thesis statement, sufficient supporting evidence, a summary statement that reinforces the essay's main idea, and all the transitions readers need to follow your discussion. Then, revise and edit your essay.

Self-Assessment Checklist: Writing a Process Essay	☐ Does your introduction indicate the process you will discuss and whether you will be explaining the process or writing instructions?
	☐ Does your thesis statement identify the process and indicate why you are writing about it?
	☐ Do you include every step readers will need to understand (or perform) the process?
	☐ Are all the steps you present necessary, or should some be deleted?
	☐ Are the steps in the process presented in strict chronological (time) order?
	☐ Are related steps grouped together in individual paragraphs?
	☐ Do topic sentences clearly identify major steps in the process and explain the function of each step or group of steps?
	☐ Do you include transitional words and phrases that clearly show how the steps in the process are related?
	☐ If you are writing instructions, have you included any necessary warnings or reminders?
	☐ Does your conclusion effectively summarize the point you are making about the process?
	☐ What problems did you experience in writing your essay? What would you do differently next time?

14e   Cause and Effect

A **cause** makes something happen; an **effect** is a result of a particular cause or event. **Cause-and-effect essays** identify causes or predict effects; sometimes, they do both.

Writing a Cause-and-Effect Essay
- Make sure your topic calls for cause and effect.
- Decide whether your essay will focus on causes, effects, or both.
- Find ideas to write about.
- Identify your main idea, and write a thesis statement.
- Choose causes or effects to support your thesis.
- Arrange causes and effects in an effective order.
- Draft your essay.
- **TEST** your essay.
- Revise your essay.
- Edit your essay.

(For detailed information on the process of writing an essay, see Chapter 12.)

Highlight: Topics for Cause and Effect

The wording of your assignment may suggest cause and effect. For example, the assignment may ask you to *explain why*, *predict the outcome*, *list contributing factors*, *discuss the consequences*, or tell what *caused* something else or how something is *affected* by something else. In a cause-and-effect essay, the thesis statement indicates why you are discussing these particular causes or effects.

Assignment	*Thesis Statement*
Women's studies: What factors contributed to the rise of the women's movement in the 1970s?	The women's movement of the 1970s had its origins in the peace and civil rights movements of the 1960s.
Public health: Discuss the possible long-term effects of smoking.	In addition to its well-known negative effects on smokers themselves, smoking also causes significant problems for those exposed to secondhand smoke.
Communication: How has the Internet affected the lives of those who have grown up with it?	The Internet has created a generation of people who learn differently from those in previous generations.

A cause-and-effect essay can focus on causes or on effects. When you write about causes, be sure to examine *all* relevant causes. You should emphasize the cause you consider the most important, but do not forget to consider other causes that may be significant. Similarly, when you write about effects, consider *all* significant effects of a particular cause, not just the first few that you think of.

If your focus is on finding causes, as it is in the first assignment in the Highlight box on the previous page, your introductory paragraph should identify the effect (the women's movement). If your focus is on predicting effects, as it is in the second and third assignments listed in the Highlight box, you should begin by identifying the cause (smoking, the Internet). In the body of your essay, you can devote a full paragraph to each cause (or effect), or you can group several related causes (or effects) together in each paragraph.

Highlight: Options for Organizing Cause-and-Effect Essays	*Identifying Causes*	*Predicting Effects*
	¶1 Introduction (identifies effect)	¶1 Introduction (identifies cause)
	¶2 First cause	¶2 First effect
	¶3 Second cause	¶3 Second effect
	¶4 Third (and most important) cause	¶4 Third (and most important) effect
	¶5 Conclusion	¶5 Conclusion

Transitions are important in cause-and-effect essays because they establish causal connections, telling readers that A caused B and not the other way around. They also make it clear that events have a *causal* relationship (A *caused* B) and not just a *sequential* relationship (A *came before* B). Remember, when one event follows another, the second is not necessarily the result of the first. For example, an earthquake may occur the day before you fail an exam, but that doesn't mean the earthquake caused you to fail.

Highlight: Transitions for Cause and Effect			
	accordingly	for	the first (second, third) effect
	another cause	for this reason	
	another effect	since	the most important cause
	as a result	so	
	because	the first (second, third) cause	the most important effect
	consequently		therefore

Model Cause-and-Effect Essay

The following student essay, "How My Parents' Separation Changed My Life" by Andrea DeMarco, examines the effects of a significant event on the writer and her family. Andrea begins by identifying the cause—the separation—and then goes on to explain its specific effects on her family and on herself. Notice how the words *because* and *effect* make the essay's causal connections clear to her readers.

How My Parents' Separation Changed My Life

Until I was eight, I lived the perfect all-American life with my perfect all-American family. I lived in a suburb of Albany, New York, with my parents, my sister and brother, and our dog, Daisy. We had a ping-pong table in the basement, a barbecue in the backyard, and two cars in the garage. My dad and mom were high school teachers, and every summer we took a family vacation. Then, it all changed. My parents' separation made everything different.

One day, just before Halloween, when my sister was twelve and my brother was fourteen (Daisy was seven), our parents called us into the kitchen for a family conference. We didn't think anything was wrong at first; they were always calling these annoying meetings. We figured it was time for us to plan a vacation, talk about household chores, or be nagged to clean our rooms. As soon as we sat down, though, we knew this was different. We could tell Mom had been crying, and Dad's voice cracked when he told us the news. They were separating—they called it a "trial separation"—and Dad was moving out of our house.

After that day, everything seemed to change. Every Halloween we always had a big jack-o'-lantern on our front porch. Dad used to spend hours at the kitchen table cutting out the eyes, nose, and mouth and hollowing out the insides. That Halloween, because he didn't live with us, things were different. Mom bought a pumpkin, and I guess she was planning to carve it up. But she never did, and we never mentioned it. It sat on the kitchen counter for a couple of weeks, getting soft and wrinkled, and then it just disappeared.

Other holidays were also different because Mom and Dad were not living together. Our first Thanksgiving without Dad was pathetic. I don't even want to talk about it. Christmas was different, too. We spent Christmas Eve with Dad and our relatives on his side and Christmas Day with Mom and her family. Of course, we got twice as many presents as usual. I realize now that both our parents were trying to make up for the pain of the separation. The worst part came when I opened my big present from Mom: Barbie's Dream House. This was something I had always wanted. Even at eight, I knew how hard it must have been for Mom to afford it. The trouble was, I had gotten the same thing from Dad the night before.

The separation affected each of us in different ways. The worst effect of my parents' separation was not any big event but the disruption in our everyday lives. Dinner used to be a family time, a chance to talk about our day and make plans. But after Dad left, Mom seemed to stop eating. Sometimes she would just have coffee while we ate, and sometimes she wouldn't eat at all. She would microwave some frozen thing for us or heat up soup or cook some hot dogs. We didn't care—after all, now she let us watch TV while we ate—but we did notice.

Other parts of our routine changed, too. Because Dad didn't live with us anymore, we had to spend every Saturday and every Wednesday night at his apartment, no matter what else we had planned. Usually, he would take us to dinner at McDonald's on Wednesdays, and then we would go back to his place and do our homework or watch TV. That wasn't too bad. Saturdays were a lot worse. We really wanted to be home, hanging out with our friends in our own rooms in our own house. Instead, we had to do some planned activity with Dad, like go to a movie or a hockey game.

By the end of the school year, my parents had somehow worked things out, and Dad was back home again. That June, at a family conference around the kitchen table, we made our summer vacation plans. We decided on Williamsburg, Virginia, the all-American vacation destination. So, things were back to normal, but I wasn't, and I'm still not. Now, ten years later, my mother and father are all right, but I still worry they'll split up again. And I worry about my own future husband and how I will ever be sure he's the one I'll stay married to. As a result of what happened in my own family, it is hard for me to believe any relationship is forever.

● Practice 14-13

1. Underline Andrea's thesis statement. Then, restate it in your own words.

2. What specific effects of her parents' separation does Andrea identify?

3. Underline the transitional words and phrases that make the causal connections in Andrea's essay clear to her readers.

4. Is Andrea's relatively long concluding paragraph effective? Why or why not? Do you think it should be shortened or divided into two paragraphs? Is her summary statement appropriate?

5. Is Andrea's straightforward title effective, or should she have used a more creative or eye-catching title? Can you suggest an alternative?

6. What is this essay's greatest strength? What is its greatest weakness?

Grammar in Context: Cause and Effect

When you write a cause-and-effect essay, you may have trouble remembering the difference between *affect* and *effect*.

        effect

The worst ˄affect of my parents' separation was not the big events

but the disruption in our everyday lives. (*effect* is a noun)

        affected

The separation ˄effected each of us in different ways. (*affect* is a verb)

For information on *affect* and *effect*, see Chapter 35.

● **Practice 14-14**

Following the writing process outlined in Chapter 12, draft a cause-and-effect essay on one of the following topics.

A teacher's positive (or negative) effect on you

Why you voted a certain way in a recent election (or why you did not vote)

Why reality shows are so popular

How your life would be different if you dropped out of school (or quit your job)

How a particular electronic device (for example, the cell phone) influences your behavior

A movie or book that changed the way you look at life

How a particular season (or day of the week) affects your mood

How having a child would change (or has changed) your life

How a particular event made you grow up

● **Practice 14-15**

Following the guidelines in 12H, **TEST** your cause-and-effect essay to make sure it includes a thesis statement, sufficient supporting evidence, a summary statement that reinforces the essay's main idea, and all the transitions readers need to follow your discussion. Then, revise and edit your essay.

Self-Assessment Checklist: Writing a Cause-and-Effect Essay

☐ Does your introduction give readers an overview of the topic you will discuss and indicate whether your essay will focus on causes or on effects?

☐ Does your thesis statement indicate why you are discussing these particular causes or effects?

☐ Do you identify all causes or effects relevant to your topic, or do you need to add any?

☐ Are all causes and effects relevant, or should some be deleted?

☐ Have you arranged causes and effects to indicate which are more important than others?

☐ Does each body paragraph identify and explain one particular cause or effect (or several closely related causes or effects)?

☐ Do you use specific words and phrases to make your essay's cause-and-effect connections clear?

☐ Does your conclusion summarize the importance of the causal relationships you discuss? If necessary, revise to make your emphasis clearer.

☐ What problems did you experience in writing your essay? What would you do differently next time?

14f   Comparison and Contrast

Comparison identifies similarities; **contrast** identifies differences. **Comparison-and-contrast essays** explain how two things are alike or how they are different; sometimes, they discuss both similarities and differences.

Writing a Comparison-and-Contrast Essay
- Make sure your topic calls for comparison and contrast.
- Find ideas to write about.
- Decide whether you want to discuss similarities, differences, or both.
- Identify your main idea, and write a thesis statement.
- Identify specific points of comparison or contrast to support your thesis.
- Decide whether to structure your essay as a point-by-point or subject-by-subject comparison.
- Draft your essay.
- **TEST** your essay.
- Revise your essay.
- Edit your essay.

(For detailed information on the process of writing an essay, see Chapter 12.)

Highlight: Topics for Comparison and Contrast

The wording of your assignment may suggest comparison and contrast—for example, by asking you to *compare*, *contrast*, *discuss similarities*, or *identify differences*. In a comparison-and-contrast essay the thesis statement indicates why you are comparing your two subjects and what point (or points) you will make about them.

Assignment	*Thesis Statement*
Philosophy: What basic similarities do you find in the beliefs of Henry David Thoreau and Martin Luther King Jr.?	Although King was more politically active, both he and Thoreau strongly supported the idea of civil disobedience.
Nutrition: How do the diets of native Japanese and Japanese Americans differ?	As they become more and more assimilated, Japanese Americans consume more fats than native Japanese do.
Literature: Contrast the two sisters in Alice Walker's short story "Everyday Use."	Unlike Maggie, Dee—her more successful, better-educated sister—has rejected her family's rural American heritage.

When you organize a comparison-and-contrast essay, you can choose either a *point-by-point* or a *subject-by-subject* arrangement. A **point-by-point** comparison alternates between the two subjects you are comparing or contrasting, moving back and forth from one subject to the other. A **subject-by-subject** comparison treats its two subjects separately, first fully discussing one subject and then moving on to discuss the other subject. In both kinds of comparison-and-contrast essays, the same points are discussed in the same order for both subjects.

Highlight: Options for Organizing Comparison-and-Contrast Essays	*Point-by-Point Comparison*	*Subject-by-Subject Comparison*
	¶1 Introduction (identifies subjects to be compared or contrasted)	¶1　Introduction (identifies subjects to be compared or contrasted)
	¶2 First point discussed for both subjects	¶s2–3 First subject discussed
	¶3 Second point discussed for both subjects	
	¶4 Third point discussed for both subjects	¶s4–5 Second subject discussed
	¶5 Conclusion	¶6　Conclusion

The transitional words and phrases you use in a comparison-and-contrast essay tell readers whether you are focusing on similarities or on differences. Transitions also help move readers through your essay from one subject to the other and from one point of similarity or difference to the next.

Highlight: Transitions for Comparison and Contrast		
	although	likewise
	but	nevertheless
	even though	on the contrary
	however	on the one hand . . . on the other hand
	in comparison	similarly
	in contrast	unlike
	instead	whereas
	like	

Model Comparison-and-Contrast Essay

The following student essay, "Another Ordinary Day" by Nisha Jani, contrasts teenage boys and girls by going through a typical day in the lives of "Johnny" and "Jane." A point-by-point comparison, Nisha's essay alternates between her two subjects, treating the same points in the same order for each. Her topic sentences identify the part of the day each paragraph will discuss, and transitional words and phrases clearly signal shifts from one subject to the next.

Another Ordinary Day

"Boys are from Jupiter and get stupider / Girls are from Mars and become movie stars / Boys take a bath and smell like trash / Girls take a shower and smell like a flower." As simple playground songs like this one suggest, the two sexes are very different. As adults, men and women have similar goals, values, and occupations, but as children and teenagers, boys and girls often seem to belong to two different species. In fact, from the first moment of the day to the last, the typical boy and girl live very different lives.

The sun rises, and the alarm clock signals the beginning of another day for Johnny and Jane, two seventh-grade classmates. Johnny, an average thirteen-year-old boy, wakes up late and has to hurry. He throws on his favorite jeans, a baggy T-shirt, and a baseball cap. Then, he has a hearty high-cholesterol breakfast and runs out of the house to school, usually forgetting some vital book or homework assignment. Jane, unlike Johnny, wakes up early and takes her time. She takes a long shower and then blow-dries her hair. For Jane, getting dressed can be a very difficult process, one that often includes taking everything out of her closet and calling friends for advice. After she makes her decision, she helps herself to some food (probably low- or no-fat) and goes off to school, making sure she has with her everything she needs.

School is a totally different experience for Johnny and Jane. Johnny will probably sit in the back of the classroom with a couple of other guys, throwing paper airplanes and spitballs. These will be directed at the males they do not like and the females they think are kind of cute. (However, if their male friends ever ask the boys about these girls, they will say girls are just losers and deny that they like any of them.) On the opposite side of the classroom, however, Jane is focused on a very different kind of activity. At first, it looks as if she is carefully copying the algebra notes that the teacher is putting on the board, but her notes have absolutely nothing to do with algebra. Instead, she is writing about boys, clothes, and other topics that are much more important to her than the square

WORD POWER
origami the Japanese art of folding paper into shapes representing birds or animals

root of one hundred twenty-one. She proceeds to fold the note into a box or other creative shape, which can often put origami to shame. As soon as the teacher turns her back, the note is passed and the process begins all over again.

Lunch, a vital part of the school day, is also very different for Johnny and Jane. On the one hand, for Johnny and his friends, it is a time to compare baseball cards, exchange sports facts, and of course tell jokes about every bodily function imaginable. In front of them on the table, their trays are filled with pizza, soda, fries, and chips, and this food is their main focus. For Jane, on the other hand, lunch is not about eating; it is a chance to exchange the latest gossip about who is going out with whom. The girls look around to see what people are wearing, what they should do with their hair, and so on. Jane's meal is quite a bit smaller than Johnny's: it consists of a small low-fat yogurt and half a bagel (if she feels like splurging, she will spread some cream cheese on the bagel).

After school, Johnny and Jane head in different directions. Johnny rushes home to get his bike and meets up with his friends to run around and play typical "guy games," like pick-up basketball or touch football. Johnny and his friends play with every boy who shows up, whether they know him or not. They may get into physical fights and arguments, but they always plan to meet up again the next day. In contrast to the boys, Jane and her friends are very selective. Their circle is a small one, and they do everything together. Some days, they go to the mall (they will not necessarily buy anything there, but they will consider the outing productive anyway because they will have spent time together). Most days, though, they just talk, with the discussion ranging from school to guys to lipstick colors. When Jane gets home, she will most likely run to the phone and talk for hours to the same three or four girls.

At the age of twelve or thirteen, boys and girls do not seem to have very much in common. Given this situation, it is amazing that boys and girls grow up to become men and women who interact as neighbors, friends, and coworkers. What is even more amazing is that so many grow up to share lives and raise families together, treating each other with love and respect.

● Practice 14-16

1. Underline Nisha's thesis statement. Then, restate it in your own words.

2. Does Nisha's opening paragraph identify the subjects she will discuss? Will she focus on similarities or on differences?

3. Nisha's essay is a point-by-point comparison. What four points does she discuss for each of her two subjects?

4. Underline some transitional words and phrases Nisha uses to move readers from one subject (Johnny) to the other (Jane).

5. Reread Nisha's topic sentences. What does each sentence contribute to the essay?

6. What is this essay's greatest strength? What is its greatest weakness?

Grammar in Context: Comparison and Contrast

When you write a comparison-and-contrast essay, you need to present the points you are comparing or contrasting in **parallel** terms to highlight their similarities or differences.

⎡ PARALLEL ⎤
Johnny, an average thirteen-year-old boy, wakes up late and has to hurry.

⎡ PARALLEL ⎤
Jane, unlike Johnny, wakes up early and takes her time.

For information on revising to make ideas parallel, see Chapter 19.

● **Practice 14-17**

Following the writing process outlined in Chapter 12, draft a comparison-and-contrast essay on one of the following topics.

An online course versus a traditional course

Two coworkers

Two movie heroes

How you expect your life to be different from the lives of your parents

Men's and women's ideas about their body images

Two ways of studying for an exam

Risk-takers and people who play it safe

Country and city living (or you can compare suburban living with either)

Two popular magazines (features, ads, target audiences, pictures)

Two actors

● Practice 14-18

Following the guidelines in 12H, **TEST** your comparison-and-contrast essay to make sure it includes a thesis statement, sufficient supporting evidence, a summary statement that reinforces the essay's main idea, and all the transitions readers need to follow your discussion. Then, revise and edit your essay.

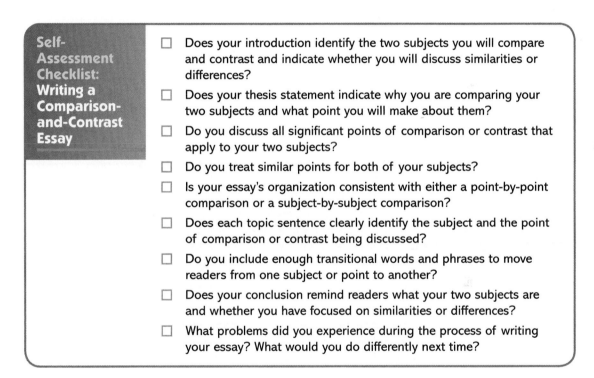

Self-Assessment Checklist: Writing a Comparison-and-Contrast Essay

☐ Does your introduction identify the two subjects you will compare and contrast and indicate whether you will discuss similarities or differences?

☐ Does your thesis statement indicate why you are comparing your two subjects and what point you will make about them?

☐ Do you discuss all significant points of comparison or contrast that apply to your two subjects?

☐ Do you treat similar points for both of your subjects?

☐ Is your essay's organization consistent with either a point-by-point comparison or a subject-by-subject comparison?

☐ Does each topic sentence clearly identify the subject and the point of comparison or contrast being discussed?

☐ Do you include enough transitional words and phrases to move readers from one subject or point to another?

☐ Does your conclusion remind readers what your two subjects are and whether you have focused on similarities or differences?

☐ What problems did you experience during the process of writing your essay? What would you do differently next time?

14g   Classification

Classification is the act of sorting items into appropriate categories. **Classification essays** divide a whole (your subject) into parts and sort various items into categories.

Writing a Classification Essay

- Make sure your topic calls for classification.
- Find ideas to write about.
- Identify your main idea, and write a thesis statement.
- Decide what categories you will discuss.
- Sort examples and details into categories.
- Arrange your categories in an effective order.
- Draft your essay.
- **TEST** your essay.
- Revise your essay.
- Edit your essay.

(For detailed information on the process of writing an essay, see Chapter 12.)

Highlight: Topics for Classification

The wording of your assignment may suggest classification. For example, you may be asked to consider *kinds*, *types*, *categories*, *components*, *segments*, or *parts of a whole*. In a classification essay, the thesis statement often lists the categories you will discuss and indicates why you are discussing them.

Assignment	*Thesis Statement*
Business: What kinds of courses are most useful for students planning to run their own businesses?	Courses dealing with accounting, management, interpersonal communication, and computer science offer the most useful skills for future business owners.
Biology: List the components of blood and explain the function of each.	Red blood cells, white blood cells, platelets, and plasma have distinct functions.
Education: Classify elementary school children according to their academic needs.	The elementary school population includes special-needs students, students with reading and math skills at or near grade level, and academically gifted students.

As a rule, each paragraph of a classification essay examines a separate category—a different part of the whole. The topic sentence identifies the category each paragraph discusses. For example, a paragraph could focus on one kind of course in the college curriculum, one component of blood, or one type of child. Within each paragraph, you discuss the individual items that you have put into a particular category—for example, accounting courses, red blood cells, or gifted students. If you consider some categories less important than others, you may decide to discuss those minor categories together in a single paragraph, devoting full paragraphs only to the most significant categories.

Highlight: Options for Organizing Classification Essays	One Category in Each Paragraph	Major Categories in Separate Paragraphs; Minor Categories Grouped Together
	¶1 Introduction (identifies whole and its major categories)	¶1 Introduction (identifies whole and its major categories)
	¶2 First category	¶2 Minor categories
	¶3 Second category	¶3 First major category
	¶4 Third category	¶4 Second (and more important) major category
	¶5 Conclusion	¶5 Conclusion

In a classification essay, topic sentences identify the category or categories discussed in each paragraph. Transitional words and phrases signal movement from one category to the next and may also tell readers which categories you consider more (or less) important.

Highlight: Transitions for Classification	one kind . . . another kind	the first (second, third) category	the most important component
	the final type	the last group	the next part

Model Classification Essay

The following student essay, "Selling a Dream" by Rob O'Neal, classifies American car names into categories on the basis of the kind of message they communicate to consumers. Notice that Rob discusses one category in each of his body paragraphs, using clear topic sentences to identify and define each kind of car name and to relate each category to the group as a whole.

Selling a Dream

The earliest automobiles were often named after the men who manufactured them—Ford, Studebaker, Nash, Olds, Chrysler, Dodge, Chevrolet, and so on. Later on, however, American car makers began competing to see what kinds of names would sell the most cars. Many car names were chosen simply for how they sounded: Alero, Corvette, Neon, Probe, Caprice. Many other names, however, were designed to sell specific dreams to consumers. Americans always seem to want to be, do, and become something different. They want to be tough and brave, to explore new places, to take risks. The names that auto manufacturers choose for their cars appeal to Americans' deepest desires.

Some American cars were named for places people dream of traveling to. Park Avenue, Malibu, Riviera, Seville, Tahoe, Yukon, Aspen, and Durango are some names that suggest escape—to New York City, California, Europe, the West. Other place names—Sebring, Daytona, and Bonneville, for example—are associated with the danger and excitement of car racing. And then there was the El Dorado, a car named for a fictional paradise: a city of gold.

Other car names were chosen to convey rough and tough, even dangerous, images. Animal names fall into this category, with models like Ram, Bronco, and Mustang suggesting powerful, untamed beasts. Other cars in the "rough and tough" category include those that suggest the wildness of the Old West: Wrangler and Rodeo, for example. Because the American auto industry was originally centered near Detroit, Michigan, where many cities have Indian names, cars named for the cities where they were manufactured inherited these names. Thus, cars called Cadillac, Pontiac, and Cherokee recalled the history of Indian nations, and these too might suggest the excitement of the untamed West.

The most interesting car names in terms of the dream they sell, however, were selected to suggest exploration and discovery. Years ago, some car names honored real explorers, like DeSoto and LaSalle. Now, model names only sell an abstract idea. Still, American car names like Blazer, Explorer, Navigator, Mountaineer, and Expedition (as well as the names of foreign cars driven by many Americans, such as Nissan's Pathfinder and Quest and Honda's Passport, Pilot, and Odyssey) have the power to make drivers feel they are blazing new trails and discovering new worlds—when in fact they may simply be carpooling their children to a soccer game or commuting to work.

Today, the car is an ordinary piece of machinery, an expensive necessity for many people. Clearly, the automobile is no longer seen as the amazing invention it once was. Despite the fact that most people take the existence of cars for granted, however, manufacturers still try to make consumers believe they are buying more than just transportation. But whether we drive a Malibu, Mustang, Cherokee, or Expedition—or even a "royal" LeBaron or Marquis—we eventually realize that we are driving cars, not magic carpets.

● **Practice 14-19**

1. What three categories of car names does Rob discuss in his essay?

2. Is Rob's treatment of the three categories similar? Does he give the same kind of information for each kind of car name?

3. What words and phrases does Rob repeat in his topic sentences to move readers from one category to the next? How do these words and phrases link the three categories?

4. Underline Rob's thesis statement. Then, restate it in your own words.

5. Should Rob have included additional examples in each category? Should he have included any additional categories?

6. What is this essay's greatest strength? What is its greatest weakness?

● **Practice 14-20**

Following the writing process outlined in Chapter 12, draft a classification essay on one of the following topics.

Your Facebook friends	Traits of oldest children, middle
Types of teachers (or bosses)	children, and youngest children
Ways to lose (or gain) weight	Kinds of desserts
Things hanging on your walls	Workers you encounter in a
Kinds of moods	typical day
Kinds of stores in your	College students' clothing choices
community shopping	Kinds of tattoos
district or mall	

Grammar in Context: Classification

When you write a classification essay, you may want to list the categories you are going to discuss or the examples in each category. If you do, use a **colon** to introduce your list, and make sure that a complete sentence comes before the colon.

Many car names were chosen simply for how they sounded: Alero, Corvette, Neon, Probe, Caprice.

For information on how to use a colon to introduce a list, see 33B.

● **Practice 14-21**

Following the guidelines in 12H, **TEST** your classification essay to make sure it includes a thesis statement, sufficient supporting evidence, a summary statement that reinforces the essay's main idea, and all the transitions readers need to follow your discussion. Then, revise and edit your essay.

Self-Assessment Checklist: Writing a Classification Essay	☐ Does your introduction identify the subject of your classification?
	☐ Does your thesis statement identify the categories you will discuss and indicate why you are discussing them?
	☐ Does each topic sentence clearly identify the category or categories the paragraph discusses?
	☐ Do all your categories support your essay's thesis?
	☐ Have you treated each major category similarly and with equal thoroughness?
	☐ Do you include enough transitional words and phrases to lead readers from one category to the next?
	☐ Does your conclusion review the major categories your essay discusses and remind readers why you discuss them?
	☐ What problems did you experience in writing your essay? What would you do differently next time?

14h Definition

Definition explains the meaning of a term or concept. A **definition essay** presents an *extended definition*, using various patterns of development to move beyond a simple dictionary definition.

Writing a Definition Essay
- Make sure your topic calls for definition.
- Find ideas to write about.
- Identify your main idea, and write a thesis statement.
- Decide what patterns of development to use to support your thesis.
    (continued)

Writing a Definition Essay (continued)
- Arrange supporting examples and details in an effective order.
- Draft your essay.
- **TEST** your essay.
- Revise your essay.
- Edit your essay.

(For detailed information on the process of writing an essay, see Chapter 12.)

Highlight: Topics for Definition

The wording of your assignment may suggest definition. For example, you may be asked to *define* or *explain* or to answer the question *What is x?* or *What does x mean?* In a definition essay, the thesis statement indicates why you are defining the term.

Assignment	Thesis Statement
Art: Explain the meaning of the term *performance art*.	Unlike more conventional forms of art, *performance art* extends beyond the canvas.
Biology: What did Darwin mean by the term *natural selection*?	*Natural selection*, popularly known as "survival of the fittest," is a good deal more complicated than most people think.
Psychology: What is *attention deficit disorder*?	*Attention deficit disorder* (ADD), once narrowly defined as a childhood problem, is now known to affect adults as well as children.

As the thesis statements above suggest, definition essays can be developed in various ways. For example, you can define something by telling how it occurred (narration), by describing its appearance (description), by giving a series of examples (exemplification), by telling how it operates (process), by telling how it is similar to or different from something else (comparison and contrast), or by discussing its parts (classification).

Some definition essays use a single pattern of development; others combine several patterns of development, perhaps using a different one in each paragraph.

Highlight: Options for Organizing Definition Essays	*Single Pattern of Development*	*Combination of Several Different Patterns of Development*
	¶1 Introduction (identifies term to be defined)	¶1 Introduction (identifies term to be defined)
	¶2 Definition by example	¶2 Definition by description
	¶3 Additional examples	¶3 Definition by example
	¶4 Additional examples	¶4 Definition by comparison and contrast
	¶5 Conclusion	¶5 Conclusion

The kinds of transitions used in a definition essay depend on the specific pattern or patterns of development in the essay.

Highlight: Transitions for Definition	also	like
	for example	one characteristic . . . another characteristic
	in addition	one way . . . another way
	in particular	specifically

Model Definition Essay

The following student essay, "Street Smart" by Kristin Whitehead, defines the term *street smart*. In the essay's introduction, Kristin defines her term briefly; in the essay's body paragraphs, she develops her definition further. Notice that the topic sentences of Kristin's three body paragraphs repeat a key phrase to remind readers of her essay's subject.

Street Smart

I grew up in a big city, so I was practically born street smart. I learned the hard way how to act and what to do, and so did my friends. To us, being *street smart* meant having common sense. We wanted to be cool, but we needed to be safe, too. Now, I go to college in a big city, and I realize that not everyone here grew up the way I did. Many students are from suburbs or rural areas, and they are either terrified of the city or totally ignorant of city life. The few suburban or rural students who are willing to venture downtown are not street smart—but they should be. Being street smart is a vital survival skill, one that everyone should learn.

For me, being street smart means knowing how to protect my possessions. Friends of mine who are not used to city life insist on wearing all their jewelry when they go downtown. I think this is asking for trouble, and I know better. I always tuck my chain under my shirt and leave my gold earrings home. Another thing that surprises me is how some of my friends wave their money around. They always seem to be standing on the street, trying to count their change or stuff dollars into their wallets. Street-smart people make sure to put their money safely away in their pockets or purses before they leave a store. A street-smart person will also carry a backpack, a purse strapped across the chest, or no purse at all. A person who is not street smart carries a purse loosely over one shoulder or dangles it by its handle. Again, these people are asking for trouble.

Being street smart also means protecting myself. It means being aware of my surroundings at all times and looking alert. A lot of times, I have been downtown with people who kept stopping on the street to talk about where they should go next or walking up and down the same street over and over again. A street-smart person would never do this. It is important that I look as if I know where I am going at all times, even if I don't. Whenever possible, I decide on a destination in advance, and I make sure I know how to get there. Even if I am not completely sure where I am headed, I make sure my body language conveys my confidence in my ability to reach my destination.

Finally, being street smart means protecting my life. A street-smart person does not walk alone, especially after dark, in an unfamiliar neighborhood. A street-smart person does not ask random strangers for directions; when lost, he or she asks a shopkeeper for help. A street-smart person takes main streets instead of side streets. When faced with danger or the threat of danger, a street-smart person knows when to run, when to scream, and when to give up money or possessions to avoid violence.

So how does someone get to be street smart? Some people think it is a gift, but I think it is something almost anyone can learn. Probably the best way to learn how to be street smart is to hang out with people who know where they are going.

● Practice 14-22

1. Underline Kristin's thesis statement. Then, restate it in your own words.

2. In your own words, define the term *street smart*. Why does this term require more than a one-sentence definition?

3. Where does Kristin use examples to develop her definition? Where does she use comparison and contrast?

4. What phrase does Kristin repeat in her topic sentences to tie her essay's three body paragraphs together?

5. Kristin's conclusion is quite a bit shorter than her other paragraphs. What, if anything, do you think she should add to this paragraph?

6. What is this essay's greatest strength? What is its greatest weakness?

Grammar in Context: Definition

When you write a definition essay, you may begin with a one-sentence definition that you expand in the rest of your essay. When you write your definition sentence, do not use the phrases *is when* or *is where*.

means knowing

For me, being street smart is when I know how to protect my possessions.

means protecting

Being street smart is also where I protect myself.

● **Practice 14-23**

Following the writing process outlined in Chapter 12, draft a definition essay on one of the following topics.

Upward mobility	Responsibility	Courage
Peer pressure	Procrastination	Happiness
Competition	Security	Home
Success		

● **Practice 14-24**

Following the guidelines in 12H, **TEST** your definition essay to make sure it includes a thesis statement, sufficient supporting evidence, a summary statement that reinforces the essay's main idea, and all the transitions readers need to follow your discussion. Then, revise and edit your essay.

Self-Assessment Checklist: Writing a Definition Essay

☐ Does your introduction identify the term your essay will define and provide a brief definition?

☐ Does your thesis statement indicate why you are defining the term?

☐ Do you use appropriate patterns of development in your definition, or should you explore other options?

☐ Do topic sentences clearly lead readers from one part of your definition to the next?

☐ Are all your details and examples clearly related to the term you are defining, or should some be deleted?

☐ Do you include enough transitional words and phrases to clearly link your ideas, or do you need to add transitions?

☐ Does your conclusion sum up your discussion and remind readers why you are defining the term?

☐ What problems did you experience in writing your essay? What would you do differently next time?

14i   Argument

Argument takes a stand on a debatable issue—that is, an issue that has two sides (and can therefore be debated). An **argument essay** uses different kinds of evidence—facts, examples, and expert opinion—to persuade readers to accept a position.

Writing an Argument Essay

- Make sure your topic calls for argument.
- Find ideas to write about.
- Decide on the position you will support, and write a thesis statement that clearly expresses this position.
- List points in support of your thesis.
- Arrange your points in an effective order.
- Support each point with evidence.
- Consider arguments against your position.
- Draft your essay.
- **TEST** your essay.
- Revise your essay.
- Edit your essay.

(For detailed information on the process of writing an essay, see Chapter 12.)

Highlight: Topics for Argument

The wording of your assignment may suggest argument. For example, you may be asked to *debate*, *argue*, *consider*, *give your opinion*, *take a position*, or *take a stand*. In an argument essay, the thesis statement states your position on the issue.

Assignment	*Thesis Statement*
Composition: Explain your position on a current issue affecting college students.	Financial aid should be based on merit, not need.
American history: Do you believe that General Lee was responsible for the South's defeat at the Battle of Gettysburg? Why or why not?	Because Lee refused to listen to the advice given to him by General Longstreet, he is largely responsible for the South's defeat at the Battle of Gettysburg.
Ethics: Should physician-assisted suicide be legalized?	Although many people think physician-assisted suicide should remain illegal, it should be legal in certain situations.

An argument essay can be organized *inductively* or *deductively*. An **inductive argument** moves from the specific to the general—that is, from a group of specific observations to a general conclusion based on these observations. An essay on the first topic in the Highlight box above, for example, could be an inductive argument. It could begin by presenting facts, examples, and expert opinion to make the case for merit-based financial aid and could end with the conclusion that it is a better strategy than need-based aid.

A **deductive argument** moves from the general to the specific. A deductive argument begins with a **major premise** (a general statement that the writer believes his or her audience will accept) and then moves to a **minor premise** (a specific instance of the belief stated in the major premise). It ends with a **conclusion** that follows from the two premises. For example, an essay on the last topic in the Highlight box above could be a deductive argument. It could begin with the major premise that all terminally ill patients who are in great pain should be given access to physician-assisted suicide. It could then go on to state and explain the minor premise that a particular patient is both terminally ill and in great pain, offering facts, examples, and the opinions of experts to support this premise. The essay could conclude that this patient should, therefore, be allowed the option of physician-assisted suicide. The deductive argument presented in the essay would have three parts.

Major Premise	All terminally ill patients who are in great pain should be allowed to choose physician-assisted suicide.
Minor Premise	John Lacca is a terminally ill patient who is in great pain.
Conclusion	Therefore, John Lacca should be allowed to choose physician-assisted suicide.

Before you present your argument, think about whether your readers are likely to be hostile toward, neutral toward, or in agreement with your position. Once you understand your audience, you can decide which points to make.

Begin each paragraph of your argument essay with a topic sentence that clearly states a point in support of your thesis. Throughout your essay, try to include specific supporting evidence that will make your argument persuasive. Keep in mind that arguments that rely just on generalizations are not as convincing as those that include vivid details and specific examples. Finally, try to use a balanced, moderate tone, and avoid name-calling or personal attacks.

Highlight: Options for Organizing Argument Essays	*Inductive Argument*	*Deductive Argument*
	¶1 Introduction	¶1 Introduction
	¶2 First point (supported by facts, examples, and expert opinion)	¶2 Major premise stated and explained
	¶3 Second point	¶3 Minor premise stated and explained
	¶4 Third point	¶4 Evidence supporting minor premise presented
	¶5 Identification and refutation of opposing arguments	¶5 Opposing arguments identified and refuted
	¶6 Conclusion	¶6 Conclusion

In addition to presenting your case, your essay should also briefly summarize arguments *against* your position and **refute** them (that is, argue against them or prove them false) by identifying factual errors or errors in logic. If an opposing argument is particularly strong, concede its strength—but try to point out some weaknesses as well. If you deal with opposing arguments in this way, your audience will see you as a fair and reasonable person.

Transitions are extremely important in argument essays because they not only signal the movement from one part of the argument to another but also relate specific points to one another and to the thesis statement.

Highlight: Transitions for Argument		
accordingly	granted	of course
admittedly	however	on the one hand . . . on the other hand
although	in addition	
because	in conclusion	since
but	indeed	so
certainly	in fact	therefore
consequently	in summary	thus
despite	meanwhile	to be sure
even so	moreover	truly
even though	nevertheless	
finally	nonetheless	
first, second . . .	now	

Model Argument Essay

WORD POWER

amnesty the overlooking or pardoning of offenses

The following student paper, "Amnesty for Undocumented Immigrants" by Peter Charron, is an argument essay. Peter takes a strong stand, supports his thesis with specific evidence, and sums up his position in his conclusion.

Amnesty for Undocumented Immigrants

More than twelve million undocumented immigrants now live in the United States. Is it practical to send them all back home? Should they be allowed to stay? Despite their illegal entry, if they have worked and raised their families in the United States for years, these people should be allowed to stay in this country and, eventually, to become American citizens.

Many people object to the idea of amnesty, an official pardon for past illegal acts. In this case, amnesty would forgive immigrants for entering the country illegally. However, this amnesty would not come without penalty. First, they would be heavily fined. In addition, they would have to show that they have jobs and can speak English. Moreover, to become American citizens, they would have to wait at least thirteen years. So, even though they would be granted amnesty, they still would be punished for entering the United States illegally.

Undocumented immigrants come to this country to work, and they often take low-wage jobs that businesses would otherwise find difficult or impossible to fill. For example, undocumented immigrants often work as migrant laborers—planting, cultivating, and picking crops like lettuce and tomatoes. In the Southwest, where there are many Mexican immigrants, laborers often work in the construction industry. The meatpacking, landscaping, and hotel industries also use immigrant workers, not all of whom are in this country legally. Finally, the health-care industry needs more and more people every year who will work for low pay as caregivers, providing personal care to the elderly and disabled. It would be very hard to fill all these jobs without illegal immigrants.

Giving amnesty to undocumented immigrants is not a perfect solution, but it would solve many problems. Now, these immigrants feel they have to hide from authorities because they are afraid they will be deported. Therefore, they may delay seeking needed medical care. As a result, they may wind up in a hospital emergency room when they are seriously ill. This is expensive for everyone. In addition, children of undocumented immigrants often cannot attend college because college scholarships require documents—and, even if students can afford the tuition, they must be legal in order to get even a part-time job. Consequently, it is very hard for undocumented immigrants to improve their lives or the lives of their children.

People who oppose immigration amnesty say that it would encourage disrespect for the law. This may be so. Nevertheless, in this case, there is no good alternative. It would be impossible to track down and deport the more than twelve million immigrants now in the United States illegally. Moreover, even if it were possible, a huge labor shortage would result. Another objection to the idea of amnesty is the claim that undocumented immigrants take jobs away from American citizens. However, according to the Department of Labor, this is not true. In fact, undocumented immigrants tend to work at jobs that citizens are unwilling to take. Finally, some say that the American way of life is being weakened by illegal immigrants. However, just the opposite is true: the United States has always been enriched by immigrants, whether legal or not. In fact, immigration is the lifeblood of the nation.

Granted, undocumented immigrants broke the law when they entered the country. However, even if it were possible to send them all back, the results would be disastrous for them and for the nation. Therefore, the best solution is to find a way to allow them to stay. By coming to America, they have shown that they want to work. They should be allowed to do so. Thus, America can continue to be a nation of immigrants.

● Practice 14-25

1. Underline the essay's thesis statement. In your own words, summarize the position Peter takes in his essay.

2. List the facts and examples Peter uses to support his thesis. Where does he include expert opinion?

3. Can you think of any supporting evidence that Peter does not mention?

4. Underline the transitional words and phrases Peter uses to move his argument along.

5. Throughout his essay, Peter acknowledges that some immigrants have broken the law. Do you think this is a good idea? Why or why not?

6. What opposing arguments does Peter address? What other arguments should he have addressed?

7. What is this essay's greatest strength? What is its greatest weakness?

Grammar in Context: Argument

When you write an argument essay, you need to show the relationships between your ideas by combining sentences to create **compound sentences** and **complex sentences**.

, and they
Undocumented immigrants come to this country to work. They often take low-wage jobs that businesses would otherwise find difficult or impossible to fill. (compound sentence)

Now, these immigrants feel they have to hide from authori-
because they
ties. They are afraid they will be deported. (complex sentence)

For information on how to create compound sentences, see Chapter 16. For information on how to create complex sentences, see Chapter 17.

● **Practice 14-26**

Following the writing process outlined in Chapter 12, draft an argument essay on one of the following topics.

Should teenagers who commit serious crimes be tried as adults?

Should citizens without criminal records be permitted to carry concealed weapons?

Should human beings be used as medical research subjects?

Should government funds be used to support the arts?

Should the minimum wage be raised?

Should college athletes be paid to play?

Should convicted felons lose the right to vote?

● **Practice 14-27**

Following the guidelines in 12H, **TEST** your argument essay to make sure it includes a thesis statement, sufficient supporting evidence, a summary statement that reinforces the essay's main idea, and all the transitions readers need to follow your discussion. Then, revise and edit your essay.

Self-Assessment Checklist: Writing an Argument Essay

☐ Is your topic debatable?

☐ Does your introduction present the issue you will discuss and clearly state your position?

☐ Does your thesis statement express your stand on the issue?

☐ Have you considered whether readers are likely to be hostile toward, neutral toward, or in agreement with your position—and have you chosen your points accordingly?

☐ Is your essay structured as either an inductive argument or a deductive argument?

☐ Have you considered and refuted arguments against your position?

☐ Do you have enough evidence to support your points?

☐ Do the points you make clearly support your position?

☐ Do you include enough transitional words and phrases?

☐ Does your conclusion follow logically from the points you have made in your essay—and does it sum up your position on the issue?

☐ What problems did you experience in writing your essay? What would you do differently next time?

Chapter Review

Although this chapter showcases student essays that are structured primarily around a single pattern of development—exemplification, narration, description, process, cause and effect, comparison and contrast, classification, definition, or argument—professional writers often combine several patterns in a single essay.

The following essay, "Color My World Burnt Sienna," by Louisa Thomas, combines several of the patterns of development illustrated in this chapter. Read the essay, and then try to identify where the writer uses each of the various patterns. Why is each pattern used, and what does it contribute to the essay? Which pattern (or patterns) dominates?

Color My World Burnt Sienna

Louisa Thomas

For a child, a box of Crayola crayons can be a wondrous thing. When I 1
was in elementary school, I was particularly taken with burnt sienna. It was neither brown nor red, but seemed taken from the earth, and it had the most beautiful name. I was reminded of my early curiosity and respect for that color recently, as I stood on top of the walls of Siena's Museo dell'Opera, high above the Piazza del Duomo, and looked out over the city spread below. At first, all I saw was a dull sea of brown, but then it began to take shape and gain heft. The brown became warmer, redder, and splintered into dozens of tones. I thought of burnt sienna, and suddenly the association between a crayon and a city did not seem silly or strange. Afterward, walking through the cramped streets of the town's historic center, I saw echoes of the color everywhere. There were the brick-red chevrons of the sloping Piazza del Campo, the town's spectacular medieval square, and the Palazzo Pubblico, burnished in afternoon light. Apartment buildings were sepia, their undulating roofs an orangey red. In the middle of such a rich but narrow chromatic range, Siena's magnificent black-and-white-striped cathedral, the Duomo di Siena, stood out even more awesomely than it would in the drabness of another city. It was a zebra amid roans, a monument to God amid the buildings of men.

Burnt sienna is elemental—it comes from roasting a pigment mined 2
from the earth. (This, of course, does not make it unusual: as anyone who's

WORD POWER

chevrons v-shaped patterns

burnished polished and smooth

undulating having a wavelike appearance or form

chromatic relating to color or colors

roans horses with chestnut or bay colored coats sprinkled with gray or white

ever gotten a grass stain knows, most colors originated not in a Crayola factory but as flower petals, or dirt, or ore.) Creating burnt sienna requires heating a particular iron-oxide pigment (*terra di Sièna*, or land of Siena). The name refers to a specific color, which the enchanted tourist's eye can glimpse in the blocks of baked clay that give Siena its consistent hue. In 14th-century Siena especially, brick was the primary material used in building, for matters of convenience, cost, esthetics—and law. The city's Council of Nine supported churches by giving them an annual allocation of bricks, established a statute in 1309 ordaining that domestic architecture should be built of brick, and paved the Campo and major streets with fired clay soon after.

WORD POWER
esthetics a sense of the beautiful

Nineteenth-century tourists, infatuated with a certain ideal of Italy, 3 were the ones to give "burnt sienna" an air of romance. In his travelogue *Pictures from Italy*, Charles Dickens—perhaps with a sly poke at the Anglo-American obsession with the exotic "other"—described "two burnt-sienna natives with naked legs and feet, who wear, each, a shirt, a pair of trousers, and a red sash, with a relic, or some sacred charm like a bonbon off a twelfth-cake, hanging round the neck." These visitors gave a pleasant but typical shade of brownish brick-red a local habitation and a name, and, with that mysterious past participle "burnt," a kind of story. They connected the color to a place with a rich history, and so gave it overtones of art, God and struggle.

In 2003, in honor of its centennial, Crayola held a contest in which 4 voters could save one of five soon-to-be-discontinued colors—burnt sienna, blizzard blue, teal blue, magic mint and mulberry—from retirement. More than 60,000 votes were cast, and burnt sienna won. The contest cannot exactly claim a place in the long line of battles fought over Siena's land, but it seemed a kind of victory, all the same.

Collaborative Activity

"Color My World Burnt Sienna" does not have a thesis statement. Still, it does convey a specific main idea to readers. Working in a group of three students, write a sentence that could serve as the thesis of the essay. Then, decide where in the essay you would place this sentence. Finally, consider what pattern or patterns of development your thesis statement suggests.

Review Checklist:
Patterns of Essay Development

☐ Exemplification essays use specific examples to support a thesis. (See 14A.)

☐ Narrative essays tell a story by presenting a series of events in chronological order. (See 14B.)

☐ Descriptive essays use details to give readers a clear, vivid picture of a person, place, or object. (See 14C.)

☐ Process essays explain the steps in a procedure, telling how something is (or was) done or how to do something. (See 14D.)

☐ Cause-and-effect essays identify causes or predict effects. (See 14E.)

☐ Comparison-and-contrast essays explain how two things are alike or how they are different. (See 14F.)

☐ Classification essays divide a whole into parts and sort various items into categories. (See 14G.)

☐ Definition essays use various patterns to develop an extended definition. (See 14H.)

☐ Argument essays take a stand on a debatable issue, using evidence to persuade readers to accept a position. (See 14I.)

Unit Four

Writing Sentences

15 Writing Simple Sentences   262
16 Writing Compound Sentences   276
17 Writing Complex Sentences   294
18 Writing Varied Sentences   308
19 Using Parallelism   326
20 Using Words Effectively   334

Chapter 15

Writing Simple Sentences

A **sentence** is a group of words that expresses a complete thought. Every sentence includes both a subject and a verb. A **simple sentence** consists of a single **independent clause**: one subject and one verb.

Chase Utley is a baseball player.

15a Subjects

Every sentence includes a subject. The **subject** of a sentence tells who or what is being talked about in the sentence. Without a subject, a sentence is not complete. In each of the three sentences below, the subject is underlined.

Derek Walcott won the 1992 Nobel Prize in literature.

He was born in the Caribbean.

St. Lucia is an island in the Caribbean.

The subject of a sentence can be a noun or a pronoun. A **noun** names a person, place, or thing—*Derek Walcott, St. Lucia.* A **pronoun** takes the place of a noun—*I, you, he, she, it, we, they,* and so on.

The subject of a sentence can be *singular* or *plural.* A **singular subject** is one person, place, or thing (*Derek Walcott, St. Lucia, he*).

A **plural subject** is more than one person, place, or thing (*readers, people, they*).

Readers admire Walcott's poems.

A plural subject that joins two subjects with *and* is called a **compound subject**.

<u>St. Lucia and Trinidad</u> are Caribbean islands.

● **Practice 15-1**

In the paragraph below, underline the subject of each sentence.

Example: The poet's <u>parents</u> were both teachers.

(1) Derek Walcott has had an interesting career. (2) His ancestors came from Africa, the Netherlands, and England. (3) Born in 1930, Walcott spent his early years on the Caribbean island of St. Lucia. (4) Writing occupied much of his time. (5) His early poems were published in Trinidad. (6) He later studied in Jamaica and in New York. (7) Walcott eventually became a respected poet. (8) He was a visiting lecturer at Harvard in 1981. (9) In 1990, he published *Omeros*. (10) This long poem about classical Greek heroes is set in the West Indies. (11) In 1992, the poet won a Nobel Prize. (12) Walcott later collaborated with songwriter Paul Simon on *The Capeman*, a Broadway musical.

● **Practice 15-2**

Underline the subject in each sentence. Then, write *S* above singular subjects and *P* above plural subjects. Remember, compound subjects are plural.

Example: <u>Farmers</u> in Afghanistan have begun planting pomegranates instead of poppies.

1. Poppy seeds are used to make opium, an illegal drug.

2. For many years, Afghanistan has been the world's largest producer of opium.

3. The pomegranate industry has always been small but profitable in Afghanistan.

4. Pomegranates look like large red onions with sweet, juicy seeds inside.

5. The fruit contains helpful antioxidants.

6. Officials in Afghanistan want their country to export healthful fruits, not dangerous drugs.

7. The United States and Europe have become large importers of pomegranates.

8. California produces most of the pomegranates in the United States.

9. The Afghan pomegranate is considered to be one of the finest in the world.

10. Pomegranate exports should improve the Afghan economy as well as the country's image.

● **Practice 15-3**

Add a subject to each of the following sentences.

    Example:　Many new _cell phones_ include a clock, a video camera, a calculator, a Web browser, and games.

1. After three weeks of stalling, _____ finally asked Jason to the party.

2. A _____ is required for travel outside the United States.

3. Each spring, _____ all forget about the horrible winter weather.

4. Every _____ must take a writing course before graduation.

5. Most _____ are not poisonous.

6. A broken-down old _____ was sitting in the driveway, with flat tires and broken windows.

7. Clean _____ is desperately needed in some of the world's poorest areas.

8. Some _____ migrate thousands of miles each year to their winter nesting sites.

9. Professional _____ are always under intense pressure from their fans, their coaches, and the media.

10. The _____ could not control the crowd outside the concert.

Focus on Writing: *Flashback*

Look back at your response to the Focus on Writing activity on page 263. Underline the subject of each of your sentences. Then, write *S* above each singular subject and *P* above each plural subject. (Remember that a compound subject is plural.)

15b   Prepositional Phrases

A **prepositional phrase** consists of a **preposition** (a word such as *on, to, in,* or *with*) and its **object** (the noun or pronoun it introduces).

Preposition	+	Object	=	Prepositional Phrase
on		the stage		on the stage
to		Nia's house		to Nia's house
in		my new car		in my new car
with		them		with them

Because the object of a preposition is a noun or a pronoun, it may seem to be the subject of a sentence. However, the object of a preposition can never be the subject of a sentence. To identify a sentence's true subject, cross out each prepositional phrase. (Remember, every prepositional phrase is introduced by a preposition.)

    subject   *prep phrase*
The <u>cost</u> of the repairs was astronomical.

  prep phrase   *prep phrase*   *subject* *prep phrase*
At the end of the novel, after an exciting chase, the <u>lovers</u> flee to Mexico.

Frequently Used Prepositions

about	among	beside	for	of
above	around	between	from	off
according to	at	beyond	in	on
across	before	by	inside	onto
after	behind	despite	into	out
against	below	during	like	outside
along	beneath	except	near	over

(continued)

Frequently Used Prepositions (*continued*)

through	toward	until	upon	within
throughout	under	up	with	without
to	underneath			

● Practice 15-4

Each of the following sentences includes at least one prepositional phrase. To identify each sentence's subject, begin by crossing out each prepositional phrase. Then, underline the subject of the sentence.

Example: In 1968, <u>George C. Wallace</u> of the American Independent Party won 13 percent of the vote.

(1) In presidential elections, third-party candidates have attracted many voters. (2) With more than 27 percent of the vote, Theodore Roosevelt was the strongest third-party presidential candidate in history. (3) In the 1912 race with Democrat Woodrow Wilson and Republican William H. Taft, Roosevelt ran second to Wilson. (4) Before Roosevelt, no third-party candidate had won a significant number of votes. (5) In recent years, however, some candidates of other parties made strong showings. (6) In 1980, John B. Anderson, an Independent, got almost 7 percent of the vote. (7) With nearly 19 percent of the popular vote, Independent Ross Perot ran a strong race against Democrat Bill Clinton and Republican George Bush in 1992. (8) In 2000, with the support of many environmentalists, Ralph Nader challenged Al Gore and George W. Bush for the presidency. (9) In 2004, Nader was also on the ballot in many states. (10) The two-party system of the United States has survived despite many challenges by third-party candidates.

Focus on Writing: *Flashback*

Look back at your response to the Focus on Writing activity on page 263. Have you used any prepositional phrases? Cross out each one you find. Then, check to make sure you have identified each sentence's subject correctly. Make any necessary changes.

15c

Verbs

In addition to its subject, every sentence includes a verb. This **verb** (also called a **predicate**) tells what the subject does or connects the subject to words that describe or rename it. Without a verb, a sentence is not complete.

Action Verbs

An **action verb** tells what the subject does, did, or will do.

> Nomar Garciaparra plays baseball.
> Renee will drive to Tampa on Friday.
> Amelia Earhart flew across the Atlantic.

Action verbs can also show mental and emotional actions.

> Travis always worries about his job.

Sometimes the subject of a sentence performs more than one action. In this case, the sentence includes two or more action verbs.

> He hit the ball and ran toward first base.

● Practice 15-5

In the following sentences, underline each action verb twice. Some sentences contain more than one action verb.

1. Many critics see one romance novel as just like another.
2. The plot usually involves a beautiful young woman in some kind of danger.
3. A handsome stranger offers his help.
4. At first, the woman distrusts him.
5. Then, another man enters the story and wins her trust.
6. Readers, however, see this man as an evil villain.
7. Almost too late, the woman too realizes the truth.
8. Luckily, the handsome hero returns and saves her from a nasty fate.

9. Many readers enjoy the familiar plots of romance novels.

10. However, most literary critics dislike these books.

Linking Verbs

A **linking verb** does not show action. Instead, it connects the subject to a word or words that describe or rename it. The linking verb tells what the subject is (or what it was, will be, or seems to be).

> A googolplex is an extremely large number.

Many linking verbs, like *is*, are forms of the verb *be*. Other linking verbs refer to the senses (*look*, *feel*, and so on).

> The photocopy looks blurry.
>
> Some students feel anxious about the future.

Frequently Used Linking Verbs

act	feel	seem
appear	get	smell
be (am, is, are, was, were)	grow	sound
	look	taste
become	remain	turn

● Practice 15-6

In the following sentences, underline each linking verb twice.

1. Urban legends are stories created to teach a lesson.

2. One familiar urban legend is the story of Hookman.

3. According to this story, a young man and woman are alone in Lovers' Lane.

4. They are in a car, listening to a radio announcement.

5. An escaped murderer is nearby.

6. The murderer's left hand is a hook.

7. The young woman becomes hysterical.

8. Suddenly, Lovers' Lane seems very dangerous.

9. Later, they are shocked to see a hook hanging from the passenger door handle.

10. The purpose of this urban legend is to frighten young people into avoiding dangerous places.

● Practice 15-7

Underline every verb in each of the following sentences twice. Remember that a verb can be an action verb or a linking verb.

Example: Some books <u>have</u> a great impact on their readers.

(1) Betty Smith's *A Tree Grows in Brooklyn* is a classic coming-of-age novel. (2) The novel tells the story of Francie Nolan. (3) Francie is very poor but seems determined to succeed. (4) She loves books and is an excellent student. (5) Francie lives with her parents and her younger brother, Neely. (6) She dreams of a better life for herself and her family. (7) Tragically, Francie's father dies. (8) Her mother supports the family and does her best for her children. (9) She works as a janitor in their apartment building. (10) Eventually, Francie graduates from high school, with a bright future ahead of her.

Helping Verbs

Many verbs consist of more than one word. For example, the verb in the following sentence consists of two words.

Minh <u>must make</u> a decision about his future.

In this sentence, *make* is the **main verb**, and *must* is a **helping verb**.

Frequently Used Helping Verbs

does	will	must	should
did	was	can	would
do	were	could	
is	have	may	
are	has	might	
am	had		

A sentence's **complete verb** is made up of a main verb and any helping verbs that accompany it. In each of the following sentences, the complete verb is underlined twice, and the helping verbs are checkmarked.

Minh should have gone earlier.

Did Minh ask the right questions?

Minh will work hard.

Minh can really succeed.

**Highlight:
Helping Verbs
with Participles**

Participles, such as *going* and *gone*, cannot stand alone as main verbs in a sentence. They need a helping verb to make them complete.

Incorrect	Minh going to the library.
Correct	Minh is going to the library.
Incorrect	Minh gone to the library.
Correct	Minh has gone to the library.

● **Practice 15-8**

The verbs in the sentences that follow consist of a main verb and one or more helping verbs. In each sentence, underline the complete verb twice, and put a check mark above each helping verb.

Example: The Salk polio vaccine <u>was given</u> to more than a million schoolchildren in 1954.

(1) By the 1950s, polio had become widespread in the United States. (2) For years, it had puzzled doctors and researchers. (3) Thousands had become ill each year in the United States alone. (4) Children should have been playing happily. (5) Instead, they would get very sick. (6) Polio was sometimes called infantile paralysis. (7) In fact, it did cause paralysis in children and in adults as well. (8) Some patients could breathe only with the help of machines called iron lungs. (9) Others would remain in wheelchairs for life. (10) By 1960, Jonas Salk's vaccine had reduced the incidence of polio in the United States by more than 90 percent.

Focus on Writing: *Flashback*

Look back at your response to the Focus on Writing activity on page 263. In each sentence, underline the complete verb twice, and put a check mark above each helping verb.

Focus on Writing: *Revising and Editing*

Look back at your response to the Focus on Writing activity on page 263. **TEST** what you have written. Then, revise and edit your work, paying special attention to your sentences' subjects and verbs.

Chapter Review

Editing Practice

Read the following student essay. Underline the subject of each sentence once, and underline the complete verb of each sentence twice. If you have trouble locating the subject, try crossing out the prepositional phrases. The first sentence has been done for you.

Hip-Hop Pioneer

Hip-Hop is extremely popular ~~among young people~~. Russell Simmons is one of the most important people in hip-hop. He started the record label Def Jam. Simmons is responsible for getting hip-hop music accepted by mainstream audiences. Simmons also showed the world a successful black-owned business.

Simmons was born in Queens, New York, in 1957. He began to promote hip-hop in 1978. Simmons started to represent rap artists with his production company, Rush Productions. One of his clients was his own brother, Joseph. Simmons called Joseph's group Run-D.M.C. With producer Rick Rubin, Simmons started the Def Jam record label. Def Jam's artists had a rebellious quality. Many listeners loved them.

Def Jam was soon known as a creative company. It introduced the work of many black artists (as well as some white groups) to a multicultural audience. Def Jam released recordings of Public Enemy, the Beastie Boys, and other hip-hop artists. The movie *Krush Groove* dramatized the founding of the company. It was a big success with fans of hip-hop. In 1991, Simmons began the HBO series *Def Comedy Jam*. This series featured the uncensored comedy of many African Americans, including Martin Lawrence, Chris Rock, and Jamie Foxx. Simmons also made some movies. One was *The Nutty Professor*. This film marked the comeback of actor Eddie Murphy.

Russell Simmons became a very successful businessman. In addition to Def Jam, Simmons started other businesses. One of them was Phat

Farm, a line of clothing for men. Phat Farm was followed by Baby Phat. This was a line of women's clothing. Simmons also started *One World*. This magazine focused on the hip-hop lifestyle. In addition, he founded an advertising agency, Rush Media Company. In 1999, Simmons sold his share of Def Jam for $100 million. By then, he was highly respected as both a music promoter and a businessman.

In the past, hip-hop was criticized as a fad. Now, however, hip-hop has entered the broader American culture. More than anyone, Russell Simmons has been responsible for hip-hop's success.

Collaborative Activities

1. Fold a sheet of paper in half lengthwise. Working in a group of three or four students, spend two minutes listing as many nouns as you can in the column to the left of the fold. When your time is up, exchange papers with another group of students. Limiting yourselves to five minutes, write an appropriate action verb beside each noun. Each noun will now be the subject of a short sentence.

2. Working in the same group, choose five short sentences from those you wrote for Collaborative Activity 1. Work together to create more fully developed sentences. First, expand each subject by adding words or prepositional phrases that give more information about the subject. (For example, you could expand *boat* to *the small, leaky boat with the red sail.*) Then, expand each sentence further, adding ideas after the verb. (For example, the sentence *The boat bounced* could become *The small, leaky boat with the red sail bounced helplessly on the water.*)

3. Work in a group of three or four students to write one original sentence for each of the linking verbs listed on page 269. When you have finished, exchange papers with another group. Now, try to add words and phrases to the other group's sentences to make them more interesting.

Review Checklist: Writing Simple Sentences

☐ A sentence expresses a complete thought. The subject tells who or what is being talked about in the sentence. (See 15A.)

☐ A prepositional phrase consists of a preposition and its object (the noun or pronoun it introduces). The object of a preposition cannot be the subject of a sentence. (See 15B.)

☐ An action verb tells what the subject does, did, or will do. (See 15C.)

☐ A linking verb connects the subject to a word or words that describe or rename it. (See 15C.)

☐ Many verbs are made up of more than one word. The complete verb in a sentence includes the main verb plus any helping verbs. (See 15C.)

The most basic kind of sentence, a **simple sentence**, consists of a single **independent clause**: one <u>subject</u> and one <u>verb</u>.

Many European <u>immigrants</u> <u>arrived</u> at Ellis Island.

A **compound sentence** is made up of two or more simple sentences (independent clauses).

<table>
<tr><td>16a</td><td></td></tr>
</table>

Using Coordinating Conjunctions

One way to form a compound sentence is by joining two independent clauses with a **coordinating conjunction** preceded by a comma.

Many European immigrants arrived at Ellis Island, <u>but</u> many Asian immigrants arrived at Angel Island.

Coordinating Conjunctions

and	for	or	yet
but	nor	so	

WORD POWER
coordinate equal in importance, rank, or degree

Coordinating conjunctions join two ideas of equal importance. They describe the relationship between two ideas, showing how and why the ideas are related. Different coordinating conjunctions have different meanings.

Focus on Writing

The picture on the opposite page shows a high school graduation with two of the graduating students holding their children. Look at the picture, and then write a letter to the president of your school explaining why your campus needs a day-care center. (If your school already has a day-care center, explain why it deserves continued—or increased—funding.)

- To indicate addition, use *and*.

    He acts like a child, <u>and</u> people think he is cute.

- To indicate contrast or contradiction, use *but* or *yet*.

    He acts like a child, <u>but</u> he is an adult.

    He acts like a child, <u>yet</u> he longs to be taken seriously.

- To indicate a cause-and-effect relationship, use *so* or *for*.

    He acts like a child, <u>so</u> we treat him like one.

    He acts like a child, <u>for</u> he craves attention.

- To present alternatives, use *or*.

    He acts like a child, <u>or</u> he is ignored.

- To eliminate alternatives, use *nor*.

    He does not act like a child, <u>nor</u> does he look like one.

Highlight: Using Commas with Coordinating Conjunctions

When you use a coordinating conjunction to link two independent clauses into a single compound sentence, always put a comma before the coordinating conjunction.

We can stand in line all night, or we can go home now.

● Practice 16-1

Fill in the coordinating conjunction—*and, but, for, nor, or, so,* or *yet*—that best links the two parts of each compound sentence. Remember to insert a comma before each coordinating conjunction.

Example: Fairy tales have been told by many people around the world , <u>but</u> the stories by two German brothers may be the most famous.

(1) Jakob and Wilhelm Grimm lived in the nineteenth century _____ they wrote many well-known fairy tales. (2) Most people think fondly of fairy tales _____ the Brothers Grimm wrote

many unpleasant and violent stories. (3) In their best-known works, children are abused _____ endings are not always happy. (4) Either innocent children are brutally punished for no reason _____ they are neglected. (5) For example, in "Hansel and Gretel," the stepmother mistreats the children _____ their father abandons them in the woods. (6) In this story, the events are horrifying _____ the ending is still happy. (7) The children outwit the evil adults _____ they escape unharmed. (8) Apparently, they are not injured physically _____ are they harmed emotionally. (9) Nevertheless, their story can hardly be called pleasant _____ it is a story of child abuse and neglect.

● **Practice 16-2**

Use a coordinating conjunction to join each of the following pairs of simple sentences into one compound sentence. Be sure to place a comma before each coordinating conjunction you add.

Example: A computer can make drafting essays easier*, and it* It also makes revision easier.

1. Training a dog to heel is difficult. Dogs naturally resist strict control.
2. A bodhran is an Irish drum. It is played with a wooden stick.
3. Students should spend two hours studying for each hour of class time. They may not do well in the course.
4. Years ago, students wrote on slates. The teacher was able to correct each student's work individually.
5. Each state in the United States has two senators. The number of representatives depends on a state's population.
6. In 1973, only 2.5 percent of those in the U.S. military were women. Today, that number is almost 20 percent.
7. A "small craft advisory" is an important warning for boaters. Bad weather conditions can be dangerous to small boats.

8. A DVD looks like a compact disc. It can hold fifteen times as much information.

9. Hip-hop fashions include sneakers and baggy pants. These styles are very popular among today's young men.

10. Multiple births have become more and more common. Even septuplets have a reasonable chance of survival today.

● **Practice 16-3**

Add coordinating conjunctions to combine some of these simple sentences. Remember to put a comma before each coordinating conjunction you add.

Example: Years ago, few Americans lived to be one hundred. Today, _, but today,_ there are over 70,000 U.S. centenarians.

(1) Diet, exercise, and family history may account for centenarians' long lives. (2) This is not the whole story. (3) One study showed surprising common traits among centenarians. (4) They did not necessarily avoid tobacco and alcohol. (5) They did not have low-fat diets. (6) In fact, they consumed relatively large amounts of fat, cholesterol, and sugar. (7) Diet could not explain their long lives. (8) They did, however, share several key survival characteristics. (9) First, all of the centenarians were optimistic about life. (10) All of them were positive thinkers. (11) They were also involved in religious life and had deep religious faith. (12) In addition, all the centenarians had continued to lead physically active lives. (13) They remained mobile even as elderly people. (14) Finally, all were able to adapt to loss. (15) They had all experienced the deaths of friends, spouses, or children. (16) They were able to get on with their lives.

● **Practice 16-4**

Write another simple sentence to follow each of the simple sentences below. Then, connect the sentences with a coordinating conjunction. Be sure to insert a comma before each coordinating conjunction.

Example: Many people need organ transplants,/ *but there is a*
serious shortage of organ donors.

1. Smoking in bed is dangerous. _____

    _____

2. Many cars are equipped with navigation systems. _____

    _____

3. Diamonds are very expensive. _____

    _____

4. Kangaroos carry their young in pouches. _____

    _____

5. Dancing is good exercise. _____

    _____

6. Motorcycle helmet laws have been dropped in some states. _____

    _____

7. Some businesses sponsor sports leagues for their employees. _____

    _____

8. Pretzels are a healthier snack than potato chips. _____

    _____

9. Many so-called juices actually contain very little real fruit juice. _____

    _____

10. Human beings tend to resist change. _____

    _____

Focus on Writing: *Flashback*

Look back at your response to the Focus on Writing activity on page 277. If you see any compound sentences, bracket them. If you see any pairs of simple sentences that could be combined into one compound sentence, try joining them with appropriate coordinating conjunctions. Be sure each of your new compound sentences includes a comma before the coordinating conjunction.

16b   Using Semicolons

Another way to create a compound sentence is by joining two simple sentences (independent clauses) with a **semicolon**. A semicolon is used to connect clauses whose ideas are closely linked.

> The AIDS Memorial quilt contains thousands of panels; each panel is a square.

Also use a semicolon to show a strong contrast between two ideas.

> With new drugs, people can live with AIDS for years; many people, however, cannot get these drugs.

Highlight: Avoiding Sentence Fragments	Remember that a semicolon can only join two complete sentences (independent clauses). A semicolon cannot join a sentence and a fragment.
	———————— FRAGMENT ————————
Incorrect	Because millions worldwide are still dying of AIDS; more research is needed.
	———————— SENTENCE ————————
Correct	Millions worldwide are still dying of AIDS; more research is needed.

● Practice 16-5

Each of the following items consists of one simple sentence. Create a compound sentence for each item by changing the period to a semicolon and then adding another simple sentence.

> **Example:** My brother is addicted to fast food*;* _he eats it every day._

1. Fast-food restaurants are an American institution. _____

   _____

2. Families often eat at these restaurants. _____

   _____

3. Many teenagers work there. _____

   _____

4. McDonald's is known for its hamburgers. _____

_____

5. KFC is famous for its fried chicken. _____

_____

6. Taco Bell serves Mexican-style food. _____

_____

7. Pizza Hut specializes in pizza. _____

_____

8. Many fast-food restaurants offer some low-fat menu items. _____

_____

9. Some offer recyclable packaging. _____

_____

10. Some even have playgrounds. _____

_____

Focus on Writing: *Flashback*

Look back at your response to the Focus on Writing activity on page 277. Do you see a pair of simple sentences that are closely linked or suggest a contrast? Try linking the sentences with a semicolon.

16c   Using Transitional Words and Phrases

Another way to create a compound sentence is by combining two simple sentences (independent clauses) with a **transitional word or phrase**. When a transitional word or phrase joins two sentences, always place a semicolon *before* the transitional word or phrase and a comma *after* it.

Some college students receive grants; <u>however</u>, others must take out loans.

He had a miserable time at the party; <u>in addition</u>, he drank too much.

Frequently Used Transitional Words

also	instead	still
besides	later	subsequently
consequently	meanwhile	then
eventually	moreover	therefore
finally	nevertheless	thus
furthermore	now	
however	otherwise	

Frequently Used Transitional Phrases

after all	in comparison
as a result	in contrast
at the same time	in fact
for example	in other words
for instance	of course
in addition	on the contrary

Adding a transitional word or phrase makes the connection between ideas in a sentence clearer and more precise than it would be if the ideas were linked with just a semicolon. Different transitional words and phrases convey different meanings.

● Some signal addition (*also, besides, furthermore, in addition, moreover,* and so on).

I have a lot on my mind; <u>also</u>, I have a lot of things to do.

● Some make causal connections (*as a result, therefore, consequently, thus,* and so on).

I have a lot on my mind; <u>as a result</u>, it is hard to concentrate.

● Some indicate contradiction or contrast (*nevertheless, however, in contrast, still,* and so on).

I have a lot on my mind; <u>still</u>, I'm trying to relax.

- Some present alternatives (*instead, on the contrary, otherwise,* and so on).

  I have a lot on my mind; <u>otherwise</u>, I could relax.

  I will try not to think; <u>instead</u>, I will relax.

- Some indicate time sequence (*at the same time, eventually, finally, later, meanwhile, now, subsequently, then,* and so on).

  I have a lot on my mind; <u>meanwhile</u>, I still have work to do.

● **Practice 16-6**

Add semicolons and commas where they are required to set off transitional words or phrases that join two simple sentences.

Example: Ketchup is a popular condiment ; therefore , it is available in almost every restaurant.

(1) Andrew F. Smith, a food historian, wrote a book about the tomato later he wrote a book about ketchup. (2) This book, *Pure Ketchup*, was a big project in fact Smith worked on it for five years. (3) The word *ketchup* may have come from a Chinese word however Smith is not certain of the word's origins. (4) Ketchup has existed since ancient times in other words it is a very old product. (5) Ketchup has changed a lot over the years for example special dyes were developed in the nineteenth century to make it red. (6) Smith's book discusses many other changes for instance preservative-free ketchup was invented in 1907. (7) Ketchup is now used by people in many cultures still salsa is more popular than ketchup in the United States. (8) Today, designer ketchups are being developed meanwhile Heinz has introduced green and purple ketchup in squeeze bottles. (9) Some of today's ketchups are chunky in addition some ketchups are spicy. (10) Ketchup continues to evolve meanwhile Smith has written a book about hamburgers.

WORD POWER
condiment something used to add flavor to food

● **Practice 16-7**

Consulting the lists of transitional words and phrases on page 284, choose a word or phrase that logically connects each pair of simple sentences below into one compound sentence. Be sure to punctuate appropriately.

> **Example:** *Time*'s Man of the Year is often a prominent politician; *however, sometimes* ~~Sometimes~~ it is not.

(1) Every year since 1927, *Time* has designated a Man of the Year. The Man of the Year has not always been a man. (2) In the 1920s and 1930s, world leaders were often chosen. Franklin Delano Roosevelt was chosen twice. (3) During World War II, Hitler, Stalin, Churchill, and Roosevelt were all chosen. Stalin was featured twice. (4) Occasionally, the Man of the Year was not an individual. In 1950, it was The American Fighting Man. (5) In 1956, The Hungarian Freedom Fighter was Man of the Year. In 1966, *Time* editors chose The Young Generation. (6) Only a few women have been selected. Queen Elizabeth II of England was featured in 1952. (7) In 1975, American Women were honored as a group. The Man of the Year has nearly always been male. (8) Very few people of color have been designated Man of the Year. Martin Luther King Jr. was honored in 1963. (9) The Man of the Year has almost always been one or more human beings. The Computer was selected in 1982 and Endangered Earth in 1988. (10) More recently, prominent politicians have once again been chosen. In 2001, New York City mayor Rudy Giuliani was *Time*'s Man of the Year (now called Person of the Year). (11) In 2003, *Time* did not choose a politician. It honored The American Soldier. (12) In 2004, *Time* selected President George W. Bush. The magazine was making a more traditional choice. (13) In 2005, *Time* wanted to honor the contributions of philanthropists. The magazine named Bill Gates, Melinda Gates, and Bono its Persons of the Year. (14) For 2006, *Time* did not choose a specific person.

WORD POWER
philanthropist
someone who tries to improve human lives through charitable aid

Its person of the year was "you." (15) For 2008, however, *Time* chose a person again. Its pick was Barack Obama.

● Practice 16-8

Add the suggested transitional word or phrase to each of the simple sentences below. Then, add a new independent clause to follow it. Be sure to punctuate correctly.

> **Example:**   Commuting students do not really experience campus life. (however)
>
> *Commuting students do not really experience campus life; however,*
>
> *there are some benefits to being a commuter.*

1. Campus residents may have a better college experience. (still)

   _____

   _____

2. Living at home gives students access to home-cooked meals. (in contrast)

   _____

   _____

3. Commuters have a wide choice of jobs in the community. (on the other hand)

   _____

   _____

4. Commuters get to live with their families. (however)

   _____

   _____

5. There are also some disadvantages to being a commuter. (for example)

   _____

   _____

6. Unlike dorm students, many commuters have family responsibilities. (in fact)

   _____

   _____

7. Commuters might have to help take care of their parents or grandparents. (in addition)

_____

_____

8. Commuters might need a car to get to school. (consequently)

_____

_____

9. Younger commuters may be under the watchful eyes of their parents. (of course)

_____

_____

10. Commuting to college has pros and cons. (therefore)

_____

_____

● Practice 16-9

Use the topics and transitional words or phrases specified below to create five compound sentences. Be sure to punctuate appropriately.

Example:

Topic: fad diets
Transitional phrase: for example

People are always trying fad diets; for example, some people eat

only pineapple to lose weight.

1. *Topic:* laws to protect people with disabilities
   Transitional phrase: in addition

_____

_____

2. *Topic:* single men and women as adoptive parents
   Transitional word: however

_____

_____

3. *Topic:* prayer in public schools
   Transitional word: therefore

   _____

   _____

4. *Topic:* high school proms
   Transitional word: also

   _____

   _____

5. *Topic:* course requirements at your school
   Transitional phrase: for instance

   _____

   _____

Focus on Writing: *Flashback*

Look back at your response to the Focus on Writing activity on page 277. Have you used any transitional words or phrases to link independent clauses? If so, check to make sure that you have punctuated them correctly. Then, check to see that you have used the transitional word or phrase that best shows the relationship between the ideas in the two independent clauses. Make any necessary changes.

Focus on Writing: *Revising and Editing*

Look back at your response to the Focus on Writing activity on page 277. **TEST** what you have written. Then, try to add one of the new compound sentences you created from a pair of simple sentences in the Flashback activities on pages 281 and 283. Finally, revise and edit your work, checking each compound sentence to make sure you have used the coordinating conjunction or transitional word or phrase that best conveys your meaning and that you have punctuated these sentences correctly.

Editing Practice

Read the following student essay. Then, create compound sentences by linking pairs of simple sentences where appropriate, joining them with a coordinating conjunction, a semicolon, or a semicolon followed by a transitional word or phrase. Remember to put commas before coordinating conjunctions and to use semicolons and commas correctly with transitional words and phrases. The first two sentences have been combined for you.

My Grandfather's Life

My great-grandparents were born in Ukraine. *, but they* They raised my grandfather in western Pennsylvania. The ninth of their ten children, he had a life I cannot begin to imagine. To me, he was my big, strong, powerful grandfather. He was also a child of poverty.

My great-grandfather worked for the American Car Foundry. The family lived in a company house. They shopped at the company store. In 1934, my great-grandfather was laid off. He went to work digging sewer lines for the government. At that time, the family was on welfare. Every week, they were entitled to get food rations. My grandfather would go to pick up the food. They desperately needed the prunes, beans, flour, margarine, and other things.

For years, my grandfather wore his brothers' hand-me-down clothes. He wore thrift-shop shoes with cardboard over the holes in the soles. He was often hungry. He would sometimes sit by the side of the railroad tracks, waiting for an engineer to throw him an orange. My grandfather would do any job to earn a quarter. He once weeded a mile-long row of tomato plants. For this work, he was paid twenty-five cents and a pack of Necco wafers.

My grandfather saved his pennies. Eventually, he was able to buy a used bicycle for two dollars. He dropped out of school at fourteen and got a job. The family badly needed his income. He woke up every day at 4 a.m. He rode his bike to his job at a meatpacking plant.

In 1943, at the age of seventeen, my grandfather joined the U.S. Navy. He discovered a new world. For the first time in his life, he had enough to eat. He was always first in line at the mess hall. He went back for seconds and thirds before anyone else. After the war ended in 1945, he was discharged from the Navy. He went to work in a meat market in New York City. The only trade he knew was the meat business. Three years later, when he had saved enough to open his own store, Pete's Quality Meats, he knew his life of poverty was finally over.

Collaborative Activities

1. Working in a small group, pair each of the simple sentences in the left-hand column below with a sentence in the right-hand column to create ten compound sentences. Use as many different coordinating conjunctions as you can to connect the independent clauses. Be sure each coordinating conjunction you choose conveys a logical relationship between ideas, and remember to put a comma before each one. You may use some of the listed sentences more than once. (Note that many different combinations—some serious and factually accurate, some humorous—are possible.)

Some dogs wear little sweaters.	Many are named Hamlet.
Pit bulls are raised to fight.	They live in groups.
Bonobos are pygmy chimpanzees.	One even sings Christmas carols.
Many people fear Dobermans.	They can wear bandanas.
Leopards have spots.	They can play Frisbee.
Dalmatians can live in firehouses.	Many live in equatorial Zaire.
Horses can wear blankets.	Some people think they are gentle.
All mules are sterile.	They don't get cold in winter.
Great Danes are huge dogs.	They are half horse and half donkey.
Parrots can often speak.	They can be unpredictable.

2. Work in a group of three or four students to create a cast of five characters for a movie, a television sitcom pilot, a reality show, or a music
video. Working on your own, write five descriptive short sentences—
one about each character. Then, exchange papers with another student.
Add a coordinating conjunction to each sentence on the list to create
five new compound sentences.

Example:

Original sentence   Mark is a handsome heartthrob.

New sentence   Mark is a handsome heartthrob, but he has
green dreadlocks.

Review Checklist: Writing Compound Sentences

☐ A compound sentence is made up of two simple sentences (independent clauses).

☐ A coordinating conjunction—*and, but, for, nor, or, so,* or *yet*—can join two independent clauses into one compound sentence. A comma always comes before the coordinating conjunction. (See 16A.)

☐ A semicolon can join two independent clauses into one compound sentence. (See 16B.)

☐ A transitional word or phrase can also join two independent clauses into one compound sentence. When it joins two independent clauses, a transitional word or phrase is always preceded by a semicolon and followed by a comma. (See 16C.)

SURGEON GENERAL'S WARNING:
Cigarette Smoke
Contains Carbon Monoxide.

SURGEON GENERAL'S WARNING: Smoking By
Pregnant Women May Result in Fetal Injury,
Premature Birth, And Low Birth Weight.

SURGEON GENERAL'S
WARNING

Identifying Complex Sentences

As you learned in Chapter 15, a simple sentence consists of a single independent clause. An **independent clause** can stand alone as a sentence.

Independent clause	The <u>exhibit</u> <u>was</u> controversial.

However, a **dependent clause** cannot stand alone as a sentence. It needs an independent clause to complete its meaning.

Dependent clause	Because the exhibit was controversial

What happened because the exhibit was controversial? To answer this question, you need to add an independent clause that completes the idea in the dependent clause. The result is a **complex sentence**—a sentence that consists of one independent clause and one or more dependent clauses.

	┌────── DEPENDENT CLAUSE ──────┐ ┌─ INDEPENDENT CLAUSE ─
Complex sentence	Because the exhibit was controversial, many people came to see the paintings.

● **Practice 17-1**

In the blank following each of the items on page 296, indicate whether the group of words is an independent clause (*IC*) or a dependent clause (*DC*).

Example: According to astrologists, the planets and stars have an effect on human lives. _____*IC*_____

Focus on Writing

In 1963, the U.S. government began requiring that all cigarette packages include a warning label. The picture on the opposite page shows some of these labels. Look at the picture, and then write a paragraph (or an essay) about a law that you think should be passed, and explain why you think this law is necessary.

1. Because astronomy and astrology both involve the study of objects in space. _____

2. People often confuse these two fields. _____

3. Even though astrology also studied the stars and other celestial bodies. _____

4. Astronomy came to be known as a more scholarly and scientific field. _____

5. Astrology began to focus only on the influence of the planets and stars on human behavior. _____

6. Although astrology is dismissed as superstition by most Western scientists. _____

7. Today, about one-third of Americans believe in astrology. _____

8. When almost two hundred scientists signed a statement objecting to astrological beliefs. _____

9. The document was not signed by the well-known scientist Carl Sagan. _____

10. Who felt that the statement would lead to controversy. _____

● **Practice 17-2**

In the blank following each of the items below, indicate whether the group of words is an independent clause (*IC*) or a dependent clause (*DC*).

> **Example:**   When novelist Toni Morrison was born in Ohio in 1931.
> _____*DC*_____

1. As a young reader, Toni Morrison liked the classic Russian novelists. _____

2. After she graduated from Howard University with a bachelor's degree in English. _____

3. Morrison based her novel *The Bluest Eye* on a childhood friend's desire for blue eyes. _____

4. While she raised two sons as a single mother and worked as an editor at Random House. _____

5. As her reputation as a novelist grew with the publication of *Song of Solomon* and *Tar Baby.* _____

6. Her picture appeared on the cover of *Newsweek* in 1981. _____

7. Before her novel *Beloved* won the 1988 Pulitzer Prize for fiction. _____

8. *Beloved* was later made into a film starring Oprah Winfrey. _____

9. In 1993, Morrison became the first African-American woman to win the Nobel Prize in Literature. _____

10. Who published the novel *Paradise* in 1998. _____

17b   Using Subordinating Conjunctions

WORD POWER
subordinate lower in rank or position; secondary in importance

One way to form a complex sentence is to use a **subordinating conjunction**—a dependent word such as *although* or *because*—to join two simple sentences (independent clauses).

Two simple sentences	Muhammad Ali was stripped of his title for refusing to go into the army. Many people admired his antiwar position.
Complex sentence	DEPENDENT CLAUSE Although Muhammad Ali was stripped of his title for refusing to go into the army, many people admired his antiwar position.

Frequently Used Subordinating Conjunctions

after	even though	since	whenever
although	if	so that	where
as	if only	than	whereas
as if	in order that	that	wherever
as though	now that	though	whether
because	once	unless	while
before	provided that	until	
even if	rather than	when	

Different subordinating conjunctions express different relationships between dependent and independent clauses.

Relationship between Clauses	Subordinating Conjunction	Example
Time	after, before, now, since, until, when, whenever, while	When the whale surfaced, Ahab threw his harpoon.
Reason or cause	as, as if, because	Scientists abandoned the project because the government cut funds.
Result or effect	in order that, in order to, so that	So that students' math scores will improve, many schools have begun special tutoring.
Condition	even if, if, unless	The rain forest may disappear unless steps are taken immediately.
Contrast	although, even though, though, whereas	Although Thomas Edison had almost no formal education, he was a successful inventor.
Location	where, wherever	Pittsburgh was built where the Allegheny and Monongahela Rivers meet.

Highlight: Punctuating with Subordinating Conjunctions

Use a comma after the dependent clause in the sentence. Do not use a comma after the independent clause.

┌──── DEPENDENT CLAUSE ────┐ ┌──── INDEPENDENT CLAUSE ────┐
Although she wore the scarlet letter, Hester carried herself proudly.

┌──── INDEPENDENT CLAUSE ────┐ ┌──── DEPENDENT CLAUSE ────┐
Hester carried herself proudly although she wore the scarlet letter.

● Practice 17-3

In the blank in each of the sentences below, write an appropriate subordinating conjunction. Look at the list of subordinating conjunctions on page 297 to help you choose a conjunction that expresses the logical relationship between the two clauses it links. (The required punctuation has been provided.)

Example: Movie cowboys are usually portrayed as white _____*although*_____ many were African American.

(1) Few people today know about black cowboys _____ they were once common. (2) _____ the transcontinental railroad was built, cowboys were in high demand. (3) The ranchers hired cowboys to drive their cattle to the Midwest, _____ the cows were loaded on trains headed to eastern cities. (4) Many former slaves became cowboys _____ they wanted a new start. (5) Many African Americans also became cowboys _____ they had experience working with horses and cattle on Southern plantations or farms. (6) However, black cowboys faced difficulties _____ they arrived in the West. (7) African-American cowboys often had to work much harder than whites _____ earn the same pay and respect. (8) _____ almost one-fourth of cowboys were black, few writers wrote about them. (9) The myth of the white-only cowboy was spread in novels, films, and television shows _____ black cowboys never existed. (10) Black cowboys did appear in some films of the 1970s _____ by this time Westerns were no longer popular. (11) Things started to change in the 1970s _____ several museums honored black, Indian, and Mexican cowboys. (12) _____ African-American cowboys have finally received some recognition, their history can now be more fully understood.

● Practice 17-4

Form one complex sentence by combining each of the following pairs of sentences. Use a subordinating conjunction from the list on page 297 to clarify the relationship between the dependent and independent clauses in each sentence. Make sure you include a comma where one is required.

although they

Example: Orville and Wilbur Wright built the first powered plane/ They had no formal training as engineers.

1. Professional midwives are used widely in Europe. In the United States, they are less common.

2. John Deere made the first steel plow in 1837. A new era began in farming.

3. Stephen Crane describes battles in *The Red Badge of Courage*. He never experienced a war.

4. Elvis Presley died suddenly in 1977. Thousands of his fans gathered in front of his mansion.

5. Edward Jenner developed the smallpox vaccine in the 1800s. The number of smallpox cases declined.

6. The salaries of baseball players rose in the 1980s. Some sportswriters predicted a drop in attendance at games.

7. The Du Ponts arrived from France in 1800. American gunpowder was not as good as French gunpowder.

8. Margaret Sanger opened her first birth-control clinic in America in 1916. She was arrested.

9. Thaddeus Stevens thought plantation land should be given to freed slaves. He disagreed with Lincoln's peace plan for the South.

10. Steven Spielberg has directed some very popular movies. He did not win an Academy Award until *Schindler's List*.

Focus on Writing: *Flashback*

Look back at your response to the Focus on Writing activity on page 295. Identify two pairs of simple sentences that could be combined with subordinating conjunctions. Combine each pair into a complex sentence by making one sentence a dependent clause. Check to make sure you have punctuated your new sentences correctly.

17c Using Relative Pronouns

Another way to form a complex sentence is to use a **relative pronoun** (a dependent word such as *who, that, which*, and so on) to join two simple sentences (independent clauses).

Two simple sentences	Pit bulls were originally bred in England. They can be very aggressive.

DEPENDENT CLAUSE

Complex sentence	Pit bulls, which were originally bred in England, can be very aggressive.

Relative Pronouns

that	which	whoever	whomever
what	who	whom	whose

Relative pronouns show the relationships between the ideas in the independent and dependent clauses that they link.

Two simple sentences	Nadine Gordimer comes from South Africa. She won the Nobel Prize in Literature in 1991.
Complex sentence	Nadine Gordimer, who won the Nobel Prize in Literature in 1991, comes from South Africa.
Two simple sentences	Last week I had a job interview. It went very well.
Complex sentence	Last week I had a job interview that went very well.
Two simple sentences	Transistors have replaced vacuum tubes in radios and televisions. They were invented in 1948.
Complex sentence	Transistors, which were invented in 1948, have replaced vacuum tubes in radios and televisions.

Note: The relative pronoun always refers to a word in the independent clause. *Who* and *whom* refer to people; *that* and *which* refer to animals or things.

● **Practice 17-5**

In each of the following complex sentences, underline the dependent clause once, and underline the relative pronoun twice. Then, draw an arrow from the relative pronoun to the word to which it refers.

Example: MTV, <u>which was the first television network devoted to popular music videos</u>, began in 1981.

1. MTV's very first music video, which was performed by a group called the Buggles, contained the lyric "Video killed the radio star."
2. The earliest videos on MTV were simple productions that recorded live studio performances.
3. Recording executives, who had been doubtful of MTV at first, soon realized the marketing potential of music videos.
4. Music videos eventually became complicated productions that featured special effects and large casts of dancers.
5. Music video directors gained recognition at MTV's Video Music Awards presentation, which first aired in September 1984.
6. *The Real World*, a reality series that featured a group of young people living together in New York City, was introduced by MTV in 1992.
7. MTV's later reality shows featured celebrities such as Jessica Simpson, who starred in *Newlyweds: Nick and Jessica* in 2003.
8. Today, MTV, which devotes less and less time to music videos, produces many hours of original programming.
9. Some of MTV's newest reality shows, which feature cast members doing good deeds, are designed to give viewers positive social messages.
10. Critics of MTV's format have included musicians such as Justin Timberlake, who challenged MTV to play more videos.

● **Practice 17-6**

Combine each of the following pairs of simple sentences into one complex sentence, using the relative pronoun that follows each pair.

Example: J. K. Rowling enjoyed writing fantasy stories as a child. She invented the character Harry Potter on a four-hour train ride. (who)

J. K. Rowling, who enjoyed writing fantasy stories as a child,

invented the character Harry Potter on a train ride.

1. The Harry Potter books follow the young wizard from age 11 to 17. They have become international best-sellers. (which)

   _____

   _____

2. Readers see Harry in some unusual situations. These situations reveal his magical powers. (that)

   _____

   _____

3. Harry faces many challenges. These challenges test his courage and willpower. (that)

   _____

   _____

4. Harry's greatest enemy is the evil Lord Voldemort. Voldemort killed his parents with dark magic. (who)

   _____

   _____

5. Harry goes to school at Hogwarts. It is a boarding school for young wizards and witches. (which)

   _____

   _____

6. At Hogwarts, Harry gets to know Ron Weasley and Hermione Granger. They become his closest friends. (who)

   _____

   _____

7. Albus Dumbledore is the headmaster of Hogwarts. He is Harry's mentor. (who)

   _____

   _____

8. The Harry Potter books are filled with magic and witchcraft. They are offensive to some people. (which)

_____

_____

9. The film adaptations of the books star Daniel Radcliffe as Harry. They have been very successful. (which)

_____

_____

10. The last of the seven books was published in 2007. It is the longest book in the Harry Potter series. (which)

_____

_____

Focus on Writing: *Flashback*

Look back at your response to the Focus on Writing activity on page 295. Identify two simple sentences that could be combined with a relative pronoun. (If you cannot find two appropriate sentences, write two new ones.) Then, combine the sentences to create a new complex sentence.

Focus on Writing: *Revising and Editing*

Look back at your response to the Focus on Writing activity on page 295. **TEST** what you have written. Then, try adding one of the new complex sentences you created from pairs of simple sentences in the Flashback activities on page 300 and above. Revise and edit your work, making sure you have no errors in your use of subordinating conjunctions and relative pronouns. Finally, make sure that you have punctuated correctly.

Editing Practice

Read the following student essay. Then, revise it by combining pairs of simple sentences with subordinating conjunctions or relative pronouns that indicate the relationship between them. Be sure to punctuate correctly. The first sentence has been revised for you.

Community Art

When a
A city has a crime problem, *the* The police and the courts try to solve it. Some cities have come up with creative ways to help young people stay out of trouble. One example is the Philadelphia Mural Arts Program. It offers free art education for high school students.

In the 1960s, Philadelphia had a serious problem. The problem was graffiti. Graffiti artists had painted their designs on buildings all over the city. A solution to the problem was the Philadelphia Anti-Graffiti Network. This offered graffiti artists an alternative. The artists would give up graffiti. They would not be prosecuted. The artists enjoyed painting. They could paint murals on public buildings instead. They could create beautiful landscapes, portraits of local heroes, and abstract designs. The graffiti artists had once been lawbreakers. They could now help beautify the city.

The Mural Arts Program began in 1984 as a part of the Philadelphia Anti-Graffiti Network. By 1996, the Philadelphia Anti-Graffiti Network was focusing on eliminating graffiti, and its Mural Arts Program was working to improve the community. It now no longer worked with graffiti offenders. It started after-school and summer programs for students. The Mural Arts Program got national recognition in 1997. That is when President Bill Clinton helped paint a mural. So far, the Mural Arts Program has completed more than 2,800 murals. This is more than any other public art program in the country.

Over 20,000 students have taken part in the Mural Arts Program. The students come from all parts of the city. In one part of the program students work alongside professional artists. The students get to paint parts of the artists' murals themselves. The artwork is on public buildings. The artwork can be seen by everyone.

The Mural Arts Programs continues to build a brighter future for students and their communities. It is now over a quarter of a century old. Students help bring people together to create a mural. They feel a stronger connection to their community and more confidence in themselves. They leave the program. They are equipped to make a positive difference in their communities and in their own lives.

Collaborative Activities

1. Working in a group of four students, make a list of three or four of your favorite television shows. Then, divide into pairs, and with your partner, write two simple sentences describing each show. Next, use subordinating conjunctions or relative pronouns to combine each pair of sentences into one complex sentence. With your group, discuss how the ideas in each complex sentence are related, and make sure you have used the subordinating conjunction or relative pronoun that best conveys this relationship.

   Example: *The Brady Bunch* portrays a 1970s family. It still appeals to many viewers.

   Although *The Brady Bunch* portrays a 1970s family, it still appeals to many viewers.

2. Imagine that you and the members of your group live in a neighborhood where workers are repairing underground power lines. As they work, the workers talk loudly and use foul language. Write a short letter of complaint to the power company in which you explain that the workers' behavior is offensive to you and to your children. Tell the company that you want the offensive behavior to end. Write the first draft of your letter in simple sentences. After you have written this draft, work as a group to combine as many sentences as you can with subordinating conjunctions and relative pronouns.

3. Assume you are in a competition to determine which student group in your class is best at writing complex sentences. Working in a group, prepare a letter to your instructor in which you present the strengths of your group. Be sure to use a subordinating conjunction or relative pronoun in each of the sentences in your letter. Finally, as a class, evaluate the letters, and choose the letter that is most convincing.

Review Checklist: Writing Complex Sentences

☐ A complex sentence consists of one independent clause (simple sentence) combined with one or more dependent clauses. (See 17A.)

☐ Subordinating conjunctions—dependent words such as *although*, *after*, *when*, *while*, and *because*—can join two independent clauses into one complex sentence. (See 17B.)

☐ Relative pronouns—dependent words such as *who*, *which*, and *that*—can also join two independent clauses into one complex sentence. The relative pronoun shows the relationship between the ideas in the two independent clauses that it links. (See 17C.)

Varying Sentence Types

Most English sentences are **statements**. Others are **questions** or **exclamations**. One way to vary your sentences is to use an occasional question or exclamation where it is appropriate.

In the following paragraph, a question and an exclamation add variety.

Jacqueline Cochran, the first woman pilot to break the sound barrier, was one of the most important figures in aviation history. In 1996, the United States Postal Service issued a stamp honoring Cochran; the words "Pioneer Pilot" appear under her name. <u>What did she do to earn this title and this tribute?</u> Cochran broke more flight records than anyone else in her lifetime and won many awards, including the United States Distinguished Service Medal in 1945 and The United States Air Force Distinguished Flying Cross in 1969. During World War II, she helped form the WASPs, the Women's Air Force Service Pilots program so that women could fly military planes to their bases (even though they were not allowed to go into combat). Remarkably, she accomplished all this with only three weeks of flying instruction. She only got her pilot's license in the first place because she wanted to start her own cosmetics business and flying would enable her to travel quickly around the country. Although she never planned to be a pilot, once she discovered flying she quickly became the best. <u>Not surprisingly, when the Postal Service honored Jacqueline Cochran, it was with an airmail stamp!</u>

Question

Exclamation

Focus on Writing

The picture on the opposite page shows items to be preserved in a time capsule at the History Center in Pittsburgh. Write a paragraph (or an essay) about a time capsule that your children will open when they are adults. What items would you include? How would you expect each item to communicate to your children what you and your world were like? Look at the picture, and then explain your decisions.

● Practice 18-1

Revise the following passage by changing one of the statements into a question and one of the statements into an exclamation.

Example: Some people pursue two different careers at the same time. (statement)

Why do some people pursue two different careers at the same time?

(question)

   (1) Many working people have more than one job. (2) For example, a police officer might moonlight as a security guard, an actor might also work as a waiter, and an artist or a writer might also teach. (3) These workers need their second jobs for survival. (4) In recent years, however, more and more successful professionals have decided to begin a second career without leaving the first one. (5) Often, the second career seems to be very different from the first one. (6) For example, a teacher might also work as a professional model. (7) Sometimes, however, the two careers really do have something in common. (8) After all, both teaching and modeling involve performing for an audience. (9) Similarly, a lawyer may be drawn to the ministry, another career that is dedicated to justice. (10) Many things motivate people to combine two seemingly different professions. (11) Those who do so say they do it not for the money but for professional satisfaction. (12) Obviously, these workers are very lucky people.

Focus on Writing: *Flashback*

Look back at your response to the Focus on Writing activity on page 309. What questions does your writing answer? On a separate sheet of paper, try writing one of these questions. (You may be able to reword a sentence that is already there.)

   If you think an exclamation would be an appropriate addition to your writing, write one on a separate sheet of paper.

18b   Varying Sentence Openings

When all the sentences in a paragraph begin in the same way, your writing is likely to seem dull and repetitive. In the following paragraph, for example, every sentence begins with the subject.

> Scientists have been observing a disturbing phenomenon. The population of frogs, toads, and salamanders has been declining. This decline was first noticed in the mid-1980s. Some reports blamed chemical pollution. Some biologists began to suspect that a fungal disease was killing these amphibians. The most reasonable explanation seems to be that the amphibians' eggs are threatened by solar radiation. This radiation penetrates the thinned ozone layer, which had shielded the eggs from the sun's rays.

Beginning with Adverbs

Instead of opening every sentence with the subject, try beginning with one or more **adverbs**, as the following paragraph illustrates.

> Scientists have been observing a disturbing phenomenon. <u>Gradually but steadily</u>, the population of frogs, toads, and salamanders has been declining. This decline was first noticed in the mid-1980s. Some reports blamed chemical pollution. Some biologists began to suspect that a fungal disease was killing these amphibians. <u>However</u>, the most reasonable explanation seems to be that the amphibians' eggs are threatened by solar radiation. This radiation penetrates the thinned ozone layer, which had shielded the eggs from the sun's rays.

● Practice 18-2

Underline the adverb in each of the following sentences. Then, rewrite the sentence so that the adverb appears at the beginning. Be sure to punctuate correctly.

> **Example:** It is <u>often</u> difficult to buy a gift for someone in a distant city.
>
> *Often, it is difficult to buy a gift for someone in a distant city.*

1. One way to deal with this problem, however, is to shop online.

2. On line shoppers must first search for the category of product they want to purchase.

3. Customer reviews are often available to help shoppers make a choice.

4. Payment is generally by credit card.

5. Online shopping now brings the world to everyone with access to a computer.

● Practice 18-3

In each of the following sentences, fill in the blank with an appropriate adverb. Be sure to punctuate correctly.

     Example: _____*Slowly,*_____ the sun crept over the horizon.

1. _____ the speeding car appeared from out of nowhere.

2. _____ it crashed into the guard rail.

3. _____ someone called 911.

4. _____ the ambulance arrived.

5. _____ emergency medical technicians went to work.

Beginning with Prepositional Phrases

As the following paragraph illustrates, you can also begin some sentences with prepositional phrases. A **prepositional phrase** (such as *along the river* or *near the diner*) is made up of a preposition and its object.

> In recent years, scientists have been observing a disturbing phenomenon. Gradually but steadily, the population of frogs, toads, and salamanders has been declining. This decline was first noticed in the mid-1980s. At first, some reports blamed chemical pollution. After a while, some biologists began to suspect that a fungal disease was killing these amphibians. However, the most reasonable explanation seems to be that the amphibians' eggs are threatened by solar radiation. This radiation penetrates the thinned ozone layer, which had shielded the eggs from the sun's rays.

● Practice 18-4

Underline the prepositional phrase in each of the following sentences, and then rewrite the sentence so that the prepositional phrase appears at the beginning. Be sure to punctuate correctly.

Example: Very few American women worked in factories <u>before</u> <u>the 1940s.</u>

Before the 1940s, very few American women worked in factories.

1. Many male factory workers became soldiers during World War II.

_____

2. The U.S. government encouraged women to take factory jobs in the war's early years.

_____

3. Over six million women took factory jobs between 1942 and 1945.

_____

4. A new female image emerged with this greater responsibility and independence.

_____

5. Most women lost their factory jobs after the war and had to return to "women's work."

_____

● **Practice 18-5**

In each of the following sentences, fill in the blank with an appropriate prepositional phrase. Be sure to punctuate correctly.

Example: *At the start of the New York marathon,* Jason felt as if he could run forever.

1. _____ he warmed up by stretching and bending.

2. _____ it was hard to move because all the runners were crowded together.

3. _____ the route became more and more steep.

4. _____ his leg muscles started to ache, and he worried that he might get a bad cramp.

5. _____ he staggered across the finish line, relieved that his first marathon was over.

● Practice 18-6

Every sentence in the following paragraph begins with the subject, but several contain prepositional phrases or adverbs that could be moved to the beginning. To vary the sentence openings, move prepositional phrases to the beginnings of four sentences, and move adverbs to the beginnings of two other sentences. Be sure to place a comma after these introductory phrases.

Example: *By the end of the 1800s,*   ~~Spain by the end of the 1800s~~ had lost most of its colonies.

(1) People in the Cuban-American community often mention José Julián Martí as one of their heroes. (2) José Martí was born in Havana in 1853, at a time when Cuba was a colony of Spain. (3) He had started a newspaper demanding Cuban freedom by the time he was sixteen years old. (4) The Spanish authorities forced him to leave Cuba and go to Spain in 1870. (5) He published his first pamphlet calling for Cuban independence while in Spain, openly continuing his fight. (6) He then lived for fourteen years in New York City. (7) He started the journal of the Cuban Revolutionary Party during his time in New York. (8) Martí's essays and poems argued for Cuba's freedom and for the individual freedom of Cubans. (9) He died in battle against Spanish soldiers in Cuba, passionately following up his words with actions.

Focus on Writing: *Flashback*

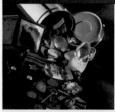

Look back at your response to the Focus on Writing activity on page 309. Identify one sentence that could begin with an adverb and one that could open with a prepositional phrase. (Note that the adverb or prepositional phrase may already appear somewhere in the sentence.) On a separate piece of paper, try revising the openings of these two sentences.

18c

Combining Sentences

You can also create sentence variety by experimenting with different ways of combining sentences.

Using *-ing* Modifiers

A **modifier** identifies or describes other words in a sentence. You can use an *-ing* modifier to combine two sentences.

Two sentences	Duke Ellington composed more than a thousand songs. He worked hard to establish his reputation as a musician.
Combined (with *-ing* modifier)	Composing more than a thousand songs, Duke Ellington worked hard to establish his reputation as a musician.

When the two sentences above are combined, the *-ing* modifier (*composing more than a thousand songs*) describes the new sentence's subject (*Duke Ellington*). Note that a comma follows the *-ing* modifier.

● Practice 18-7

Use an *-ing* modifier to combine each of the following pairs of sentences into a single sentence. Eliminate any unnecessary words, and place a comma after each *-ing* modifier.

> **Example:**   Many American colleges are setting an example for the rest of the country. They are going green.
>
> Setting an example for the rest of the country, many American
>
> colleges are going green.

1. Special lamps in the dorms of one Ohio college change from green to red. They warn of rising energy use.

   _____

   _____

2. A Vermont college captures methane from dairy cows. It now needs less energy from other sources.

   _____

   _____

3. Student gardeners at a North Carolina college tend a campus vegetable plot. They supply the cafeteria with organic produce.

_____

_____

4. A building on a California campus proves that recycled materials can be beautiful. It is built from redwood wine casks.

_____

_____

5. Some colleges offer courses in sustainability. They are preparing students to take the green revolution beyond campus.

_____

_____

Using -ed Modifiers

You can also use an -ed modifier to combine two sentences.

Two sentences	Nogales is located on the border between Arizona and Mexico. It is a bilingual city.
Combined (with -ed modifier)	Located on the border between Arizona and Mexico, Nogales is a bilingual city.

When the sentences are combined, the -ed modifier (*located on the border between Arizona and Mexico*) describes the new sentence's subject (*Nogales*). Note that a comma follows the -ed modifier.

● Practice 18-8

Use an -ed modifier to combine each of the pairs of sentences into a single sentence. Eliminate any unnecessary words, and place a comma after each -ed modifier.

Example: Sacajawea was born in about 1787. She lived among her Shoshone tribespeople until she was eleven.

Born in about 1787, Sacajawea lived among her Shoshone tribespeople

until she was eleven.

1. She was captured as a young girl by a rival tribe. Sacajawea was later sold into slavery.

   _____

   _____

2. She was saved by a French Canadian fur trader named Charbonneau. Sacajawea became his wife.

   _____

   _____

3. The explorers Lewis and Clark hired Charbonneau in 1806. He brought his pregnant wife along on their westward expedition.

   _____

   _____

4. Sacajawea was skilled in several Native-American languages. She helped Lewis and Clark on their journey.

   _____

   _____

5. A U.S. dollar coin was created in 2000. It shows her picture.

   _____

   _____

Using a Series of Words

Another way to vary your sentences is to combine a group of sentences into one sentence that includes a **series** of words (nouns, verbs, or adjectives). Combining sentences in this way eliminates a boring string of similar sentences and repetitive phrases and also makes your writing more concise.

Group of sentences	College presidents want to improve athletes' academic performance. Coaches too want to improve athletes' academic performance. The players themselves also want to improve their academic performance.
Combined (series of nouns)	College presidents, coaches, and the players themselves want to improve athletes' academic performance.

Group of sentences	In 1997, Arundhati Roy published her first novel, *The God of Small Things*. She won the Pulitzer Prize. She became a literary sensation.
Combined (series of verbs)	In 1997, Arundhati Roy <u>published</u> her first novel, *The God of Small Things*, <u>won</u> the Pulitzer Prize, and <u>became</u> a literary sensation.
Group of sentences	As the tornado approached, the sky grew dark. The sky grew quiet. The sky grew threatening.
Combined (series of adjectives)	As the tornado approached, the sky grew <u>dark</u>, <u>quiet</u>, and <u>threatening</u>.

● **Practice 18-9**

Combine each of the following groups of sentences into one sentence that includes a series of nouns, verbs, or adjectives.

Example: Many years ago, Pacific Islanders from Samoa settled in Hawaii. Pacific Islanders from Fiji also settled in Hawaii. Pacific Islanders from Tahiti settled in Hawaii, too.

Many years ago, Pacific Islanders from Samoa, Fiji, and Tahiti settled

in Hawaii.

1. In the eighteenth century, the British explorer Captain Cook came to Hawaii. Other explorers also came to Hawaii. European travelers came to Hawaii too.

   _____

   _____

2. Explorers and traders brought commerce to Hawaii. They brought new ideas. They brought new cultures.

   _____

   _____

3. Missionaries introduced the Christian religion. They introduced a Hawaiian-language bible. Also, they introduced a Hawaiian alphabet.

   _____

   _____

4. In the mid-nineteenth century, pineapple plantations were established in Hawaii. Sugar plantations were established there as well. Other industries were also established.

_____

_____

5. By 1900, Japanese people were working on the plantations. Chinese people were also working on the plantations. In addition, native Hawaiians were working there.

_____

_____

6. People of many different races and religions now live in Hawaii. People of many different races and religions now go to school in Hawaii. People of many different races and religions now work in Hawaii.

_____

_____

7. Schoolchildren still study the Hawaiian language. They learn about the Hawaiian kings and queens. They read about ancient traditions.

_____

_____

8. Today, Hawaii is well known for its tourism. It is well known too for its weather. It is especially well known for its natural beauty.

_____

_____

9. Tourists can swim. They can surf. They can play golf. They can ride in outrigger canoes.

_____

_____

10. Today, the state of Hawaii remains lively. It remains culturally diverse. It remains very beautiful.

_____

_____

Using Appositives

An **appositive** is a word or word group that identifies, renames, or describes a noun or pronoun. Creating an appositive is often a good way to combine two sentences about the same subject.

Two sentences   C. J. Walker was the first American woman to become a self-made millionaire. She marketed a line of hair-care products for black women.

Combined (with   C. J. Walker, the first American woman to become
appositive)   a self-made millionaire, marketed a line of hair-care products for black women.

In the example above, the appositive appears in the middle of the sentence. However, an appositive can also come at the beginning or at the end of a sentence.

The first American woman to become a self-made millionaire, C. J. Walker marketed a line of hair-care products for black women. (appositive at the beginning)

Several books have been written about C. J. Walker, the first American woman to become a self-made millionaire. (appositive at the end)

When you combine sentences with an appositive, always set off the appositive with commas. (See 31C.)

● Practice 18-10

Combine each of the following pairs of sentences into one sentence by creating appositives. Note that the appositive may appear at the beginning, in the middle, or at the end of the sentence. Be sure to use commas appropriately.

Example: Lorraine Hansberry's *A Raisin in the Sun* was one of the first American plays to focus on the experiences of African Americans. It was produced on Broadway in 1959.

(1) Lorraine Hansberry was born in Chicago in 1930. She was a playwright who wrote the prize-winning *A Raisin in the Sun*.

(2) Hansberry's father was a successful businessman. He moved the family from the south side of Chicago to a predominantly white neighborhood when Hansberry was eight. (3) Hostile neighbors there threw a brick through a window of their house. This was an act Hansberry never forgot. (4) Such experiences inspired *A Raisin in the Sun*. It is the story of a family's struggle to escape a cramped apartment in a poor Chicago neighborhood.

Focus on Writing: *Flashback*

Look back at your response to the Focus on Writing activity on page 309. Find two pairs of sentences that you think could be combined. On a separate sheet of paper, try combining each pair of sentences into a single sentence, using one of the methods discussed in 18C. Use a different method for each pair of sentences.

18d   Varying Sentence Length

A paragraph of short, choppy sentences—or a paragraph of long, rambling sentences—can be monotonous. By mixing long and short sentences, perhaps combining some simple sentences to create compound and complex sentences, you can create a more interesting paragraph.

In the following paragraph, the sentences are all short, and the result is a dull passage.

> The world's first drive-in movie theater opened on June 6, 1933. This drive-in was in Camden, New Jersey. Automobiles became more popular. Drive-ins did, too. By the 1950s, there were more than four thousand drive-ins in the United States. Over the years, the high cost of land led to a decline in the number of drive-ins. So did the rising popularity of television. Soon, the drive-in movie theater had almost disappeared. It was replaced by the multiplex. In 1967, there were forty-six drive-ins in New Jersey. Today, only one is still open. That one is the Delsea Drive-in in Vineland, New Jersey.

The revised paragraph that follows is more interesting because it mixes long and short sentences.

> The world's first drive-in movie theater opened on June 6, 1933, in Camden, New Jersey. As automobiles became more popular, drive-ins did too, and by the 1950s, there were more than four thousand drive-ins in the United States. Over the years, the high cost of land and the rising popularity of television led to a decline in the number of drive-ins. Soon, the drive-in movie theater had almost disappeared, replaced by the multiplex. In 1967, there were forty-six drive-ins in New Jersey, but today, only one is still open: the Delsea Drive-in in Vineland, New Jersey.

● **Practice 18-11**

The following paragraph contains a series of short, choppy sentences that can be combined. Revise it so that it mixes long and short sentences. Be sure to use commas and other punctuation appropriately.

Example: Kente cloth has special significance for many African
                                    , *but some*
Americans./Some other people do not understand this significance.

(1) Kente cloth is made in western Africa. (2) It is produced primarily by the Ashanti people. (3) It has been worn for hundreds of years by African royalty. (4) They consider it a sign of power and status. (5) Many African Americans wear kente cloth. (6) They see it as a link to their heritage. (7) Each pattern on the cloth has a name. (8) Each color has a special significance. (9) For example, red and yellow suggest a long and healthy life. (10) Green and white suggest a good harvest. (11) African women may wear kente cloth as a dress or head wrap. (12) African-American women, like men, usually wear strips of cloth around their shoulders. (13) Men and women of African descent wear kente cloth as a sign of racial pride. (14) It often decorates college students' gowns at graduation.

Focus on Writing: *Flashback*

Look back at your response to the Focus on Writing activity on page 309. Count the number of words in each sentence. Then, on a separate sheet of paper, write a new short sentence to follow your longest sentence.

Focus on Writing: *Revising and Editing*

Look back at your response to the Focus on Writing activity on page 309. **TEST** what you have written. Then, using any strategies from this chapter that seem appropriate, revise your work so that your sentences are varied, interesting, and smoothly connected. (You may want to incorporate some of the sentences you wrote for the Flashback activities on pages 310, 314, 321, and above.) Finally, edit your work.

Chapter Review

Editing Practice

The following student essay lacks sentence variety. All of its sentences are statements beginning with the subject, and it includes a number of short, choppy sentences. Using the strategies discussed in this chapter, revise the essay to achieve greater sentence variety. The first sentence has been edited for you.

Toys by Accident

Many popular toys and games are discovered by accident. ~~People~~ try *when people*
to invent one thing but discover something else instead. Sometimes they are not trying to invent anything at all. They are completely surprised to find a new product.

Play-Doh is one example of an accidental discovery. Play-Doh is a popular preschool toy. Play-Doh first appeared in Cincinnati. A company made a compound to clean wallpaper. They sold it as a cleaning product.

The company then realized that this compound could be a toy. Children could mold it like clay. They could use it again and again. The new toy was an immediate hit. Play-Doh was first sold in 1956. Since then, more than two billion cans of Play-Doh have been sold.

The Slinky was discovered by Richard James. He was an engineer. He was trying to invent a spring to keep ships' instruments steady at sea. He tested hundreds of springs of varying sizes, metals, and tensions. None of them worked. One spring fell off the desk. It "walked" down a pile of books. It fell end over end onto the floor. He thought his children might enjoy playing with it. James took the spring home. They loved it. Every child in the neighborhood wanted one. The first Slinky was demonstrated at Gimbel's Department Store in Philadelphia in 1945. All four hundred Slinkys on hand were sold within ninety minutes. The Slinky is simple and inexpensive. The Slinky is still popular with children.

The Frisbee was discovered by accident, too. According to one story, some Yale University students were eating pies from a local bakery. The bakery was called Frisbies. They finished eating the pies. They started throwing the empty pie tins around. A carpenter in California made a plastic version. He called it the Pluto Platter. The Wham-O company bought the patent on the product. Wham-O renamed it the Frisbee after the bakery. Wham-O started selling it.

Some new toys are not developed by toy companies. Play-Doh, the Frisbee, and the Slinky are examples of very popular toys that resulted from accidental discoveries. Play-Doh started as a cleaning product. The Slinky was discovered by an engineer who was trying to invent something else. The Frisbee was invented by students having fun. The toys were discovered unexpectedly. All three toys have become classics.

Collaborative Activities

1. Read the following list of sentences. Working in a small group, add to the list one related sentence that is a question or an exclamation. Then, add appropriate adverbs or prepositional phrases at the beginning of several of the sentences on the list.

> Many well-known African-American writers left the United States in the years following World War II.
>
> Many went to Paris.
>
> Richard Wright was a novelist.
>
> He wrote *Native Son* and *Black Boy*.
>
> He wrote *Uncle Tom's Children*.
>
> He left the United States for Paris in 1947.
>
> James Baldwin wrote *Another Country*, *The Fire Next Time*, and *Giovanni's Room*.
>
> He also wrote essays.
>
> He went to Paris in 1948.
>
> Chester Himes was a detective story writer.
>
> He arrived in Paris in 1953.
>
> William Gardner Smith was a novelist and journalist.
>
> He also left the United States for Paris.
>
> These expatriates found Paris more hospitable than America.
>
> They also found it less racist.

2. Continuing to work in your group, combine all the sentences on the list to create a varied and interesting paragraph. Use the strategies illustrated in 18C as a guide.

3. When your group's revisions are complete, trade paragraphs with another group and further revise the other group's paragraph to improve sentence variety.

Review Checklist: Achieving Sentence Variety

- ☐ Vary sentence types. (See 18A.)
- ☐ Vary sentence openings. (See 18B.)
- ☐ Combine sentences. (See 18C.)
- ☐ Vary sentence length. (See 18D.)

Recognizing Parallel Structure

Parallelism means using matching words, phrases, and clauses to emphasize similar items in a sentence. When you use parallelism, you are telling readers that certain items or ideas are related. By repeating similar grammatical patterns to express similar ideas, you create sentences that are clearer and easier to read.

In the following examples, the parallel sentences emphasize elements that are similar; the other sentences do not.

Not Parallel	*Parallel*
Please leave your name, your number, and you should also leave a message.	Please leave your name, your number, and a message.
I plan to graduate from high school and then becoming a nurse would be a good idea.	I plan to graduate from high school and to become a nurse.
The grass was soft, green, and the smell was sweet.	The grass was soft, green, and sweet smelling.
Making the team was one thing; to stay on it was another.	Making the team was one thing; staying on it was another.
We can register for classes in person, or registering by email is another option.	We can register for classes in person, or we can register by email.

Focus on Writing

The picture on the opposite page shows children playing in a fountain in a public park in Portland, Oregon. Look at the picture, and then write a paragraph (or an essay) about three positive things in your own neighborhood, school, or workplace. Support your statements with specific examples.

• Practice 19-1

In the following sentences, decide whether the underlined words and phrases are parallel. If so, write *P* in the blank. If not, rewrite the sentences so that the underlined ideas are presented in parallel terms.

Examples: The missing dog had <u>brown fur</u>, <u>a red collar</u>, and <u>a long tail</u>. _____*P*_____

Signs of drug abuse in teenagers include <u>falling grades</u>, <u>mood swings</u>, and <u>they lose weight</u>. _____
loss.

1. The food in the cafeteria is <u>varied</u>, <u>tasty</u>, and <u>it is healthy</u>. _____

2. Do you want the job done <u>quickly</u>, or do you want it done <u>well</u>? _____

3. Last summer <u>I worked at the library</u>, <u>babysat my neighbor's daughter</u>, and <u>there was a soup kitchen where I volunteered</u>. _____
volunteered at

4. Pandas <u>eat bamboo leaves</u> and <u>eucalyptus leaves are eaten by koalas</u>. _____
koalas eat

5. Skydiving is <u>frightening</u> but <u>fun</u>. _____

6. A number of interesting people work at the co-op with me, including <u>an elderly German man</u>, <u>there is a middled-aged Chinese woman</u>, and <u>a teenaged Mexican boy</u>. _____

7. <u>The bell rang</u>, and <u>the students stood up</u>. _____

8. To conserve energy while I was away, I <u>unplugged the television</u>, <u>closed the curtains</u>, and <u>the thermostat was set at 65 degrees</u>. _____
set   at

9. I <u>put away the dishes</u>. Will you <u>put away the laundry</u>? _____

10. For several weeks after the storm, the supermarkets had <u>no eggs</u>, <u>they were out of</u> milk, and <u>they did not have any</u> bread. _____
no   no

Focus on Writing: *Flashback*

Look back at your response to the Focus on Writing activity on page 327, and underline the parallel words, phrases, and clauses. Revise if necessary so that similar elements are presented in parallel terms.

19b   Using Parallel Structure

Use parallel structure to emphasize similar elements in *paired items, comparisons,* and *items in a series.*

Paired Items

Use parallel structure when you connect ideas with a coordinating conjunction—*and, but, for, nor, or, so,* and *yet.*

> George believes in <u>doing a good job</u> and <u>minding his own business.</u>
> You can <u>pay me now</u> or <u>pay me later.</u>

Also use parallel structure for paired items joined by *both . . . and, not only . . . but also, either . . . or, neither . . . nor,* and *rather . . . than.*

> Jan is both <u>artistically talented</u> and <u>mechanically inclined.</u>
> The group's new recording not only <u>has a dance beat</u> but also <u>has good lyrics.</u>
> I'd rather <u>eat one worm by itself</u> than <u>eat ten with ice cream.</u>

Items in a Series

Use parallel structure for items in a series—words, phrases, or clauses. (Be sure to use commas to separate three or more items in a series.)

> Every Wednesday I have <u>English</u>, <u>math</u>, and <u>psychology</u>. (Three words)
> <u>Increased demand</u>, <u>high factory output</u>, and <u>a strong dollar</u> all help the economy. (Three phrases)

She is a champion because <u>she stays in excellent physical condition</u>, <u>she puts in long hours of practice</u>, and <u>she has an intense desire to win</u>. (Three clauses)

Items in a List or in an Outline

Use parallel structure for items in a numbered or bulleted list.

> You should open an Individual Retirement Account (IRA) for the following reasons:
> - To save money
> - To pay fewer taxes
> - To be able to retire

Use parallel structure for the elements in an outline.

> A. Basic types of rocks
>   1. Igneous
>   2. Sedimentary
>   3. Metamorphic

● Practice 19-2

Fill in the blanks in the following sentences with parallel words, phrases, or clauses of your own that make sense in context.

Example: At the lake, we can ___*go for a swim*___ , ___*paddle a canoe*___ , and ___*play volleyball*___ .

1. When I get too little sleep, I am _____ , _____ , and _____ .

2. I am good at _____ but not at _____ .

3. My ideal vacation would be _____ and _____ .

4. I define success not only as _____ but also as _____ .

5. I use my computer for both _____ and _____ .

6. I like _____ and _____ .

7. You need three qualities to succeed at college: _____ , _____ , and _____ .

8. I enjoy not only _____ but also _____ .

9. I would rather _____ than _____ .

10. Classical music _____ , but jazz _____ .

Focus on Writing: *Flashback*

Look back at your response to the Focus on Writing activity on page 327. Write two new sentences that you could add to your response, and then revise them as follows: (1) In one sentence, use a coordinating conjunction, such as *and* or *but*; (2) in a second sentence, present items in a series. When you have finished, check to make sure that you have used parallel structure in each sentence and that you have punctuated correctly.

Focus on Writing: *Revising and Editing*

Look back at your response to the Focus on Writing activity on page 327, and try to add one or more of the sentences you wrote for the Flashback activity above. Then, **TEST** what you have written. Finally, revise and edit your work, making sure to correct faulty parallelism and to add parallel constructions to highlight relationships or increase clarity. When you are finished, do the same for another assignment you are currently working on.

Chapter Review

Editing Practice

Read the following student essay, which contains some elements that are not parallel. Identify the sentences you think need to be corrected, and make the changes required to achieve parallelism. Add punctuation as needed. The first error has been edited for you.

Questionable Heroes

The heroes we learn about in school are usually historical figures. We look up to them for their outstanding achievements / and their personal qualities ~~are also admired.~~ Our heroes include our country's first leaders, American colonists, and soldiers who were thought of as brave. After the terrorist attacks on September 11, 2001, we realized that anyone who helps in a disaster can also be a hero. However, some people confuse heroes with people who are celebrities. It is much harder to be a hero than becoming famous. For example, many entertainers and people who play professional sports are famous, but they should not be thought of as heroes.

To be a real hero, a person should be a model for others. A genuine hero like George Washington was brave and showed determination throughout his life. Soldiers often risk their lives to save other people, and sometimes death even results. During the terrorist attacks of September 11, 2001, firefighters climbed up the stairs of the burning World Trade Center buildings, and many lives were able to be saved. Even the thousands of Americans who pitched in to help during the cleanup were heroes. They brought supplies to the rescue workers, and in addition, food was brought.

On the other hand, to be famous does not always mean that people are heroes. Some athletes, for example, get a lot of attention for their misbehavior. Sometimes they fight with their coaches, the media may be cursed at, drug tests may be failed, and they may even get arrested. Similarly, some entertainers get news coverage for their worst behavior. Sometimes they get married many times, or very provocative clothes are worn by them. Although sports superstars can earn millions of dollars, and so can entertainers, many parents do not see them as role models for their children.

Clearly, the definition of a hero has changed over time. The heroes of the past were dedicated leaders and acted with courage. Now, these individuals have been replaced by superstars who are famous for all the wrong reasons—for example, selfishness and they cannot control their own actions. These people may be fascinating, but they are not heroic.

Collaborative Activities

1. Working in a group, list three or four qualities that you associate with each word in the following pairs.

   Brothers / sisters
   Teachers / students
   Parents / children
   City / country
   Fast food / organic food
   Movies / TV shows
   Work / play

2. Write a compound sentence comparing each of the above pairs of words. Use a coordinating conjunction to join the clauses, and make sure each sentence uses clear parallel structure, mentions both words, and includes the qualities you listed for the words in Collaborative Activity 1.

3. Choose the three best sentences your group has written for Collaborative Activity 2. Assign one student from each group to write these sentences on the board so the entire class can read them. The class can then decide which sentences use parallelism most effectively.

Review Checklist: Using Parallelism

☐ Use matching words, phrases, and clauses to highlight similar items or ideas. (See 19A.)

☐ Use parallel structure with paired items. (See 19B.)

☐ Use parallel structure for items in a series. (See 19B.)

☐ Use parallel structure for items in a list and for the elements in an outline. (See 19B.)

Using Specific Words

Specific words refer to particular people, places, things, ideas, or qualities; **general** words refer to entire classes or groups. Sentences that contain specific words are more precise and vivid—and often more memorable—than those that contain only general words. The following sentences use just general words.

Sentences with General Words

While walking in the woods, I saw an <u>animal</u>.

<u>Someone</u> decided to run for Congress.

<u>Weapons</u> are responsible for many murders.

Denise bought new <u>clothes</u>.

I really enjoyed my <u>meal</u>.

Darrell had always wanted a <u>classic car</u>.

Specific words make the following revised sentences clearer and more precise.

Sentences with Specific Words

While walking in the woods, I saw a <u>baby skunk</u>.

<u>Rebecca</u> decided to run for Congress.

<u>Cheap imported handguns</u> are responsible for many murders.

Denise bought a new <u>blue dress</u>.

I really enjoyed my <u>pepperoni pizza with extra cheese</u>.

Darrell had always wanted a <u>black 1969 Chevrolet Camaro</u>.

Focus on Writing

The picture on the opposite page shows a father reading to his children. Look at the picture, and then think about the books you liked best when you were a child. Write a paragraph (or an essay) that explains what you liked about these books and what you remember most about them.

| **Highlight: Using Specific Words** | One way to strengthen your writing is to avoid **utility words**—general words like *good*, *nice*, or *great*. Instead, take the time to think of more specific words. For example, when you say the ocean looked *pretty*, do you really mean that it *sparkled*, *glistened*, *rippled*, *foamed*, *surged*, or *billowed*? |

● Practice 20-1

In the following passage, underline the specific words that help you imagine the scene the writer describes. The first sentence has been done for you.

Last summer, I spent three weeks backpacking through <u>the remote rural province of Yunnan in China</u>. One day, I came across four farm women playing a game of mahjong on a patch of muddy ground. Squatting on rough wooden stools around a faded green folding table, the women picked up and discarded the smooth ivory mahjong tiles as if they were playing cards. In the grassy field around them, their chestnut-colored horses grazed with heavy red and black market bags tied to their backs. A veil of shimmering white fog hung over a nearby hill, and one woman sat under a black umbrella to shelter herself from the sun. A fifth woman watched, with her wrinkled hands on her hips and a frown on her face. The only sound was the sharp click of the tiles and the soft musical talk of the women as they played.

● Practice 20-2

For each of the five general words below, write a more specific word. Then, use the more specific word in a sentence.

Example: child _____six-year-old_____

All through dinner, my six-year-old chattered excitedly about his first

day of school.

1. emotion _____

2. building _____

3. said _____

4. animal _____

5. went _____

● Practice 20-3

The following job-application letter uses general words. Rewrite the paragraph, substituting specific words for the general words of the original and adding details where necessary. Start by making the first sentence, which identifies the job, more specific (for example, "I would like to apply for the sales position you advertised on March 15 in the *Post*"). Then, add specific information about your background and qualifications, expanding the original paragraph into a three-paragraph letter.

> I would like to apply for the position you advertised in today's paper. I graduated from high school and am currently attending college. I have taken several courses that have prepared me for the duties the position requires. I also have several personal qualities that I think you would find useful in a person holding this position. In addition, I have had certain experiences that qualify me for such a job. I would appreciate the opportunity to meet with you to discuss your needs as an employer. Thank you.

Focus on Writing: *Flashback*

Look back at your response to the Focus on Writing activity on page 335. Find several general words, and write those words on a sheet of paper. For each word, substitute another word that is more specific.

20b   Using Concise Language

Concise language says what it has to say in as few words as possible. Too often, writers use words and phrases that add nothing to a sentence's meaning. A good way to test a sentence for these words is to see if crossing them out changes the sentence's meaning. If the sentence's meaning does not change, you can assume that the words you crossed out are unnecessary.

~~It is clear that the~~ *The* United States was not ready to fight World War II.

~~In order to~~ *To* follow the plot, you must make an outline.

Sometimes, you can replace several unnecessary words with a single word.

~~Due to the fact that~~ *Because* I was tired, I missed my first class.

Highlight: Using Concise Language

The following wordy phrases add nothing to a sentence. You can usually delete or condense them with no loss of meaning.

Wordy	Concise
It is clear that	(delete)
It is a fact that	(delete)
The reason is because	Because
The reason is that	Because
It is my opinion that	I think / I believe
Due to the fact that	Because
Despite the fact that	Although
At the present time	Today / Currently
At that time	Then
In most cases	Usually
In order to	To
In the final analysis	Finally
Subsequent to	After

Unnecessary repetition—saying the same thing twice for no reason—can also make your writing wordy. When you revise, delete repeated words and phrases that add nothing to your sentences.

My instructor told me the book was ~~old-fashioned and~~ outdated. (An old-fashioned book *is* outdated.)

The ~~terrible~~ tragedy of the fire could have been avoided. (A tragedy is *always* terrible.)

• Practice 20-4

To make the following sentences more concise, delete or condense wordy expressions, and eliminate any unnecessary repetition.

Example: The ~~old~~ historic home of poet Robert Frost is located in Franconia, New Hampshire.

(1) Despite the fact that Robert Frost's home is a national landmark, local teenagers from the area broke into the house in 2007 in order to have a party. (2) By the time the party was over and done, the teens had caused about roughly $10,000 worth of damage. (3) Due to the fact that a hiker soon discovered the break-in, the police were quickly able to find and track down the suspects in the crime. (4) Subsequent to their arrest, the teenagers were found guilty, and the judge in the case had an unusual idea for their sentence that was different from typical rulings. (5) After discussing and talking over his idea with a local college professor, the judge required the teenagers to take a course in Robert Frost's poetry as part of their sentence. (6) At first the professor was not absolutely sure or certain that poetry should be used as a form of punishment or penalty, but in the final analysis he decided that it might do some good. (7) The instructor, who had been teaching poetry for many years, knew that usually students in most cases could relate to two of Frost's poems: "Out, Out—" and "The Road Not Taken." (8) The reason that "Out, Out—" catches students' attention is because it is somewhat startling or shocking in its portrayal of a mill worker's death. (9) "The Road Not Taken" is suitable for these teens due to the fact that they would always face or encounter choices in life, and in this case, they had taken the wrong road, making a bad choice. (10) This story shows that sometimes the punishment really can fit the crime.

Focus on Writing: *Flashback*

Look back at your response to the Focus on Writing activity on page 335. Underline a sentence that contains unnecessary repetition. Then, rewrite the sentence to make it more concise.

20c   Avoiding Slang

Slang is nonstandard language that calls attention to itself. It is usually associated with a particular social group—musicians, computer users, or college students, for example. Often, it is used for emphasis or to produce a surprising or original effect. Because it is very informal, slang has no place in your college writing.

> *easy*
> My psychology exam was really ~~sweet~~.

> *relax*
> On the weekends, I like to ~~chill~~ and watch old movies on TV.

If you have any question about whether a term is slang or not, look it up in a dictionary. If the term is identified as *slang* or *informal*, find a more suitable term.

● Practice 20-5

Edit the following sentences, replacing the slang expressions with clearer, more precise words and phrases.

> *yelled at me*
> **Example:**   My father ~~lost it~~ when I told him I crashed the car.

1. Whenever I get bummed, I go outside and jog.

2. Tonight I'll have to leave by 11 because I'm wiped out.

3. I'm not into movies or television.

4. Whenever we get into an argument, my boyfriend knows how to push my buttons.

5. I really lucked out when I got this job.

Focus on Writing: *Flashback*

Look back at your response to the Focus on Writing activity on page 335. See if any sentences contain slang. If they do, replace the slang terms with more suitable words or phrases.

20d   Avoiding Clichés

Clichés are expressions—such as "easier said than done" and "last but not least"—that have been used so often they have lost their meaning. These worn-out expressions do little to create interest; in fact, they may even get in the way of communication.

When you identify a cliché in your writing, replace it with a direct statement—or, if possible, with a fresher expression.

Cliché   When school was over, she felt ~~free as a bird~~.

Cliché   These days, you have to be ~~sick as a dog~~ *seriously ill* before you are admitted to a hospital.

Highlight: Avoiding Clichés

Here are examples of some clichés you should avoid in your writing.

better late than never	play God
beyond a shadow of a doubt	pushing the envelope
break the ice	raining cats and dogs
broad daylight	selling like hotcakes
face the music	the bottom line
give 110 percent	think outside the box
happy as a clam	tried and true
hard as a rock	water under the bridge
it goes without saying	what goes around comes around

● Practice 20-6

Cross out any clichés in the following sentences, and either substitute a fresher expression or restate the idea more directly.

Example: Lottery winners often think they will be ~~on easy street~~ for the rest of their lives.

free of financial worries

(1) Many people think that a million-dollar lottery jackpot allows the winner to stop working like a dog and start living high on the hog. (2) All things considered, however, the reality for lottery winners is quite different. (3) For one thing, lottery winners who hit the jackpot do not always receive their winnings all at once; instead, payments— for example, $50,000—can be spread out over twenty years. (4) Of that $50,000 a year, close to $20,000 goes to taxes and anything else the lucky stiff owes the government, such as student loans. (5) Next come relatives and friends with their hands out, leaving winners between a rock and a hard place. (6) They can either cough up gifts and loans or wave bye-bye to many of their loved ones. (7) Adding insult to injury, many lottery winners have lost their jobs because employers thought that once they were "millionaires," they no longer needed the salary. (8) Many lottery winners wind up way over their heads in debt within a few years. (9) In their hour of need, many might like to sell their future payments to companies that offer lump-sum payments of forty to forty-five cents on the dollar. (10) This is easier said than done, however, because most state lotteries do not allow winners to sell their winnings.

Focus on Writing: *Flashback*

Look back at your response to the Focus on Writing activity on page 335. If you have used any clichés, circle them. Then, either replace each cliché with a more direct statement, or think of a more original way of expressing the idea.

20e   Using Similes and Metaphors

A **simile** is a comparison of two unlike things that uses *like* or *as*.

> His arm hung at his side <u>like</u> a broken branch.
>
> He was <u>as</u> content <u>as</u> a cat napping on a windowsill.

A **metaphor** is a comparison of two unlike things that does *not* use *like* or *as*.

> Invaders from another world, the dandelions conquered my garden.
>
> He was a beast of burden, hauling cement from the mixer to the building site.

The force of similes and metaphors comes from the surprise of seeing two seemingly unlike things being compared and, as a result, seeing a hidden or unnoticed similarity between them. Used in moderation, similes and metaphors can make your writing more lively and more interesting.

● Practice 20-7

Use your imagination to complete each of the following items by creating three original similes.

Example: A boring class is like *toast without jam.*

a four-hour movie.

a bedtime story.

1. A good friend is like _____

_____

_____

2. A thunderstorm is like _____

_____

_____

3. A workout at the gym is like _____

_____

_____

● **Practice 20-8**

Think of a person you know well. Using that person as your subject, fill in each of the following blanks to create metaphors. Try to complete each metaphor with more than a single word, as in the example.

Example: If ___my baby sister___ were an animal, ___she___ would be _a curious little kitten._

1. If _____ were a musical instrument, ____ would be _____
   _____

2. If _____ were a food, ____ would be _____
   _____

3. If _____ were a means of transportation, ____ would be _____
   _____

4. If _____ were a natural phenomenon, ____ would be _____
   _____

5. If _____ were a toy, ____ would be _____
   _____

Focus on Writing: *Flashback*

Look back at your response to the Focus on Writing activity on page 335. Find two sentences that could be enriched with a simile or a metaphor. Rewrite these two sentences, adding a simile to one sentence and a metaphor to the other.

20f

Avoiding Sexist Language

Sexist language refers to men and women in insulting terms. Sexist language is not just words like *stud* or *babe*, which many people find objectionable. It can also be words or phrases that unnecessarily call attention to gender or that suggest a job or profession is held only by a man (or only by a woman) when it actually is not (for example, *male model* or *woman doctor*).

You can avoid sexist language by using a little common sense. There is almost always an acceptable nonsexist alternative for a sexist term.

Sexist	Nonsexist
man, mankind	humanity, humankind, the human race
businessman	executive, business person
fireman, policeman, mailman	firefighter, police officer, letter carrier

Sexist	Nonsexist
male nurse, woman engineer	nurse, engineer
congressman	member of Congress, representative
stewardess, steward	flight attendant
man and wife	man and woman, husband and wife
manmade	synthetic
chairman	chair, chairperson
anchorwoman, anchorman	anchor
actor, actress	actor

Highlight: Avoiding Sexist Language

Do not use *he* when your subject could be either male or female.

Everyone should complete his assignment by next week.

You can correct this problem in three ways:

- *Use* he or she *or* his or her.

  Everyone should complete his or her homework by next week.
- *Use plural forms.*

  Students should complete their homework by next week.
- *Eliminate the pronoun.*

  Everyone should complete the homework by next week.

● **Practice 20-9**

Edit the following sentences to eliminate sexist language.

Example: A doctor should be honest with his patients.
or her (or omit "his")

1. Many people today would like to see more policemen patrolling the streets.

2. The attorneys representing the plaintiff are Geraldo Diaz and Mrs. Barbara Wilkerson.

3. Every soldier picked up his weapons.

4. Jane Fox is the female mayor of Port London, Maine.

5. Travel to other planets will be a significant step for man.

Focus on Writing: *Flashback*

Look back at your response to the Focus on Writing activity on page 335. Have you used any words or phrases that unnecessarily call attention to gender? Have you used *he* when your subject could be either male or female? Cross out any sexist language, and substitute acceptable non-sexist alternatives.

Focus on Writing: *Revising and Editing*

Look back at your response to the Focus on Writing activity on page 335. **TEST** what you have written. Then, revise and edit your work, making sure your language is as specific as possible and that you have not used clichés or sexist expressions. Be sure to incorporate the revisions you made in this chapter's Flashback activities.

Chapter Review

Editing Practice

Read the following student essay carefully, and then revise it. Make sure that your revision is concise, uses specific words, and includes no slang, sexist language, or clichés. If you can, add an occasional simile or metaphor to increase interest. The first sentence has been edited for you.

Unexpected Discoveries

When we hear the word "accident," we think of bad things. ~~like dented fenders and broken glass.~~ But

accidents can be good, too. Modern science has made important advances

as a result of lucky accidents. It is a fact that a scientist sometimes works like a dog for years in his laboratory, only to make a weird discovery because of a mistake.

The most famous example of a good, beneficial accident is the discovery of penicillin. A scientist, Alexander Fleming, had seen many soldiers die of infections after they were wounded in World War I. All things considered, many more soldiers died due to the fact that infections occurred than from wounds. Fleming wanted to find a drug that could put an end to these terrible, fatal infections. One day in 1928, Fleming went on vacation, leaving a pile of dishes in the lab sink. As luck would have it, he had been growing bacteria in those dishes. When he came back, he noticed that one of the dishes looked moldy. What was strange was that near the mold, the bacteria were dead as a doornail. It was crystal clear to Fleming that the mold had killed the bacteria. He had discovered penicillin, the first antibiotic.

Everyone has heard the name "Goodyear." It was Charles Goodyear who made a discovery that changed and revolutionized the rubber industry and made our modern tires last so long. In the early nineteenth century, rubber products became thin and runny in hot weather and cracked in cold weather. One day in 1839, Goodyear accidentally dropped some rubber mixed with sulfur on a hot stove. It changed color and turned black, but after being cooled, it could be stretched, and it would return to its original size and shape. This kind of rubber is now used in tires and in many other products.

Another thing was discovered because of a lab accident involving rubber. In 1953, Patsy Sherman, a female chemist for the 3M company, was trying to find a new type of rubber. She created a man-made, synthetic liquid compound. Some of the liquid accidentally spilled onto a lab assistant's new white canvas sneaker. According to one story, her assistant used everything but the kitchen sink to clean the shoe, but nothing worked. Over time, the rest of the shoe became dirty, but the part where the spill had hit was still clean as a whistle. Sherman realized that she had found something that could actually keep fabrics clean by doing a number on dirt. The 3M company named this new product Scotchguard.

A scientist can sometimes be careless, but sometimes his mistakes lead to great and significant discoveries. Penicillin, long-lasting tires, and Scotchguard are examples of successful products that were the result of scientific accidents.

Collaborative Activities

1. Photocopy two or three paragraphs of description from a romance novel, a western novel, or a mystery novel, and bring your paragraphs to class. Working in a group, choose one paragraph that seems to need clearer, more specific language.

2. As a group, revise the paragraph you chose for Collaborative Activity 1, making it as clear and specific as possible and eliminating any clichés or sexist language.

3. Exchange your revised paragraph from Collaborative Activity 2 with the paragraph revised by another group, and check the other group's work. Make any additional changes you think your paragraph needs.

Review Checklist: Using Words Effectively	☐ Use specific words that convey your ideas clearly and precisely. (See 20A.) ☐ Use concise language that says what it has to say in the fewest possible words. (See 20B.) ☐ Avoid slang. (See 20C.) ☐ Avoid clichés. (See 20D.) ☐ Whenever possible, use similes and metaphors to make your writing more lively and more interesting. (See 20E.) ☐ Avoid sexist language. (See 20F.)

Unit Review

Editing Practice

Some of the following sentences have problems with parallelism and ineffective word use. Others are pairs of simple sentences that can be combined with coordinating conjunctions, semicolons, transitional words or phrases, subordinating conjunctions, or relative pronouns. Identify the problems, and correct them.

1. Many women of infant children work outside the home. They hire babysitters or bring their babies to day-care centers.

2. After Donald got out of jail, he was sadder but wiser and was determined never to break the law again.

3. I left work at 5:00 p.m. I was late getting home because of a bad accident on I-70.

4. Some parents feel that their children should attend school. Others feel just as strongly that they should be taught at home.

5. Volunteers bring pets to hospitals and nursing homes. The patients benefit both physically and emotionally.

6. It was very hot. Yosemite National Park was very crowded.

7. Caroline lived in an apartment with her parents. Then she got married.

8. Hurricane Wilma devastated some parts of Florida. It hit in October 2005.

9. With a computer, it is possible to communicate by email, to do research, and spelling can be checked.

10. In most cases, people gain weight because they eat like horses, even though they deny it.

Editing Practice: Essay

Read the following student essay, which has problems with sentence variety, parallelism, and word use. It also contains pairs of simple sentences that can be combined. Identify the sentences that need to be corrected, and edit them. The first editing change has been made for you.

Dangerous Animals

Lately, a number of people have been attacked and sometimes they have been killed by wild animals. Alligators, bears, and even cats that are large have carried out these attacks. There is no guarantee of safety. There are actions that people can take to make these attacks less likely.

During the past fifty years, alligators have attacked more than 350 people in Florida. Twenty-five people have been killed. Three women were killed in the spring of 2006. Their bodies were found near canals or ponds. Most alligator attacks happen in water, where these animals can move quickly. The most dangerous time is when it is getting dark. This is when alligators are usually looking for food. It is not the time to swim in water in which alligators are found. People take a big risk when they clean fish and then throw away the unwanted parts. Alligators are attracted by these remains. Golfers should not put their feet or hands into ponds to retrieve balls because alligators are attracted by motion. They can pull a golfer into the water. If an alligator attacks a golfer, the best thing he can do is make noise. The alligator believes that its victim is larger and more powerful than it expected. It may let the victim go.

Wild bears have also been tough to deal with. Avoiding these animals is the best strategy. Sometimes, however, this is not a piece of cake because bears may live in some areas that overlap neighborhoods where people live. Hikers and campers sometimes encounter bears in the wild. To keep safe from bears, hikers should keep certain guidelines in mind. First, it is important not to surprise a bear or make it feel threatened. It is also important not to come between a mother bear and its cubs due to the fact that mother bears will attack someone who seems to threaten their babies. Making a lot of noise while moving through bear country is a good way to avoid taking this dangerous animal by surprise. Walking backwards slowly is better than running away. This only encourages the bear to attack. The bear may attack. The best thing to do is to curl up on the ground. Pretending to be dead is good.

Large cats are sometimes reported in certain areas. They may be escaped pets. They may be wild animals. These cats are usually cougars. They can be dangerous to livestock and occasionally to humans. Cougars are also called mountain lions, panthers, or pumas. They eat raccoons and deer. Cougars, like bears, chase whatever runs away. In the West, mountain bikers and hikers are endangered. Joggers are also at risk. Hiking alone is especially dangerous. This is because cougars only attack hikers without companions. People who are attacked by a cougar can shout and make themselves look bigger by putting up their hands or opening their coats. The cougar may be frightened and run away. Finally, cougars are nocturnal. People should keep their pets and small livestock protected at night.

Wild animals can be a danger to a human being and to his or her pets. Alligators, bears, and cougars have injured and killed people in recent years. However, people can protect themselves by knowing about the habits of these animals.

Unit Five

Solving Common Sentence Problems

21 Run-Ons   354
22 Sentence Fragments   370
23 Subject-Verb Agreement   394
24 Illogical Shifts   410
25 Dangling and Misplaced Modifiers   420

Chapter 21

Run-Ons

21a

Recognizing Run-Ons

A **sentence** consists of at least one independent clause — one subject and one verb.

> College costs are rising.

A **run-on** is an error that occurs when two sentences are joined incorrectly. There are two kinds of run-ons: *fused sentences* and *comma splices*.

- A **fused sentence** occurs when two sentences are joined without any punctuation.

WORD POWER
fused melted together

  Fused sentence   [College costs are rising] [many students are worried.]

WORD POWER
splice to join together at the ends

- A **comma splice** occurs when two sentences are joined with just a comma.

  Comma splice   [College costs are rising], [many students are worried.]

Highlight: Grammar Checkers

Grammar checkers sometimes identify a long sentence as a run-on. However, a long sentence can be correct. Before you make any changes, be sure you have actually made an error.

Focus on Writing

The picture on the opposite page shows chocolate-glazed donuts, a popular snack food. Many people believe such foods are to blame for our nation's overweight children. Why do you think so many American children are overweight? What do you think can be done about this problem? Look at the picture, and then write a paragraph (or essay) in which you answer these questions.

● Practice 21-1

Some of the sentences below are correct, but others are fused sentences or comma splices. In the blank after each sentence, write *C* if the sentence is correct, *CS* if it is a comma splice, and *FS* if it is a fused sentence.

> **Example:** Cynthia has new jeans, they look good on her. __CS__

1. My neighborhood is never quiet it is even noisy at midnight. __FS__

2. Some professional Italian soccer clubs were accused of fixing games, other teams were not accused. __CS__

3. Many people in big cities ride the subway, it is a fast way to get to work. __CS__

4. Sonia hung the mirror in the hall, near the coats and shoes. __C__

5. I like to walk in the park, it is always full of people playing soccer and kickball. __CS__

6. The movie isn't rated yet maybe it isn't suitable for children. __FS__

7. In 2006, Merriam-Webster's dictionary added the word *Google*. __C__

8. My favorite meal is fried chicken, black-eyed peas, and greens, both of my grandmothers are from the South. __CS__

9. Heather took a home-repair course she wanted to learn basic carpentry. __FS__

10. I had to take my cat to the veterinarian, he was in a lot of pain. __FS__

● Practice 21-2

Some of the sentences in the following paragraph are correct, but others are fused sentences or comma splices. In the blank after each sentence, write *C* if the sentence is correct, *CS* if it is a comma splice, and *FS* if it is a fused sentence.

Example: "Race movies" had all-black casts, they were intended for African-American audiences. <u>CS</u>

(1) Oscar Micheaux has an important place in film history, he is considered the first African-American film director. _____ (2) In 1919, Micheaux filmed *Within Our Gates* this movie examined black life in Chicago. _____ (3) The film included scenes of violence, it even depicted two lynchings. _____ (4) It also treated interracial relationships white censors banned it. _____ (5) Race riots had occurred in Chicago that year, the censors feared violence. _____ (6) The movie was finally shown, twelve hundred feet of film were omitted. _____ (7) Most of Micheaux's movies were not socially conscious films like *Within Our Gates*. _____ (8) He made many low-budget musicals and melodramas, few of them survive today. _____ (9) Micheaux died in 1951. _____ (10) In 1990, an uncut version of *Within Our Gates* was discovered in Madrid, it was shown in Chicago for the first time in 1992. _____

Focus on Writing: *Flashback*

Look back at your response to the Focus on Writing activity on page 355. Do you see any run-ons? If so, underline them.

21b Correcting Run-Ons

You can correct run-ons in five ways.

1. *Use a period to create two separate sentences.*

   College costs are rising. Many students are worried.

2. *Use a coordinating conjunction (*and, but, or, nor, for, so, *or* yet*) to connect ideas.*

   College costs are rising, and many students are worried.

3. *Use a semicolon to connect ideas.*

   College costs are rising; many students are worried.

4. *Use a semicolon followed by a transitional word or phrase to connect ideas.*

   College costs are rising; as a result, many students are worried.

5. *Use a dependent word (*although, because, when, *and so on) to connect ideas.*

   Because college costs are rising, many students are worried.

1. Use a period to create two separate sentences. Be sure each sentence begins with a capital letter and ends with a period.

Incorrect (fused sentence)	Gas prices are very high some people are buying hybrid cars.
Incorrect (comma splice)	Gas prices are very high, some people are buying hybrid cars.
Correct	Gas prices are very high. Some people are buying hybrid cars. (two separate sentences)

● Practice 21-3

Correct each of the following run-ons by using a period to create two separate sentences. Be sure both of your sentences begin with a capital letter and end with a period.

Example: In 2005, Hurricane Katrina hit the Gulf Coast hard~~,~~ ~~many~~ . Many people lost everything.

1. Hurricane Katrina destroyed many homes in New Orleans it destroyed many businesses, too.
2. The city was flooded, high winds damaged the Mississippi and Alabama coasts.
3. Americans watched the terrible scenes, hundreds died waiting for rescuers.
4. Many police officers, soldiers, and firefighters acted heroically, ordinary citizens also took action.
5. Residents of flooded communities vowed to return they knew it would not be easy.

2. Use a coordinating conjunction to connect ideas. If you want to indicate a particular relationship between ideas—for example, cause and effect or contrast—you can connect two independent clauses with a coordinating conjunction (*and*, *but*, *or*, *nor*, *for*, *so*, or *yet*) that makes this relationship clear. Always place a comma before the coordinating conjunction.

Incorrect (fused sentence)	Some schools require students to wear uniforms other schools do not.
Incorrect (comma splice)	Some schools require students to wear uniforms, other schools do not.
Correct	Some schools require students to wear uniforms, but other schools do not. (clauses connected with the coordinating conjunction *but*, preceded by a comma)

● Practice 21-4

Correct each of the following run-ons by using a coordinating conjunction (*and*, *but*, *or*, *nor*, *for*, *so*, or *yet*) to connect ideas. Be sure to put a comma before each coordinating conjunction.

Example: Many TV shows focus on war, but some are more realistic than others.

1. Right after World War II, some television programs showed actual scenes of war, *Victory at Sea* and *The Big Picture* were two of those programs.

2. *Hogan's Heroes* was a 1960s comedy set in a German prisoner-of-war camp this show was bound to be very unrealistic.

3. In the 1970s, *M*A*S*H* depicted a Korean War medical unit, the show was really about the Vietnam War.

4. The 1980s drama *China Beach* was set in Vietnam, the main character was an army nurse.

5. The contemporary drama *Army Wives* focuses on the home front, it occasionally shows scenes of the Iraq War.

3. Use a semicolon to connect ideas. If you want to indicate a particularly close connection—or a strong contrast—between two ideas, use a semicolon.

Incorrect (fused sentence)	Most professional basketball players go to college most professional baseball players do not.
Incorrect (comma splice)	Most professional basketball players go to college, most professional baseball players do not.
Correct	Most professional basketball players go to college; most professional baseball players do not. (clauses connected with a semicolon)

● Practice 21-5

Correct each of the following run-ons by using a semicolon to connect ideas. Do not use a capital letter after the semicolon unless the word that follows it is a proper noun.

Example: Many successful people in the United States have Hispanic backgrounds ; Supreme Court Justice Sonia Sotomayor is a notable example.

1. New Mexico governor Bill Richardson has been a U.N. ambassador and a congressman he also served as U.S. energy secretary.

2. César Chávez was a leader of the United Farm Workers Union, Dolores Huerta also became known as a union leader.

3. Roberto Clemente was a professional baseball player, Oscar de la Hoya achieved fame as a professional boxer.

4. Oscar Hijuelos wrote *The Mambo Kings Play Songs of Love*, Julia Alvarez wrote *How the Garcia Girls Lost Their Accents*.

5. Luis Valdez is a noted playwright and film director his plays include *Los Vendidos* and *The Zoot Suit*.

4. Use a semicolon followed by a transitional word or phrase to connect ideas. To indicate a specific relationship between two closely related ideas, add a transitional word or phrase after the semicolon. Always place a comma after the transitional word or phrase.

Incorrect (fused sentence)	Finding a part-time job can be challenging sometimes it is even hard to find an unpaid internship.
Incorrect (comma splice)	Finding a part-time job can be challenging, sometimes it is even hard to find an unpaid internship.
Correct	Finding a part-time job can be challenging; in fact, sometimes it is even hard to find an unpaid internship. (clauses connected with a semicolon followed by the transitional phrase *in fact*)

Some Frequently Used Transitional Words and Phrases

as a result	in addition	now
finally	in fact	still
for example	moreover	therefore
for instance	nevertheless	thus
however		

For complete lists of transitional words and phrases, see 16C.

● Practice 21-6

Correct each of the following run-ons by using a semicolon, followed by the transitional word or phrase in parentheses, to connect ideas. Be sure to put a comma after the transitional word or phrase.

Example: High schools prepare students for college and jobs*; in addition,* they can prepare students for life. (in addition)

1. High schools have always taught subjects like English and math many also teach personal finance and consumer education. (now)

2. Personal-finance courses prepare students for life, students learn about money management, online banking, and identity theft. (for example)

3. Consumer-education courses can be very practical students can learn how to buy, finance, and insure a car. (for instance)

4. Some high schools teach students how to avoid credit card debt, they teach students how to invest their money. (in addition)

5. Academic subjects will always dominate the high school curriculum, courses focusing on practical life skills are becoming increasingly important. (however)

Highlight: Connecting Ideas with Semicolons

Run-ons often occur when you use a transitional word or phrase to join two independent clauses *without also using a semicolon.*

Incorrect (fused sentence)	It is easy to download information from the Internet however it is not always easy to evaluate the information.
Incorrect (comma splice)	It is easy to download information from the Internet, however it is not always easy to evaluate the information.

To correct this kind of run-on, put a semicolon before the transitional word or phrase, and put a comma after it.

Correct	It is easy to download information from the Internet; however, it is not always easy to evaluate the information.

---

5. Use a dependent word to connect ideas. When one idea is dependent on another, you can connect the two ideas by adding a dependent word, such as *when, who, although,* or *because.*

Incorrect (fused sentence)	American union membership was high in the mid-twentieth century it has declined in recent years.

Incorrect (comma splice)	American union membership was high in the mid-twentieth century, it has declined in recent years.
Correct	Although American union membership was high in the mid-twentieth century, it has declined in recent years. (clauses connected with the dependent word *although*)
Correct	American union membership, which was high in the mid-twentieth century, has declined in recent years. (clauses connected with the dependent word *which*)

Some Frequently Used Dependent Words

after	if
although	instead
as	unless
because	until
before	when
even though	which
eventually	

For complete lists of dependent words, including **subordinating conjunctions** and **relative pronouns**, see 17B and 17C.

● Practice 21-7

Correct each run-on in the following paragraph by adding a dependent word. Consult the list above to help you choose a logical dependent word. Be sure to add correct punctuation where necessary.

Example: Harlem was a rural area until the nineteenth century
when
improved transportation linked it to lower Manhattan.
    ^

(1) Contemporary historians have written about the Harlem Renaissance, its influence is still not widely known. (2) Harlem was populated mostly by European immigrants at the turn of the last century, it saw an influx of African Americans beginning in 1910. (3) This migration

from the South continued Harlem became one of the largest African-American communities in the United States. (4) Many black artists and writers settled in Harlem during the 1920s. African-American art flowered. (5) This "Harlem Renaissance" was an important era in American literary history it is not even mentioned in some textbooks. (6) Scholars recognize the great works of the Harlem Renaissance, they point to the writers Langston Hughes and Countee Cullen and the artists Henry Tanner and Sargent Johnson. (7) Zora Neale Hurston moved to Harlem from her native Florida in 1925, she began a book of African-American folklore. (8) Harlem was an exciting place in the 1920s people from all over the city went there to listen to jazz and to dance. (9) The white playwright Eugene O'Neill went to Harlem to audition actors for his play *The Emperor Jones*, he made an international star of the great Paul Robeson. (10) The Great Depression occurred in the 1930s it led to the end of the Harlem Renaissance.

● Practice 21-8

Correct each of the run-ons below in one of the following four ways: by creating two separate sentences, by using a coordinating conjunction, by using a semicolon, or by using a semicolon followed by a transitional word or phrase. Be sure punctuation is correct. Remember to put a semicolon before, and a comma after, each transitional word or phrase.

> **Example:** Some people believe chronic sex offenders should be given therapy /however others believe they should be jailed indefinitely.

1. Nursing offers job security and high pay, therefore many people are choosing nursing as a career.

2. Anne Boleyn was the second wife of Henry VIII her daughter was Elizabeth I.

3. The Democratic Republic of the Congo was previously known as Zaire it was previously called the Belgian Congo.

4. Housewife Jean Nidetch started Weight Watchers in 1961 she sold the company for $100 million in 1978.

5. Millions of Jews were murdered during the Holocaust, in addition Catholics, Gypsies, homosexuals, and other "undesirables" were killed.

6. Sojourner Truth was born a slave she eventually became a leading abolitionist and feminist.

7. Japanese athletes now play various positions on American baseball teams at first all the Japanese players were pitchers.

8. Oliver Wendell Holmes Jr. was a Supreme Court justice, his father was a physician and writer.

9. Père Noël is the French name for Santa Claus, he is also known as Father Christmas and St. Nicholas.

10. Latin is one classical language Greek is another.

● Practice 21-9

Correct each run-on in the following paragraph in the way that best indicates the relationship between ideas. Be sure you use appropriate punctuation. (Note that not every sentence is a run-on.)

> **Example:** *Although*
> Pluto was once considered the ninth planet in our solar system it was removed from the official list of planets in 2006.

(1) Scientists suspected the existence of Pluto as early as 1846, they believed it was causing the changes they observed in Neptune's orbit. (2) However, Pluto was not discovered until much later. (3) Percival Lowell founded the Lowell Observatory in 1894, he began searching for a ninth planet in 1906. (4) Telescopes caught images of Pluto in 1915, it was not named a planet until 1930. (5) The newly discovered ninth planet made international headlines, in fact, thousands of people sent in ideas for names. (6) "Pluto" was suggested by a British girl, the name refers to the Greek god of the underworld. (7) Scientists

at the Lowell Observatory liked the name the planet is cold and far away like the underworld. (8) They also chose it in honor of Percival Lowell, his initials are the first two letters of the name. (9) Later, Walt Disney borrowed the name for a new cartoon character, in addition, a new element was named plutonium. (10) Recently, scientists learned that Pluto does not have enough mass to maintain a stable orbit, it was reclassified as a dwarf planet in 2006.

Focus on Writing: *Flashback*

Look at the run-ons that you identified in the Flashback activity on page 357, and try correcting each one in two different ways.

Focus on Writing: *Revising and Editing*

Look back at your response to the Focus on Writing activity on page 355. **TEST** what you have written. Then, look again at the Flashback activities on page 357 and above. For each run-on you found, choose the revision that best conveys your meaning, and revise your Focus on Writing activity accordingly. Finally, edit your work. (If you do not find any run-ons, work with a classmate to correct his or her errors.)

Editing Practice: Paragraph

Read the following student paragraph, and revise it to eliminate run-ons. Correct each run-on in the way that best indicates the relationship between ideas. The first error has been corrected for you.

Cold Cases

Cold cases are criminal investigations that have not been solved$\overset{, so}{\wedge}$ they are not officially closed. New evidence is found, cold cases may be reexamined. DNA tests might provide new clues, a witness may come forward with new testimony. The new evidence might lead to new suspects it might change the nature of the crime. In some cases, an accident might be reclassified a homicide, in other cases a murder might be ruled a suicide. Sometimes a person who was convicted of a crime is found to be innocent. Cold cases usually involve violent crimes, rape and murder are two examples. Investigators sometimes reopen very old cold cases, they usually focus on more recent cases with living suspects. For serious crimes, there is no limit on how much time may pass before a suspect is brought to justice, a criminal may be convicted many years after the crime was committed. When cold cases are solved, the crime is not undone, nevertheless victims' families finally feel that justice has been served.

Editing Practice: Essay

Read the following student essay, and revise it by eliminating run-ons and correcting them to indicate the relationships between ideas. Be sure punctuation is correct. The first error has been corrected for you.

Dollars and Cents

Although most
Most of us handle money every day, we rarely look closely at it or think much about what goes into producing it. However, the U.S. Treasury Department thinks about our money all the time. The Treasury Department is always looking for ways to make money more interesting to consumers

and collectors, it is also constantly trying to make money harder for counterfeiters to copy.

In recent years, some major changes have been made to our money. Between 2004 and 2006, the U.S. Mint produced a new series of nickels these nickels feature new images on both the front and back. The fronts of the new nickels include new images of Thomas Jefferson's face, the backs now show several images related to the explorers Lewis and Clark. In 1999, the Mint introduced a series of new quarters each quarter shows an image from one of the fifty states. A similar series of coins was issued in 2009 the Mint produced six new quarters for the District of Columbia and five American territories, including Puerto Rico and Guam. All of the new coins have been very popular, in fact, many people are collecting sets of coins.

The Mint has also recently produced new pennies. Abraham Lincoln's face remains on the front of the new pennies, the backs have changed. The new pennies show five scenes from Lincoln's life, one coin shows an image of the log cabin in Kentucky where Lincoln was born. Another depicts his youth in Indiana, a third coin shows his professional life in Illinois. The fourth penny shows an image from the time of his presidency. The image on the last new penny of the series represents the unity of the country, this is what Lincoln fought very hard to preserve.

The U.S. Treasury is always trying to stay ahead of counterfeiters. In 2008, it began circulating new five-dollar bills, these are similar to the recently redesigned ten-, twenty-, and fifty-dollar bills. All the new bills are multicolored, the portraits on the fronts of the bills are larger and slightly off-center. The paper includes watermarks and security threads, these are very difficult for counterfeiters to reproduce. The Treasury plans to change these bills every seven to ten years to make them even harder to copy, eventually, the one hundred-dollar bill will also be printed in color and have additional security features.

Changes in our money may be hard to get used to, these changes serve two important purposes. They help to prevent counterfeiting, they also provide us with attractive currency to collect—or to spend.

Collaborative Activities

1. Find an interesting paragraph in a newspaper or magazine article. Retype the paragraph, creating several run-ons.

2. Exchange paragraphs with another student, and correct the run-ons in the paragraph you received. When you have finished, return the paragraph to the student who created it.

3. Evaluate the student's corrections to your paragraph, comparing it to the original newspaper or magazine paragraph. Pay particular attention to punctuation.

Review Checklist: Run-Ons

☐ A run-on is an error that occurs when two sentences are joined incorrectly. (See 21A.)

☐ A fused sentence occurs when two sentences are incorrectly joined without any punctuation. (See 21A.)

☐ A comma splice occurs when two sentences are incorrectly joined with just a comma. (See 21A.)

☐ Correct a run-on by using a period to create two separate sentences or by connecting ideas with a coordinating conjunction, a semicolon, a semicolon followed by a transitional word or phrase, or a dependent word. (See 21B.)

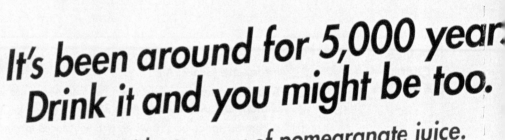

Recognizing Fragments

A **sentence fragment** is an incomplete sentence. Every sentence must include at least one subject and one verb, and every sentence must express a complete thought. If a group of words does not do *all* these things, it is a fragment and not a sentence — even if it begins with a capital letter and ends with a period.

The following is a complete sentence.

Sentence	The <u>actors</u> in the play <u>were</u> very talented. (includes both a subject and a verb and expresses a complete thought)

Because a sentence must have both a subject and a verb and express a complete thought, the following groups of words are not complete sentences; they are fragments.

Fragment (no verb)	The actors in the play. (What point is being made about the actors?)
Fragment (no subject)	Were very talented. (Who were very talented?)
Fragment (no subject or verb)	Very talented. (Who was very talented?)
Fragment (does not express a complete thought)	Because the actors in the play were very talented. (What happened because they were very talented?)

Focus on Writing

The picture on the opposite page shows a billboard advertising Pom pomegranate juice. Look at the picture, and then write a paragraph (or an essay) that discusses what appeals to you about your favorite beverage, brand of footwear, or health or beauty product.

**Highlight:
Identifying
Fragments**

Sentence fragments almost always appear next to complete sentences.

┌─ COMPLETE SENTENCE ─┐┌──── FRAGMENT ────┐
Celia took two electives. Physics 320 and Spanish 101.

The fragment above does not have a subject or a verb. The complete sentence that precedes it, however, has both a subject (*Celia*) and a verb (*took*).

Often, you can correct a sentence fragment that appears in your own writing by attaching it to a nearby sentence that supplies the missing words. (This sentence will usually appear before the fragment.)

Celia took two electives, Physics 320 and Spanish 101.

● Practice 22-1

Some of the following items are fragments, and others are complete sentences. On the line following each item, write *F* if it is a fragment and *S* if it is a complete sentence.

Example: At the beginning of the test. ___*F*___

1. The students in the classroom. _____

2. Some students were very nervous about the test. _____

3. With a number-two pencil. _____

4. Opened their test booklets. _____

5. After twenty-five minutes. _____

6. The second part of the test was very hard. _____

7. The last set of questions. _____

8. It was finally over. _____

9. Breathed a sigh of relief. _____

10. The students ran out into the hallway. _____

● Practice 22-2

In the following paragraph, some of the numbered groups of words are missing a subject, a verb, or both. Identify each fragment by labeling it *F*. Then, decide how each fragment could be attached to a nearby word group to create a complete new sentence. Finally, rewrite the entire paragraph, using complete sentences, on the lines provided.

Example: Martha Grimes, Ruth Rendell, and Deborah Crombie write detective novels. _____ Set in England. __*F*__

Martha Grimes, Ruth Rendell, and Deborah Crombie write detective

novels set in England.

_____

(1) Sara Paretsky writes detective novels. _____ (2) Such as *Hardball* and *Guardian Angel*. _____ (3) These novels are about V. I. Warshawski. _____ (4) A private detective. _____ (5) V. I. lives and works in Chicago. _____ (6) The Windy City. _____ (7) Every day as a detective. _____ (8) V. I. takes risks. _____ (9) V. I. is tough. _____ (10) She is also a woman. _____

Rewrite:

_____

_____

_____

_____

_____

_____

Focus on Writing: *Flashback*

Look back at your response to the Focus on Writing activity on page 371. Do all your sentences seem complete? Underline any that you think are not complete.

22b   Missing-Subject Fragments

Every sentence must include a subject and a verb. If the subject is left out, the sentence is incomplete. In the following example, the first word group is a sentence. It includes a subject (*He*) and a verb (*packed*). However, the second word group is a fragment. It includes a verb (*took*) but no subject.

```
┌────────── SENTENCE ──────────┐ ┌──────── FRAGMENT ────────┐
```
He packed his books and papers. And also took an umbrella.

The best way to correct this kind of fragment is usually to attach it to the sentence that comes right before it. This sentence often contains the missing subject.

Correct   He packed his books and papers and also took an umbrella.

Another way to correct this kind of fragment is to add a new subject.

Correct   He packed his books and papers. He also took an umbrella.

● **Practice 22-3**

Each of the following items includes a missing-subject fragment. Using one of the two methods explained above, correct each fragment.

Example: Many schools give out summer reading lists. And also assign summer homework.

Many schools give out summer reading lists and also assign

summer homework.

Many schools give out summer reading lists. They also assign

summer homework.

1. Spelling bees help children learn to love words. And teach them to be good sports.

   Spelling bees help children learn to love word, I Also
   teachs them to be good

2. Some celebrities have their own charities. And give away millions of dollars.

   Some celebrities have there own charities and give away
   millions of dollars

3. The Peace Corps was a popular choice for college graduates in the 1960s. And it is a popular choice today as well.

   The peace corps was a populer

4. Johnny Depp starred in *Pirates of the Caribbean.* And also starred in its sequels.

   _____

5. People can find information on the Internet. Or learn by reading, observing, and asking questions.

   _____

(handwritten margin note:) Fix Frag / - Add info / - Blend

6. Some wealthy people retire to relax and play golf. But still help others by volunteering.

---

7. Hybrid cars can save their owners money. And help the environment.

---

8. Some credit cards earn miles. Or earn other rewards, such as hotel stays.

---

9. In Madrid, people eat dinner at ten or eleven o'clock. But snack on tapas earlier in the evening.

---

10. To protect your body from the sun, you should use sunscreen. And wear long-sleeved shirts.

Focus on Writing: *Flashback*

Look back at your response to the Focus on Writing activity on page 371. Does every word group that is punctuated as a sentence include a subject? Correct any missing-subject fragments you find.

22c   Phrase Fragments

Every sentence must include a subject and a verb. A **phrase** is a group of words that is missing a subject or a verb or both. When you punctuate a phrase as if it is a sentence, you create a fragment.

Appositive Fragments

An **appositive** identifies, renames, or describes a noun or a pronoun. An appositive cannot stand alone as a sentence.

To correct an appositive fragment, attach it to the sentence that comes right before it. (This sentence usually includes the noun or pronoun that the appositive describes.)

Incorrect	He decorated the room in his favorite colors. Brown and black.
Correct	He decorated the room in his favorite colors, brown and black.

Sometimes a word or expression like *especially, except, including, such as, for example,* or *for instance* introduces an appositive. Even if an appositive is introduced by one of these expressions, it is still a fragment.

Incorrect	A balanced diet should include high-fiber foods. Such as leafy vegetables, fruits, beans, and whole-grain bread.
Correct	A balanced diet should include high-fiber foods, such as leafy vegetables, fruits, beans, and whole-grain bread.

● **Practice 22-4**

Each of the following items includes an appositive fragment. In each case, correct the fragment by attaching it to the sentence that comes before it.

Example: The Pledge of Allegiance was written in 1892 by Francis Bellamy. A Baptist minister.

The Pledge of Allegiance was written in 1892 by Francis Bellamy, a

Baptist minister.

1. The U.S. flag was designed by Francis Hopkinson. A New Jersey delegate to the Continental Congress.

   The U.S flag was dessned by Francis lin

2. The first flag may have been sewn by Betsy Ross, A Philadelphia seamstress.

3. Congress officially recognized the Pledge of Allegiance in 1942, The year the United States entered World War II.

4. In 1814, Francis Scott Key composed "The Star-Spangled Banner." The U.S. national anthem.

_____

_____

5. Some people wanted a different national anthem, Such as "America" or "America the Beautiful."

_____

_____

Prepositional Phrase Fragments

A **prepositional phrase** consists of a preposition and its object. A prepositional phrase cannot stand alone as a sentence.

To correct a prepositional phrase fragment, attach it to the sentence that comes right before it.

┌────── FRAGMENT ──────┐

Incorrect   She promised to stand by him. In sickness and in health.

Correct   She promised to stand by him in sickness and in health.

See page 266

● Practice 22-5

Each of the following items includes a prepositional phrase fragment. In each case, correct the fragment by attaching it to the sentence that comes before it.

Example: Birth order has a strong influence. On personality.

Birth order has a strong influence on personality.

1. First-born children are reliable, serious, and goal-oriented; In most cases.

_____

2. More than half of U.S. presidents have been first-born or only children. In their families.

_____

_____

3. In large families, middle children often form close relationships, Outside of the family.

_____

_____

4. The youngest child is always trying to get attention. From the older members of the family.

_____

_____

5. Youngest children often take a while to settle down. Into careers and marriages.

_____

_____

● **Practice 22-6**

Each of the following items is a phrase fragment, not a sentence. Turn each fragment into a sentence by adding any words needed to complete it. (You may add words before or after the fragment.)

Example: During World War I. _During World War I, a flu epidemic_
killed millions of people. or A flu epidemic killed millions of people
during World War I.

1. The best player on the Yankees. _____

_____

2. From a developing nation in Africa. _____

_____

3. Such as tulips or roses. _____

_____

4. Behind door number 3. _____

_____

5. Including my parents and grandparents. _____

_____

6. With a new car in the driveway. _____

_____

7. A very small animal. _____

_____

8. For a long time. _____

_____

9. Turkey, stuffing, potatoes, and cranberry sauce. _____

_____

10. In less than a year. _____

_____

Focus on Writing: *Flashback*

Look back at your response to the Focus on Writing activity on page 371. Are any phrases incorrectly punctuated as sentences? Correct each phrase fragment you find. (Hint: In many cases, you will be able to correct the fragment by attaching it to the sentence that comes right before it.)

22d　Incomplete-Verb Fragments

Every sentence must include a subject and a verb. If the verb is missing or incomplete, a word group is a fragment, not a sentence.

-ing Fragments

An *-ing* verb cannot be a complete verb. It needs a **helping verb** to complete it. An *-ing* verb, such as *looking*, cannot stand alone in a sentence without a helping verb (*is looking*, *was looking*, *were looking*, and so on). When you use an *-ing* verb without a helping verb, you create a fragment.

FRAGMENT

Incorrect　　The twins are full of mischief. Always looking for trouble.

The best way to correct an *-ing* fragment is usually to attach it to the sentence that comes right before it.

Correct　　The twins are full of mischief, always looking for trouble.

Another way to correct this kind of fragment is to add a subject and a helping verb.

Correct　　The twins are full of mischief. They are always looking for trouble.

Highlight: Incomplete-Verb Fragments with *Being*	The *-ing* verb *being* is often used incorrectly as if it were a complete verb.

Incorrect　I decided to take a nap. The outcome being that I slept through calculus class.

To correct this kind of fragment, substitute a form of the verb *be* that can stand alone in a sentence — for example, *is, was, are,* or *were.*

Correct　I decided to take a nap. The outcome was that I slept through calculus class.

● **Practice 22-7**

Each of the following items includes an *-ing* fragment. In each case, correct the fragment by attaching it to the sentence that comes before it.

Example: Certain tips can help grocery shoppers. Saving them a lot of money.

Certain tips can help grocery shoppers, saving them a lot of money.

_____

1. Always try to find a store brand. Costing less than the well-known and widely advertised brands.

_____

_____

2. Look for a product's cost per pound. Comparing it to the cost per pound of similar products.

_____

_____

3. Examine sale-priced fruits and vegetables. Checking carefully for damage or spoilage.

_____

_____

4. Use coupons whenever possible. Keeping them all in one place until they are needed.

_____

_____

5. Buy different brands of the same product. Trying each one to see which brand you like best.

_____

_____

● **Practice 22-8**

Each of the following items is an *-ing* fragment. Turn each fragment into a sentence by adding the words needed to complete it. (You can either add a subject and a helping verb or add a new sentence before or after the fragment.)

> **Example:** Hoping she would be lucky. *We were all hoping she would*
> *be lucky or Hoping she would be lucky, she bet her last few dollars*
> *on the lottery.*

1. Knowing that he was qualified for the job. _____

_____

2. Leaving for an extended trip to Russia. _____

_____

3. Worrying about money every day. _____

_____

4. Trying to complete the loan application. _____

_____

5. Staying inside during the three-day snowstorm. _____

_____

6. Tossing and turning during a sleepless night. _____

_____

7. Really feeling optimistic about the future. _____

_____

8. Wanting to get better grades. _____

_____

9. Wondering what would happen next. _____

_____

10. Hoping to meet the man of her dreams. _____

_____

Infinitive Fragments

An **infinitive**, which consists of *to* plus the base form of the verb (*to be, to go, to write*), is not a complete verb. An infinitive phrase (*to be free, to go home, to write a novel*) cannot stand alone as a sentence because it does not include a subject or a complete verb.

┌── FRAGMENT ──┐

Incorrect Eric considered dropping out of school. To start his own business.

Often, you can correct an infinitive fragment simply by attaching it to the sentence that comes right before it.

Correct Eric considered dropping out of school to start his own business.

Another way to correct an infinitive fragment is to add a subject and a complete verb.

Correct Eric considered dropping out of school. He wanted to start his own business.

● Practice 22-9

Each of the following items includes an infinitive fragment. Correct each fragment by attaching it to the sentence that comes right before it.

Example: Some people require surgery. To bring their weight down to a healthy level.

Some people require surgery to bring their weight down to a

healthy level.

1. Psychologists need advanced degrees. To practice as licensed therapists.

_____

_____

2. Schools sometimes close during a flu outbreak. To prevent the disease from spreading.

   _____

   _____

3. In 1941, Japan attacked the United States naval base at Pearl Harbor. To weaken America's position in the Pacific.

   _____

   _____

4. You should always back up your computer files. To avoid losing valuable work.

   _____

   _____

5. Scientists sent remote-controlled robots, called "rovers," to Mars. To take photographs of the planet's surface.

   _____

   _____

● Practice 22-10

Each of the following items is an infinitive fragment. Correct each fragment by adding a subject and a complete verb.

Example: To say good-bye.

It was not easy to say good-bye. _____

1. To complete the loan application. _____

   _____

2. To take the most scenic route through the mountains. _____

   _____

3. To help his best friend. _____

   _____

4. To become a good photographer. _____

   _____

5. To eat a plate of nachos. _____

   _____

Focus on Writing: *Flashback*

Look back at your response to the Focus on Writing activity on page 371. Underline any *-ing* verbs or infinitives you find. Are the sentences in which they appear complete? Correct each incomplete-verb fragment you find.

22e   Dependent Clause Fragments

Every sentence must include a subject and a verb. A sentence must also express a complete thought.

A **dependent** clause is a group of words that is introduced by a dependent word, such as *although*, *because*, *that*, or *after*. A dependent clause includes a subject and a verb, but it does not express a complete thought. Therefore, it cannot stand alone as a sentence. To correct a dependent clause fragment, you must complete the thought.

The following dependent clause is incorrectly punctuated as if it were a sentence.

Fragment   After Simon won the lottery.

This sentence fragment includes both a subject (*Simon*) and a complete verb (*won*), but it does not express a complete thought. What happened after Simon won the lottery? To turn this fragment into a sentence, you need to complete the thought.

Sentence   After Simon won the lottery, <u>he quit his night job</u>.

- Some dependent clauses are introduced by dependent words called **subordinating conjunctions**.

Fragment   Although Marisol had always dreamed of coming to America.

This sentence fragment includes a subject (*Marisol*) and a complete verb (*had dreamed*), but it is not a sentence; it is a dependent clause introduced by the subordinating conjunction *although*.

To correct this kind of fragment, attach it to an **independent clause** (a simple sentence) to complete the thought. (You can usually find the independent clause you need right before or right after the fragment.)

Sentence Although Marisol had always dreamed of coming to America, <u>she did not have enough money for the trip until 1985</u>.

Highlight: Subordinating Conjunctions				
	after	even though	since	whenever
	although	if	so that	where
	as	if only	than	whereas
	as if	in order that	that	wherever
	as though	now that	though	whether
	because	once	unless	while
	before	provided that	until	
	even if	rather than	when	

For information on how to use subordinating conjunctions, see 17B.

Highlight: Correcting Dependent Clause Fragments	The simplest way to correct a dependent clause fragment is just to cross out the dependent word that makes the idea incomplete.
	~~Although~~ Marisol had always dreamed of coming to America.
	However, when you delete the dependent word, readers may have trouble seeing the connection between the new sentence and the one before or after it. A better way to revise is to attach the dependent clause fragment to an independent clause.

- Other dependent clauses are introduced by dependent words called **relative pronouns**.

Fragment Novelist Richard Wright, <u>who</u> came to Paris in 1947.

Fragment A quinceañera, <u>which</u> celebrates a Latina's fifteenth birthday.

> **Fragment**   A key World War II battle <u>that</u> was fought on the Pacific island of Guadalcanal.

Each of the above sentence fragments includes a subject (*Richard Wright, quinceañera, battle*) and a complete verb (*came, celebrates, was fought*). However, they are not sentences because they do not express complete thoughts. In each case, a relative pronoun creates a dependent clause.

To correct each of these fragments, add the words needed to complete the thought.

> **Sentence**   Novelist Richard Wright, who came to Paris in 1947, <u>spent the rest of his life there.</u>

> **Sentence**   A quinceañera, which celebrates a Latina's fifteenth birthday, <u>signifies her entrance into womanhood.</u>

> **Sentence**   A key World War II battle that was fought on the Pacific island of Guadalcanal <u>took place in 1943</u>.

Highlight: Relative Pronouns	that	whoever
	what	whom
	which	whomever
	who	whose

For information on how to use relative pronouns, see 17C.

● Practice 22-11

Correct each of the following dependent clause fragments by attaching it to the sentence before or after it. If the dependent clause comes at the beginning of a sentence, place a comma after it.

Example: Before it became a state. West Virginia was part of Virginia.

Before it became a state, West Virginia was part of Virginia.

1. Because many homeless people are mentally ill. It is hard to find places for them to live. *It's herd to fins nacitally ill peeple pleces to live*

2. People do not realize how dangerous raccoons can be. Even though they can be found in many parts of the United States. _____

_____

_____

3. I make plans to be a better student. Whenever a new semester begins.

When ever a new Semester begins I plan on being a better student

4. Until something changes. We will just have to accept the situation. ____

_____

5. Because it is a very controversial issue. My parents and I have agreed not to discuss it. _____

_____

● Practice 22-12

Correct each of these dependent clause fragments by adding the words needed to complete the idea.

Example: Many minor species of animals, which are rapidly disappearing.

Many minor species of animals, which are rapidly disappearing,

need to be protected.

1. The film that frightened me. _____

_____

2. People who drink and drive. _____

_____

3. Some parents who are very strict with their children. _____

_____

4. The Vietnam War, which many Americans did not support. _____

_____

5. Animals that are used in medical research. _____

_____

● Practice 22-13

Each of the following is a fragment. Some are missing a subject, some are phrases incorrectly punctuated as sentences, others do not have a complete verb, and still others are dependent clauses incorrectly punctuated as sentences. Turn each fragment into a complete sentence, writing your revised sentence on the line below the fragment. Whenever possible, create two different correct sentences. Be sure to punctuate correctly.

Example: Waiting in the dugout.
Revised: _Waiting in the dugout, the players chewed tobacco._
Revised: _The players were waiting in the dugout._

1. Because three-year-olds are still very attached to their parents.

   Revised: _____

   Revised: _____

2. Going around in circles.

   Revised: _____

   Revised: _____

3. To win the prize for the most unusual costume.

   Revised: _____

   Revised: _____

4. Students who thought they could not afford to go to college.

   Revised: _____

   Revised: _____

5. On an important secret mission.

   Revised: _____

   Revised: _____

6. Although many instructors see cheating as a serious problem.

   Revised: _____

   Revised: _____

7. Hoping to get another helping of chocolate fudge cake.

   Revised: _____

   Revised: _____

8. The rule that I always felt was the most unfair.

   Revised: _____

   Revised: _____

9. A really exceptional worker.

   Revised: _____

   Revised: _____

10. And finished in record time.

   Revised: _____

   Revised: _____

Focus on Writing: *Flashback*

Look back at your response to the Focus on Writing activity on page 371. Underline every subordinating conjunction you find, and underline *which*, *that*, and *who* wherever you find them. Do any of these words introduce a dependent clause that is punctuated as if it is a sentence? Correct each dependent clause fragment you find by adding the words needed to complete the thought.

Focus on Writing: *Revising and Editing*

Look back at your response to the Focus on Writing activity on page 371. **TEST** what you have written. Then, revise your work, incorporating corrections from all the Flashback activities in this chapter, and check one more time to make sure every sentence is complete. Finally, edit your work. (If you do not find any fragments, work with a classmate to correct his or her errors.)

Chapter Review

Editing Practice: Paragraph

Read the following student paragraph, which includes incomplete sentences. Underline each fragment. Then, correct the fragment by attaching it to a nearby sentence that completes the thought. The first fragment has been underlined and corrected for you.

The Hidden Costs of Knockoffs

Fake designer clothing and bags seem inexpensive, *but they* ~~But come~~ with
hidden costs. The first cost is to the workers. Who are often children
earning only pennies for each item they make. The second cost is to the
buyer. Of the bargain purse or shirt. Counterfeit goods fall apart easily.
Because they are made quickly from cheap materials. The third cost is
to society. Profits from knockoffs are not taxed. And in some cases even
support crime. The good news is that it is illegal. To sell a product with
a fake designer label. Unfortunately, however, it is not illegal to buy
counterfeit goods. Therefore, it is up to shoppers to consider the hidden
costs of knockoffs. Before giving in to that "designer" deal.

Editing Practice: Essay

Read the following student essay, which includes incomplete sentences. Underline each fragment. Then, correct it by attaching it to a nearby sentence that completes the thought. The first fragment has been underlined and corrected for you.

Not in My Backyard

There are many benefits to living in a modern society, *including* ~~Including~~ safe
streets, affordable electricity, and efficient transportation systems. These
benefits, however, come at a cost. Modern society also needs places to
put criminals. To dispose of nuclear waste. And to build train tracks. Many
people want to enjoy the benefits society offers. Without experiencing
any of the problems. The expression "NIMBY," which stands for "not in my
backyard," refers to people who take this view.

NIMBYs are people who protest against things like prisons, nuclear waste sites, or train tracks in their communities. Even though these projects may lead to safer streets, cheaper electricity, and more convenient commutes. NIMBYs do not want controversial projects coming to their communities. Because they might have a negative impact on their lives. For example, NIMBYs worry that their children might be at risk. From possible prison breaks, water contamination, or train accidents. In addition, these people may believe that their quality of life will decline. Construction of various projects can take months or years. Causing noise and traffic disruptions. NIMBYs also fear that their property values will go down. Because of the changes being made in their community.

NIMBYs fight unwanted projects with several strategies. Such as with petitions, protests, and letters to politicians. Their main goal is to raise public awareness. So that the project will not be approved. A politician who wants to be re-elected needs to vote against unpopular projects. Or come up with alternative solutions.

In many cases, a compromise can be reached between NIMBYs and politicians. That allows a project to move forward. One of the most common ways to convince NIMBYs to agree to a controversial project is to offer a tax break. Politicians can also promise to construct new schools or roads. In exchange for community support for an unpopular project.

Individuals sometimes need to make sacrifices. In order to create a safe, clean, and productive society. Politicians are often faced with the challenge of striking a balance. Between the needs of the many and the requests of a few. Often, however, compromises can be reached. That will make everybody happy.

Collaborative Activities

1. Exchange workbooks with another student, and read each other's responses to the Focus on Writing activity on page 371. On a separate sheet of paper, list five fragments that describe the product your partner has written about. When your own paper is returned to you, revise each fragment written by your partner, creating a complete sentence for each one. Finally, try to add one of these new sentences to your own Focus on Writing activity.

2. Working in a group of three or four students, add different subordinating conjunctions to sentences *a* through *d* below to create several different fragments. (See page 385 for a list of subordinating conjunctions.) Then, turn each of the resulting fragments into a complete sentence by adding words that complete the thought.

   Example:

Sentence	*Fragment*	*New Sentence*
I left the party.	As I left the party	As I left the party, I fell.
	After I left the party	After I left the party, the fun stopped.
	Until I left the party	Until I left the party, I had no idea it was so late.

   Sentences
   a. My mind wanders.
   b. She caught the ball.
   c. He made a wish.
   d. Disaster struck.

3. Working in a group of three or four students, create as many sentences as you can from the fragments listed on the following page. Use your imagination to generate as many creative sentences as you can.

   Example:

   Fragment   Known for his incredible memory

   Sentences   Zack, known for his incredible memory, has somehow managed to forget everything he learned about chemistry.

   Known for his incredible memory, Monty the Magnificent captivated audiences.

Fragments
a. wandering in the desert
b. stranded in the jungle
c. looking for his ideal mate
d. always using as much ketchup as possible

Review Checklist: Sentence Fragments

☐ A sentence fragment is an incomplete sentence. Every sentence must include a subject and a verb and express a complete thought. (See 22A.)

☐ Every sentence must include a subject. (See 22B.)

☐ Phrases cannot stand alone as sentences. (See 22C.)

☐ Every sentence must include a complete verb. (See 22D.)

☐ Dependent clauses cannot stand alone as sentences. (See 22E.)

Understanding Subject-Verb Agreement

A sentence's subject (a noun or pronoun) and its verb must **agree**: singular subjects take singular verbs, and plural subjects take plural verbs.

      S   V

The <u>museum</u> <u>opens</u> at ten o'clock. (singular noun subject *museum* takes singular verb *opens*)

      S   V

Both <u>museums</u> <u>open</u> at ten o'clock. (plural noun subject *museums* takes plural verb *open*)

  S   V

<u>She</u> always <u>watches</u> the eleven o'clock news. (singular pronoun subject *she* takes singular verb *watches*)

  S   V

<u>They</u> always <u>watch</u> the eleven o'clock news. (plural pronoun subject *they* takes plural verb *watch*)

Subject-Verb Agreement with Regular Verbs

	Singular	*Plural*
First person	I play	Molly and I/we play
Second person	you play	you play
Third person	he/she/it plays	they play
	the man plays	the men play
	Molly plays	Molly and Sam play

Focus on Writing

On October 25, 1990, after the *New York Daily News* demanded millions of dollars in concessions from its workers, the newspaper locked them out. Employees picketed for 148 days before returning to work after the unions agreed to salary reductions and major job cuts.

The picture on the opposite page, by the artist Ralph Fasanella, depicts the *Daily News* strike. Look at the picture, and then write a paragraph (or an essay) that describes what you see. (Use **present tense** in your response.)

● Practice 23-1

Underline the correct form of the verb in each of the following sentences.
Make sure the verb agrees with its subject.

Example: Radio stations (broadcast/broadcasts) many kinds of music.

(1) Most music fans (know/knows) about salsa, but they may not
be familiar with other popular styles of Latin music. (2) For example,
many fans (need/needs) a little education when it comes to ranchera,
a blend of several traditional forms of Mexican music. (3) These forms
(include/includes) mariachi music as well as ballads and waltz-like
tunes. (4) Ranchera (appeal/appeals) to a wide audience of Americans
of Mexican descent. (5) Its performers (sell/sells) millions of records
a year, and often they (top/tops) *Billboard*'s Latin charts. (6) In fact,
Mexican recordings (outsell/outsells) any other form of Latin music in
the United States. (7) Older ranchera lovers (tend/tends) to be first-
generation, working-class immigrants, but more and more young listeners (seem/seems) drawn to ranchera. (8) When one Los Angeles
nightclub (host/hosts) a ranchera night, it (draw/draws) a large number of English-speaking fans in their twenties. (9) Clearly, ranchera
musicians (deserve/deserves) more attention from the music industry.

● Practice 23-2

Fill in the blank with the correct present tense form of the verb.

Example: Everyone ___*knows*___ that the Internet is full of
information. (know)

(1) Internet users often _____ useful sites. (overlook) (2) For
example, many people _____ the online encyclopedia Wikipedia.
(use) (3) However, they _____ more specialized encyclopedias available on the Web. (ignore) (4) In many cases, experts _____ such specialized encyclopedias, so they are usually more detailed and up-to-date
than Wikipedia. (maintain) (5) For example, at baseball-reference.com,

baseball experts _____ frequent updates to a huge database of statistics. (make) (6) Similarly, at the Encyclopedia of Life (eol.org), biology researchers _____ the latest information about the Earth's species, with pages for everything from Spanish moss to the "jewelled blenny" fish. (post) (7) Many people _____ the video site YouTube when they need instructions—for example, how to bake bread or how to tie a bow tie. (visit) (8) However, YouTube users often _____ the thousands of useful and fun how-to's on instructables.com. (miss) (9) On this site, projects _____ from the ordinary to the weird and wild. (range) (10) For example, the site _____ instructions not just for baking white bread and tying a standard bow tie, but for capturing wild yeast for sourdough and building a bow tie from tiny lightbulbs. (include) (11) Many other specialized sites _____ advice, information, and assistance to the online public. (offer)

Focus on Writing: *Flashback*

Look back at your response to the Focus on Writing activity on page 395. Choose two sentences that contain present tense verbs, and rewrite them on a sheet of paper. Underline the subject of each sentence once and the verb twice. If the subject and verb of each sentence do not agree, correct them.

23b   Compound Subjects

The subject of a sentence is not always a single word. It can also be a **compound subject**, a subject that consists of two or more words. To avoid subject-verb agreement problems with compound subjects, follow these rules.

- When the parts of a compound subject are connected by *and*, the compound subject takes a plural verb.

                s   v

John and Marsha share an office.

• When the parts of a compound subject are connected by *or*, the verb agrees with the part of the subject that is closer to it.

The mayor or the council members <u>meet</u> with community groups.

The council members or the mayor <u>meets</u> with community groups.

● Practice 23-3

Underline the correct form of the verb in each of the following sentences. Make sure that the verb agrees with its compound subject.

> **Example:** Every summer, wind and rain (<u>pound</u>/pounds) the small shack on the beach.

1. Trophies and medals (fill/fills) my sister's bedroom.

2. Mashed potatoes and gravy (come/comes) with all our chicken dinners.

3. The instructor or his graduate students (grade/grades) the final exams.

4. A voice coach and a piano instructor (teach/teaches) each of the students.

5. Pollen or cat hair (trigger/triggers) allergies in many people.

6. Psychologists or social workers (provide/provides) crisis counseling.

7. Exercise and healthy eating habits (lead/leads) to longer lives.

8. Both parents or only the father (walk/walks) the bride down the aisle.

9. The restaurant owner and his daughters (greet/greets) customers as they enter.

10. Flowers or a get-well balloon (cheer/cheers) people up when they are ill.

Focus on Writing: *Flashback*

Look at the two sentences you wrote for the Flashback activity on page 397. Rewrite them with compound subjects. In each sentence, make sure the compound subject agrees with the verb.

23c   Be, Have, and Do

The verbs *be*, *have*, and *do* are irregular in the present tense. For this reason, they can present problems with subject-verb agreement. Memorizing their forms is the only sure way to avoid such problems.

Subject-Verb Agreement with *Be*

	Singular	Plural
First person	I am	we are
Second person	you are	you are
Third person	he/she/it is	they are
	Tran is	Tran and Ryan are
	the boy is	the boys are

Subject-Verb Agreement with *Have*

	Singular	Plural
First person	I have	we have
Second person	you have	you have
Third person	he/she/it has	they have
	Shana has	Shana and Robert have
	the student has	the students have

Subject-Verb Agreement with *Do*

	Singular	Plural
First person	I do	we do
Second person	you do	you do
Third person	he/she/it does	they do
	Ken does	Ken and Mia do
	the book does	the books do

● **Practice 23-4**

Fill in the blank with the correct present tense form of the verb *be*, *have*, or *do*.

Example: Sometimes, people __*do*__ damage without really meaning to. (do)

(1) Biologists _____ serious worries about the damage that invading species of animals can cause. (have) (2) The English sparrow _____ one example. (be) (3) It _____ a role in the decline in the number of bluebirds. (have) (4) On the Galapagos Islands, cats _____ another example. (be) (5) Introduced by early explorers, they currently _____ much damage to the eggs of the giant tortoises that live on the islands. (do) (6) Scientists today _____ worried about a new problem. (be) (7) This _____ a situation caused by wildlife agencies that put exotic fish into lakes and streams. (be) (8) They _____ this to please those who enjoy fishing. (do) (9) Although popular with people who fish, this policy _____ major drawbacks. (have) (10) It _____ one drawback in particular: many species of fish have been pushed close to extinction. (have)

Focus on Writing: *Flashback*

Look back at your response to the Focus on Writing activity on page 395. Have you used a form of *be*, *have*, or *do* in any of your sentences? If so, have you used the correct forms of *be*, *have*, and *do*? Correct any agreement errors you find.

23d   Words between Subject and Verb

Remember, a verb must always agree with its subject. Don't be confused when a group of words (for example, a prepositional phrase) comes between the subject and the verb. These words do not affect subject-verb agreement.

                                    S   V
Correct   High levels of mercury occur in some fish.

                              S   V
Correct   Water in the fuel lines causes an engine to stall.

                             S   V
Correct   Food between the teeth results in decay.

An easy way to identify the subject of the sentence is to cross out the words that come between the subject and the verb.

High levels ~~of mercury~~ occur in some fish.

Water ~~in the fuel lines~~ causes an engine to stall.

Food ~~between the teeth~~ results in decay.

Highlight: Words between Subject and Verb

Look out for words and phrases such as *in addition to*, *along with*, *together with*, *as well as*, *except*, and *including*. When they come between the subject and the verb, phrases introduced by these expressions do not affect subject-verb agreement.

                      S   V
St. Thomas, ~~along with St. Croix and St. John,~~ is part of the United States Virgin Islands.

● **Practice 23-5**

In each of the following sentences, cross out the words that separate the subject and the verb. Then, underline the subject of the sentence once and the verb that agrees with the subject twice.

Example: The apartments ~~on the top floor~~ (cost / costs) the most money.

1. The roses along the side of the house (bloom / blooms) all summer long.

2. Workers in the city (pay / pays) a high wage tax.

3. The tools in my garage (belong / belongs) to a friend.

4. Refrigerators, especially those with the freezer on one side, (use / uses) most of the energy in a typical home.

5. A tropical storm with heavy rain and strong winds (move / moves) quickly.

6. Approximately one out of every four high school students (drop / drops) out before graduation.

7. Workers with a college degree (earn / earns) more money than those without a degree.

8. The president of the company (get / gets) a large bonus.

9. Vegetarians, especially those who do not eat eggs or cheese, (need / needs) to be careful to get enough vitamins in their diets.

10. A doctor, along with two nurses, (staff / staffs) the neighborhood clinic.

Focus on Writing: *Flashback*

Look back at your response to the Focus on Writing activity on page 395. Can you find any sentences in which a prepositional phrase comes between the subject and the verb? If so, cross out the prepositional phrase, and then correct any subject-verb agreement errors you find.

23e   Collective Noun Subjects

Collective nouns are words (like *family* and *audience*) that name a group of people or things. These words are usually singular and take singular verbs.

$$\overset{\text{S}}{\underline{}} \quad \overset{\text{V}}{\underline{}}$$

The <u>team</u> <u>practices</u> five days a week in the gym.

Frequently Used Collective Nouns

army	club	corporation	group
association	committee	family	jury
band	company	gang	team
class	congregation	government	union

● Practice 23-6

Fill in the blank with the correct present tense form of the verb.

> **Example:** Our government __*is*__ democratically elected by the
> people. (be)

1. The Caribbean Culture Club _____ on the first Thursday of every
   month. (meet)

2. The company no longer _____ health insurance for part-time
   employees. (provide)

3. The basketball team _____ competing in the division finals next
   week. (be)

4. After two days, the jury _____ been unable to reach a verdict.
   (have)

5. The union _____ its members to have guaranteed salary
   increases. (want)

Focus on Writing: *Flashback*

Look back at your response to the Focus on Writing activity on page
395. Can you find any sentences that have collective nouns as subjects?
If so, check carefully to make sure the subjects and verbs agree. If they
do not, revise any incorrect sentences.

23f   Indefinite Pronoun Subjects

Indefinite pronouns—*anybody*, *everyone*, and so on—do not refer to a
particular person, place, or idea.

   Most indefinite pronouns are singular and take singular verbs.

>   S   V
> No one likes getting up early.

>   S   V
> Everyone likes to sleep late.

>   S   V
> Somebody likes beets.

Singular Indefinite Pronouns

another	either	neither	one
anybody	everybody	nobody	somebody
anyone	everyone	no one	someone
anything	everything	nothing	something
each	much		

A few indefinite pronouns (*both, many, several, few, others*) are plural and take plural verbs.

S V
Many were left homeless by the storm.

Highlight: Indefinite Pronouns as Subjects	If a prepositional phrase comes between the indefinite pronoun and the verb, crossing out the prepositional phrase will help you identify the sentence's subject.

S   V
Each ~~of the boys~~ has a bike.

S   V
Many ~~of the boys~~ have bikes.

● **Practice 23-7**

Underline the correct verb in each sentence.

Example: As my friends and I know, anything (helps / help) when it comes to paying for college.

1. One of my friends (has / have) an academic scholarship.

2. Another (relies / rely) entirely on loans.

3. Several of us (works / work) on weekends.

4. Everybody (says / say) that work-study jobs are best.

5. Many of the most interesting work-study jobs (is / are) located on campus.

6. Others (places / place) students off campus with nonprofits or government agencies.

Focus on Writing: *Flashback*

Look back at your response to the Focus on Writing activity on page 395. Do any of the sentences contain indefinite pronoun subjects? Do the verbs in these sentences agree with the indefinite pronoun subjects? If you find any that do not, rewrite the sentences.

7. Some of the work-study jobs available (tends / tend) to be better than a regular job.

8. Not everyone (understands / understand) the demands of school, but work-study employers do.

9. Nobody (says / say) juggling work and school is simple, but work-study makes it easier.

10. Each of my work-study friends (is / are) glad to have this option.

23g   Verbs before Subjects

A verb always agrees with its subject—even if the verb comes *before* the subject. In questions, for example, word order is reversed, with the verb coming before the subject or with the subject coming between two parts of the verb.

>   V   S
> Where is the bank?

> V   S   V
> Are you going to the party?

If you have trouble identifying the subject of a question, answer the question with a statement.

>   V   S   S V
> Where is the bank? The bank is on Walnut Street.

> **Highlight:**
> ***There Is* and**
> ***There Are***
>
> When a sentence begins with *there is* or *there are*, the word *there* can never be the subject of the sentence. The subject comes after the form of the verb *be*.
>
>   V   S
> There is one chief justice on the Supreme Court.
>
>   V   S
> There are nine justices on the Supreme Court.

● Practice 23-8

Underline the subject of each sentence, and circle the correct form of the verb.

Example: Who (is / are) the writer who won the 2007 Nobel Prize in Literature?

1. Where (is / are) the Bering Strait?
2. Why (do / does) the compound change color when it is exposed to light?
3. (Is / Are) the twins identical or fraternal?
4. How (do / does) Congress override a presidential veto?
5. What (have / has) this got to do with me?
6. There (is / are) only one working computer in the writing center.
7. There (is / are) more than nine million people living in Mexico City.
8. There (is / are) several reference books in this library that can help you with your research.
9. There (is / are) four reasons why we should save the spotted owl from extinction.
10. There (is / are) more than one way to answer the question.

Focus on Writing: *Flashback*

Look back at your response to the Focus on Writing activity on page 395. Do you have any sentences in which the verb comes before the subject? If so, check carefully to make sure the subjects and verbs agree. Revise any incorrect sentences you find.

Focus on Writing: *Revising and Editing*

Look back at your response to the Focus on Writing activity on page 395. **TEST** what you have written. Then, revise and edit your work, checking to make sure all your verbs agree with their subjects. (Don't forget to incorporate the changes and corrections you made in this chapter's Flashback activities.)

Chapter Review

Editing Practice: Paragraph

Read the following student paragraph, which includes errors in subject-verb agreement. Decide whether each of the underlined verbs agrees with its subject. If it does not, cross out the verb, and write in the correct form. If it does, write *C* above the verb. The first sentence has been done for you.

Popular Dogs' Names

reflect
Dogs' names reflects how humans view their canine companions.
C   *see*
Many owners give their dogs human names, perhaps because they sees
them as friends or children instead of pets. Toby, Jake, Max, Charlie,
and Oscar is among the most popular names for male dogs. Popular
names for female dogs includes Maggie, Lucy, Sophie , Holly, and Zoe.
Some owners name their dogs for a physical or personality trait, maybe
because they admires the special characteristic. For example, a dark
coat inspires the popular name Shadow, while a strong, rough-and-
tumble dog get the name Rocky. Likewise, although Fido (Latin for
"faithfulness") no longer make the list of top-50 dog names, some loyal
dogs earn the name Buddy. Owners of small dogs often considers their
dogs cute and sweet, even when the dogs is high-strung and unfriendly.
As a result, the common names Baby, Missy, Sugar, and Angel
sometimes says more about the owner than about the dog. Whether or
not a dog lives up to its name, human owners reveals something about
themselves when they name their dogs.

Editing Practice: Essay

Read the following student essay, which includes errors in subject-verb agreement. Decide whether each of the underlined verbs agrees with its subject. If it does not, cross out the verb, and write in the correct form. If it does, write *C* above the verb. The first sentence has been done for you.

Party in the Parking Lot

Fun at football games *is* <u>are</u> not limited to cheering for the home team. Many people <u>arrives</u> four or five hours early, <u>sets</u> up grills in the parking lot, and <u>start</u> cooking. Typically, fans <u>drives</u> to the stadium in a pickup truck, a station wagon, or an SUV. They <u>open</u> up the tailgate, <u>puts</u> out the food, and <u>enjoys</u> the atmosphere with their friends. In fact, tailgating <u>is</u> so popular that, for some fans, it's more fun than the game itself.

What <u>do</u> it take to tailgate? First, most tailgaters <u>plan</u> their menus in advance. To avoid forgetting anything, they <u>makes</u> lists of what to bring. Disposable paper plates, along with a set of plastic cups, <u>make</u> it unnecessary to bring home dirty dishes. Jugs of water <u>is</u> essential, and damp towels <u>helps</u> clean up hands and faces. Also, lightweight chairs or another type of seating <u>is</u> important.

At the game, parking near a grassy area or at the end of a parking row <u>are</u> best. This strategy <u>give</u> tailgaters more space to cook and eat. If the food <u>are</u> ready two hours before the game <u>start</u>, there <u>is</u> plenty of time to put out the fire in the grill and to clean up.

Some tailgaters <u>buys</u> expensive equipment. The simple charcoal grill <u>have</u> turned into a combination grill, cooler, and fold-out table with a portable awning. There <u>is</u> grills with their own storage space. Other grills <u>swings</u> out from the tailgate to provide access to the vehicle's storage area. Some deluxe grills even <u>has</u> their own beer taps, stereo systems, and sinks.

Whatever equipment tailgaters <u>brings</u> to the game, the most important things <u>is</u> food and companionship. There <u>is</u> a tradition of sharing food and swapping recipes with other tailgaters. Most tailgaters <u>loves</u> to meet and <u>compares</u> notes on recipes. For many, the tailgating experience <u>is</u> as important as the game itself.

Collaborative Activities

1. Working in a group of four students, list ten nouns (five singular and five plural) — people, places, or things — on the left-hand side of a sheet of paper. Beside each noun, write the present tense form of a verb that could logically be used with the noun. Exchange papers with another group, and check to see that singular nouns have singular verbs and plural nouns have plural verbs.

2. Working with your group, expand each noun-and-verb combination you listed in Collaborative Activity 1 into a complete sentence. Next, write a sentence that could logically follow each of these sentences, using a pronoun as the subject of the new sentence. Make sure the pronoun you choose refers to the noun in the previous sentence, as in this example: *Alan watches three movies a week. He is addicted to films.* Check to be certain the subjects in your sentences agree with the verbs.

3. Exchange the final version of your edited Focus on Writing activity with another student in your group. Answer the following questions about each sentence in your partner's work:

   ● Does the sentence contain a compound subject?
   ● Does the sentence contain words that come between the subject and the verb?
   ● Does the sentence contain an indefinite pronoun used as a subject?
   ● Does the sentence contain a verb that comes before the subject?

As you answer these questions, check to make sure all the verbs agree with their subjects. When your own work is returned to you, make any necessary corrections.

Review Checklist: Subject-Verb Agreement

☐ Singular subjects (nouns and pronouns) take singular verbs, and plural subjects take plural verbs. (See 23A.)

☐ Special rules govern subject-verb agreement with compound subjects. (See 23B.)

☐ The irregular verbs *be, have,* and *do* often present problems with subject-verb agreement in the present tense. (See 23C.)

☐ Words that come between the subject and the verb do not affect subject-verb agreement. (See 23D.)

☐ Collective nouns are usually singular and take singular verbs. (See 23E.)

☐ Most indefinite pronouns, such as *no one* and *everyone*, are singular and take singular verbs. A few are plural and take plural verbs. (See 23F.)

☐ A sentence's subject and verb must always agree, even if the verb comes before the subject. (See 23G.)

A **shift** occurs whenever a writer changes **tense**, **person**, or **voice**. As you write and revise, be sure that any shifts you make are **logical**—that is, that they occur for a reason.

24a

Shifts in Tense

Tense is the form a verb takes to show when an action takes place or when a situation occurs. Some shifts in tense are necessary—for example, to indicate a change from past time to present time.

Logical shift	When they first came out, cell phones were large and bulky, but now they are small and compact.

An **illogical shift in tense** occurs when a writer shifts from one tense to another for no apparent reason.

Illogical shift in tense	The dog walked to the fireplace. Then, he circles twice and lies down in front of the fire. (shift from past tense to present tense)
Revised	The dog walked to the fireplace. Then, he circled twice and lay down in front of the fire. (consistent use of past tense)
Revised	The dog walks to the fireplace. Then, he circles twice and lies down in front of the fire. (consistent use of present tense)

Focus on Writing

The picture on the opposite page shows a mansion in Florida. Look at the picture, and then write a paragraph (or an essay) that describes your dream house. Would it resemble the house in the picture, or would it be different? What would be inside the house? Be as specific as possible.

● Practice 24-1

Edit the following sentences to correct illogical shifts in tense. If a sentence is correct, write *C* in the blank.

Examples:

During World War II, the 100th Battalion of the 442nd Combat Infantry Regiment was made up of young Japanese Americans who are *were* eager to serve in the U.S. Army. _____

The 100th Battalion of the 442nd Infantry is the only remaining United States Army Reserve ground combat unit that fought in World War II.
  C
_____

(1) At the start of World War II, 120,000 Japanese Americans are sent to relocation camps because the government feared that they might be disloyal to the United States. _____ (2) However, in 1943, the United States needed more soldiers, so it sends recruiters to the camps to ask for volunteers. _____ (3) The Japanese-American volunteers are organized into the 442nd Combat Infantry Regiment. _____ (4) The soldiers of the 442nd Infantry fought in some of the bloodiest battles of the war, including the invasion of Italy at Anzio and a battle in Bruyeres, France, where they capture over two hundred enemy soldiers. _____ (5) When other U.S. troops are cut off by the enemy, the 442nd Infantry soldiers were sent to rescue them. _____ (6) The Japanese-American soldiers suffered the highest casualty rate of any U.S. unit and receive over eighteen thousand individual decorations. _____ (7) Former senator Daniel Inouye of Hawaii, a Japanese American, who was awarded the Distinguished Service Cross for his bravery in Italy, has to have his arm amputated. _____ (8) The 442nd Infantry received more decorations than any other combat unit of its size and earns eight Presidential Unit citations. _____ (9) Today, the dedication and sacrifice of the 442nd Infantry was evidence that Japanese Americans were patriotic and committed to freedom and democracy. _____ (10) The bravery

of the 442nd Infantry during World War II paved the way for today's desegregated American military. _____

Focus on Writing: *Flashback*

Look back at your response to the Focus on Writing activity on page 411. Check each sentence to make sure it includes no illogical shifts from one tense to another. If you find an error, correct it.

24b   Shifts in Person

Person is the form a pronoun takes to show who is speaking, spoken about, or spoken to.

Person

	Singular	Plural
First person	I	we
Second person	you	you
Third person	he, she, it	they

An **illogical shift in person** occurs when a writer shifts from one person to another for no apparent reason.

Illogical shift in person	The hikers were told that you had to stay on the trail. (shift from third person to second person)
Revised	The hikers were told that they had to stay on the trail. (consistent use of third person)
Illogical shift	Anyone can learn to cook if you practice. (shift from third person to second person)
Revised	You can learn to cook if you practice. (consistent use of second person)

Revised   Anyone can learn to cook if <u>he or she</u> practices. (consistent use of third person)

● Practice 24-2

The sentences in the following paragraph contain illogical shifts. Edit each sentence so that it uses pronouns consistently. Be sure to change any verbs that do not agree with the new subjects.

Example: Before a person can find a job in the fashion industry,
he or she has
~~you~~ have to have some experience.

(1) Young people who want careers in the fashion industry do not always realize how hard you will have to work. (2) They think that working in the world of fashion will be glamorous and that you will quickly make a fortune. (3) In reality, no matter how talented you are, a recent college graduate entering the industry is paid less than $30,000 a year. (4) The manufacturers who employ new graduates expect you to work for three years or more at this salary before you are promoted. (5) A young designer may receive a big raise if you are very talented, but this is unusual. (6) New employees have to pay their dues, and you soon realize that most of your duties are boring. (7) An employee may be excited to land a job as an assistant designer but then find that you have to color in designs that have already been drawn. (8) Other beginners discover that you spend most of your time sewing or typing up orders. (9) If a person is serious about working in the fashion industry, you have to be realistic. (10) For most newcomers to the industry, the ability to do what you are told to do is more important than your artistic talent.

Focus on Writing: *Flashback*

Look back at your response to the Focus on Writing activity on page 411. Check each sentence to make sure it includes no illogical shifts in person. If you find an error, correct it.

24c   Shifts in Voice

Voice is the form a verb takes to indicate whether the subject is acting or is acted upon. When the subject of a sentence is acting, the sentence is in the **active voice**. When the subject of a sentence is acted upon, the sentence is in the **passive voice**.

Active voice	Nat Turner organized a slave rebellion in August 1831. (Subject *Nat Turner* is acting.)
Passive voice	A slave rebellion was organized by Nat Turner in 1831. (Subject *rebellion* is acted upon.)

An **illogical shift in voice** occurs when a writer shifts from active to passive voice or from passive to active voice for no apparent reason.

Illogical shift in voice	J. D. Salinger wrote *The Catcher in the Rye*, and *Franny and Zooey* was also written by him. (active to passive)
Revised	J. D. Salinger wrote *The Catcher in the Rye*, and he also wrote *Franny and Zooey*. (consistent use of active voice)
Illogical shift in voice	Radium was discovered by Marie Curie in 1910, and she won a Nobel Prize in chemistry in 1911. (passive to active)
Revised	Marie Curie discovered radium in 1910, and she won a Nobel Prize in chemistry in 1911. (consistent use of active voice)

Highlight: Changing from Passive to Active Voice	You should generally use the active voice in your college writing because it is stronger and more direct than the passive voice. To change a sentence from the passive to the active voice, determine who or what is acting, and make this noun the subject of the new active voice sentence.

Passive voice	The campus escort service is used by my friends. (*My friends* are acting.)
Active voice	My friends use the campus escort service.

● Practice 24-3

The following sentences contain illogical shifts in voice. Revise each sentence by changing the underlined passive-voice verb to the active voice.

Example:

Several researchers are interested in leadership qualities, so a study of decision making <u>was conducted</u> by them.

Several researchers are interested in leadership qualities, *so they* *conducted a study of decision making.*

1. A local university funded the study, and the research team <u>was led</u> by Dr. Alicia Flynn.

   A local university funded the study, _____

   _____

2. The researchers developed a series of questions about decision making, and then one hundred subjects <u>were interviewed</u> by them.

   The researchers developed a series of questions about decision making,

   _____

3. Intuition <u>was relied on</u> by two-thirds of the subjects, and only one-third used logic.

   _____, and only one-third

   used logic.

4. After the researchers completed the study, a report <u>was written</u> about their findings.

   After the researchers completed the study, _____

   _____

5. The report <u>was read</u> by many experts, and most of them found the results surprising.

   _____, and most

   of them found the results surprising.

Focus on Writing: *Flashback*

Look back at your response to the Focus on Writing activity on page 411. Check each sentence to make sure it includes no illogical shifts in voice. If you find an error, correct it.

Focus on Writing: *Revising and Editing*

Look back at your response to the Focus on Writing activity on page 411. **TEST** what you have written. Then, revise and edit, paying particular attention to any illogical shifts in tense, person, or voice. (Don't forget to incorporate the changes and corrections you made in this chapter's Flashback activities.)

Chapter Review

Editing Practice: Paragraph

Read the following student paragraph, which includes illogical shifts in tense, person, and voice. Edit the passage to eliminate the unnecessary shifts, making sure subjects and verbs agree. The first error has been corrected for you.

The Origin of Baseball Cards

The first baseball cards appeared in the late 1800s. These cardboard

pictures ~~are~~ *were* inserted in packs of cigarettes. Some people collected the

cards, and the cigarette companies use the cards to encourage people to

buy their products. By the early twentieth century, it was found by candy

makers that they could use baseball cards to sell candy to children, so

they developed new marketing plans. For example, each Cracker Jack box

contains a baseball card. In 1933, gum manufacturers packaged bubble gum with baseball cards to make "bubble gum cards." Children could trade these cards. Sometimes, children would put cards in the spokes of their bike wheels. The cards made noise when the wheels turns. Eventually, the bubble gum is dropped by the card manufacturers, and people just collected the cards. Still, collecting baseball cards was seen as just a hobby for children until the 1970s, when dealers began to sell their rarest cards at high prices. Today, baseball-card collectors were mainly adults who are interested in investment, not baseball. For example, in 2007, a rare Honus Wagner baseball card sells for a record 2.6 million dollars.

Editing Practice: Essay

Read the following essay, which includes illogical shifts in tense, person, and voice. Edit the passage to eliminate the illogical shifts, making sure subjects and verbs agree. The first sentence has been edited for you.

A Different Kind of Vacation

During our upcoming winter break, my sister and I ~~were~~ are going to Belize to help build a school. Like many people, we want to travel and see new places, but we did not want to be tourists who only see what is in a guidebook. We also want to help people who are less fortunate than we were. Volunteering gives us the opportunity to combine travel with community service and to get to know a different culture at the same time.

These days, many people are using his or her vacation time to do volunteer work. Lots of charitable organizations offer short-term projects that coincide with school or holiday breaks. For most projects, no particular experience was necessary. All people need is his or her interest in other people and a desire to help.

For example, last year my aunt goes to Tanzania to work in a health clinic. She loved her experience volunteering in a poor rural community where you help local doctors. She also loved the generous host family who shared their modest house with her. Before she left Tanzania, she and some of the other volunteers climb Mount Kilimanjaro. She said it was the best vacation she had ever had.

Although many volunteer vacations focus on improving schools or health care, a wide range of projects was available. Everyone can find work that suits their interests. For instance, people can volunteer to help conserve the environment, or you can work to protect women's rights. Countries all over the world welcome volunteers because help is needed by a lot of people.

My sister and I decided to help with the school in Belize because we believe a clean and safe place to learn is deserved by everyone. We are also eager to do some construction, get to know the local people, and enjoy the warm weather. If we have enough time, we hoped to visit some Mayan ruins as well. All in all, we are looking forward to a rewarding and unforgettable experience.

Collaborative Activities

1. Write five sentences that include shifts from present to past tense, some logical and some illogical. Exchange sentences with another student, and revise any errors you find.

2. As a group, make up a test with five sentences containing illogical shifts in tense, person, and voice. Exchange tests with another group in the class. After you have taken their test, compare your answers with theirs.

Review Checklist: Illogical Shifts

☐ An illogical shift in tense occurs when a writer shifts from one tense to another for no apparent reason. (See 24A.)

☐ An illogical shift in person occurs when a writer shifts from one person to another for no apparent reason. (See 24B.)

☐ An illogical shift in voice occurs when a writer shifts from active to passive voice or from passive to active voice for no apparent reason. (See 24C.)

Harrietts Tomato: - Mozilla Firefox

File Edit View History Bookmarks Tools Help

http://harriettstomato.typepad.com/foodlog/2005/05/index.html

Google

Harriett's Tomato

...all food, all the time

Main | June 2005 »

OCTOBER 2009

Sun	Mon	Tue	Wed	Thu	Fri	Sat
				1	2	3
4	5	6	7	8	9	10
11	12	13	14	15	16	17
18	19	20	21	22	23	24
25	26	27	28	29	30	31

Kitchen feeling bland? Try spicing up your kitchenware with bold colored plates and fun patterns!

Subscribe to this blog's feed

SUBSCRIBE WITH WIKIO

Subscribe With Wikio

Subscribe

Add me to your TypePad People list

RECENT POSTS

Would A Couple Tons of Hummus Take Care of Your Craving...

Denver's WESTWORD Piece About Antarctic Bloggers

Sunrise Dinner at the South Pole

William Thackeray on Food

Yodelling Pickle

Inevitable: Operatic Recipes

Lady Mary Wortley Montagu on Food

MONDAY, MAY 30, 2005

Beet, New Potato and Feta Salad

BEET, NEW POTATO AND FETA SALAD

serves 6

1 pound new potatoes, red or white
1/2 red onion, finely chopped
1/2 pound crumbly feta cheese
1/2 bunch Italian parsley, finely chopped

vinaigrette:
1 tablespoon dijon mustard
1/4 cup red wine or sherry vinegar
1/2 cup olive oil
salt and freshly ground pepper to taste

Cut beets from their greens and rinse off. Steam the beets in their skins. If some are really bigger than others, take them out as they cook. Cook them until still crunchy inside, about 25 or 30 minutes for a medium to large beet. Alternatively, you can roast them, covered in foil, about an hour for medium beets at 400 F, with a little olive oil, salt and pepper, thyme sprigs and a little water. Let cool completely to room temperature and peel off skins. They should come off easily.

ABOUT

Email Me

PUBLISHED WRITING & PHOTOGRAPHY

Wall Street Journal

Nation's Restaurant News

Christian Science Monitor

Public Radio: Here On Earth

New York Times T:Living

New York Times: T-Living

FOOD VIDEOS WITH H.TOMATO

potato galette

stovetop espresso

A **modifier** is a word or word group that **modifies** (identifies or describes) another word in a sentence. To avoid confusion, a modifier should be placed as close as possible to the word it modifies—ideally, directly before or directly after it.

Correcting Dangling Modifiers

A **dangling modifier** "dangles" because the word it is supposed to modify does not appear in the sentence. Often, a dangling modifier comes at the beginning of a sentence and seems to modify the noun or pronoun that follows it.

Using my computer, the report was finished in two days.

In the sentence above, the modifier *Using my computer* seems to be modifying *the report*. But this makes no sense. (How can the report use a computer?) The word the modifier should logically modify is missing. To correct this sentence, you need to supply the missing word.

Using my computer, I finished the report in two days.

To correct a dangling modifier, supply the noun or pronoun that the dangling modifier should actually modify.

Incorrect   Moving the microscope's mirror, the light can be directed onto the slide. (Did the light move the mirror?)

Correct   Moving the microscope's mirror, you can direct the light onto the slide.

Focus on Writing

On the opposite page is a recipe that appeared on a food blog. Read this recipe, and then write a recipe of your own. Begin by discussing the dish to be prepared; then, list the ingredients; and finally, explain how to prepare the dish.

Incorrect   Paid in advance, the furniture was delivered. (Was the furniture paid in advance?)

Correct   Paid in advance, the movers delivered the furniture.

● Practice 25-1

Each of the following sentences contains a dangling modifier. To correct each sentence, add a noun or pronoun that the modifier can logically identify or describe.

Example: Waiting inside, my bus passed by.

Waiting inside, I missed my bus.

1. Paid by the school, the books were sorted in the library.

   _____

2. Pushing on the brakes, my car would not stop for the red light.

   _____

3. Lacking money, my trip was canceled.

   _____

4. Working overtime, his salary almost doubled.

   _____

5. Angered by the noise, the concert was called off.

   _____

6. Using the correct formula, the problem was easily solved.

   _____

7. Exhausted and hungry, the assignment was finished by midnight.

   _____

8. Jogging through the park, the pigeons were fed.

   _____

9. Staying in bed on Sunday, the newspaper was read from beginning to end.

   _____

10. Driving for a long time, my leg began to hurt.

   _____

● **Practice 25-2**

Complete the following sentences, making sure to include a noun or pronoun that each modifier can logically identify or describe.

Example: Dancing with the man of her dreams, *she decided that it*
was time to wake up.

1. Begging for forgiveness, _____

2. Soaked by the rain, _____

3. Seeing a strange light in the sky, _____

4. Running down the steps at midnight, _____

5. Alerted by a sound from outside, _____

6. Sent to fight in a foreign land, _____

7. Swinging from the chandelier, _____

8. Disgusted by the horrible meal, _____

9. Wanting desperately to go to the concert, _____

10. Distrusting the advice he got from his friends, _____

Focus on Writing: *Flashback*

Look back at your response to the Focus on Writing activity on page 421. Do any of your sentences contain dangling modifiers? Rewrite any sentence that contains a dangling modifier, making sure to include a word that the modifier can logically identify or describe.

25b   Correcting Misplaced Modifiers

A modifier should be placed as close as possible to the word it modifies. A **misplaced modifier** is a modifier that appears to modify the wrong word because it is placed incorrectly in the sentence. To correct this problem, move the modifier so it is as close as possible to the word it is supposed to modify (usually directly before or after it).

Incorrect	Sarah fed the dog wearing her pajamas. (Was the dog wearing Sarah's pajamas?)
Correct	Wearing her pajamas, Sarah fed the dog.
Incorrect	Dressed in a raincoat and boots, I thought my son was prepared for the storm. (Who was dressed in a raincoat and boots?)
Correct	I thought my son, dressed in a raincoat and boots, was prepared for the storm.
Incorrect	At the wedding, she danced with the groom in a beautiful white gown. (Was the groom wearing a white gown?)
Correct	At the wedding, she danced in a beautiful white gown with the groom.

● Practice 25-3

Rewrite the following sentences, which contain misplaced modifiers, so that each modifier clearly refers to the word it should actually modify.

Example: I tried to remember my password sitting at the computer.

Sitting at the computer, I tried to remember my password.

1. My brother was surprised to see a bear driving to work on Interstate 5.

   _____

2. I saw the dark shape approach frozen with fear.

   _____

3. Tagged with metal bracelets, the volunteers easily identified the hawks.

   _____

4. My sister found a job with a degree in electrical engineering.

   _____

5. Molly went outside to look for her dog wearing her warmest coat.

   _____

6. Powered by a 250-watt battery, Oscar rides to school on a bike.

   _____

7. The brick house is still on the market at the corner of Huron and Willow.

   _____

8. Sammy auditioned for the role of King Lear hoping to be chosen.

   _____

9. Yelling from the stands, the Detroit Tigers were cheered on by fans.

   _____

10. The contestant won the competition with the loudest voice.

    _____

Focus on Writing: *Flashback*

Look back at your response to the Focus on Writing activity on page 421. Does any sentence contain a misplaced modifier? Rewrite any such sentence by placing the modifier as close as possible to the word it should actually modify.

Focus on Writing: *Revising and Editing*

Look back at your response to the Focus on Writing activity on page 421. **TEST** what you have written. Then, revise and edit your work, paying particular attention to modifiers.

Editing Practice: Paragraph

Read the following paragraph. Rewrite sentences to correct dangling and misplaced modifiers. In some cases, you may have to supply a noun or pronoun that the modifier can logically identify or describe. The first incorrect sentence has been corrected for you.

Wyclef Jean: Musician and Humanitarian

Known for hip-hop, rap, reggae, and folk,
Wyclef Jean is a musician with diverse interests and talents ~~known for hip-hop, rap, reggae, and folk.~~ Born in Haiti in 1972, Jean's family moved to the United States when he was nine. Here, he started his musical career as a member of the Fugees. With musicians Lauryn Hill and Pras Michel, the hip-hop group was formed in 1994. However, after selling millions of albums, a split-up occurred a few years later. Choosing to collaborate with many different artists, a successful solo career was launched. Some of his music reflects his Haitian roots. For example, on his 2004 album *Sak Pasé Presents: Welcome to Haiti (Creole 101)*, Jean sings primarily in Haitian Creole. Although best known for his work as a musician and a producer, humanitarian work in his native country also keeps him busy. In 2004, Jean created the Yéle Haiti Foundation. Dedicated to Haiti's development, scholarships and food are just two of the benefits the foundation provides. Altogether, Wyclef Jean's many accomplishments are remarkable. In addition to creating Grammy Award–winning music, he acts as a Goodwill Ambassador to Haiti and helped raise money for relief efforts after the 2010 earthquake.

Editing Practice: Essay

Read the following student essay, which contains modification errors. Rewrite sentences to correct dangling and misplaced modifiers. In some cases, you may have to supply a noun or pronoun that the modifier can logically identify or describe. The first incorrect sentence has been corrected for you.

Dumb Laws

Did you know ~~in Los Angeles~~ that it is illegal to lick a toad? Many *in Los Angeles*
cities and states have surprisingly "dumb laws" on their books in
America. Some laws are simply out of date and are no longer enforced.
Other "dumb laws" prohibit behavior that probably happened once
but is unlikely to happen again, describing very specific and peculiar
circumstances. Forbidding behavior that is either impossible to control
or pointless to regulate, there are still other "dumb laws" that are simply
laughable. Whether we ignore them or appreciate their absurdity, "dumb
laws" seem to be a fact of life.

One of the most common types of outdated law is the Sunday law.
Written before it was common to do business seven days a week, most
states forbid certain activities on Sunday. For example, playing dominoes
on Sunday is illegal in Alabama. In Washington, a person can be arrested
by authorities buying meat or a mattress.

Other laws have stories to tell. Carrying a sloshing fishbowl onto
a bus, an irritated Seattle passenger must have complained because
now the city forbids fishbowls on buses. In Texas, unhampered by law, a
buffalo was shot from the second story of a hotel. Now, it is illegal to do
this. In Louisiana, there are limits on the uses of toy guns; as a result of
someone's prank, a person is forbidden from shooting a bank teller with a
water pistol robbing a bank.

Trying to control some kinds of behavior, failure is certain. For
instance, the city of Los Angeles prohibits crying on the witness stand,
but holding back tears is not always possible. Los Angeles residents
also risk arrest by police bathing two babies in the same tub at the same
time. However, enforcing this law would be as ridiculous and impractical
as enforcing the Oregon law requiring residents to drip-dry their dishes.

"Dumb laws" are everywhere. Hearing about these bizarre regulations,
the wisdom of lawmakers might be questioned. However, it is better to go

easy on legislators, recognizing how slow and complicated the process of lawmaking is. Eventually, the silliest laws will be removed. In the meantime, if you are ever in Canton, Ohio, and you lose your pet tiger, be sure to notify the police within one hour.

Collaborative Activities

1. Working in a group of three or four students, make a list of five modifiers. Exchange your list with another group, and complete one another's sentences.

   Example:

   Typing as fast as he could, *John could not wait to finish his screenplay.*

2. Working in a team of three students, compete with other teams to compose sentences that contain outrageous and confusing dangling or misplaced modifiers. As a class, correct the sentences. Then, vote on which group wrote the best sentences.

3. In a group of four or five students, find examples of confusing dangling and misplaced modifiers in magazines and newspapers. Rewrite the sentences, making sure each modifier is placed as close as possible to the word it describes.

Review Checklist: Dangling and Misplaced Modifiers

☐ A modifier is a word or word group that identifies or describes another word in a sentence. Modifiers should be placed near the words they modify.

☐ Correct a dangling modifier by supplying the noun or pronoun that the dangling modifier can logically identify or describe. (See 25A.)

☐ Correct a misplaced modifier by moving the modifier as close as possible to the word it should actually modify. (See 25B.)

Editing Practice: Sentences

Read the following sentences, which contain run-ons, sentence fragments, errors in subject-verb agreement, illogical shifts, and dangling and misplaced modifiers. Identify the errors, and then correct them. Some sentences may have more than one error.

1. Driving up Mt. Washington in winter, the road was closed at 3,500 feet because of huge snowdrifts.

2. Each of the graduates are planning to come to the event.

3. The floor plans for the new house was not impressive. Because the rooms were very small.

4. Public transportation can be cheap and fast, many people prefer to drive their cars to work.

5. There was too many students in my biology class to fit in the room.

6. I couldn't get to class yesterday. The reason being that my car had a flat tire.

7. Anyone who visits a new city should take a bus tour so that you can get a quick view of the most important sights.

8. It is traditional for brides to wear red because it is considered a lucky color. In China and Japan.

9. After a series of questions were asked by the lawyers and the judge. The jury were chosen.

10. A chemistry book lay open on the desk that Michael had read.

Editing Practice: Essay

Read the following student essay, which contains run-ons, sentence fragments, errors in subject-verb agreement, illogical shifts, and dangling and misplaced modifiers. Identify the errors, and then correct them. The first sentence has been edited for you.

New Trends in Street Food

In the past, buying a quick lunch on the street *meant* ~~means~~ getting a hot dog. These days, people in most large American cities enjoys a wide range of street foods. Parking in strategic locations around mealtimes, these foods are sold from carts or trucks. Most items are inexpensive, quick to prepare, and easy to eat, in addition, the food offerings are diverse. Reflecting a city's ethnic make-up. Street food give visitors a convenient way to try new foods and gave residents an easy way to enjoy their own ethnic specialties.

Some of the most common dishes are Mexican prepared in mobile kitchens. Given its large Latino population, it is not surprising that Los Angeles boasted countless "taco trucks." Taco truck vendors offer a variety of hand-held foods. Such as burritos, tamales, tortas, empanadas and, of course, tacos. However, Mexican is by no means the only ethnicity. Customers can also find kebabs. Falafel, noodles, barbecue, panini, sushi, and plenty more. If you are hungry and curious, the streets of Los Angeles is a good place to be.

Several new trends in street food are making eating-on-the-go even more exciting. In Los Angeles, for example, Chinese-Mexican and Korean-Mexican fusion foods are becoming very popular most notable is the Kogi Korean BBQ taco truck. The creators of this mobile business fills corn tortillas with Korean-style barbecued meat, and a variety of Korean and Mexican sauces and accompaniments is added. Another Los Angeles street vendor, Don Chow Tacos, combine Mexican food with Chinese food one of Don Chow's popular inventions are the "chimale," a Chinese-flavored tamale.

In addition to creating exciting new flavor combinations, street-food vendors are now using Twitter to increase its business this trend has caught on quickly. Vendors can communicate with customers via Twitter and let them know where the truck or cart will be. And when it will be there. One big advantage to having a restaurant on wheels is that it can move wherever there are a large number of hungry people. Twitter allows food trucks to move around without customers losing track of it. Twitter offers an additional advantage it helps create hype. Businesses like Kogi Korean BBQ have developed an almost cult-like following among Twitter users. Many other street-food vendors have followed Kogi's lead and good results have been seen by them.

Street food in the United States used to be a strictly local phenomenon with limited offerings. Today, street-food fans have access to a wide variety of cuisines. If someone is looking for new tastes, exciting combinations of ethnic flavors, and lively communities. Street food has much to offer them. Though hot dog carts still have their place, it is nice to know there are other options.

Unit Six

Understanding Basic Grammar

26 Verbs: Past Tense   434

27 Verbs: Past Participles   446

28 Nouns and Pronouns   462

29 Adjectives and Adverbs   488

30 Grammar and Usage for ESL Writers   500

A Star Idolized and Haunted, Michael Jackson Dies at 50

June 26, 2009

Michael Jackson, whose quintessentially American tale of celebrity and excess took him from musical boy wonder to global pop superstar to sad figure haunted by lawsuits, paparazzi and failed plastic surgery, was pronounced dead on Thursday afternoon at U.C.L.A. Medical Center after arriving in a coma, a city official said. Mr. Jackson was 50, having spent 40 of those years in the public eye he loved. . . .

From his days as the youngest brother in the Jackson 5 to his solo career in the 1980s and early 1990s, Mr. Jackson was responsible for a string of hits like . . . "I'll Be There" . . . "Billie Jean" and "Black or White" that exploited his high voice, infectious energy and ear for irresistible hooks.

As a solo performer, Mr. Jackson ushered in the age of pop as a global product — not to mention an age of spectacle and pop culture celebrity. He became more character than singer: his sequined glove, his whitened face, his moonwalk dance move became embedded in the cultural firmament.

His entertainment career hit high-water marks with the release of "Thriller," from 1982 . . . and with the "Victory" world tour that reunited him with his brothers in 1984.

Tense is the form a verb takes to show when an action or situation takes place. The **past tense** indicates that an action occurred in the past.

26a

Regular Verbs

Regular verbs form the past tense by adding either *-ed* or *-d* to the **base form** of the verb (the present tense form of the verb that is used with *I*).

> I <u>registered</u> for classes yesterday.
>
> Walt Disney <u>produced</u> short cartoons in 1928.

Regular verbs that end in *-y* form the past tense by changing the *y* to *i* and adding *-ed*.

tr<u>y</u>	tr<u>ied</u>
appl<u>y</u>	appl<u>ied</u>

● **Practice 26-1**

Change the verbs in the sentences at the top of page 436 to the past tense. Cross out the present tense form of each underlined verb, and write the past tense form above it.

Focus on Writing

The obituary on the opposite page tells about the life of singer Michael Jackson. Read the obituary, and then write your own obituary. As you write, assume that you have led a long life and have achieved almost everything you hoped you would. Be sure to include the accomplishments for which you would most like to be remembered. Remember to use transitional words and phrases that clearly show how one event in your life relates to another. (Refer to yourself by name or by *he* or *she*.)

visited
Example: Every year, my mother ~~visits~~ her family in Bombay, India.
                                              ∧

(1) My mother always <u>returns</u> from India with intricate designs on her hands and feet. (2) In India, women called henna artists <u>create</u> these complex patterns. (3) Henna <u>originates</u> in a plant found in the Middle East, India, Indonesia, and northern Africa. (4) Many women in these areas <u>use</u> henna to color their hands, nails, and parts of their feet. (5) Men <u>dye</u> their beards, as well as the manes and hooves of their horses, with henna. (6) They also <u>color</u> animal skins with henna. (7) In India, my mother always <u>celebrates</u> the end of the Ramadan religious fast by going to a "henna party." (8) A professional henna artist <u>attends</u> the party to apply new henna decorations to the palms and feet of the women. (9) After a few weeks, the henna designs <u>wash</u> off. (10) In the United States, my mother's henna designs <u>attract</u> the attention of many people.

Focus on Writing: *Flashback*

Look back at your response to the Focus on Writing activity on page 435. Underline the past tense verbs that end in *-ed* and *-d*.

26b

Irregular Verbs

Unlike regular verbs, whose past tense forms end in *-ed* or *-d*, **irregular verbs** have irregular forms in the past tense. In fact, their past tense forms may look very different from their present tense forms.

The following chart lists the base form and past tense form of many of the most commonly used irregular verbs.

Irregular Verbs in the Past Tense

Base Form	Past	Base Form	Past
awake	awoke	hold	held
be	was, were	hurt	hurt
beat	beat	keep	kept
become	became	know	knew
begin	began	lay (to place)	laid
bet	bet	lead	led
bite	bit	leave	left
blow	blew	let	let
break	broke	lie (to recline)	lay
bring	brought	light	lit
build	built	lose	lost
buy	bought	make	made
catch	caught	meet	met
choose	chose	pay	paid
come	came	quit	quit
cost	cost	read	read
cut	cut	ride	rode
dive	dove (dived)	ring	rang
do	did	rise	rose
draw	drew	run	ran
drink	drank	say	said
drive	drove	see	saw
eat	ate	sell	sold
fall	fell	send	sent
feed	fed	set	set
feel	felt	shake	shook
fight	fought	shine	shone (shined)
find	found	sing	sang
fly	flew	sit	sat
forgive	forgave	sleep	slept
freeze	froze	speak	spoke
get	got	spend	spent
give	gave	spring	sprang
go (goes)	went	stand	stood
grow	grew	steal	stole
have	had	stick	stuck
hear	heard	sting	stung
hide	hid	swear	swore

→

Irregular Verbs in the Past Tense *(continued)*

Base Form	Past	Base Form	Past
swim	swam	throw	threw
take	took	understand	understood
teach	taught	wake	woke
tear	tore	wear	wore
tell	told	win	won
think	thought	write	wrote

● **Practice 26-2**

In the following sentences, fill in the correct past tense form of the irregular verb in parentheses. Use the chart on page 437 and above to help you find the correct irregular verb form. If you do not find a verb on the chart, look it up in the dictionary.

Example: Dr. David Ho and his research team ___*found*___ (find) ways to treat AIDS at a time when many patients were dying of the disease.

(1) David Ho _____ (come) to the United States from Taiwan when he _____ (be) twelve years old. (2) He _____ (know) no English at first, but he _____ (keep) studying hard. (3) He _____ (go) to M.I.T. for one year. (4) Then, he _____ (get) a B.S. in physics from Caltech. (5) Soon, he _____ (become) interested in molecular biology and gene splicing. (6) While studying for his medical degree at the Harvard–M.I.T. School of Medicine, he _____ (see) some of the first cases of AIDS. (7) Dr. Ho _____ (think) that he could fight the disease by strengthening patients' immune systems. (8) He _____ (have) the idea of treating patients in the early stages of the disease with an AIDS "cocktail," which combined several AIDS medications. (9) Because of his work, deaths from AIDS _____ (begin) to decline. (10) In 1996, *Time* magazine _____ (give) Dr. Ho the honor of being named its Man of the Year.

Focus on Writing: *Flashback*

Look back at your response to the Focus on Writing activity on page 435. Circle each irregular past tense verb you find. Then, list all the irregular past tense verbs on a sheet of paper. Beside each past tense verb, write its base form. (If necessary, consult the list of irregular verbs on pages 437–38 or a dictionary.)

26c   Problem Verbs: *Be*

The irregular verb *be* can cause problems for writers because it has two different past tense forms—*was* for singular subjects and *were* for plural subjects.

> Carlo <u>was</u> interested in becoming a city planner. (singular)
>
> They <u>were</u> happy to help out at the school. (plural)

Past Tense Forms of the Verb *Be*

	Singular	*Plural*
First person	I <u>was</u> tired.	We <u>were</u> tired.
Second person	You <u>were</u> tired.	You <u>were</u> tired.
Third person	He <u>was</u> tired.	
	She <u>was</u> tired.	They <u>were</u> tired.
	It <u>was</u> tired.	
	The man <u>was</u> tired.	Frank and Billy <u>were</u> tired.

● Practice 26-3

Edit the following passage for errors in the use of the verb *be*. Cross out any underlined verbs that are incorrect, and write the correct forms above them. If a verb form is correct, label it *C*.

Example: In 1947, the National Guard <u>were</u> divided into two parts:
the Army National Guard and the Air National Guard.

(1) Long before the United States became a country, the National Guard <u>was</u> here. (2) The colonial militias of the 17th century <u>was</u> not called by that name. (3) However, their purpose <u>were</u> essentially the same as that of today's National Guard. (4) As a "citizens' army," the colonial militia's job <u>was</u> to protect and defend its community. (5) Later, its duties <u>was</u> specified in the Constitution. (6) The militia <u>was</u> "to execute the laws of the Union, suppress insurrections, and repel invasions." (7) In 1903, the United States National Guard <u>were</u> officially created as a reserve force for the country's military. (8) National Guardsmen and women <u>were</u> to serve their states but also be prepared to serve the nation in times of war. (9) For years, recruiters used the phrase "one weekend a month, two weeks a year" to advertise the commitment that <u>was</u> required. (10) However, because of the increased demands on National Guard troops in the 21st century, the military <u>were</u> forced to abandon that slogan.

Focus on Writing: *Flashback*

Look back at your response to the Focus on Writing activity on page 435. Find all the sentences in which you use the past tense of *be*. Then, identify the subject of each *be* verb. Make sure you have used the correct form of the verb in each case.

26d Problem Verbs: *Can/Could* and *Will/Would*

The helping verbs *can/could* and *will/would* present problems because their past tense forms are sometimes confused with their present tense forms.

Can/Could

Can, a present tense verb, means "is able to" or "are able to."

First-year students <u>can</u> apply for financial aid.

Could, the past tense of *can*, means "was able to" or "were able to."

> Escape artist Harry Houdini claimed that he <u>could</u> escape from any prison.

Will / Would

Will, a present tense verb, talks about the future from a point in the present.

> A solar eclipse <u>will</u> occur in ten months.

Would, the past tense of *will*, talks about the future from a point in the past.

> I told him yesterday that I <u>would</u> think about it.

Would is also used to express a possibility or wish.

> If we stuck to our budget, we <u>would</u> be better off.
> Laurie <u>would</u> like a new stuffed animal.

Highlight:
Will* and *Would

Note that *will* is used with *can* and that *would* is used with *could*.

I will feed the cats if I can find their food.

I would feed the cats if I could find their food.

● Practice 26-4

Underline the appropriate helping verb from the choices in parentheses.

Example: Before enrolling at Michigan State, Jacob decided that the benefits of getting an education (will/<u>would</u>) outweigh the burden of going into debt.

(1) The cost of higher education is greater than ever, and, without financial help, few of today's students (can/could) afford to get a college degree. (2) To pay for school, most people (will/would) take out student loans. (3) These days, two-thirds of college students

(will/would) be in debt when they graduate. (4) On average, a student (will/would) owe $22,500. (5) A generation ago, if a student wanted a college degree, he or she (can/could) often pay for it by working at a part-time job. (6) Today's students (can/could) barely manage to keep up with living expenses, much less cover tuition costs. (7) In response, schools who (can/could) afford to are eliminating loans from their student aid packages and offering grants and work-study jobs instead. (8) Unfortunately, only the wealthiest schools, such as Harvard, Yale, Stanford, and Duke, (can/could) offer students such generous support. (9) For most graduates, paying back loans (will/would) continue to be a burden. (10) However, by learning about debt consolidation and alternate repayment plans, students (can/could) keep this burden under control.

Focus on Writing: *Flashback*

Look back at your response to the Focus on Writing activity on page 435. On a separate sheet of paper, write a few sentences that describe what you would have accomplished in your lifetime if you had had the chance. Be sure to use *could* and *would* in your sentences. (Don't forget to refer to yourself by name or as *he* or *she*.)

Focus on Writing: *Revising and Editing*

Look back at your response to the Focus on Writing activity on page 435. TEST what you have written. Then, revise and edit your work, making sure you have used the correct past tense form for each of your verbs.

Chapter Review

Editing Practice

Read the following student essay, which includes errors in past tense verb forms. Decide whether each of the underlined past tense verbs is correct. If the verb is correct, write *C* above it. If it is not, cross out the verb, and write in the correct past tense form. The first sentence has been corrected for you. (If necessary, consult the list of irregular verbs on pages 437–38.)

Healing

                                    was
The window seat <u>were</u> our favorite place to sit. I piled comfortable

pillows on the ledge and <u>spended</u> several minutes rearranging them.

Then, my friend and I <u>lied</u> on our backs and propped our feet on the

wall. We <u>sat</u> with our arms around our legs and <u>thinked</u> about the

mysteries of life.

We stared at the people on the street below and <u>wonder</u> who

they <u>was</u> and where they <u>was</u> going. We imagined that they <u>can</u> be

millionaires, foreign spies, or ruthless drug smugglers. We believed

that everyone except us <u>leaded</u> wonderful and exciting lives.

I <u>heard</u> a voice call my name. Reluctantly, I <u>standed</u> up, tearing

myself away from my imaginary world. My oldest and dearest friend—my

teddy bear—and I came back to the real world. I grabbed Teddy and

<u>brung</u> him close to my chest. Together we <u>go</u> into the cold sitting

room, where twelve other girls <u>sit</u> around a table eating breakfast.

None of them looked happy.

In the unit for eating disorders, meals <u>was</u> always tense. Nobody

<u>wants</u> to eat, but the nurses watched us until we <u>eated</u> every crumb.

I <u>set</u> Teddy on the chair beside me and stared gloomily at the food on

my plate. I closed my eyes and <u>taked</u> the first bite. I <u>feeled</u> the calories

adding inches of ugly fat. Each swallow <u>were</u> like a nail being ripped

from my finger. At last, it <u>was</u> over. I had survived breakfast.

Days passed slowly; each passing minute <u>was</u> a victory. After a

while, I learned how to eat properly. I learned that other people had problems too. I also learned that people loved me. Eventually, even Teddy stopped feeling sorry for me. I <u>begun</u> to smile—and laugh. Sometimes I even considered myself happy. My doctors challenged me—and, surprisingly, I <u>rised</u> to the occasion.

Collaborative Activities

1. Working in a group of three or four students, choose a famous living figure—an actor, a sports star, or a musician, for example—and brainstorm together to list details about this person's life. Then, working on your own, use the details to write a profile of the famous person.

2. Working in a group, list several contemporary problems that you think will be solved within ten or fifteen years. Each member of the group should then select a problem from the list and write a paragraph or two describing how the problem could be solved. As a group, arrange the paragraphs so that they form the body of an essay. Develop a thesis statement, write an introduction and a conclusion, and then revise the body paragraphs of the essay.

3. Form a group with three other students. What national or world events do you remember most vividly? Take ten minutes to list news events that you think have defined the last five years. On your own, write a paragraph in which you discuss the significance of the event that the members of your group agree was the most important.

Review Checklist: Verbs: Past Tense

- [ ] The past tense is the form a verb takes to show that an action occurred in the past.
- [ ] Regular verbs form the past tense by adding *-ed* or *-d* to the base form of the verb. (See 26A.)
- [ ] Irregular verbs have irregular forms in the past tense. (See 26B.)
- [ ] *Be* has two different past tense forms—*was* for singular subjects and *were* for plural subjects. (See 26C.)
- [ ] *Could* is the past tense of *can*. *Would* is the past tense of *will*. (See 26D.)

Chapter 27

Verbs: Past Participles

Regular Past Participles

Every verb has a past participle form. The **past participle** form of a **regular verb** is identical to its past tense form. Both are formed by adding *-d* or *-ed* to the **base form** of the verb (the present tense form of the verb that is used with the pronoun *I*).

PAST TENSE

He <u>earned</u>.

PAST PARTICIPLE

He has <u>earned</u>.

● **Practice 27-1**

Fill in the correct past participle form of each verb in parentheses.

Example: Recently, vacationers have ___*discovered*___ (discover) some new opportunities to get away from it all and to do good at the same time.

　(1) Volunteering vacationers have _____ (visit) remote locations to help build footpaths, cabins, and shelters. (2) Groups such as Habitat for Humanity have _____ (offer) volunteers a chance to help build homes in low-income areas. (3) Habitat's Global Village trips have _____ (raise) awareness about the lack of

Focus on Writing

The picture on the opposite page, from the 2005 film *Mad Hot Ballroom*, shows children practicing ballroom dancing. Look at the picture, and then write about an activity—a hobby or a sport, for example—that you have been involved in for a relatively long time.

Begin by identifying the activity and stating why it has been important to you. Write a paragraph (or an essay) about an activity, paying particular attention to what you have gained from it over the years.

affordable housing in many countries. (4) Participants in Sierra Club programs have _____ (donate) thousands of work hours to groups all over the United States. (5) Sometimes these volunteers have _____ (join) forest service workers to help restore wilderness areas. (6) They have _____ (clean) up trash and campsites. (7) They have also _____ (remove) nonnative plants. (8) Some vacationers have _____ (travel) to countries such as Costa Rica, Russia, and Thailand to help with local projects. (9) Other vacationers have _____ (serve) as teachers of English. (10) Volunteering vacations have _____ (help) to strengthen cross-cultural understanding.

Focus on Writing: *Flashback*

Look back at your response to the Focus on Writing activity on page 447, and identify each use of *have* or *has* that is followed by a regular past participle (ending in *-ed* or *-d*). Underline the past participle.

27b   Irregular Past Participles

Irregular verbs nearly always have irregular past participles. **Irregular verbs** do not form the past participle by adding *-ed* or *-d* to the base form of the verb. (Note that the past participle of an irregular verb is not necessarily the same as its past tense form.)

Base Form	Past Tense	Past Participle
buy	bought	bought
choose	chose	chosen
ride	rode	ridden

The following chart lists the base form, the past tense, and the past participle of the most commonly used irregular verbs.

Irregular Past Participles

Base Form	Past Tense	Past Participle
awake	awoke	awoken
be (am, are)	was (were)	been
beat	beat	beaten
become	became	become
begin	began	begun
bet	bet	bet
bite	bit	bitten
blow	blew	blown
break	broke	broken
bring	brought	brought
build	built	built
buy	bought	bought
catch	caught	caught
choose	chose	chosen
come	came	come
cost	cost	cost
cut	cut	cut
dive	dove, dived	dived
do	did	done
draw	drew	drawn
drink	drank	drunk
drive	drove	driven
eat	ate	eaten
fall	fell	fallen
feed	fed	fed
feel	felt	felt
fight	fought	fought
find	found	found
fly	flew	flown
forgive	forgave	forgiven
freeze	froze	frozen
get	got	got, gotten
give	gave	given
go	went	gone
grow	grew	grown
have	had	had
hear	heard	heard
hide	hid	hidden
hold	held	held
hurt	hurt	hurt

Irregular Past Participles (continued)

Base Form	Past Tense	Past Participle
keep	kept	kept
know	knew	known
lay (to place)	laid	laid
lead	led	led
leave	left	left
let	let	let
lie (to recline)	lay	lain
light	lit	lit
lose	lost	lost
make	made	made
meet	met	met
pay	paid	paid
quit	quit	quit
read	read	read
ride	rode	ridden
ring	rang	rung
rise	rose	risen
run	ran	run
say	said	said
see	saw	seen
sell	sold	sold
send	sent	sent
set	set	set
shake	shook	shaken
shine	shone, shined	shone, shined
sing	sang	sung
sit	sat	sat
sleep	slept	slept
speak	spoke	spoken
spend	spent	spent
spring	sprang	sprung
stand	stood	stood
steal	stole	stolen
stick	stuck	stuck
sting	stung	stung
swear	swore	sworn
swim	swam	swum
take	took	taken
teach	taught	taught

→

Irregular Past Participles *(continued)*

Base Form	Past Tense	Past Participle
tear	tore	torn
tell	told	told
think	thought	thought
throw	threw	thrown
understand	understood	understood
wake	woke, waked	woken, waked
wear	wore	worn
win	won	won
write	wrote	written

● **Practice 27-2**

Fill in the correct past participle of each verb in parentheses. Refer to the chart on pages 449–51 as needed. If you cannot find a verb on the chart, look it up in the dictionary.

Example: American teachers have ____*taught*____ (teach) their students about the defenders of the Alamo during Texas's battle for independence from Mexico.

(1) Since 1836, the Alamo has _____ (be) one of the most famous American historical sites, but recently its importance has _____ (be) questioned. (2) Americans have _____ (hear) about how 189 Texans held off a Mexican army of thousands for thirteen days. (3) Many children have _____ (build) models of the Alamo, which was once a home for Spanish missionaries. (4) Visitors have _____ (come) to see the place where many American heroes, including Davy Crockett and Jim Bowie, died. (5) The slogan "Remember the Alamo" has _____ (become) famous. (6) Now, however, one historian has _____ (make) a startling claim. (7) Dr. Will Fowler, of St. Andrews University in Scotland, has _____ (write) a book that suggests that we were wrong about the Alamo. (8) According to Fowler, the story that many people have

_____ (read) may not be accurate. (9) He has _____ (say) that the Texans wanted to take land away from Mexico and to preserve slavery in that territory. (10) Those who have always _____ (see) the defenders of the Alamo as heroes strongly disagree with Fowler's position.

● **Practice 27-3**

Edit the following passage for errors in irregular past participles. Cross out any underlined past participles that are incorrect, and write in the correct form above them. If the verb form is correct, label it *C*.

> **Example:** In recent years, some people have ~~standed~~ up against over- $\overset{stood}{\underset{\wedge}{}}$ seas sweatshops.

(1) Buying products from overseas sweatshops has <u>became</u> controversial over the last few decades. (2) American manufacturers have <u>sended</u> their materials to developing countries where employees work under terrible conditions for very low wages. (3) Violations of basic U.S. labor laws—such as getting extra pay for overtime and being paid on time—have <u>lead</u> to protests. (4) Low-wage workers in developing countries have <u>finded</u> themselves facing dangerous working conditions as well as verbal and sexual abuse. (5) Even well-known retailers—such as Sears, Tommy Hilfiger, and Target—have <u>gotten</u> in trouble for selling items made in sweatshops. (6) Recently, colleges have <u>be</u> criticized for using overseas sweatshops to make clothing featuring school names. (7) Students have <u>spoke</u> out against such practices, and schools have <u>had</u> to respond. (8) Even though manufacturers have sometimes <u>losed</u> money by increasing wages for overseas workers, they have <u>understanded</u> that this was the right thing to do. (9) They have <u>made</u> a promise to their customers that they will not employ sweatshop labor. (10) Still, many consumers have not <u>forgave</u> manufacturers who have a history of such practices.

Focus on Writing: *Flashback*

Look back at your response to the Focus on Writing activity on page 447, and identify each use of *have* or *had* that is followed by an irregular past participle. Then, underline the irregular past participle.

27c ## The Present Perfect Tense

The past participle is combined with the present tense forms of *have* to form the **present perfect tense**.

The Present Perfect Tense (*have* or *has* + past participle)

Singular

I have gained.

You have gained.

He has gained.

She has gained.

It has gained.

Plural

We have gained.

You have gained.

They have gained.

- Use the present perfect tense to indicate an action that began in the past and continues into the present.

  Present perfect   The nurse has worked at the clinic for two years. (The working began in the past and continues into the present.)

- Use the present perfect tense to indicate that an action has just occurred.

  Present perfect   I have just eaten. (The eating has just occurred.)

● **Practice 27-4**

Circle the appropriate verb tense (past tense or present perfect) from the choices in parentheses.

Example: When I was in Montreal, I (heard, have heard) both English and French.

(1) When I (visited, have visited) Montreal, I was surprised to discover a truly bilingual city. (2) Montreal (kept, has kept) two languages as a result of its history. (3) Until 1763, Montreal (belonged, has belonged) to France. (4) Then, when France (lost, has lost) the Seven Years War, the city (became, has become) part of England. (5) When I was there last year, most people (spoke, have spoken) both French and English. (6) Although I (knew, have known) no French, I (found, have found) that I was able to get along quite well. (7) For example, all the museums (made, have made) their guided tours available in English. (8) Most restaurants (offered, have offered) bilingual menus. (9) There (were, have been) even English radio and television stations and English newspapers. (10) In Montreal, I (felt, have felt) both at home and in a foreign country.

● **Practice 27-5**

Fill in the appropriate tense (past tense or present perfect) of the verb in parentheses.

Example: Bath towels and mattresses are just two of the many things that _have increased_ (increase) in size over the last few years.

(1) In recent years, the size of many everyday items _____ (change) drastically. (2) Cell phones and computers _____ (undergo) the biggest changes. (3) There was a time, not long ago, when a single computer _____ (fill) an entire room. (4) Likewise, the first cell phones were more than a foot long and

_____ (weigh) as much as two pounds. (5) Since then, we _____ (develop) sophisticated machines that fit in a pocket and weigh as little as a few ounces. (6) However, while these items have shrunk, other things _____ (get) bigger. (7) In 1980, when 7-Eleven _____ (invent) the 32-ounce Big Gulp, it was the largest drink on the market. (8) Now, the Big Gulp looks small to most of us because the average size of a fountain soda _____ (increase) significantly. (9) Television screens _____ (grow) as well. (10) While twenty years ago most viewers _____ (watch) TV on a 20-inch screen, many of today's viewers are demanding screens that are 60 inches or larger.

Focus on Writing: *Flashback*

Look back at your response to the Focus on Writing activity on page 447. Choose three sentences with past tense verbs, and rewrite them on a separate sheet of paper, changing past tense to present perfect tense. How does your revision change the meaning of each sentence?

27d The Past Perfect Tense

The past participle is also used to form the **past perfect tense**, which consists of the past tense of *have* plus the past participle.

The Past Perfect Tense (*had* + past participle)

Singular	Plural
I had returned.	We had returned.
You had returned.	You had returned.
He had returned.	They had returned.
She had returned.	
It had returned.	

Use the past perfect tense to show that one past action occurred before another past action.

PAST
PERFECT TENSE   PAST TENSE

Chief Sitting Bull <u>had fought</u> many battles before <u>he</u> <u>defeated</u> General Custer. (The fighting done by Sitting Bull occurred before he defeated Custer.)

● Practice 27-6

Underline the appropriate verb tense (present perfect or past perfect) from the choices in parentheses.

Example: Although he (has missed / <u>had missed</u>) his second free throw, the crowd cheered for him anyway.

1. Meera returned to Bangladesh with the money she (has raised / had raised).

2. Her contributors believe that she (has shown / had shown) the ability to spend money wisely.

3. The planner told the commission that she (has found / had found) a solution to the city's traffic problem.

4. It seems clear that traffic cameras (have proven / had proven) successful in towns with similar congestion problems.

5. Emily says she (has saved / had saved) a lot of money by driving a motor scooter instead of a car.

6. She sold the car she (has bought / had bought) three years before.

7. Because they are huge fans, Esteban and Tina (have camped / had camped) out in front of the theater to buy tickets.

8. The people who (have waited / had waited) all night were the first to get tickets.

9. Sam and Ryan volunteer at Habitat for Humanity where they (have learned / had learned) many useful skills.

10. After they (have completed / had completed) 500 hours of work, they were eligible to get their own house.

Focus on Writing: *Flashback*

Look back at your response to the Flashback activity on page 455. On a separate sheet of paper, rewrite the three present perfect tense sentences you wrote for the Flashback activity, this time using the past perfect tense. How do your revisions change the meaning of each sentence?

27e Past Participles as Adjectives

In addition to functioning as verbs, past participles can also function as adjectives modifying nouns that follow them.

I cleaned up the broken glass.

The exhausted runner finally crossed the finish line.

Past participles are also used as adjectives after **linking verbs**, such as *seemed* or *looked*.

Jason seemed surprised.

He looked shocked.

● Practice 27-7

Edit the following passage for errors in past participle forms used as adjectives. Cross out any underlined participles that are incorrect, and write the correct form above them. If the participle form is correct, label it *C*.

> **Example:** College students are often strapped for cash.

(1) College students are surprise when they receive preapprove applications for credit cards. (2) Credit-card companies also recruit targeted students through booths that are locate at events they attend. (3) They also post ads on social-networking sites that are design to

attract new customers. (4) Why have companies gone to all this trouble to attract <u>qualified</u> students? (5) Most older Americans already have at least five credit cards that are <u>stuff</u> in their wallets. (6) Banks and credit-card companies see younger college students as a major <u>untapped</u> market. (7) According to experts, students are a good credit risk because <u>concern</u> parents usually bail them out when they cannot pay a bill. (8) Finally, people tend to feel <u>tie</u> to their first credit card. (9) Companies want to be the first card that is <u>acquire</u> by a customer. (10) For this reason, credit-card companies target <u>uninform</u> college students.

Focus on Writing: *Flashback*

Look back at your response to the Focus on Writing activity on page 447. Choose three nouns you used in your writing, and list them on a sheet of paper. Then, list a past participle that can modify each noun. Finally, use each noun and its past participle modifier in a new sentence.

Focus on Writing: *Revising and Editing*

Look back at your response to the Focus on Writing activity on page 447. **TEST** what you have written. Then, revise and edit your work, paying particular attention to present perfect and past perfect tense verb forms.

Chapter Review

Editing Practice

Read the following student essay, which includes errors in the use of past participles and in the use of the perfect tenses. Decide whether each of the underlined verbs or participles is correct. If it is correct, write *C* above it. If it is not, write in the correct verb form. The first error has been corrected for you.

Using Technology to Get Out the Vote

These days, the Internet <u>became</u> *has become* one of the most common ways for political candidates to reach voters and to raise money for election campaigns. In addition, social networking sites and text-messaging <u>have allow</u> candidates to connect more easily with young people. In the past, far too many young voters <u>have</u> not <u>took</u> part in U.S. elections. Recently, however, young voters <u>had participated</u> in greater numbers, perhaps thanks to their familiarity with technology.

Over the last few years, political campaigns <u>have finded</u> that they can attract voters and election workers by using the Internet. Both Democrats and Republicans <u>used</u> email and online advertising to persuade voters to support candidates and to provide vote-by-mail ballots. At the same time, their Web sites and blogs <u>had stimulate</u> interest in politics and <u>have provide</u> ways for young people to meet each other and work for their candidates.

In 2004, both major political parties <u>have used</u> the Internet to gain young voters' support. Hoping to draw young people to the campaign trail, John Kerry's camp <u>has worked</u> with Moveon.org to organize and publicize a tour of popular musicians. GeorgeWBush.com <u>offered</u> young Republicans ways to use the Internet to create a pro-Bush poster, download pro-Bush screensavers, and order pro-Bush items. With these online promotions, both parties definitely <u>have catched</u> the interest of young people. However, the use of technology <u>had played</u> an even greater role in the 2008 presidential election.

459

In addition to using the Internet, 2008 candidates have discover new ways of reaching young voters: text-messaging, social networking, and YouTube. Candidates have keeped supporters informed by texting them with up-to-the-minute campaign news. They have use sites like Facebook to link up and unite supporters. Candidates also had recognized the potential that YouTube have provided. This popular video-sharing site had not existed in 2004. However, in 2008, most of the presidential candidates have had political ads, short talks, and debate clips on YouTube. Posting videos there had enable them to reach millions of voters without paying a cent.

After the 2008 presidential election, many experts have suggested that young voters' technological competence had gave them more political strength. Commentators also credited young voters, in part, for the election of Barack Obama. Twice as many 18- to 29-year-olds have voted for Obama as voted for John McCain. Many had acknowledge that the Obama campaign's use of texting, emailing, and blogging has most likely helped the candidate win young people's support. In the years to come, the use of technology will certainly influence future U.S. elections, and young voters, even more profoundly.

Collaborative Activities

1. Exchange Focus on Writing activities with another student. Read each other's work, making sure that past participles and perfect tenses are used correctly.

2. Assume that you are a restaurant employee who has been nominated for the Employee of the Year Award. To win this award (along with a thousand-dollar prize), you have to explain in writing what you have done during the past year to deserve this honor. Write a letter to your supervisor and the awards committee. When you have finished, trade papers with another student and edit his or her letter. Read all the letters to the class, and have the class decide which is the most convincing.

Review Checklist: Verbs: Past Participles

☐ The past participle of regular verbs is formed by adding -*ed* or -*d* to the base form. (See 27A.)

☐ Irregular verbs usually have irregular past participles. (See 27B.)

☐ The past participle is combined with the present tense forms of *have* to form the present perfect tense. (See 27C.)

☐ The past participle is used to form the past perfect tense, which consists of the past tense of *have* plus the past participle. (See 27D.)

☐ The past participle can function as an adjective. (See 27E.)

Identifying Nouns

A **noun** is a word that names a person *(singer, Jay-Z)*, an animal *(dolphin, Flipper)*, a place *(downtown, Houston)*, an object *(game, Scrabble)*, or an idea *(happiness, Darwinism)*.

A **singular noun** names one thing. A **plural noun** names more than one thing.

Highlight: Common and Proper Nouns

Most nouns, called **common nouns**, begin with lowercase letters.

    character   holiday

Some nouns, called **proper nouns**, name particular people, animals, places, objects, or events. A proper noun always begins with a capital letter.

    Homer Simpson   Labor Day

Forming Plural Nouns

Most nouns that end in consonants add *-s* to form plurals. Other nouns form plurals with *-es*. For example, most nouns that end in *-o* add *-es* to form plurals. Other nouns, whose singular forms end in *-s*, *-ss*, *-sh*, *-ch*, *-x*, or *-z*, add *-es* to form plurals. (Some nouns that end in *-s* or *-z* double the *s* or *z* before adding *-es*.)

Focus on Writing

The picture on the opposite page shows Bruce Springsteen and E Street Band members giving a performance. Look at the picture, and then write a paragraph (or an essay) about why you like a particular musician or group, TV show, or movie. Assume your readers are not familiar with the subject you are writing about.

Singular	*Plural*
street	streets
hero	heroes
gas	gases
class	classes
bush	bushes
church	churches
fox	foxes
quiz	quizzes

Irregular Noun Plurals

Some nouns form plurals in unusual ways.

- Nouns whose plural forms are the same as their singular forms

Singular	*Plural*
a deer	a few deer
this species	these species
a television series	two television series

- Nouns ending in *-f* or *-fe*

Singular	*Plural*
each half	both halves
my life	our lives
a lone thief	a gang of thieves
one loaf	two loaves
the third shelf	several shelves

Exceptions: *roof* (plural *roofs*), *proof* (plural *proofs*), *belief* (plural *beliefs*)

- Nouns ending in *-y*

Singular	*Plural*
another baby	more babies
every worry	many worries

Note that when a vowel (*a, e, i, o, u*) comes before the *y*, the noun has a regular plural form: *monkey* (plural *monkeys*), *day* (plural *days*).

Irregular Noun Plurals *(continued)*

• Hyphenated compound nouns

Singular	*Plural*
Lucia's sister-in-law	Lucia's two favorite sisters-in-law
a mother-to-be	twin mothers-to-be
the first runner-up	all the runners-up

• Miscellaneous irregular plurals

Singular	*Plural*
that child	all children
a good man	a few good men
the woman	lots of women
my left foot	both feet
a wisdom tooth	my two front teeth
this bacterium	some bacteria

● **Practice 28-1**

Next to each of the following singular nouns, write the plural form of the noun. Then, circle the irregular noun plurals.

Examples: bottle _____*bottles*_____   child _____*children*_____

1. headache _____
2. life _____
3. foot _____
4. chain _____
5. deer _____
6. honey _____
7. bride-to-be _____
8. woman _____
9. loaf _____
10. kiss _____

11. beach _____
12. duty _____
13. son-in-law _____
14. species _____
15. wife _____
16. city _____
17. elf _____
18. tooth _____
19. catalog _____
20. patty _____

● Practice 28-2

Proofread the underlined nouns in the following paragraph, checking to make sure singular and plural forms are correct. If a correction needs to be made, cross out the noun, and write the correct form above it. If the noun is correct, write *C* above it.

airports
Example: Getting through security lines at ~~airportes~~ has become difficult.
                                                            ^

(1) Since September 11, 2001, traveler-to-bes need to think carefully about what they pack in their carry-on luggage. (2) All airlines have to protect the lifes of the men and woman who fly on their planes. (3) On some days, long delayes in the security lines occur as screeners carry out their dutys. (4) Most people understand that they should never carry weapons and explosives onto a plane. (5) Hunters have to accept the fact that all firearms must be unloaded and checked in at the gate and that boxs of ammunition should be packed separately. (6) Most people are aware that items like nail clippers and tweezerz are now permitted but that other sharp tooles, like knifes and razor blades, are still forbidden. (7) However, some individuals forget that most shampoos, lotiones, and drinkes are only allowed in very small quantitys. (8) When packing liquides or gels in their carry-on luggage, traveleres must be sure that each container holds no more than three ounces and that all containers fit in a quart-size plastic bag. (9) Emptying the contentes of water bottles and coffee cupps can seem frustrating and unnecessary to many passengers. (10) However, most passengers accept these small inconveniences and minor irritations because they want to fly safely.

Focus on Writing: *Flashback*

Look back at your response to the Focus on Writing activity on page 463. Underline each noun. Write *P* above any plural nouns, and circle any irregular plurals.

28c   Identifying Pronouns

A **pronoun** is a word that refers to and takes the place of a noun or another pronoun.

> Michelle was really excited because <u>she</u> had finally found a job that made <u>her</u> happy. (*She* refers to *Michelle*; *her* refers to *she*.)

In the sentence above, the pronouns *she* and *her* take the place of the noun *Michelle*.

Pronouns, like nouns, can be singular or plural.

- Singular pronouns (*I*, *he*, *she*, *it*, *him*, *her*, and so on) are always singular and take the place of singular nouns or pronouns.

  > Geoff left his jacket at work, so <u>he</u> went back to get <u>it</u> before <u>it</u> could be stolen. (*He* refers to *Geoff*; *it* refers to *jacket*.)

- Plural pronouns (*we*, *they*, *our*, *their*, and so on) are always plural and take the place of plural nouns or pronouns.

  > Jessie and Dan got up early, but <u>they</u> still missed <u>their</u> train. (*They* refers to *Jessie and Dan*; *their* refers to *they*.)

- The pronoun *you* can be either singular or plural.

  > When the volunteers met the mayor, they said, "We really admire <u>you</u>." The mayor replied, "I admire <u>you</u>, too." (In the first sentence, *you* refers to *the mayor*; in the second sentence, *you* refers to *the volunteers*.)

**Highlight:
Demonstrative
Pronouns**

Demonstrative pronouns—*this*, *that*, *these*, and *those*—point to one or more items.

- *This* and *that* point to one item: <u>This</u> is a work of fiction, and <u>that</u> is a nonfiction book.

- *These* and *those* point to more than one item: <u>These</u> are fruits, but <u>those</u> are vegetables.

● **Practice 28-3**

In the following sentences, fill in each blank with an appropriate pronoun.

Example: I was looking for part-time work when ___*I*___ saw an ad for jobs with the 2010 U.S. Census.

(1) My friend Michelle and _____ decided to apply for temporary jobs as census takers. (2) _____ are students, so _____ was important that _____ find jobs with flexible hours that fit our class schedules. (3) Also, _____ wanted work that involved talking to people and being outside. (4) This job would let us do both, so _____ seemed perfect. (5) _____ did not hurt that _____ speak Spanish and that _____ is fluent in French. (6) Being bilingual helped _____ get hired. (7) The job required walking through neighborhoods, talking to people and verifying _____ addresses. (8) During our training, _____ learned how important _____ is to get accurate information. (9) The census data are critical because _____ help determine how much government funding and representation _____ will receive in our state. (10) All in all, _____ enjoyed being a census taker, and Michelle says _____ did, too.

Focus on Writing: *Flashback*

Look back at your response to the Focus on Writing activity on page 463. Draw a line down the middle of a sheet of paper, creating two columns. In the column on the left, list all the pronouns (*I, he, she, it, we, you, they*) you used. In the column on the right, list the noun or pronoun each pronoun takes the place of.

28d Pronoun-Antecedent Agreement

The word that a pronoun refers to is called its **antecedent**. In the following sentence, the noun *leaf* is the antecedent of the pronoun *it*.

The leaf turned yellow, but it did not fall.

A pronoun must always agree in **number** with its antecedent. If an antecedent is singular, as it is in the preceding sentence, the pronoun must be singular. If the antecedent is plural, as it is in the sentence below, the pronoun must also be plural.

The leaves turned yellow, but they did not fall.

Highlight: Vague Pronoun References

WORD POWER
inevitable something that cannot be avoided; unavoidable

A pronoun should always refer to a specific antecedent.

Vague　On the evening news, they said a baseball strike was inevitable. (Who said a strike was inevitable?)

Revised　On the evening news, the sportscaster said a baseball strike was inevitable. (noun replaces vague pronoun)

● **Practice 28-4**

In the following sentences, circle the antecedent of each underlined pronoun. Then, draw an arrow from the pronoun to the antecedent it refers to.

Example:　College students today often fear they will be the victims of crime on campus.

(1) Few campuses are as safe as they should be, experts say. (2) However, crime on most campuses is probably no worse than it is in any other community. (3) Still, students have a right to know how safe their campuses are. (4) Some students never set foot on campus without their cans of Mace. (5) These students believe they must be prepared for the worst. (6) Other students take self-defense courses, which they say are very helpful. (7) Most students do not let fear of crime keep them from enjoying the college experience. (8) They know that their schools are doing all they can to provide a safe environment.

Focus on Writing: *Flashback*

Look back at your response to the Focus on Writing activity on page 463. Draw an arrow from each pronoun to its antecedent. Do all your pronouns agree with their antecedents? If not, correct your pronouns.

28e   Special Problems with Agreement

Certain kinds of antecedents can present challenges for writers because they cannot be easily identified as singular or plural.

Compound Antecedents

A **compound antecedent** consists of two or more words connected by *and* or *or*.

- Compound antecedents connected by *and* are plural, and they are used with plural pronouns.

  During World War II, Belgium and France tried to protect their borders.

- Compound antecedents connected by *or* may take a singular or a plural pronoun. The pronoun always agrees with the word that is closer to it.

  Is it possible that European nations or Russia may send its [not *their*] troops?

  Is it possible that Russia or European nations may send their [not *its*] troops?

● Practice 28-5

In each of the following sentences, underline the compound antecedent, and circle the connecting word (*and* or *or*). Then, circle the appropriate pronoun in parentheses.

Example: Bill Gates (and) Paul Allen founded (his /(their)) company, Microsoft, in 1975.

1. Mary-Kate and Ashley sell (her / their) clothing line at Wal-Mart.

2. Was it a doctor or a nurse who told you (her / their) life story?

3. Chinese and Arabic are seeing (its / their) popularity rise on college campuses.

4. Bert and Ernie have always had (his / their) differences.

5. It sounds as if either Homer or Bart has lost (his / their) temper.

6. Either chocolate or oranges will lose (its / their) flavor if not eaten right away.

7. Adam and Nathan rarely wear (his / their) coats, even in the middle of winter.

8. Either the chips or the salsa spilled on (its / their) way home from the store.

9. Robins and finches are building (its / their) nests in our yard.

10. Will the White Sox or the Cubs finally make (its / their) way to the World Series this year?

Indefinite Pronoun Antecedents

Most pronouns refer to a specific person or thing. However, **indefinite pronouns** do not refer to any particular person or thing.

Most indefinite pronouns are singular.

Singular Indefinite Pronouns

another	everybody	no one
anybody	everyone	nothing
anyone	everything	one
anything	much	somebody
each	neither	someone
either	nobody	something

When an indefinite pronoun antecedent is singular, use a singular pronoun to refer to it.

Everything was in its place. (*Everything* is singular, so it is used with the singular pronoun *its*.)

Highlight: Indefinite Pronouns with *Of*

The singular indefinite pronouns *each*, *either*, *neither*, and *one* are often used in phrases with *of*—*each of*, *either of*, *neither of*, or *one of*— followed by a plural noun. Even in such phrases, these indefinite pronoun antecedents are always singular and take singular pronouns.

Each of the routes has its [not *their*] own special challenges.

A few indefinite pronouns are plural.

Plural Indefinite Pronouns

both	others
few	several
many	

When an indefinite pronoun antecedent is plural, use a plural pronoun to refer to it.

They all wanted to graduate early, but few received their diplomas in January. (*Few* is plural, so it is used with the plural pronoun *their*.)

Highlight: Using *His* or *Her* with Indefinite Pronouns

Even though the indefinite pronouns *anybody*, *anyone*, *everybody*, *everyone*, *somebody*, *someone*, and so on are singular, many people use plural pronouns to refer to them.

Everyone must hand in their completed work before 2 p.m.

This usage is widely accepted in spoken English. Nevertheless, indefinite pronouns like *everyone* are singular, and written English requires a singular pronoun.

However, using the singular pronoun *his* to refer to *everyone* suggests that *everyone* refers to a male. Using *his or her* is more accurate because the indefinite pronoun may refer to either a male or a female.

Everyone must hand in his or her completed work before 2 p.m.

**Highlight:
Using *His
or Her* with
Indefinite
Pronouns**
continued

When used over and over again, *he or she*, *him or her*, and *his or her* make sentences wordy and awkward. To avoid this problem, try to use plural forms.

All students must hand in <u>their</u> completed work before 2 p.m.

● **Practice 28-6**

In each of the following sentences, first circle the indefinite pronoun. Then, circle the pronoun or pronouns in parentheses that refer to the indefinite pronoun antecedent.

Example: (Each) of the artists will have ((his or her)/their) own exhibit.

1. Either of those paintings will be sold with (its / their) frame.
2. Each of the artist's brushes has (its / their) own use.
3. Everything in the room made (its / their) contribution to the setting.
4. Everyone must remember to take (his or her / their) paint box.
5. Neither of my sisters wanted (her / their) painting displayed.
6. Many of the men brought (his / their) children to the exhibit.
7. Several of the colors must be mixed with (its / their) contrasting colors.
8. When someone compliments your work, be sure to tell (him or her / them) that it is for sale.
9. Anyone can improve (his or her / their) skills as an artist.
10. Both of these workrooms have (its / their) own advantages.

● **Practice 28-7**

Edit the following sentences for errors in pronoun-antecedent agreement. When you edit, you have two options: either substitute *his or her* for *their* to refer to the singular antecedent, or replace the singular antecedent with a plural word.

Examples:

                                        his or her
Everyone will be responsible for ~~their~~ own transportation.
                                        ^
All
~~Each of~~ the children took their books out of their backpacks.
^

1. Everyone has the right to their own opinion.

2. Everyone can eat their lunches in the cafeteria.

3. Somebody forgot their backpack.

4. Each of the patients had their own rooms, with their own televisions and their own private baths.

5. Someone has left their car headlights on.

6. Simone keeps everything in her kitchen in their own little container.

7. Each of the applicants must have their driver's license.

8. Anybody who has ever juggled a job and children knows how valuable their free time can be.

9. Either of those coffeemakers comes with their own filter.

10. Almost everyone waits until the last minute to file their income tax returns.

Collective Noun Antecedents

Collective nouns are words (such as *band* and *team*) that name a group of people or things but are singular. Because they are singular, collective noun antecedents are used with singular pronouns.

The band played for hours, but it never played our song.

Frequently Used Collective Nouns

army	committee	gang	orchestra
band	company	government	posse
class	congregation	group	team
club	family	jury	union

● Practice 28-8

Circle the collective noun antecedent in the following sentences. Then, circle the correct pronoun in parentheses.

Example: The jury returned with (its / their) verdict.

1. The company offers generous benefits to (its / their) employees.

2. All five study groups are supposed to hand in (its / their) projects by Tuesday.

3. Any government should care about the welfare of (its / their) citizens.

4. Every family has (its / their) share of problems.

5. To join the electricians' union, applicants had to pass (its / their) test.

● Practice 28-9

Edit the following passage for correct pronoun-antecedent agreement. First, circle the antecedent of each underlined pronoun. Then, cross out any pronoun that does not agree with its antecedent, and write the correct form above it. If the pronoun is correct, write *C* above it.

> **Example:**   The history of woman suffrage in the United States shows
> that (women) were determined to achieve her equal rights.
>   *their*

(1) Before 1920, most American women were not allowed to vote for the candidates they preferred. (2) Men ran the government, and a woman could not express their views at the ballot box. (3) However, in the mid-1800s, women began to demand her right to vote—or "woman suffrage." (4) Supporters of woman suffrage believed everyone, regardless of their gender, should be able to vote. (5) At the first woman suffrage convention, Elizabeth Cady Stanton and Lucretia Mott gave speeches explaining his or her views. (6) Susan B. Anthony started the National Woman Suffrage Association, which opposed the Fifteenth Amendment to the Constitution because it gave the vote to black men but not to women. (7) The first state to permit women to vote was Wyoming, and soon other states became more friendly to her cause. (8) Many women participated in marches where he or she carried banners and posters for their cause. (9) During World War I, the U.S. government found that the cooperation of women was essential to their military success. (10) Finally,

in 1919, the House of Representatives and the states gave <u>its</u> approval to the Nineteenth Amendment, which gave American women the right to vote.

Focus on Writing: *Flashback*

Look back at your response to the Focus on Writing activity on page 463. Does your paragraph include any antecedents that are compounds, indefinite pronouns, or collective nouns? Have you used the correct pronoun to refer to each of these antecedents? If not, correct your pronouns.

28f   Pronoun Case

A **personal pronoun** refers to a particular person or thing. Personal pronouns change form according to their function in a sentence. Personal pronouns can be *subjective*, *objective*, or *possessive*.

Personal Pronouns

Subjective Case	Objective Case	Possessive Case
I	me	my, mine
he	him	his
she	her	her, hers
it	it	its
we	us	our, ours
you	you	your, yours
they	them	their, theirs

Subjective Case

When a pronoun is a subject, it is in the **subjective case**.

Finally, <u>she</u> realized that dreams could come true.

Objective Case

When a pronoun is an object, it is in the **objective case**.

> If Joanna hurries, she can stop h<u>im</u>. (The pronoun *him* is the object of the verb *can stop*.)
>
> Professor Miller sent u<u>s</u> information about his research. (The pronoun *us* is the object of the verb *sent*.)
>
> Marc threw the ball to <u>them</u>. (The pronoun *them* is the object of the preposition *to*.)

Possessive Case

When a pronoun shows ownership, it is in the **possessive case**.

> Hieu took <u>his</u> lunch to the meeting. (The pronoun *his* indicates that the lunch belongs to Hieu.)
>
> Debbie and Kim decided to take <u>their</u> lunches, too. (The pronoun *their* indicates that the lunches belong to Debbie and Kim.)

● Practice 28-10

In the following passage, fill in the blank after each pronoun to indicate whether the pronoun is subjective (*S*), objective (*O*), or possessive (*P*).

Example: Famous criminals Bonnie and Clyde committed their ___P___ crimes in broad daylight.

(1) Bonnie Parker and Clyde Barrow are remembered today because they _____ were the first celebrity criminals. (2) With their _____ gang, Bonnie and Clyde robbed a dozen banks as well as many stores and gas stations. (3) In small towns, they _____ terrorized the police. (4) Capturing them _____ seemed impossible. (5) To many Americans, however, their _____ crimes seemed exciting. (6) Because Bonnie was a woman, she _____ was especially fascinating to them _____. (7) During their _____ crimes, Bonnie and Clyde would often carry a camera, take photographs of themselves, and then send them

_____ to the newspapers, which were happy to publish them _____.
(8) By the time they _____ were killed in an ambush by Texas and Louisiana law officers, Bonnie and Clyde were famous all over the United States.

Focus on Writing: *Flashback*

Look back at your response to the Focus on Writing activity on page 463. First, list all the personal pronouns you have used. Then, divide a sheet of paper into three columns labeled *subjective*, *objective*, and *possessive*. Finally, copy the pronouns from your own work in the appropriate columns. Have you used correct pronoun case in every sentence? Make any necessary corrections.

28g   Special Problems with Case

When you are trying to determine which pronoun case to use, three kinds of pronouns can present challenges: pronouns in compounds, pronouns in comparisons, and the relative pronouns *who* and *whom*.

Pronouns in Compounds

Sometimes a pronoun is linked to a noun or to another pronoun with *and* or *or* to form a **compound**.

> The teacher and I met for an hour.
> She and I had a good meeting.

To determine whether to use the subjective or objective case for a pronoun in a compound, follow the same rules that apply for a pronoun that is not part of a compound.

- If the compound is a subject, use the subjective case.

> Toby and I [not *me*] like jazz.
> He and I [not *me*] went to the movies.

● If the compound is an object, use the objective case.

The school sent <u>my father and me</u> [not <i>I</i>] the financial aid forms.

This fight is between <u>Kate and me</u> [not <i>I</i>].

Highlight: Choosing Pronouns in Compounds

To determine which pronoun case to use in a compound that joins a noun and a pronoun, rewrite the sentence with just the pronoun.

Toby and [<i>I</i> or <i>me</i>?] like jazz.

I like jazz. [not <i>Me like jazz</i>]

Toby and I like jazz.

● **Practice 28-11**

In the following sentences, the underlined pronouns are part of compound constructions. Check them for correct subjective or objective case. If a correction needs to be made, cross out the pronoun, and write the correct form above it. If the pronoun is correct, write *C* above it.

Example: My sister and *I*
~~me~~ heard a strange sound one night last year.

(1) Julia and <u>me</u> were about to go to sleep when we heard eerie howls. (2) At first, we thought that our parents had forgotten to turn off the television, but then we remembered that <u>they</u> had gone away for the weekend. (3) Alone in the house, Julia and <u>me</u> were in a panic. (4) Deciding what to do was up to <u>she</u> and <u>I</u>. (5) We considered calling 911, but we thought the police wouldn't believe us when we described the strange howls heard by my sister and <u>me</u>. (6) <u>Them</u> and the 911 operators might just think that Julia and <u>me</u> were playing a trick on them. (7) Finally, we decided to wait until morning, when <u>her</u> and <u>me</u> would be able to figure out what had frightened us. (8) During the night, we remembered that our cat Annie and Sam, her kitten, were

outside, and we began to worry about <u>she</u> and <u>he</u>. (9) The next morning, we found traces of blood and scraps of fur in our backyard, but we never found <u>she</u> or her kitten. (10) Now, we suspect that coyotes had been prowling around our neighborhood and that <u>them</u> or other wild animals may have carried off our pets.

Pronouns in Comparisons

Sometimes a pronoun appears after the word *than* or *as* in a comparison.

> John is luckier <u>than I</u>.
> The inheritance changed Raymond as much <u>as her</u>.

- If the pronoun is a subject, use the subjective case.

> John is luckier <u>than</u> I [am].

- If the pronoun is an object, use the objective case.

> The inheritance changed Raymond as much <u>as</u> [it changed] her.

Highlight: Choosing Pronouns in Comparisons	Sometimes the pronoun you use can change your sentence's meaning. For example, if you say, "I like Cheerios more than *he*," you mean that you like Cheerios more than the other person likes them.

> I like Cheerios more than he [does].

If, however, you say, "I like Cheerios more than *him*," you mean that you like Cheerios more than you like the other person.

> I like Cheerios more than [I like] him.

● Practice 28-12

Each of the following sentences includes a comparison with a pronoun following the word *than* or *as*. Write in each blank the correct form (subjective or objective) of the pronoun in parentheses. In brackets, add the word or words needed to complete the comparison.

Example: Many people are better poker players than ___I [am]___ (I / me).

1. The survey showed that most people like the candidate's wife as much as _____ (he / him).

2. No one enjoys shopping more than _____ (she / her).

3. My brother and Aunt Cecile were very close, so her death affected him more than _____ (I / me).

4. My neighbor drives better than _____ (I / me).

5. That jacket fits you better than _____ (I / me).

Who and Whom

To determine which **relative pronoun**—*who* or *whom* (or *whoever* or *whomever*)—to use, you need to know how the pronoun functions within the clause in which it appears.

- When the pronoun is the subject of the clause, use *who*.

  I wonder <u>who</u> wrote that song. (*Who* is the subject of the clause *who wrote that song*.)

- When the pronoun is the object, use *whom*.

  <u>Whom</u> do the police suspect? (*Whom* is the object of the verb *suspect*.)

  I wonder <u>whom</u> the song is about. (*Whom* is the object of the preposition *about* in the clause *whom the song is about*.)

Highlight: Who and Whom	To determine whether to use *who* or *whom*, try substituting another pronoun for *who* or *whom* in the clause. If you can substitute *he* or *she*, use *who*; if you can substitute *him* or *her*, use *whom*. [Who / Whom] wrote a love song? He wrote a love song. [Who / Whom] was the song about? The song was about her.

● **Practice 28-13**

Circle the correct form of *who* or *whom* in parentheses in each sentence.

Example: With (who /whom) did Rob collaborate?

1. For (who / whom) was the witness going to testify?
2. It will take time to decide (who / whom) the record holder is.
3. (Who / Whom) did Kobe take to the prom?
4. We saw the man (who / whom) fired the shots.
5. To (who / whom) am I speaking?

Focus on Writing: *Flashback*

Look back at your response to the Focus on Writing activity on page 463. Can you find any pronouns used in compounds or comparisons? If so, box them. Then, box any uses of *who* and *whom*. Have you used these pronouns correctly?

28h ## Reflexive Pronouns

Reflexive pronouns always agree with their antecedents in person and number.

Reflexive pronouns always end in *-self* (singular) or *-selves* (plural). The pronouns indicate that people or things did something to themselves or for themselves.

Rosanna lost herself in the novel.

You need to watch yourself when you mix those solutions.

Mehul and Paul made themselves cold drinks.

Reflexive Pronouns

Singular Forms

Antecedent	Reflexive Pronoun
I	myself
you	yourself
he	himself
she	herself
it	itself

Plural Forms

Antecedent	Reflexive Pronoun
we	ourselves
you	yourselves
they	themselves

● **Practice 28-14**

Fill in the correct reflexive pronoun in each of the following sentences.

Example: My aunt welcomed her visitors and told them to make
_____*themselves*_____ at home.

1. Mysteriously, migrating birds can direct _____ through clouds, storms, and moonless nights.

2. We all finished the marathon without injuring _____.

3. Sometimes, he finds _____ daydreaming in class.

4. The guide warned her to watch _____ because the path was slippery.

5. You should give _____ a manicure.

Focus on Writing: *Flashback*

Look back at your response to the Focus on Writing activity on page 463. Have you used any reflexive pronouns? If so, label each one. If not, write a new sentence that includes a reflexive pronoun.

Focus on Writing: *Revising and Editing*

Look back at your response to the Focus on Writing activity on page 463. **TEST** what you have written. Then, revise and edit your work, incorporating the corrections you made for this chapter's Flashback activities.

Chapter Review

Editing Practice

Read the following student essay, which includes noun and pronoun errors. Check for errors in plural noun forms, pronoun case, and pronoun-antecedent agreement. Then, make any editing changes you think are necessary. The first sentence has been edited for you.

Cell Phone Misbehavior

manners
Good ~~manneres~~ used to mean using the right fork and holding the

door open for others. Today, however, people may find that good manners

are more complicated than ~~it~~ they used to be. New inventions have led to new

challenges. Cell phones, in particular, have created some problems.

One problem is the "cell yell," which is the tendency of ~~a person~~ *people* to shout while they are using their cell phones. Why do we do this? Maybe we do not realize how loud we are talking. Maybe we yell out of frustration. Anyone can become angry when ~~they~~ *he or she* lose a call. Dead batterys can be infuriating. Unfortunately, the yeller annoys everyone around them.

Even if the cell-phone user speaks normally, other people can hear them. My friends and me are always calling each other, and we do not always pay attention to whom can hear us. The result is that other people are victims of "secondhand conversations." These conversations are not as bad for people's health as secondhand smoke, but ~~it is~~ *They* just as annoying. Whom really wants to hear about the private lifes of strangers? Restrooms used to be private; now, anyone in the next stall can overhear a person's private conversation and learn their secrets.

Also, some cell-phone user seem to think that getting ~~his~~ calls is more important than anything else that might be going on. Phones ring, chirp, or play silly tunes at concertes, in classrooms, at weddings, in churchs, and even at funerals. Can you picture a grieving family at a cemetery having their service interrupted by a ringing phone? People should have enough sense to turn off his or her cell phones at times like ~~these.~~ *This.*

In the United States, there are more than 150 million cell phones. Many people hate their cell phones, but they do not think they can live without *They* ~~it~~. The problem is that cell phones became popular before there were any rules for its use. However, even if the government passed laws about cell-phone behavior, they would have a tough time enforcing it. It seems obvious that us cell-phone users should not need laws to make us behave ourself and use ordinary courtesy.

Collaborative Activities

1. Working in a group, fill in the following chart, writing one noun on each line. If the noun is a proper noun, be sure to capitalize it.

Cars	Trees	Foods	Famous Couples	Cities
_____	_____	_____	_____	_____
_____	_____	_____	_____	_____
_____	_____	_____	_____	_____

Now, using as many of the nouns listed above as you can, write a one-paragraph news article that describes an imaginary event. Exchange your work with another group, and check the other group's article to be sure the correct pronoun refers to each noun. Return the articles to their original groups for editing.

2. Working in a group, write a silly story that uses each of these nouns at least once: *Martians, eggplant, MTV, toupee, kangaroo, Iceland, bat, herd,* and *kayak.* Then, exchange stories with another group. After you have read the other group's story, edit it so that it includes all of the following pronouns: *it, its, itself, they, their, them, themselves.* Return the edited story to its authors. Finally, reread your group's story, and check to make sure pronoun-antecedent agreement is clear and correct.

**Review Checklist:
Nouns and Pronouns**

☐ A noun is a word that names something. A singular noun names one thing; a plural noun names more than one thing. (See 28A.)

☐ Most nouns add -s or -es to form plurals. Some nouns have irregular plural forms. (See 28B.)

☐ A pronoun is a word that refers to and takes the place of a noun or another pronoun. (See 28C.)

☐ The word a pronoun refers to is called the pronoun's antecedent. A pronoun and its antecedent must always agree in number. (See 28D.)

☐ Compound antecedents connected by *and* are plural and are used with plural pronouns. Compound antecedents connected by *or* may take singular or plural pronouns. (See 28E.)

☐ Most indefinite pronoun antecedents are singular and are used with singular pronouns; some are plural and are used with plural pronouns. (See 28E.)

☐ Collective noun antecedents are singular and are used with singular pronouns. (See 28E.)

☐ Personal pronouns can be subjective, objective, or possessive. (See 28F.)

☐ Choosing the correct pronoun to use in compounds and comparisons can be challenging. The relative pronouns *who* and *whom* can also present difficulties. (See 28G.)

☐ Reflexive pronouns must agree with their antecedents in person and number. (See 28H.)

Chapter 29

Adjectives and Adverbs

Identifying Adjectives and Adverbs

Adjectives and adverbs are words that **modify** (identify or describe) other words. They help make sentences clearer and more specific.

An **adjective** answers the question *What kind? Which one?* or *How many?* Adjectives modify nouns or pronouns.

The Turkish city of Istanbul spans two continents. (*Turkish* modifies the noun *city*, and *two* modifies the noun *continents*.)

It is fascinating because of its location and history. (*Fascinating* modifies the pronoun *it*.)

Highlight: Demonstrative Adjectives

Demonstrative adjectives—*this, that, these,* and *those*—do not describe other words. They simply identify particular nouns.

This and *that* identify singular nouns and pronouns.

This Web site is much more up-to-date than that one.

These and *those* identify plural nouns.

These words and phrases are French, but those expressions are Creole.

Focus on Writing

The picture on the opposite page shows children being home schooled by their mother. Look at the picture, and then write a paragraph (or an essay) about the advantages and disadvantages of being educated at home by parents instead of at school by professional teachers.

An **adverb** answers the question *How? Why? When? Where?* or *To what extent?* Adverbs modify verbs, adjectives, or other adverbs.

Traffic moved steadily. (*Steadily* modifies the verb *moved*.)

Still, we were quite impatient. (*Quite* modifies the adjective *impatient*.)

Very slowly, we moved into the center lane. (*Very* modifies the adverb *slowly*.)

Highlight: Distinguishing Adjectives from Adverbs	Many adverbs are formed when *-ly* is added to an adjective.

Adjective	Adverb
slow	slowly
nice	nicely
quick	quickly
real	really

Adjective	Let me give you one quick reminder. (*Quick* modifies the noun *reminder*.)
Adverb	He quickly changed the subject. (*Quickly* modifies the verb *changed*.)

Note: Some adjectives—*lovely*, *friendly*, and *lively*, for example—end in *-ly*. Do not mistake these words for adverbs.

● Practice 29-1

In the following sentences, circle the correct form (adjective or adverb) from the choices in parentheses.

Example: Beatles enthusiasts all over the world have formed tribute bands devoted to the (famous/ famously) group's music.

(1) To show appreciation for their favorite musicians, tribute bands go to (great / greatly) lengths. (2) Fans who have a (real / really) strong affection for a particular band may decide to play its music and copy its style. (3) Sometimes they form their own groups and have successful

careers (simple / simply) performing that band's music. (4) These groups are (usual / usually) called "tribute bands." (5) Most tribute bands are (passionate / passionately) dedicated to reproducing the original group's work. (6) They not only play the group's songs but (careful / carefully) imitate the group's look. (7) They study the band members' facial expressions and body movements and create (exact / exactly) copies of the band's costumes and instruments. (8) Some more (inventive / inventively) tribute bands take the original band's songs and interpret them (different / differently). (9) For example, by performing Beatles songs in the style of Metallica, the tribute band "Beatallica" has created a (unique / uniquely) sound. (10) Some believe such tributes are the (ultimate / ultimately) compliment to the original band; others feel (sure / surely) that tribute groups are just copycats who (serious / seriously) lack imagination.

Highlight: Good and Well

Be careful not to confuse *good* and *well*. Unlike regular adjectives, whose adverb forms add *-ly*, the adjective *good* is irregular. Its adverb form is *well*.

| **Adjective** | Fred Astaire was a good dancer. (*Good* modifies the noun *dancer*.) |
| **Adverb** | He danced especially well with Ginger Rogers. (*Well* modifies the verb *danced*.) |

Always use *well* when you are describing a person's health.

He really didn't feel well [not *good*] after eating two pizzas.

● **Practice 29-2**

Circle the correct form (*good* or *well*) in the sentences below.

Example: It can be hard for some people to find a (good)/ well) job that they really like.

(1) Some people may not do (good / well) sitting in an office. (2) Instead, they may prefer to find jobs that take advantage of the (good / well) physical condition of their bodies. (3) Such people might consider becoming smoke jumpers—firefighters who are (good / well) at parachuting from small planes into remote areas to battle forest fires. (4) Smoke jumpers must be able to work (good / well) even without much sleep. (5) They must also handle danger (good / well). (6) They look forward to the (good / well) feeling of saving a forest or someone's home. (7) As they battle fires, surrounded by smoke and fumes, smoke jumpers may not feel very (good / well). (8) Sometimes, things go wrong; for example, when their parachutes fail to work (good / well), jumpers may be injured or even killed. (9) Smoke jumpers do not get paid (good / well). (10) However, they are proud of their strength and endurance and feel (good / well) about their work.

Focus on Writing: *Flashback*

Look back at your response to the Focus on Writing activity on page 489. Underline each adjective and adverb, and draw an arrow from each to the word it describes or identifies. Do all adjectives modify nouns or pronouns? Do all adverbs modify verbs, adjectives, or other adverbs? Have you used *good* and *well* correctly? Revise any sentences that use adjectives or adverbs incorrectly.

29b   Comparatives and Superlatives

The **comparative** form of an adjective or adverb compares two people or things. Adjectives and adverbs form the comparative with *-er* or *more*. The **superlative** form of an adjective or adverb compares more than two things. Adjectives and adverbs form the superlative with *-est* or *most*.

Adjectives	This film is <u>dull</u> and <u>predictable</u>.
Comparative	The film I saw last week was even <u>duller</u> and <u>more predictable</u> than this one.
Superlative	The film I saw last night was the <u>dullest</u> and <u>most predictable</u> one I've ever seen.

Adverb	For a beginner, Jane did needlepoint <u>skillfully</u>.
Comparative	After she had watched the demonstration, Jane did needlepoint <u>more skillfully</u> than Rosie.
Superlative	Of the twelve beginners, Jane did needlepoint the <u>most skillfully</u>.

Forming Comparatives and Superlatives

Adjectives

● One-syllable adjectives generally form the comparative with *-er* and the superlative with *-est*.

　　great　　greater　　greatest

● Adjectives with two or more syllables form the comparative with *more* and the superlative with *most*.

　　wonderful　　more wonderful　　most wonderful

Exception: Two-syllable adjectives ending in *-y* add *-er* or *-est* after changing the *y* to an *i*.

　　funny　　funnier　　funniest

Adverbs

● All adverbs ending in *-ly* form the comparative with *more* and the superlative with *most*.

　　efficiently　　more efficiently　　most efficiently

● Some other adverbs form the comparative with *-er* and the superlative with *-est*.

　　soon　　sooner　　soonest

Solving Special Problems with Comparatives and Superlatives

The following rules will help you avoid errors with comparatives and superlatives.

● Never use both *-er* and *more* to form the comparative or both *-est* and *most* to form the superlative.

Nothing could have been <u>more awful</u>. (not *more awfuller*)

Space Mountain is the <u>most frightening</u> (not *most frighteningest*) ride at Disney World.

- Never use the superlative when you are comparing only two things.

  This is the <u>more serious</u> (not *most serious*) of the two problems.

- Never use the comparative when you are comparing more than two things.

  This is the <u>worst</u> (not *worse*) day of my life.

● Practice 29-3

Fill in the correct comparative form of the word supplied in parentheses.

Example: Children tend to be _____*noisier*_____ (noisy) than adults.

1. Traffic always moves _____ (slow) during rush hour than late at night.

2. The weather report says temperatures will be _____ (cold) tomorrow.

3. Some elderly people are _____ (healthy) than younger people.

4. It has been proven that pigs are _____ (intelligent) than dogs.

5. When someone asks you to repeat yourself, you usually answer _____ (distinct).

6. The _____ (tall) of the two buildings was damaged by the fire.

7. They want to teach their son to be _____ (respectful) of women than many young men are.

8. Las Vegas is _____ (famous) for its casinos than for its natural resources.

9. The WaterDrop is _____ (wild) than any other ride in the park.

10. You must move _____ (graceful) if you expect to be a good ballroom dancer.

● **Practice 29-4**

Fill in the correct superlative form of the word supplied in parentheses.

Example: Today, tattoos are created __*most frequently*__ (frequently) by a professional using an electric tattoo machine.

(1) Getting a tattoo used to be one of the _____ (sure) and _____ (shocking) ways to show one's individuality. (2) Today, however, only the _____ (daring) tattoos cause a stir. (3) According to the _____ (recent) polls, 36 percent of 18- to 25-year-olds in the United States have at least one tattoo. (4) Tattoos are _____ (common) among people between 26 and 40, 40 percent of whom have one or more. (5) One might expect people in the _____ (competitive) years of their careers not to get tattoos that might limit their job opportunities. (6) However, now that so many people have tattoos, only the _____ (conventional) employers find them shocking. (7) People still tend to place their tattoos in the _____ (safe) and _____ (easily) hidden spots, like the back or the upper arm. (8) That trend is starting to change, though; getting a hand or neck tattoo is one of the _____ (late) fads. (9) In the past, prisoners and gang members were the _____ (likely) people to get tattoos in the _____ (visible) locations. (10) Today, however, some of the _____ (popular) media stars and sports heroes have prominent tattoos.

Highlight: *Good/Well* and *Bad/Badly*	Most adjectives and adverbs form the comparative with *-er* or *more* and the superlative with *-est* or *most*. The adjectives *good* and *bad* and their adverb forms *well* and *badly* are exceptions.

Adjective	Comparative Form	Superlative Form
good	better	best
bad	worse	worst

Adverb	Comparative Form	Superlative Form
well	better	best
badly	worse	worst

● Practice 29-5

Fill in the correct comparative or superlative form of *good*, *well*, *bad*, or *badly*.

Example: She is at her _____*best*_____ (good) when she is under pressure.

1. Today in track practice, Luisa performed _____ (well) than she has in weeks.

2. In fact, she ran her _____ (good) time ever in the fifty meter.

3. When things are bad, we wonder whether they will get _____ (good) or _____ (bad).

4. I've had some bad meals before, but this is the _____ (bad).

5. The world always looks _____ (good) when you're in love than when you're not.

6. Athletes generally play the _____ (badly) when their concentration is poorest.

7. The Sport Shop's prices may be good, but Athletic Attic's are the _____ (good) in town.

8. There are _____ (good) ways to solve conflicts than by fighting.

9. People seem to hear _____ (well) when they agree with what you're saying than when they don't agree with you.

10. Of all the children, Manda took the _____ (good) care of her toys.

Focus on Writing: *Flashback*

Look back at your response to the Focus on Writing activity on page 489. Divide a sheet of paper into three columns. Copy all the adjectives and adverbs from your writing activity in the column on the left. Then, write the comparative and superlative forms for each adjective or adverb in the other columns. (If you use a comparative or superlative in your writing, list it in the appropriate column.)

Focus on Writing: *Revising and Editing*

Look back at your response to the Focus on Writing activity on page 489. **TEST** what you have written. Then, revise your work, beginning by adding or replacing adjectives and adverbs as needed to make your writing clearer and more interesting and deleting any unnecessary adjectives and adverbs. When you are finished, edit your work.

Chapter Review

Editing Practice

Read the following student essay, which includes errors in the use of adjectives and adverbs. Make any changes necessary to correct adjectives incorrectly used for adverbs and adverbs incorrectly used for adjectives. Also correct any errors in the use of comparatives and superlatives and in the use of demonstrative adjectives. Finally, try to add some adjectives and adverbs that you feel would make the writer's ideas clearer or more specific. The first sentence has been edited for you.

Starting Over

A wedding can be the ~~joyfullest~~ *most joyful* occasion in two people's lives, the beginning of a couple's ~~most~~ happiest years. For some unlucky women, however, a wedding can be the worse thing that ever happens; it is the beginning not of their happiness but of their battered lives. As I went through the joyful day of my wedding, I wanted bad to find happiness for the rest of my life, but what I hoped and wished for did not come true.

I was married in the savannah belt of the Sudan in the eastern part of Africa, where I grew up. I was barely twenty-two years old. The first two years of my marriage progressed peaceful, but problems started as soon as our first child was born.

Many American women say, "If my husband gave me just one beating, that would be it. I'd leave." But those attitude does not work in cultures where tradition has overshadowed women's rights and divorce is not accepted. All women can do is accept their sadly fate. Battered women give many reasons for staying in their marriages, but fear is the commonest. Fear immobilizes these women, ruling their decisions, their actions, and their very lives. This is how it was for me.

Of course, I was real afraid whenever my husband hit me. I would run to my mother's house and cry, but she would always talk me into going back and being more patiently with my husband. Our tradition discourages divorce, and wife-beating is taken for granted. The situation is really quite ironic: the religion I practice sets harsh punishments for abusive husbands, but tradition has so overpowered religion that the laws do not work very good.

One night, after nine years of unhappiness, I asked myself whether life had treated me fair. True, I had a high school diploma and two of the beautifullest children in the world, but it was not enough. I realized that to stand up to the husband who treated me so bad, I would have to achieve a more better education than he had. That night, I decided to get a college education in the United States. My husband opposed my decision, but with the support of my father and mother, I was able to change my life. My years as a student and single parent in the United States have been real difficult for me, but I know I made the right choice.

Collaborative Activities

1. Working in a small group, write a one-paragraph plot summary of a scene in an imaginary film. Begin with one of the following three sentences:

   - Dirk and Clive were sworn enemies, but that night on Boulder Ridge they vowed to work together just this once, for the good of their country.

   - Genevieve entered the room in a cloud of perfume, and when she spoke, her voice was like velvet.

   - The desert sun beat down on her head, but Susanna was determined to protect what was hers, no matter what the cost.

2. Trade plot summaries with another group. Add as many adjectives and adverbs as you can to the other group's summary. Make sure each modifier is appropriate. Then, return the summary to the group that wrote it.

3. Reread your own group's plot summary, and edit it carefully, paying special attention to the way adjectives and adverbs are used.

Review Checklist: Adjectives and Adverbs

☐ Adjectives modify nouns or pronouns. (See 29A.)

☐ Demonstrative adjectives—*this*, *that*, *these*, and *those*—identify particular nouns. (See 29A.)

☐ Adverbs modify verbs, adjectives, or other adverbs. (See 29A.)

☐ To compare two people or things, use the comparative form of an adjective or adverb. To compare more than two people or things, use the superlative form of an adjective or adverb. Adjectives and adverbs form the comparative with *-er* or *more* and the superlative with *-est* or *most*. (See 29B.)

☐ The adjectives *good* and *bad* and their adverb forms *well* and *badly* have irregular comparative and superlative forms. (See 29B.)

Chapter 30

Grammar and Usage for ESL Writers

Learning English as a second language involves more than just learning grammar. In fact, if you have been studying English as a second language, you may know more about English grammar than many native speakers do. However, you will still need to learn the conventions and rules that most native speakers already know.

30a   Subjects in Sentences

English requires that every sentence state its subject. In addition, every dependent clause must also have a subject.

Incorrect	Elvis Presley was only forty-two years old when died. (When who died?)
Correct	Elvis Presley was only forty-two years old when <u>he</u> died.

When the real subject follows the verb and the normal subject position before the verb is empty, it must be filled by a "dummy" subject, such as *it* or *there*.

Incorrect	Is hot in this room.
Correct	It is hot in this room.
Incorrect	Are many rivers in my country.
Correct	There are many rivers in my country.

Focus on Writing

The image on the opposite page, a painting by Childe Hassam, shows American flags displayed on the Fourth of July, Independence Day. Look at the picture, and then write a paragraph (or an essay) in which you explain how you and your family celebrate a holiday that is important to you.

Standard English also does not permit a two-part subject in which the second part of the subject is a pronoun referring to the same person or thing as the first part.

Incorrect   The Caspian Sea it is the largest lake in the world.

Correct   The Caspian Sea is the largest lake in the world.

● Practice 30-1

Each of the following sentences is missing the subject of a dependent or an independent clause. On the lines after each sentence, rewrite it, adding an appropriate subject. Then, underline the subject you have added.

Example: Reality TV programs are very popular, but some people believe are going too far.

Reality TV programs are very popular, but some people believe they
are going too far.

1. When the first season of the reality show *Survivor* aired, was an immediate hit.

   _____

   _____

2. Millions of Americans planned their evening so that could be sure not to miss the next episode.

   _____

   _____

3. Was not surprising to see the many other reality shows that suddenly appeared on the air.

   _____

   _____

4. A recent poll asked viewers: "Do enjoy reality TV, or has it gone too far?"

   _____

   _____

5. Most viewers thought that reality TV had gone too far even though enjoyed shows like *Jon and Kate Plus 8* and *So You Think You Can Dance*.

_____

_____

_____

● Practice 30-2

The following sentences contain incorrect two-part subjects. Cross out the unnecessary pronoun. Then, rewrite each sentence correctly on the lines provided.

> **Example:**   Travelers to China ~~they~~ often visit the Great Wall.
>
> *Travelers to China often visit the Great Wall.*

1. The first parts of the Great Wall they were built around 200 A.D.

_____

2. The Great Wall it was built to keep out invading armies.

_____

3. The sides of the Great Wall they are made of stone, brick, and earth.

_____

4. The top of the Great Wall it is paved with bricks, forming a roadway.

_____

5. The Great Wall it is so huge that it can be seen by astronauts in space.

_____

Focus on Writing: *Flashback*

Look back at your response to the Focus on Writing activity on page 501. Does every sentence state its subject? Underline the subject of each sentence. If a sentence does not have a subject, add one. If any sentence has a two-part subject, cross out the unnecessary pronoun.

30b   Plural Nouns

In English, most nouns add *-s* or *-es* to form plurals. Every time you use a noun, ask yourself whether you are talking about one item or more than one, and choose a singular or plural form accordingly. Consider this sentence.

Correct   The <u>books</u> in both <u>branches</u> of the <u>library</u> are out of date.

The three nouns in this sentence are underlined: one is singular (*library*), and the other two are plural (*books, branches*). The word *both* is not enough to indicate that *branch* is plural even though it might be obvious that there are many books in any branch of a library. But even if a sentence includes information that tells you that a noun is plural, you must always use a form of the noun that shows that it is plural.

● Practice 30-3

Underline the plural nouns in the following sentences. (Not all the sentences contain plural nouns.)

Example: Some blind <u>people</u> are finding that miniature <u>horses</u> make very effective guide <u>animals</u>.

1. Blind people first began using guide dogs after World War I.
2. Since then, it has become common to train animals to assist humans with essential tasks.
3. One of the benefits of having a service animal is that it is available 24 hours a day.
4. Guide dogs are the most familiar kind of service animal but not the only kind.
5. Monkeys, parrots, pigs, and horses can all learn to assist people with disabilities.
6. For example, a quadriplegic person needs help turning on light switches and opening containers.
7. A specially trained monkey can perform these chores easily and provide companionship at the same time.

8. An experienced parrot can help an epileptic person by anticipating a seizure before it happens.

9. In addition, with a service animal's help, someone with severe anxiety is sometimes able to avoid frequent panic attacks.

10. Today, fish and insects are some of the only creatures not trained to provide personal assistance to humans.

Focus on Writing: *Flashback*

Look back at your response to the Focus on Writing activity on page 501. List all the plural nouns you used. Does each plural noun have a form that shows the noun is plural? Correct any errors you find.

30c   Count and Noncount Nouns

A **count noun** names one particular thing or a group of particular things that can be counted: *a teacher, a panther, a bed, an ocean, a cloud, an ice cube; two teachers, many panthers, three beds, two oceans, several clouds, some ice cubes.* A **noncount noun**, however, names things that cannot be counted: *gold, cream, sand, blood, smoke, water.*

Count nouns usually have a singular form and a plural form: *cube, cubes.* Noncount nouns usually have only a singular form: *water.* Note how the nouns *cube* and *water* differ in the way they are used in sentences.

Correct	The glass is full of ice cubes.
Correct	The glass is full of water.
Incorrect	The glass is full of waters.
Correct	The glass contains five ice cubes.
Correct	The glass contains some water.
Incorrect	The glass contains five waters.

Often, the same idea can be represented with either a count noun or a noncount noun.

Count	Noncount
people (plural of *person*)	humanity [*not* humanities]
tables, chairs, beds	furniture [*not* furnitures]
letters	mail [*not* mails]
supplies	equipment [*not* equipments]
facts	information [*not* informations]

Some words can be either count or noncount, depending on the meaning intended.

Count   He had many interesting <u>experiences</u> at his first job.

Noncount   It is often difficult to get a job if you do not have <u>experience</u>.

Highlight: Count and Noncount Nouns

Here are some guidelines for using count and noncount nouns.

- Use a count noun to refer to a living animal, but use a noncount noun to refer to the food that comes from that animal.

  Count   There are three live <u>lobsters</u> in the tank.

  Noncount   This restaurant specializes in <u>lobster</u>.

- If you use a noncount noun for a substance or class of things that can come in different varieties, you can often make that noun plural if you want to talk about those varieties.

  Noncount   <u>Cheese</u> is a rich source of calcium.

  Count   Many different <u>cheeses</u> come from Italy.

- If you want to shift attention from a concept in general to specific examples of it, you can often use a noncount noun as a count noun.

  Noncount   You have a great deal of <u>talent</u>.

  Count   My <u>talents</u> do not include singing.

● **Practice 30-4**

In each of the following sentences, decide if the underlined word is being used as a count or a noncount noun. If it is being used as a noncount noun, circle the *N* following the sentence. If it is being used as a count noun, circle the *C*.

Examples: As a Peace Corps <u>volunteer</u> in Ecuador, Dave Schweidenback realized how important bicycles could be.   N Ⓒ

Using his <u>imagination</u>, Dave figured out an effective way to recycle America's unwanted bicycles.   Ⓝ C

1. Pedals for Progress is an American nonprofit <u>organization</u>.   N   C
2. Founded in 1991 by Dave Schweidenback, the <u>group</u> collects and repairs old bicycles and sends them to countries where they are needed.   N   C
3. Pedals for Progress aims to reduce the amount of bicycle <u>waste</u> that ends up in American landfills.   N   C
4. People in the United States throw away millions of bikes and bike parts every <u>year</u>.   N   C
5. At the same time, lack of <u>transportation</u> is a serious problem for many people in developing countries.   N   C
6. Without an efficient and affordable way to get to work, a person cannot hold a <u>job</u>.   N   C
7. A working bicycle provides an easy and environmentally friendly <u>way</u> to get around.   N   C
8. Bicycles from Pedals for Progress only cost the user a small amount of <u>money</u>.   N   C
9. To help maintain these recycled bikes, the organization also helps to establish local repair <u>shops</u>.   N   C
10. By making it easier for people to work, Pedals for Progress hopes to reduce <u>poverty</u>.   N   C

30d   Determiners with Count and Noncount Nouns

Determiners are adjectives that *identify* rather than describe the nouns they modify. Determiners may also *quantify* nouns (that is, indicate an amount or a number).

Determiners include the following words.

● Articles: *a, an, the*
● Demonstrative pronouns: *this, these, that, those*
● Possessive pronouns: *my, our, your, his, her, its, their*
● Possessive nouns: *Sheila's, my friend's,* and so on
● *Whose, which, what*
● *All, both, each, every, some, any, either, no, neither, many, most, much, a few, a little, few, little, several, enough*
● All numerals: *one, two,* and so on

When a determiner is accompanied by one or more other adjectives, the determiner always comes first. For example, in the phrase *my expensive new gold watch, my* is a determiner; you cannot put *expensive, new, gold,* or any other adjective before *my.*

A singular count noun must always be accompanied by a determiner—for example, *my watch* or *the new gold watch,* not just *watch* or *new gold watch.* However, noncount nouns and plural count nouns sometimes have determiners but sometimes do not. *This honey is sweet* and *Honey is sweet* are both acceptable, as are *These berries are juicy* and *Berries are juicy.* (In each case, the meaning is different.) You cannot say, *Berry is juicy,* however; instead, say *This berry is juicy, Every berry is juicy,* or *A berry is juicy.*

Highlight: Determiners	Some determiners can be used only with certain types of nouns:

● *This* and *that* can be used only with singular nouns (count or noncount): *this berry, that honey.*

● *These, those, a few, few, many, both,* and *several* can be used only with plural count nouns: *these berries, those apples, a few ideas, few people, many students, both sides, several directions.*

● *Much, little,* and *a little* can be used only with noncount nouns: *much affection, little time, a little honey.*

● *Some, enough, all,* and *most* can be used only with noncount or plural count nouns: *some honey, some berries; enough trouble, enough problems; all traffic, all roads; most money, most coins.*

● *A, an, every, each, either,* and *neither* can be used only with singular count nouns: *a berry, an elephant, every possibility, each citizen, either option, neither candidate.*

● Practice 30-5

In each of the following sentences, circle the correct choice from each pair of words or phrases in parentheses.

Examples:

Volcanoes are among the most destructive of (all)/ every) natural forces on Earth.

People have always been fascinated and terrified by (this)/ these) force of nature.

1. Not (all / every) volcano is as dangerous as Mt. Vesuvius, which destroyed the ancient city of Pompeii in 79 A.D.

2. In (major some / some major) volcanic eruptions, huge clouds rise over the mountain.

3. (A few violent / Violent a few) eruptions are so dramatic that they blow the mountain apart.

4. (Many / Much) volcanic eruptions, like the deadly 1980 eruption of Mt. St. Helens in Washington State, cannot be predicted.

5. Since the 1400s, (many / much) people—almost 200,000—have lost their lives in volcanic eruptions.

6. When a volcano erupts, (little / a little) can be done to prevent property damage.

7. (Many / Much) lives can be saved, however, if people in the area are evacuated in time.

8. Unfortunately, by the time people realize an eruption is about to take place, there rarely is (every / enough) time to escape.

9. Volcanoes can be dangerous, but they also produce (a little / some) benefits.

10. For example, (a few / a little) countries use energy from underground steam in volcanic areas to produce electric power.

Focus on Writing: *Flashback*

Look back at your response to the Focus on Writing activity on page 501. Divide a sheet of paper into two columns, and list all the count nouns in one column and all the noncount nouns in another column. Then, check to see that you have used count and noncount nouns correctly. Correct any errors you find.

30e   Articles

The **definite article** *the* and the **indefinite articles** *a* and *an* are determiners that tell readers whether the noun that follows is one they can identify (*the book*) or one they cannot yet identify (*a book*).

The Definite Article

When the definite article *the* is used with a noun, the writer is saying to readers, "You can identify which particular thing or things I have in mind. The information you need to make that identification is available to you. Either you have it already, or I am about to give it to you."

Readers can find the necessary information in the following ways.

- By looking at other information in the sentence

    Meet me at the corner of Main Street and Lafayette Road.

    In this example, *the* is used with the noun *corner* because other words in the sentence tell readers which particular corner the writer has in mind: the one located at Main and Lafayette.

- By looking at information in other sentences

    Aisha ordered a slice of pie and a cup of coffee. The pie was delicious. She asked for a second slice.

    Here, *the* is used before the word *pie* in the second sentence to indicate that it is the same pie identified in the first sentence. Notice, however, that the noun *slice* in the third sentence is preceded by an indefinite article (*a*) because it is not the same slice referred to in the first sentence.

- By drawing on general knowledge

    The Earth revolves around the sun.

    Here, *the* is used with the nouns *Earth* and *sun* because readers are expected to know which particular things the writer is referring to.

**Highlight:
The Definite
Article**

Always use *the* (rather than *a* or *an*) in the following situations.

- Before the word *same*: *the same day*
- Before the superlative form of an adjective: *the youngest son*
- Before a number indicating order or sequence: *the third time*

Indefinite Articles

When an indefinite article is used with a noun, the writer is saying to readers, "I don't expect you to have enough information right now to identify a particular thing that I have in mind. I do, however, expect you to recognize that I'm referring to only one item."

Consider the following sentences.

    We need a table for our computer.

    I have a folding table; maybe you can use that.

In the first sentence, the writer is referring to a hypothetical table, not an actual one. Because the table is indefinite to the writer, it is clearly indefinite to the reader, so *a* is used, not *the*. The second sentence refers to an actual table, but because the writer does not expect the reader to be able to identify the table specifically, it is also used with *a* rather than *the*.

**Highlight:
Indefinite
Articles**

Unlike the definite article (*the*), the indefinite articles *a* and *an* occur only with singular count nouns. *A* is used when the next sound is a consonant, and *an* is used when the next sound is a vowel. In choosing *a* or *an*, pay attention to sound rather than to spelling: *a house, a year, a union,* but *an hour, an uncle.* (See the box on p. 599 for a review of vowels and consonants.)

No Article

Only noncount and plural count nouns can stand without articles: *butter, chocolate, cookies, strawberries* (but *a cookie* or *the strawberry*).

Nouns without articles can be used to make generalizations.

Infants need affection as well as food.

In the sentence above, the absence of articles before the nouns *infants, affection,* and *food* indicates that the statement is not about particular infants, affection, or food but about infants, affection, and food in general. Remember not to use *the* in such sentences; in English, a sentence like *The infants need affection as well as food* can only refer to particular, identifiable infants, not to infants in general.

Articles with Proper Nouns

Proper nouns can be divided into two classes: names that take *the* and names that take no article.

- Names of people usually take no article unless they are used in the plural to refer to members of a family, in which case they take *the*: *Napoleon, Mahatma Gandhi,* but *the Parkers.*
- Names of places that are plural in form usually take *the*: *the Andes, the United States.*
- The names of most places on land (cities, states, provinces, and countries) take no article: *Salt Lake City, Mississippi, Alberta, Japan.* The names of most bodies of water (rivers, seas, and oceans, although not lakes or bays) take *the*: *the Mississippi, the Mediterranean, the Pacific* (but *Lake Erie, San Francisco Bay*).
- Names of streets take no article: *Main Street.* Names of unnumbered highways take *the*: *the Belt Parkway.*

● **Practice 30-6**

In the following paragraph, decide whether each blank needs a definite article (*the*), an indefinite article (*a* or *an*), or no article. If a definite or indefinite article is needed, write it in the space provided. If no article is needed, leave the space blank.

Example: Adopted in 2007, Vietnamese-born Pax is __*the*__ third child whom _____ Angelina Jolie brought back to __*the*__ United States from __*a*__ foreign country.

(1) _____ number of American celebrities have adopted children from _____ other countries. (2) Two of _____ best-known parents of foreign children are Madonna and _____ Angelina Jolie. (3) These famous mothers have drawn attention to _____ practice of international adoption and prompted _____ heated debate on _____ topic. (4) Critics argue that taking _____ child from his or her native country and culture is _____ selfish act. (5) Some of _____ most vocal opponents of _____ international adoptions are _____ organizations Save the Children and UNICEF. (6) These groups believe that _____ money spent on adopting _____ single child should go toward improving _____ welfare of all children. (7) Many children in _____ countries like _____ Malawi, where Madonna's son was born, suffer from poverty and are in need of _____ basic social services. (8) _____ tens of thousands of dollars that adoptive parents give to international adoption agencies could go _____ long way toward improving _____ lives of these children. (9) Opponents also make _____ point that _____ agencies involved in these adoptions are often corrupt. (10) However, supporters of international adoption say that providing _____ child with _____ stable, loving family should be _____ first priority. (11) _____ orphanage simply cannot provide _____ opportunities and personal attention that _____ adoptive parent can. (12) Supporters of _____ practice say that celebrity adoptions, in particular, have _____ positive impact because they draw attention to _____ struggles of _____ world's children. (13) Ultimately, people on _____ both sides of _____ debate share _____ same belief: no child should have to suffer from _____ poverty and neglect.

Focus on Writing: *Flashback*

Look back at your response to the Focus on Writing activity on page 501. Circle each definite article (*the*) and indefinite article (*a* or *an*) you have used. Have you used articles correctly? Correct any errors you find.

30f

Negative Statements and Questions

Negative Statements

To form a negative statement, add the word *not* directly after the first helping verb of the complete verb.

> Global warming has been getting worse.
>
> Global warming has <u>not</u> been getting worse.

When there is no helping verb, a form of the verb *do* must usually be inserted before *not*.

> Automobile traffic contributes to pollution.
>
> Automobile traffic <u>does not</u> contribute to pollution.

However, if the main verb is *am*, *is*, *are*, *was*, or *were*, do not insert a form of *do* before *not*: *Harry <u>was</u> late. Harry <u>was not</u> late.*

Remember that when *do* is used as a helping verb, the form of *do* used must match the tense and number of the original main verb. Note that in the negative statement above, the main verb loses its tense and appears in the base form (*contribute*, not *contributes*).

Questions

To form a question, move the helping verb that follows the subject to the position directly before the subject.

> The governor <u>is</u> trying to compromise.
>
> <u>Is</u> the governor trying to compromise?

The governor <u>is</u> working on the budget.

<u>Is</u> the governor working on the budget?

The same rule applies even when the verb is in the past or future tense.

The governor <u>was</u> trying to lower state taxes.

<u>Was</u> the governor trying to lower state taxes?

The governor <u>will</u> try to get reelected.

<u>Will</u> the governor try to get reelected?

As with negatives, when the verb does not include a helping verb, you must usually supply a form of *do*. To form a question, put the correct form of *do* directly before the subject.

The governor <u>works</u> hard.

<u>Does</u> the governor <u>work</u> hard?

The governor <u>improved</u> life in his state.

<u>Did</u> the governor <u>improve</u> life in his state?

However, if the main verb is *am, is, are, was,* or *were,* do not insert a form of *do* before the verb. Instead, move the main verb so it comes before the subject (*Harry <u>was</u> late. <u>Was</u> Harry late?)*

Note: The helping verb never comes before the subject if the subject is a question word (such as *who* or *which*).

<u>Who</u> is talking to the governor?

<u>Which</u> bills have been vetoed by the governor?

● Practice 30-7

Rewrite each of the following sentences in two ways: first, turn the sentence into a question; then, rewrite the original sentence as a negative statement.

Example:　Her newest album is selling as well as her first one.

Question: Is her newest album selling as well as her first one?

Negative statement: Her newest album is not selling as well as her first one.

1. Converting metric measurements to the system used in the United States is difficult.

   Question: _____

   _____

   Negative statement: _____

   _____

2. The early frost damaged many crops.

   Question: _____

   Negative statement: _____

3. That family was very influential in the early 1900s.

   Question: _____

   Negative statement: _____

   _____

4. Most stores in malls are open on Sundays.

   Question: _____

   Negative statement: _____

5. Choosing the right gift is a difficult task.

   Question: _____

   Negative statement: _____

6. Some great artists are successful during their lifetimes.

   Question: _____

   Negative statement: _____

   _____

7. The lawyer can verify the witness's story.

   Question: _____

   Negative statement: _____

8. American cities are as dangerous as they were thirty years ago.

   Question: _____

   _____

   Negative statement: _____

   _____

9. The British royal family is loved by most British people.

   Question: _____

   Negative statement: _____

   _____

10. Segregation in the American South ended with the Civil War.

    Question: _____

    Negative statement: _____

    _____

Focus on Writing: *Flashback*

Look back at your response to the Focus on Writing activity on page 501. Do you see any negative statements? If so, check to make sure you have formed them correctly. Then, on the line below, write a question that you could add to your Focus on Writing activity.

Question: _____

_____

Check carefully to make sure you have formed the question correctly.

30g   Verb Tense

In English, a verb's form indicates its **tense**—when an action took place (for instance, in the past or in the present). Use the appropriate tense of the verb, even if the time is obvious or if the sentence includes other indications of time (such as *two years ago* or *at present*).

Incorrect	Albert Einstein emigrate from Germany in 1933.
Correct	Albert Einstein emigrated from Germany in 1933.

Focus on Writing: *Flashback*

Look back at your response to the Focus on Writing activity on page 501. Are all your verbs in the appropriate tense? Correct any errors you find.

30h Stative Verbs

Stative verbs indicate that someone or something is in a state that will not change, at least for a while.

> Hiro <u>knows</u> American history very well.

Most English verbs show action, and these action verbs can be used in the progressive tenses. The **present progressive** tense consists of the present tense of *be* plus the present participle (*I am going*). The **past progressive** tense consists of the past tense of *be* plus the present participle (*I was going*). Unlike other verbs, however, stative verbs are rarely used in the progressive tenses.

> **Incorrect**　Hiro is knowing American history very well.
>
> **Correct**　　Hiro knows American history very well.

Highlight: Stative Verbs

Verbs that are stative—such as *know*, *understand*, *think*, *believe*, *want*, *like*, *love*, and *hate*—often refer to mental states. Other stative verbs include *be*, *have*, *need*, *own*, *belong*, *weigh*, *cost*, and *mean*. Certain verbs of sense perception, like *see* and *hear*, are also stative even though they can refer to momentary events as well as to unchanging states.

Many verbs have more than one meaning, and some of these verbs are active with one meaning but stative with another. An example is the verb *weigh*.

> **Active**　　The butcher <u>weighs</u> the meat.
>
> **Stative**　The meat <u>weighs</u> three pounds.

In the first of these two sentences, the verb *weigh* means "to put on a scale"; it is active, not stative. In the second sentence, however, the same verb means "to have weight," so it is stative, not active. It would be unacceptable to say, "The meat is weighing three pounds," but "The butcher is weighing the meat" would be correct.

● Practice 30-8

In each of the following sentences, circle the verb or verbs. Then, correct any problems with stative verbs by crossing out the incorrect verb tense and writing the correct verb tense above the line. If the verb is correct, write *C* above it.

> *know*
> **Example:**   Police officers ~~are knowing~~ that fingerprint identification is
> one of the best ways to catch criminals.

1. As early as 1750 B.C., ancient Babylonians were signing their identities on clay tablets.

2. By 220 A.D., the Chinese were becoming aware that ink fingerprints could identify people.

3. However, it was not until the late 1800s that anyone was believing that criminal identification was possible with fingerprints.

4. Today, we know that each person is having unique patterns on the tips of his or her fingers.

5. When police study a crime scene, they want to see whether the criminals have left any fingerprint evidence.

6. There is always a layer of oil on the skin, and police are liking to use it to get fingerprints.

7. Crime scene experts are often seeing cases where the criminals are touching their hair and pick up enough oil to leave a good fingerprint.

8. The police are needing to judge whether the fingerprint evidence has been damaged by sunlight, rain, or heat.

9. In the courtroom, juries often weigh fingerprint evidence before they are deciding on their verdict.

10. Now, the FBI is collecting millions of fingerprints, which police departments can compare with the fingerprints they find at crime scenes.

Focus on Writing: *Flashback*

Look back at your response to the Focus on Writing activity on page 501. Can you identify any stative verbs? Check carefully to be sure you have not used any of these verbs in a progressive tense. Correct any errors you find.

30i ## Modal Auxiliaries

A **modal auxiliary** (such as *can*, *may*, *might*, or *must*) is a helping verb that is used with a sentence's main verb to express ability, possibility, necessity, intent, obligation, and so on. In the following sentence, *can* is the modal auxiliary, and *imagine* is the main verb.

> I *can imagine* myself in Hawaii.

Modal auxiliaries usually intensify the main verb's meaning.

> I *must run* as fast as I can.
> You *ought to lose* some weight.

Modal Auxiliaries

can	ought to
could	shall
may	should
might	will
must	would

Highlight: Modal Auxiliaries

Modal auxiliaries can be used to do the following.

- Express physical ability

    I can walk faster than my brother.

- Express the possibility of something occurring

    He might get the job if his interview goes well.

**Highlight:
Modal
Auxiliaries**
continued

- Express or request permission

  May I use the restroom in the hallway?

- Express necessity

  I must get to the train station on time.

- Express a suggestion or advice

  To be healthy, you should [or ought to] exercise and eat balanced meals.

- Express intent

  I will try to study harder next time.

- Express a desire

  Would you please answer the telephone?

● **Practice 30-9**

In the exercise below, circle the correct modal auxiliary.

Example: (May /Would) you help me complete the assignment?

1. It doesn't rain very often in Arizona, but today it looks like it (can / might).
2. I know I (will / ought to) call my aunt on her birthday, but I always find an excuse.
3. Sarah (should / must) study for her math exam, but she would rather spend time with her friends.
4. John (can / would) be the best person to represent our class.
5. After the close presidential election of 2000, many people began to realize they (could / should) vote in every election.
6. All students (will / must) bring two pencils, a notebook, and a dictionary to class every day.
7. (Would / May) you show me the way to the post office?
8. I (could / should) not ask for more than my family, my job, and my health.

9. Do you think they (could / can) come back tomorrow to finish the painting job?

10. A dog (should / might) be a helpful companion for your disabled father.

30j   Gerunds

A **gerund** is a verb form ending in -*ing* that always acts as a noun.

<u>Reading</u> the newspaper is one of my favorite things to do on Sundays.

Just like a noun, a gerund can be used as a subject, a direct object, a subject complement, or the object of a preposition.

Highlight: Gerunds

● A gerund can be the subject of a sentence.

    Playing tennis is one of my hobbies.

● A gerund can be a direct object.

    My brother influenced my racing.

● A gerund can be a subject complement.

    The most important thing is winning.

● A gerund can be the object of a preposition.

    The teacher rewarded him for passing.

● Practice 30-10

To complete the sentences below, fill in the blanks with the gerund form of the verb provided in parentheses.

Example: _____*Typing*_____ (type) is a skill that used to be taught in high school.

1. _____ (eat) five or six smaller meals throughout the day is healthier than eating two or three big meals.

2. In the winter, there is nothing better than _____ (skate) outdoors on a frozen pond.

3. The household task I dread the most is _____ (clean).

4. The fish avoided the net by _____ (swim) faster.

5. _____ (quit) is easier than accomplishing a goal.

6. Her parents praised her for _____ (remember) their anniversary.

7. Her favorite job is _____ (organize) the files.

8. I did not like his _____ (sing).

9. For me, _____ (cook) is relaxing.

10. The best way to prepare for the concert is by _____ (practice).

30k

Placing Modifiers in Order

Adjectives and other modifiers that come before a noun usually follow a set order.

Required Order

- Determiners always come first in a series of modifiers: *these fragile glasses*. The determiners *all* or *both* always precede any other determiners: *all these glasses*.
- If one of the modifiers is a noun, it must come directly before the noun it modifies: *these wine glasses*.
- Descriptive adjectives are placed between the determiners and the noun modifiers: *these fragile wine glasses*. If there are two or more descriptive adjectives, the following order is preferred.

Preferred Order

- Adjectives that show the writer's attitude generally precede adjectives that merely describe: *these lovely fragile wine glasses*.
- Adjectives that indicate size generally come early: *these lovely large fragile wine glasses*.

● Practice 30-11

Arrange each group of modifiers in the correct order, and rewrite the complete phrase in the blank.

> **Example:** (annual, impressive, the, publisher's) report
> *the publisher's impressive annual report*

1. (brand-new, a, apartment, high-rise) building

   _____

2. (gifted, twenty-five-year-old, Venezuelan, this) author

   _____

3. (successful, short-story, numerous) collections

   _____

4. (her, all, intriguing, suspense) novels

   _____

5. (publisher's, best-selling, the, three) works

   _____

6. (main, story's, two, this) characters

   _____

7. (young, a, strong-willed) woman

   _____

8. (middle-aged, shy, the, British) poet

   _____

9. (exquisite, wedding, an, white) gown

   _____

10. (elaborate, wedding, an) reception

    _____

Focus on Writing: *Flashback*

Look back at your response to the Focus on Writing activity on page 501. Have you used more than one modifier before a single noun? If so, list here all the modifiers you used and the noun that follows them.

Modifiers: _____ _____ _____ Noun: _____

Modifiers: _____ _____ _____ Noun: _____

Have you arranged the modifiers in the correct order? Make any necessary corrections.

30I

Choosing Prepositions

A **preposition** introduces a noun or pronoun and links it to other words in the sentence. The word the preposition introduces is called the **object** of the preposition.

A preposition and its object combine to form a **prepositional phrase**: *on the table, near the table, under the table.*

> I thought I had left the book <u>on</u> the table or somewhere <u>near</u> the table, but I found it <u>under</u> the table.

The prepositions *at, in,* and *on* sometimes cause problems for nonnative speakers of English. For example, to identify the location of a place or an event, you can use *at, in,* or *on.*

- The preposition *at* specifies an exact point in space or time.

  > The museum is <u>at</u> 1000 Fifth Avenue. Let's meet there <u>at</u> 10:00 tomorrow morning.

- Expanses of space or time are treated as containers and therefore require *in.*

  > Women used to wear long skirts <u>in</u> the early 1900s.

- *On* must be used in two cases: with names of streets (but not with exact addresses), and with days of the week or month.

  > We will move into our new office <u>on</u> 18th Street either <u>on</u> Monday or <u>on</u> March 12.

30m   Prepositions in Familiar Expressions

Many familiar expressions end with prepositions. Learning to write clearly and **idiomatically** means learning which preposition is used in such expressions. Even native speakers of English sometimes have trouble choosing the correct preposition.

The sentences that follow illustrate idiomatic use of prepositions in various expressions. Note that sometimes different prepositions are used with the same word. For example, both *on* and *for* can be used with *wait* to form two different expressions with two different meanings (*He waited on their table*; *She waited for the bus*). Which preposition you choose depends on your meaning. (In the list that follows, pairs of similar expressions that end with different prepositions are bracketed.)

Expression with Preposition	Sample Sentence
acquainted with	During orientation, the university offers workshops to make sure that students are acquainted with its rules and regulations.
addicted to	I think Abby is becoming addicted to pretzels.
agree on (a plan or objective)	It is vital that all members of the school board agree on goals for the coming year.
agree to (a proposal)	Striking workers finally agreed to the terms of management's offer.
angry about or at (a situation)	Taxpayers are understandably angry about (or at) the deterioration of city recreation facilities.
angry with (a person)	When the mayor refused to hire more police officers, his constituents became angry with him.
approve of	Amy's adviser approved of her decision to study in Guatemala.
bored with	Salah got bored with economics, so he changed his major to psychology.
capable of	Hannah is a good talker, but she is not capable of acting as her own lawyer.
consist of	The deluxe fruit basket consisted of five pathetic pears, two tiny apples, a few limp bunches of grapes, and one lonely kiwi.

contrast with	Coach Pauley's relaxed style <u>contrasts</u> <u>with</u> Coach Morgan's more formal approach.
convenient for	The proposed location of the new day-care center is <u>convenient for</u> many families.
deal with	Many parents and educators believe it is possible to <u>deal with</u> the special needs of children with autism in a regular classroom.
depend on	Children <u>depend on</u> their parents for emotional as well as <u>financial</u> support.
differ from (something else)	A capitalist system <u>differs from</u> a socialist system in its view of private ownership.
differ with (someone else)	When Miles realized that he <u>differed with</u> his boss on most important issues, he handed in his resignation.
emigrate from	My grandfather and his brother <u>emigrated from</u> the part of Russia that is now Ukraine.
grateful for (a favor)	If you can arrange an interview next week, I will be very <u>grateful for</u> your time and trouble.
grateful to (someone)	Jerry Garcia was always <u>grateful to</u> his loyal fans.
immigrate to	Many Cubans want to leave their country and <u>immigrate to</u> the United States.
impatient with	Keshia often gets <u>impatient with</u> her four younger brothers.
interested in	Tomiko had always been <u>interested in</u> computers, so no one was surprised when she became a Web designer.
interfere with	College athletes often find that their dedication to sports <u>interferes with</u> their schoolwork.
meet with	I hope I can <u>meet with</u> you soon to discuss my research project.
object to	The defense attorney <u>objected to</u> the prosecutor's treatment of the witness.
pleased with	Most of the residents are <u>pleased with</u> the mayor's crackdown on crime.
protect against	Nobel Prize winner Linus Pauling believed that large doses of vitamin C could <u>protect</u> people <u>against</u> the common cold.
reason with	When two-year-olds have tantrums, it is nearly impossible to <u>reason with</u> them.

reply to	If no one <u>replies to</u> our ad within two weeks, we will advertise again.
responsible for	Should teachers be held <u>responsible for</u> their students' low test scores?
similar to	The blood sample found at the crime scene was remarkably <u>similar to</u> one found in the suspect's residence.
specialize in	Dr. Casullo is a dentist who <u>specializes in</u> periodontal surgery.
succeed in	Lisa hoped her M.B.A. would help her <u>succeed in</u> a business career.
take advantage of	Some consumer laws are designed to prevent door-to-door salespeople from <u>taking advantage of</u> buyers.
wait for (something to happen)	Many parents of teenagers experience tremendous anxiety while <u>waiting for</u> their children to come home at night.
wait on (in a restaurant)	We sat at the table for twenty minutes before someone <u>waited on</u> us.
worry about	Why <u>worry about</u> things you cannot change?

Highlight: Using Prepositions in Familiar Expressions: Synonyms

Below is a list of familiar expressions that have similar meanings. They can often be used in the same contexts.

acquainted with, familiar with

addicted to, hooked on

angry with (a person), upset with

approve of, authorize

bored with, tired of

capable of, able to

consists of, has, contains, includes

deal with (a problem), address

depend on, rely on

differ from (something else), be different from

differ with (someone else), disagree

emigrate from, move from (another country)

grateful for (a favor), thankful for

immigrate to, move to (another country)

interested in, fascinated by

interfere with, disrupt

meet with, get together with

object to, oppose

Highlight: Using Prepositions in Familiar Expressions: Synonyms continued	pleased with, happy with	succeed in, attain success, reach a goal
	protect against, guard against	take advantage of, use an opportunity
	reply to, answer	
	responsible for, accountable for	wait for (something to happen), expect
	similar to, almost the same as	
	specialize in, devote oneself to (a special area of work)	wait on (in a restaurant), serve

● Practice 30-12

In the following paragraph, fill in each blank with the correct preposition.

Example: Tony Bartoli is ____*in*____ his second year ____*at*____ a large state college.

(1) There have been many changes _____ Tony Bartoli's life _____ the past few years. (2) _____ 2009, Tony's family emigrated _____ Argentina. (3) Although Tony had studied English _____ Argentina, he was amazed _____ how little he seemed to know when he got _____ the States. (4) _____ his first day _____ high school, he met _____ a guidance counselor who convinced him to take advantage _____ the special English classes that were being offered _____ the vocational-technical school. (5) Since Tony was very interested _____ improving his English (and knew he would have to do that if he wanted to succeed _____ his new world), he enrolled _____ a class. (6) Now, Tony is grateful not only _____ his guidance counselor but also _____ all the teachers who supported him and showed him that he was capable _____ succeeding. (7) Adjusting _____ a new life _____ a new country and getting acquainted _____ a culture that differs greatly _____ the one that he was used _____ were challenges that

he met _____ enthusiasm and _____ success. (8) Last year, when Tony first arrived _____ Florida State, he was worried _____ taking regular college courses _____ his second language, English. (9) Some of the first-year classes were difficult, but he was pleased _____ his grades _____ the end _____ the year. (10) This year, he went back _____ campus early so that he could look _____ a part-time job and a place to live. (11) When he found the apartment _____ College Avenue, he called his parents _____ the phone. (12) _____ first, they objected _____ his decision to live on his own, but they finally agreed _____ the idea. (13) It is going to be a great year, and Tony is looking forward _____ it.

Focus on Writing: *Flashback*

Look back at your response to the Focus on Writing activity on page 501. Have you used any of the idiomatic expressions listed on pages 526–28? If so, have you used the correct prepositions with these expressions? Make any necessary corrections.

30n   Prepositions in Phrasal Verbs

A **phrasal verb** consists of two words, a verb and a preposition, that are joined to form an idiomatic expression. Many phrasal verbs are **separable**. This means that a direct object can come between the verb and the preposition. However, some phrasal verbs are **inseparable**; that is, the preposition must always come immediately after the verb.

Separable Phrasal Verbs

In many cases, phrasal verbs may be split, with the direct object coming between the two parts of the verb. When the direct object is a noun, the second word of the phrasal verb can come either before or after the object.

In the sentences below, *fill out* is a phrasal verb. Because the object of the verb *fill out* is a noun (*form*), the second word of the verb can come either before or after the verb's object.

Correct   Please fill out the form.

Correct   Please fill the form out.

When the object is a pronoun, however, these phrasal verbs must be split, and the pronoun must come between the two parts of the verb.

Incorrect   Please fill out it.

Correct   Please fill it out.

Some Common Separable Phrasal Verbs

ask out	give away	put back	throw away
bring up	hang up	put on	try out
call up	leave out	set aside	turn down
carry out	let out	shut off	turn off
drop off	make up	take down	wake up
fill out	put away	think over	

Remember, when the object of the verb is a pronoun, these phrasal verbs must be split, and the pronoun must come between the two parts (for example, *take it down*, *put it on*, *let it out*, and *make it up*).

Inseparable Phrasal Verbs

Some phrasal verbs, however, cannot be separated; that is, the preposition cannot be separated from the verb. This means that a direct object cannot come between the verb and the preposition.

Incorrect   Please go the manual over carefully.

Correct   Please go over the manual carefully.

Notice that in the correct sentence above, the direct object (*manual*) comes right after the preposition (*over*).

> **Some Common Inseparable Phrasal Verbs**
>
> | | | |
> | --- | --- | --- |
> | come across | run across | show up |
> | get along | run into | stand by |
> | go over | see to | |

● **Practice 30-13**

Consulting the lists of separable and inseparable phrasal verbs on page 531 and above, decide whether the preposition is placed correctly in each of the following sentences. If a sentence is correct, write *C* in the blank after the sentence. If it is not correct, edit the sentence.

Example: These days, Stephenie Meyer's vampire novels are so popular that it is difficult to enter a bookstore and not come across one. __*C*__

1. Most fans of the characters in Stephenie Meyer's popular *Twilight* series know that Meyer first thought up them in a dream. _____

2. One night in 2003, Meyer dreamed of a shy teenage girl and the vampire who loved her and stood her by even though he wanted to suck her blood. _____

3. Because Meyer immediately knew their story and just needed to put on paper it, she was able to complete her first book, *Twilight*, in just three months. _____

4. Once her imagination got going, it seemed Meyer could not turn off it. _____

5. After completing four books from the teenager Bella's point of view, Meyer wanted to try out a new perspective. _____

6. So, she began writing *Midnight Sun*, a book that went the same events over but told them from the vampire's point of view. _____

7. Unfortunately, the first twelve chapters of *Midnight Sun* showed online up after an unexplained leak. _____

8. Frustrated, Meyer set the project aside and worked on other books for a while. _____

9. She promised to return to the draft and assured fans that she was not throwing away it. _____

10. In the meantime, carrying out her plan to publish a book for adults, Meyer released a science-fiction novel, *The Host*. _____

Focus on Writing: *Flashback*

Look back at your response to the Focus on Writing activity on page 501. Have you used any phrasal verbs? Have you placed the preposition correctly in each case? Make any necessary corrections.

Focus on Writing: *Revising and Editing*

Look back at your response to the Focus on Writing activity on page 501. **TEST** what you have written. Then, revise and edit your work, reviewing all your Flashback activities to be sure you have made all necessary corrections in grammar and usage.

Editing Practice

Read the following student essay, which includes errors in the use of subjects, nouns, articles and determiners, and stative verbs, as well as errors with prepositions in idiomatic expressions. Check each underlined word or phrase. If it is not used correctly, write in any necessary changes. If the underlined word or phrase is correct, write *C* above it. The title of the essay has been edited for you.

in
How to Succeed ~~on~~ Multinational Business

Success in multinational business often <u>depends in</u> the ability to understand other countries' cultures. Understanding how cultures <u>differ to</u> our own, however, is only one key to <u>these</u> success. Also, <u>is</u> crucial that businesses learn to adapt to different cultures. <u>The ethnocentrism</u> is the belief that one's own culture has <u>a</u> best way of doing things. In international business, <u>is</u> necessary to <u>set aside</u> this belief. A company cannot <u>be using</u> the same methods or sell the same products overseas as it does at home. Though making these changes requires a lot of work, companies that choose to adjust to new <u>market</u> are usually <u>happy with</u> their decision.

<u>It is</u> many aspects of a country that must be understood before <u>successful international business</u> can be <u>carried out</u>. To protect itself <u>from</u> legal errors, a company needs to understand the country's legal system, which may be very different from its home country's legal system. <u>May be</u> necessary to get licenses to export products <u>onto</u> other countries. The role of women is also likely to be different; without knowing this, businesspeople might unintentionally offend people. Also, <u>much</u> personal interactions in other countries may give the wrong impression to someone who is inexperienced. For example, in Latin American countries, people <u>are often standing</u> close together and touch each other when they are talking. Americans may feel uncomfortable in such a situation <u>unless understand</u> it.

To succeed in international business, companies are also needing to understand what people buy and why. To avoid problems, a company that wants to sell its product internationally it should do a few market research. For example, when McDonald's opened restaurants on India, realized that beef burgers would not work in a country where many people believe that cows are sacred. Instead, burgers were made from ground chickens. For India's many vegetarians, McDonald's created several different vegetable patty. McDonald's understood that both the religious and cultural characteristic of India had to be considered if its new restaurants were going to succeed.

Looking to attract new customer in today's international market, companies they are noticing a growing demand for *halal* goods and services. The word *halal* indicates the object or action that is permissible by Islamic law. Businesses are realizing that world's Muslims depend in companies to provide acceptable *halal* foods, banks, hotels, magazines, and other services. Nestlé, Kentucky Fried Chicken, Subway, LG, and Nokia are just a few of the well-known companies that have been successfully remaking their products to appeal in Muslim consumers. Because these ethical, high-quality items also appeal to non-Muslims, many of this companies are discovering that meeting cultural needs and desires are simply good business.

Over time, the marketplace is becoming more global. In those setting, individuals from numerous cultures come together. To take advantage from opportunities and perform effectively, an international company must hire people with the right experiences. To deal with other cultures, multinational companies inside today's global market must have good informations and show other cultures the highest respects.

Collaborative Activities

1. Working in a small group, make a list of ten prepositional phrases that include the prepositions *above, around, at, between, from, in, on, over, under,* and *with.* Use specific nouns as objects of these prepositions, and use as many modifying words as you wish. (Try, for example, to write something like *above their hideous wedding portrait,* not just *above the picture.*)

2. Exchange lists with another group. Still working collaboratively, compose a list of ten sentences, each including one of the other group's ten prepositional phrases. Give your list of ten sentences to another group.

3. Working with this new list of ten sentences, substitute a different prepositional phrase for each one that appears in a sentence. Make sure each sentence still makes sense.

Review Checklist: Grammar and Usage for ESL Writers

☐ All English sentences must state their subjects. (See 30A.)

☐ In English, most nouns add *-s* or *-es* to form plurals. When a noun refers to more than one person or thing, always use a form that indicates that a noun is plural. (See 30B.)

☐ English nouns may be count nouns or noncount nouns. A count noun names one particular thing or a group of particular things (*a teacher, oceans*). A noncount noun names something that cannot be counted (*gold, sand*). (See 30C.)

☐ Determiners are adjectives that identify rather than describe the nouns they modify. Determiners may also indicate amount or number. (See 30D.)

☐ The definite article *the* and the indefinite articles *a* and *an* are determiners that indicate whether the noun that follows is one readers can identify (*the book*) or one they cannot yet identify (*a book*). (See 30E.)

☐ To form a negative statement, add the word *not* directly after the first helping verb of the complete verb. To form a question, move the helping verb that follows the subject to the position directly before the subject. (See 30F.)

☐ A verb's form must indicate when an action took place. (See 30G.)

→

Review Checklist: Grammar and Usage for ESL Writers
continued

☐ Stative verbs indicate that someone or something is in a state that will not change, at least for a while. Stative verbs are rarely used in the progressive tenses. (See 30H.)

☐ A modal auxiliary is a helping verb that is used with a sentence's main verb to express ability, possibility, necessity, intent, obligation, and so on. (See 30I.)

☐ A gerund is a verb form ending in -ing that always acts as a noun. (See 30J.)

☐ Adjectives and other modifiers that come before a noun usually follow a set order. (See 30K.)

☐ A preposition introduces a noun or pronoun and links it to other words in the sentence. The prepositions at, in, and on can present challenges for nonnative speakers of English. (See 30L.)

☐ Many familiar expressions end with prepositions. (See 30M.)

☐ A phrasal verb consists of two words, a verb and a preposition, that are joined to form an idiomatic expression. (See 30N.)

Editing Practice: Sentences

Read the following sentences, which contain errors in basic grammar. Identify errors in the use of the past tense, past participles, nouns, pronouns, adjectives, and adverbs, and edit the faulty sentences. Some sentences have more than one error.

1. Whenever I went fishing with my brother, he catched fewer fish than me.
2. Before Kylie typed her English essay, she has never used a computer; however, she finded it more easier than she expected.
3. After the news conference, the soccer team (including the two heros of the game) boarded their bus and went home.
4. When I visited them last summer, neither my aunt nor her two childs can meet me at the train station.
5. After the power outage, everything in the freezer had to be threw away because it was not froze solid.
6. Airport security officers told everyone in line to remove their shoes.
7. Me and my roommate met for the first time during the summer.
8. The person whom was working late last night forgets to lock the office door.
9. As soon as I saw the first question, I knew I would do bad on the test.
10. When a person needs help, you should ask for it.

Editing Practice: Essay

Read the following student essay, which contains errors in the use of the past tense, past participles, nouns, pronouns, and adjectives and adverbs. Identify the sentences that need to be corrected, and edit the faulty sentences. The first sentence has been edited for you.

Banning Soft Drinks and Snacks in Schools

Americans' weight problems ~~usual~~ *usually* start in childhood. Almost one-third of American childrens are more heavier than children of past generations, and the number is increasing. Since a child spent much of their time in school, what they eat and drink there is important. As a result, some person have sayed that soft drinks and snacks are real bad and should not be sold in schools. They say students would have more healthier lifes as adults if they did not eat so much snack food. Banning such products would reduce the number of calories consume by students. However, those whom opposed such rules say that school budgets would suffer bad from the loss of profits from vending machines.

By the time they are adults, almost 65 percent of Americans are either obese or overweight. In the past, adult-onset diabetes is a disease that has affected overweight peoples over age forty-five; now, it has became common among the young. Also, obesity is related to other diseases, such as cancer, high blood pressure, and heart disease. Obesity leads to more than $100 billion in health-care costs in the United States every year. Obviously, anyone who cares about this problem should do whatever they can to make it better. We all want each child to live the most longest, healthiest life possible.

One solution to the problem is to limit the amount of sugary soft drinks and snacks that children consume every day. These drink are a major source of extra calories. Two out of three children consume these drinks every day. Each can of soda provide about 50 grams of sugar, and consumption is growing. More than 10 percent of a children's daily calories comes from soft drinks. For each can of sugar-sweetened soda a child drinks each day, their chance of becoming obese grows by 60 percent. Sugary snacks, such as candy, package cakes, and cookies, also increase the number of calories. School vending machines usually offer soda and sugary snacks, so students buy them. Students who were offered more healthier drinks and snacks, such as bottled water, orange juice, and popcorn would buy them instead.

Those who oppose a ban on sugary soft drinks and snacks in schools are concern about the schools finances. Many schools have contracts with large companyes like Pepsi and Coke to place its vending machines in prominent locations. In fact, the schools earn a percentage of the profits. When vending machines offer lower-calorie drinks and healthier snacks, students do not buy them, so the schools' profits are reduce. Because many schools depend on what they earn from vending machines to pay for extras like field trips, SAT fees, and band uniforms, its budgets suffer.

Nevertheless, those who support the ban seem to be doing good. Many school districts have started its own programs to ban sugary soft drinks and snacks. In 2006, former president Bill Clinton and Governor Mike Huckabee of Arkansas used his fame to negotiate agreementes with soft-drink manufacturers like Coke and Pepsi. This agreements banned the sale of high-calorie soft drinks in Arkansas schools and limited the size of more healthier drinks. By 2008, studies showed that obesity rates among children in Arkansas had stop climbing.

Unit Seven

Understanding Punctuation, Mechanics, and Spelling

31 Using Commas   542

32 Using Apostrophes   560

33 Using Other Punctuation Marks   570

34 Understanding Mechanics   578

35 Understanding Spelling   596

Chapter 31

Using Commas

A **comma** is a punctuation mark that separates words or groups of words within sentences. In this way, commas keep ideas distinct from one another.

In earlier chapters, you learned to use a comma between two simple sentences (independent clauses) linked by a coordinating conjunction to form a compound sentence.

> Some people are concerned about global warming, but others are not.

You also learned to use a comma after a dependent clause that comes before an independent clause in a complex sentence.

> Although bears in the wild can be dangerous, hikers can take steps to protect themselves.

In addition, commas are used to set off directly quoted speech or writing from the rest of the sentence.

> John F. Kennedy said, "Ask not what your country can do for you; ask what you can do for your country."

As you will learn in this chapter, commas have several other uses as well.

31a   Commas in a Series

Use commas to separate all elements in a **series** of three or more words, phrases, or clauses.

> Leyla, Zack, and Kathleen campaigned for Representative Lewis.
> Leyla, Zack, or Kathleen will be elected president of Students for Lewis.

Focus on Writing

The picture on the opposite page shows volunteers building housing units in New Orleans. Look at the picture, and then write a paragraph (or an essay) about an ideal public housing complex for families in need. What should the individual houses or apartments look like? What kinds of buildings should be constructed? What facilities and services should be offered to residents?

Leyla <u>made phone calls</u>, <u>stuffed envelopes</u>, and <u>ran errands</u> for the campaign.

Leyla <u>is president</u>, <u>Zack is vice president</u>, and <u>Kathleen is treasurer</u>.

Highlight: Using Commas in a Series

Newspapers and magazines usually omit the comma before the coordinating conjunction in a series. However, in college writing you should always use a comma before the coordinating conjunction.

Leyla, Zack, and Kathleen worked on the campaign.

● Practice 31-1

Edit the following sentences for the use of commas in a series. If the sentence is correct, write *C* in the blank.

Examples:

Costa Rica produces bananas, cocoa, and sugarcane. ___*C*___

The pool rules state that there is no running , jumping , or diving. _____

1. The musician plays guitar bass and drums. _____

2. The organization's goals are feeding the hungry, housing the homeless and helping the unemployed find work. _____

3. *The Price Is Right*, *Let's Make a Deal*, and *Jeopardy* are three of the longest-running game shows in television history. _____

4. In native Hawaiian culture, yellow was worn by royalty red was worn by priests and a mixture of the two colors was worn by others of high rank. _____

5. The diary Anne Frank kept while her family hid from the Nazis is insightful, touching and sometimes humorous. _____

6. A standard bookcase is 60 inches tall 36 inches wide and 9 inches deep. _____

7. Most coffins manufactured in the United States are lined with bronze, copper, or lead. _____

8. Young handsome and sensitive, Leonardo DiCaprio was the 1990s answer to the 1950s actor James Dean. _____

9. California's capital is Sacramento, its largest city is Los Angeles and its oldest settlement is San Diego. _____

10. Watching television, playing video games, and riding a bicycle are the favorite pastimes of many young boys. _____

Focus on Writing: *Flashback*

Look back at your response to the Focus on Writing activity on page 543. Have you included a series of three or more words or word groups in any of your sentences? Have you used commas correctly to separate elements in the series? If not, correct your punctuation.

31b   Commas with Introductory Phrases and Transitional Words and Phrases

Introductory Phrases

Use a comma to set off an **introductory phrase** from the rest of the sentence.

> In the event of a fire, proceed to the nearest exit.
> Walking home, Nelida decided to change her major.
> To keep fit, people should try to exercise regularly.

● Practice 31-2

Edit the following sentences for the use of commas with introductory phrases. If the sentence is correct, write *C* in the blank.

Examples:

From professionals to teenagers, many athletes have used steroids.
_____

Regulated by the Drug Enforcement Administration, steroids are a controlled substance and can be legally obtained only with a prescription. __C__

    (1) In the past few years many Olympic athletes have been disqualified because they tested positive for banned drugs. _____ (2) At the 2008 Beijing Games, organizers adopted the slogan "Zero Tolerance for Doping." _____ (3) In the past banned steroids were the most common cause of positive drug tests. _____ (4) In recent years other banned substances have also been used. _____ (5) For example, athletes have tested positive for male hormones and human growth hormones. _____ (6) Among track and field athletes doping has been especially common. _____ (7) In some cases athletes' drug use was not uncovered until the games were long over. _____ (8) More than seven years after winning five medals at the 2000 Sydney Olympics, runner Marion Jones admitted to having used banned drugs. _____ (9) Having witnessed many scandals and disappointments today's fans are suspicious of extraordinary athletic feats. _____ (10) For instance, many suspected record-breaking sprinter Usain Bolt of doping at the 2008 Beijing Olympics. _____

Transitional Words and Phrases

Use commas to set off **transitional words and phrases** whether they appear at the beginning, in the middle, or at the end of a sentence.

In fact, Thoreau spent only one night in jail.
He was, of course, bailed out by a friend.
He did spend more than two years at Walden Pond, however.

**Highlight:
Using Commas
in Direct
Address**

Always use commas to set off the name of someone whom you are **addressing** (speaking to) directly, whether the name appears at the beginning, in the middle, or at the end of a sentence.

Molly, come here and look at this.

Come here, Molly, and look at this.

Come here and look at this, Molly.

● **Practice 31-3**

Edit the following sentences for the use of commas with transitional words and phrases. If the sentence is correct, write *C* in the blank.

Example: Many holidays, of course, have been celebrated for generations.

(1) Some holidays are fairly new; the African-American celebration of Kwanzaa for example, was only introduced in the 1960s. _____ (2) This holiday celebrating important African traditions has, however attracted many people over its short life. _____ (3) By the way the word *Kwanzaa* means "first fruits" in Swahili. _____ (4) In other words, Kwanzaa stands for renewal. _____ (5) This of course can be demonstrated in some of the seven principles of Kwanzaa. _____ (6) Kwanzaa is, in fact celebrated over seven days to focus on each of these seven principles. _____ (7) The focus first of all is on unity (*umoja*). _____ (8) Also Kwanzaa focuses on personal self-determination (*kujichagulia*). _____ (9) In addition Kwanzaa celebrations emphasize three kinds of community responsibility (*ujima, ujamaa,* and *nia*). _____ (10) The other principles of Kwanzaa are creativity (*kuumba*) and finally, faith (*imani*). _____

Focus on Writing: *Flashback*

Look back at your response to the Focus on Writing activity on page 543. Have you used any introductory phrases or transitional words and phrases? Have you set off each of these with commas where appropriate? Revise any incorrect sentences by adding commas where needed.

31c   Commas with Appositives

Use commas to set off an **appositive**—a word or word group that identifies, renames, or describes a noun or pronoun.

I have visited only one country, Canada, outside the United States. (*Canada* is an appositive that identifies the noun *country*.)

Carlos Santana, leader of the group Santana, played at Woodstock in 1969. (*Leader of the group Santana* is an appositive that identifies *Carlos Santana*.)

A really gifted painter, he is also a wonderful father. (*A really gifted painter* is an appositive that describes the pronoun *he*.)

Highlight: Using Commas with Appositives

Appositives are set off by commas whether they fall at the beginning, in the middle, or at the end of a sentence.

A dreamer, he spent his life thinking about what he could not have.

He always wanted to build a house, a big white one, overlooking the ocean.

He finally built his dream house, a log cabin.

● Practice 31-4

Edit the following sentences for the correct use of commas to set off appositives. If the sentence is correct, write *C* in the blank.

Examples:

The Buccaneers have not joined the Cheese League, the group

of NFL teams that holds summer training in Wisconsin. _____

Edward A. Filene the son of the Boston merchant who founded Filene's department store, invented the concept of the "bargain basement." _____

1. Traditional Chinese medicine is based on meridians channels of energy believed to run in regular patterns through the body. _____

2. Acupuncture the insertion of thin needles at precise points in the body, stimulates these meridians. _____

3. Herbal medicine the basis of many Chinese healing techniques requires twelve years of study. _____

4. Gary Larson, creator of the popular *Far Side* cartoons ended the series in 1995. _____

5. A musician at heart, Larson said he wanted to spend more time practicing the guitar. _____

6. *Far Side* calendars and other product tie-ins earned Larson over $500 million a lot of money for guitar lessons. _____

7. Nigeria the most populous country in Africa is also one of the fastest-growing nations in the world. _____

8. On the southwest coast of Nigeria lies Lagos a major port. _____

9. The Yoruba people the Nigerian settlers of Lagos, are unusual in Africa because they tend to form large urban communities. _____

10. A predominantly Christian people the Yoruba have incorporated many native religious rituals into their practice of Christianity. _____

Focus on Writing: *Flashback*

Look back at your response to the Focus on Writing activity on page 543. Have you used any appositives? Have you set off appositives with commas? Revise any incorrect sentences by adding commas where needed.

31d   Commas with Nonrestrictive Clauses

WORD POWER
restrict to keep within limits
restrictive limiting

Clauses are used to add information within a sentence. In some cases, you need to add commas to set off these clauses; in other cases, commas are not required.

Use commas to set off **nonrestrictive clauses**, clauses that are not essential to a sentence's meaning. Do not use commas to set off **restrictive clauses**.

● A **nonrestrictive** clause does *not* contain essential information. Nonrestrictive clauses are set off from the rest of the sentence by commas.

> Credit-card fraud, <u>which costs consumers and banks billions of dollars each year</u>, is increasing.

Here, the clause between the commas (underlined) provides extra information to help readers understand the sentence, but the sentence would communicate the same idea without this information.

> Credit-card fraud is increasing.

● A **restrictive** clause contains information that is essential to a sentence's meaning. Restrictive clauses are *not* set off from the rest of the sentence by commas.

> Many rock stars <u>who recorded hits in the 1950s</u> made little money from their songs.

In the sentence above, the clause *who recorded hits in the 1950s* supplies specific information that is essential to the idea the sentence is communicating: it tells readers which group of rock stars made little money. Without the clause, the sentence does not communicate the same idea because it does not tell which rock stars made little money.

> Many rock stars made little money from their songs.

Highlight:
Which, That,
and Who

- *Which* always introduces a nonrestrictive clause.

    The job, which had excellent benefits, did not pay well. (clause set off by commas)

- *That* always introduces a restrictive clause.

    He accepted the job that had the best benefits. (no commas)

- *Who* can introduce either a restrictive or a nonrestrictive clause.

    Restrictive   Many parents who work feel a lot of stress. (no commas)

    Nonrestrictive   Both of my parents, who have always wanted the best for their children, have worked two jobs for years. (clause set off by commas)

● Practice 31-5

Edit the following sentences so that commas set off all nonrestrictive clauses. (Remember, commas are *not* used to set off restrictive clauses.) If a sentence is correct, write *C* in the blank.

Example: A museum exhibition that celebrates the Alaska highway tells the story of its construction. ___*C*___

(1) During the 1940s, a group of African-American soldiers who defied the forces of nature and human prejudice were shipped to Alaska. _____ (2) They built the Alaska highway which stretches twelve hundred miles across Alaska. _____ (3) The troops who worked on the highway have received little attention in most historical accounts. _____ (4) The highway which cut through some of the roughest terrain in the world was begun in 1942. _____ (5) The Japanese had just landed in the Aleutian Islands which lie west of the tip of the Alaska Peninsula. _____ (6) Military officials, who oversaw the project, doubted the ability of the African-American troops. _____ (7) As a result, they made them work under conditions, that made construction difficult. _____ (8) The

troops who worked on the road proved their commanders wrong by finishing the highway months ahead of schedule. _____ (9) In one case, white engineers, who surveyed a river, said it would take two weeks to bridge. _____ (10) To the engineers' surprise, the soldiers who worked on the project beat the estimate by half a day. _____ (11) A military report that was issued in 1945 praised them. _____ (12) It said the goals that the African-American soldiers achieved would be remembered through the ages. _____

Focus on Writing: *Flashback*

Look back at your response to the Focus on Writing activity on page 543. Make sure you have included commas to set off nonrestrictive clauses and have *not* set off restrictive elements with commas. Correct any errors you find.

31e   Commas in Dates and Addresses

Dates

Use commas in dates to separate the day of the week from the month and the day of the month from the year.

> The first Cinco de Mayo we celebrated in the United States was Tuesday, May 5, 1998.

When a date that includes commas falls in the middle of a sentence, place a comma after the date.

> Tuesday, May 5, 1998, was the first Cinco de Mayo we celebrated in the United States.

Addresses

Use commas in addresses to separate the street address from the city and the city from the state or country.

The office of the famous fictional detective Sherlock Holmes was located at 221b Baker Street, London, England.

When an address that includes commas falls in the middle of a sentence, place a comma after the state or country.

The office at 221b Baker Street, London, England, belonged to the famous fictional detective Sherlock Holmes.

● Practice 31-6

Edit the following sentences for the correct use of commas in dates and addresses. Add any missing commas, and cross out any unnecessary commas. If the sentence is correct, write *C* in the blank.

Examples:

June 3, 1985 is the day my parents were married. _____

Their wedding took place in Santiago, Chile. _____

1. The American Declaration of Independence was approved on July 4 1776. _____

2. The Pelican Man's Bird Sanctuary is located at 1705 Ken Thompson Parkway, Sarasota Florida. _____

3. At 175 Carlton Avenue Brooklyn New York is the house where Richard Wright began writing *Native Son*. _____

4. The article originally appeared in the February 12, 2009 issue of the *New York Times*. _____

5. The Mexican hero Father Miguel Hidalgo y Costilla was shot by a firing squad on June 30, 1811. _____

6. The Palacio de Gobierno at Plaza de Armas, Guadalajara, Mexico houses a mural of the famous revolutionary. _____

7. The Pueblo Grande Museum is located at 1469 East Washington Street Phoenix Arizona. _____

8. Brigham Young led the first settlers into the valley that is now Salt Lake City, Utah, in July, 1847. _____

9. St. Louis Missouri was the birthplace of writer Maya Angelou, but she spent most of her childhood in Stamps Arkansas. _____

10. Some records list the writer's birthday as May 19 1928 while others indicate she was born on April 4 1928. _____

31f   Unnecessary Commas

In addition to knowing where commas are required, it is also important to know when *not* to use commas.

- Do not use a comma before the first item in a series.

Incorrect	*Duck Soup* starred, Groucho, Chico, and Harpo Marx.
Correct	*Duck Soup* starred Groucho, Chico, and Harpo Marx.

- Do not use a comma after the last item in a series.

Incorrect	Groucho, Chico, and Harpo Marx, starred in *Duck Soup*.
Correct	Groucho, Chico, and Harpo Marx starred in *Duck Soup*.

- Do not use a comma between a subject and a verb.

Incorrect	Students and their teachers, should try to respect one another.
Correct	Students and their teachers should try to respect one another.

- Do not use a comma before the coordinating conjunction that separates the two parts of a compound predicate.

Incorrect	The transit workers voted to strike, and walked off the job.
Correct	The transit workers voted to strike and walked off the job.

- Do not use a comma before the coordinating conjunction that separates the two parts of a compound subject.

Incorrect	The transit workers, and the sanitation workers voted to strike.
Correct	The transit workers and the sanitation workers voted to strike.

● Do not use a comma to set off a restrictive clause.

Incorrect	People, who live in glass houses, should not throw stones.
Correct	People who live in glass houses should not throw stones.

● Finally, do not use a comma before a dependent clause that follows an independent clause.

Incorrect	He was exhausted, because he had driven all night.
Correct	He was exhausted because he had driven all night.

● Practice 31-7

Some of the following sentences contain unnecessary commas. Edit to eliminate unnecessary commas. If the sentence is correct, write *C* in the blank following it.

Example: Both the Dominican Republic, and the republic of Haiti occupy the West Indian island of Hispaniola. _____

1. The capital of the Dominican Republic, is Santo Domingo. _____

2. The country's tropical climate, generous rainfall, and fertile soil, make the Dominican Republic suitable for many kinds of crops. _____

3. Some of the most important crops are, sugarcane, coffee, cocoa, and rice. _____

4. Mining is also important to the country's economy, because the land is rich in many ores. _____

5. Spanish is the official language of the Dominican Republic, and Roman Catholicism is the state religion. _____

6. In recent years, resort areas have opened, and brought many tourists to the country. _____

7. Tourists, who visit the Dominican Republic, remark on its tropical beauty. _____

8. Military attacks, and political unrest have marked much of the Dominican Republic's history. _____

9. Because the republic's economy has not always been strong, many Dominicans have immigrated to the United States. _____

10. However, most Dominican immigrants maintain close ties to their home country, and return often to visit. _____

Focus on Writing: *Flashback*

Look back at your response to the Focus on Writing activity on page 543. Check your work carefully to make sure you have not used commas in any of the situations listed in 31F. Make any necessary corrections.

Focus on Writing: *Revising and Editing*

Look back at your response to the Focus on Writing activity on page 543. **TEST** what you have written. Then, make the following additions.

1. Add a sentence that includes a series of three or more words, phrases, or clauses.

2. Add introductory phrases to two of your sentences.

3. Add an appositive to one of your sentences.

4. Add a transitional word or phrase to one of your sentences (at the beginning, in the middle, or at the end).

5. Add a nonrestrictive clause to one of your sentences.

Now, revise and edit your work, paying particular attention to your use of commas with the new material.

Chapter Review

Editing Practice

Read the following student essay, which includes errors in comma use. Add commas where necessary between items in a series and with introductory phrases, transitional words and phrases, appositives, and nonrestrictive clauses. Cross out any unnecessary commas. The first sentence has been edited for you.

Brave Orchid

One of the most important characters in *The Woman Warrior,* Maxine Hong Kingston's autobiographical work, is Brave Orchid, Kingston's mother. Brave Orchid was a strong woman, but not a happy one. Through Kingston's stories about her mother, readers learn a lot about Kingston herself.

Readers are introduced to Brave Orchid, a complex character as an imaginative storyteller, who tells her daughter vivid tales of China. As a young woman she impresses her classmates with her intelligence. She is a traditional woman. However she is determined to make her life exactly what she wants it to be. Brave Orchid strongly believes in herself; still, she considers herself a failure.

In her native China Brave Orchid trains to be a midwife. The other women in her class envy her independence brilliance and courage. One day Brave Orchid bravely confronts the Fox Spirit, and tells him he will not win. First of all she tells him she can endure any pain that he inflicts on her. Next she gathers together the women in the dormitory to burn the ghost away. After this event the other women admire her even more.

Working hard Brave Orchid becomes a midwife in China. After coming to America however she cannot work as a midwife. Instead she works in a Chinese laundry, and picks tomatoes. None of her classmates in China would have imagined this outcome. During her later years in America Brave Orchid becomes a woman, who is overbearing and domineering. She bosses her children around, she tries to ruin her sister's life and she criticizes everyone and everything around her. Her daughter, a straight-A student is the object of her worst criticism.

Brave Orchid's intentions are good. Nevertheless she devotes her energy to the wrong things. She expects the people around her to be as strong as she is. Because she bullies them however she eventually loses them. In addition she is too busy criticizing her daughter's faults to see all her accomplishments. Brave Orchid an independent woman and a brilliant student never achieves her goals. She is hard on the people around her, because she is disappointed in herself.

Collaborative Activities

1. Bring a homemaking, sports, or fashion magazine to class. Working in a small group, look at the people pictured in the ads. In what roles are men most often depicted? In what roles are women most often presented? Identify the three or four most common roles for each sex, and give each kind of character a descriptive name—*jock* or *mother*, for example.

2. Working on your own, choose one type of character from the list your group made in Collaborative Activity 1. Then, write a paragraph in which you describe this character's typical appearance and habits. Refer to the appropriate magazine pictures to support your characterization.

3. Collaborating with other members of your group, write two paragraphs, one discussing how men are portrayed in ads and one discussing how women are portrayed.

4. Circle every comma in the paragraphs you wrote for Collaborative Activity 3. Then, work with your group to explain why each comma is used. If no one in your group can justify a particular comma's use, cross it out.

**Review
Checklist:
Using Commas**

☐ Use commas to separate all elements in a series of three or more words or word groups. (See 31A.)

☐ Use commas to set off introductory phrases and transitional words and phrases from the rest of the sentence. (See 31B.)

☐ Use commas to set off appositives from the rest of the sentence. (See 31C.)

☐ Use commas to set off nonrestrictive clauses. (See 31D.)

☐ Use commas to separate parts of dates and addresses. (See 31E.)

☐ Avoid unnecessary commas. (See 31F.)

An **apostrophe** is a punctuation mark that is used in two situations: to form a contraction and to form the possessive of a noun or an indefinite pronoun.

32a   Apostrophes in Contractions

A **contraction** is a word that uses an apostrophe to combine two words. The apostrophe takes the place of the omitted letters.

I <u>didn't</u> (*did not*) realize how late it was.

<u>It's</u> (*it is*) not right for cheaters to go unpunished.

Frequently Used Contractions

I + am = I'm	are + not = aren't
we + are = we're	can + not = can't
you + are = you're	do + not = don't
it + is = it's	will + not = won't
I + have = I've	should + not = shouldn't
I + will = I'll	let + us = let's
there + is = there's	that + is = that's
is + not = isn't	who + is = who's

Focus on Writing

Traditionally, certain jobs have been considered "men's work," and others have been viewed as "women's work." Although the workplace has changed considerably in recent years, some things have remained the same.

The picture on the opposite page shows Dr. Mae Jemison at her job as a NASA astronaut.

Look at the picture, and then write a paragraph (or an essay) about the tasks that are considered "men's work" and "women's work" at your job or in your current household. Be sure to give examples of the responsibilities of the different people you are discussing. (Note: Contractions, such as *isn't* or *don't*, are acceptable in this informal response.)

● Practice 32-1

In the following sentences, add apostrophes to contractions if needed. If the sentence is correct, write *C* in the blank.

Example: $\overset{What's}{\underset{\wedge}{\text{Whats}}}$ the deadliest creature on Earth? _____

(1) Bacteria and viruses, which we cant see without a microscope, kill many people every year, but they are not the only deadly creatures. _____ (2) When we speak about the deadliest creatures, usually were talking about creatures that cause illness or death from their poison, which is called venom. _____ (3) After your bitten, stung, or stuck, how long does it take to die? _____ (4) The fastest killer is a creature called the sea wasp, but it isn't a wasp at all. _____ (5) The sea wasp is actually a fifteen-foot-long jellyfish, and although its not aggressive, it can be deadly. _____ (6) People who've gone swimming off the coast of Australia may have encountered this creature. _____ (7) While jellyfish found off the Atlantic coast of the United States can sting, they arent as dangerous as the sea wasp, whose venom is deadly enough to kill sixty adults. _____ (8) A person whos been stung by a sea wasp has anywhere from thirty seconds to four minutes to get help or die. _____ (9) Oddly, it's been found that something as thin as pantyhose worn over the skin will prevent these stings. _____ (10) Also, theres an antidote to the poison that can save the lives of victims. _____

Focus on Writing: *Flashback*

Look back at your response to the Focus on Writing activity on page 561. Have you used apostrophes correctly to replace the missing letters in contractions? Make any necessary corrections.

32b   Apostrophes in Possessives

Possessive forms indicate ownership. Nouns and indefinite pronouns do not have special possessive forms. Instead, they use apostrophes to indicate ownership.

Singular Nouns and Indefinite Pronouns

To form the possessive of **singular nouns** (including names) and **indefinite pronouns**, add an apostrophe plus an *s*.

> Cesar Chavez's goal (*the goal of Cesar Chavez*) was justice for American farm workers.
>
> The strike's outcome (*the outcome of the strike*) was uncertain.
>
> Whether it would succeed was anyone's guess (*the guess of anyone*).

Note: Even if a singular noun already ends in *-s*, add an apostrophe plus an *s* to form the possessive: *The class's next assignment was a research paper; Dr. Ramos's patients are participating in a clinical trial.*

Plural Nouns

Most plural nouns end in *-s*. To form the possessive of **plural nouns ending in -s** (including names), add just an apostrophe (not an apostrophe plus an *s*).

> The two drugs' side effects (*the side effects of the two drugs*) were quite different.
>
> The Johnsons' front door (*the front door of the Johnsons*) is red.

Some irregular noun plurals do not end in *-s*. With plural nouns that do not end in *-s*, add an apostrophe plus an *s* to form the possessive.

> The men's room is right next to the women's room.

● Practice 32-2

Rewrite the following phrases, changing the noun or indefinite pronoun that follows *of* to the possessive form. Be sure to distinguish between singular and plural nouns.

Examples:

the mayor of the city   *the city's mayor* _____

the uniforms of the players   *the players' uniforms* _____

1. the video of the singer _____

2. the test scores of the students _____

3. the favorite band of everybody _____

4. the office of the boss _____

5. the union of the players _____

6. the specialty of the restaurant _____

7. the bedroom of the children _____

8. the high cost of the tickets _____

9. the dreams of everyone _____

10. the owner of the dogs _____

Focus on Writing: *Flashback*

Look back at your response to the Focus on Writing activity on page 561. Underline any possessive forms of nouns or indefinite pronouns. Then, check to make sure you have used apostrophes correctly to form these possessives, and make any necessary corrections.

32c Incorrect Use of Apostrophes

Be careful not to confuse a plural noun (*boys*) with the singular possessive form of the noun (*boy's*). Never use an apostrophe with a plural noun unless the noun is possessive.

Termites can be dangerous <u>pests</u> [not *pest's*].

The <u>Velezes</u> [not *Velez's*] live on Maple Drive, right next door to the <u>Browns</u> [not *Brown's*].

Also be careful not to use apostrophes with possessive pronouns that end in -s: *theirs* (not *their's*), *hers* (not *her's*), *its* (not *it's*), *ours* (not *our's*), and *yours* (not *your's*).

Highlight:
Possessive
Pronouns

Be especially careful not to confuse possessive pronouns with sound-alike contractions. Possessive pronouns never include apostrophes.

Possessive Pronoun	*Contraction*
The dog bit its master.	It's (*it is*) time for breakfast.
The choice is theirs.	There's (*there is*) no place like home.
Whose house is this?	Who's (*who is*) on first base?
Is this your house?	You're (*you are*) late again.

● **Practice 32-3**

Check the underlined nouns and pronouns in the following sentences for correct use of apostrophes. If a correction needs to be made, cross out the word, and write the correct version above it. If the noun or pronoun is correct, write *C* above it.

> **Example:** The <u>president's</u> views were presented after several other
> speaker's first presented <u>their's</u>.
> (*C* above president's; *speakers* above speaker's; *theirs.* above their's.)

1. <u>Parent's</u> should realize that when it comes to disciplining children, the responsibility is <u>their's</u>.

2. <u>It's</u> also important that parents offer praise for a <u>child's</u> good behavior.

3. In <u>it's</u> first few <u>week's</u> of life, a dog is already developing a personality.

4. His and <u>her's</u> towels used to be popular with <u>couple's</u>, but <u>it's</u> not so common to see them today.

5. All the <u>Ryan's</u> spent four <u>year's</u> in college and then got good jobs.

6. From the radio came the lyrics "<u>You're</u> the one <u>who's</u> love I've been waiting for."

7. If you expect to miss any <u>class's</u>, you will have to make arrangements with someone <u>who's</u> willing to tell you <u>you're</u> assignment.

8. No other <u>school's</u> cheerleading squad ever tried as many challenging moves as <u>our's</u> did.

9. Surprise <u>test's</u> are common in my economics class.

10. <u>Jazz's</u> influence on many mainstream <u>musician's</u> is one of the <u>book's</u> main <u>subject's</u>.

Focus on Writing: *Flashback*

Look back at your response to the Focus on Writing activity on page 561. Circle each plural noun. Then, circle each possessive pronoun that ends in *-s*. Have you incorrectly used an apostrophe with any of the circled words? Make any necessary corrections.

Focus on Writing: *Revising and Editing*

Look back at your response to the Focus on Writing activity on page 561. **TEST** what you have written.

Because this is an informal exercise, contractions are acceptable; in fact, they may be preferable because they give your writing a conversational tone. Revise so that you have used contractions in all possible situations.

Now, add two sentences—one that includes a singular possessive noun and one that includes a plural possessive noun. Make sure these two new sentences fit smoothly into your writing and that these two sentences use contractions wherever possible.

Finally, revise and edit your work.

Chapter Review

Editing Practice

Read the following student essay, which includes errors in the use of apostrophes. Edit it to eliminate errors by crossing out incorrect words and writing corrections above them. (Note that this is an informal response paper, so contractions are acceptable.) The first sentence has been edited for you.

The Women of Messina

In William ~~Shakespeares'~~ *Shakespeare's* play *Much Ado about Nothing*, the women of Messina, whether they are seen as love objects or as ~~shrew's~~ *shrews,* have very few options. A womans role is to please a man. She can try to resist, but she will probably wind up giving in.

The plays two women, Hero and Beatrice, are very different. Hero is the obedient one. Heroes cousin, Beatrice, tries to challenge the rules of the mans world in which she lives. However, in a place like Messina, even women like Beatrice find it hard to get the respect that should be their's.

Right from the start, we are drawn to Beatrice. Shes funny, she has a clever comment for most situation's, and she always speaks her mind about other peoples behavior. Unlike Hero, she tries to stand up to the men in her life, as we see in her and Benedicks conversations. But even though Beatrice's intelligence is obvious, she often mocks herself. Its clear that she doesn't have much self-esteem. In fact, Beatrice is'nt the strong woman she seems to be.

Ultimately, Beatrice does get her man, and she will be happy—but at what cost? Benedicks' last word's to her are "Peace! I will stop your mouth." Then, he kisses her. The kiss is a symbolic end to their bickering. It is also the mark of Beatrices defeat. She has lost. Benedick has silenced her. Now, she will be Benedick's wife and do what he wants her to do. Granted, she will have more say in her marriage than Hero will have in her's, but she is still defeated.

Shakespeares audience might have seen the plays ending as a happy one. For contemporary audience's, however, the ending is disappointing. Even Beatrice, the most rebellious of Messinas women, finds it impossible to achieve anything of importance in this male-dominated society.

Collaborative Activities

1. Working in a group of four students and building on your individual responses to the Focus on Writing activity at the beginning of the chapter, consider which specific occupational and professional roles are still associated largely with men and which are associated primarily with women. Make two lists, heading one "women's jobs" and one "men's jobs."

2. Now, work in pairs, with one pair of students in each group of four concentrating on men and the other pair on women. Write a paragraph that attempts to justify why the particular jobs you listed should or should not be restricted to one gender. In your discussion, list the various qualities men or women possess that qualify (or disqualify) them for particular jobs. Use possessive forms whenever possible—for example, *women's energy* (not *women have energy*).

3. Bring to class a magazine or newspaper whose style is informal—for example, *TV Guide*, your school newspaper, or even a comic book. Working in a group, circle every contraction you can find on one page of each publication, and substitute for each contraction the words it combines. Are your substitutions an improvement? (You may want to read a few paragraphs aloud before you reach a conclusion.)

Review Checklist: Using Apostrophes

☐ Use apostrophes to form contractions. (See 32A.)

☐ Use an apostrophe plus an *s* to form the possessive of singular nouns and indefinite pronouns, even when a noun ends in *-s*. (See 32B.)

☐ Use an apostrophe alone to form the possessive of plural nouns ending in *-s*, including names. If a plural noun does not end in *-s*, add an apostrophe plus an *s*. (See 32B.)

☐ Do not use apostrophes with plural nouns unless they are possessive. Do not use apostrophes with possessive pronouns. (See 32C.)

Chapter 33

Using Other Punctuation Marks

Punctuation marks tell readers to slow down, to look ahead, or to pause. To write clear sentences, you need to use appropriate punctuation.

Every sentence ends with a punctuation mark.

- If a sentence is a statement, it ends with a **period**.

  Eight planets revolve around the sun.

- If a sentence is a question, it ends with a **question mark**.

  Is Venus the planet closest to the sun?

- If a sentence is an exclamation, it ends with an **exclamation point**.

  Look out! An asteroid is about to fall on Sioux Falls!

Other important punctuation marks are the **comma**, discussed in Chapter 31, and the **apostrophe**, discussed in Chapter 32. Four additional punctuation marks—*semicolons, colons, dashes,* and *parentheses*—are discussed and illustrated in this chapter.

33a   Semicolons

Use a **semicolon** to join two simple sentences (independent clauses) into one compound sentence.

Sandra Day O'Connor was the first woman to sit on the United States Supreme Court; Ruth Bader Ginsburg was the second.

Focus on Writing

The picture on the opposite page shows a child playing with a hula hoop, a popular toy of the 1960s. Look at the picture, and write a paragraph (or an essay) about the games you used to play outdoors when you were a child. Describe some of your favorite outdoor toys and games.

Highlight:
Semicolons

Never use a semicolon between a phrase and an independent clause.
Use a comma instead.

Incorrect   I voted for the winning candidate; the Democrat.

Correct   I voted for the winning candidate, the Democrat.

Never use a semicolon between a dependent clause and an independent clause. Use a comma instead.

Incorrect   When Bob was in high school; he had shoulder-
length hair.

Correct   When Bob was in high school, he had shoulder-
length hair.

● **Practice 33-1**

Each of the following sentences includes errors in the use of semicolons. Correct any errors you find. If a sentence is correct, write *C* on the line after the sentence.

Example: A marsupial is a mammal; many kinds of marsupials live in
Australia today. _____

1. Marsupials have pouches mothers carry their young in these pouches.
   _____

2. Marsupials are covered with hair; and nursed by their mothers. _____

3. The opossum is the only marsupial now found in the United States; in prehistoric times, however, there were many others. _____

4. Marsupials include the koala; the kangaroo, and the wombat. _____

5. Many thousands of years ago, marsupials were common in South America now, they are extinct. _____

Focus on Writing: *Flashback*

Look back at your response to the Focus on Writing activity on page 571. Have you used any semicolons in your writing? Have you used them correctly? Correct any errors you find.

33b   Colons

Colons are used to introduce quotations, explanations, clarifications, examples, and lists. A complete sentence always comes before the colon.

- Use a colon to introduce a quotation.

  Our family motto is simple: "accept no substitutes."

- Use a colon to introduce an explanation, a clarification, or an example.

  Only one thing kept him from climbing Mt. Everest: fear of heights.

- Use a colon to introduce a list. (Note that all items in a list are expressed in **parallel** terms.)

  I left my job for four reasons: boring work, poor working conditions, low pay, and a terrible supervisor.

● Practice 33-2

The following sentences include errors in the use of colons to introduce quotations, examples, lists, and so on. Correct any errors you find. (Remember that every colon must be preceded by a complete sentence.) If a sentence is correct, write *C* on the line after the sentence.

Example: A new kind of amusement park is appearing the amuse-
                                                                                  ^:
ment park with a religious theme. _____

1. Four parks with religious themes are: the Holy Land Experience, Dinosaur Adventure Land, Ganga-Dham, and City of Revelation. _____

2. The Holy Land Experience is near another popular attraction, which is: Disney World. _____

3. An advertisement for Dinosaur Adventure Land describes it in these words "where dinosaurs and the Bible meet!" _____

4. India's Ganga-Dham is billed as: "the world's first spiritual theme park." _____

5. In central Florida, another park is being planned: City of Revelation. _____

Focus on Writing: *Flashback*

Look back at your response to the Focus on Writing activity on page 571. Can you add a quotation, an example, or a list to your writing? Write your possible new material on the lines below.

Quotation: _____

Example: _____

List: _____

Now, try adding the quotation, example, or list to your writing. Be sure to introduce this new material with a colon, and make sure the colon is preceded by a complete sentence.

33c   Dashes and Parentheses

Dashes and parentheses set words off from the rest of the sentence. Dashes call attention to the material they set off; parentheses do just the opposite.

• Use **dashes** to set off important information.

   She parked her car—a red Firebird—in a towaway zone.

• Use **parentheses** to enclose information that is relatively unimportant.

   The weather in Portland (a city in Oregon) was overcast.

● Practice 33-3

Add dashes or parentheses to the following sentences where you think they are necessary to set off material from the rest of the sentence. Remember that dashes tend to emphasize the material they set off, while parentheses tend to deemphasize the enclosed material.

Example: The National Basketball Association (NBA) was founded in the 1940s.

1. In the 1950s, Bob Cousy was a star player for the Boston Celtics. Cousy an "old man" at age thirty-four led his team to their fifth NBA championship in 1963.

2. During the 1960s, the legendary Wilt "the Stilt" Chamberlain played for the Philadelphia Warriors.

3. Many people still consider game 5 of the 1976 NBA finals which the Celtics won in triple overtime the greatest basketball game ever played.

4. During the 1980s, five truly outstanding players Magic Johnson, Kareem Abdul-Jabbar, Larry Bird, Julius "Dr. J" Erving, and Michael Jordan dominated the NBA.

5. Today, young players some joining the NBA right out of high school dream of making names for themselves as their heroes did.

Focus on Writing: *Flashback*

Look back at your response to the Focus on Writing activity on page 571. If you see any material that could be set off with dashes or parentheses, add the punctuation that is necessary to set it off.

Focus on Writing: *Revising and Editing*

Look back at your response to the Focus on Writing activity on page 571. **TEST** what you have written. Then, revise and edit your work, checking carefully to make sure all the punctuation marks discussed in this chapter are used correctly.

Chapter Review

Editing Practice

The following student essay includes errors in the use of semicolons, colons, dashes, and parentheses. (Some are used incorrectly; others have been omitted where they are needed.) Correct any errors you find. The first sentence has been corrected for you.

Just Right

In the fairy tale "Goldilocks and the Three Bears," a little girl called Goldilocks wanders away from home, and discovers an empty house in the forest. When she sees no one is home, she tries out different things in the house; bowls of cereal, chairs, and beds. When she tries the beds; one is too small, and one is too big. The third one is just right. As Goldilocks knew: finding the "just right" size is not easy.

In the United States today, many things are much too big. For example, food stores—and food portions—are often huge. The "mom and pop" grocery stores are gone; replaced by giant supermarkets. Many fast-food restaurants offer double or triple hamburgers convenience stores sell 32-ounce cups of soda. At any diner; portions are so big that food hangs off the edges of the plate.

Other things we encounter daily are also too big. Even with gas so expensive, some people still have to drive big vehicles, such as: huge SUVs, vans, and pickups. Parents push baby strollers the size of Humvees, and some suburban houses are so big that they are called McMansions. Televisions have grown into "home theaters" with 60-inch screens; movie theaters are now multiplexes—that look like airport terminals.

At the same time so many things are getting bigger and bigger; many other things particularly electronics are getting smaller. Cameras are one example; cell phones are another. Some MP3 players are smaller than credit cards. Even M&Ms come in a mini version. Recently, the tiny Smart car has been attracting a lot of attention; especially in cities. And, of course, families have been getting smaller for years.

What is the right size? That is not an easy question to answer. As Goldilocks knew; sometimes you have to try out the "too big" and "too small" version before you find the "just right" one.

Collaborative Activities

1. Write five original compound sentences, each composed of two simple sentences connected with *and*. Then, exchange papers with another student, and edit each compound sentence so that it uses a semicolon instead of *and* to connect the independent clauses.

2. Compile three lists, each with three or four items (people, places, or things). Then, working in a group, compose a sentence that could introduce each of your lists. Use a colon after each introductory sentence.

Review Checklist: Using Other Punctuation Marks

☐ Use semicolons to join two simple sentences (independent clauses) into one compound sentence. (See 33A.)

☐ Use colons to introduce quotations, explanations, clarifications, examples, and lists. (See 33B.)

☐ Use dashes and parentheses to set off material from the rest of the sentence. (See 33C.)

Capitalizing Proper Nouns

A **proper noun** names a particular person, animal, place, object, or idea. Proper nouns are always capitalized. The list that follows explains and illustrates rules for capitalizing proper nouns.

- Always capitalize the names of **races, ethnic groups, tribes, nationalities, languages,** and **religions.**

  The census data revealed a diverse community of Caucasians, African Americans, and Asian Americans, with a few Latino and Navajo residents. Native languages included English, Korean, and Spanish. Most people identified themselves as Catholic, Protestant, or Muslim.

- Capitalize names of **specific people** and the **titles that accompany them.** In general, do not capitalize titles used without a name.

  In 1994, President Nelson Mandela was elected to lead South Africa.

  The newly elected fraternity president addressed the crowd.

- Capitalize names of **specific family members and their titles.** Do not capitalize words that identify family relationships, including those introduced by possessive pronouns.

  The twins, Aunt Edna and Aunt Evelyn, are Dad's sisters.

  My aunts, my father's sisters, are twins.

Focus on Writing

The picture on the opposite page shows a scene from *Spider-Man 3*. Look at the picture, and then describe a memorable scene from your favorite movie. Begin by giving the film's title and listing the names of the major stars and the characters they play. Then, tell what happens in the scene, quoting a few words of dialogue if possible.

- Capitalize names of **specific countries, cities, towns, bodies of water, streets,** and so on. Do not capitalize words that do not name specific places.

  The Seine runs through Paris, France.

  The river runs through the city.

- Capitalize names of **specific geographical regions**. Do not capitalize such words when they specify direction.

  William Faulkner's novels are set in the South.

  Turn right at the golf course, and go south for about a mile.

- Capitalize names of **specific buildings and monuments**. Do not capitalize general references to buildings and monuments.

  He drove past the Liberty Bell and looked for a parking space near City Hall.

  He drove past the monument and looked for a parking space near the government building.

- Capitalize names of **specific groups, clubs, teams,** and **associations**. Do not capitalize general references to such groups.

  The Teamsters Union represents workers who were at the stadium for the Republican Party convention, the Rolling Stones concert, and the Phillies-Astros game.

  The union represents workers who were at the stadium for the political party's convention, the rock group's concert, and the baseball teams' game.

- Capitalize names of **specific historical periods, events,** and **documents**. Do not capitalize nonspecific references to periods, events, or documents.

  The Emancipation Proclamation was signed during the Civil War, not during Reconstruction.

  The document was signed during the war, not during the postwar period.

- Capitalize names of **businesses, government agencies, schools,** and **other institutions**. Do not capitalize nonspecific references to such institutions.

  The Department of Education and Apple Computer have launched a partnership project with Central High School.

A government agency and a computer company have launched a partnership project with a high school.

- Capitalize **brand names**. Do not capitalize general references to kinds of products.

    While Jeff waited for his turn at the Xerox machine, he drank a can of Coke.

    While Jeff waited for his turn at the copier, he drank a can of soda.

- Capitalize **titles of specific academic courses**. Do not capitalize names of general academic subject areas, except for proper nouns—for example, a language or a country.

    Are Introduction to American Government and Biology 200 closed yet?

    Are the introductory American government course and the biology course closed yet?

- Capitalize **days of the week, months of the year**, and **holidays**. Do not capitalize the names of seasons.

    The Jewish holiday of Passover usually falls in April.

    The Jewish holiday of Passover falls in the spring.

• Practice 34-1

Edit the following sentences, capitalizing letters or changing capitals to lowercase where necessary.

Example: The third largest City in the united states is chicago, illinois.

(1) Located in the midwest on lake Michigan, chicago is an important port city, a rail and highway hub, and the site of o'hare international airport, one of the Nation's busiest. (2) The financial center of the city is Lasalle street, and the lakefront is home to Grant park, where there are many Museums and monuments. (3) To the North of the city, soldier field is home to the chicago bears, the city's football team, and wrigley field is home to the chicago cubs, a national league Baseball

Team. (4) In the mid-1600s, the site of what is now Chicago was visited by father jacques marquette, a catholic missionary to the ottawa and huron tribes, who were native to the area. (5) By the 1700s, the city was a trading post run by john kinzie. (6) The city grew rapidly in the 1800s, and immigrants included germans, irish, italians, poles, greeks, and chinese, along with african americans who migrated from the south. (7) In 1871, much of the city was destroyed in one of the worst fires in united states history; according to legend, the fire started when mrs. O'Leary's Cow kicked over a burning lantern. (8) Today, Chicago's skyline has many Skyscrapers, built by businesses like the john hancock company, sears, and amoco. (9) I know Chicago well because my Mother grew up there and my aunt jean and uncle amos still live there. (10) I also got information from the Chicago Chamber of Commerce when I wrote a paper for introductory research writing, a course I took at Graystone high school.

Focus on Writing: *Flashback*

Look back at your response to the Focus on Writing activity on page 579. Check carefully to make sure each proper noun you have used begins with a capital letter, and correct any that do not.

34b ## Punctuating Quotations

A **direct quotation** reproduces the *exact* words of a speaker or writer. Direct quotations are always placed in quotation marks. A direct quotation is usually accompanied by an **identifying tag**, a phrase that names the person being quoted. In the following sentences, the identifying tag is underlined.

Lauren said, "My brother and Tina have gotten engaged."

A famous salesman wrote, "Don't sell the steak; sell the sizzle."

When a quotation is a complete sentence, it begins with a capital letter and ends with a period, a question mark, or an exclamation point. When a quotation falls at the end of a sentence (as in the two examples above), the period is placed *inside* the quotation marks.

If the quotation is a question or an exclamation, the question mark or exclamation point is also placed *inside* the quotation marks.

The instructor asked, "Has anyone read *Sula*?"

Officer Warren shouted, "Hold it right there!"

If the quotation itself is not a question or an exclamation, the question mark or exclamation point goes *outside* the quotation marks.

Did Joe really say, "I quit"?

I can't believe he really said, "I quit"!

Highlight: Indirect Quotations	Be careful not to confuse direct and indirect quotations. A direct quotation reproduces someone's *exact* words, but an **indirect quotation** simply summarizes what was said or written. Do not use quotation marks with indirect quotations.
	Direct quotation Martin Luther King Jr. said, "I have a dream."
	Indirect quotation Martin Luther King Jr. said that he had a dream.

The rules for punctuating direct quotations with identifying tags are summarized below.

● **Identifying tag at the beginning**   When the identifying tag comes *before* the quotation, it is followed by a comma.

Alexandre Dumas wrote, "Nothing succeeds like success."

- **Identifying tag at the end**   When the identifying tag comes at the *end* of the sentence, it is followed by a period. A comma (or sometimes a question mark or exclamation point) inside the closing quotation marks separates the quotation from the identifying tag.

   "Life is like a box of chocolates," <u>stated Forrest Gump</u>.

   "Is that so?" <u>his friends wondered</u>.

- **Identifying tag in the middle**   When the identifying tag comes in the *middle* of the quoted sentence, it is followed by a comma. The first part of the quotation is also followed by a comma, placed inside the quotation marks. (Because the part of the quotation that follows the tag is not a new sentence, it does not begin with a capital letter.)

   "This is my life," <u>Bette insisted</u>, "and I'll live it as I please."

- **Identifying tag between two sentences**   When the identifying tag comes *between two* quoted sentences, it is preceded by a comma and followed by a period. (The second quoted sentence begins with a capital letter.)

   "Berry Gordy is an important figure in the history of music," <u>Tony explained</u>. "He was the creative force behind Motown records."

● Practice 34-2

The following sentences contain direct quotations. First, underline the identifying tag. Then, punctuate the quotation correctly, adding capital letters as necessary.

   Example: "Why <u>Darryl asked</u> "are teachers so strict about deadlines?"

1. The bigger they are said boxer John L. Sullivan the harder they fall.

2. Do you take Michael to be your lawfully wedded husband asked the minister.

3. Lisa Marie replied I do.

4. If you believe the *National Enquirer* my friend always says then you'll believe anything.

5. Yabba dabba doo Fred exclaimed this brontoburger looks great.

● **Practice 34-3**

The following quotations are followed in parentheses by the names of the people who wrote or spoke them. On the blank lines, write a sentence that includes the quotation and places the identifying tag in the position specified. Be sure to punctuate and capitalize correctly.

> **Example:** "Education is not the filling of a pail, but the lighting of a fire." (written by poet William Butler Yeats)
>
> **Identifying tag in the middle** *"Education is not the filling of a pail,"*
> *wrote poet William Butler Yeats, "but the lighting of a fire."*

1. "Revenge only engenders violence, not clarity and true peace. I think liberation must come from within." (written by Mexican-American author Sandra Cisneros)

   Identifying tag between two sentences _____

   _____

2. "Luck is a matter of preparation meeting opportunity." (spoken by talk-show host Oprah Winfrey)

   Identifying tag at the beginning _____

3. "Imagination is more important than knowledge." (spoken by physicist Albert Einstein)

   Identifying tag at the end _____

4. "May the force be with you." (spoken by at least one character in every *Star Wars* movie)

   Identifying tag at the beginning _____

5. "I hate admitting that my enemies have a point." (written by British novelist Salman Rushdie)

   Identifying tag at the end _____

Focus on Writing: *Flashback*

Look back at your response to the Focus on Writing activity on page 579. If you have quoted dialogue from the film you wrote about, make sure that you have enclosed it in quotation marks, placed other punctuation correctly, capitalized where necessary, and included identifying tags. Revise any incorrectly punctuated quotations. (If you did not quote any dialogue, try adding some now.)

34c   Setting Off Titles

Some titles are typed in *italics*. Others are enclosed in quotation marks. The following box shows how to set off different kinds of titles.

Italicized Titles	*Titles in Quotation Marks*
Books: *How the García Girls Lost Their Accents*	Book chapters: "Understanding Mechanics"
Newspapers: *Miami Herald*	Short stories: "The Tell-Tale Heart"
Magazines: *People*	
Long poems: *John Brown's Body*	Essays and articles: "Orange Crush"
Plays: *Death of a Salesman*	Short poems: "Richard Cory"
Films: *The Rocky Horror Picture Show*	Songs and speeches: "America the Beautiful"; "The Gettysburg Address"
Television or radio series: *Star Trek: The Next Generation*	
Web sites: *CNN.com*, *Google Maps*	Individual episodes of television or radio series: "The Montgomery Bus Boycott" (an episode of the PBS series *Eyes on the Prize*)

● Practice 34-4

In the following sentences, underline (to indicate italics) or insert quotation marks around titles. (Remember that titles of books and other long works are italicized, and titles of stories, essays, and other shorter works are enclosed in quotation marks.)

Example: An article in the <u>New York Times</u> called "It's Not Easy Being Green" is a profile of former Chicago Bulls player Dennis Rodman, who once had green hair.

1. Sui Sin Far's short story The Wisdom of the New, from her book Mrs. Spring Fragrance, is about the clash between Chinese and American cultures in the early twentieth century.

2. Major league baseball games traditionally open with fans taking their hats off and singing The Star-Spangled Banner.

3. Interesting information about fighting skin cancer can be found in the article Putting Sunscreens to the Test, which appeared in the magazine Consumer Reports.

4. One of the best-known poems of the twentieth century is Robert Frost's The Road Not Taken.

5. Ang Lee has directed several well-received films, including Crouching Tiger, Hidden Dragon, and Brokeback Mountain.

6. It is surprising how many people enjoy reruns of two 1960s television series: Bewitched and I Dream of Jeannie.

7. The title of Lorraine Hansberry's play A Raisin in the Sun comes from Langston Hughes's poem Harlem.

8. In his autobiography, Breaking the Surface, Olympic diving champion Greg Louganis wrote about his struggle with AIDS.

Highlight: Capital Letters in Titles

Capitalize the first letters of all important words in a title. Do not capitalize an **article** (*a, an, the*), a **preposition** (*of, around,* and so on), or a **coordinating conjunction** (*and, but,* and so on)—unless it is the first or last word of the title or subtitle (*On the Road*; "To an Athlete Dying Young"; *No Way Out*; *And Quiet Flows the Don*).

● Practice 34-5

Edit the following sentences, capitalizing letters as necessary in titles.

Example: *New york times* bestseller *three cups of tea* is about coauthor Greg Mortenson's work building schools in Pakistan and Afghanistan.

1. When fans of the television show *lost* voted for their favorite episodes, "through the looking glass," "the shape of things to come," and "the incident" were in the top ten.

2. In 1948, Eleanor Roosevelt delivered her famous speech "the struggle for human rights" and published an article titled "toward human rights throughout the world."

3. Before being elected president, Barack Obama wrote and published two books: *dreams from my father* and *the audacity of hope.*

4. English actor Daniel Craig plays secret agent James Bond in the films *casino royale* and *quantum of solace.*

5. *janis joplin's greatest hits* includes songs written by other people, such as "piece of my heart," as well as songs she wrote herself, such as "mercedes benz."

Focus on Writing: *Flashback*

Look back at your response to the Focus on Writing activity on page 579. Have you italicized the title of the film you discussed (or underlined the title to indicate italics)? Have you used capital letters in the title where necessary? Make any necessary corrections.

34d   Hyphens

A hyphen has two uses: to divide a word at the end of a line, and to join words in compounds.

- Use a **hyphen** to divide a word at the end of a line. If you need to divide a word, divide it between syllables. (Check your dictionary to see how a word is divided into syllables.) Never break a one-syllable word, no matter how long it is.

   When the speaker began his talk, all the people seated in the audi-torium grew very quiet.

- Use a hyphen in a **compound**—a word that is made up of two or more words.

   This theater shows first-run movies.

● Practice 34-6

Add hyphens to join words in compounds in the following sentences.

   Example: The course focused on nineteenth-century American literature.

1. The ice skating rink finally froze over.
2. We should be kind to our four legged friends.
3. The first year students raised money for charity.
4. The under prepared soldiers were at a real disadvantage.
5. The hand carved sculpture looked like a pair of doves.

34e   Abbreviations

An **abbreviation** is a shortened form of a word. Although abbreviations are generally not used in college writing, it is acceptable to abbreviate the following.

- Titles—such as Mr., Ms., Dr., and Jr.—that are used along with names.
- a.m. and p.m.
- BC and AD (in dates such as 43 BC)
- Names of organizations (NRA, CIA) and technical terms (DNA). Note that some abbreviations, called **acronyms**, are pronounced as words: AIDS, FEMA.

Keep in mind that it is *not* acceptable to abbreviate days of the week, months, names of streets and places, names of academic subjects, or titles that are not used along with names.

● Practice 34-7

Edit the incorrect use of abbreviations in the following sentences.

> **Example:**   In leap years, Feb. has twenty-nine days.
> *(February)*

1. The dr. diagnosed a case of hypertension.
2. Nov. 11 is a federal holiday.
3. Derek registered for Eng. literature and a psych elective.
4. The museum was located at the corner of Laurel Ave. and Neptune St.
5. The clinic is only open Tues. through Thurs. and every other Sat.

34f   Numbers

In college writing, most numbers are spelled out (*forty-five*) rather than written as **numerals** (*45*). However, numbers more than two words long are always written as numerals (*4,530*, not *four thousand five hundred thirty*).

In addition, you should use numerals in the following situations.

Dates	January 20, 1976
Addresses	5023 Schuyler Street
Exact times	10:00 (If you use *o'clock*, spell out the number: *ten o'clock*)

Percentages and decimals	80% 8.2
Divisions of books	Chapter 3 Act 4 Page 102

Note: Never begin a sentence with a numeral. Either use a spelled-out number, or reword the sentence so the numeral does not come at the beginning.

● Practice 34-8

Edit the incorrect use of numbers in the following sentences.

> **Example:**   The population of the United States is over ~~three hundred~~ ³⁰⁰ million.

1. Only 2 students in the 8 o'clock lecture were late.

2. More than seventy-five percent of the class passed the exit exam.

3. Chapter six begins on page 873.

4. The wedding took place on October twelfth at 7:30.

5. Meet me at Sixty-five Cadman Place.

Focus on Writing: *Flashback*

Look back at your response to the Focus on Writing activity on page 579. Have you used any hyphens, numbers, or abbreviations in your writing? If so, have you used them correctly? Make any necessary corrections.

Focus on Writing: *Revising and Editing*

Look back at your response to the Focus on Writing activity on page 579. **TEST** what you have written. Then, revise your work, editing for proper use of capital letters, quotation marks, and italics.

Editing Practice

Read the following student essay, which includes errors in capitalization and in punctuation with direct quotations as well as errors in the use of titles, abbreviations, and numbers. Edit the passage to correct any such errors. The first sentence has been edited for you.

The World of Gary Soto

My favorite Author is Gary Soto, a mexican-american poet and fiction writer whose first book of poetry, The Elements of San Joaquin, was published in 1977. Soto was born in 1952 in fresno, california, and grew up in a large spanish-speaking family. His Father, who died when Soto was 5, worked in a factory, and his Mother picked grapes and other crops in the farms of the san joaquin valley. Much of Soto's writing is influenced by childhood memories. "These are the pictures I take with me when I write", he once said. "they stir the past, the memories that are so vivid."

Soto attended fresno city college and later studied at the U. of California at fresno, where he originally majored in Geol. There, according to Soto, "One day I came across a book of poetry on a shelf in the college library. I read it, liked it, and began to write poems of my own".

One of Soto's best poems is Oranges, from his 1985 book "Black Hair." In this poem, he describes the events of a cold december afternoon when a boy takes his Girlfriend into a drugstore to buy her a treat. She wants a chocolate that costs a Dime, but he only has a Nickel. He gives the Saleslady the coin plus an orange he has in his pocket, and she lets him pay for the candy this way.

This theme of money is picked up again in the Title of one of Soto's books of stories, "Nickel And Dime." The first story is called "We Ain't

Asking Much and is about Roberto, who loses his job, cannot pay his rent, and ends up on the Street, trying to sell christmas ornaments made of twigs to rich people. Silver, a Character in another story, has something in common with Soto (he is a poet), but he also has trouble making enough money to live on.

Does Soto write from Personal Experience? He admits that this is partly true. He says, however, "Although the experiences in my stories, poems, and novels may seem autobiographical, much of what I write is the stuff of imagination".

Collaborative Activities

1. Work in a small group to list as many items in each of the following five categories as you can: planets, islands, musicians or bands, automobile models, sports teams. Be sure all your items are proper nouns, and use capital letters where necessary.

    On a separate sheet of paper, write five original sentences using one proper noun from each category in each sentence. When you are finished, exchange papers with another group, and check for the correct use of capital letters.

2. Imagine that you and the other members of your group are the nominations committee for this year's Emmy, Oscar, or Grammy Awards. Work together to compile a list of categories and several nominees for each category, deciding as a group when to use capital letters.

    Trade lists with another group. From each category, select the individual artist or work you believe deserves to win the award. Write a sentence about each winner, explaining why it is the best in its category.

    When you have finished, exchange papers with another group. Check one another's papers for correct use of capitals, quotation marks, and underlining (to indicate italics).

3. Working in pairs, write a conversation between two characters, real or fictional, who have very different positions on a particular issue. Place all direct quotations within quotation marks, and include identifying

tags that clearly indicate which character is speaking. (Begin a new paragraph each time a new person speaks.)

Exchange your conversations with another pair of students, and check their work to see that all directly quoted speech is set within quotation marks and that capital letters and all other punctuation are used correctly.

Review Checklist: Understanding Mechanics

- ☐ Capitalize proper nouns. (See 34A.)
- ☐ Always place direct quotations in quotation marks. (See 34B.)
- ☐ In titles, capitalize all important words. Use italics or quotation marks to set off titles. (See 34C.)
- ☐ Use hyphens to divide words at the end of a line and to join words in compounds. (See 34D.)
- ☐ Use abbreviations for titles used along with names, for names of organizations and technical terms, and in other conventional situations. (See 34E.)
- ☐ Spell out numbers that can be expressed in fewer than three words. Use numerals in most other cases. (See 34F.)

Becoming a Better Speller

Improving your spelling may take time, but the following steps can make this task a lot easier.

1. **Use a spell checker.** When you write on a computer, use your spell checker. It will correct most misspelled words and also identify many typos, such as transposed or omitted letters. Keep in mind, however, that spell checkers do not identify typos that create other words (*then/than*, *form/from*, or *big/beg*, for example). They also do not identify words that have been used incorrectly (*their/there* or *its/it's*, for example).

2. **Proofread carefully.** Even if you have used a spell checker, always proofread your papers for spelling before you hand them in.

3. **Use a dictionary.** As you proofread your papers, circle words whose spellings you are unsure of. After you have finished, look up these words in a print or online dictionary.

4. **Keep a personal spelling list.** Write down all the words you misspell. Whenever your instructor returns one of your papers, look for misspelled words—usually circled and marked *sp*. Add these to your personal spelling list.

5. **Look for patterns in your misspelling.** Do you consistently misspell words with *ei* combinations? Do you have trouble forming plurals? Once you figure out which errors you make most frequently, you can take steps to eliminate them.

Focus on Writing

In an effort to improve discipline and boost self-esteem, a number of schools across the country require students to wear uniforms. The picture on the opposite page shows two students at an elementary school that requires uniforms. Look at the picture, and then write a paragraph (or an essay) about whether or not you think students should be required to wear uniforms such as the ones in the picture.

6. **Learn the basic spelling rules.** Memorize the spelling rules in this chapter, especially those that apply to areas in which you are weak. Remember that each rule can help you spell many words correctly.

7. **Review the list of commonly confused words in 35E.** If you have problems with any of these word pairs, add them to your personal spelling list.

8. **Use memory cues.** Memory cues help you remember how to spell certain words. For example, remembering that *definite* contains the word *finite* will help you remember that *definite* is spelled with an *i*, not an *a*.

9. **Learn to spell some of the most frequently misspelled words.** Identify those on the list below that give you trouble, and add them to your personal spelling list.

Frequently Misspelled Words

across	disappoint	loneliness	reference
all right	early	medicine	restaurant
a lot	embarrass	minute	roommate
already	entrance	necessary	secretary
argument	environment	noticeable	sentence
beautiful	everything	occasion	separate
becoming	exercise	occur	speech
beginning	experience	occurred	studying
believe	finally	occurrences	surprise
benefit	forty	occurring	tomato
calendar	fulfill	occurs	tomatoes
cannot	generally	personnel	truly
careful	government	possible	until
careless	grammar	potato	usually
cemetery	harass	potatoes	Wednesday
certain	height	prejudice	weird
conscience	holiday	prescription	window
definite	integration	privilege	withhold
definitely	intelligence	probably	woman
dependent	interest	professor	women
describe	interfere	receive	writing
develop	judgment	recognize	written

Because English pronunciation is not always a reliable guide for spelling, most people find it useful to memorize some spelling rules.

Highlight: Vowels and Consonants	Knowing which letters are vowels and which are consonants will help you understand the spelling rules presented in this chapter.

Vowels: *a, e, i, o, u*

Consonants: *b, c, d, f, g, h, j, k, l, m, n, p, q, r, s, t, v, w, x, y, z*

The letter *y* may be considered either a vowel or a consonant, depending on how it is pronounced. In *young*, *y* acts as a consonant because it has the sound of *y*; in *truly*, it acts as a vowel because it has the sound of *ee*.

35b   *ie* and *ei*

Memorize this rule: *i* comes before *e* except after *c* or when the *ei* sound is pronounced *ay*.

i *before* e	*except after* c	*or when* ei *is pronounced* ay
achieve	ceiling	eight
believe	conceive	freight
friend	deceive	neighbor
		weigh

Highlight: Exceptions to the "*i* before *e*" Rule	The exceptions to the "*i* before *e*" rule follow no pattern, so you must memorize them.

ancient	either	leisure	seize
caffeine	foreign	neither	species
conscience	height	science	weird

● **Practice 35-1**

Proofread the underlined words in the following sentences for correct spelling. If a correction needs to be made, cross out the incorrect word, and write the correct spelling above it. If the word is spelled correctly, write *C* above it.

Example: It was a <u>relief</u> to <u>recieve</u> the good news.

C *receive*

1. Be sure to <u>wiegh</u> the pros and cons before making important decisions, particularly those involving <u>friends</u>.

2. When your <u>beliefs</u> are tested, you may be able to <u>acheive</u> a better understanding of yourself.

3. In our <u>society</u>, many people <u>decieve</u> themselves into <u>beleiving</u> that they are better than everyone else.

4. It is <u>cheifly</u> because they have been lucky that they have reached a certain <u>height</u> in the world.

5. They think that the blood running through <u>their</u> <u>viens</u> makes them belong to a higher <u>species</u> than the average person.

Focus on Writing: *Flashback*

Look back at your response to the Focus on Writing activity on page 597. Underline any words that have *ie* or *ei* combinations, and check a dictionary to make sure they are spelled correctly. Correct any spelling errors you find.

35c Prefixes

A **prefix** is a group of letters added at the beginning of a word that changes the word's meaning. Adding a prefix to a word never affects the spelling of the original word.

dis + service = disservice	pre + heat = preheat
un + able = unable	un + natural = unnatural
co + operate = cooperate	over + rate = overrate

● Practice 35-2

Write in the blanks the new words that result when the specified prefix is added to each of the following words.

Example: dis + respect = <u>disrespect</u>

1. un + happy = _____
2. tele + vision = _____
3. pre + existing = _____
4. dis + satisfied = _____
5. un + necessary = _____

6. non + negotiable = _____
7. im + patient = _____
8. out + think = _____
9. over + react = _____
10. dis + solve = _____

Focus on Writing: *Flashback*

Look back at your response to the Focus on Writing activity on page 597. Underline any words that have prefixes, and check a dictionary to make sure each word is spelled correctly. Correct any spelling errors you find.

35d

Suffixes

A **suffix** is a group of letters added to the end of a word that changes the word's meaning or its part of speech. Adding a suffix to a word can change the spelling of the original word.

Words Ending in Silent *e*

If a word ends with a silent (unpronounced) *e*, drop the *e* if the suffix begins with a vowel.

Drop the *e*

hope + <u>ing</u> = hoping
continue + <u>ous</u> = continuous

dance + <u>er</u> = dancer
insure + <u>able</u> = insurable

Exceptions

change + able = changeable
notice + able = noticeable

courage + ous = courageous
replace + able = replaceable

Keep the *e* if the suffix begins with a consonant.

Keep the *e*

hope + ful = hopeful   bore + dom = boredom

excite + ment = excitement   same + ness = sameness

Exceptions

argue + ment = argument   true + ly = truly

judge + ment = judgment   nine + th = ninth

● **Practice 35-3**

Write in the blanks the new words that result when the specified suffix is added to each of the following words.

Examples:

insure + ance = _____*insurance*_____

love + ly = _____*lovely*_____

1. lone + ly = _____   6. microscope + ic = _____

2. use + ful = _____   7. prepare + ation = _____

3. revise + ing = _____   8. nine + th = _____

4. base + ment = _____   9. indicate + ion = _____

5. desire + able = _____   10. effective + ness = _____

Words Ending in -y

When you add a suffix to a word that ends in *-y*, change the *y* to an *i* if the letter before the *y* is a consonant.

Change *y* to *i*

beauty + ful = beautiful   busy + ly = busily

try + ed = tried   friendly + er = friendlier

Exceptions

● Keep the *y* if the suffix starts with an *i*.

cry + ing = crying   baby + ish = babyish

- Keep the *y* when you add a suffix to certain one-syllable words.

  shy + er = shyer   dry + ness = dryness

When you add a suffix to a word that ends in *-y*, keep the *y* if the letter before the *y* is a vowel.

Keep the *y*

annoy + ance = annoyance   enjoy + ment = enjoyment

play + ful = playful   display + ed = displayed

Exceptions

day + ly = daily   say + ed = said

gay + ly = gaily   pay + ed = paid

● Practice 35-4

Write in the blanks the new words that result when the specified suffix is added to each of the following words.

Examples:

study + ed = _____*studied*_____

employ + ment = _____*employment*_____

1. happy + ness = _____
2. convey + or = _____
3. deny + ing = _____
4. carry + ed = _____
5. ready + ness = _____
6. annoy + ing = _____
7. destroy + er = _____
8. twenty + eth = _____
9. lonely + ness = _____
10. spy + ing = _____

Doubling the Final Consonant

When you add a suffix that begins with a vowel—for example, *-ed*, *-er*, or *-ing*—sometimes you need to double the final consonant in the original word. Do this (1) if the last three letters of the word have a consonant-vowel-consonant (cvc) pattern *and* (2) if the word has one syllable (or if the last syllable is stressed).

Final consonant doubled

drum   +   ing   =   drumming (cvc—one syllable)

bat   +   er   =   batter (cvc—one syllable)

pet	+	ed	=	petted (cvc—one syllable)
commit	+	ed	=	committed (cvc—stress is on last syllable)
occur	+	ing	=	occurring (cvc—stress is on last syllable)

Final consonant not doubled

answer	+	ed	=	answered (cvc—stress is not on last syllable)
happen	+	ing	=	happening (cvc—stress is not on last syllable)
act	+	ing	=	acting (no cvc)

● Practice 35-5

Write in the blanks the new words that result when the specified suffix is added to each of the following words.

Examples:

rot + ing = _____rotting_____

narrow + er = _____narrower_____

1. hope + ed = _____
2. shop + er = _____
3. rest + ing = _____
4. combat + ed = _____
5. reveal + ing = _____

6. open + er = _____
7. unzip + ed = _____
8. trap + ed = _____
9. cram + ing = _____
10. omit + ed = _____

Focus on Writing: *Flashback*

Look back at your response to the Focus on Writing activity on page 597. Underline any words that have suffixes, and check a dictionary to make sure each word is spelled correctly. Correct any spelling errors you find.

35e   Commonly Confused Words

Accept/Except   *Accept* means "to receive something." *Except* means "with the exception of" or "to leave out or exclude."

> "I <u>accept</u> your challenge," said Alexander Hamilton to Aaron Burr.
>
> Everyone <u>except</u> Darryl visited the museum.

Affect/Effect   *Affect* is a verb meaning "to influence." *Effect* is a noun meaning "result."

> Carmen's job could <u>affect</u> her grades.
>
> Overexposure to sun can have a long-term <u>effect</u> on skin.

All ready/Already   *All ready* means "completely prepared." *Already* means "previously, before."

> Serge was <u>all ready</u> to take the history test.
>
> Gina has <u>already</u> been to Italy.

Brake/Break   *Brake* is a noun that means "a device to slow or stop a vehicle." *Break* is a verb meaning "to smash" or "to detach" and sometimes a noun meaning either "a gap or an interruption" or "a stroke of luck."

> Peter got into an accident because his foot slipped off the <u>brake</u>.
>
> Babe Ruth thought no one would ever <u>break</u> his home run record.
>
> The baseball game was postponed until there was a <u>break</u> in the bad weather.

Buy/By   *Buy* means "to purchase." *By* is a preposition meaning "close to" or "next to" or "by means of."

> The Stamp Act forced colonists to <u>buy</u> stamps for many public documents.
>
> He drove <u>by</u> but did not stop.
>
> He stayed <u>by</u> her side all the way to the hospital.
>
> Malcolm X wanted "freedom <u>by</u> any means necessary."

● **Practice 35-6**

Proofread the underlined words in the following sentences for correct spelling. If a correction needs to be made, cross out the incorrect word, and write the correct spelling above it. If the word is spelled correctly, write *C* above it.

Example: We must ~~except~~ the fact that the human heart can break.
                      accept   *C*

1. The affects of several new AIDS drugs have all ready been reported.

2. *Consumer Reports* gave high ratings to the breaks on all the new cars tested accept one.

3. Advertisements urge us to by a new product even if we already own a similar item.

4. If you except the charges for a collect telephone call, you will probably have to brake your piggy bank to pay the bill.

5. Cigarette smoking affects the lungs by creating deposits of tar that make breathing difficult.

Conscience/Conscious   *Conscience* is a noun that refers to the part of the mind that urges a person to choose right over wrong. *Conscious* is an adjective that means "aware" or "deliberate."

   After he cheated at cards, his conscience started to bother him.

   As she walked through the woods, she became conscious of the hum of insects.

   Elliott made a conscious decision to stop smoking.

Everyday/Every day   *Everyday* is a single word that means "ordinary" or "common." *Every day* is two words that mean "occurring daily."

   I Love Lucy was a successful comedy show because it appealed to everyday people.

   Every day, Lucy and Ethel would find a new way to get into trouble.

Fine/Find   *Fine* means "superior quality" or "a sum of money paid as a penalty." *Find* means "to locate."

He sang a <u>fine</u> solo at church last Sunday.

Demi had to pay a <u>fine</u> for speeding.

Some people still use a willow rod to <u>find</u> water.

Hear/Here *Hear* means "to perceive sound by ear." *Here* means "at or in this place."

I moved to the front so I could <u>hear</u> the speaker.

My great-grandfather came <u>here</u> in 1883.

Its/It's *Its* is the possessive form of *it*. *It's* is the contraction of *it is* or *it has*.

The airline canceled <u>its</u> flights because of the snow.

<u>It's</u> twelve o'clock, and we're late.

Because <u>it's</u> been in an accident, the car rattles when I drive.

● **Practice 35-7**

Proofread the underlined words in the following sentences for correct spelling. If a correction needs to be made, cross out the incorrect word, and write the correct spelling above it. If the word is spelled correctly, write *C* above it.

Example: <u>It's</u> often difficult for celebrities to adjust to <u>every day</u> ^*everyday*^ life.
(C above It's)

1. <u>Hear</u> at Simonson's Fashions, we try to make our customers feel that <u>everyday</u> is a sale day.

2. My uncle was a <u>find</u> person, and <u>its</u> a shame that he died so young.

3. That inner voice you <u>hear</u> is your <u>conscious</u> telling you how you should behave.

4. In the <u>every day</u> world of work and school, it can be hard to <u>fine</u> the time to relax and enjoy life.

5. By the time I became <u>conscience</u> of the leaking pipe, <u>it's</u> damage had run to more than a hundred dollars.

Know/No/Knew/New *Know* means "to have an understanding of" or "to have fixed in the mind." *No* means "not any," "not at all," or "not one." *Knew* is the past tense form of the verb *know*. *New* means "recent or never used."

I <u>know</u> there will be a lunar eclipse tonight.

You have <u>no</u> right to say that.

He <u>knew</u> how to install a <u>new</u> light switch.

Lie / Lay   *Lie* means "to rest or recline." The past tense of *lie* is *lay. Lay* means "to put or place something down." The past tense of *lay* is *laid.*

Every Sunday, I <u>lie</u> in bed until noon.

They <u>lay</u> on the grass until it began to rain, and then they went home.

Tammy told Carl to <u>lay</u> his cards on the table.

Brooke and Cassia finally <u>laid</u> down their hockey sticks.

Loose / Lose   *Loose* means "not fixed or rigid" or "not attached securely." *Lose* means "to mislay" or "to misplace."

In the 1940s, many women wore <u>loose</u>-fitting pants.

I don't gamble because I hate to <u>lose</u>.

Passed / Past   *Passed* is the past tense of the verb *pass*. It means "moved by" or "succeeded in." *Past* is a noun meaning time "earlier than the present time."

The car that <u>passed</u> me was doing more than eighty miles an hour.

David finally <u>passed</u> his driving test.

The novel was set in the <u>past</u>.

Peace / Piece   *Peace* means "the absence of war" or "calm." *Piece* means "a part of something."

The British prime minister thought he had achieved <u>peace</u> with honor.

My <u>peace</u> of mind was destroyed when the flying saucer landed.

"Have a <u>piece</u> of cake," said Marie.

● **Practice 35-8**

Proofread the underlined words in the following sentences for correct spelling. If a correction needs to be made, cross out the incorrect word, and write the correct spelling above it. If the word is spelled correctly, write *C* above it.

Example: Although the soldiers stopped fighting, a <u>piece</u> *peace* treaty was never signed.

1. Because he was late for the job interview, he was afraid he would <u>loose</u> his chance to work for the company.

2. While she <u>laid</u> down to rest, her children cooked dinner and cleaned the house.

3. There will be <u>know</u> wool sweaters on sale before the holidays.

4. The committee <u>past</u> three resolutions.

5. The blade found in the trash turned out to be a <u>peace</u> of the murder weapon.

Principal/Principle   *Principal* means "first" or "highest" or "the head of a school." *Principle* means "a law or basic assumption."

> She had the <u>principal</u> role in the movie.
>
> I'll never forget the day the <u>principal</u> called me into his office.
>
> It was against his <u>principles</u> to lie.

Quiet/Quite   *Quiet* means "free of noise" or "still." *Quite* means "actually" or "very."

> Jane looked forward to the <u>quiet</u> evenings at the lake.
>
> "You haven't <u>quite</u> got the hang of it yet," she said.
>
> After practicing all summer, Tamika got <u>quite</u> good at tennis.

Raise/Rise   *Raise* means "to elevate" or "to increase in size, quantity, or worth." The past tense of *raise* is *raised. Rise* means "to stand up" or "to move from a lower position to a higher position." The past tense of *rise* is *rose.*

> Carlos <u>raises</u> his hand whenever the teacher asks for volunteers.
>
> They finally <u>raised</u> the money for the down payment.
>
> The crowd <u>rises</u> every time their team scores a touchdown.
>
> Aurea <u>rose</u> before dawn so she could see the eclipse.

Sit/Set   *Sit* means "to assume a sitting position." The past tense of *sit* is *sat. Set* means "to put down or place" or "to adjust something to a desired position." The past tense of *set* is *set.*

> I usually <u>sit</u> in the front row at the movies.
>
> They <u>sat</u> at the clinic waiting for their names to be called.

Elizabeth <u>set</u> the mail on the kitchen table and left for work.

Every semester I <u>set</u> goals for myself.

Suppose / Supposed   *Suppose* means "to consider" or "to assume." *Supposed* is both the past tense and the past participle of *suppose*. *Supposed* also means "expected" or "required." (Note that when *supposed* has this meaning, it is followed by *to*.)

Suppose researchers were to find a cure for cancer.

We <u>supposed</u> the movie would be over by ten o'clock.

You were <u>supposed</u> to finish a draft of the report by today.

● **Practice 35-9**

Proofread the underlined words in the following sentences for correct spelling. If a correction needs to be made, cross out the incorrect word, and write the correct spelling above it. If the word is spelled correctly, write *C* above it.

C

Example: Boarding took <u>quite</u> a long time because of the security process.

1. Jackie was <u>suppose</u> to mow the lawn and trim the bushes last weekend.
2. It is important to <u>sit</u> the computer in a place where the on-off switch can be easily reached.
3. If you <u>raise</u> the window, a pleasant breeze will blow into the bedroom.
4. The <u>principle</u> reason for her <u>raise</u> to the position of <u>principal</u> of the school was hard work.
5. We were all told to <u>sit</u> and wait for the crowd to become <u>quite</u>.

Their / There / They're   *Their* is the possessive form of the pronoun *they*. *There* means "at or in that place." *There* is also used in the phrases *there is* and *there are*. *They're* is the contraction of "they are."

They wanted to improve <u>their</u> living conditions.

I put the book over <u>there</u>.

<u>There</u> are three reasons I will not eat meat.

<u>They're</u> the best volunteer firefighters I've ever seen.

Then/Than   *Then* means "at that time" or "next in time." *Than* is used in comparisons.

> He was young and naive <u>then</u>.
>
> I went to the job interview and <u>then</u> stopped off for a chocolate shake.
>
> My dog is smarter <u>than</u> your dog.

Threw/Through   *Threw* is the past tense of *throw*. *Through* means "in one side and out the opposite side" or "finished."

> Satchel Paige <u>threw</u> a baseball more than ninety-five miles an hour.
>
> It takes almost thirty minutes to go <u>through</u> the tunnel.
>
> "I'm <u>through</u>," said Clark Kent, storming out of Perry White's office.

To/Too/Two   *To* means "in the direction of." *Too* means "also" or "more than enough." *Two* denotes the numeral 2.

> During spring break, I am going <u>to</u> Disney World.
>
> My roommates are coming <u>too</u>.
>
> The microwave popcorn is <u>too</u> hot to eat.
>
> "If we get rid of the Tin Man and the Cowardly Lion, the <u>two</u> of us can go to Oz," said the Scarecrow to Dorothy.

Use/Used   *Use* means "to put into service" or "to consume." *Used* is both the past tense and past participle of *use*. *Used* also means "accustomed." (Note that when *used* has this meaning, it is followed by *to*.)

> I <u>use</u> a soft cloth to clean my glasses.
>
> "Hey! Who <u>used</u> all the hot water?" he yelled from the shower.
>
> Marisol had <u>used</u> all the firewood during the snowstorm.
>
> After two years in Alaska, they got <u>used</u> to the short winter days.

● **Practice 35-10**

Proofread the underlined words in the following sentences for correct spelling. If a correction needs to be made, cross out the incorrect word, and write the correct spelling above it. If the word is spelled correctly, write *C* above it.

> **Example:** Because of good nutrition, people are taller <u>then</u> they <u>use</u>
> to be in the past.

(above "then": than; above "use": used)

1. The power went out in the dorms, and many students <u>then</u> went <u>too</u> the library to study.

2. Whenever he <u>through</u> out the trash, he walked <u>threw</u> the backyard on his way <u>two</u> the alley.

3. Get your tickets before <u>their</u> all gone.

4. I <u>use</u> to think that my ancestors all came from northern Europe, but I recently learned that one of my great-grandparents <u>used</u> to live in South Africa.

5. The countries that signed the peace treaty have not lived up to <u>they're</u> responsibilities.

Weather/Whether   *Weather* refers to temperature, humidity, precipitation, and so on. *Whether* is used to introduce alternative possibilities.

The *Farmer's Almanac* says that the <u>weather</u> this winter will be severe.
<u>Whether</u> or not this prediction will be correct is anyone's guess.

Where/Were/We're   *Where* means "at or in what place." *Were* is the past tense of *are*. *We're* is the contraction of "we are."

<u>Where</u> are you going, and <u>where</u> have you been?
Charlie Chaplin and Mary Pickford <u>were</u> popular stars of silent movies.
<u>We're</u> doing our back-to-school shopping early this year.

Whose/Who's   *Whose* is the possessive form of *who*. *Who's* is the contraction of either "who is" or "who has."

My roommate asked, "<u>Whose</u> book is this?"
"<u>Who's</u> there?" squealed the second little pig as he leaned against the door.
<u>Who's</u> left a yellow 1957 Chevrolet blocking the driveway?

Your/You're   *Your* is the possessive form of *you*. *You're* is the contraction of "you are."

"You should have worn <u>your</u> running shoes," said the hare as he passed the tortoise.
"<u>You're</u> too kind," said the tortoise sarcastically.

● **Practice 35-11**

Proofread the underlined words in the following sentences for correct spelling. If a correction needs to be made, cross out the incorrect word, and write the correct spelling above it. If the word is spelled correctly, write *C* above it.

> **Example:**   As citizens, <u>were</u> all concerned with <u>where</u> our country is going.
> *we're* above "were"; *C* above "where"

1. Authorities are attempting to discover <u>who's</u> fingerprints <u>were</u> left at the scene of the crime.

2. Cancer does not care <u>weather</u> <u>your</u> rich or poor, young or old; it can strike anyone.

3. Santa Fe, <u>were</u> I lived for many years, has better <u>weather</u> than New Jersey has.

4. Whenever we listen to politicians debate, <u>were</u> likely to wonder <u>whose</u> telling the truth.

5. You should take <u>your</u> time before deciding <u>weather</u> to focus <u>your</u> energy on school or on work.

Focus on Writing: *Flashback*

Look back at your response to the Focus on Writing activity on page 597. Identify any words that appear in the list of commonly confused words in 35E, and check to make sure you have spelled them correctly.

Focus on Writing: *Revising and Editing*

Type your response to the Focus on Writing activity on page 597 if you have not already done so. **TEST** what you have written. Then, revise and edit your work, paying particular attention to spelling errors your computer identified when you ran a spell check as well as to those that you found while proofreading.

Editing Practice

Read the following student essay, which includes spelling errors. Identify the words you think are misspelled; then, look them up in a dictionary. Finally, cross out each incorrectly spelled word, and write the correct spelling above the line. The first sentence has been edited for you.

The Guardian Angels

The Guardian Angels are volunteers ~~who's~~ *whose* aim is to promote public ~~saftey~~ *safety*. Organizzed in New York City in 1979, the Angels originaly got together to fight crime on New York's subways. Unnarmed, they patroled the streets, hoping to prevent violence before it happened. Since than, the group has expanded it's reach to include other cities and other methods of violence prevention. The organizetion now has chapters in more than 100 cities all over the world, and in addition to doing there Safety Patrols, the Guardian Angels offer youth programs and promote Internet safety.

All Guardian Angel patrollers are volunteers who recieve training in first aid and CPR. Before going out on the streets, they also learn how to communicate effectivelly and resolve conflicts piecefully. Their distinctive red jackets and red berets make them noticable whereever they go. When they first appeared more than thirty years ago, the Safety Patrols rised quiet a stir. Many goverment officials where opposed to them. Today, however, many chapters are welcomed by local police and city leadders, who except that buy trying to prevent nieghborhood violence, the Angels are providing a usefull service.

From the begining, the Guardian Angels have tryed to include young people in their programs. Founder Curtis Sliwa beleives that his organization gives urban youth a positive way to be involved in there communities. Although people under 16 can not join the Safety Patrols, the Guardian Angels have groups specifically designed for young teenagers and children. Accordding to the organization's Web site, the Urban Angels program offers 12- to 16-year-olds an alternative to gangs and drugs.

Urban Angels learn about violence prevention threw working with peers on community-service projects. The Junior Angels program is suppose to give 7- to 11-year-olds a way to build self-esteem and fine a sense of purpose. Junior Angels also learn about nonviolent ways to ressolve conflicts.

In 1995, to detect online threats and to educate people about the risks of the Internet, the Guardian Angels creatted a knew group, the CyberAngels. These Angels aim to teach people how to protect themselves from online harasment, identity theft, computer viruses, and other online dangers. This group is also intrested in helping parents and schools to reconize the particlar problems children face when they spend time online and to protect children from Internet threats. Often, parents spend alot of time argueing with their children about appropriate limits on Internet use. The CyberAngels advice parents about how to monitor use effectively without interferring too much in their children's lives.

Although they're are people who do not approve of evrything the Guardian Angels do, most acknowledge that the Angels' aims are honorible. These volunteers are committed to understanding and improving their own communities. In addition, the Guardian Angels have shown they can change with the times. Because they have developped a diverse range of usefull programs, its likely they will be around for years to come.

Collaborative Activities

1. Working in pairs, compare responses to the Focus on Writing activity on page 597. How many misspelled words did each of you find? How many of these errors did you and your partner both find?

2. Exchange books with a classmate. Are there any patterns of misspelling in your Flashback activities? What types of spelling errors seem most common?

3. Collaborate with your partner to make a spelling list for the two of you, and then work with other groups to create a spelling list for the whole class. When you have finished, determine which types of errors are most common.

Review Checklist: Understanding Spelling

☐ Follow the steps to becoming a better speller. (See 35A.)

☐ *I* comes before *e*, except after *c* or in any *ay* sound, as in *neighbor*. (See 35B.)

☐ Adding a prefix to a word never affects the word's spelling. (See 35C.)

☐ Adding a suffix to a word may change the word's spelling. (See 35D.)

☐ When a word ends with silent *e*, drop the *e* if the suffix begins with a vowel. Keep the *e* if the suffix begins with a consonant. (See 35D.)

☐ When you add a suffix to a word that ends with a *y*, change the *y* to an *i* if the letter before the *y* is a consonant. Keep the *y* if the letter before the *y* is a vowel. (See 35D.)

☐ When you add a suffix that begins with a vowel, double the final consonant in the original word (1) if the last three letters of the word have a consonant-vowel-consonant (cvc) pattern *and* (2) if the word has one syllable (or if the last syllable is stressed). (See 35D.)

☐ Memorize the spellings of the most commonly confused words. (See 35E.)

Unit Review

Editing Practice: Sentences

Read the following sentences, which contain errors in punctuation, mechanics, and spelling. Identify the sentences that need to be corrected, and edit the faulty sentences. Some sentences have more than one error.

1. There are fourty restuarants within 5 miles of my house but the most popular place is: Golden Crown a Chinese buffet.

2. Mr Glass my middle school principle, retired last year; after he turned 65.

3. Mike has lived in Chicago Illinois since he was born on Aug. eleventh 1986.

4. When we moved into our new apartment Tony said, their were alot of ants in the kitchen and the front door lock didnt work.

5. There are several ways too keep a computer secure; install spam blocking software change your email adress frequently and keep your're real name a secret.

6. What kind of vaccum cleaner is Jins grandmother using.

7. Its clear that the clerk at the registration desk one of the first people guests see when they check in needs better comunication skills.

8. Stan and his wife spent part of their Summer vacation in Philadelphia, visiting Constitution center, and independance hall.

9. At first, readers thought that in his book *The Painted Bird*, writter Jerzy Kosinski was discribeing his own dificult life as a young boy in Nazi-occupied poland, but now they're are doubts about weather he ever had those experiances or even wrote the book himself.

10. Lenders say that families should spend no more then 35% of there total income on housing, but many familyies are spending almost 50%.

Editing Practice: Essay

Read the following student essay, which contains errors in the use of punctuation, mechanics, and spelling. Identify the sentences that need to be corrected, and edit the faulty sentences. (Underline to indicate italics where necessary.) The first sentence has been edited for you.

Telenovelas

What is the most-watched kind of television program in Spanish-speaking countries⸮ It's the telenovela, a Spanish language soap opera. Televised in the prime evenning hours telenovelas started in the early nineteen hundred fifties and are still popular today. In fact more telenovelas are shown in central America and South america than any other type of TV drama. In a 1998 study, more than half the population of Latin American countries said "that they watch these shows." Telenovelas are different from american soap operas in the way they are planed and scheduled. Also they dont have the same kind of plots. Telenovela's popularity can be seen in there Web sites and buy their growth in countries that do not speak spanish.

Telenovelas are quiet different from American Soap Operas. In the United States, there have been some evening soap opera dramas (dallas and dynasty are good examples but they have usually been televised once a week, however telenovelas usually appear Mon. through Fri. In the United States soap operas' genneraly continue for months and years, until viewers stop watching and ratings fall. The writters of an american soap opera, do not no how the plot will develope or when it will end. In contrast telenovela's are usually completely planned at the beggining. In general a telenovela continues for about 8 months and then it is finished. A new telenovela takes it's place.

The plots may seem wierd to american viewers. In a typical telenovela the beautiful heroine is a girl who has no money but has a good heart. The hero—a rich handsome man, rejects his rich but evil girlfreind in favor of the heroine. Eventualy the heroine may turn out too be the secret child of a wealthy family. The unnhappy villains may wind up in the cemetary and the heroine and her hero will live happily ever after. Other telenovelas occurr in the passed or may deal with modern social problems such as drug abuse, or predjudice. Some telenovelas are really cereal comedies and are more like American sitcoms.

Telenovelas are becomeing more and more popular. There are even Web sites dedicated to popular telenovelas and there actors. For example viewers can go to the Web site called topnovelas to access plot summaries lists of the most popular shows and downloads of episodes. Although telenovelas started in Spanish-speaking countries they have spread to other countries. The first telenovela to be translated into another language was "The Rich Cry too" (Los Ricos También Lloran) which was first produced in Mexico in nineteen seventy-nine and was brought to, China, the Soviet Union and the United States. Other places where telenovelas are popular include the following countries; france israel japan, malaysia Singapore and indonesia.

The popularity of the telenovela in the United states is only partly a reflection of its' millions of spanish speaking people. While it is true that networks want hispanic viewers it is also true that the format and subject matter truely interrest English-speaking viewers. Its quite possable that the once a week format of most american TV shows may be a thing of the past and that telenovelas in English will soon appear every night.

Unit Eight

Reading Essays

36 Reading Critically   622

37 Readings for Writers   634

Chapter 36 Reading Critically

Reading is essential to all your college courses. To get the most out of your reading, you should approach the books and articles you read in a practical way, always asking yourself what information they can offer you. You should also approach assigned readings critically, just as you approach your own writing.

Reading critically does not mean challenging or arguing with every idea, but it does mean wondering, commenting, questioning, and judging. Most of all, it means being an active rather than a passive reader. Being an **active reader** means approaching a reading assignment with a clear understanding of your purpose, previewing a selection, highlighting and annotating it, and perhaps outlining it—all *before* you begin to respond in writing to what you have read.

To gain an understanding of your **purpose**—your reason for reading—you should start by answering some questions.

Questions about Your Purpose

- Why are you reading?
- Will you be expected to discuss what you are reading? If so, will you discuss it in class or in a conference with your instructor?
- Will you have to write about what you are reading? If so, will you be expected to write an informal response (for example, a journal entry) or a more formal one (for example, an essay)?
- Will you be tested on the material?

Once you understand your purpose, you are ready to begin reading.

36a Previewing

Your first step is to preview the material you have been assigned to read. When you **preview**, you try to get a sense of the writer's main idea and key supporting points as well as his or her general emphasis. You can begin by focusing on the title, the first paragraph (which often contains a thesis statement or overview), and the last paragraph (which often contains a summary of the writer's points). You should also look for clues to the writer's message in other **visual signals** (headings, boxes, and so on) as well as in

verbal signals (the words and phrases the writer uses to convey order and emphasis).

Using Visual Signals

- Look at the title.
- Look at the opening and closing paragraphs.
- Look at each paragraph's first sentence.
- Look at headings.
- Look at *italicized* and **boldfaced** words.
- Look at numbered lists.
- Look at bulleted lists (like this one).
- Look at graphs, charts, tables, photographs, and so on.
- Look at any information that is boxed.
- Look at any information that is in color.

Using Verbal Signals

- Look for phrases that signal emphasis ("The *primary* reason"; "The *most important* idea").
- Look for repeated words and phrases.
- Look for words that signal addition (*also, in addition, furthermore*).
- Look for words that signal time sequence (*first, after, then, next, finally*).
- Look for words that identify causes and effects (*because, as a result, for this reason*).
- Look for words that introduce examples (*for example, for instance*).
- Look for words that signal comparison (*likewise, similarly*).
- Look for words that signal contrast (*unlike, although, in contrast*).
- Look for words that signal contradiction (*however, on the contrary*).
- Look for words that signal a narrowing of the writer's focus (*in fact, specifically, in other words*).
- Look for words that signal summaries or conclusions (*to sum up, in conclusion*).

When you have finished previewing the material, you should have a general sense of what the writer wants to communicate.

● Practice 36-1

"No Comprendo" ("I Don't Understand") is a newspaper article by Barbara Mujica, a professor of Spanish at Georgetown University in Washington,

WORD POWER

bilingual able to communicate in two languages

D.C. In this article, which was published in the *New York Times*, Mujica argues against bilingual education (teaching students in their native language as well as in English).

In preparation for class discussion and for other activities that will be assigned later in this chapter, preview the article. As you read, try to identify the writer's main idea and key supporting points, which you will be asked to write on the lines that follow the article, on page 626.

No Comprendo

Last spring, my niece phoned me in tears. She was graduating from high school and had to make a decision. An outstanding soccer player, she was offered athletic scholarships by several colleges. So why was she crying? 1

My niece came to the United States from South America as a child. Although she had received good grades in her schools in Miami, she spoke English with a heavy accent, and her comprehension and writing skills were deficient. She was afraid that once she left the Miami environment, she would feel uncomfortable and, worse still, have difficulty keeping up with class work. 2

Programs that keep foreign-born children in Spanish-language classrooms for years are only part of the problem. During a visit to my niece's former school, I observed that all business, not just teaching, was conducted in Spanish. In the office, secretaries spoke to the administrators and the children in Spanish. Announcements over the public-address system were made in an English so fractured that it was almost incomprehensible. 3

WORD POWER

Spanglish a mixture of Spanish and English

I asked my niece's mother why, after years in public schools, her daughter had poor English skills. "It's the whole environment," she replied. "All kinds of services are available in Spanish or Spanglish. Sports and after-school activities are conducted in Spanglish. That's what the kids hear on the radio and in the street." 4

Until recently, immigrants made learning English a priority. But even when they didn't learn English themselves, their children grew up speaking it. Thousands of first-generation Americans still strive to learn English, but others face reduced educational and career opportunities because they have not mastered this basic skill they need to get ahead. 5

According to the 1990 census, 40 percent of the Hispanics born in the United States do not graduate from high school, and the Department of Education says that a lack of proficiency in English is an important factor in the drop-out rate. 6

People and agencies that favor providing services only in foreign languages want to help people who do not speak English, but they may be 7 doing these people a disservice by condemning them to a linguistic ghetto from which they cannot easily escape.

And my niece? She turned down all of her scholarship opportunities, 8 deciding instead to attend a small college in Miami, where she will never have to put her English to the test.

Writer's main idea

_____

_____

Key supporting points

1. _____

2. _____

3. _____

4. _____

36b   Highlighting

After you have previewed the assigned material, read through it carefully, highlighting as you read. **Highlighting** means using underlining and symbols to identify key ideas. This active reading strategy will help you understand the writer's ideas and make connections among these ideas when you reread. Be selective; don't highlight too much. Remember, you will eventually be rereading every highlighted word, phrase, and sentence—so highlight only the most important, most useful information.

Using Highlighting Symbols

- Underline key ideas—for example, topic sentences.
- Box or circle words or phrases you want to remember.
- Place a check mark (✔) or star (✱) next to an important idea.
- Place a double check mark (✔✔) or double star (✱✱) next to an especially significant idea.
- Draw lines or arrows to connect related ideas.
- Put a question mark (?) beside a word or idea that you need to look up.
- Number the writer's key supporting points or examples.

Highlight: Knowing What to Highlight	You want to highlight what's important—but how do you *know* what's important? As a general rule, you should look for the same **visual signals** you looked for when you did your previewing. Many of the ideas you will need to highlight will probably be found in material that is visually set off from the rest of the text—opening and closing paragraphs, lists, and so on. Also, continue to look for **verbal signals**—words and phrases like *however, therefore, another reason, the most important point,* and so on—that often introduce key points. Together, these visual and verbal signals will give you clues to the writer's meaning and emphasis.

Here is how a student highlighted an excerpt from a newspaper column, "Barbie at Thirty-Five" by Anna Quindlen.

But consider the recent study at the University of Arizona investigating the attitudes of white and black teenage girls toward body image. The attitudes of the white girls were a nightmare. Ninety percent expressed dissatisfaction with their own bodies, and many said they saw dieting as a kind of all-purpose panacea. "I think the reason I would diet would be to gain self-confidence," said one. "I'd feel like it was a way of getting control," said another. And they were curiously united in their description of the perfect girl. She's 5 feet 7 inches, weighs just over 100 pounds, has long legs and flowing hair. The researchers concluded, "The ideal girl was a living manifestation of the Barbie doll."

While white girls described an impossible ideal, black teenagers talked about appearance in terms of style, attitude, pride, and personality. White respondents talked "thin," black ones "shapely." Seventy percent of the black teenagers said they were satisfied with their weight, and there was little emphasis on dieting. "We're all brought up and taught to be realistic about life," said one, "and we don't look at things the way you want them to be. You look at them the way they are."

The student who highlighted this passage was preparing to write an essay about eating disorders. She began her highlighting by underlining and starring the writer's main idea. She then boxed the names of the two key groups the passage compares—*white girls* and *black teenagers*—and underlined two phrases that illustrate how the attitudes of the two groups differ (*dissatisfaction with their own bodies* and *satisfied with their weight*). Check marks in the margin remind the student of the importance of these two phrases, and arrows connect each phrase to the appropriate group of girls.

The student also circled three related terms that characterize white girls' attitudes—*perfect girl*, *Barbie doll*, and *impossible ideal*—drawing lines to connect them. Finally, she circled the unfamiliar word *panacea* and put a question mark above it to remind herself to look up the word's meaning.

● Practice 36-2

Review the highlighted passage on page 627. How would your own highlighting of this passage be similar to or different from the sample student highlighting?

● Practice 36-3

Reread "No Comprendo" (pp. 625–26). As you reread, highlight the article by underlining and starring main ideas, boxing and circling key words, checkmarking important points, and, if you wish, drawing lines and arrows to connect related ideas. Be sure to circle each unfamiliar word and put a question mark above it.

36c ▸ Annotating

As you highlight, you should also *annotate* what you are reading. **Annotating** a passage means reading critically and making notes—of questions, reactions, reminders, and ideas for writing or discussion—in the margins or between the lines. Keeping a record of your reactions will prepare you for class discussion and for writing.

As you read a passage, asking the following questions will help you make useful annotations.

Questions for Critical Reading

- What is the writer saying? What do you think the writer is suggesting or implying?
- What is the writer's purpose (his or her reason for writing)?

→

> **Questions for Critical Reading** *(continued)*
> - What kind of audience is the writer addressing?
> - Is the writer discussing another writer's ideas?
> - What is the writer's main idea?
> - What examples and explanations does the writer use to support his or her points?
> - Does the writer include enough examples and explanations?
> - Do you understand the writer's vocabulary?
> - Do you understand the writer's ideas?
> - Do you agree with the points the writer is making?
> - How are the ideas presented here like (or unlike) those explored in other things you have read?

The following passage, which reproduces the student's highlighting from page 627, also illustrates her annotations.

But consider the recent study at the University of Arizona investigating the attitudes of white and black teenage girls toward body image. The attitudes of the white girls were a nightmare. Ninety percent expressed dissatisfaction with their own bodies, and many said they saw dieting as a kind of all-purpose panacea. "I think the reason I would diet would be to gain self-confidence," said one. "I'd feel like it was a way of getting control," said another. And they were curiously united in their description of the perfect girl. She's 5 feet 7 inches, weighs just over 100 pounds, has long legs and flowing hair. The researchers concluded, "The ideal girl was a living manifestation of the Barbie doll."

While white girls described an impossible ideal, black teenagers talked about appearance in terms of style, attitude, pride, and personality. White respondents talked "thin," black ones "shapely." Seventy percent of the black teenagers said they were satisfied with their weight, and there was little emphasis on dieting. "We're all brought up and taught to be realistic about life," said one, "and we don't look at things the way you want them to be. You look at them the way they are."

cure-all

Need for control, perfection. Why? Media? Parents?

Barbie doll = plastic, unreal

"Thin" vs. "shapely"

Only 30% dissatisfied — but 90% of white girls

vs. Barbie doll (= unrealistic)   *overgeneralization?*

In her annotations, this student wrote down the meaning of the word *panacea*, put the study's conclusions and the contrasting statistics into her own words, and recorded questions she intended to explore further.

● Practice 36-4

Reread "No Comprendo" (pp. 625–26). As you reread, refer to the Questions for Critical Reading (pp. 628–29), and use them as a guide while you write down your own thoughts and questions in the margins of the article. Note where you agree or disagree with the writer, and briefly explain why. Briefly summarize any points you think are particularly important. Take time to look up any unfamiliar words you have circled and to write short definitions. Think of these annotations as your preparation for discussing the article in class and eventually writing about it.

● Practice 36-5

Trade books with another student, and read over his or her highlighting and annotating of "No Comprendo." How are your written responses similar to the other student's? How are they different? Do your classmate's responses help you to see anything new about the article?

36d Outlining

Outlining is another technique you can use to help you understand a reading assignment. Unlike a **formal outline**, which follows strict conventions, an **informal outline** enables you to record a writer's ideas in the order in which they are presented. After you have finished an informal outline, you should be able to see the writer's emphasis (which ideas are more important than others) as well as how the ideas are related.

**Highlight:
Making an
Informal
Outline**

1. Write or type the writer's main idea at the top of a sheet of paper. (This will remind you of the writer's focus and help keep your outline on track.)
2. At the left margin, write down the most important idea of the first body paragraph or first part of the reading.

<table>
<tr>
<td>

**Highlight:
Making an
Informal
Outline**

continued
</td>
<td>

3. Indent the next line a few spaces, and list the examples or details that support this idea. (You can use your computer's Tab key to help you set up your outline.)

4. As ideas become more specific, indent further. (Ideas that have the same degree of importance are indented the same distance from the left margin.)

5. Repeat the process with each body paragraph or part of the passage.
</td>
</tr>
</table>

The student who highlighted and annotated the excerpt from Anna Quindlen's "Barbie at Thirty-Five" made the following informal outline to help her understand the writer's ideas.

Main idea: Black and white teenage girls have very different attitudes about their body images.

White girls dissatisfied
      90% dissatisfied with appearance
      Dieting = cure-all
          —self-confidence
          —control
      Ideal = unrealistic
          —tall and thin
          —Barbie doll
Black girls satisfied
      70% satisfied with weight
      Dieting not important
      Ideal = realistic
          —shapely
          —not thin

● Practice 36-6

Working on your own or in a small group, make an informal outline of "No Comprendo" (pp. 625–26). Refer to your highlighting and annotations as you construct your outline. When you have finished, check to make certain your outline accurately represents the writer's emphasis and the relationships among her ideas.

36e   Summarizing

Once you have highlighted, annotated, and outlined a passage, you may want to try summarizing it to help you understand it better. A **summary** retells, *in your own words*, what a passage is about. A summary condenses a passage, so it leaves out all but the main idea and perhaps the key supporting points. A summary omits examples and details, and it does *not* include your own ideas or opinions.

Highlight: Writing a Summary	1. Review your outline. 2. Consulting your outline, restate the passage's main idea in your own words. 3. Consulting your outline, restate the passage's key supporting points in your own words. 4. Add transitional words and phrases between sentences where necessary. 5. Reread the original passage to make sure you haven't left out anything significant. Note: To avoid accidentally using the exact language of the original, do not look at the passage while you are writing your summary. Later, if you decide to add a distinctive word or phrase from the original passage, put it in quotation marks.

The student who highlighted, annotated, and outlined the excerpt from "Barbie at Thirty-Five" wrote the following summary.

> As Anna Quindlen reports in "Barbie at Thirty-Five," a University of Arizona study found that black and white teenage girls have very different attitudes about their body images. Almost all white girls said they were dissatisfied with their appearance. To them, the "perfect girl" would look like a Barbie doll (tall and very thin). Quindlen sees this attitude as unrealistic. African-American girls in the study, however, were generally satisfied with their appearance. In fact, most said that they were happy with their weight. They did not say they wanted to be thin; they said they wanted to be "shapely."

● Practice 36-7

Write a brief summary of "No Comprendo" (pp. 625–26). Use your outline to guide you, and keep your summary short and to the point. Your summary should be about one-quarter to one-third the length of the original article.

36f   Writing a Response Paragraph

Once you have highlighted and annotated a reading selection, you are ready to write about it—perhaps in a **response paragraph** in which you record your informal reactions to the writer's ideas.

Because a response paragraph is informal, conversational style and personal opinions are acceptable. As in any paragraph, however, you should include a topic sentence, evidence (examples and details) to support the topic sentence, appropriate transitions, and a summary statement.

The student who highlighted, annotated, outlined, and summarized the Quindlen passage wrote this response paragraph.

> Why are white and black girls' body images so different? Why do African-American girls think it's okay to be "shapely" while white girls want to be thin? Maybe it's because music videos and movies and fashion magazines show so many more white models, all half-starved, with perfect hair and legs. Or maybe white girls get different messages from their parents or from the people they date. Do white and black girls' attitudes about their bodies stay the same when they get older? And what about *male* teenagers' self-images? Do white and black *guys* have different body images, too? These are questions that really need to be answered.

The process of writing this paragraph was very helpful to the student. The questions she asked suggested some interesting ideas that she could explore in class discussion or in a more fully developed piece of writing.

● Practice 36-8

Write an informal response paragraph expressing your reactions to "No Comprendo" (pp. 625–26) and to the issue of bilingual education.

Review Checklist: Reading Critically

- ☐ Preview the material. (See 36A.)
- ☐ Highlight the material. (See 36B.)
- ☐ Annotate the material. (See 36C.)
- ☐ Outline the material. (See 36D.)
- ☐ Summarize the material. (See 36E.)
- ☐ Write a response paragraph. (See 36F.)

This chapter introduces you to nineteen essays by professional writers. These essays offer interesting material to read, react to, think critically about, discuss, and write about. They are grouped according to the patterns of essay development discussed in Chapter 14. Each essay is accompanied by a short introduction that tells you something about the reading and its author. Definitions of some of the words used in the essay appear in Word Power boxes in the margins.

Each essay is followed by discussion questions and writing prompts.

- **Focus on Meaning** questions assess your understanding of the basic ideas the writer communicates.
- **Focus on Strategy** questions ask you to consider the writer's purpose, the essay's intended audience, the essay's thesis statement, and the writer's stylistic and rhetorical choices.
- **Focus on the Pattern** questions emphasize how the essay's ideas are arranged in one or more patterns of development.
- **Focus on Critical Thinking** questions encourage you to form judgments about the writer's choices. Sometimes these questions ask you to move beyond what is on the page to consider the essay's wider implications for your own life.

Two or three **Writing Practice** assignments, which can be used as prompts for essays or paragraphs, also follow each essay.

As you read these essays, you should **highlight** and **annotate** them to help you understand what you are reading. (Highlighting and annotating are discussed in Chapter 36.) Then, you should reread them more carefully in preparation for class discussion and writing.

Exemplification
"Don't Call Me a Hot Tamale," Judith Ortiz Cofer 636

"Volunteer Workers of the World, Unite," Nicols Fox 640

Narration
"Orange Crush," Yiyun Li 643

"Pick One," David Matthews 646

Description

"An American in Mexico," Alex Espinoza 650

"A Fable for Tomorrow," Rachel Carson 653

Process

"Mummy Arts," Adam Goodheart 656

"My Grandmother's Dumpling," Amy Ma 659

Cause and Effect

"The Poncho Bearer," John Schwartz 667

"At the Heart of a Historic Movement," John Hartmire 670

Comparison and Contrast

"My Two Lives," Jhumpa Lahiri 674

"The Transaction," William Zinsser 678

Classification

"But What Do You Mean?" Deborah Tannen 681

"The Dog Ate My Disk, and Other Tales of Woe," Carolyn Foster Segal 689

Definition

"The Wife-Beater," Gayle Rosenwald Smith 693

"Triskaidekaphobia," Paul Hoffman 696

Argument

"Don't Hang Up, That's My Mom Calling," Bobbi Buchanan 702

"For Most People, College Is a Waste of Time," Charles Murray 704

"Impounded Fathers," Edwidge Danticat 708

37a

Exemplification

An **exemplification** essay uses examples to support a thesis statement. The two selections that follow, "Don't Call Me a Hot Tamale" by Judith Ortiz Cofer and "Volunteer Workers of the World, Unite" by Nicols Fox, are exemplification essays. Both writers use a series of short examples to support a thesis.

Don't Call Me a Hot Tamale

Judith Ortiz Cofer

Award-winning poet, novelist, and essayist Judith Ortiz Cofer often writes about her experiences as a Latina—a Hispanic woman—living in a non-Hispanic culture. In "Don't Call Me a Hot Tamale," she discusses how being Puerto Rican has affected her life in the world beyond Puerto Rico. Note that her examples illustrate the stereotypes she encounters from people reacting to both her heritage and her gender.

On a bus to London from Oxford University, where I was earning some [1] graduate credits one summer, a young man, obviously fresh from a pub, approached my seat. With both hands over his heart, he went down on his knees in the aisle and broke into an Irish tenor's rendition of "Maria" from *West Side Story*. I was not amused. "Maria" had followed me to London, reminding me of a prime fact of my life: You can leave the island of Puerto Rico, master the English language, and travel as far as you can, but if you're a Latina, especially one who so clearly belongs to Rita Moreno's[1] gene pool, the island travels with you.

WORD POWER
rendition performance of a song

Growing up in New Jersey and wanting most of all to belong, I lived in [2] two completely different worlds. My parents designed our life as a microcosm of their *casas* on the island—we spoke in Spanish, ate Puerto Rican food bought at the *bodega*, and practiced strict Catholicism complete with Sunday mass in Spanish.

I was kept under tight surveillance by my parents, since my virtue [3] and modesty were, by their cultural equation, the same as their honor. As teenagers, my friends and I were lectured constantly on how to behave as proper *señoritas*. But it was a conflicting message we received, since our Puerto Rican mothers also encouraged us to look and act like women by dressing us in clothes our Anglo schoolmates and their mothers found too "mature" and flashy. I often felt humiliated when I appeared at an American friend's birthday party wearing a dress more suitable for a semiformal. At Puerto Rican festivities, neither the music nor the colors we wore could be too loud.

WORD POWER
surveillance constant observation

I remember Career Day in high school, when our teachers told us to [4] come dressed as if for a job interview. That morning, I agonized in front of my closet, trying to figure out what a "career girl" would wear, because the

---

1. A Puerto Rican actress, dancer, and singer. She is well known for her role in the movie musical *West Side Story*, a version of Shakespeare's *Romeo and Juliet* featuring Anglos and Puerto Ricans in New York City.

only model I had was Marlo Thomas[2] on TV. To me and my Puerto Rican girlfriends, dressing up meant wearing our mother's ornate jewelry and clothing.

At school that day, the teachers assailed us for wearing "everything at once"—meaning too much jewelry and too many accessories. And it was painfully obvious that the other students in their tailored skirts and silk blouses thought we were hopeless and vulgar. The way they looked at us was a taste of the cultural clash that awaited us in the real world, where prospective employers and men on the street would often misinterpret our tight skirts and bright colors as a come-on. 5

WORD POWER

chromosomes strands of DNA containing genetic information

provocatively in a way that attracts attention

machismo pride in masculinity

It is custom, not chromosomes, that leads us to choose scarlet over pale pink. Our mothers had grown up on a tropical island where the natural environment was a riot of primary colors, where showing your skin was one way to keep cool as well as to look sexy. On the island, women felt freer to dress and move provocatively since they were protected by the traditions and laws of a Spanish / Catholic system of morality and machismo, the main rule of which was: *You may look at my sister, but if you touch her I will kill you*. The extended family and church structure provided them with a circle of safety on the island; if a man "wronged" a girl, everyone would close in to save her family honor. 6

Off-island, signals often get mixed. When a Puerto Rican girl who is dressed in her idea of what is attractive meets a man from the mainstream culture who has been trained to react to certain types of clothing as a sexual signal, a clash is likely to take place. She is seen as a Hot Tamale, a sexual firebrand. I learned this lesson at my first formal dance when my date leaned over and painfully planted a sloppy, overeager kiss on my mouth. When I didn't respond with sufficient passion, he said in a resentful tone: "I thought you Latin girls were supposed to mature early." It was only the first time I would feel like a fruit or vegetable—I was supposed to *ripen*, not just grow into womanhood like other girls. 7

These stereotypes, though rarer, still surface in my life. I recently stayed at a classy metropolitan hotel. After having dinner with a friend, I was returning to my room when a middle-aged man in a tuxedo stepped directly into my path. With his champagne glass extended toward me, he exclaimed, "Evita!"[3] 8

Blocking my way, he bellowed the song "Don't Cry for Me, Argentina." Playing to the gathering crowd, he began to sing loudly a ditty to the tune 9

2. Star of a 1966–71 television comedy about a young woman living on her own in New York City.

3. Eva Perón, wife of Juan Perón, president of Argentina in the 1940s and 1950s. She is the subject of the musical *Evita*.

of "La Bamba"[4]—except the lyrics were about a girl named Maria whose exploits all rhymed with her name and gonorrhea.

I knew that this same man—probably a corporate executive, even 10 worldly by most standards—would never have regaled a white woman with a dirty song in public. But to him, I was just a character in his universe of "others," all cartoons.

Still, I am one of the lucky ones. There are thousands of Latinas without 11 the privilege of the education that my parents gave me. For them every day is a struggle against the misconceptions perpetuated by the myth of the Latina as whore, domestic worker or criminal.

Rather than fight these pervasive stereotypes, I try to replace them 12 with a more interesting set of realities. I travel around the U.S. reading from my books of poetry and my novel. With the stories I tell, the dreams and fears I examine in my work, I try to get my audience past the particulars of my skin color, my accent or my clothes.

I once wrote a poem in which I called Latinas "God's brown daughters." 13 It is really a prayer, of sorts, for communication and respect. In it, Latin women pray "in Spanish to an Anglo God / with a Jewish heritage," and they are "fervently hoping / that if not omnipotent, / at least He be bilingual."

WORD POWER
perpetuated caused to continue

WORD POWER
omnipotent all-powerful

Focus on Meaning

1. Cofer states her thesis in paragraph 1: "You can leave the island of Puerto Rico, master the English language, and travel as far as you can, but if you're a Latina, . . . the island travels with you." What does she mean? Restate this thesis in your own words.

2. What two worlds did Cofer grow up in? Why?

3. What happened to Cofer on Career Day? What did she learn from this experience?

4. According to Cofer, why do Latinas tend to "choose scarlet over pale pink" (6)?

5. How, according to Cofer, are the signals sent by dress interpreted differently in Puerto Rico and "off-island" (7)? How does this difference create problems for her?

6. Why does Cofer consider herself "one of the lucky ones" (11)?

7. How does Cofer try to counter the stereotypes she encounters?

Focus on Strategy

1. Cofer begins her essay with an anecdote. Do you think this is an effective opening strategy? Why or why not? How else could she have begun her essay?

---

4. A song with Spanish lyrics popular in the late 1950s.

2. This essay is directed not at Latinas but at a wider general audience. How can you tell?

3. Cofer closes her essay by quoting a poem she wrote. How is this poem related to the rest of her essay? Would a more conventional conclusion — for example, restating her thesis and closing with a strong summary statement — be more effective? Why or why not?

Focus on the Pattern

1. What examples does Cofer use to support her thesis? Do you think she supplies enough examples to convince readers that her thesis is reasonable?

2. Cofer uses phrases such as "On a bus to London . . ."(1) and "I remember Career Day in high school. . . ."(4) to introduce the examples that support her thesis. Identify the phrases she uses to introduce her other examples. Do you think she needs to add transitional words and phrases such as "Another example . . ." or "One more incident . . ."? Or, do you think her supporting examples are clearly identified?

Focus on Critical Thinking

1. Do you think there is anything Cofer could do to avoid the problems she describes? Do you think she *should* do anything — for example, change the way she dresses?

2. Where in her essay does Cofer define the phrase *hot tamale*? What does this term really mean? What does it suggest? Can you think of other words or phrases that convey the same meaning?

3. Do you think the problem Cofer identifies applies only to Latinas or also to members of other ethnic groups? Do you think it also applies to Latinos? Explain.

4. Do you think Cofer should do more to "fight [the] pervasive stereotypes" (12) she encounters? What actions might she take?

5. Do you think Cofer herself is guilty of stereotyping? Why or why not?

Writing Practice

1. What positive examples can you think of to counteract the stereotype of the Latina as "whore, domestic worker or criminal" (11)? Write a proposal to a television network in which you suggest the addition of several different Latina characters to actual programs in which they might appear.

2. What do you think Cofer can do to avoid being stereotyped? Give examples of specific things she might do to change the way others see her. In your thesis, state why she should (or should not) make these changes.

3. Do you think others stereotype you because of your heritage — or because of your age, your gender, your dress, or where you live? Discuss some specific examples of such stereotyping.

Volunteer Workers of the World, Unite

Nicols Fox

Nicols Fox, who received her MFA from Bennington College, lives on the coast of Maine. Her books include *Against the Machine: The Hidden Luddite Tradition in Literature, Art, and Individual Lives* and *Spoiled: Why Our Food Is Making Us Sick and What We Can Do about It*. Note how multiple examples illustrate the concept of "volunteer workers" in this essay, which first appeared as an opinion piece in the *New York Times*.

Bass Harbor, Me.—It began in the 1970s. Or at least that's when I 1 became conscious of it. People began cleaning up after themselves in fast-food restaurants. I had been living abroad and didn't know about such things, but my children, faster to pick up on American cultural expectations, made sure I took back my tray and put my trash in the appropriate bin.

Cleverly, the restaurants made this choice not only easy but gratifying. 2 Customers were given the sense of being good citizens or helping out the teenage minimum-wage workers who wiped off the tables.

I was never fooled. I knew what was going on. We were doing the res- 3 taurant's work and if we didn't we felt guilty. My children would shrink into their coats while people stared disapprovingly if I tried to abandon a cluttered table.

In fact, it was a manifestation of the Great Labor Transfer. Companies 4 that had already applied every possible efficiency to their businesses were looking for other ways to cut costs and saw an entirely new pool of workers who didn't have to be paid. Call them consumers.

In the 1940s—virtually the pre-history of the Labor Transfer Move- 5 ment—it had been discovered that people could dial numbers without the help of an operator. It was a momentous illumination. What else might they be able to do?

In the 50s, people proved stunningly capable of finding what they 6 wanted in the open shelves of a store without assistance, and clerks everywhere hung up their aprons and filed for unemployment. It was a rudimentary start, but businesses realized that the potential transfer of labor was unlimited.

Ordinary people, it seemed, could operate gas pumps without causing 7 explosions. They could check their own oil. They could fill their tires. They could then be persuaded to complete their purchases with the swipe of a card and be quickly out of the way with no help from any human being at all. And some of them even seemed to prefer to do the work themselves—or, curiously in a country so adamantly anti-Socialist, people began to take pride in doing it, and to look down upon those who still wanted to be served.

WORD POWER
rudimentary basic, not very advanced
adamantly stubbornly; insistently

In some cases consumers were given no option other than to do it or 8 do without. Sometimes these new consumer-employees could be convinced that doing the work gave them more freedom, or that magic word, "choices." It was all in the way the company phrased it. They could even be made to believe, in a triumph of psychological marketing, that taking on the extra work was for their own convenience.

The consumer as worker had tremendous appeal for employers. Not just 9 no pay, but no health insurance, no taxes, no forms, no personal days, no sexual harassment lawsuits, no problems at all. If these new workers were slow or inept or confused, well, they were only making things more difficult for themselves. And the Great Labor Transfer could and would go even further.

Consumers were found to be more medically skilled than anyone had 10 given them credit for. They could take their own blood pressure, give themselves injections and enemas, and starve themselves before surgery. Then they could find someone to drive them to the hospital at 6 a.m., wait, and then take their tottering bodies, still exhaling anesthesia, back to their beds at home where another friend could care for them. In short, they could do what nurses had once done, allowing hospitals to concentrate on investing more heavily in machines to do what doctors once did.

But the greatest labor transfer was yet to come. It began, as no one needs 11 reminding, with the invention of the touch-tone phone and the subsequent, tauntingly named "voice mail" system, in which a voice is the thing precisely never heard. Consumers became the unpaid receptionists for business everywhere, traversing the unfamiliar and mysterious territory of multiple inappropriate choices as their time slipped away and their blood pressure mounted. Now we have robots that promise to listen closely, and to which we find ourselves speaking slowly and carefully in third-grade sentences only to hear: "I couldn't understand you. Will you repeat the message?"

What on earth are we doing and who's making us do it? I can't be the 12 only one who feels like a fool talking to a machine.

So where does this leave us economically? A good part of the increase 13 in productivity during the past two decades can be credited to the Great Labor Transfer. We've taken on more than anyone thought possible. But it can't last.

Someday, consumers will become passive refuseniks or revolt. Or they 14 will simply collapse with exhaustion, unable to take on one more task. I don't know when that point will come, but when it does, expect a fierce downturn in the economy. Happily, it should be followed by an upsurge when companies have to hire people to do what we've been doing and everyone once again has money to spend.

For my part I'm frustrated, irritated and exhausted. And I don't think 15 I'm alone.

Focus on Meaning

1. When did Fox first notice the trend her essay discusses?

2. What is the Great Labor Transfer? How does Fox explain its emergence?

3. In what sense does Fox see the "potential transfer of labor" she describes as "unlimited" (6)?

4. How, according to Fox, did companies get consumers to "volunteer" to do more work themselves?

5. What advantages does the "consumer as worker" (9) have for employers?

6. What, according to Fox, is "the greatest labor transfer" (11)?

Focus on Strategy

1. What is Fox's opinion of the Great Labor Transfer? Does she state this opinion directly? If so, where?

2. Does Fox seem to expect her readers to be aware of the trend she describes? If so, do you think she expects them to object to it, to accept it as normal, or to embrace it enthusiastically?

3. In paragraphs 12 and 13, Fox asks two **rhetorical questions**—questions that she does not expect readers to answer. Can you answer these two questions?

4. In paragraph 14, Fox makes a prediction. What is this prediction? Do you think she really expects the scenario she outlines to occur? Does she see this as a positive outcome? Do you?

5. Evaluate the last sentence of this essay. Do you think it is an effective way to connect with readers?

Focus on the Pattern

1. What specific examples does Fox use to illustrate the Great Labor Transfer?

2. Fox gives a series of examples in paragraph 7, another group of examples in paragraph 10, and a third series of examples in paragraph 11. What does each group of examples illustrate?

Focus on Critical Thinking

1. What does the word *volunteer* usually suggest? How are the volunteers Fox discusses different from conventional volunteers?

2. Do you think Fox is presenting a genuine problem, or do you think she is exaggerating its extent—or even manufacturing a nonexistent issue? Explain your view.

3. Reread paragraph 10. Do you think Fox is being serious here, or do you think she is being **sarcastic**—that is, saying the opposite of what she means?

4. What effects—both positive and negative—do you think the Great Labor Transfer will have on our lives if it continues? Do you think it *will* continue? Why or why not?

Writing Practice

1. Write an email to a fast-food restaurant, office, or business you know well. In your message, give examples of all the "volunteering" you do there, and explain why it is unfair, inefficient, or dishonest for the establishment to expect you to perform all of these tasks.

2. Write a defense of the Great Labor Transfer, giving examples to illustrate the point that the shift has improved your life and the lives of those around you.

⟨37b⟩ # Narration

A **narrative** essay tells a story by presenting a series of events in chronological order. In the first of the two essays that follow, "Orange Crush," Yiyun Li tells a story about the role the drink Tang played in her family. In the second essay, "Pick One," David Matthews tells the story of his adjustment to a new school.

Orange Crush

Yiyun Li

At age twenty-four, Yiyun Li moved from Beijing, China, to the United States to study biology. Before long, however, she enrolled in the Iowa Writers' Workshop, where she wrote a collection of stories, *A Thousand Years of Good Prayers*. In the following essay, she recalls her childhood desire for a trendy Western drink that her family in China could not afford.

During the winter in Beijing, where I grew up, we always had orange and tangerine peels drying on our heater. Oranges were not cheap. My father, who believed that thrift was one of the best virtues, saved the dried peels in a jar; when we had a cough or cold, he would boil them until the water took on a bitter taste and a pale yellow cast, like the color of water drizzling out of a rusty faucet. It was the best cure for colds, he insisted. 1

I did not know then that I would do the same for my own children, preferring nature's provision over those orange- and pink- and purple-colored medicines. I just felt ashamed, especially when he packed it in my lunch for the annual field trip, where other children brought colorful flavored fruit drinks—made with "chemicals," my father insisted. 2

The year I turned 16, a new product caught my eye. Fruit Treasure, as Tang was named for the Chinese market, instantly won everyone's heart. 3

WORD POWER
provision something that is supplied

WORD POWER

assess to measure

Imagine real oranges condensed into a fine powder! Equally seductive was the TV commercial, which gave us a glimpse of a life that most families, including mine, could hardly afford. The kitchen was spacious and brightly lighted, whereas ours was a small cube—but at least we had one; half the people we knew cooked in the hallways of their apartment buildings, where every family's dinner was on display and their financial status assessed by the number of meals with meat they ate every week. The family on TV was beautiful, all three of them with healthy complexions and toothy, carefree smiles (the young parents I saw on my bus ride to school were those who had to leave at 6 or even earlier in the morning for the two-hour commute and who had to carry their children, half-asleep and often screaming, with them because the only child care they could afford was that provided by their employers).

The drink itself, steaming hot in an expensive-looking mug that was   4
held between the child's mittened hands, was a vivid orange. The mother talked to the audience as if she were our best friend: "During the cold winter, we need to pay more attention to the health of our family," she said. "That's why I give my husband and my child hot Fruit Treasure for extra warmth and vitamins." The drink's temperature was the only Chinese aspect of the commercial; iced drinks were considered unhealthful and believed to induce stomach disease.

WORD POWER

induce to cause, to bring about

As if the images were not persuasive enough, near the end of the ad an   5
authoritative voice informed us that Tang was the only fruit drink used by NASA for its astronauts—the exact information my father needed to prove his theory that all orange-flavored drinks other than our orange-peel water were made of suspicious chemicals.

Until this point, all commercials were short and boring, with catchy   6
phrases like "Our Product Is Loved by People Around the World" flashing on screen. The Tang ad was a revolution in itself: the lifestyle it represented—a more healthful and richer one, a Western luxury—was just starting to become legitimate in China as it was beginning to embrace the West and its capitalism.

Even though Tang was the most expensive fruit drink available, its   7
sales soared. A simple bottle cost 17 yuan, a month's worth of lunch money. A boxed set of two became a status hostess gift. Even the sturdy glass containers that the powder came in were coveted. People used them as tea mugs, the orange label still on, a sign that you could afford the modern American drink. Even my mother had an empty Tang bottle with a snug orange nylon net over it, a present from one of her fellow schoolteachers. She carried it from the office to the classroom and back again as if our family had also consumed a full bottle.

WORD POWER

covet to desire something that belongs to someone else

WORD POWER

melancholy sadness, depression

The truth was, our family had never tasted Tang. Just think of how 8 many oranges we could buy with the money spent on a bottle, my father reasoned. His resistance sent me into a long adolescent melancholy. I was ashamed by our lack of style and our life, with its taste of orange-peel water. I could not wait until I grew up and could have my own Tang-filled life.

To add to my agony, our neighbor's son brought over his first girlfriend, 9 for whom he had just bought a bottle of Tang. He was five years older and a college sophomore; we had nothing in common and had not spoken more than 10 sentences. But this didn't stop me from having a painful crush on him. The beautiful girlfriend opened the Tang in our flat and insisted that we all try it. When it was my turn to scoop some into a glass of water, the fine orange powder almost choked me to tears. It was the first time I had drunk Tang, and the taste was not like real oranges but stronger, as if it were made of the essence of all the oranges I had ever eaten. This would be the love I would seek, a boy unlike my father, a boy who would not blink to buy a bottle of Tang for me. I looked at the beautiful girlfriend and wished to replace her.

My agony and jealousy did not last long, however. Two months later 10 the beautiful girlfriend left the boy for an older and richer man. Soon after, the boy's mother came to visit and was still outraged about the Tang. "What a waste of money on someone who didn't become his wife!" she said.

"That's how it goes with young people," my mother said. "Once he has 11 a wife, he'll have a better brain and won't throw his money away."

"True. He's just like his father. When he courted me, he once invited 12 me to an expensive restaurant and ordered two fish for me. After we were married, he wouldn't even allow two fish for the whole family for one meal!"

That was the end of my desire for a Tangy life. I realized that every 13 dream ended with this bland, ordinary existence, where a prince would one day become a man who boiled orange peels for his family. I had not thought about the boy much until I moved to America 10 years later and discovered Tang in a grocery store. It was just how I remembered it—fine powder in a sturdy bottle—but its glamour had lost its gloss because, alas, it was neither expensive nor trendy. To think that all the dreams of my youth were once contained in this commercial drink! I picked up a bottle and then returned it to the shelf.

Focus on Meaning

1. What does Tang represent for Li and for her family and friends? Why is it so appealing? How does paragraph 3 help you answer this question?
2. Why doesn't Li's family drink Tang?

3. What does Li learn from her family's experiences with Tang?

4. What do you think Li means in paragraph 13 by "a Tangy life"?

Focus on Strategy

1. Do you think Li is writing for a Chinese audience, a Chinese-American audience, or an American audience? How can you tell?

2. What is the thesis of this essay? Is it actually stated? How does paragraph 7 support this thesis?

3. Why do you think Li opens her essay by describing her father's cold remedy? Is this a good opening strategy for this essay?

4. In paragraphs 10–12, Li quotes dialogue between her mother and another woman. What does this exchange of dialogue add to the essay?

5. Li uses first-person pronouns (*I, we,* and so on) in this essay. What does she gain by doing this? What, if anything, does she lose?

Focus on the Pattern

1. This is a narrative essay. List some of the transitions Li uses to move her reader from one event or time period to another.

2. What other patterns of development does Li use in this essay? Where?

Focus on Critical Thinking

1. What products do you think hold the same fascination for children today that Tang held for Li? Why?

2. Why do you think Tang eventually loses its appeal for Li?

3. What do Li's comments about Tang tell readers about her attitude toward her parents? Toward her culture?

Writing Practice

1. Write about a food that was considered a luxury in your family when you were growing up, communicating to readers why it was so important to you.

2. Part of the appeal of Tang to Li was the fact that it was glamorous (13) and foreign. What products from other countries have this kind of appeal for you? Recount a situation in which you first encountered one such product.

Pick One

David Matthews

David Matthews's memoir, *Ace of Spades*, was published in 2007. He grew up in Baltimore, Maryland, and now lives in New York City. In the following essay, he remembers a series of events in his childhood that challenged his sense of his own identity.

In 1977, when I was 9, my father and I moved away from the protected 1
Maryland suburbs of Washington — and away from his latest wife, my latest
stepmother — to my grandmother's apartment in inner-city Baltimore. I had
never seen so many houses connected to one another, block after block,
nor so many people on streets, marble stoops and corners. Many of those
people, I could not help noticing, were black. I had never seen so many
black people in all my life.

I was black, too, though I didn't look it; and I was white, though I wasn't 2
quite. My mother, a woman I'd never really met, was white and Jewish,
and my father was a black man who, though outwardly hued like weak coffee, was — as I grew to learn — stridently black nationalist in his views and
counted Malcolm X and James Baldwin[1] among his friends. I was neither
blessed nor cursed, depending on how you looked at it, with skin milky
enough to classify me as white or swarthy enough to render me black. But
before moving from our integrated and idyllic neighborhood, I really knew
nothing of "race." I was pretty much just a kid, my full-time gig. And though
I was used to some measure of instability — various apartments, sundry
stepmothers and girlfriends — I had always gone to the same redbrick
single-level school. Nothing prepared me for walking into that public-school
classroom, already three weeks into fourth grade. I had never felt so utterly
on my own.

Mrs. Eberhard, my new homeroom teacher, made an introduction of 3
sorts, and every student turned around to study me. The black kids, who
made up more than 80 percent of the school's population, ranged in shades
from butterscotch to Belgian chocolate, but none had my sallow complex-
ion, nor my fine, limp hair. And the white kids, a salting of red and alabaster
faces, had noses that were tapered and blunted, free of the slightly equine
flare of my own, and lips that unobtrusively parted their mouths, in contrast
to the thickened slabs I sucked between my teeth.

In the hallway, on the way to class, black and white kids alike herded 4
around me. Then the question came: "What are you?"

I was stumped. No one had ever asked what I was before. It came buzz- 5
ing at me again, like a hornet shaken from its hive. The kids surrounded
me, pressing me into a wall of lockers. *What are you? Hey, he won't answer
us. Look at me. What are you? He's black. He looks white! No way, he's too
dark. Maybe he's Chinese!*

They were rigidly partisan. The only thing that unified them was their 6
inquisitiveness. And I had a hunch, based on their avidity, that the question
had a wrong answer. There was black or white. Pick one. Nowhere in their

---

1. Malcolm X and James Baldwin: Mid-twentieth century African-American civil rights
   activist and writer, respectively.

WORD POWER

sallow yellowish
alabaster white
equine horse-like

WORD POWER

partisan divided,
taking sides

ringing questions was the elastic clause, mixed. The choice was both necessary and impossible: identify myself or have it done for me. I froze, and said nothing—for the time being.

At lunchtime that first day, teetering on the edge of the cafeteria, my eyes scanned the room and saw an island of white kids in a sea of black faces. I didn't contemplate the segregation; it was simply part of the new physical geography, and I was no explorer; I was a weak-kneed outsider, a yellowed freak.

In some way I wasn't fully aware of, urban black people scared me. I didn't know how to play the dozens[2] or do double Dutch. I didn't know the one about how your mama's so dumb she failed her pap test. I didn't know that with the wrong intonation, or the wrong addressee, any mention of one's mama could lead to a table-clearing brawl. The black kids at school carried a loose, effortless charge that crackled through their interactions. They were alive and cool. The only experience I had with cool had been vicarious, watching my father and his bebop-era revolutionary friends, and feeling their vague sense of disappointment when I couldn't mimic their behavior. The black kids reminded me of home, but the white kids reminded me of myself, the *me* I saw staring back in the mirror. On that day, I came to believe that if I had said I was black, I would have had to spend the rest of my life convincing my own people.

Lunch tray in hand, I made a final and (at least I like to tell myself) psychologically logical choice, one I would live with, and wrestle with, for a full decade to come: I headed toward the kids who looked most like me. Goofy bell-bottoms and matching Garanimals?[3] Check. Seventies mop-top? Check. Then a ruddy boy with blond bangs lopped off at the eyebrows looked up from his Fantastic Four comic book, caught my eye across the cafeteria, scooched over in his seat and nodded me over.

That was it. By the code of the cafeteria table, which was just as binding in that time and place as the laws of Jim Crow or Soweto,[4] I was white.

Focus on Meaning

1. How is Matthews's new home different from his old one?

2. Why is his new school such a shock to him?

---

2. Dozens: An African-American tradition of verbal fighting whose objective is to outdo the opponent with words instead of physical force. The tradition can express humor as well as hostility.

3. Garanimals: A popular children's clothing line known for its "mix-and-match" garments.

4. Jim Crow or Soweto: *Jim Crow* was a system of legalized segregation in the American South from 1866 to the mid-1960s. Black Americans were denied access to schools, voting, public restrooms, and transportation and were often subjected to violence. *Soweto* is the most populous black area of Johannesburg, South Africa, noted for its riots during the time of white rule under apartheid.

WORD POWER
vicarious indirect, through others

3. How is Matthews's appearance different from that of the other African-American students in his new class? Does he look like the white students?

4. What choices does Matthews face in the cafeteria? What does he decide to do? Why does he make this decision?

5. Why does Matthews fear urban blacks? Why does he envy them?

6. What is the "code of the cafeteria table" (10)? Why, according to this code, is Matthews white?

Focus on Strategy

1. How do you suppose Matthews expected his readers to react to the following two statements: "I had never seen so many black people in all my life" (1); "I had never felt so utterly on my own" (2)? How do these two statements predict what decision he will make?

2. What does Matthews mean when, contemplating the "new physical geography," he says, "I was no explorer" (7)?

3. Do you think white and African-American readers would be likely to have different reactions to this essay? Explain.

4. What central idea does Matthews communicate in this essay? Does he state this idea in the form of a thesis statement? If so, where?

5. Evaluate this essay's conclusion. Do you think the summary statement is appropriate? Do you think it is effective?

6. In paragraph 9, Matthews suggests the choice he made troubled him for years. Do you think he should have continued his story, explaining how the choice he made affected the rest of his school experience (and his life outside of school), or do you accept his statement, "That was it" (10)?

Focus on the Pattern

1. How much time passes in this narrative?

2. Where do the various events Matthews discusses take place?

3. How does Matthews move readers through his story from one time and place to another? Do you think he needs to add transitions to connect events? Explain.

4. Where in his narrative does Matthews use dialogue? Would adding more dialogue add interest or power to this essay? Whose voices would you like to hear?

Focus on Critical Thinking

1. In paragraph 2, Matthews says, "I was black, too, though I didn't look it; and I was white, though I wasn't quite." Based on the factual information in this essay and on your own experience, do you consider Matthews black or white—or something else?

2. In paragraph 6, Matthews presents the choice he had to make as a simple one: "There was black or white. Pick one." Do you see this choice, as Matthews did at the time, as "both necessary and impossible" (6)?

3. Matthews describes experiences that occurred in 1977. Do you think he would still have to "pick one" today? Why or why not?

Writing Practice

1. Write a narrative about a time when you had to identify yourself with one group over another. You can focus on childhood or adulthood and on school, work, or personal relationships. Explain the choice presented to you, explain what you decided and why, and tell how you now feel about the decision you made.

2. Matthews writes as an adult looking back at a childhood experience. Rewrite his narrative from the point of view of Matthews as a younger child—either as a nine-year-old or as a high school student looking back at his experience.

37c # Description

A **descriptive** essay tells what something looks, sounds, smells, tastes, or feels like, giving readers a picture of a person, place, or object. In "An American in Mexico," Alex Espinoza describes his first impression of his family's home in Mexico. In the classic 1962 essay "A Fable for Tomorrow," Rachel Carson describes an environmental disaster.

An American in Mexico
Alex Espinoza

Alex Espinoza, author of the novel *Stillwater Saints* (2007), moved from Mexico to California with his family when he was two years old. He teaches creative writing at California State University in Fresno. In this essay, he uses specific details to create a vivid picture of his family's original home.

When my father came to the United States to work as a day laborer many years ago, he intended to move back to the village in Michoacán where my mother and seven of my siblings lived. He wired my mother money, some of which she used to build a house there in El Ojo de Agua, on a parcel of land that has been in her family since before the Mexican Revolution. But at some point my mother had enough of waiting for my father's return. She packed up what little she had and, with her children, traveled to Tijuana to be closer to him and to make visits easier. She stayed in Tijuana for several years—I was born there, the youngest of 11 children. Eventually we moved to the three-bedroom house outside Los Angeles where I grew up.

My childhood was different from the childhood of most of my siblings. 2
I rode my BMX bike through vacant lots, watched cable and collected "Star
Wars" action figures. They climbed mesquite trees, made handmade dolls
from old rags and stole chicken eggs from a neighbor's henhouse to sell for
candy. They also shared hardships and misfortunes—hunger, long hours
of working in the fields at young ages, the loss of two infant sisters.

Their connection to Mexico was close, deep and also painful, something 3
I simply could not grasp. Growing up, I felt no ties to El Ojo de Agua. I traveled into Mexico with my family as a child a few times, but I felt disconnected
and uninterested during those trips—and was always eager to return to my
American life. But as I grew older, I began to want to see the place most of
my family called home, the place my siblings had talked about with such
complicated feelings. Two years ago, at 33, I finally decided to go. I took my
mother along; it had been more than 25 years since she had returned.

We flew into Mexico City, where we stayed for one day—strolling 4
through parks and museums and visiting the Basilica of Our Lady of Gua-
dalupe; there we watched the steady flow of devotees making their pilgrim-
ages to the altar on their knees, their hands clasped in prayer. The next day,
we traveled by bus to the city of La Piedad, where my uncle picked us up at
the depot.

After many years in the U.S., my uncle had recently returned home to 5
sell agricultural equipment to local farmers. He employed a maid named
Chavela, who lived in one of the nearby villages. Chavela told me that her
boyfriend had left for the United States about a month before, but that
weeks had gone by without news of his whereabouts. She said she hoped to
save enough money to be able to go and find him. It made me think of the
trip my mother took more than three decades earlier, traveling by train to
Tijuana with her children to be near my father.

It was threatening to rain the afternoon my uncle drove us out over 6
unpaved roads to the old house. Many of the houses along the main road of
the village were empty and dark, with overgrown weeds and broken fences.
Now and again, I'd spot one with dim lights illuminating the small windows.
Tricycles and toys might be scattered around the front yard, and a column
of white smoke threaded out through a hole in the corrugated-metal roof.

Gradually the houses vanished, giving way to tall cornstalks, and we 7
reached the wooden fence marking the entrance to my grandfather's property. We drove up a short distance before stopping and getting out. I spotted
a reservoir behind some trees, and the water glistened when the clouds
broke enough to allow a few beams of sunlight to touch the surface.

The house my mother built was nothing more than four walls made of 8
orange bricks surrounded by thickets of wild shrubs and grass. The windows had no glass, and the front door had been ripped from its hinges. My

uncle said that the house was sometimes used as a stable for the livestock that grazed in the hills not far away. There were broken bottles on the dirt floor, and it smelled of urine and manure.

"I lived here," my mother said to me, as if she couldn't believe it herself. 9 "Right here."

This was a place that had, over the years, become mythic in my mind. 10 But it was real. I touched the brick walls, and I saw the trees my siblings had climbed, the fields where they had worked. The soft mud gave way underneath my shoes. A clean set of my footprints remained.

I took many pictures, and after the film was developed I sat on the floor 11 of my apartment back in California and took the photos out. I looked at each one and tried piecing them together, assembling a memory. I really wanted to connect to that land the way my brothers and sisters had—to get a better sense of our shared past. I thought I could understand things like sacrifice, the small traces of ourselves we are forced to leave behind. But all that the pictures showed were indistinguishable sections of walls, windows and dark doorways.

Focus on Meaning

1. How was Espinoza's childhood different from that of his siblings? *Why* was it different?

2. Why did Espinoza finally decide to visit "the place most of [his] family called home" (3)?

3. What does Espinoza mean when he says the house "had, over the years, become mythic in my mind" (10)?

4. What do Espinoza's photos reveal? What is missing from these pictures?

5. In the last sentence of this essay, Espinoza evaluates his visit. Does he think it has been successful? Do you think it has?

Focus on Strategy

1. Why does Espinoza provide such a long introduction before he begins his description? What information does he supply in paragraphs 1–3? Why do readers need this information?

2. Does this essay have an explicitly stated thesis? If so, where is it? If not, write one.

3. Do you think this essay's subject matter and "message" are likely to appeal to a wide audience or only to readers who have family members born in Mexico (or in other countries outside the United States)? Explain.

Focus on the Pattern

1. Paragraphs 6 and 7 describe Espinoza's journey to the house in which his family lived; paragraphs 8 through 10 describe the house itself. What dominant impression of the house do these paragraphs convey?

2. How does Espinoza organize his description? For example, does he move from side to side? From near to far? From outside to inside?

3. Do you think Espinoza includes enough transitional words and phrases to move readers from one part of the subject he describes to the next? Where, if anywhere, would you add transitions?

4. Is this a subjective or an objective description? How can you tell?

Focus on Critical Thinking

1. Espinoza calls his essay "An American in Mexico," suggesting he sees himself as American, not Mexican. Do you see him as American? Does he see his family as American?

2. In paragraph 3, Espinoza says that his siblings talked about their childhood home with "complicated feelings." What do you think these "complicated feelings" were?

3. What kind of "complicated feelings" do you think Espinoza's mother felt? (Reread paragraph 9 before you answer this question.)

4. After his visit, do you think Espinoza felt more connected to his family or less connected? Why?

Writing Practice

1. Write about a time when you visited a place you had often heard of but never seen—or a place you visited long ago and have not returned to since. Describe this place, and then describe your reaction to it. Were you surprised, or disappointed, in any way?

2. Write a letter to your children describing the house you lived in when you were a child.

A Fable for Tomorrow

Rachel Carson

Rachel Carson (1907–1964) is often credited with starting the modern-day environmental movement. Her book *Silent Spring* (1962) exposed the devastating effects of pesticides on the environment. In the excerpt that follows, part of the introduction to this book, Carson uses specific details to create a powerful picture of the place she describes.

There was once a town in the heart of America where all life seemed 1 to live in harmony with its surroundings. The town lay in the midst of a checkerboard of prosperous farms, with fields of grain and hillsides of orchards where, in spring, white clouds of bloom drifted above the green fields. In autumn, oak and maple and birch set up a blaze of color that flamed and flickered across a backdrop of pines. Then foxes barked in the hills and deer silently crossed the fields, half hidden in the mists of the fall mornings.

WORD POWER
viburnum a type of shrub with large, bright flower clusters

Along the roads, laurel, viburnum and alder, great ferns and wildflowers 2 delighted the traveler's eye through much of the year. Even in winter the roadsides were places of beauty, where countless birds came to feed on the berries and on the seed heads of the dried weeds rising above the snow. The countryside was, in fact, famous for the abundance and variety of its bird life, and when the flood of migrants was pouring through in spring and fall people traveled from great distances to observe them. Others came to fish the streams, which flowed clear and cold out of the hills and contained shady pools where trout lay. So it had been from the days many years ago when the first settlers raised their houses, sank their wells, and built their barns.

Then a strange blight crept over the area and everything began to 3 change. Some evil spell had settled on the community: mysterious maladies swept the flocks of chickens; the cattle and sheep sickened and died. Everywhere was a shadow of death. The farmers spoke of much illness among their families. In the town the doctors had become more and more puzzled by new kinds of sickness appearing among their patients. There had been several sudden and unexplained deaths, not only among adults but even among children, who would be stricken suddenly while at play and die within a few hours.

There was a strange stillness. The birds, for example—where had they 4 gone? Many people spoke of them, puzzled and disturbed. The feeding stations in the backyards were deserted. The few birds seen anywhere were moribund; they trembled violently and could not fly. It was a spring without voices. On the mornings that had once throbbed with the dawn chorus of robins, catbirds, doves, jays, wrens, and scores of other bird voices there was now no sound; only silence lay over the fields and woods and marsh.

WORD POWER
moribund dying

On the farms the hens brooded, but no chicks hatched. The farmers 5 complained that they were unable to raise any pigs—the litters were small and the young survived only a few days. The apple trees were coming into bloom but no bees droned among the blossoms, so there was no pollination and there would be no fruit.

The roadsides, once so attractive, were now lined with browned and 6 withered vegetation as though swept by fire. These, too, were silent, deserted by all living things. Even the streams were now lifeless. Anglers no longer visited them, for all the fish had died.

In the gutters under the eaves and between the shingles of the roofs, a 7 white granular powder still showed a few patches; some weeks before it had fallen like snow upon the roofs and the lawns, the fields and streams.

No witchcraft, no enemy action had silenced the rebirth of new life in 8 this stricken world. The people had done it themselves.

This town does not actually exist, but it might easily have a thousand 9 counterparts in America or elsewhere in the world. I know of no community that has experienced all the misfortunes I describe. Yet every one of these disasters has actually happened somewhere, and many real communities have already suffered a substantial number of them. A grim specter has crept upon us almost unnoticed, and this imagined tragedy may easily become a stark reality we all shall know. . . .

Focus on Meaning

1. What is a fable? In what sense was this essay—written for the introduction to Carson's 1962 book *Silent Spring*, which exposed the dangerous effects of pesticides on the environment—a "fable for tomorrow"?
2. What is the "strange blight" (3) that comes to the town?
3. What signs are there that the town has changed?
4. How do the townspeople react to the changes?
5. What does Carson mean when she says, "The people had done it themselves" (8)?
6. What "stark reality" (9) is Carson warning against in this essay?

Focus on Strategy

1. Why do you suppose Carson opened her book with this story? How do you think she expected readers to react? Do you think today's readers would be likely to react differently from those reading the essay in 1962? If so, how?
2. Do you think Carson expected her story to enlighten readers? To entertain them? To frighten them? To persuade them? Explain.
3. Carson's essay is called "A Fable for Tomorrow," but (except for the last paragraph) it is written in past tense. What does Carson achieve with this strategy?
4. In paragraph 9, Carson admits that the town she has been describing does not exist. Do you think this admission weakens her essay?
5. Throughout this essay, Carson uses strong language, such as "evil spell" (3) and "grim specter" (9), to get her point across. Identify other examples of such language. Do you think these expressions are effective, or do you think she goes too far?

Focus on the Pattern

1. Where does Carson describe the town in positive terms? What positive features does she identify?
2. Where does Carson describe the town in negative terms? What negative features does she identify?

3. How does Carson indicate to readers that she is moving from positive to negative description?

4. Is this a subjective or an objective description? How can you tell?

Focus on Critical Thinking

1. Where is the town "in the heart of America" (1) actually located? Why do you think the author doesn't give more identifying information about this town?

2. Do you think Carson's predictions have come true?

3. Is there a situation affecting our environment that you see as just as alarming as the one Carson writes about? In what sense do you see this situation as a threat?

Writing Practice

1. Write your own "fable for tomorrow" describing the likely effects on our environment of the unchecked piling up of non-biodegradable garbage and trash in our landfills. In the thesis statement of your descriptive essay, encourage readers to recycle to avoid the outcome you describe.

2. Many people see climate change as a destructive environmental problem of epic proportions—as an even greater problem than the pesticides whose use Carson warned against. Write a "fable for tomorrow" in which you describe an extreme scenario that could possibly result from increased global warming.

37d   Process

A **process** essay explains the steps in a procedure, telling how something is (or was) done. In "Mummy Arts," Adam Goodheart presents a set of instructions for mummifying a body. In "My Grandmother's Dumpling," Amy Ma explains the stages in the process of making dumplings with her family.

Mummy Arts

Adam Goodheart

Adam Goodheart is a writer, editor, and historian. One of the founders of *Civilization* magazine, where this piece originally appeared, he has published widely on subjects including travel, anthropology, science, and history. In this essay, he explains the steps required for making a mummy.

Old pharaohs never died—they just took long vacations. Ancient Egyptians believed that at death a person's spirit, or *ka*, was forcibly separated from the body. But it returned now and then for a visit, to snack on the food that had been left in the tomb. It was crucial that the body stay as life-like as possible for eternity—that way, the *ka* (whose life was hard enough already) would avoid reanimating the wrong corpse. These days, dead pharaohs are admittedly a bit hard to come by. If you decide to practice mummification on a friend or relative, please make sure that the loved one in question is fully deceased before you begin.

1. Evisceration Made Easy. The early stages of the process can be a bit malodorous, so it's recommended that you follow the ancient custom of relocating to a well-ventilated tent. (You'll have trouble breathing anyway, since tradition also prescribes that you wear a jackal-head mask in honor of Anubis, god of the dead.) After cleansing the body, break the nose by pushing a long iron hook up the nostrils. Then use the hook to remove the contents of the skull. You can discard the brain (the ancient Egyptians attributed no special significance to it). 2

Next, take a flint knife and make a long incision down the left side of the abdomen. Actually, it's best to have a friend do this, since the person who cuts open the body must be pelted with stones to atone for the profanation. After you've stoned your friend, use a bronze knife to remove the internal organs through the incision. Wash them in palm wine as a disinfectant and set them aside to inter later in separate alabaster jars. Leave the heart in place (Egyptians believed it was the seat of consciousness). 3

2. Salting and Stuffing. Once the abdominal cavity is empty, fill it with natron, a natural salt found at the Wadi Natrun in the western Nile delta. Heap more natron on top of the body until it is completely covered. According to a papyrus in the Louvre, it should then be left for 42 days, after which it will be almost totally desiccated. Having removed the natron, anoint the head with frankincense and the body with sacred oil. Pack the skull and abdomen with myrrh and other spices, and cover the incision with a sheet of gold. 4

For an extra-lifelike effect, you can stuff the corpse's skin with a compound of sawdust, butter, and mud. Don't overdo it, though. Queen Henettowey, wife of Pinedjem I, was so overstuffed that when archaeologists found her, her face had split open like an old sofa. 5

3. Wrapping Up. If you thought mummies wrapped in bedsheets were the stuff of B movies, think again: Even pharaohs were usually wound in strips cut from household linens. Pour molten pine resin over the body; in the course of centuries this will turn the flesh black, glassy, and rock-hard. While the resin's still tacky, bandage each of the extremities separately, including fingers and toes. Then brush on another coat and repeat. (Go easy on the resin—Tutankhamen stuck to his coffin and had to be chipped out piece by piece.) Amulets can be placed between the layers of bandages; a scarab over the heart is the minimum. The last layers should secure the 6

WORD POWER

evisceration removal of organs

WORD POWER

profanation disrespectful act

WORD POWER

desiccated dry

WORD POWER

amulet a charm worn around the neck to ward off evil

scarab a decorative item in the shape of the scarab beetle

arms and legs to the body. Your mummy is now ready to be entombed in grand style.

A note on sarcophagi: Careful labeling will prevent embarrassing mix-   7 ups later on. A mummy long thought to be Princess Mutemhet of the 21st dynasty was recently x-rayed and found to be a pet baboon.

Focus on Meaning

1. Why did the ancient Egyptians practice mummification?
2. What equipment is needed for the process Goodheart describes?
3. What steps are included in the "evisceration" stage of the process?
4. What are the individual steps in the "salting and stuffing" stage of the process?
5. What does the "wrapping up" stage of the process involve?

Focus on Strategy

1. Goodheart knows that his readers will never be called upon to mummify their friends or relatives. Why, then, does he use commands and "you," telling readers how to perform this process?
2. Do you think this essay's primary purpose is informational—or even educational? Or, do you think Goodheart had another purpose, or purposes, in mind?
3. Is this essay meant to be a serious treatment of the subject? How can you tell? Do you think the writer's tone is appropriate for his subject?
4. This essay does not include a thesis statement. Write one that would be suitable. Where should this new sentence be located?
5. Do you think the essay's last paragraph is necessary, or should the essay have ended with the last sentence of paragraph 6? Explain.
6. What does the title "Mummy Arts" suggest about this essay's purpose? What other titles might work for this essay?

Focus on the Pattern

1. How can you tell this essay is a set of instructions rather than an explanation of a process?
2. Where does Goodheart include cautions and reminders for those undertaking the process? Are these really necessary?
3. Goodheart numbers and names three key stages of the process. Do you think his names are effective? If not, what names would you use instead?
4. List the individual steps in the process. Are they all presented in chronological order?
5. What transitional words and phrases does Goodheart use to link the steps in the process?

Focus on Critical Thinking

1. Many of the details in this essay are extremely graphic. Why do you think the writer chose to include such harsh—even disgusting—details? Do you think these details add to the essay's appeal, or do you think they do just the opposite?

2. What factual information did you learn from this essay? Do you think you would have learned more if the information on mummification had been presented in a more serious, straightforward way? Explain.

3. Some steps, such as throwing stones at a friend (3), are clearly not part of the actual process. Can you identify other such "steps"? Do they add something to the essay, or do they just get in the way?

Writing Practice

1. Write a straightforward description of the process of mummifying a body. Aim at an audience of middle-school students. Your purpose is to educate these readers about the process, making it sound as interesting as possible.

2. Think of another "art," one you practice yourself—for example, the art of creating a perfect CD mix or using computer software to edit your photos. Write a set of instructions for this process.

My Grandmother's Dumpling

Amy Ma

Amy Ma is a writer who lives in Hong Kong. This article, which first appeared in the *Wall Street Journal*, provides both information about how to make dumplings and the story of several generations of Ma's family.

There was no denying a dumpling error. If the meat tumbled out of a poorly made one as it cooked, Grandmother could always tell who made it because she had personally assigned each of us a specific folding style at the onset of our dumpling-making education. In our house, a woman's folding style identified her as surely as her fingerprints.

"From now on, you and only you will fold it in this way," she instructed me in our Taipei kitchen in 1994, the year I turned 13. That is when I had reached a skill level worthy of joining the rest of the women—10 in all, from my 80-year-old grandmother, Lu Xiao-fang, to my two middle-aged aunts, my mother and the six children of my generation—in the folding of *jiao zi*, or dumplings, for Chinese New Year. Before then I had been relegated to prep work: mixing the meat filling or cutting the dough and flattening it.

WORD POWER
relegated assigned
[to a lower position]

Cousin Mao Mao, the eldest daughter of my grandmother's first son, 3 had been away for four years at college in the U.S. But with casual ease, she fashioned her dumplings in the style of the rat, tucking in the creases and leaving a small tail that pinched together at one end. Two distinct pleats in a fan-shaped dumpling marked the work of Aunt Yee, Mao Mao's mother, who had just become a grandmother herself with the birth of a grandson. A smaller purse-like dumpling with eight folds toward the center was my mother's. Grandmother's dumplings were the simplest of the bunch— flat, crescent-shaped with no creases and a smooth edge. And as I was the youngest in my generation, she'd thought it appropriate to make my signature design a quirky variation of her own, with an added crimping to create a rippling *hua bian*, or flower edge.

WORD POWER
requisite necessary

"A pretty little edge, for a pretty little girl," she said. 4

While dumplings graced our tables year-round, they were a requisite dish 5 during the Lunar New Year holidays. The Spring Festival, as it is known in China—*chun jie*—is arguably the most important celebration of the year: It is a time to be with family, to visit friends and start life anew—and eat dumplings.

The length of observance varies. Today in Taiwan, the national holiday 6 stretches to nine days—including two weekends—with all businesses and government offices closed. In mainland China, officials rearrange the working calendar to give the public seven consecutive days off, while in Hong Kong there are three public holidays and in Singapore, two. Unofficially, many Chinese people consider the traditional period of the first 15 days appropriate to welcome the new year.

My family celebrated the first three days of the Spring Festival in a 7 traditional way: Everyone came "home," which meant to my grandfather's house. We were already home—my father, mother, brother and I lived in Taipei with my father's parents, who had moved from China in the late 1940s. Most of my father's family lived nearby. On *chu yi*, the first day of the new year, friends came to our house to extend greetings. For *chu er*, the second day, married women returned to their parents' house. The third day, *chu san*, was always celebrated united, as a family. And on each of those days, dumplings were the main food served during lunch and dinner. There might be other side dishes—leftovers from New Year's Eve—but no other food was prepared from scratch during the holiday. It was considered bad luck to do any work during this time; to ensure a peaceful year ahead, you had to rest and that meant no cooking.

Though it isn't known exactly when dumplings came into being, author 8 and Chinese food expert Fuchsia Dunlop says *jiao zi* date as far back as 1,100 years ago. "In the city of Turpan, a tomb was uncovered that had boiled dumplings from the Tang dynasty (618–907) preserved in much the same shape with similar fillings as they are today," says Ms. Dunlop.

WORD POWER
ingots solid metal bars

Many people believe the practice of eating these dumplings on Chinese 9 New Year became popular in the Yuan and Ming dynasties, which stretched from 1271 to 1644, when *yuan bao*—gold and silver ingots—began to take hold as currency in China; the dumplings take the shape of those coins. During new year celebrations, filling your stomach with edible replicas of ingots was thought to ensure a year of prosperity ahead. The packaged bites also celebrated a letting go of the past, since the word "*jiao*" also means "the end of something."

Traditions have relaxed: Not every family eats only dumplings for three 10 days. They also vary regionally: In the south of China, *nian gao*, or rice cakes, are often served instead of these dough-swaddled morsels at Chinese New Year. Still, hefty portions of dumplings undoubtedly remain a big attraction this time of year in many Chinese households.

WORD POWER
redolent fragrant

Even now, that initial bite of any dumpling transports me back to our 11 Taipei kitchen: the women packed like sardines working on their craft with a Zen-like rhythm, the flour-dusted countertops, the air redolent with the scent of dough, and the faded brown ceramic tiles on the floor polished smooth by countless footsteps over the years.

The great dumpling cook-off commenced each year following Lunar 12 New Year's Eve dinner, a family meal of Grandmother's best dishes—sweet soy-braised pork, *ru yi cai* (10 vegetables tossed together with a soy-sauce vinaigrette), and always steamed fish since its term in Mandarin, "*yu*," is a homonym for "plenty." By 9 p.m., the plates were cleared and washed, and the women were clustered in the kitchen.

The men, forbidden to enter the cooking area, dispersed to their sepa- 13 rate corners to talk politics and play dice or mahjong while awaiting the countdown to midnight. Every room of the house swelled with festivity as the whole family of more than 30 members—four generations—gathered for this night in my grandparents' house.

Amid the bustle, the kitchen alone had an air of serenity and purpose 14 as the women worked through the night. Before dawn of the next morning, there would be enough dumplings to cover two large dining room tables and every kitchen countertop.

To start, Grandmother unloaded from the refrigerator the large ball 15 of dough made from flour, cold water and a dash of egg white (her secret ingredient) that she had prepared the day before. Setting it onto the butcher block with her plump and sturdy hands, she ripped off two large balls and rolled each into a log, starting her gentle kneading from the center and stretching out to both sides. The remaining dough she kept covered under a damp towel.

Meanwhile, the rest of the women—my mother and two aunts and 16 my cousins and me—picked over bunches of coriander and peeled off the wilted layers of scallions and cabbages. A liberal douse of salt sprinkled over the cabbage drew out the excess water, and the chopped confetti-like bits were hand-squeezed to prevent a watery dumpling filling. The butcher knife rocked repeatedly back and forth on the ginger and garlic until it was almost a paste. Likewise, the vegetables had to be diced as finely as possible so they would be evenly spread through every bite of the final product.

17   Ignoring the slew of innovative options for fillings popular in contemporary restaurants—shrimp and chives, shark's fin and vermicelli—we filled our no-frills dumplings with minced pork. Into the pink ground meat went the chopped speckles of vegetables and herbs along with sesame oil, Shaoxin wine, salt, soy sauce, a pinch of sugar, white pepper, five-spice powder and an egg. Nothing was measured, yet it always tasted the same.

18   "That's enough mixing," Grandmother cautioned. My mother was using a pair of wooden chopsticks to combine the ingredients in large circular motions. Grandmother insisted on only combing through the filling in one direction—clockwise—so as to not over-mix, which would make it tough.

19   Then like a carefully orchestrated master plan, a natural assembly line formed. First, Grandmother cut off equal-size segments of her log of dough and then passed them to my mother, who used a wooden roller to flatten them into circles, a process called *gan mien*. Two aunts continued to fashion new dough into logs on one end of the kitchen counter, and three cousins lined up on the other end to begin filling and folding dumplings. The positions would alternate periodically, and makers would move up the line over the years as their skills improved. At 5 years old, my job had been the menial task of pressing the just-cut dough segments into flat disks so they would be easier to roll out, but I had since graduated to a dumpling folder. All together, we women stood, each ready to play her part in this culinary theater.

20   "Every step requires its own *kung fu*," Grandmother instructed in Mandarin. She was short, but her chubby silhouette held the solid stance of a symphony conductor. The process was tedious, but a mere mention of serving a frozen dumpling from a supermarket would be confronted with a gaze that screamed: uncultured, unbelievable, un-*Chinese*. The matriarch in her kitchen was doing more than just cooking; she was training the next generation of wives, daughters and mothers as her mother-in-law had taught her.

21   "Use your palm to control the roller, not your fingertips," she barked. "Keep a steady rhythm, consistent like your pulse." The dumpling skins weren't flattened in one fell swoop like a pie crust. Each one had to be rolled just around the rim and rotated so that the resulting circle was thinner on the edges than in the center. When folded in half the two sides met; the dumpling skin was uniform in thickness. It was a painstaking task when

repeated over the span of many hours, and my mother once showed me her swollen palms after a night of *gan mien*.

The amount of meat filling had to be just right. Not too much—"too greedy!"—and not too little: "too stingy!" 22

And dumplings had to be folded with both hands. "It's a superstition," 23 Grandmother told us. "Women who fold dumplings with one hand won't have children. Your right and left hand have to work together to be a good mother." Grandmother demonstrated how she used the fleshy part of the index finger and thumb to press together the dough. Fresh dough, unlike frozen dough, didn't need water to seal the seams. Only a firm pinch.

"Beautifully folded," Grandmother commented on the dumpling of the 24 newest granddaughter-in-law, Mei Fang. "But it took you too long to make. What good is a wife who makes lovely dumplings if there's not enough to feed everyone?" Grandmother asked.

The women smirked at the acrid words—she had been equally harsh 25 to all of them when they first joined the family. Grandmother had taken her lumps, too: After she married grandfather, her mother-in-law had harrassed her on the ways of making a proper dumpling. Now, Grandmother reigned over her kitchen; it was a classroom and crucible we all endured.

"It's better that I am more strict on you girls now," she sighed. "Lest 26 you get criticized by someone else even worse than me." My mother looked over her shoulder to check on me, her only daughter, and smiled when I gave her an assuring nod.

When no one was looking, Grandmother washed a small coin and hid 27 it in one of the dumplings to be discovered by a lucky winner, who was said to be blessed with extra good fortune for the new year. Despite my best efforts, I never chanced upon it.

Working until the early hours of the next morning in the kitchen 28 brought out the juicier stories, ones laced with family secrets, scandals, gossips and tall tales, all soaked up by my youthful ears.

"Did you hear? Second uncle's daughter got a tattoo." 29

"So-and-so's sister is really her daughter." 30

By the time the echoes of popping firecrackers filled the streets sig- 31 naling the stroke of midnight, hundreds of dumplings, ready for boiling, were lined up on the kitchen sheet pans like tiny soldiers pending a final command.

With only the boiling of the dumplings left to do, the women then took 32 turns cleaning up and bathing, all the while trailing after their children and lulling them to bed. But the majority of the family didn't sleep. The custom of *shou sui*, or staying up all night to symbolize having unlimited energy for the upcoming year, was usually followed.

Around 5 a.m., the tables were set in preparation for the midmorning 33 dumpling brunch. But there was no counting of bowls or chopsticks. "You're not allowed to count anything during the first day of the year," reminded Grandmother. "If you don't count anything today, then the amount of possessions you have will be countless for next year." So we grabbed chopsticks by the handfuls—some wooden, some metal, all mixed in a pile—and laid them on the table alongside stacks of blue and white porcelain bowls and plates.

Before long, the first doorbell rang, and along with it came the boisterous greetings from guests, friends and neighbors. The words *gong xi fa cai* ("congratulations and be prosperous") were audible even from inside the kitchen, and they drew out the younger girls, who were eager for their *hong bao*, or red packets. These waxy packets stuffed with money were given by elders to children as a gift, and the youngest in the house could often rack up what seemed to them a small fortune. Their flour-covered fingerprints dotted the envelopes as they calculated the year's gains. 34

At 9 a.m. or when the guest count reached 10—enough to fill a table—we slid the dumplings into the stainless steel pot, careful not to let the boiling water splatter onto our bare toes, peeking out from house slippers. Grandmother insisted on never stirring the pot, and to ensure the dumplings wouldn't stick together, she slid a spatula through the bubbling broth just once in a pushing motion. Thrice the water came to a boil and each time we added more water. By the fourth time, the dumplings bobbed merrily on the surface. They were done. 35

Grandmother fished out the broken dumplings before turning to Cousin Jia Yin, often the culprit, in half jest. "Ah . . . thanks to you, the dumpling soup will be especially tasty this year since you've flavored it with all the filling that busted out." The casualties were fished out and quickly disposed of; broken dumplings are considered bad luck if served. To save Jia Yin's face, her father, grandmother's second son, often said at the table, "Dumplings are great, but my favorite is still the dumpling soup," ladling up another bowl. 36

Guests and grandparents ate first and the two large tables in the dining room were seated by gender. My grandfather took the head seat at one table with his friends, and my grandmother with hers at the other. After they ate, the tables were reset and the second generation took its turn, with my father and uncles at one table, my mother and aunts at the other. The third and fourth generations had less strict table assignments and took whatever empty chairs opened up—it could be two or three hours before it was our turn to eat. 37

Steaming plates were heaped high with dumplings still glistening from their hot-water bath. Diners readied themselves with their own taste-tinkering rituals in concocting the perfect dipping sauce—a combination of soy sauce, vinegar, minced garlic and sometimes sesame oil or chili paste. Grandmother's special *la ba* vinegar, marinated with whole garlic cloves, was the most coveted condiment. 38

Before the first bite, everyone gathered around Grandfather, who 39 made a toast—usually with tea though sometimes he would sneak in some Chinese wine—to ring in the new year. Then, he took the first pick of the dumplings—something of an honor among the women, who held their breath in hopes that his choice of the perfect dumpling would be their own. It would have to have the ideal skin-to-filling ratio, every bite an equal portion of meat and dough, and expert craftsmanship—a balanced and symmetrical shape with firmly sealed seams.

"This one looks good to me," my grandfather decided, gently lifting the 40 plump parcel with the tips of his chopsticks. It was Grandmother's dumpling, and she stood poker-faced next to him, not revealing her triumph.

She remembered a time when her dumplings were the only ones on the 41 platter. As her family grew, so too did the styles of dumplings until the plate resembled an eclectic family tree, and each doughy pouch carried within it the cross-generational memoirs of its maker. The dumpling ritual slowly faded after Grandmother's passing in 1999; Grandfather died soon after and the family scattered. But every Chinese New Year, I still make dumplings in Grandmother's way, repeating her lessons in my head.

"Eat more! Eat more! There's magic in these dumplings," Grandmother 42 would say. And she meant it truly.

Focus on Meaning

1. What different kinds of dumpling "folding style" do the various women have? Why are these differences important?

2. What significance do dumplings have in Chinese culture? What significance do dumplings (and the dumpling-making process) have to Ma?

3. In paragraph 20, Ma says that her grandmother is "training the next generation of wives, daughters and mothers as her mother-in-law had taught her." What, besides dumpling making, does this "training" involve?

4. Reread this essay's conclusion. In what sense does Ma herself see "magic in these dumplings"?

Focus on Strategy

1. What kind of information does Ma provide in paragraphs 1–11 (before she focuses on the process)? Why do you think she provides all this information?

2. Why do you think Ma wrote this essay? What did she want to convey to her readers?

3. At various points, Ma quotes her grandmother. What purpose do these quotations serve? What do the quoted words tell you about the grandmother? About Ma?

4. Whom do you think Ma expected to read her essay? For example, do you see her target audience as largely male or female? Chinese or American? Her age or her grandmother's age? Explain.

5. What do paragraphs 5–10 tell you about Ma's purpose in writing this essay? About her intended audience?

Focus on the Pattern

1. How can you tell this is an explanation of a process rather than a set of instructions?

2. Where does Ma begin explaining the process she calls "the great dumpling cook-off"? Where does the process conclude?

3. Why do you think Ma did not write this essay as a set of instructions? If it were written as instructions, what cautions or reminders might she have had to add?

4. What are the main steps in the process Ma explains? If you can, group the steps in this long process into stages.

5. What transitional words and phrases does Ma use to move readers from one step to the next?

Focus on Critical Thinking

1. This essay's title is "My Grandmother's Dumpling," but it also discusses other people (and other people's dumplings). Who, or what, do you think is the essay's central focus? What makes you think so? Do you think the essay should have a different title? Explain.

2. In paragraph 41, Ma refers to the dumplings on the plate as "an eclectic family tree" and says that "each doughy pouch carried within it the cross-generational memoirs of its maker." What does she mean? Do you think she is making too much of the significance of the ritual she describes? Why or why not?

Writing Practice

1. Explain the process of preparing a meal or dish that is traditional in your culture or in your family. Begin with several paragraphs of background to help readers to understand what the preparation process means to you.

2. Rewrite Ma's process explanation as a set of instructions to be followed by her daughters. Remember to include any necessary cautions and reminders.

37e   Cause and Effect

A **cause-and-effect** essay identifies cause or predicts effects; sometimes it does both. In "The Poncho Bearer," John Schwartz examines the reasons his son wore a poncho every Friday throughout high school. In "At the Heart of a Historic Movement," John Hartmire considers the impact an important historic figure had on his family.

The Poncho Bearer

John Schwartz

A former science writer for the *Washington Post*, John Schwartz now writes about technology for the *New York Times*. In this article, Schwartz reflects on his son's decision to wear a poncho to school every Friday and considers the effects of his son's behavior on his school, his family, and himself. Note how the causes and effects of the poncho-wearing shift as they become accepted by the school and as Schwartz learns more about his son's motives.

Sam wears a Mexican poncho to school every Friday. 1

Like a number of things about our middle child, the "why" of it is a 2 mystery. When he started wearing it about two years ago, I guessed that he was perhaps reinterpreting the idea of casual Friday for high school. Or he might have just thought, "I will wear the poncho to school on Friday. See what happens."

"Thought" may be too strong a word. The poncho appeared in our 3 home when a boy gave it to our oldest child, Elizabeth. She had no interest in it, but Sammy did. It is brightly colored, or more accurately, blinding. By all rights, he should look stupid. In a weird way, he looks good.

As we all know, high school for most teenagers is a time of intense pres- 4 sure to conform. But at 16, Sam has become something of a quiet joker, a subversive with a smile.

Sam has often found ways to stand out in situations where others try to 5 fit in. When we first moved to our little town in New Jersey six years ago, he was entering fifth grade. After watching his new school for a while, he came home one day and told us that there were three kinds of kids: the straight-A kids, the kids who were always in trouble and the class clowns. "I think I have a shot," he said, "at class clown."

And so he's always made his own path. He dyed his dark blond hair 6 Corvette red one year, got a buzz cut the next. Always changing, always distinctive, and always with that knowing smile. Then he donned the poncho. And then again. And again. Before long, he was known more as Poncho than Sam in the halls of his school.

A couple of his coaches didn't like it; one warned Sam that people 7 would not take him seriously if he continued to wear it. As a compromise during football season, he threw his serape over his jersey, which players are required to wear on game days. Even he seemed to think the combination looked stupid, and ultimately he left the poncho home a couple of days in favor of the team colors.

Sam let us know about the coaches' displeasure—not because he 8 wanted us to intervene, just F.Y.I.

WORD POWER
subversive a person who opposes authority

WORD POWER
intervene get involved

Now, I am not a parent who's going to get upset if my son dresses 9 funny. My parents taught me that lesson in the early 1970s in Galveston, Tex., when the principal of Ball High School suspended my brother Dick for having long hair.

My brother thought there was a First Amendment issue at stake, and 10 my dad decided to back him up—literally, to make a federal case of it. Dick and Dad took the school district to court. It was a risky move; my father was a state senator, and it was not a popular stand. People called our home—the number was always listed—and shouted obscenities and hung up.

We lost the case. And I ended up thinking my father was the kind of guy 11 who would stand up for his children no matter what.

So I never gave Sam any trouble about the poncho. For his part, Sam 12 showed his coaches that he was every bit as serious about sports as he was silly in his choice of Friday attire. They've seen his determination when he pushes through the offensive line to take down an opposing quarterback. He shows the same drive on the wrestling mat and the lacrosse field.

With achievement came acceptance. The wrestling team gave out 13 knit caps at the end of the season with the player's name embroidered on the back. Sam's said "Poncho." At the end of lacrosse season, one of the coaches gave a speech about all the funny things he had learned that year. The collection of inside jokes had the players rolling, but the best line was the last: "I have learned it's O.K. to wear a poncho."

Sammy decided to write an essay for an English class about the poncho. 14 Many mysteries were revealed. He wrote that he started wearing it because, when he tried it on at home, it made him laugh. He also acknowledged that it has become something of an obligation.

"Despite the amount of fun I've had with this whole experiment, I do 15 tire of it from time to time. I didn't know what I was getting myself into at the start, and now it's escalated to the point where if I stop more than half the school will forget that the weekend is about to come up. I feel obligated. I must fulfill my duty in this strange society of learners to remind them of the good times ahead, even if they only last a few precious days."

He also included a haiku: 16
A blur of color
I stride as poncho billows
In the strong wind gusts.

The essay concluded with his plan to pass his poncho along "to a pre- 17 determined underclassman who upholds all of the standards necessary to become the next Poncho Bearer" and who will "Remember that the Poncho Bearer does not own the Poncho, but is merely holding onto it and taking care of it for future generations."

O.K., he seems to have cribbed that from the Patek Philippe ads, but it 18
still brought a lump to my throat. The process of finding yourself only starts
in high school; it goes on through the college years.

Defining yourself is the central question of adolescence. We ask, Am 19
I a jock or a geek? A joker or a hippie? Am I smart? Good looking? Am I
enough like everyone else? Am I distinctive? We are pulled in every direction. Sam has asked the question and, I think, begun to answer it well.

And so I have felt pretty good about my own light touch as a parent. 20
That good feeling lasted about a week, until I got an instant message from
my daughter at college:

I got a tattoo today.   21

Focus on Meaning

1. In paragraph 2, Schwartz says that he wants to know why his son Sam started
   wearing a poncho to school, stating, "the 'why' of it is a mystery." Do you understand "the 'why' of it"?

2. Look again at Sam's own words, which his father quotes from conversation and
   from Sam's essay (15–17). What do these words tell you about Sam?

3. What effect did his brother Dick's experience have on Schwartz?

4. In paragraph 19, Schwartz says that Sam has "asked the question" and "begun
   to answer it well." What does he mean? Do you think he is right about Sam?

Focus on Strategy

1. In paragraphs 9–11, Schwartz discusses his brother Dick. Why? What is the
   connection between these paragraphs and the rest of the essay?

2. Is this essay directed at parents? At high school students? At high school
   teachers? What makes you think so?

3. What is this essay's thesis—the point Schwartz is trying to get across to
   readers? Does he convey this message successfully?

4. What does the word *bearer* (used in the essay's title) mean? Why do you suppose Schwartz uses this word?

5. Evaluate the essay's last line. Is it an effective conclusion? Why or why not?

Focus on the Pattern

1. Is this essay's emphasis on causes, on effects, or on both causes and effects?
   Explain.

2. List the reasons Sam gives for wearing the poncho. Then, list the reasons
   Schwartz suggests. Which reason do you think best explains Sam's actions?

3. What effects does Sam's decision to wear the poncho have on his parents? On
   his classmates and teammates? On Sam himself?

Focus on Critical Thinking

1. What details about Sam's background and family life do you think might explain his decision to wear the poncho?

2. A **haiku** is a three-line poem with seventeen syllables. Because it is so short and focuses on a single vivid image, each word must be carefully chosen. Read Sam's haiku in paragraph 16. What does it tell you about Sam? About his reasons for wearing the poncho?

3. Where does Schwartz describe what the poncho looked like? Do you think he should have described the poncho in more detail? What more would you like to know about the appearance of the poncho, and why?

4. Do you think this essay is really about Sam, or do you think it is about Schwartz himself? Explain.

Writing Practice

1. Suppose you are Schwartz's son Sam, now a college student. Assuming your audience is your composition class, explain your motives for wearing the poncho in high school.

2. Assume you are the new "Poncho Bearer" to whom Sam has entrusted his poncho. Write a speech for your fellow high school students in which you accept this honor and explain how it will affect you.

3. As this essay acknowledges, the high school years can be a difficult time, and fitting in is not always easy. Explain what can cause young teenagers to feel out of place and what the possible effects—both positive and negative—of this situation can be. Conclude with some recommendations for helping high school students feel that they belong.

At the Heart of a Historic Movement

John Hartmire

As executive director of the National Farmworker Ministry, John Hartmire's father worked closely with César Chávez to fight for social justice for farmworkers. However, his father's dedication to the cause meant that he was absent for most of Hartmire's childhood. In this essay, Hartmire discusses what it is like to make a personal sacrifice for a social cause.

When my friend's daughter asked me if I knew anything about the 1 man her school was named after, I had to admit that I did. I told her that in California there are at least twenty-six other schools, seventeen streets, seven parks, and ten scholarships named after César Chávez. Not only that, I said, I once hit a ground ball through his legs during a softball game, and I watched his two dogs corner my sister's rabbit and, quite literally, scare it to death. I used to curse his name to the sun gods while I marched through one sweltering valley or another knowing my friends were at the beach staring at Carrie Carbajal and her newest bikini.

During those years I wasn't always sure of how I felt about the man, 2 but I did believe César Chávez was larger than life. The impact he had on my family was at once enriching and debilitating. He was everywhere. Like smoke and cobwebs, he filled the corners of my family's life. We moved to California from New York in 1961 when my father was named executive director of the National Farmworker Ministry, and for the next thirty-plus years our lives were defined by César and the United Farm Workers.

During those years my father was gone a lot, traveling with, or for, 3 César. I "understood" because the struggle to organize farmworkers into a viable union was the work of a lifetime, and people would constantly tell me how much they admired what Dad was doing. Hearing it made me proud. It also made me lonely. He organized the clergy to stand up for the union, went to jail defying court injunctions, and was gone from our house for days on end, coming home, my mother likes to say, only for clean underwear. It was my father who fed the small piece of bread to César ending his historic twenty-five-day fast in 1968. It's no wonder Dad missed my first Little League home run.

The experience of growing up in the heart of a historic movement has 4 long been the stuff of great discussions around our dinner table. The memories are both vibrant and difficult. There were times when César and the union seemed to be more important to my father than I was, or my mother was, or my brothers and sister were. It is not an easy suspicion to grow up with, or to reconcile as an adult.

While my friends surfed, I was dragged to marches in the Coachella 5 and San Joaquin valleys. I was taken out of school to attend union meetings and rallies that interested me even less than geometry class. I spent time in supermarket parking lots reluctantly passing out leaflets and urging shoppers not to buy nonunion grapes and lettuce. I used to miss Sunday-afternoon NFL telecasts to canvass neighborhoods with my father. Since my dad wanted his family to be a part of his life, I marched and slept and ate and played with César Chávez's kids. When we grew older his son, Paul, and I would drink beer together and wonder out loud how our lives would have been different had our fathers been plumbers or bus drivers.

But our fathers were fighting to do something that had never been done 6 before. Their battle to secure basic rights for migrant workers evolved into a moral struggle that captured the nation's attention. I saw it all, from the union's grape strike in 1965, to the signing of the first contracts five years

WORD POWER
debilitate to take away strength

WORD POWER
viable able to survive

WORD POWER
orchestrate to arrange

WORD POWER
transcend to be
greater than; to go
beyond

later, to the political power gained then lost because, for César, running a union was never as natural as orchestrating a social movement.

My father and César parted company four years before Chávez died in 1993. Chávez, sixty-six at the time of his death, father of eight, grandfather of twenty-seven, leader of thousands, a Hispanic icon who transcended race, left the world a better place than he found it. He did it with the help of a great many good people, and the sacrifice of their families, many of whom believed in his cause but didn't always understand what he was asking of, or taking from, them.   7

So as students here attend César Chávez Elementary School, as families picnic in a Sacramento park named after him and public employees opt to take off March 31 in honor of his birthday, I try to remember César Chávez for what he was—a quiet man, the father of friends, a man intricately bound with my family—and not what he took from my childhood. Namely, my father. I still wrestle with the cost of my father's commitment, understanding that social change does not come without sacrifice. I just wonder if the price has to be so damn high.   8

Do I truly know César Chávez? I suppose not. He was like a boat being driven by some internal squall, a disturbance he himself didn't always understand, and that carried millions right along with him, some of us kicking and screaming.   9

Focus on Meaning

1. When he was a child, why did Hartmire "curse [César Chávez's] name to the sun gods" (paragraph 1)?

2. Hartmire says that Chávez was "larger than life. The impact he had on my family was at once enriching and debilitating. He was everywhere" (2). What does he mean?

3. What is the "historic movement" Hartmire mentions in his title and in paragraph 4?

4. What does Hartmire believe he has lost because of his father's involvement with César Chávez? What, if anything, does he suggest he has gained?

5. How has Hartmire's opinion of Chávez changed over the years? Has his opinion of his father also changed?

6. Does Hartmire still feel bitterness about his childhood? If so, at whom is this bitterness directed?

Focus on Strategy

1. Hartmire begins and ends with a question asked of him by the daughter of a friend. Why is her question significant? Why is repeating the question an effective strategy?

2. This essay first appeared in *Newsweek*, a weekly magazine with a national audience. How does Hartmire appeal to this wide audience?

3. How much does Hartmire assume that readers already know about César Chávez and about the causes he championed? Do those assumptions seem fair? Do you think readers unfamiliar with the history of migrant farm workers in the United States can understand the point of this essay?

4. What information does Hartmire reveal about his own background and political activities? How might his personal experiences have shaped his thoughts about the "price" (8) of social change?

5. Why, in paragraph 3, does Hartmire put the word *understood* in quotation marks? Did he truly understand his father's absences? Does he understand them now? How can you tell?

6. What seems to be Hartmire's purpose for writing? Why, in an essay about an important historic figure, would the author focus so much on personal details and his own intimate feelings? How do those personal elements help you to understand his point?

Focus on the Pattern

1. According to Hartmire, what caused his family to become involved with César Chávez, the National Farmworker Ministry, and the United Farm Workers?

2. What effects of that involvement does Hartmire identify? Does he identify any positive outcomes, or are they all negative?

3. Can you think of any causes or effects Hartmire doesn't mention? Are they negative or positive, or are they both positive and negative?

4. Is the emphasis of this essay more on causes or more on effects? Explain.

Focus on Critical Thinking

1. Hartmire writes about events that took place half a century ago. Why bring them up now? What makes his subject relevant today?

2. Do you think Hartmire's father would agree with his son's descriptions of their experiences together in the 1960s and 1970s? How might his father's memories, and his interpretation of them, be different from Hartmire's?

3. In paragraph 5, Hartmire says that he and Paul Chávez used to try to imagine how their lives might have been different if their fathers had been "plumbers or bus drivers." How do you think their lives would have been different?

4. Hartmire comments that "there were times when César and the union seemed to be more important to my father than I was, or my mother was, or my brothers and sister were" (4). Do you agree with Hartmire's suggestion that family should always come first, or could you argue that social justice is, in fact, more important than family? Explain your answer.

Writing Practice

1. What historical or political figure was "larger than life" for your family? Write an essay explaining the impact that this person had on you.

2. Who is your greatest living hero? Write an essay about your hero's personal qualities and contributions to society. (If you like, you may write a recommendation for an award, addressing your remarks to the awards committee.)

3. If your middle school or high school was named after a person, write an article for the school newspaper in which you explain why this individual deserves (or does not deserve) this honor.

37f   Comparison and Contrast

A **comparison-and-contrast** essay explains how two things are alike or how they are different. Sometimes it discusses both similarities and differences. In "My Two Lives," Jhumpa Lahiri compares the two different worlds she confronts as an "Indian American." In "The Transaction," William Zinsser compares his writing methods to those of another writer.

My Two Lives

Jhumpa Lahiri

Jhumpa Lahiri was born in London in 1967 and moved to the United States with her family when she was three. Her first book, *Interpreter of Maladies*, won the Pulitzer Prize for Fiction in 2000. In this essay, she considers how she understood her identity when she was a child and how she understands it now, as an adult.

I have lived in the United States for almost 37 years and anticipate growing old in this country. Therefore, with the exception of my first two years in London, "Indian-American" has been a constant way to describe me. Less constant is my relationship to the term. When I was growing up in Rhode Island in the 1970s I felt neither Indian nor American. Like many immigrant offspring I felt intense pressure to be two things, loyal to the old world and fluent in the new, approved of on either side of the hyphen. Looking back, I see that this was generally the case. But my perception as a young girl was that I fell short at both ends, shuttling between two dimensions that had nothing to do with one another.

At home I followed the customs of my parents, speaking Bengali and eating rice and dal with my fingers. These ordinary facts seemed part of a secret, utterly alien way of life, and I took pains to hide them from my American friends. For my parents, home was not our house in Rhode Island but Calcutta, where they were raised. I was aware that the things they lived for — the Nazrul songs they listened to on the reel-to-reel, the family they missed, the clothes my mother wore that were not available in any store in any mall — were at once as precious and as worthless as an outmoded currency.

I also entered a world my parents had little knowledge or control of: 3 school, books, music, television, things that seeped in and became a fundamental aspect of who I am. I spoke English without an accent, comprehending the language in a way my parents still do not. And yet there was evidence that I was not entirely American. In addition to my distinguishing name and looks, I did not attend Sunday school, did not know how to ice-skate, and disappeared to India for months at a time. Many of these friends proudly called themselves Irish-American or Italian-American. But they were several generations removed from the frequently humiliating process of immigration, so that the ethnic roots they claimed had descended underground whereas mine were still tangled and green. According to my parents I was not American, nor would I ever be no matter how hard I tried. I felt doomed by their pronouncement, misunderstood and gradually defiant. In spite of the first lessons of arithmetic, one plus one did not equal two but zero, my conflicting selves always canceling each other out.

When I first started writing I was not conscious that my subject was 4 the Indian-American experience. What drew me to my craft was the desire to force the two worlds I occupied to mingle on the page as I was not brave enough, or mature enough, to allow in life. My first book was published in 1999, and around then, on the cusp of a new century, the term "Indian-American" has become part of this country's vocabulary. I've heard it so often that these days, if asked about my background, I use the term myself, pleasantly surprised that I do not have to explain further. What a difference from my early life, when there was no such way to describe me, when the most I could do was to clumsily and ineffectually explain.

As I approach middle age, one plus one equals two, both in my work 5 and in my daily existence. The traditions on either side of the hyphen dwell in me like siblings, still occasionally sparring, one outshining the other depending on the day. But like siblings they are intimately familiar with one another, forgiving and intertwined. When my husband and I were married five years ago in Calcutta we invited friends who had never been to India, and they came full of enthusiasm for a place I avoided talking about in my childhood, fearful of what people might say. Around non-Indian friends, I no longer feel compelled to hide the fact that I speak another language. I speak Bengali to my children, even though I lack the proficiency to teach

WORD POWER

cusp edge, turning point

them to read or write the language. As a child I sought perfection and so denied myself the claim to any identity. As an adult I accept that a bicultural upbringing is a rich but imperfect thing.

While I am American by virtue of the fact that I was raised in this country, I am Indian thanks to the efforts of two individuals. I feel Indian not because of the time I've spent in India or because of my genetic composition but rather because of my parents' steadfast presence in my life. They live three hours from my home; I speak to them daily and see them about once a month. Everything will change once they die. They will take certain things with them—conversations in another tongue, and perceptions about the difficulties of being foreign. Without them, the back-and-forth life my family leads, both literally and figuratively, will at last approach stillness. An anchor will drop, and a line of connection will be severed.

I have always believed that I lack the authority my parents bring to being Indian. But as long as they live they protect me from feeling like an impostor. Their passing will mark not only the loss of the people who created me but the loss of a singular way of life, a singular struggle. The immigrant's journey, no matter how ultimately rewarding, is founded on departure and deprivation, but it secures for the subsequent generation a sense of arrival and advantage. I can see a day coming when my American side, lacking the counterpoint India has until now maintained, begins to gain ascendancy and weight. It is in fiction that I will continue to interpret the term "Indian-American," calculating that shifting equation, whatever answers it may yield.

WORD POWER
ascendancy
dominance

Focus on Meaning

1. When she was a child, Lahiri's world was different from the world her parents inhabited. How? How was she different from her Irish-American and Italian-American friends (3)?

2. How has Lahiri's attitude toward her "two lives" changed since she was a child? How do you account for this change?

3. In paragraph 3, Lahiri says that as a child confronting her two lives, she felt that "one plus one did not equal two but zero." In paragraph 5, however, she observes, "As I approach middle age, one plus one equals two." What does she mean by each of these statements?

4. Lahiri says that a bicultural upbringing is "a rich but imperfect thing" (5). In what sense does she see her upbringing as "rich"? In what respects does she see it as "imperfect"?

5. In what respects does Lahiri feel American? In what respects does she feel Indian?

6. What does Lahiri mean when she says of her parents, "as long as they live they protect me from feeling like an impostor" (7)?

Focus on Strategy

1. Which of these two statements comes closer to what you see as this essay's thesis?

   - As a young girl, Lahiri felt torn between two cultures, and she still struggles with her "two lives."

     - As a young girl, Lahiri felt torn between two cultures, but today she is secure in her cultural identity.

   If neither of these statements is acceptable, suggest an alternative thesis statement.

2. Explain what Lahiri means by this statement: "The immigrant's journey, no matter how ultimately rewarding, is founded on departure and deprivation, but it secures for the subsequent generation a sense of arrival and advantage" (7). How does this statement apply to Lahiri's struggle to define herself?

3. Do you think Lahiri is writing here as a daughter, as a mother, or as a writer?

4. Do you think Lahiri's purpose is to explain her two roles to others in her position, to those who identify with only one culture or nationality, or to both groups? Why?

Focus on the Pattern

1. What two subjects is Lahiri comparing in this essay? For example, is she comparing her past with her present? Herself and her parents? Indians and Americans?

2. Is this a subject-by-subject comparison or a point-by-point comparison? Make an informal outline of the essay to help you decide.

Focus on Critical Thinking

1. Do you think it is possible for someone to be truly bicultural—"Loyal to the old world and fluent in the new, approved of on either side of the hyphen"(1)? Why or why not?

2. What do you imagine Lahiri's parents might say about her "two lives"? Which might they see as the more important world for her as a daughter? As a mother? As a writer?

3. Do you think it is easier for a writer to maintain a dual identity than it is for other people? Why or why not?

Writing Practice

1. In what sense are you, like Lahiri, torn between two identities? Choosing two different roles you play—for example, student and employee, child and parent, "American" and member of a particular cultural or ethnic group—compare and contrast your two roles.

2. Compare Lahiri's view of her dual identity with that of Judith Ortiz Cofer (p. 636) or David Matthews (p. 646). How are their problems alike, and how are they different?

WORD POWER

transaction an exchange or transfer of goods, services, or money; an exchange of thoughts and feelings

The Transaction

William Zinsser

William Zinsser has written many articles and books on improving writing and study skills. He has also had a long career as a professional newspaper and magazine writer, drama and film critic, and author of nonfiction books on subjects ranging from jazz to baseball. This excerpt is from his book *On Writing Well: An Informal Guide to Writing Nonfiction.*

WORD POWER

vocation an occupation; regular employment

avocation a hobby or interest pursued for enjoyment rather than for money

arduous difficult and tiring

1   A school in Connecticut once held "a day devoted to the arts," and I was asked if I would come and talk about writing as a vocation. When I arrived, I found that a second speaker had been invited—Dr. Brock (as I'll call him), a surgeon who had recently begun to write and had sold some stories to magazines. He was going to talk about writing as an avocation. That made us a panel, and we sat down to face a crowd of students, teachers, and parents, all eager to learn the secrets of our glamorous work.

2   Dr. Brock was dressed in a bright red jacket, looking vaguely bohemian, as authors are supposed to look, and the first question went to him. What was it like to be a writer?

3   He said it was tremendous fun. Coming home from an arduous day at the hospital, he would go straight to his yellow pad and write his tensions away. The words just flowed. It was easy. I then said that writing wasn't easy and it wasn't fun. It was hard and lonely, and the words seldom just flowed.

4   Next, Dr. Brock was asked if it was important to rewrite. Absolutely not, he said. "Let it all hang out," he told us, and whatever form the sentences take will reflect the writer at his most natural. I then said that rewriting is the essence of writing. I pointed out that professional writers rewrite their sentences over and over and then rewrite what they have rewritten.

5   "What do you do on days when it isn't going well?" Dr. Brock was asked. He said he just stopped writing and put the work aside for a day when it would go better. I then said that the professional writer must establish a daily schedule and stick to it. I said that writing is a craft, not an art, and that the man who runs away from his craft because he lacks inspiration is fooling himself. He is also going broke.

6   "What if you're feeling depressed or unhappy?" a student asked. "Won't that affect your writing?"

7   Probably it will, Dr. Brock replied. Go fishing. Take a walk. Probably it won't, I said. If your job is to write every day, you learn to do it like any other job.

8   A student asked if we found it useful to circulate in the literary world. Dr. Brock said he was greatly enjoying his new life as a man of letters, and he told several stories of being taken to lunch by his publisher and his agent

at Manhattan restaurants where writers and editors gather. I said that professional writers are solitary drudges who seldom see other writers.

"Do you put symbolism in your writing?" a student asked me.   9

"Not if I can help it," I replied. I have an unbroken record of missing the   10
deeper meaning in any story, play, or movie, and as for dance and mime, I have never had any idea of what is being conveyed.

"I *love* symbols!" Dr. Brock exclaimed, and he described with gusto the   11
joys of weaving them through his work.

So the morning went, and it was a revelation to all of us. At the end Dr.   12
Brock told me he was enormously interested in my answers—it had never occurred to him that writing could be hard. I told him I was just as interested in *his* answers—it had never occurred to me that writing could be easy. Maybe I should take up surgery on the side.

As for the students, anyone might think we left them bewildered. But in   13
fact we probably gave them a broader glimpse of the writing process than if only one of us had talked. For there isn't any "right" way to do such personal work. There are all kinds of writers and all kinds of methods, and any method that helps you to say what you want to say is the right method for you. Some people write by day, others by night. Some people need silence, others turn on the radio. Some write by hand, some by word processor, some by talking into a tape recorder. Some people write their first draft in one long burst and then revise; others can't write the second paragraph until they have fiddled endlessly with the first.

But all of them are vulnerable and all of them are tense. They are driven   14
by a compulsion to put some part of themselves on paper, and yet they don't just write what comes naturally. They sit down to commit an act of literature, and the self who emerges on paper is far stiffer than the person who sat down to write. The problem is to find the real man or woman behind all the tension.

Ultimately, the product that any writer has to sell is not the subject   15
being written about, but who he or she is. I often find myself reading with interest about a topic I never thought would interest me—some scientific quest, perhaps. What holds me is the enthusiasm of the writer for his field. How was he drawn into it? What emotional baggage did he bring along? How did it change his life? It's not necessary to want to spend a year alone at Walden Pond[1] to become deeply involved with a writer who did.

This is the personal transaction that's at the heart of good nonfiction   16
writing. Out of it come two of the most important qualities that this book

WORD POWER

symbolism the use of a symbol (something that stands for something else) in a work of art or literature

gusto an enthusiasm; a lively enjoyment

---

1. The place where Henry David Thoreau (1817–1862), an American writer, naturalist, and political activist, lived for two years in a cabin he built himself. He wrote about the experience in his most famous book, *Walden*.

will go in search of: humanity and warmth. Good writing has an aliveness that keeps the reader reading from one paragraph to the next, and it's not a question of gimmicks to "personalize" the author. It's a question of using the English language in a way that will achieve the greatest strength and the least clutter.

Can such principles be taught? Maybe not. But most of them can be learned.   17

Focus on Meaning

1. What two or three adjectives would you use to describe Dr. Brock's approach to writing? What adjectives could describe Zinsser's approach?

2. What product does Zinsser believe a writer "has to sell"?

3. Zinsser states that "humanity and warmth" are two important qualities of non-fiction writing. What other characteristics of writing does he say or imply that he values?

4. Why does Zinsser mention that Dr. Brock was dressed in a bright red jacket (2)? What does he aim to show about Dr. Brock by noting this detail?

Focus on Strategy

1. Why do you think Zinsser chose to use an interview format to compare and contrast his own writing methods and experiences with those of Dr. Brock?

2. Zinsser does not state his thesis until late in the essay, when he says that "any method that helps you to say what you want to say is the right method for you." Why do you think he decided not to state his thesis earlier? Were you able to understand it as you read the essay?

3. Zinsser and Dr. Brock hold opposite views on each question Zinsser mentions. Do you think Zinsser exaggerated the difference between the two writers, perhaps by leaving out points of agreement or slight disagreement? If so, do you think this was a good decision?

4. Explain what Zinsser means by this statement: "The problem is to find the real man or woman behind all the tension" (14). How does this statement relate to the essay's title, "The Transaction"?

Focus on the Pattern

1. The first half of the essay (1–11) is a point-by-point comparison. How can you tell?

2. What is Zinsser comparing in paragraph 13? Explain how this paragraph relates to the point-by-point comparison developed in paragraphs 1–11.

Focus on Critical Thinking

1. Zinsser claims that "rewriting is the essence of writing" (4). Use your own experience to support or challenge this statement.

2. Zinsser says that "the self who emerges on paper is far stiffer than the person who sat down to write" (14). Is this true in your experience?

3. How do you imagine Dr. Brock would respond to Zinsser's essay? Would he agree with Zinsser's conclusions?

Writing Practice

1. Suppose that you have been asked some of the same questions as Zinsser and Dr. Brock—but about your own experience as a college student. How would you respond? Be sure to include answers to the following questions: What is it like to be a student? What do you do when schoolwork or classes are not going well? Does being depressed or unhappy affect your performance in the classroom? How?

2. In paragraph 13, Zinsser writes, "There are all kinds of writers and all kinds of methods." Describe the kind of writer you are. Do you find writing easy, as Dr. Brock does, or difficult, as Zinsser does? What methods do you use to come up with ideas or to get through a particularly difficult assignment? Do you use any of the methods that Zinsser describes in paragraph 13?

3. Zinsser claims that the most successful pieces of writing are produced when the writer really cares about his or her subject. Identify three or four topics that interest you—for example, a book, a sport, a famous person, a political opinion, or a religous belief. Then, try to explain why each of these topics interests you.

`37g`

Classification

A **classification** essay divides a whole into parts and sorts various items into categories. In "But What Do You Mean?" Deborah Tannen considers different categories of communication. In "The Dog Ate My Disk, and Other Tales of Woe," Carolyn Foster Segal classifies student excuses.

But What Do You Mean?

Deborah Tannen

Linguistics professor and best-selling author Deborah Tannen writes about communication differences across gender, age, and other divides. Her books include *You Just Don't Understand: Women and Men in Conversation* (1990) and *You're Wearing That?: Understanding Mothers and Daughters in Conversation* (2006). In the following essay, Tannen uses anecdotes about dialogue in the workplace to illustrate differences between men's and women's communication styles.

Conversation is a ritual. We say things that seem obviously the thing to 1
say, without thinking of the literal meaning of our words, any more than we
expect the question "How are you?" to call forth a detailed account of aches
and pains.

Unfortunately, women and men often have different ideas about what's 2
appropriate, different ways of speaking. Many of the conversational rituals common among women are designed to take the other person's feelings into account, while many of the conversational rituals common among
men are designed to maintain the one-up position, or at least avoid appearing one-down. As a result, when men and women interact—especially at
work—it's often women who are at the disadvantage. Because women are
not trying to avoid the one-down position, that is unfortunately where they
may end up.

Here, the biggest areas of miscommunication. 3

1. Apologies

WORD POWER

self-deprecating
critical of oneself

Women are often told they apologize too much. The reason they're told 4
to stop doing it is that, to many men, apologizing seems synonymous with
putting oneself down. But there are many times when "I'm sorry" isn't self-
deprecating, or even an apology; it's an automatic way of keeping both
speakers on an equal footing. For example, a well-known columnist once
interviewed me and gave me her phone number in case I needed to call
her back. I misplaced the number and had to go through the newspaper's
main switchboard. When our conversation was winding down and we'd
both made ending-type remarks, I added, "Oh, I almost forgot—I lost your
direct number, can I get it again?" "Oh, I'm sorry," she came back instantly,
even though she had done nothing wrong and *I* was the one who'd lost the
number. But I understood she wasn't really apologizing; she was just automatically reassuring me she had no intention of denying me her number.

Even when "I'm sorry" *is* an apology, women often assume it will be the 5
first step in a two-step ritual: I say "I'm sorry" and take half the blame, then
you take the other half. At work, it might go something like this:

A: When you typed this letter, you missed this phrase I inserted.

B: Oh, I'm sorry. I'll fix it.

A: Well, I wrote it so small it was easy to miss.

When both parties share blame, it's a mutual face-saving device. But 6
if one person, usually the woman, utters frequent apologies and the other
doesn't, she ends up looking as if she's taking the blame for mishaps that
aren't her fault. When she's only partially to blame, she looks entirely in the
wrong.

I recently sat in on a meeting at an insurance company where the sole 7 woman, Helen, said "I'm sorry" or "I apologize" repeatedly. At one point she said, "I'm thinking out loud. I apologize." Yet the meeting was intended to be an informal brainstorming session, and *everyone* was thinking out loud.

The reason Helen's apologies stood out was that she was the only per- 8 son in the room making so many. And the reason I was concerned was that Helen felt the annual bonus she had received was unfair. When I interviewed her colleagues, they said that Helen was one of the best and most productive workers—yet she got one of the smallest bonuses. Although the problem might have been outright sexism, I suspect her speech style, which differs from that of her male colleagues, masks her competence.

Unfortunately, not apologizing can have its price too. Since so many 9 women use ritual apologies, those who don't may be seen as hard-edged. What's important is to be aware of how often you say you're sorry (and why), and to monitor your speech based on the reaction you get.

2. Criticism

A woman who cowrote a report with a male colleague was hurt when 10 she read a rough draft to him and he leapt into a critical response—"Oh, that's too dry! You have to make it snappier!" She herself would have been more likely to say, "That's a really good start. Of course, you'll want to make it a little snappier when you revise."

Whether criticism is given straight or softened is often a matter of con- 11 vention. In general, women use more softeners. I noticed this difference when talking to an editor about an essay I'd written. While going over changes she wanted to make, she said, "There's one more thing. I know you may not agree with me. The reason I noticed the problem is that your other points are so lucid and elegant." She went on hedging for several more sentences until I put her out of her misery: "Do you want to cut that part?" I asked—and of course she did. But I appreciated her tentativeness. In contrast, another editor (a man) I once called summarily rejected my idea for an article by barking, "Call me when you have something new to say."

Those who are used to ways of talking that soften the impact of criti- 12 cism may find it hard to deal with the right-between-the-eyes style. It has its own logic, however, and neither style is intrinsically better. People who prefer criticism given straight are operating on an assumption that feelings aren't involved: "Here's the dope. I know you're good; you can take it."

3. Thank-Yous

A woman manager I know starts meetings by thanking everyone for 13 coming, even though it's clearly their job to do so. Her "thank-you" is simply a ritual.

WORD POWER
convention accepted practice

WORD POWER
intrinsically naturally

A novelist received a fax from an assistant in her publisher's office; 14 it contained suggested catalog copy for her book. She immediately faxed him her suggested changes and said, "Thanks for running this by me," even though her contract gave her the right to approve all copy. When she thanked the assistant, she fully expected him to reciprocate: "Thanks for giving me such a quick response." Instead, he said, "You're welcome." Suddenly, rather than an equal exchange of pleasantries, she found herself positioned as the recipient of a favor. This made her feel like responding, "Thanks for nothing!"

Many women use "thanks" as an automatic conversation starter and 15 closer; there's nothing literally to say thank you for. Like many rituals typical of women's conversation, it depends on the goodwill of the other to restore the balance. When the other speaker doesn't reciprocate, a woman may feel like someone on a seesaw whose partner abandoned his end. Instead of balancing in the air, she has plopped to the ground, wondering how she got there.

4. Fighting

Many men expect the discussion of ideas to be a ritual fight—explored 16 through verbal opposition. They state their ideas in the strongest possible terms, thinking that if there are weaknesses someone will point them out, and by trying to argue against those objections, they will see how well their ideas hold up.

Those who expect their own ideas to be challenged will respond to 17 another's ideas by trying to poke holes and find weak links—as a way of *helping.* The logic is that when you are challenged you will rise to the occasion: Adrenaline makes your mind sharper; you get ideas and insights you would not have thought of without the spur of battle.

But many women take this approach as a personal attack. Worse, they 18 find it impossible to do their best work in such a contentious environment. If you're not used to ritual fighting, you begin to hear criticism of your ideas as soon as they are formed. Rather than making you think more clearly, it makes you doubt what you know. When you state your ideas, you hedge in order to fend off potential attacks. Ironically, this is more likely to *invite* attack because it makes you look weak.

Although you may never enjoy verbal sparring, some women find it 19 helpful to learn how to do it. An engineer who was the only woman among four men in a small company found that as soon as she learned to argue she was accepted and taken seriously. A doctor attending a hospital staff meeting made a similar discovery. She was becoming more and more angry with a male colleague who'd loudly disagreed with a point she'd made. Her better judgment told her to hold her tongue, to avoid making an enemy of this powerful senior colleague. But finally she couldn't hold it in any longer, and

WORD POWER
reciprocate return the favor

WORD POWER
adrenaline a hormone released during stress

she rose to her feet and delivered an impassioned attack on his position. She sat down in a panic, certain she had permanently damaged her relationship with him. To her amazement, he came up to her afterward and said, "That was a great rebuttal. I'm really impressed. Let's go out for a beer after work and hash out our approaches to this problem."

5. Praise

A manager I'll call Lester had been on his new job six months when he 20 heard that the women reporting to him were deeply dissatisfied. When he talked to them about it, their feelings erupted; two said they were on the verge of quitting because he didn't appreciate their work, and they didn't want to wait to be fired. Lester was dumbfounded: He believed they were doing a fine job. Surely, he thought, he had said nothing to give them the impression he didn't like their work. And indeed he hadn't. That was the problem. He had said *nothing*—and the women assumed he was following the adage "If you can't say something nice, don't say anything." He thought he was showing confidence in them by leaving them alone.

Men and women have different habits in regard to giving praise. For 21 example, Deirdre and her colleague William both gave presentations at a conference. Afterward, Deirdre told William, "That was a great talk!" He thanked her. Then she asked, "What did you think of mine?" and he gave her a lengthy and detailed critique. She found it uncomfortable to listen to his comments. But she assured herself that he meant well, and that his honesty was a signal that she, too, should be honest when he asked for a critique of his performance. As a matter of fact, she had noticed quite a few ways in which he could have improved his presentation. But she never got a chance to tell him because he never asked—and she felt put down. The worst part was that it seemed she had only herself to blame, since she *had* asked what he thought of her talk.

But had she really asked for his critique? The truth is, when she asked 22 for his opinion, she was expecting a compliment, which she felt was more or less required following anyone's talk. When he responded with criticism, she figured, "Oh, he's playing 'Let's critique each other'"—not a game she'd initiated, but one which she was willing to play. Had she realized he was going to criticize her and not ask her to reciprocate, she would never have asked in the first place.

It would be easy to assume that Deirdre was insecure, whether she was 23 fishing for a compliment or soliciting a critique. But she was simply talking automatically, performing one of the many conversational rituals that allow us to get through the day. William may have sincerely misunderstood Deirdre's intention—or may have been unable to pass up a chance to one-up her when given the opportunity.

WORD POWER
soliciting asking for

6. Complaints

"Troubles talk" can be a way to establish rapport with a colleague. You 24 complain about a problem (which shows that you are just folks) and the other person responds with a similar problem (which puts you on equal footing). But while such commiserating is common among women, men are likely to hear it as a request to *solve* the problem.

One woman told me she would frequently initiate what she thought 25 would be pleasant complaint-airing sessions at work. She'd talk about situations that bothered her just to talk about them, maybe to understand them better. But her male office mate would quickly tell her how she could improve the situation. This left her feeling condescended to and frustrated. She was delighted to see this very impasse in a section in my book *You Just Don't Understand*, and showed it to him. "Oh," he said, "I see the problem. How can we solve it?" Then they both laughed, because it had happened again: He short-circuited the detailed discussion she'd hoped for and cut to the chase of finding a solution.

Sometimes the consequences of complaining are more serious: A man 26 might take a woman's lighthearted griping literally, and she can get a reputation as a chronic malcontent. Furthermore, she may be seen as not up to solving the problems that arise on the job.

7. Jokes

I heard a man call in to a talk show and say, "I've worked for two women 27 and neither one had a sense of humor. You know, when you work with men, there's a lot of joking and teasing." The show's host and the guest (both women) took his comment at face value and assumed the women this man worked for were humorless. The guest said, "Isn't it sad that women don't feel comfortable enough with authority to see the humor?" The host said, "Maybe when more women are in authority roles, they'll be more comfortable with power." But although the women this man worked for *may* have taken themselves too seriously, it's just as likely that they each had a terrific sense of humor, but maybe the humor wasn't the type he was used to. They may have been like the woman who wrote to me: "When I'm with men, my wit or cleverness seems inappropriate (or lost!) so I don't bother. When I'm with my women friends, however, there's no hold on puns or cracks and my humor is fully appreciated."

The types of humor women and men tend to prefer differ. Research 28 has shown that the most common form of humor among men is razzing, teasing, and mock-hostile attacks, while among women it's self-mocking. Women often mistake men's teasing as genuinely hostile. Men often mistake women's mock self-deprecation as truly putting themselves down.

Women have told me they were taken more seriously when they learned to joke the way the guys did. For example, a teacher who went to a national conference with seven other teachers (mostly women) and a group of administrators (mostly men) was annoyed that the administrators always found reasons to leave boring seminars, while the teachers felt they had to stay and take notes. One evening, when the group met at a bar in the hotel, the principal asked her how one such seminar had turned out. She retorted, "As soon as you left, it got much better." He laughed out loud at her response. The playful insult appealed to the men—but there was a trade-off. The women seemed to back off from her after this. (Perhaps they were put off by her using joking to align herself with the bosses.) 29

There is no "right" way to talk. When problems arise, the culprit may be style differences—and *all* styles will at times fail with others who don't share or understand them, just as English won't do you much good if you try to speak to someone who knows only French. If you want to get your message across, it's not a question of being "right"; it's a question of using language that's shared—or at least understood. 30

Focus on Meaning

1. What does Tannen mean by "conversational rituals" (2)?

2. What different categories of conversational rituals does Tannen identify?

3. Why, according to Tannen, is it important to understand the differences between men's and women's conversational styles?

4. Why are women who apologize too much at a disadvantage? What is the danger for women of *not* apologizing?

5. What two styles of criticism does Tannen identify? What are their advantages and disadvantages?

6. In paragraph 15, Tannen says of women's use of automatic thank-yous, "Like many rituals typical of women's conversation, it depends on the goodwill of the other to restore the balance." What does she mean?

7. How do men and women differ when it comes to "verbal sparring" (19)?

8. How do men and women differ in terms of giving praise? In terms of making complaints?

9. How are men's and women's use of humor different?

Focus on Strategy

1. This essay's title is in the form of a question. Why do you think Tannen chose this kind of title? What other title would work for this essay?

2. What is this essay's thesis?

3. Tannen supports her thesis with a series of informal anecdotes drawn from her observations and communications with others about workplace interaction between men and women. Do you think this kind of supporting evidence is convincing enough, or do you think she should have included a different kind of evidence—for example, reports of research studies?

4. Do you think this essay is aimed at men or at women? At employees or at managers? What kind of publication might it appear in?

5. In her conclusion, Tannen says, "There is no 'right' way to talk" (30). Do you think her essay supports or contradicts this statement? Why?

Focus on the Pattern

1. Tannen is contrasting men's and women's conversational styles, but she structures her essay as a classification rather than as a comparison and contrast. What are the advantages and disadvantages of this decision?

2. The headings Tannen uses for her categories are straightforward and descriptive but not particularly interesting or eye-catching. Would you change them—for example, rewriting them in the form of quotations or phrasing them as questions—or are they effective as they are?

3. Do you think Tannen needs to add transitions to move readers from one category to the next, or do her numbered headings do the job?

Focus on Critical Thinking

1. Which of Tannen's categories do you think is likely to be most problematic for women in the workplace? Why?

2. Does your own experience support Tannen's point about the differences between men's and women's "conversational rituals"? Or, do you think she exaggerates the extent—or the importance—of these differences?

3. Do you think Tannen's observations apply only to the workplace, or do you believe they apply to other situations as well—for example, to your college classes?

Writing Practice

1. Tannen's essay focuses on the workplace, but the conversational rituals she identifies also exist in other contexts. Choose three or four of Tannen's seven categories, and illustrate each category with examples of conversational behavior in the college classroom.

2. Focusing on one of Tannen's categories—for example, "Fighting"—discuss the differences between men's and women's conversational rituals. Divide your subject into the following four categories: conversations at work, conversations in class, conversations with friends, and conversations at home.

The Dog Ate My Disk, and Other Tales of Woe

Carolyn Foster Segal

Carolyn Foster Segal, associate professor of English at Cedar Crest College in Pennsylvania, has heard practically every student excuse for handing in late papers. In this humorous essay, she divides student excuses into categories. This article appeared in *The Chronicle of Higher Education*, a periodical for college teachers and administrators.

WORD POWER
woe sadness

WORD POWER
feline (noun) a member of the cat family; (adjective) catlike

Taped to the door of my office is a cartoon that features a cat explaining 1 to his feline teacher, "The dog ate my homework." It is intended as a gently humorous reminder to my students that I will not accept excuses for late work, and it, like the lengthy warning on my syllabus, has had absolutely no effect. With a show of energy and creativity that would be admirable if applied to the (missing) assignments in question, my students persist, week after week, semester after semester, year after year, in offering excuses about why their work is not ready. Those reasons fall into several broad categories: the family, the best friend, the evils of dorm life, the evils of technology, and the totally bizarre.

WORD POWER
veracity truthfulness

The Family   The death of the grandfather / grandmother is, of course, 2 the grandmother of all excuses. What heartless teacher would dare to question a student's grief or veracity? What heartless student would lie, wishing death on a revered family member, just to avoid a deadline? Creative students may win extra extensions (and days off) with a little careful planning and fuller plot development, as in the sequence of "My grandfather / grandmother is sick"; "Now my grandfather / grandmother is in the hospital"; and finally, "We could all see it coming — my grandfather / grandmother is dead."

WORD POWER
conjure up to bring to mind

Another favorite excuse is "the family emergency," which (always) goes 3 like this: "There was an emergency at home, and I had to help my family." It's a lovely sentiment, one that conjures up images of Louisa May Alcott's little women rushing off with baskets of food and copies of *Pilgrim's Progress*, but I do not understand why anyone would turn to my most irresponsible students in times of trouble.

WORD POWER
adjunct an instructor at a college or university who is not a permanent staff member; any temporary employee

The Best Friend   This heartwarming concern for others extends 4 beyond the family to friends, as in, "My best friend was up all night and I had to (a) stay up with her in the dorm, (b) drive her to the hospital, or (c) drive to her college because (1) her boyfriend broke up with her, (2) she was throwing up blood [no one catches a cold anymore; everyone throws up blood], or (3) her grandfather / grandmother died."

At one private university where I worked as an adjunct, I heard an 5 interesting spin that incorporated the motifs of both best friend and dead relative: "My best friend's mother killed herself." One has to admire the cleverness here: A mysterious woman in the prime of her life has allegedly committed suicide, and no professor can prove otherwise! And I admit I was moved, until finally I had to point out to my students that it was amazing how the simple act of my assigning a topic for a paper seemed to drive large numbers of otherwise happy and healthy middle-aged women to their deaths. I was careful to make that point during an off week, during which no deaths were reported.

The Evils of Dorm Life　These stories are usually fairly predict- 6 able; they almost always feature the evil roommate or hallmate, with my student in the role of the innocent victim; and can be summed up as follows: My roommate, who is a horrible person, likes to party, and I, who am a good person, cannot concentrate on my work when he or she is partying. Variations include stories about the two people next door who were running around and crying loudly last night because (a) one of them had boyfriend / girlfriend problems; (b) one of them was throwing up blood; or (c) someone, somewhere, died. A friend of mine in graduate school had a student who claimed that his roommate attacked him with a hammer. That, in fact, was a true story; it came out in court when the bad roommate was tried for killing his grandfather.

The Evils of Technology　The computer age has revolutionized the 7 student story, inspiring almost as many new excuses as it has Internet businesses. Here are just a few electronically enhanced explanations.

- The computer wouldn't let me save my work.
- The printer wouldn't print.
- The printer wouldn't print this disk.
- The printer wouldn't give me time to proofread.
- The printer made a black line run through all my words, and I know you can't read this, but do you still want it, or wait, here, take my disk. File name? I don't know what you mean.
- I swear I attached it.
- It's my roommate's computer, and she usually helps me, but she had to go to the hospital because she was throwing up blood.
- I did write to the newsgroup, but all my messages came back to me.
- I just found out that all my other newsgroup messages came up under a different name. I just want you to know that its really me who wrote all those messages, you can tel which ones our mine because I didnt use the spelcheck! But it was yours truely :) Anyway, just in case you missed those messages or dont belief its my writting. I'll

repeat what I sad: I thought the last movie we watched in clas was borring.

The Totally Bizarre I call the first story "The Pennsylvania Chain 8 Saw Episode." A commuter student called to explain why she had missed my morning class. She had gotten up early so that she would be wide awake for class. Having a bit of extra time, she walked outside to see her neighbor, who was cutting some wood. She called out to him, and he waved back to her with the saw. Wouldn't you know it, the safety catch wasn't on or was broken, and the blade flew right out of the saw and across his lawn and over her fence and across her yard and severed a tendon in her right hand. So she was calling me from the hospital, where she was waiting for surgery. Luckily, she reassured me, she had remembered to bring her paper and a stamped envelope (in a plastic bag, to avoid bloodstains) along with her in the ambulance, and a nurse was mailing everything to me even as we spoke.

That wasn't her first absence. In fact, this student had missed most 9 of the class meetings, and I had already recommended that she withdraw from the course. Now I suggested again that it might be best if she dropped the class. I didn't harp on the absences (what if even some of this story were true?). I did mention that she would need time to recuperate and that making up so much missed work might be difficult. "Oh, no," she said, "I can't drop this course. I had been planning to go on to medical school and become a surgeon, but since I won't be able to operate because of my accident, I'll have to major in English, and this course is more important than ever to me." She did come to the next class, wearing—as evidence of her recent trauma—a bedraggled Ace bandage on her left hand.

You may be thinking that nothing could top that excuse, but in fact I have 10 one more story, provided by the same student, who sent me a letter to explain why her final assignment would be late. While recuperating from her surgery, she had begun corresponding on the Internet with a man who lived in Germany. After a one-week, whirlwind Web romance, they had agreed to meet in Rome, to rendezvous (her phrase) at the papal Easter Mass. Regrettably, the time of her flight made it impossible for her to attend class, but she trusted that I—just this once—would accept late work if the pope wrote a note.

Focus on Meaning

1. Why does Segal see a grandparent's death as "the grandmother of all excuses" (2)?

2. What problems do students' friends always seem to have?

3. What are some of "the evils of dorm life"?

4. What problems do computers cause for students?

5. What are some of "the totally bizarre" excuses students come up with?

WORD POWER

harp on to repeat over and over again

WORD POWER

rendezvous (verb) to meet at a prearranged place and time; (noun) a prearranged meeting

Focus on Strategy

1. This essay originally appeared in the *Chronicle of Higher Education*, a weekly newspaper for college faculty and administrators. How can you tell?

2. Why does Segal begin her essay by describing a cartoon?

3. In her first paragraph, Segal includes a sentence that lists the five categories she will discuss. Do you think she needs this sentence?

4. **Sarcastic** remarks mean the opposite of what they say and are usually meant to make fun of someone or something. Where does Segal use sarcasm? Considering her audience, do you think this is an effective strategy?

5. Do you think this essay needs a formal conclusion, or does the story in its last paragraph serve as an effective ending? Explain.

Focus on the Pattern

1. What categories of excuses does Segal identify?

2. Are Segal's categories arranged in random order? If not, what determines the order in which she presents them?

3. The "totally bizarre" category is broader than the others. Do you think it needs to be divided into smaller categories? If so, what would you call these new subcategories?

Focus on Critical Thinking

1. What other excuses for handing in late assignments can you think of? Do they fit into the categories Segal has established? If not, what new category (or categories) would you add to Segal's?

2. Do you see all the excuses Segal lists as valid reasons for handing in a late paper or asking for more time to complete an assignment? Why or why not?

3. Do you think this essay is funny? Do you find it offensive in any way? How do you suppose your instructors would react to Segal's ideas?

4. What is Segal's attitude toward her students? What might explain this attitude?

5. What would Segal have to change if she were to rewrite this essay for her campus's student newspaper? Why?

Writing Practice

1. Write about the strangest excuse you have ever been given by someone for not doing something he or she was supposed to do. Explain the circumstances of this excuse in a humorous manner.

2. Discuss one of the following topics (or a similar topic of your own choice):
   - Types of unacceptable behavior by a teacher
   - Types of students at your school
   - Kinds of tattoos

3. Write a letter to Carolyn Foster Segal explaining why your English paper will be late. Explain that you have read her essay about various categories of student excuses but that *your* excuse is valid.

Definition

A **definition** essay presents an extended definition, using other patterns of development to move beyond a simple dictionary definition. In "The Wife-Beater," Gayle Rosenwald Smith defines an item of clothing. In "Triskai-dekaphobia," Paul Hoffman defines a superstition.

The Wife-Beater

Gayle Rosenwald Smith

Philadelphia lawyer Gayle Rosenwald Smith, who specializes in family law, coauthored *What Every Woman Should Know about Divorce and Custody* (1998). Her articles have been published in newspapers such as the *Chicago Tribune* and the *Philadelphia Inquirer* (where this essay appeared). As you read, think about the connotations of violence and masculinity in Smith's definition of a "wife-beater."

WORD POWER
lavished decorated to excess

Everybody wears them. The Gap sells them. Fashion designers Dolce and Gabbana have lavished them with jewels. Their previous greatest resurgence occurred in the 1950s, when Marlon Brando's Stanley Kowalski wore one in Tennessee Williams' *A Streetcar Named Desire*. They are all the rage.   1

What are they called?   2

The name is the issue. For they are known as "wife-beaters."   3

WORD POWER
gusto enthusiastic enjoyment

A Web search shows that kids nationwide are wearing the skinny-ribbed white T-shirts that can be worn alone or under another shirt. Women have adopted them with the same gusto as men. A search of boutiques shows that these wearers include professionals who wear them, adorned with designer accessories, under their pricey suits. They are available in all colors, sizes and price ranges.   4

Wearers under 25 do not seem to be disturbed by the name. But I sure am.   5

It's an odd name for an undershirt. And even though the ugly stereotypes behind the name are both obvious and toxic, it appears to be cool to say the name without fear of (or without caring about) hurting anyone.   6

That the name is fueled by stereotype is now an academically estab- 7
lished fact, although various sources disagree on exactly when shirt and
name came together. The *Oxford Dictionary* defines the term *wife-beater* as:

"1. A man who physically abuses his wife and

2. Tank-style underwear shirts. Origin: based on the stereotype that
physically abusive husbands wear that particular type of shirt."

The *World Book Dictionary* locates the origin of the term *wife-beater* in 8
the 1970s, from the stereotype of the Midwestern male wearing an undershirt while beating his wife. The shirts are said to have been popular in
the 1980s at all types of sporting events, especially ones at which one sits
in the sun and develops "wife-beater marks." The undershirts also attained
popularity at wet T-shirt contests, in which the wet, ribbed tees accentuated
contestants' breasts.

In an article in the style section of the *New York Times*, Jesse Sheidlower, 9
principal editor of the *Oxford English Dictionary*'s American office, says the
association of the undershirt and the term *wife-beater* arose in 1997 from varied sources, including gay and gang subcultures and rap music.

In the article, some sources argued that the reference in the term was 10
not to spousal abuse per se but to popular-culture figures such as Ralph
Cramden and Tony Soprano. And what about Archie Bunker?[1]

It's not just the name that worries me. Fashion headlines reveal 11
that we want to overthrow '90s grunge and return to shoulder pads and
hardware-studded suits. Am I reading too much into a fashion statement
that the return is also to male dominance where physical abuse is acceptable as a means of control?

There has to be a better term. After all, it's a pretty rare piece of cloth- 12
ing that can make both men and women look sexier. You'd expect a term
connoting flattery—not violence.

Wearers under 25 may not want to hear this, but here it is. More than 13
4 million women are victims of severe assaults by boyfriends and husbands
each year. By conservative estimate, family violence occurs in 2 million families each year in the United States. Average age of the batterer: 31.

Possibly the last statistic is telling. Maybe youth today would rather 14
ignore the overtones of the term *wife-beater*. It is also true, however, that the
children of abusers often learn the behavior from their elders.

Therein lies perhaps the worst difficulty: that this name for this shirt 15
teaches the wrong thing about men. Some articles quote women who felt

WORD POWER
connoting implying;
suggesting

---

1. Characters in the 1950s sitcom *The Honeymooners*, the HBO series *The Sopranos* (1999–
2007), and the 1970s sitcom *All in the Family*.

the shirts looked great, especially on guys with great bodies. One woman stated that it even made guys look "manly."

So *manly* equals *violent*? Not by me, and I hope not by anyone on any   16 side of age 25.

Focus on Meaning

1. According to Smith, who wears wife-beaters?
2. What is it about the shirts that Smith most objects to?
3. In paragraph 11, Smith says, "It's not just the name that worries me." What else concerns her?
4. According to Smith, what is the "worst difficulty" (15) with the shirt's name?
5. What course of action does Smith propose or recommend to her readers? For example, does she think people should stop wearing wife-beater shirts?

Focus on Strategy

1. Smith's essay opens with the sentence, "Everybody wears them." Do you think this is an effective way for her to begin? Why or why not?
2. Smith uses informal words and phrases—for example, *kids* (4), *pricey* (4), and *Not by me* (16)—as well as contractions. Do you think this informal style weakens the impact of her serious message? Explain your views.
3. Beyond defining the term *wife-beater*, what is Smith's purpose for writing this essay? How can you tell? Does she express this purpose as a thesis statement?
4. Do you think men and women are likely to react differently to this essay? Why or why not?
5. Do you think readers under and over 25 might react differently to Smith's points? Does Smith seem to think so?
6. Given what Smith hopes to accomplish, some readers might think this essay's conclusion is not strong enough. Rewrite the conclusion, including a forceful summary statement.

Focus on the Pattern

1. Where does Smith present a formal (dictionary) definition of *wife-beater*?
2. Where does Smith supply information about the origin of the term she defines? Why do you think she includes this information?
3. Where does Smith use examples to develop her definition? Where does she use description? Does she use any other patterns of development?

Focus on Critical Thinking

1. In paragraph 11, Smith asks, "Am I reading too much into a fashion statement . . . ?" How would you answer her question?

2. Smith's major complaint is not with the item of clothing she describes but with its name. In paragraph 12, she says, "There has to be a better term." Can you suggest an alternative name for this kind of shirt? In what sense is your alternative a "better term"?

3. Can you think of other items of clothing that have similarly negative associations? Do you think the problem is with the clothing item itself or with its name?

4. Do you think there is a relationship between wife-beater shirts and domestic violence? If so, how would you characterize that relationship?

Writing Practice

1. Define another article of clothing that, like the wife-beater undershirt, has taken on some special significance. (For example, you could write about hoodies, baggy jeans, or baseball caps.) Focus on the garment and its wearers (not on its name), discussing the impression the article of clothing makes and the associations it has for its wearers and for others. You can use description and either exemplification or classification to develop your essay.

2. Define a particular type of student on your campus. Develop your definition with a description of the person's typical dress and accessories and examples of his or her habits. If you like, you may also include a brief narrative that illustrates this type of student's typical behavior. Be sure to provide a one-sentence definition that identifies the person you are discussing.

Triskaidekaphobia

Paul Hoffman

Paul Hoffman, a journalist and television personality, has written for such diverse publications as *Discover* magazine, the *New York Times*, and the *Encyclopaedia Britannica*. In this essay, he explores the historical roots of the superstitions surrounding the number 13.

The dark forces have triumphed again. They have made the thirteenth 1 of the month fall on a Friday—and not only this month but last month and next November, too. Those who suffer from triskaidekaphobia, morbid fear of the number 13, will want to go into hiding because three Friday the thirteenths is the maximum number the sinister forces can serve up in any one year. Although there is at least one Friday the thirteenth every year, the fainthearted will be spared another triple dose of calendrical evil until 1998.

Even in our seemingly rational age, the number 13 is still often avoided 2 in the labeling of high-rise floors and hospital rooms. Moreover, latent (and not-so-latent) superstition undoubtedly contributed to the appeal of the gory cult film *Friday the 13th*, a summer-camp dismemberment extravaganza in which fun-loving youngsters are slaughtered at Camp Crystal Lake, where a Down syndrome child once drowned. Fear of the number 13 is also fueled by newspaper tabloids; when the thirteenth Apollo mission, launched at 1313 hours central time from pad 39 (the third multiple of 13), had to be aborted on the thirteenth of April 1970, the wicked number was implicated.

Triskaidekaphobes can muster ample historical evidence in support of 3 their affliction. After all, Jesus was the thirteenth at the Last Supper and look what happened to him. The belief that 13 people cannot dine together at the same table without fatal consequences actually goes back even further than Christ's betrayal. In Nordic mythology, the demonic god Loki crashed a dinner party of benevolent deities, making their number 13 and in the process causing the death of Balder, the god of light.

The fear of dining 13 at a table plagued Napoléon, J. Paul Getty, Herbert 4 Hoover, and Franklin Delano Roosevelt. In Paris, a *quatorzième*, or professional fourteenth guest, can be hired on short notice to round out an otherwise ill-fated dinner party. Roosevelt drafted secretary Grace Tully to be a *quatorzième* at White House functions. In her memoirs, *FDR My Boss*, Tully writes: "The Boss was superstitious, particularly about the number thirteen and the practice of lighting three cigarettes on a single match. On several occasions I received last-minute summonses to attend a lunch or a dinner party because a belated default or a late addition had brought the guest list to thirteen." Tully also recalls how Roosevelt went to great pains to avoid departing by train on the thirteenth of the month, even if that "meant pulling a train out at 11:50 p.m. on the twelfth or 12:10 a.m. on the fourteenth. Even in death he escaped the day of ill omen, the end coming on the afternoon of Thursday, April 12, less than twelve hours before that bugaboo of all days, a Friday the thirteenth."

The idea that numbers are not mere instruments of enumeration but 5 are sacred, perfect, friendly, lucky, or evil goes back to antiquity. In the sixth century BC Pythagoras, whom schoolchildren associate with the famous theorem that in a right triangle the square of the hypotenuse always equals the sum of the squares of its sides, not only performed brilliant mathematics but made a religion out of numbers. In numerology, the number 12 has always represented completeness, as in the 12 months of the year, the 12 signs of the zodiac, the 12 hours of the day, the 12 gods of Olympus, and 12 labors of Hercules, the 12 tribes of Israel, the 12 apostles of Jesus, the 12 days of Christmas, and, more recently perhaps, the 12 eggs in an egg carton. Since 13 exceeds 12 by only one, the number lies just beyond completeness and, hence, is restless to the point of being evil.

Friday the thirteenth is doubly potent, drawing on the evil power of the 6 number 13 as well as Friday's reputation as a day of bad luck. Since Christ

WORD POWER

bugaboo source of concern

enumeration counting

antiquity ancient times

was crucified on a Friday, the day is a time for endings, not beginnings. Accordingly, it is not the day to get married, set sail, embark on a journey, move into a new house, start a new job, wean a child, cut your nails, or turn over a mattress. Moreover, Friday was the day reserved for capital executions.

On Friday the thirteenth, January 1882, 13 stout-hearted men in New York City had had enough of this foolishness. Although the sky was reportedly black and murky, and "the wind wailed through the leafless trees with a mournful sound, which, to the superstitious mind, suggested the banshee's cry," these 13 intrepid founders of the Thirteen Club dined in room 13 of Knickerbocker Cottage at 454 Sixth Avenue from 13 minutes past seven until the thirteenth hour. They offered toasts to the health of Trismegistus, an ancient Egyptian who was the thirteenth son of a thirteenth mother (though they did not say how this could be). Having set the club's initiation fee at $1.13, monthly dues at 13 cents, and a life membership at $13, the members pledged to continue dining together 13 at a table on the thirteenth of every month.

As they freely spilled salt at these sumptuous feasts and cheerfully took post-prandial walks under ladders, they recounted stories about the number 13. One such tale was of an old Englishman, who, it was said, feared the consequences of dining 13 at a table and always insisted on eating alone. He persisted in this habit for many years, until one day he died, and his friends concluded that on the whole it was safer not to dine at all.

Club membership soon swelled to 1,300, including the likes of President Chester Arthur and P. T. Barnum. Branch clubs, which paid a charter fee of $13.13, sprang up in London and in cities across the United States. By writing to judges and legislators, New York's Thirteen Club succeeded in freeing Friday from the slur of being "hangman's day." Decius S. Wade, the chief justice of Montana, wrote back, describing how he had sentenced a murderer to be hanged on a Thursday: "I could not see but the fellow enjoyed it just as well as though Friday had been the day appointed, and I thought poor, abused Friday looked a little brighter the next morning."

Not to be outdone by the home club in New York, the London branch carried its thirteenth-of-the-month dinners to a funereal extreme. The salt shakers were shaped like coffins and the dim lights like skulls. For badges each member wore in his buttonhole a small coffin from which a tiny skeleton dangled. Cross-eyed waiters made sure the knives and forks were crossed, and mirrors were freely broken. So defiant was the club in challenging the dark forces that a neighborhood undertaker and funeral arranger sent over his black-edged business card.

What is more, a few of the club's own members, overcome by sheer fright, failed to show up. Writing in *Confessions of a Caricaturist*, Harry

Furniss, the famous *Punch*-magazine cartoonist who presided over the club's dinner on January 13, 1894, shares a letter from an absent member: "At the last moment my courage fails me, and I return the dinner ticket you have so kindly sent me. If I had only myself to think of, I would gladly come and defy the fates. . . . But I have others to think of—dogs and cats and horses—who if anything happened to me would be alone in the world. For their sakes I must not run the risks that a faithful carrying out of your program implies. Trusting that nothing very terrible will happen to any of you in after life . . ."

To counter triskaidekaphobia the various Thirteen Clubs collected and 12 promoted lucky stories about the number 13. This practice, however, was frowned upon by the clubs' more skeptical members who feared that they were not merely undoing a superstition but reversing it. One of the more curious "lucky" stories was the unsolicited testimony of a man in Christiana, Norway: "In 1873, March 20th, I left Liverpool in the steamship *Atlantic*, then bound for New York. On the 13th day, the 1st of April, we went on the rocks near Halifax, Nova Scotia. Out of nearly 1,000 human beings, 580 were frozen to death or drowned. The first day out from Liverpool some ladies at my table discovered that we were thirteen, and in their consternation requested their gentleman-companion to move to another table. Out of the entire thirteen, I was the only one that was saved. I was asked at the time if I did not believe in the unlucky number thirteen. I told them I did not. In this case the believers were all lost and the unbelievers saved."

In its crusade to vindicate 13, one of the New York club's finest 13 moments came in 1886, when it persuaded Maria Cristina, queen regent of Spain, to ignore the pleas of her triskaidekaphobic ministers and christen her son Alfonso XIII, after his dead father, Alfonso XII. But this rational act did not mark the end of royal superstition. On August 21, 1930, when Queen Elizabeth's sister, Princess Margaret, was born in Scotland's Glamis Castle, palace officials did not immediately record the birth because the next registration number was 13; they waited three days for another birth, so they could assign Margaret the harmless number 14. And in 1965, when Elizabeth herself was touring Germany, she was scheduled to depart by train from platform 13 in Duisburg railroad station. Nervous officials hastily changed the platform number to 12a.

Since queens and presidents go out of their way to avoid the number 14 13, it's no wonder that the common man does, too. A Columbia University study of 403 psychology students found that 40 of them, or 10 percent, thought it was unlucky to have anything to do with the number 13—and who knows how many more may have believed this but were embarrassed to admit it. Professional skeptics, like the James Randises of the world, have hardly made an effort to counter triskaidekaphobia, concentrating their

WORD POWER

innocuous harmless

efforts instead on exposing spontaneous human combustion and mental spoon-bending as flimflam. They may think that fear of the number 13 is innocuous, and perhaps it is. But one account estimates that triskaideka-phobia costs American business a billion dollars a year in absenteeism, cancellations, and reduced commerce on the thirteenth of the month.

I, for one, am hardly impressed by the historical evidence in favor 15 of 13's wickedness. After all, for every sinister association of 13—say, the 13 witches in a coven—I can cite a good association—for example, the 13 states that formed the Union. I am, however, distressed by the mathematical evidence. If you were the diabolical number 13, you'd want to wreak havoc on the human race as often as possible. Therefore, you'd want the thirteenth of the month to fall on a Friday more often than it falls on any other day. That, indeed, turns out to be the case. If you don't believe me, consult the elegant paper, "To Prove That the 13th Day of the Month Is More Likely to Be a Friday Than Any Other Day of the Week," in *Mathematical Gazette* (volume 53; pages 127–129). It was written by an Eton schoolboy, S. R. Baxter, at the age of 13.

Focus on Meaning

1. What is triskaidekaphobia?

2. According to Hoffman, what evidence of triskaidekaphobia can be found in "our seemingly rational age" (2)?

3. What historical figures suffered from triskaidekaphobia?

4. Where does Hoffman think the fear of the number 13 originated?

5. Why was the first Thirteen Club founded? What did the Thirteen Clubs around the world hope to accomplish? How? Were they successful?

Focus on Strategy

1. What is this essay's thesis—that is, what point is Hoffman making about fear of the number 13? Does this thesis appear in the essay? If not, state it in your own words.

2. Do you think Hoffman is presenting a neutral view of his subject, or does he seem to be sympathetic to—or critical of—"triskaidekaphobes"? (Read the essay's last paragraph before you answer this question.)

3. Hoffman presents many historical examples of triskaidekaphobia. Which examples are most convincing, and why?

4. In paragraph 14, Hoffman mentions that one authority believes triskaidekaphobia "costs American business a billion dollars a year." Why does he include this information? Should he have developed this idea further?

5. Do you think Hoffman expects his readers to be superstitious about the number 13—or, at least, to be sympathetic to those who are? Or, do you

think he expects his audience to be scornful of those who suffer from triskaidekaphobia?

Focus on the Pattern

1. This definition is developed primarily by means of exemplification. What other patterns does Hoffman use?

2. Write a one-sentence definition of the term *triskaidekaphobia*. Then, write a one-paragraph definition, incorporating some of Hoffman's key examples.

3. What do paragraphs 7 through 13 contribute to this definition essay? Are they necessary?

Focus on Critical Thinking

1. Why do you think people in modern society are superstitious about the number 13? Do you think Hoffman should have spent more time focusing on contemporary society and less on history? Explain your viewpoint.

2. Do you think Hoffman spends too much time discussing the Thirteen Clubs? Why or why not?

3. What other kinds of information do you think Hoffman could have added to this essay? For example, should he have explored how regional differences or childhood experiences influence fear of the number 13?

Writing Practice

1. Define a common fear that you suffer from—for example, fear of flying or fear of the dentist. (You might begin by Googling *phobias* to get some ideas.) Give your phobia a name, and develop your definition with anecdotes and examples from your own experience. Your essay can be humorous or serious.

2. Do you believe in superstitions? Write about why you do—or do not—believe in a particular superstition. (Common examples include opening an umbrella indoors, throwing salt over your shoulder, and having bad luck if you break a mirror.)

37i

Argument

An **argument** essay takes a stand on a debatable issue, using supporting evidence to convince readers to accept the writer's position. The writers of the three essays that follow—Bobbi Buchanan in "Don't Hang Up, That's My Mom Calling," Charles Murray in "For Most People, College Is a Waste of Time," and Edwidge Danticat in "Impounded Fathers"—all try to convince readers to accept their arguments.

Don't Hang Up, That's My Mom Calling

Bobbi Buchanan

Telemarketers' sales calls often interrupt our already hectic lives. Bobbi Buchanan's article reminds us that there is a real, and sometimes familiar, person on the other end of every telemarketing call. Buchanan, whose writing has appeared in the *New York Times* and the *Louisville Review*, is the editor of the online journal *New Southerner*.

1   The next time an annoying sales call interrupts your dinner, think of my 71-year-old mother, LaVerne, who works as a part-time telemarketer to supplement her Social Security income. To those Americans who have signed up for the new national do-not-call list, my mother is a pest, a nuisance, an invader of privacy. To others, she's just another anonymous voice on the other end of the line. But to those who know her, she's someone stuggling to make a buck, to feed herself and pay her utilities—someone who personifies the great American way.

2   In our family, we think of my mother as a pillar of strength. She's survived two heart surgeries and lung cancer. She stayed at home her whole life to raise the seven of us kids. She entered the job market unskilled and physically limited after my father's death in 1998, which ended his pension benefits.

WORD POWER
viable capable of success or effectiveness

3   Telemarketing is a viable option for my mother and the more than six million other Americans who work in the industry. According to the American Teleservices Association, the telemarketing work force is mostly women; 26 percent are single mothers. More than 60 percent are minorities; about 5 percent are disabled; 95 percent are not college graduates; more than 30 percent have been on welfare or public assistance. This is clearly a job for those used to hardship.

WORD POWER
exempt to free from an obligation

4   Interestingly enough, the federal list exempts calls from politicians, pollsters, and charities, and companies that have existing business relationships with customers can keep calling. Put this in perspective. Are they not the bulk of your annoying calls? Telemarketing giants won't be as affected by the list but smaller businesses that rely on this less costly means of sales will. The giants will resort to other, more expensive forms of advertisement and pass those costs along to you, the consumer.

WORD POWER
impervious impossible to affect

5   My mother doesn't blame people for wanting to be placed on the do-not-call list. She doesn't argue the fairness of its existence or take offense when potential clients cut her off in mid-sentence. All her parenting experience has made her impervious to rude behavior and snide remarks, and she is not discouraged by hang-ups or busy signals. What worries my mother is

that she doesn't know whether she can do anything else at her age. As it is, sales are down and her paycheck is shrinking.

So when the phone rings at your house during dinnertime and you can't 6 resist picking it up, relax, breathe deeply and take a silent oath to be polite. Try these three painless words: "No, thank you."

Think of the caller this way: a hard-working, first-generation American; 7 the daughter of a Pittsburgh steelworker; a survivor of the Great Depression; the widow of a World War II veteran; a mother of seven, grandmother of eight, great-grandmother of three. It's my mother calling.

Focus on Meaning

1. According to Buchanan, what kind of people work as telemarketers? What does Buchanan mean in paragraph 3 when she says, "This is clearly a job for those used to hardship"?

2. How does the federal do-not-call list favor big businesses? How does it negatively affect small businesses?

3. Why has Buchanan's mother become a telemarketer? What concerns does she have about her future?

4. What image does Buchanan want readers to keep in mind when a telemarketer calls?

Focus on Strategy

1. What preconceptions about telemarketers does Buchanan believe readers have? How can you tell?

2. This essay's thesis appears at the end of paragraph 1. How does the paragraph prepare readers for this thesis?

3. In paragraph 3, Buchanan presents several statistics. What is she trying to establish with these statistics? How do they support the essay's thesis?

4. In paragraph 5, Buchanan says that her mother "doesn't blame people for wanting to be placed on the do-not-call list." She also says that her mother doesn't blame people when they are rude. Why does Buchanan include this information about her mother?

5. Buchanan ends her essay by speaking directly to readers. What does she hope to accomplish? How effective is this strategy?

Focus on the Pattern

1. What arguments does Buchanan make to support her thesis?

2. Where in the essay does Buchanan address arguments against her thesis? How effectively does she deal with these opposing arguments?

3. What patterns of development does Buchanan use to construct her argument?

Focus on Critical Thinking

1. Is Buchanan's argument in support of telemarketers convincing? What are its strengths? What are its weaknesses?

2. In paragraph 2, Buchanan says that the people in her family consider her mother "a pillar of strength." Do you agree with this characterization?

3. At various points in her essay, Buchanan encourages readers to identify with her mother. Does she achieve her goal?

Writing Practice

1. Have you ever had a job that people do not understand or appreciate? Write an essay in which you, like Buchanan, argue that people ought to take the time to consider the challenges this job presents. Be sure to include a clear thesis and support it with specific arguments.

2. Write an editorial for your local newspaper in which you argue for or against the national do-not-call list. Do you think such a list is warranted, or do you believe it is unfair to the six million Americans who work in the telemarketing industry? Use your own experience with telemarketers to support your position.

For Most People, College Is a Waste of Time

Charles Murray

Charles Murray, a political scientist, writes about social policy and our education system. His books include *Real Education: Four Simple Truths for Bringing America's Schools Back to Reality* (2008) and, with Richard J. Hernstein, *The Bell Curve: Intelligence and Class Structure in American Life* (1994). In this essay, Murray questions the value of the traditional four-year college degree program and proposes creating apprenticeship programs that lead to industry certification.

Imagine that America had no system of post-secondary education, and 1 you were a member of a task force assigned to create one from scratch. One of your colleagues submits this proposal:

First, we will set up a single goal to represent educational success, which 2 *will take four years to achieve no matter what is being taught. We will attach an economic reward to it that seldom has anything to do with what has been learned. We will urge large numbers of people who do not possess adequate ability to try to achieve the goal, wait until they have spent a lot of time and money, and then deny it to them. We will stigmatize everyone who doesn't meet the goal. We will call the goal a "BA."*

You would conclude that your colleague was cruel, not to say insane. 3 But that's the system we have in place.

WORD POWER
stigmatize label as an outcast

Finding a better way should be easy. The BA acquired its current 4 inflated status by accident. Advanced skills for people with brains really did get more valuable over the course of the 20th century, but the acquisition of those skills got conflated with the existing system of colleges, which had evolved the BA for completely different purposes.

Outside a handful of majors—engineering and some of the sciences—a 5 bachelor's degree tells an employer nothing except that the applicant has a certain amount of intellectual ability and perseverance. Even a degree in a vocational major like business administration can mean anything from a solid base of knowledge to four years of barely remembered gut courses.

The solution is not better degrees, but no degrees. Young people enter- 6 ing the job market should have a known, trusted measure of their qualifica- tions they can carry into job interviews. That measure should express what they know, not where they learned it or how long it took them. They need a certification, not a degree.

The model is the CPA exam that qualifies certified public accountants. 7 The same test is used nationwide. It is thorough—four sections, timed, totaling 14 hours. A passing score indicates authentic competence (the pass rate is below 50%). Actual scores are reported in addition to pass/fail, so that employers can assess where the applicant falls in the distribution of accounting competence. You may have learned accounting at an anonymous online university, but your CPA score gives you a way to show employers you're a stronger applicant than someone from an Ivy League school.

The merits of a CPA-like certification exam apply to any college major 8 for which the BA is now used as a job qualification. To name just some of them: criminal justice, social work, public administration and the many sep- arate majors under the headings of business, computer science and educa- tion. Such majors accounted for almost two-thirds of the bachelor's degrees conferred in 2005. For that matter, certification tests can be used for purely academic disciplines. Why not present graduate schools with certifications in microbiology or economics—and who cares if the applicants passed the exam after studying in the local public library?

Certification tests need not undermine the incentives to get a traditional 9 liberal-arts education. If professional and graduate schools want students who have acquired one, all they need do is require certification scores in the appropriate disciplines. Students facing such requirements are likely to get a much better liberal education than even our most elite schools require now.

Certification tests will not get rid of the problems associated with differ- 10 ences in intellectual ability: People with high intellectual ability will still have an edge. Graduates of prestigious colleges will still, on average, have higher certification scores than people who have taken online courses—just because prestigious colleges attract intellectually talented applicants.

But that's irrelevant to the larger issue. Under a certification system, 11 four years is not required, residence is not required, expensive tuitions are not required, and a degree is not required. Equal educational opportunity means, among other things, creating a society in which it's what you know that makes the difference. Substituting certifications for degrees would be a big step in that direction.

The incentives are right. Certification tests would provide all employ- 12 ers with valuable, trustworthy information about job applicants. They would benefit young people who cannot or do not want to attend a traditional four-year college. They would be welcomed by the growing post-secondary online educational industry, which cannot offer the halo effect of a BA from a traditional college, but can realistically promise their students good training for a certification test—as good as they are likely to get at a traditional college, for a lot less money and in a lot less time.

Certification tests would disadvantage just one set of people: Students 13 who have gotten into well-known traditional schools, but who are coasting through their years in college and would score poorly on a certification test. Disadvantaging them is an outcome devoutly to be wished.

No technical barriers stand in the way of evolving toward a system 14 where certification tests would replace the BA. Hundreds of certification tests already exist, for everything from building code inspectors to advanced medical specialties. The problem is a shortage of tests that are nationally accepted, like the CPA exam.

But when so many of the players would benefit, a market opportunity 15 exists. If a high-profile testing company such as the Educational Testing Service were to reach a strategic decision to create definitive certification tests, it could coordinate with major employers, professional groups and nontraditional universities to make its tests the gold standard. A handful of key decisions could produce a tipping effect. Imagine if Microsoft announced it would henceforth require scores on a certain battery of certification tests from all of its programming applicants. Scores on that battery would acquire instant credibility for programming job applicants throughout the industry.

An educational world based on certification tests would be a better place 16 in many ways, but the overarching benefit is that the line between college and noncollege competencies would be blurred. Hardly any jobs would still have the BA as a requirement for a shot at being hired. Opportunities would be wider and fairer, and the stigma of not having a BA would diminish.

Most important in an increasingly class-riven America: The demonstra- 17 tion of competency in business administration or European history would,

WORD POWER

incentives motivating factors

appropriately, take on similarities to the demonstration of competency in cooking or welding. Our obsession with the BA has created a two-tiered entry to adulthood, anointing some for admission to the club and labeling the rest as second-best.

Here's the reality: Everyone in every occupation starts as an apprentice. Those who are good enough become journeymen. The best become master craftsmen. This is as true of business executives and history professors as of chefs and welders. Getting rid of the BA and replacing it with evidence of competence—treating post-secondary education as apprenticeships for everyone—is one way to help us to recognize that common bond.

Focus on Meaning

1. What does Murray mean in paragraph 5 when he says, "a bachelor's degree tells an employer nothing except that the applicant has a certain amount of intellectual ability and perseverance"?

2. Why is the CPA exam a good model for the certification tests that Murray advocates?

3. According to Murray, what are the advantages of certification tests? What are the disadvantages?

4. In paragraph 16, Murray says that certification tests would blur the line between "college and noncollege competencies." What does he mean? Why does he think this outcome would be a good one?

5. What does Murray mean in paragraph 17 when he says, "Our obsession with the BA has created a two-tiered entry into adulthood"?

Focus on Strategy

1. Does Murray think that readers will be receptive, hostile, or neutral to his proposal? How do you know?

2. Murray states his thesis in paragraph 6. Why does he wait so long? How do paragraphs 1–5 prepare readers for his thesis?

3. What are the main points Murray makes to support his thesis?

4. What evidence does Murray present to support his points? Would more evidence have strengthened his case? What other evidence could he have provided?

5. What objections to his ideas does Murray mention? Are there any other objections he should have addressed?

6. What ideas does Murray emphasize in his conclusion? Is this an effective strategy, or do you think he should have emphasized different ideas? Explain.

Focus on the Pattern

1. Look at several paragraphs in the body of Murray's essay. Do the topic sentences unify the paragraphs? Do the topic sentences help readers follow the discussion as they move from one paragraph to another?

2. List the transitions Murray uses to move readers from one point to another. Should he have used more transitions?

Focus on Critical Thinking

1. Do you think that Murray's proposal has merit, or do you think it is too impractical to work?

2. Murray says that certification tests would hurt only one group: students who "are coasting through their years in college" (13). Do you think any other groups of students would also be hurt?

3. In paragraph 9, Murray says, "Certification tests need not undermine the incentives to get a traditional liberal-arts education." Do you agree?

Writing Practice

1. Write an email to Murray in which you respond to his proposal for certification tests. Do you agree with Murray that a bachelor's degree does not tell an employer much about an applicant's ability to do a job? Or, do you think that a bachelor's degree gives an employer valuable information about a candidate? Make sure that your email has a clear thesis and that you support your points with information from your own experience.

2. What is the purpose of a college education? Is it to prepare students for the workforce? Is it to expose them to ideas that help them to develop intellectually? Or, is it supposed to do something else? Write an argument in which you support your position on this issue.

Impounded Fathers

Edwidge Danticat

Edwidge Danticat was born in Haiti in 1969. Her books, which explore Haitian culture and identity, include *Breath, Eyes, Memory* (1994), *Krik? Krak!* (1995), and *Brother, I'm Dying* (2007). Consider how the examples of deported fathers and abandoned children in this essay—first published in the *New York Times* on Father's Day 2007—support Danticat's argument for fairer immigration policies.

My father died in May 2005, after an agonizing battle with lung disease. 1 This is the third Father's Day that I will spend without him since we started celebrating together in 1981. That was when I moved to the United States from Haiti, after his own migration here had kept us apart for eight long years.

My father's absence, then and now, makes all the more poignant for 2 me the predicament of the following fathers who also deserve to be remembered today.

There is the father from Honduras who was imprisoned, then deported, 3 after a routine traffic stop in Miami. He was forced to leave behind his wife, who was also detained by immigration officials, and his 5- and 7-year-old sons, who were placed in foster care. Not understanding what had happened, the boys, when they were taken to visit their mother in jail, asked why their father had abandoned them. Realizing that the only way to reunite his family was to allow his children to be expatriated to Honduras, the father resigned himself to this, only to get caught up in a custody fight with American immigration officials who have threatened to keep the boys permanently in foster care on the premise that their parents abandoned them.

There is also the father from Panama, a cleaning contractor in his 50s, 4 who had lived and worked in the United States for more than 19 years. One morning, he woke to the sound of loud banging on his door. He went to answer it and was greeted by armed immigration agents. His 10-year asylum case had been denied without notice. He was handcuffed and brought to jail.

There is the father from Argentina who moves his wife and children 5 from house to house hoping to remain one step ahead of the immigration raids. And the Guatemalan, Mexican and Chinese fathers who have quietly sought sanctuary from deportation at churches across the United States.

There's the Haitian father who left for work one morning, was picked 6 up outside his apartment and was deported before he got a chance to say goodbye to his infant daughter and his wife. There's the other Haitian father, a naturalized American citizen, whose wife was deported three weeks before her residency hearing, forcing him to place his 4-year-old son in the care of neighbors while he works every waking hour to support two households.

These families are all casualties of a Department of Homeland Security 7 immigration crackdown cheekily titled Operation Return to Sender. The goals of the operation, begun last spring, were to increase the enforcement of immigration laws in the workplace and to catch and deport criminals. Many women and men who have no criminal records have found themselves in its crosshairs. More than 18,000 people have been deported since the operation began last year.

So while politicians debate the finer points of immigration reform, the 8 Department of Homeland Security is already carrying out its own. Unfortunately, these actions can not only plunge families into financial decline, but sever them forever. One such case involves a father who was killed soon after he was deported to El Salvador last year.

"Something else could be done," his 13-year-old son Junior pleaded to 9 the New York-based advocacy group Families for Freedom, "because kids need their fathers."

WORD POWER
sanctuary shelter
from danger

Right now the physical, emotional, financial and legal status of 10
American-born minors like Junior can neither delay nor prevent their
parents' detention or deportation. Last year, Representative José E.
Serrano, a Democrat from New York, introduced a bill that would allow
immigration judges to take into consideration the fates of American-born
children while reviewing their parents' cases. The bill has gone nowhere,
while more and more American-citizen children continue to either lose
their parents or their country.

Where are our much-touted family values when it comes to these chil- 11
dren? Today, as on any other day, they deserve to feel that they have not
been abandoned — by either their parents or their country.

Focus on Meaning

1. Why did Danticat choose to write this essay to commemorate Father's Day?

2. Why, in paragraph 2, does Danticat say that the predicament of other fathers—
   men she doesn't know—is "poignant" for her?

3. Why does Danticat include paragraphs 3–6? What do all the fathers described in
   these paragraphs have in common?

4. Why does Danticat criticize the actions of the Department of Homeland Security? According to her, how are its policies harmful to families?

5. In paragraph 11, Danticat says, "Where are our much-touted family values when
   it comes to these children?" What does she mean? How would you answer this
   question?

Focus on Strategy

1. Does Danticat think her readers will be receptive to her ideas? How can you
   tell?

2. How does Danticat try to influence readers to sympathize with the plight of
   undocumented immigrants? Is she successful?

3. Where, if anywhere, does Danticat address arguments against her position?
   What opposing arguments can you think of? How would you refute them?

4. At what point does Danticat state her thesis? Why does she wait so long to
   state it?

5. When making her argument, Danticat appeals both to logic and to emotion.
   Which parts of her argument appeal primarily to logic? Which appeal primarily
   to emotion? Which of these appeals do you think is more effective? Why?

Focus on the Pattern

1. Is Danticat's argument inductive? deductive? Or, does she use both induction
   and deduction to develop her argument?

2. What determines the order in which Danticat presents her points? How effective do you think this order is? What other order could she have used?

Focus on Critical Thinking

1. According to Danticat, many innocent immigrants are caught in the "cross-hairs" of Operation Return to Sender. Do you agree with her that because these immigrants have no criminal records, they are "innocent"?

2. Do you agree with Representative José E. Serrano that judges should take into consideration the fates of American-born children—who by law are United States citizens—when reviewing their parents' cases?

3. Why do you think the Department of Homeland Security instituted Operation Return to Sender? Do think that this policy is fair? Do you think that it has out-lived its usefulness? Explain.

4. Do you think the devastation in Haiti as a result of the 2010 earthquake (which occurred after this essay was written) strengthens Danticat's argument in any way, or do you think it is irrelevant? Explain.

Writing Practice

1. Write an argument for or against Danticat's position. Make the case that deporting undocumented immigrants who have no criminal records is (or is not) in the best interests of the United States.

2. Write an email to Representative José E. Serrano in which you argue for or against his bill.

Appendix A | Strategies for College Success

A1 Orientation Strategies

Some strategies come in handy even before school begins, as you orient yourself to life as a college student. In fact, you may already have discovered some of them.

1. **Make sure you have everything you need:** a college catalog, a photo ID, a student handbook, a parking permit, and any other items that entering students at your school are expected to have.

2. **Read your school's orientation materials** (distributed as handouts and posted on the school Web site) carefully. These materials will help you familiarize yourself with campus buildings and offices, course offerings, faculty members, extracurricular activities, and so on.

3. **Be sure you know your academic adviser's name** (and how to spell it), email address, and office location. Enter this information into your address book.

4. **Get a copy of your library's orientation materials.** These will tell you about the library's hours and services and explain procedures such as how to use the online catalog.

5. **Be sure you know where things are**—not just how to find the library and the parking lot but also where you can do photocopying or buy a newspaper.

A2 First-Week Strategies

College can seem like a confusing place at first, but from your first day as a college student, there are steps you can take to help you get your bearings.

1. **Make yourself at home.** Find places on campus where you can get something to eat or drink, and find a good place to study or relax before or between classes. As you explore the campus, try to locate all the things you need to feel comfortable—for example, ATMs, rest rooms, and vending machines.

2. **Know where you are going and when you need to be there.** Check the building and room number for each of your classes and the days and hours the class meets. Copy this information onto the front cover of the appropriate notebook. Pay particular attention to classes with irregular schedules (for example, a class that meets from 9 a.m. to 10 a.m. on Tuesdays but from 11 a.m. to noon on Thursdays).

3. **Get to know your fellow students.** Networking with other students is an important part of the college experience. Get the name, phone number, and email address of at least one student in each of your classes. If you miss class, you will need to get in touch with someone to find out what material you missed.

4. **Familiarize yourself with each course's syllabus.** At the first meeting of every course, your instructor will hand out a **syllabus**, an outline or summary of course requirements, policies, and procedures. (The syllabus may also be posted on the course's Web page.) A syllabus gives you three kinds of useful information:

   - Practical information, such as the instructor's office location and phone number and what books and supplies to buy
   - Information that can help you plan a study schedule—for example, when assignments are due and when exams are scheduled
   - Information about the instructor's policies on absences, grading, class participation, and so on

   Read each syllabus carefully, ask questions about anything you do not understand, and refer to all your course syllabi regularly.

5. **Buy books and supplies.** When you buy your books and supplies, be sure to keep the receipts, and do not write your name in your books until you are certain that you are not going to drop a course. (If you write in a book, you will not be able to return it.) If your schedule of courses is not definite, wait a few days to buy your texts. You should, however, buy some items right away: a separate notebook and folder for each course you are taking, a college dictionary, and a pocket organizer (see A4). In addition to the books and other items required for a particular course (for example, a lab notebook, a programmable

WORD POWER
networking interacting with others to share information

calculator, art supplies), you should buy pens and pencils in different colors, paper clips or a stapler, self-stick notes, highlighter pens, and so on. Finally, you will need to buy a backpack or bookbag in which to keep all these items.

Highlight: Using a Dictionary

Even though your computer has a spell checker, you still need to buy a dictionary. A college dictionary tells you not only how to spell words but also what words mean and how to use them.

---

6. **Set up your notebooks.** Establish a separate notebook (or a separate section of a divided notebook) for each of your classes. Write your instructor's name, email address, phone number, and office hours and location on the inside front cover of the notebook; write your own name and email address or phone number on the outside, along with the class location and meeting times. (Notebooks with pocket folders can help you keep graded papers, handouts, and the class syllabus all in one place, near your notes.)

A3   Day-to-Day Strategies

As you get busier and busier, you may find that it is hard to keep everything under control. Here are some strategies to help you as you move through the semester.

1. **Find a place to study.** As a college student, you will need your own private place to work and study. This space should include everything you will need to make your work easier—quiet, good lighting, a comfortable chair, a clean work surface, storage for supplies, and so on.

2. **Set up a bookshelf.** Keep your textbooks, dictionary, calculator, supplies, and everything else you use regularly for your coursework in one place—ideally, in your own workspace. That way, when you need something, you will know exactly where it is.

3. **Set up a study schedule.** Identify thirty- to forty-five-minute blocks of free time before, between, and after classes. Set this time aside for reviewing your notes and assigned reading. Remember, studying

Highlight: Skills Check	Don't wait until you have a paper to write to discover that your computer skills need improvement. Be sure your basic word-processing skills are at the level you need for your work. If you need help, get it right away. Your school's computer lab should be the first place you turn to for help with word processing, but writing center and library staff members may also be able to help you.

should be part of your regular routine, not something you do only the night before an exam.

WORD POWER

priorities things considered more important than others

4. **Establish priorities.** It is very important that you understand what your priorities are. Before you can establish priorities, however, you have to know which assignments are due first, which ones can be done in steps, and which tasks or steps will be most time consuming. Then, you must decide which tasks are most pressing. For example, studying for a test to be given the next day is more pressing than reviewing notes for a test scheduled for the following week. Finally, you have to decide which tasks are more important than others. For example, studying for a midterm is more important than studying for a quiz, and the midterm for a course you are in danger of failing is more important than the midterm for a course in which you are doing well. Remember, you cannot do everything at once; you need to decide what must be done immediately and what can wait.

5. **Check your mail.** Check your campus email regularly—if possible, several times a day. If you miss a message, you may miss important last-minute information about changes in assignments, canceled classes, or rescheduled quizzes.

6. **Schedule conferences.** Try to meet with each of your instructors during the semester even if you are not required to do so. You might schedule one conference during the second or third week of the semester and another a week or two before a major exam or paper is due. Your instructors will respect your initiative.

7. **Become familiar with the student services available on your campus.** There is nothing wrong with getting help from your school's writing center or tutoring center or from the center for disabled students (which serves students with learning disabilities as well as physical challenges), the office of international students, or the counseling center as well as from your adviser or course instructors. Think of yourself as a consumer. You are paying for your education, and you should take advantage of all the available services you need.

Highlight: Asking for Help	Despite all your careful planning, you may still run into trouble. For example, you may miss an exam and have to make it up; you may miss several days of classes in a row and fall behind in your work; you may have trouble understanding the material in one of your courses; or a family member may get sick. Do not wait until you are overwhelmed to ask for help. If you have an ongoing personal problem or a family emergency, let your instructors and the dean of students know immediately.

A4

Time-Management Strategies

Learning to manage your time is very important for success in college. Here are some strategies you can adopt to make this task easier.

1. **Use an organizer.** Whether you prefer a print organizer or an electronic one, you should certainly use one—and use it consistently. If you are most comfortable with paper and pencil, purchase a "week-on-two-pages" academic year organizer (one that begins in September, not January); the "week-on-two-pages" format (see pp. 717 and 718) gives you more writing room for Monday through Friday than for the weekend, and it also lets you view an entire week at once.

   Carry your organizer with you at all times. At the beginning of the semester, copy down key pieces of information from each course syllabus—for example, the date of every quiz and exam and the due date of every paper. As the semester progresses, continue to write in assignments and deadlines. In addition, enter information such as days when a class will be canceled or will meet in the computer lab or in the library, reminders to bring a particular book or piece of equipment to class, and appointments with instructors or other college personnel.

   If you like, you can also jot down reminders and appointments that are not related to school—for example, changes in your work hours, a dental appointment, or lunch with a friend. (In addition to writing notes on the pages for each date, some students like to keep a separate month-by-month "to do" list. Crossing out completed items can give you a feeling of accomplishment—and make the road ahead look shorter.)

   The sample organizer pages on page 717 show how you can use an organizer to keep track of deadlines, appointments, and reminders. The sample organizer pages on page 718 include not only this

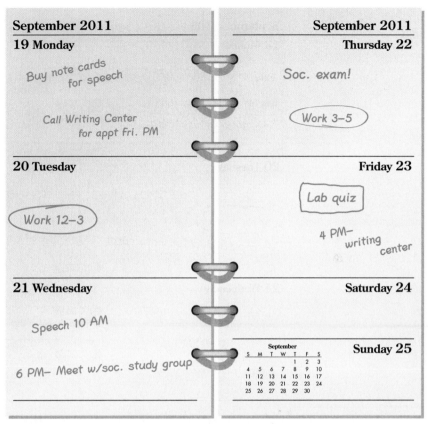

Sample organizer page: deadlines, appointments, and reminders only

information but also a study schedule, with notes about particular tasks to be done each day.

2. **Use a calendar.** Buy a large calendar, and post it where you will see it every morning—on the wall above your desk, on the refrigerator, or wherever you keep your keys and your ID. At the beginning of the semester, fill in important dates such as school holidays, work commitments, exam dates, and due dates for papers and projects. When you return from class each day, update the calendar with any new information you have entered into your organizer.

3. **Plan ahead.** If you think you will need help from a writing-center tutor to revise a paper that is due in two weeks, don't wait until day thirteen to make an appointment; all the tutoring slots may be filled by then. To be safe, make an appointment for help about a week in advance.

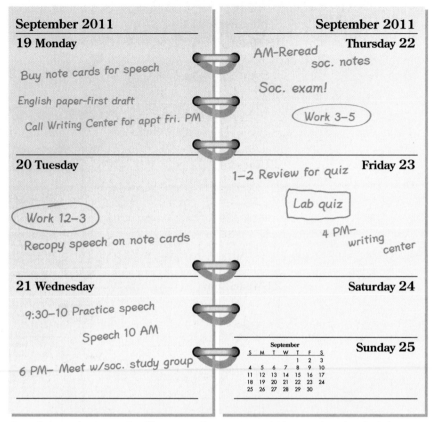

Sample organizer page: deadlines, appointments, reminders, and study schedule

4. **Learn to enjoy downtime.** One final—and important—point to remember is that you are entitled to "waste" a little time. When you have a free minute, take time for yourself—and don't feel guilty about it.

A5   Note-Taking Strategies

Learning how to take notes in a college class takes practice, but taking good notes is essential for success in college. Here are some basic guidelines that will help you develop and improve your note-taking skills.

During Class

1. **Come to class.** If you miss class, you miss notes—so come to class, and come on time. Sit where you can see the board or screen and hear the instructor. Do not feel you have to sit in the same place in each class every day; change your seat until you find a spot that is comfortable for you.

2. **Date your notes.** Begin each class by writing the date at the top of the page. Instructors frequently identify material that will be on a test by dates. If you do not date your notes, you may not know what to study.

3. **Know what to write down.** You cannot possibly write down everything an instructor says. If you try, you will miss a lot of important information. Listen carefully *before* you write, and watch for cues to what is important. For example, sometimes the instructor will tell you that something is important or that a particular piece of information will be on a test. If the instructor emphasizes an idea or underlines it on the board, you should do the same in your notes. (Of course, if you have done the assigned reading before class, you will recognize important topics and know to take especially careful notes when these topics are introduced in class.)

4. **Include examples.** Try to write down an example for each important concept introduced in class—something that will help you remember what the instructor was talking about. (If you do not have time to include examples as you take notes during class, add them when you review your notes.) For instance, if your world history instructor is explaining *nationalism*, you should write down not only a definition but also an example, such as "Germany in 1848."

5. **Write legibly, and use helpful signals.** Use dark (blue or black) ink for your note-taking, but keep a red or green pen handy to highlight important information, jot down announcements (such as a change in a test date), note gaps in your notes, or question confusing points. Do not take notes in pencil, which is hard to read and not as permanent as ink.

6. **Ask questions.** If you do not hear (or do not understand) something your instructor said, or if you need an example to help you understand something, *ask!* Do not immediately turn to another student for clarification. Instead, wait to see if the instructor explains further, or if he or she pauses to ask if anyone has a question. If you are not comfortable asking a question during class, make a note of the question and ask the instructor—or send an email—after class.

After Class

1. **Review your notes.** After every class, try to spend ten or fifteen minutes rereading your notes, filling in gaps and adding examples while the material is still fresh in your mind.

2. **Recopy information.** When you have a break between classes, or when you get back from class, recopy important pieces of information from your notes. (Some students even find it helpful to recopy their notes after every class to reinforce what they have learned.)

   - Copy announcements (such as quiz dates) onto your calendar.
   - Copy reminders (for example, a note to schedule a conference before your next paper is due) into your organizer.
   - Copy questions you want to ask the instructor onto the top of the next blank page in your class notebook.

Before the Next Class

1. **Reread your notes.** Leave time to skim the previous class's notes just before each class. This strategy will get you oriented for the class to come and will remind you of anything that needs clarification or further explanation. (You might want to give each day's notes a title so you can remember the topic of each class. This strategy can also help you find information when you study.)

2. **Ask for help.** Call or email a classmate if you need to fill in missing information; if you still need help, see the instructor during his or her office hours, or come to class early to ask your question before class begins.

A6

Homework Strategies

Doing homework is an important part of your education. Homework gives you a chance to practice your skills and measure your progress. If you are having trouble with the homework, chances are you are having trouble with the course. Ask the instructor or teaching assistant for help *now*; do not wait until the day before the exam. Here are some tips for getting the most out of your homework.

1. **Write down the assignment.** Do not expect to remember an assignment; copy it down. If you are not sure exactly what you are supposed to do, check with your instructor or with another student.

2. **Do your homework, and do it on time.** Teachers assign homework to reinforce classwork, and they expect homework to be done on a regular basis. It is easy to fall behind in college, but trying to do three—or five—nights' worth of homework in one night is not a good idea. If you do several assignments at once, you not only overload yourself but also miss important day-to-day connections with classwork.

3. **Be an active reader.** Get into the habit of highlighting your textbooks and other material as you read.

4. **Join study groups.** A study group of three or four students can be a valuable support system for homework as well as for exams. If your schedule permits, do some homework assignments—or at least review your homework—with other students on a regular basis. In addition to learning information, you will learn different strategies for doing assignments.

A7   Exam-Taking Strategies

Preparation for an exam should begin well before the exam is announced. In a sense, you begin this preparation on the first day of class.

Before the Exam

1. **Attend every class.** Regular attendance in class—where you can listen, ask questions, and take notes—is the best possible preparation for exams. If you do have to miss a class, arrange to copy (and read) another student's notes *before the next class* so you will be able to follow the discussion.

2. **Keep up with the reading.** Read every assignment, and read it before the class in which it will be discussed. If you do not, you may have trouble understanding what is going on in class.

3. **Take careful notes.** Take careful, thorough notes, but be selective. If you can, compare your notes on a regular basis with those of other students in the class; working together, you can fill in gaps or correct

errors. Establishing a buddy system will also force you to review your notes regularly instead of just on the night before the exam.

4. **Study on your own.** When an exam is announced, adjust your study schedule—and your priorities—so you have time to review everything. (This is especially important if you have more than one exam in a short period of time.) Over a period of several days, review all your material (class notes, readings, and so on), and then review it again. Make a note of anything you do not understand, and keep track of topics you need to review. Try to predict the most likely questions, and—if you have time—practice answering them.

5. **Study with a group.** If you can, set up a study group. Studying with others can help you understand the material better. However, do not come to group sessions unprepared and expect to get all the information you need from the other students. You must first study on your own.

6. **Make an appointment with your instructor.** Make a conference appointment with the instructor or with the course's teaching assistant a few days before the exam. Bring to this meeting any specific questions you have about course content and about the format of the upcoming exam. (Be sure to review all your material before the conference.)

7. **Review the material one last time.** The night before the exam is not the time to begin your studying; it is the time to review. When you have finished your review, get a good night's sleep.

Highlight: Writing Essay Exams

If an exam question asks you to write an essay, remember that what you are really being asked to do is write a **thesis-and-support essay**. Chapter 12 tells you how to do this.

During the Exam

By the time you walk into the exam room, you will already have done all you could to get ready for the test. Your goal now is to keep the momentum going and not do anything to undermine all your hard work.

1. **Read through the entire exam.** Be sure you understand how much time you have, how many points each question is worth, and exactly what each question is asking you to do. Many exam questions call for

just a short answer—*yes* or *no*, *true* or *false*. Others ask you to fill in a blank with a few words, and still others require you to select the best answer from among several choices. If you are not absolutely certain what kind of answer a particular question calls for, ask the instructor or the proctor *before* you begin to write.

2. **Budget your time.** Once you understand how much each section of the exam and each question are worth, plan your time and set your priorities, devoting the most time to the most important questions.

3. **Reread each question.** Carefully reread each question *before* you start to answer it. Underline the **key words**—the words that give specific information about how to approach the question and how to phrase your answer.

    Remember, even if everything you write is correct, your response is not acceptable if you do not answer the question. If a question asks you to *compare* two novels, writing a *summary* of one of them will not be acceptable.

Highlight: Key Words

Here are some helpful key words to look for on exams.

analyze	explain	suggest results, effects, outcomes
argue	give examples	
compare	identify	summarize
contrast	illustrate	support
define	recount	take a stand
demonstrate	suggest causes, origins, contributing factors	trace
describe		
evaluate		

---

4. **Brainstorm to help yourself recall the material.** If you are writing a paragraph or an essay, look frequently at the question as you brainstorm. (You can write your brainstorming notes on the inside cover of the exam book.) Quickly write down all the relevant points you can think of—what the textbook had to say, your instructor's comments in class, and so on. The more information you can think of now, the more you will have to choose from when you write your answer.

5. **Write down the main idea.** Looking closely at the way the question is worded and at your brainstorming notes, write a sentence that expresses the main idea of your answer. If you are writing a paragraph,

this sentence will be your **topic sentence**; if you are writing an essay, it will be your **thesis statement**.

6. **List your main points.** You do not want to waste your limited (and valuable) time making a detailed outline, but an informal outline that lists just your key points is worth the little time it takes. An informal outline will help you plan a clear direction for your paragraph or essay.

7. **Draft your answer.** You will spend most of your time actually writing the answers to the questions on the exam. Follow your outline, keep track of time, and consult your brainstorming notes when you need to—but stay focused on your writing.

8. **Reread, revise, and edit.** When you have finished drafting your answer, reread it carefully to make sure it says everything you want it to say—and that it answers the question.

Highlight: Academic Honesty

Academic honesty—the standard for truth and fairness in work and behavior—is very important in college. Understanding academic honesty goes beyond simply knowing that it is dishonest to cheat on a test. To be sure you are conforming to the rules of academic honesty, you need to pay attention to the following situations:

- Don't reuse papers you wrote in high school. The written work you are assigned in college is designed to help you learn, and your instructors expect you to do the work for the course when it is assigned.

- Don't copy information from a book or article or paste material from a Web site directly into your papers. Using someone else's words or ideas without proper acknowledgment constitutes **plagiarism**, a very serious offense.

- Don't ask another student (or your parents) to help you write or revise a paper. If you need help, ask your instructor or a writing center tutor.

- Don't allow another student to copy your work on a test.

- Don't allow another student to turn in a paper you wrote (or one you helped him or her write).

- Don't work with other students on a take-home exam unless your instructor gives you permission to do so.

- Never buy a paper. Even if you edit it, it is still not your own work.

Appendix B Using Research in Your Writing

In many writing assignments, you use your own ideas to support your points. In other essays—such as argument essays—you may need to supplement your own ideas with **research**: information from outside sources, such as books, periodicals (journals, magazines, and newspapers), and the Internet. You will have an easier time writing your essay if you follow the steps discussed below.

B1 Choosing a Topic

The first step in writing an essay that calls for research is finding a topic to write about. Before you choose a topic, ask the following questions.

- What is your page limit?
- When is your paper due?
- How many sources are you expected to use?
- What kind of sources are you expected to use?

These questions will help you tell if your topic is too broad or too narrow.

When May Compton, a student in a composition course, was asked to write a three- to four-page essay that was due in five weeks, she decided that she wanted to write about the counterfeit designer goods that she saw for sale everywhere. She knew, however, that the general topic "counterfeit designer goods" would be too broad to cover in a short essay.

May was used to seeing sidewalk vendors selling brand-name sunglasses and jewelry. Recently, she and her friends had been invited to a "purse party," where they were able to buy designer handbags at extremely low prices. Even though these handbags were not identified as fakes, she was sure that they were. Because May was a marketing major, she wondered how these copies were marketed and sold. She also wondered if these counterfeits had any negative effects on consumers. May decided to narrow her topic to the problems that occur when consumers buy counterfeit designer merchandise. She thought she could discuss this topic in the required number of pages and would be able to finish her paper within the five-week time limit.

B2 Doing Research

Finding Information in the Library

The best place to start your research is with the resources of your college library: print and electronic resources that you cannot find anywhere else—including on the Internet. For the best results, you should do your library research systematically. Begin by searching the library's online catalog and electronic databases; then, look for any additional facts or statistics that you need to support your ideas.

Remember, once you find information in the library, you still have to **evaluate** it—that is, to determine its usefulness and reliability. For example, an article in a respected newspaper such as the *New York Times*

Highlight: The Resources of the Library

WORD POWER
periodical a magazine or newspaper published regularly—for example, daily or weekly

The Online Catalog

Once you get a general sense of your topic, you can consult the library's catalog. Libraries have **online catalogs** that enable you to use your computer to search all the resources held by the library. By typing in words or phrases related to your topic, you can find books, periodicals, and other materials that you can use in your paper.

Electronic Databases

After consulting the online catalog, you should look at the **electronic databases** that your library subscribes to. These databases enable you to access information from newspapers, magazines, and journals. Some databases list just citations, while others enable you to retrieve the full text of articles. (You can usually search your library's databases from home or from your dorm room.)

Sources for Facts and Statistics

As you write your paper, you may find that you need certain facts or statistics to support particular points. Sources like *Facts on File*, the *Information Please Almanac*, and the *Statistical Abstract of the United States* can help you find such information. These and similar sources (which your reference librarian can recommend) are available online.

WORD POWER

tabloid a newspaper that focuses on stories with sensational content

or the *Wall Street Journal* is more trustworthy and believable than one in a tabloid such as the *National Enquirer* or the *Sun*. You should also look at the date of publication to decide if a book or article is up to date. Finally, consider the author. Is he or she an expert? Does the author have a particular point of view to advance? Your instructor or college librarian can help you select sources that are both appropriate and reliable.

Finding Information on the Internet

The Internet can give you access to a great deal of information that can help you support your points and develop your essay. To use the Internet, you need a **search engine**, software that helps you find information by sorting through the millions of documents that are available on the Internet. Among the most popular search engines are *Google* and *Yahoo!*.

There are three ways to use a search engine to find information.

1. **You can enter a Web site's URL.** All search engines have a box in which you can enter a Web site's electronic address, or **uniform resource locator (URL)**. When you click on the URL or hit your computer's Enter or Return key, the search engine connects you to the Web site.

2. **You can do a keyword search.** All search engines let you do a **keyword search**. You type a term into a box, and the search engine looks for documents that contain the term, listing all the **hits** (documents containing one or more of the words you entered) that it found.

3. **You can do a subject search.** Some search engines, such as *Yahoo!*, let you do a **subject search**. First, you choose a broad subject from a list of subjects: The Humanities, The Arts, Entertainment, Business, and so on. Each of these general subjects leads you to more specific subjects, until eventually you get to the subtopic that you want.

Highlight: Avoiding Plagiarism	When you transfer information from Web sites into your notes, you may be tempted to "cut and paste" text without recording where the text came from. If you then copy this text into a draft of your paper, you are committing **plagiarism**—that is, stealing someone else's ideas. Every college has rules that students must follow when using words, ideas, and visuals from books, periodical articles, and Internet sources. Consult your writing center's Web site or your school's student handbook for information on the appropriate use of such information.

Not every site you access will turn out to be a valuable source of information. Just as you would with a print source, you should determine whether information you find on the Internet is believable and useful.

May Compton began her research by doing a subject search of her library's online catalog to see what books it listed on her topic. Under the general subject of *counterfeits*, she found the headings *counterfeit coins* and *counterfeit money*. She did not, however, find any books on counterfeit designer goods. She thought that her topic might be too recent for any books to have been published on the subject, so she turned to her library's databases.

A quick look at the *Infotrac* database showed May that many recent articles had been written about counterfeit designer merchandise. Although some articles only reported police raids on local counterfeiting operations, a few discussed the reasons for counterfeiting and the negative effects of counterfeit goods.

Because May's topic was so current, however, she found that the Internet was her best source of information. Using the keywords *counterfeit designer goods* and *designer handbags knockoffs*, she located several recent newspaper and magazine articles about her topic. For example, using *Google* to search for the term *counterfeit designer goods*, she found a site maintained by the Resource for Security Executives that gave recent statistics of counterfeit seizures by the Department of Homeland Security. Using the same search terms on *Yahoo!*, May found an article in the *Arizona Republic* that discussed the purse parties that are often used to sell counterfeit designer handbags.

B3   Taking Notes

Once you have gathered the source material you will need, read it carefully, recording any information you think you can use in your paper. (Record your notes on index cards, or in computer files you have created for this purpose.)

In your notes, you will *paraphrase*, *summarize*, and *quote* your sources. As you do so, keep your topic in mind; this will help you decide what material is useful.

Paraphrasing

When you **paraphrase**, you use your own words to create a detailed restatement of the main ideas of a source. You paraphrase when you want detailed information from the source but not the author's exact words. Paraphrase is useful when you want to make a complex discussion easier to understand while still giving readers a clear sense of the original.

Highlight: Writing a Paraphrase	1. Read the passage until you understand it.
	2. Jot down the main idea of the passage, and list all key supporting points.
	3. Draft your paraphrase, beginning with the main idea and then presenting the source's key supporting points.
	4. When you revise, make sure you have used your own words and phrasing, and not the words or sentence structure of the original. Use quotation marks to identify any unique terms or phrases that you have borrowed from the source.
	5. Document your source.

Here is a passage from the article "Hot Fakes," by Joanie Cox, followed by May's paraphrase.

Original

Always pay close attention to the stitching. On a Kate Spade bag, the logo is stitched perfectly straight; it's not a sticker. Most designers stitch a simple label to the inside of their purses. On Chanel bags, however, the interior label is usually stamped and tends to match the color of the exterior. Study the material the bag is made from. A real Chanel Ligne Cambon multipocket bag, for example, is constructed from buttery lambskin leather, not vinyl.

Paraphrase

It is often possible to tell a fake designer handbag from a genuine one by looking at the details. For example, items such as logos should not be crooked. You should also look for the distinctive features of a particular brand of handbag. Counterfeiters will not take the time to match colors, and they may use vinyl instead of expensive leather (Cox).

Summarizing

Unlike a paraphrase, which restates the ideas of a source in detail, a **summary** is a general restatement, in your own words, of the main idea of a passage. For this reason, a summary is always much shorter than the original.

Highlight: Writing a Summary	1. Read the passage until you understand it.
	2. Jot down the main idea of the passage.
	3. Draft your summary, being careful to use your own words, not those of your source.
	4. When you revise, make sure your summary expresses the source's main idea.
	5. Document your source.

Here is May's summary of the original passage on page 729.

Summary

Buyers who want to identify fake handbags should check details such as the way the label is sewn and the material the item is made from (Cox).

Quoting

When you **quote**, you use the author's exact words as they appear in the source, including all punctuation and capitalization. Enclose all words from your source in quotation marks—*followed by appropriate documentation.* Because quotations can distract readers, use them only when you think that the author's exact words will add something to your discussion.

Highlight: When to Quote	1. Quote when the words of a source are unique or so memorable that to put them into your own words would lessen their impact.
	2. Quote when the words of a source are so concise that a paraphrase or summary would change the meaning of the original.
	3. Quote when the words of a source add authority to your discussion. The words of a recognized expert can help you make your point convincingly.

Here is how May incorporated a quotation from the original passage on page 729 into her notes.

Quotation

Someone who wants to buy an authentic designer handbag should look carefully at the material the purse is made from. For example, there is a big difference between vinyl and Chanel's "buttery lambskin leather" (Cox).

B4   Watching Out for Plagiarism

As a rule, you must **document** (give source information for) all words, ideas, or statistics from an outside source. You must also document all visuals—tables, graphs, photographs, and so on—that you do not create yourself. (It is not necessary, however, to document **common knowledge**, factual information widely available in various reference works.)

When you present information from another source as if it is your own (whether you do it intentionally or unintentionally), you commit **plagiarism**—and plagiarism is theft. You can avoid plagiarism by understanding what you must document and what you do not have to document.

Highlight: What to Document

You should document

- All word-for-word quotations from a print or electronic source
- All summaries and paraphrases of material from a source
- All ideas—opinions, judgments, and insights—that are not your own
- All tables, graphs, charts, and statistics from a source

You do not need to document

- Your own ideas
- Common knowledge
- Familiar quotations

Read the following paragraph from "The Facts on Fakes!" (an unsigned article on the National Association of Resale & Thrift Shops Web site) and the four rules that follow the paragraph. These rules will help you understand the most common causes of plagiarism and show you how to avoid it.

Original

Is imitation really the sincerest form of flattery? Counterfeiting deceives the consumer and tarnishes the reputation of the genuine manufacturer. Brand value can be destroyed when a trademark is imposed on counterfeit products of inferior quality—hardly a form of flattery! Therefore, prestigious companies who are the targets of counterfeiters have begun to battle an industry that copies and sells their merchandise. They have filed lawsuits and in some cases have employed private investigators across the nation to combat the counterfeit trade. A quick search of the Internet brings up dozens of press releases from newspapers throughout the country, all reporting instances of law enforcement cracking down on sellers of counterfeit goods by confiscating bogus merchandise and imposing fines.

Rule 1. Document Ideas from Your Sources

Plagiarism

When counterfeits are sold, the original manufacturer does not take it as a compliment.

Even though the student writer does not actually quote from her source, she must still identify the article as the source of this material because it expresses the article's ideas, not her own.

Correct

When counterfeits are sold, the original manufacturer does not take it as a compliment ("Facts").

Rule 2. Place Borrowed Words in Quotation Marks

Plagiarism

It is possible to ruin the worth of a brand by selling counterfeit products of inferior quality — hardly a form of flattery ("Facts").

Although the student writer cites the source, the passage incorrectly uses the source's exact words without placing them in quotation marks. (All borrowed words must be placed in quotation marks.)

Correct (Borrowed Words in Quotation Marks)

It is possible to ruin the worth of a brand by selling "counterfeit products of inferior quality — hardly a form of flattery!" ("Facts").

Rule 3. Use Your Own Phrasing

Plagiarism

Is copying a design a compliment? Not at all. The fake design not only fools the buyer but also harms the original company. It can ruin the worth of a brand. Because counterfeits are usually of poor quality, they pay the original no compliment. As a result, companies whose products are often copied have started to fight back. They have sued the counterfeiters and have even used private detectives to identify phony goods. Throughout the United States, police have fined people who sell counterfeits and have seized their products ("Facts").

Even though the student writer acknowledges "The Facts on Fakes!" as her source, and even though she does not generally use the source's exact words, her passage closely follows the order, emphasis, sentence structure, and phrasing of the original.

In the following passage, the writer uses her own wording, quoting one distinctive phrase from the source.

Correct

According to "The Facts on Fakes!" it is not a compliment when an original design is copied by a counterfeiter. The poor quality of most fakes is "hardly a form of flattery!" The harm to the image of the original manufacturers has caused them to fight back against the counterfeiters, sometimes using their own detectives. As a result, lawsuits and criminal charges have led to fines and confiscated merchandise ("Facts").

Rule 4. Distinguish Your Ideas from the Source's Ideas

Plagiarism

Counterfeit goods are not harmless. Counterfeiting not only fools the consumer, but it also destroys consumer confidence in the quality of the real item. Manufacturers know this and have begun to fight back. A number have begun to sue "and in some cases have employed private investigators across the nation to combat the counterfeit trade" ("Facts").

In the passage above, only the quotation in the last sentence seems to be borrowed from the article "The Facts on Fakes!" In fact, however, the ideas in the second sentence also come from this article.

In the following passage, the writer uses an identifying phrase to acknowledge the borrowed material in this sentence.

Correct

Counterfeit goods are not harmless. According to the article "The Facts on Fakes!" counterfeiting not only fools the consumer, but it also destroys consumer confidence in the quality of the real item. Manufacturers know this and have begun to fight back. A number have begun to sue "and in some cases have employed private investigators across the nation to combat the counterfeit trade" ("Facts").

B5   Developing a Thesis

After you have taken notes, review the information you have gathered, and develop a thesis statement. Your **thesis statement** is a single sentence that states the main idea of your paper and tells readers what to expect. After reviewing her notes, May Compton came up with the following thesis statement for her paper on counterfeit designer goods.

Thesis Statement

People should not buy counterfeit designer merchandise, no matter how tempted they are to do so.

B6   Making an Outline

Once you have a thesis statement, you are ready to make an outline. Your outline, which covers just the body paragraphs of your paper, can be either a **topic outline** (in which each idea is expressed in a word or a short phrase) or a **sentence outline** (in which each idea is expressed in a complete sentence). After reviewing her notes, May Compton wrote the following sentence outline for her paper.

I. Real designer goods are too expensive.
   A. Genuine designer merchandise costs ten times more than it costs to make it.
   B. Even people who can afford it buy fakes.
II. Buying designer knockoffs is a form of stealing.
   A. The buyer is stealing the work of the original designer.
   B. Counterfeiting operations take jobs away from legitimate workers.
   C. The buyer is stealing the sales taxes that would be paid by the original designer.

III. Buying designer knockoffs supports organized crime.
    A. The production of designer knockoffs requires money and organization.
    B. Buying knockoffs supports illegal activities.
        1. The profits of selling knockoffs support murder, prostitution, and drugs.
        2. Knockoffs are made in shops that violate the law.
IV. There is evidence that designer knockoffs support terrorism.
    A. The 1993 World Trade Center bombing has been connected to a counterfeit operation.
    B. The 2001 World Trade Center terrorist attack has been connected to counterfeiting.
    C. The 2004 Madrid train bombing has been connected to counterfeiting.

B7   Writing Your Paper

Once you have decided on a thesis and written an outline, you are ready to write a draft of your essay.

- Begin with an **introduction** that includes your thesis statement. Usually, your introduction will be a single paragraph, but sometimes it will be longer.

- In the **body** of your essay, support your thesis statement with specific evidence. Each body paragraph should develop a single point, and these paragraphs should have clear topic sentences so that your readers will know exactly what points you are making. Use transitional words and phrases to help readers follow your ideas.

- Finally, write a **conclusion** that gives readers a sense of completion. Like your introduction, your conclusion will usually be a single paragraph, but it can be longer. It should include a summary statement that reinforces your thesis statement.

Remember, you will probably write several drafts of your essay before you hand it in. You can use the **TEST** checklist on page 181 to make sure your essay includes all necessary elements. You can also use the Self-Assessment Checklists in 12I and 12J to help you revise and edit your paper.

May Compton's completed essay on counterfeit designer goods begins on page 743.

B8 Documenting Your Sources

When you **document** your sources, you tell readers where you found the information you used in your essay. The Modern Language Association (MLA) recommends the following documentation style for essays that use sources. This format consists of *parenthetical references* in the body of the paper that refer to a *works-cited list* at the end of the paper.

Parenthetical References in the Text

A parenthetical reference should include enough information to lead readers to a specific entry in your works-cited list. A typical parenthetical reference consists of the author's last name and the page number (Brown 2). If you use more than one work by the same author, include a shortened form of the title in the parenthetical reference (Brown, "Demand" 2). Notice that there is no comma and no *p* or *p.* before the page number.

Whenever possible, introduce information from a source with a phrase that includes the author's name. (If you do this, include only the page number in parentheses.) Place documentation so that it does not interrupt the flow of your ideas, preferably at the end of a sentence.

> As Jonathan Brown observes in "Demand for Fake Designer Goods Is Soaring," as many as 70 percent of buyers of luxury goods are willing to wear designer brands alongside of fakes (2).

In the four special situations listed below, the format for parenthetical references departs from these guidelines.

1. *When You Are Citing a Work by Two Authors*

   Instead of buying nonbranded items of similar quality, many customers are willing to pay extra for the counterfeit designer label (Grossman and Shapiro 79).

2. *When You Are Citing a Work without Page Numbers*

   A seller of counterfeited goods in California "now faces 10 years in prison and $20,000 in fines" (Cox).

3. *When You Are Citing a Work without a Listed Author or Page Numbers*

   More counterfeit goods come from China than from any other country ("Counterfeit Goods").

Note: Material from the Internet or from a library's electronic databases frequently lacks publication information—for example, page numbers. For this reason, the parenthetical references that cite it may contain just the author's name (as in example 2 on p. 736) or just a shortened title (as in example 3 on p. 736) if the article appears without an author.

4. When You Are Citing a Statement by One Author That Is Quoted in a Work by Another Author

Speaking of consumers' buying habits, designer Miuccia Prada says, "There is a kind of an obsession with bags" (qtd. in Thomas 23).

Highlight: Formatting Quotations

- **Short quotations** Quotations of no more than four typed lines are run in with the text of your paper. End punctuation comes after the parenthetical reference (which follows the quotation marks).

  According to Dana Thomas, customers often "pick up knockoffs for one-tenth the legitimate bag's retail cost, then pass them off as real" ("Terror's Purse Strings").

- **Long quotations** Quotations of more than four lines are set off from the text of your paper. Begin a long quotation one inch from the left-hand margin, and do not enclose it in quotation marks. Do not indent the first line of a single paragraph. If a quoted passage has more than one paragraph, indent the first line of each paragraph (including the first) an extra one-quarter inch. Introduce a long quotation with a complete sentence followed by a colon, and place the parenthetical reference one space *after* the end punctuation.

  In her article, Dana Thomas describes a surprise visit to a factory that makes counterfeit purses:

  > On a warm winter afternoon in Guangzhao, I accompanied Chinese police officers on a raid in a decrepit tenement. We found two dozen children, ages 8 to 13, gluing and sewing together fake luxury-brand handbags. The police confiscated everything, arrested the owner and sent the children out. Some punched their timecards, hoping to still get paid. ("Terror's Purse Strings")

The Works-Cited List

The works-cited list includes all the works you **cite** (refer to) in your essay. Use the guidelines in the box on pages 741–42 to help you prepare your list.

The following sample works-cited entries cover the situations you will encounter most often. Follow the sample entries exactly as they appear here.

Books

Books by One Author

List the author with last name first. Italicize the title. Include the city of publication and a shortened form of the publisher's name—for example, *Bedford* for *Bedford/St. Martin's*. Use the abbreviation *UP* for *University Press*, as in *Princeton UP* and *U of Chicago P.* Include the date of publication. End with the medium of publication, such as *Print* or *Web*.

> Russo, Richard. *Bridge of Sighs*. New York: Knopf, 2007. Print.

Note: MLA recommends that you put book titles in italics.

Books by Two or Three Authors

List second and subsequent authors with first name first, in the order in which they are listed on the book's title page.

> Mooney, Chris, and Sheril Kirshenbaum. *Unscientific America: How Scientific Illiteracy Threatens Our Future*. New York: Basic, 2009. Print.

Books by More than Three Authors

List only the first author, followed by the abbreviation *et al.* ("and others").

> Beer, Andrew, et al. *Consuming Housing?: Transitions through the Housing Market in the 21st Century*. Bristol: Policy, 2010. Print.

Two or More Books by the Same Author

List two or more books by the same author in alphabetical order according to title. In each entry after the first, use three unspaced hyphens (followed by a period) instead of the author's name.

> Alda, Alan. *Never Have Your Dog Stuffed*. New York: Arrow, 2007. Print.
>
> ---. *Things I Overheard While Talking to Myself*. New York: Random, 2007. Print.

Edited Book

Thompson, Hunter S. *Gonzo*. Ed. Steve Crist. Los Angeles: Ammo, 2007. Print.

Translation

Garcia Marquez, Gabriel. *Living to Tell the Tale*. Trans. Edith Grossman. New York: Knopf, 2004. Print.

Revised Edition

Roberts, Cokie. *We Are Our Mothers' Daughters*. Rev. ed. New York: Collins, 2010. Print.

Anthology

Adler, Frances P., Debra Busman, and Diana Garcia, eds. *Fire and Ink: An Anthology of Social Action Writing*. Tucson: U of Arizona P, 2009. Print.

Essay in an Anthology

Welty, Eudora. "Writing and Analyzing a Story." *Signet Book of American Essays*. Ed. M. Terry Weiss and Helen Weiss. New York: Signet, 2006. 21-30. Print.

Section or Chapter of a Book

Mueenuddin, Daniyal. "Lily." *In Other Rooms, Other Wonders*. New York: Norton, 2010. Print.

Periodicals

Journals

A **journal** is a periodical aimed at readers who know a lot about a particular subject—literature or history, for example. The articles that journals contain can sometimes be challenging.

Some scholarly journals have continuous pagination; that is, one issue might end on page 234, and the next issue would then begin with page 235. Others have separate pagination in each issue. For both types of journals, include the volume number, followed by a period and the issue number. Leave no space after the period.

Article in a Journal with Continuous Pagination throughout Annual Volume

Kessler-Harris, Alice. "Why Biography?" *American Historical Review* 114.3 (2009): 625-30. Print.

Article in a Journal with Separate Pagination in Each Issue

> Favret, Mary A. "Jane Austen at 25: A Life in Numbers." *English Language Notes* 46.1 (2008): 9-20. Print.

Magazines

A **magazine** is a periodical aimed at general readers. For this reason, it contains articles that are easier to understand than those in scholarly journals. Frequently, an article in a magazine is not printed on consecutive pages. For example, it may begin on page 40, skip to page 47, and continue on page 49. If this is the case, your citation should include only the first page, followed by a plus sign.

Article in a Monthly or Bimonthly Magazine

> McLean, Bethany. "Fannie Mae's Last Stand." *Vanity Fair* Feb. 2009: 118+. Print.

> Larmer, Brook. "The Real Price of Gold." *National Geographic* Jan. 2009: 34-61. Print.

Article in a Weekly or Biweekly Magazine

> Weisberg, Jacob. "All Lobbyists Are Not Created Equal." *Newsweek* 27 Apr. 2009: 35. Print.

Newspapers

Article in a Newspaper

> Campoy, Ana. " 'Water Hog' Label Haunts Dallas." *Wall Street Journal* 15 July 2009: A4. Print.

Editorial

> "Waiting Game." Editorial. *New York Times* 15 July 2009: A24. Print.

Internet Sources

Full source information is not always available for Internet sources. When citing Internet sources, include whatever information you can find—ideally, the name of the author (or authors), the title of the article or other document (in quotation marks), the title of the site (italicized), the sponsor or publisher, the date of publication or last update, and the date on which you accessed the source. Include the medium of publication (*Web*) between the publication date and the access date.

It is not necessary to include a Web address (URL) when citing an electronic source. Readers can usually find the source merely by typing the author, title, and other identifying information into a search engine or database. However, you should include a URL if your instructor requires that you do so or if you think readers might not be able to locate the source without it. In these cases, enclose the URL in angle brackets at the end of your citation (as illustrated in the "Personal Site" entry below).

Document within a Web Site

Baker, Fred W. "Army Lab Works to Improve Soldier Health, Performance." *DefenseLINK*. U.S. Department of Defense, 25 June 2009. Web. 15 August 2009.

Personal Site

Bricklin, Dan. Home page. Dan Bricklin, 7 July 2009. Web. 15 July 2009. <www.bricklin.com>.

Article in an Online Reference Book or Encyclopedia

"Sudan." *Infoplease World Atlas and Map Library*. Pearson Education, 2009. Web. 29 Apr. 2009.

Article in a Newspaper

Wilbon, Michael. "The 'One and Done' Song and Dance." *Washington Post*. The Washington Post Company, 25 June 2009. Web. 1 Sept. 2009.

Editorial

"Innovation and the LAUSD." Editorial. *Los Angeles Times*. Los Angeles Times, 14 July 2009. Web. 31 July 2009.

Article in a Magazine

Chen, Brian X. "Microsoft to Open Retail Stores Next to Apple's." *Wired*. CondéNet, 15 July 2009. Web. 15 July 2009.

Highlight: Preparing the Works-Cited List

- Begin the works-cited list on a new page after the last page of your paper.
- Number the works-cited page as the next page of your paper.
- Center the heading *Works Cited* one inch from the top of the page; do not italicize the heading or place it in quotation marks.
- Double-space the list.
- List entries alphabetically according to the author's last name.

Highlight: Preparing the Works-Cited List
continued

- Alphabetize unsigned articles according to the first major word of the title.
- Begin typing each entry at the left-hand margin.
- Indent second and subsequent lines one-half inch.
- Separate major divisions of each entry—author, title, and publication information—by a period and one space.

Sample MLA-Style Paper

On the pages that follow is May Compton's completed essay on the topic of counterfeit designer goods. The paper uses MLA documentation style and includes a works-cited page.

Compton 1

May Compton

Professor DiSalvo

English 100

29 April 2009

The True Price of Counterfeit Goods

At purse parties in city apartments and suburban homes, customers can buy "designer" handbags at impossibly low prices. On street corners, sidewalk vendors sell name-brand perfumes and sunglasses for much less than their list prices. On the Internet, buyers can buy fine watches for a fraction of the prices charged by manufacturers. Is this too good to be true? Of course it is. All of these "bargains" are knockoffs—copies of the real thing. What the people who buy these items do not know (or prefer not to think about) is that the money they are spending supports organized crime—and, sometimes, terrorism. For this reason, people should not buy counterfeit designer merchandise, no matter how tempted they are to do so.

People who buy counterfeit designer merchandise defend their actions by saying that designer products cost too much. This is certainly true. According to Dana Thomas, the manufacturers of genuine designer merchandise charge more than ten times what it costs to make it. A visitor from Britain, who bought an imitation Gucci purse in New York City for fifty dollars, said, "The real thing is so overpriced. To buy a genuine Gucci purse, I would have to pay over a thousand dollars" (qtd. in "Counterfeit Goods"). Even people who can easily afford to pay the full amount buy fakes. For example, movie stars like Jennifer Lopez openly wear counterfeit goods, and many customers think that if it is all right for celebri-

ties like Lopez to buy fakes, it must also be all right for them too

(Malone). However, as the well-known designer Giorgio Armani

points out, counterfeiters create a number of problems for legiti-

mate companies because they use the brand name but do not

maintain quality control ("10 Questions").

What most people ignore is that buying counterfeit items is

really stealing. The FBI estimates that in the United States alone,

companies lose about $250 billion as a result of counterfeits

(Wallace). In addition, buyers of counterfeit items avoid the state

and local sales taxes that legitimate companies pay. Thus, New York

City alone loses about a billion dollars every year as a result of the

sale of counterfeit merchandise ("Counterfeit Goods"). When this

happens, everyone loses. After all, a billion dollars would pay for a

lot of police officers and teachers, would fill a lot of potholes, and

would pave a lot of streets. Buyers of counterfeit designer goods

do not think of themselves as thieves, but that is exactly what they

really are.

Buyers of counterfeit merchandise also do not realize that the

sale of knockoffs supports organized crime. Most of the profits go

to the criminal organization that either makes or imports the coun-

terfeit goods—not to the person who sells the items. In fact, the

biggest manufacturer and distributor of counterfeit items is orga-

nized crime (Nellis). Michael Kessler, who heads a company that

investigates corporate crime, makes this connection clear when

he describes the complicated organization that is needed to make

counterfeit perfume:

Paragraph contains
May's own ideas
combined with para-
phrases of material
from two articles

Compton 3

Long quotation is set
off one inch from the
text

> They need a place that makes bottles, a factory with
>
> pumps to fill the bottles, a printer to make the labels,
>
> and a box manufacturer to fake the packaging. Then,
>
> they need a sophisticated distribution network, as well
>
> as all the cash to set everything up. (qtd. in Malone)

Kessler concludes that only an organized crime syndicate—not
any individual—has the money to support this illegal activity. For
this reason, anyone who buys counterfeits may also be supporting activities such as prostitution, drug distribution, smuggling of
illegal immigrants, gang warfare, extortion, and murder (Nellis). In
addition, the workers who make counterfeits often work in sweatshops where labor and environmental laws are ignored. The illegal
factories are often located in countries where children usually work
long hours for very low pay (Malone). In fact, as Dana Thomas
points out, a worker in China who makes counterfeits earns only a
fraction of the salary of a worker who makes the real thing.

Paragraph contains
May's own ideas as
well as a paraphrase
and a quotation

Finally, and perhaps most shocking, is the fact that some of
the money earned from the sale of counterfeit designer goods also
supports international terrorism. For example, Kim Wallace reports
that during Al-Qaeda training, terrorists are advised to sell fakes to
get money for their operations. According to Interpol, an international police organization, the bombing of the World Trade Center
in 1993 was paid for in part by the sale of counterfeit T-shirts.
Also, evidence suggests that associates of the 2001 World Trade
Center terrorists may have been involved with the production of
imitation designer goods (Malone). Finally, the 2004 bombing of
commuter trains in Madrid was financed in part by the sale of

Compton 4

counterfeits. In fact, an intelligence source states, "It would be more shocking if Al Qaeda *wasn't* involved in counterfeiting. The sums involved are staggering—it would be inconceivable if money were not being raised for their terrorist activities" (qtd. in Malone). Most people would never consciously support terrorism, but customers who buy counterfeit purses or fake perfume may be doing just that.

Consumers should realize that when they buy counterfeits, they are actually breaking the law. By doing so, they are making it possible for organized crime syndicates and terrorists to earn money for their illegal activities. Although buyers of counterfeit merchandise justify their actions by saying that the low prices are impossible to resist, they might reconsider if they knew the uses to which their money was going. The truth of the matter is that counterfeit designer products, such as handbags, sunglasses, jewelry, and T-shirts, are "luxuries" that people could do without. By resisting the temptation to buy knockoffs, consumers could help to eliminate the companies that hurt legitimate manufacturers, exploit workers, and even finance international terrorism.

Conclusion contains May's original ideas, so no documentation is necessary

Compton 5

Works Cited

Armani, Giorgio. "10 Questions for Giorgio Armani." *Time*. Time,

12 Feb. 2009. Web. 24 Mar. 2009.

"Counterfeit Goods Are Linked to Terror Groups." *International*

Herald Tribune. International Herald Tribune, 12 Feb. 2007.

Web. 24 Mar. 2009.

Malone, Andrew. "Revealed: The True Cost of Buying Cheap Fake

Goods." *Mail Online*. Daily Mail, 29 July 2007. Web. 25 Mar.

2009.

Nellis, Cynthia. "Faking it: Counterfeit Fashion." *About.com:*

Women's Fashion. About.com, 2009. Web. 24 Mar. 2009.

Thomas, Dana. "Terror's Purse Strings." Editorial. *New York Times*

30 Aug. 2007, late ed.: A23. Print.

Wallace, Kim. "A Counter-Productive Trade." *TimesDaily.com*. Times

Daily, 29 July 2007. Web. 31 Mar. 2009.

This Internet source has no listed author.

Answers to Odd-Numbered Exercise Items

Chapter 15

● Practice 15-1, page 264

Answers: 1. Derek Walcott **3.** Walcott **5.** poems
7. Walcott **9.** he **11.** poet

● Practice 15-2, page 264

Answers: 1. seeds; plural **3.** industry; singular
5. fruit; singular **7.** The United States and Europe;
plural **9.** pomegranate; singular

● Practice 15-3, page 265

Possible answers: 1. I **3.** we **5.** snakes
7. water **9.** athletes

● Practice 15-4, page 267

Answers: 1. ~~In presidential elections,~~ third-party
candidates have attracted many voters. **3.** ~~In the~~
~~1912 race with Democrat Woodrow Wilson and~~
~~Republican William H. Taft,~~ Roosevelt ran second
~~to Wilson.~~ **5.** ~~In recent years,~~ however, some
candidates ~~of other parties~~ made strong showings.
7. ~~With nearly 19 percent of the popular vote,~~
Independent Ross Perot ran a strong race ~~against~~
~~Democrat Bill Clinton and Republican George Bush~~
~~in 1992.~~ **9.** ~~In 2004,~~ Nader was also ~~on the ballot~~
~~in many states.~~

● Practice 15-5, page 268

Answers: 1. see **3.** offers **5.** enters; wins
7. realizes **9.** enjoy

● Practice 15-6, page 269

Answers: 1. are **3.** are **5.** is **7.** becomes
9. are

● Practice 15-7, page 270

Answers: 1. is **3.** is; seems **5.** lives **7.** dies
9. works

● Practice 15-8, page 271

Answers: 1. Complete verb: had become; helping
verb: had **3.** Complete verb: had become; helping

verb: had **5.** Complete verb: would get; helping
verb: would **7.** Complete verb: did cause;
helping verb: did **9.** Complete verb: would remain;
helping verb: would

Chapter 16

● Practice 16-1, page 278

Possible answers: 1. and **3.** and **5.** and
7. so/and **9.** for

● Practice 16-2, page 279

Possible answers: 1. Training a dog to heel is
difficult, for dogs naturally resist strict control.
3. Students should spend two hours studying for
each hour of class time, or they may not do well in
the course. **5.** Each state in the United States has
two senators, but the number of representatives
depends on a state's population. **7.** A "small craft
advisory" is an important warning for boaters, for
bad weather conditions can be dangerous to small
boats. **9.** Hip-hop fashions include sneakers and
baggy pants, and these styles are very popular
among today's young men.

● Practice 16-3, page 280

Possible edits: Diet, exercise, and family history
may account for centenarians' long lives, but this is
not the whole story. One study showed surprising
common traits among centenarians. They did not
necessarily avoid tobacco and alcohol, nor did they
have low-fat diets. In fact, they consumed relatively
large amounts of fat, cholesterol, and sugar, so diet
could not explain their long lives. They did, however,
share several key survival characteristics. First, all of
the centenarians were optimistic about life, and all of
them were positive thinkers. They were also involved
in religious life and had deep religious faith. In
addition, all the centenarians had continued to lead
physically active lives, and they remained mobile
even as elderly people. Finally, all were able to adapt
to loss. They had all experienced the deaths of

748

friends, spouses, or children, but they were able to get on with their lives.

● Practice 16-4, page 280

Answers will vary.

● Practice 16-5, page 282

Answers will vary.

● Practice 16-6, page 285

Answers: **1.** Andrew F. Smith, a food historian, wrote a book about the tomato; later, he wrote a book about ketchup.   **3.** The word *ketchup* may have come from a Chinese word; however, Smith is not certain of the word's origins.   **5.** Ketchup has changed a lot over the years; for example, special dyes were developed in the nineteenth century to make it red.   **7.** Ketchup is now used by people in many cultures; still, salsa is more popular than ketchup in the United States.   **9.** Some of today's ketchups are chunky; in addition, some ketchups are spicy.

● Practice 16-7, page 286

Possible answers: **1.** Every year since 1927, *Time* has designated a Man of the Year; however, the Man of the Year has not always been a man.   **3.** During World War II, Hitler, Stalin, Churchill, and Roosevelt were all chosen; in fact, Stalin was featured twice. **5.** In 1956, The Hungarian Freedom Fighter was Man of the Year; then, in 1966, *Time* editors chose The Young Generation.   **7.** In 1975, American Women were honored as a group; nevertheless, the Man of the Year has nearly always been male.   **9.** The Man of the Year has almost always been one or more human beings; however, The Computer was selected in 1982 and Endangered Earth in 1988.   **11.** In 2003, *Time* did not choose a politician; instead, it honored The American Soldier.   **13.** In 2005, *Time* wanted to honor the contributions of philanthropists; thus, the magazine named Bill Gates, Melinda Gates, and Bono its Persons of the Year.   **15.** For 2008, however, *Time* chose a person again; then, its pick was Barack Obama.

● Practice 16-8, page 287

Possible answers: **1.** Campus residents may have a better college experience; still, being a commuter has its advantages.   **3.** Commuters have a wide choice of jobs in the community; on the other hand, students living on campus may have to take on-campus jobs. **5.** There are also some disadvantages to being a commuter; for example, commuters may have trouble joining study groups.   **7.** Commuters might have to help take care of their parents or grandparents; in addition, they might have to babysit for younger siblings.   **9.** Younger commuters may be under the watchful eyes of their parents; of course, parents are likely to be stricter than resident advisors.

Practice 16-9, page 288

Answers will vary.

Chapter 17

● Practice 17-1, page 295

Answers: **1.** DC   **3.** DC   **5.** IC   **7.** IC   **9.** IC

● Practice 17-2, page 296

Answers: **1.** IC   **3.** IC   **5.** DC   **7.** DC   **9.** IC

● Practice 17-3, page 299

Possible answers: **1.** even though   **3.** where **5.** because   **7.** in order to   **9.** as if   **11.** when

● Practice 17-4, page 299

Possible answers: **1.** Although professional midwives are used widely in Europe, in the United States, they are less common.   **3.** Stephen Crane describes battles in *The Red Badge of Courage* even though he never experienced a war.   **5.** After Edward Jenner developed the smallpox vaccine in the 1800s, the number of smallpox cases declined. **7.** Before the Du Ponts arrived from France in 1800, American gunpowder was not as good as French gunpowder.   **9.** Because Thaddeus Stevens thought plantation land should be given to freed slaves, he disagreed with Lincoln's peace plan for the South.

● Practice 17-5, page 302

Possible answers: **1.** Dependent clause: which was performed by a group called the Buggles; relative pronoun: which; noun: video   **3.** Dependent clause: who had been doubtful of MTV at first; relative pronoun: who; noun: executives   **5.** Dependent clause: which first aired in September 1984; relative pronoun: which; noun: presentation   **7.** Dependent clause: who starred in *Newlyweds: Nick and Jessica* in 2003; relative pronoun: who; noun: Jessica Simpson **9.** Dependent clause: which feature cast members doing good deeds; relative pronoun: which; noun: shows

● Practice 17-6, page 302

Possible answers: 1. The Harry Potter books, which follow the young wizard from age 11 to 17, have become international best-sellers.   **3.** Harry faces many challenges that test his courage and willpower.   **5.** Harry goes to school at Hogwarts, which is a boarding school for young wizards and witches.   **7.** Albus Dumbledore, who is the head-master of Hogwarts, is Harry's mentor.   **9.** The film adaptations of the books, which star Daniel Radcliffe as Harry, have been very successful.

Chapter 18

● Practice 18-1, page 310

Answers will vary.

● Practice 18-2, page 311

Revised sentences will vary. Adverbs: 1. however **3.** often   **5.** now

● Practice 18-3, page 312

Answers will vary.

● Practice 18-4, page 312

Revised sentences will vary. Prepositional phrases: 1. during World War II   **3.** between 1942 and 1945 **5.** after the war

● Practice 18-5, page 313

Answers will vary.

● Practice 18-6, page 314

Possible answers: 1. In the Cuban-American community, people often mention José Julián Martí as one of their heroes.   **3.** By the time he was sixteen years old, he had started a newspaper demanding Cuban freedom.   **5.** Openly continuing his fight, he published his first pamphlet calling for Cuban independence while in Spain.   **7.** During his time in New York, he started the journal of the Cuban Revolutionary party.   **9.** Passionately following up his words with action, he died in battle against Spanish soldiers in Cuba.

● Practice 18-7, page 315

Possible answers: 1. Changing from green to red, special lamps in the dorms of one Ohio college warn of rising energy use.   **3.** Tending a campus vegetable plot, student gardeners at a North Carolina college

supply the cafeteria with organic produce.   **5.** Offering courses in sustainability, some colleges are preparing students to take the green revolution beyond campus.

● Practice 18-8, page 316

Possible answers: 1. Captured as a young girl by a rival tribe, Sacajawea was later sold into slavery. **3.** Hired by the explorers Lewis and Clark in 1806, Charbonneau brought his pregnant wife along on their westward expedition.   **5.** Created in 2000, a U.S. dollar coin shows her picture.

● Practice 18-9, page 318

Answers will vary.

● Practice 18-10, page 320

Possible answers: 1. A playwright who wrote the prize-winning *A Raisin in the Sun*, Lorraine Hansberry was born in Chicago in 1930.   **3.** Hostile neighbors there threw a brick through a window of their house, an act Hansberry never forgot.

● Practice 18-11, page 322

Possible edits: Kente cloth is made in western Africa and produced primarily by the Ashanti people. It has been worn for hundreds of years by African royalty, who consider it a sign of power and status. Many African Americans wear kente cloth because they see it as a link to their heritage. Each pattern on the cloth has a name, and each color has a special significance. For example, red and yellow suggest a long and healthy life while green and white suggest a good harvest. Although African women may wear kente cloth as a dress or head wrap, African-American women, like men, usually wear strips of cloth around their shoulders. Men and women of African descent wear kente cloth as a sign of racial pride; in fact, it often decorates college students' gowns at graduation.

Chapter 19

● Practice 19-1, page 328

Answers: 1. The food in the cafeteria is varied, tasty, and healthy.   **3.** Last summer I worked at the library, babysat my neighbor's daughter, and volunteered at a soup kitchen.   **5.** P   **7.** P   **9.** P

● Practice 19-2, page 330

Answers will vary.

Chapter 20

● Practice 20-1, page 336

Answers: 1. a game of mahjong; a patch of muddy ground   **3.** the grassy field; chestnut-colored horses; heavy red and black market bags   **5.** wrinkled hands; a frown

● Practice 20-2, page 336

Answers will vary.

● Practice 20-3, page 337

Answers will vary.

● Practice 20-4, page 339

Possible edits: 1. Although Robert Frost's home is a national landmark, local teenagers broke into the house in 2007 to have a party.   **3.** Because a hiker soon discovered the break-in, the police were quickly able to find the suspects.   **5.** After discussing his idea with a local college professor, the judge required the teenagers to take a course in Robert Frost's poetry as part of their sentence.   **7.** The instructor, who had been teaching poetry for many years, knew that usually students could relate to two of Frost's poems: "Out, Out—" and "The Road Not Taken."
9. "The Road Not Taken" is suitable for these teens because they would always face choices in life, and in this case, they had taken the wrong road.

● Practice 20-5, page 340

Answers will vary.

● Practice 20-6, page 342

Possible answers: 1. Many people think that a million-dollar lottery jackpot allows the winner to stop working long hours and start living a comfortable life.   **3.** For one thing, lottery winners who win big prizes do not always receive their winnings all at once; instead, payments—for example, $50,000—can be spread out over twenty years.   **5.** Next come relatives and friends who ask for money, leaving winners with difficult choices to make.   **7.** Even worse, many lottery winners have lost their jobs because employers thought that once they were "millionaires," they no longer needed the salary.
9. Faced with financial difficulties, many might like to sell their future payments to companies that offer lump-sum payments of forty to forty-five cents on the dollar.

● Practice 20-7, page 343

Answers will vary.

● Practice 20-8, page 344

Answers will vary.

● Practice 20-9, page 345

Possible edits: 1. Many people today would like to see more police officers patrolling the streets.
3. All the soldiers picked up their weapons.
5. Travel to other planets will be a significant step for humanity.

Chapter 21

● Practice 21-1, page 356

Answers: 1. FS   **3.** CS   **5.** CS   **7.** C   **9.** FS

● Practice 21-2, page 356

Answers: 1. CS   **3.** CS   **5.** CS   **7.** C   **9.** C

● Practice 21-3, page 358

Answers: 1. Hurricane Katrina destroyed many homes in New Orleans. It destroyed many businesses, too.   **3.** Americans watched the terrible scenes. Hundreds died waiting for rescuers.
5. Residents of flooded communities vowed to return. They knew it would not be easy.

● Practice 21-4, page 359

Answers: 1. Right after World War II, some television programs showed actual scenes of war, and *Victory at Sea* and *The Big Picture* were two of those programs.   **3.** In the 1970s, *M*A*S*H* depicted a Korean War medical unit, yet the show was really about the Vietnam War.   **5.** The contemporary drama *Army Wives* focuses on the home front, but it occasionally shows scenes of the Iraq War.

● Practice 21-5, page 360

Answers: 1. New Mexico governor Bill Richardson has been a U.N. ambassador and a congressman; he also served as U.S. energy secretary.   **3.** Roberto Clemente was a professional baseball player; Oscar de la Hoya achieved fame as a professional boxer.
5. Luis Valdez is a noted playwright and film director; his plays include *Los Vendidos* and *The Zoot Suit*.

● Practice 21-6, page 361

Answers: **1.** High schools have always taught subjects like English and math; now, many also teach personal finance and consumer education.   **3.** Consumer-education courses can be very practical; for instance, students can learn how to buy, finance, and insure a car.   **5.** Academic subjects will always dominate the high school curriculum; however, courses focusing on practical life skills are becoming increasingly important.

● Practice 21-7, page 363

Possible answers: **1.** Even though contemporary historians have written about the Harlem Renaissance, its influence is still not widely known.   **3.** As this migration from the South continued, Harlem became one of the largest African-American communities in the United States.   **5.** This "Harlem Renaissance" was an important era in American literary history although it is not even mentioned in some textbooks.   **7.** After Zora Neale Hurston moved to Harlem from her native Florida in 1925, she began a book of African-American folklore.   **9.** When the white playwright Eugene O'Neill went to Harlem to audition actors for his play *The Emperor Jones*, he made an international star of the great Paul Robeson.

● Practice 21-8, page 364

Possible answers: **1.** Nursing offers job security and high pay; therefore, many people are choosing nursing as a career.   **3.** The Democratic Republic of the Congo was previously known as Zaire; it was previously called the Belgian Congo.   **5.** Millions of Jews were murdered during the Holocaust; in addition, Catholics, Gypsies, homosexuals, and other "undesirables" were killed.   **7.** Japanese athletes now play various positions on American baseball teams; at first, all the Japanese players were pitchers.   **9.** Père Noël is the French name for Santa Claus; he is also known as Father Christmas and St. Nicholas.

● Practice 21-9, page 365

Possible answers: **1.** Scientists suspected the existence of Pluto as early as 1846. They believed it was causing the changes they observed in Neptune's orbit.   **3.** Percival Lowell founded the Lowell Observatory in 1894, and he began searching for a ninth planet in 1906.   **5.** The newly discovered ninth planet made international headlines; in fact, thousands of people sent in ideas for names.   **7.** Scientists at the Lowell Observatory liked the name because the planet is cold and far away like the underworld.   **9.** Later, Walt Disney borrowed the name for a new cartoon character; in addition, a new element was named plutonium.

Chapter 22

● Practice 22-1, page 372

Answers: **1.** F   **3.** F   **5.** F   **7.** F   **9.** F

● Practice 22-2, page 372

Answers: Items 2, 4, 6, and 7 are fragments. *Rewrite:* Sara Paretsky writes detective novels, such as *Hardball* and *Guardian Angel*. These novels are about V. I. Warshawski, a private detective. V. I. lives and works in Chicago, the Windy City. Every day as a detective, V. I. takes risks. V. I. is tough. She is also a woman.

● Practice 22-3, page 374

Answers will vary.

● Practice 22-4, page 376

Answers: **1.** The U.S. flag was designed by Francis Hopkinson, a New Jersey delegate to the Continental Congress.   **3.** Congress officially recognized the Pledge of Allegiance in 1942, the year after the United States entered World War II.   **5.** Some people wanted a different national anthem, such as "America" or "America the Beautiful."

● Practice 22-5, page 377

Answers: **1.** First-born children are reliable, serious, and goal-oriented in most cases.   **3.** In large families, middle children often form close relationships outside of the family.   **5.** Youngest children often take a while to settle down into careers and marriages.

● Practice 22-6, page 378

Answers will vary.

● Practice 22-7, page 380

Answers: **1.** Always try to find a store brand costing less than the well-known and widely advertised brands.   **3.** Examine sale-priced fruits and vegetables, checking carefully for damage or spoilage.   **5.** Buy different brands of the same product, trying each one to see which brand you like best.

● Practice 22-8, page 381

Answers will vary.

● Practice 22-9, page 382

Answers: 1. Psychologists need advanced degrees to practice as licensed therapists.   **3.** In 1941, Japan attacked the United States naval base at Pearl Harbor to weaken America's position in the Pacific. **5.** Scientists sent remote-controlled robots, called "rovers," to Mars to take photographs of the planet's surface.

● Practice 22-10, page 383

Answers will vary.

● Practice 22-11, page 386

Answers will vary.

● Practice 22-12, page 387

Answers will vary.

● Practice 22-13, page 388

Answers will vary.

Chapter 23

● Practice 23-1, page 396

Answers: 1. know   **3.** include   **5.** sell; top **7.** tend; seem   **9.** deserve

● Practice 23-2, page 396

Answers: 1. overlook   **3.** ignore   **5.** make **7.** visit   **9.** range   **11.** offer

● Practice 23-3, page 398

Answers: 1. fill   **3.** grade   **5.** triggers   **7.** lead **9.** greet

● Practice 23-4, page 400

Answers: 1. have   **3.** has   **5.** do   **7.** is   **9.** has

● Practice 23-5, page 401

Answers: 1. The <u>roses</u> ~~along the side of the house~~ <u>bloom</u> all summer long.   **3.** The <u>tools</u> ~~in my garage~~ <u>belong</u> to a friend.   **5.** A tropical <u>storm</u> ~~with heavy rain and strong winds~~ <u>moves</u> quickly.   **7.** <u>Workers</u>

~~with a college degree~~ <u>earn</u> more money than those without a degree.   **9.** <u>Vegetarians,</u> ~~especially those who do not eat eggs or cheese,~~ <u>need</u> to be careful to get enough vitamins in their diets.

● Practice 23-6, page 403

Answers: 1. meets   **3.** is   **5.** wants

● Practice 23-7, page 404

Answers: 1. has   **3.** work   **5.** are   **7.** tend **9.** says

● Practice 23-8, page 406

Answers: 1. Subject: Bering Strait; verb: is **3.** Subject: twins; verb: Are   **5.** Subject: this; verb: has   **7.** Subject: people; verb: are   **9.** Subject: reasons; verb: are

Chapter 24

● Practice 24-1, page 412

Answers: 1. At the start of World War II, 120,000 Japanese Americans were sent to relocation camps because the government feared that they might be disloyal to the United States.   **3.** The Japanese-American volunteers were organized into the 442nd Combat Infantry Regiment.   **5.** When other U.S. troops were cut off by the enemy, the 442nd Infantry soldiers were sent to rescue them.   **7.** Former senator Daniel Inouye of Hawaii, a Japanese American who was awarded the Distinguished Service Cross for his bravery in Italy, had to have his arm amputated.   **9.** Today the dedication and sacrifice of the 442nd Infantry is evidence that Japanese Americans were patriotic and committed to freedom and democracy.

● Practice 24-2, page 414

Answers: 1. Young people who want careers in the fashion industry do not always realize how hard they will have to work.   **3.** In reality, no matter how talented he or she is, a recent college graduate entering the industry is paid less than $30,000 a year.   **5.** A young designer may receive a big raise if he or she is very talented, but this is unusual. **7.** An employee may be excited to land a job as an assistant designer but then find that he or she has to color in designs that have already been drawn. **9.** If a person is serious about working in the fashion industry, he or she has to be realistic.

● Practice 24-3, page 416

Answers: 1. A local university funded the study, and Dr. Alicia Flynn led the research team.   **3.** Two-thirds of the subjects relied on intuition, and only one-third used logic.   **5.** Many experts read the report, and most of them found the results surprising.

Chapter 25

● Practice 25-1, page 422

Answers will vary.

● Practice 25-2, page 423

Answers will vary.

● Practice 25-3, page 424

Possible answers: 1. Driving to work on Interstate 5, my brother was surprised to see a bear.   **3.** The volunteers easily identified the hawks tagged with metal bracelets.   **5.** Wearing her warmest coat, Molly went outside to look for her dog.   **7.** The brick house at the corner of Huron and Willow is still on the market.   **9.** Yelling from the stands, fans cheered on the Detroit Tigers.

Chapter 26

● Practice 26-1, page 435

Answers: 1. My mother always returned from India with intricate designs on her hands and feet.
3. Henna originated in a plant found in the Middle East, India, Indonesia, and northern Africa.   **5.** Men dyed their beards, as well as the manes and hooves of their horses, with henna.   **7.** In India, my mother always celebrated the end of the Ramadan religious fast by going to a "henna party."   **9.** After a few weeks, the henna designs washed off.

● Practice 26-2, page 438

Answers: 1. came; was   **3.** went   **5.** became
7. thought   **9.** began

● Practice 26-3, page 439

Answers: 1. Correct   **3.** was   **5.** were   **7.** was
9. Correct

● Practice 26-4, page 441

Answers: 1. can   **3.** will   **5.** could   **7.** can
9. will

Chapter 27

● Practice 27-1, page 447

Answers: 1. visited   **3.** raised   **5.** joined
7. removed   **9.** served

● Practice 27-2, page 451

Answers: 1. been; been   **3.** built   **5.** become
7. written   **9.** said

● Practice 27-3, page 452

Answers: 1. become   **3.** led   **5.** Correct
7. spoken; Correct   **9.** Correct

● Practice 27-4, page 454

Answers: 1. visited   **3.** belonged   **5.** spoke
7. made   **9.** were

● Practice 27-5, page 454

Answers: 1. has changed   **3.** filled   **5.** have developed   **7.** invented   **9.** have grown

● Practice 27-6, page 456

Answers: 1. had raised   **3.** had found   **5.** has saved   **7.** have camped   **9.** have learned

● Practice 27-7, page 457

Answers: 1. surprised; preapproved   **3.** designed
5. stuffed   **7.** concerned   **9.** acquired

Chapter 28

● Practice 28-1, page 465

Answers: 1. headaches (regular)   **3.** feet (irregular)   **5.** deer (irregular)   **7.** brides-to-be (irregular)   **9.** loaves (irregular)   **11.** beaches (regular)   **13.** sons-in-law (irregular)   **15.** wives (irregular)   **17.** elves (irregular)   **19.** catalogs (regular)

● Practice 28-2, page 466

Answers: 1. travelers-to-be   **3.** Correct; delays; duties   **5.** Correct; boxes   **7.** Correct; lotions; drinks; quantities   **9.** contents; Correct; cups

● Practice 28-3, page 468

Answers: 1. I   **3.** we   **5.** It; I; she   **7.** their
9. they; we

● Practice 28-4, page 469

Answers: **1.** Antecedent: campuses; pronoun: they   **3.** Antecedent: students; pronoun: their   **5.** Antecedent: students; pronoun: they   **7.** Antecedent: students; pronoun: them

● Practice 28-5, page 470

Answers: **1.** Compound antecedent: Mary-Kate and Ashley; connecting word: and; pronoun: their   **3.** Compound antecedent: Chinese and Arabic; connecting word: and; pronoun: their   **5.** Compound antecedent: Homer or Bart; connecting word: or; pronoun: his   **7.** Compound antecedent: Adam and Nathan; connecting word: and; pronoun: their   **9.** Compound antecedent: Robins and finches; connecting word: and; pronoun: their

● Practice 28-6, page 473

Answers: **1.** Indefinite pronoun: Either; pronoun: its   **3.** Indefinite pronoun: Everything; pronoun: its   **5.** Indefinite pronoun: Neither; pronoun: her   **7.** Indefinite pronoun: Several; pronoun: their   **9.** Indefinite pronoun: Anyone; pronoun: his or her

● Practice 28-7, page 473

Possible answers: **1.** Everyone has the right to his or her own opinion.   **3.** Somebody forgot his or her backpack.   **5.** Someone has left his or her car headlights on.   **7.** Each of the applicants must have his or her driver's license.   **9.** Either of the coffee-makers comes with its own filter.

● Practice 28-8, page 474

Answers: **1.** Collective noun antecedent: company; pronoun: its   **3.** Collective noun antecedent: government; pronoun: its   **5.** Collective noun antecedent: union; pronoun: its

● Practice 28-9, page 475

Answers: **1.** Antecedent: women; pronoun: Correct   **3.** Antecedent: women; pronoun: their   **5.** Antecedent: Elizabeth Cady Stanton and Lucretia Mott; pronoun: their   **7.** Antecedent: women; pronoun: their   **9.** Antecedent: the U.S. government; pronoun: its

● Practice 28-10, page 477

Answers: **1.** Subjective   **3.** Subjective   **5.** Possessive   **7.** Possessive; Objective; Objective

● Practice 28-11, page 479

Answers: **1.** I   **3.** I   **5.** Correct   **7.** she; I   **9.** her

● Practice 28-12, page 480

Answers: **1.** [they like] him   **3.** [it affected] me   **5.** [it fits] me

● Practice 28-13, page 482

Answers: **1.** whom   **3.** Whom   **5.** whom

● Practice 28-14, page 483

Answers: **1.** themselves   **3.** himself   **5.** yourself

Chapter 29

● Practice 29-1, page 490

Answers: **1.** great   **3.** simply   **5.** passionately   **7.** exact   **9.** unique

● Practice 29-2, page 491

Answers: **1.** well   **3.** good   **5.** well   **7.** well   **9.** well

● Practice 29-3, page 494

Answers: **1.** more slowly   **3.** healthier   **5.** more distinctly   **7.** more respectful   **9.** wilder

● Practice 29-4, page 495

Answers: **1.** surest; most shocking   **3.** most recent   **5.** most competitive   **7.** safest; most easily   **9.** most likely; most visible

● Practice 29-5, page 496

Answers: **1.** better   **3.** better; worse   **5.** better   **7.** best   **9.** better

Chapter 30

● Practice 30-1, page 502

Answers: **1.** When the first season of the reality show *Survivor* aired, <u>it</u> was an immediate hit.   **3.** <u>It</u> was not surprising to see the many other reality shows that suddenly appeared on the air.   **5.** Most viewers thought that reality TV had gone too far even though <u>they</u> enjoyed shows like *Jon and Kate Plus 8* and *So You Think You Can Dance*.

● Practice 30-2, page 503

Possible answers: **1.** The first parts of the Great Wall were built around 200 A.D. **3.** The sides of the Great Wall are made of stone, brick, and earth. **5.** The Great Wall is so huge that it can be seen by astronauts in space.

● Practice 30-3, page 504

Answers: **1.** people; dogs **3.** benefits; hours **5.** monkeys; parrots; pigs; horses; people; disabilities **7.** chores **9.** attacks

● Practice 30-4, page 506

Answers: **1.** Count **3.** Noncount **5.** Noncount **7.** Count **9.** Count

● Practice 30-5, page 509

Answers: **1.** every **3.** A few violent **5.** many **7.** Many **9.** some

● Practice 30-6, page 512

Answers: **1.** A; No article needed **3.** the; a; the **5.** the; No article needed; the **7.** No article needed; No article needed; No article needed **9.** the; the **11.** An; the; an **13.** No article needed; the; the; No article needed

● Practice 30-7, page 515

Answers will vary.

● Practice 30-8, page 519

Answers: **1.** were signing: Correct **3.** was: Correct; was believing: believed; was: Correct **5.** study: Correct; want: Correct; have left: Correct **7.** are often seeing: often see; are touching: touch; pick up: Correct **9.** weigh: Correct; are deciding: decide

● Practice 30-9, page 521

Answers: **1.** might **3.** should **5.** should **7.** Would **9.** can

● Practice 30-10, page 522

Answers: **1.** Eating **3.** cleaning **5.** Quitting **7.** organizing **9.** cooking

● Practice 30-11, page 524

Answers: **1.** a brand-new high-rise apartment building **3.** numerous successful short-story collections **5.** the publisher's three best-selling

works **7.** a strong-willed young woman **9.** an exquisite white wedding gown

● Practice 30-12, page 529

Answers: **1.** in; in **3.** in; at; to **5.** in; in; in **7.** to; in; with; from; to; with; with **9.** with; at; of **11.** on; on **13.** to

● Practice 30-13, page 532

Answers: **1.** Most fans of the characters in Stephenie Meyer's popular *Twilight* series know that Meyer first thought them up in a dream. **3.** Because Meyer immediately knew their story and just needed to put it on paper, she was able to complete her first book, *Twilight*, in just three months. **5.** Correct **7.** Unfortunately, the first twelve chapters of *Midnight Sun* showed up online after an unexplained leak. **9.** She promised to return to the draft and assured fans that she was not throwing it away.

Chapter 31

● Practice 31-1, page 544

Answers: **1.** The musician plays guitar, bass, and drums. **3.** Correct **5.** The diary Anne Frank kept while her family hid from the Nazis is insightful, touching, and sometimes humorous. **7.** Correct **9.** California's capital is Sacramento, its largest city is Los Angeles, and its oldest settlement is San Diego.

● Practice 31-2, page 545

Answers: **1.** In the past few years, many Olympic athletes have been disqualified because they tested positive for banned drugs. **3.** In the past, banned steroids were the most common cause of positive drug tests. **5.** Correct **7.** In some cases, athletes' drug use was not uncovered until the games were long over. **9.** Having witnessed many scandals and disappointments, today's fans are suspicious of extraordinary athletic feats.

● Practice 31-3, page 547

Answers: **1.** Some holidays are fairly new; the African-American celebration of Kwanzaa, for example, was only introduced in the 1960s. **3.** By the way, the word *Kwanzaa* means "first fruits" in Swahili. **5.** This, of course, can be demonstrated in some of the seven principles of Kwanzaa. **7.** The focus, first of all, is on unity (*umoja*). **9.** In addition,

Kwanzaa celebrations emphasize three kinds of community responsibility (*ujima, ujamaa,* and *nia*).

● Practice 31-4, page 548

Answers: 1. Traditional Chinese medicine is based on meridians, channels of energy believed to run in regular patterns through the body. **3.** Herbal medicine, the basis of many Chinese healing techniques, requires twelve years of study. **5.** Correct **7.** Nigeria, the most populous country in Africa, is also one of the fastest-growing nations in the world. **9.** The Yoruba people, the Nigerian settlers of Lagos, are unusual in Africa because they tend to form large urban communities.

● Practice 31-5, page 551

Answers: 1. Correct **3.** Correct **5.** The Japanese had just landed in the Aleutian Islands, which lie west of the tip of the Alaska Peninsula. **7.** As a result, they made them work under conditions that made construction difficult. **9.** In one case, white engineers who surveyed a river said it would take two weeks to bridge. **11.** Correct

● Practice 31-6, page 553

Answers: 1. The American Declaration of Independence was approved on July 4, 1776. **3.** At 175 Carlton Avenue, Brooklyn, New York, is the house where Richard Wright began writing *Native Son*. **5.** Correct **7.** The Pueblo Grande Museum is located at 1469 East Washington Street, Phoenix, Arizona. **9.** St. Louis, Missouri, was the birthplace of writer Maya Angelou, but she spent most of her childhood in Stamps, Arkansas.

● Practice 31-7, page 555

Answers: 1. The capital of the Dominican Republic is Santo Domingo. **3.** Some of the most important crops are sugarcane, coffee, cocoa, and rice. **5.** Correct **7.** Tourists who visit the Dominican Republic remark on its tropical beauty. **9.** Correct

Chapter 32

● Practice 32-1, page 562

Answers: 1. Bacteria and viruses, which we can't see without a microscope, kill many people every year, but they are not the only deadly creatures. **3.** After you're bitten, stung, or stuck, how long does

it take to die? **5.** The sea wasp is actually a fifteen-foot-long jellyfish, and although it's not aggressive, it can be deadly. **7.** While jellyfish found off the Atlantic coast of the United States can sting, they aren't as dangerous as the sea wasp, whose venom is deadly enough to kill sixty adults. **9.** Correct

● Practice 32-2, page 563

Answers: 1. the singer's video **3.** everybody's favorite band **5.** the players' union **7.** the children's bedroom **9.** everyone's dreams

● Practice 32-3, page 565

Answers: 1. Parents; theirs **3.** its; weeks **5.** Ryans; years **7.** classes; Correct; your **9.** tests

Chapter 33

● Practice 33-1, page 572

Answers: 1. Marsupials have pouches; mothers carry their young in these pouches. **3.** Correct **5.** Many thousands of years ago, marsupials were common in South America; now, they are extinct.

● Practice 33-2, page 573

Answers: 1. Four parks with religious themes are the Holy Land Experience, Dinosaur Adventure Land, Ganga-Dham, and City of Revelation. **3.** An advertisement for Dinosaur Adventure Land describes it in these words: "where dinosaurs and the Bible meet!" **5.** Correct

● Practice 33-3, page 575

Possible answers: 1. In the 1950s, Bob Cousy was a star player for the Boston Celtics. Cousy (an "old man" at age thirty-four) led his team to their fifth NBA championship in 1963. **3.** Many people still consider game 5 of the 1976 NBA finals—which the Celtics won in triple overtime—the greatest basketball game ever played. **5.** Today, young players (some joining the NBA right out of high school) dream of making names for themselves as their heroes did.

Chapter 34

● Practice 34-1, page 581

Answers: 1. Midwest; Lake; Chicago; O'Hare International Airport; nation's **3.** north; Soldier

Field; Chicago Bears; Wrigley Field; Chicago Cubs; National League baseball team   **5.** John Kinzie
7. United States; Mrs.; cow   **9.** mother; Aunt Jean; Uncle Amos

● Practice 34-2, page 584

Answers: **1.** "The bigger they are," said boxer John L. Sullivan, "the harder they fall."   **3.** Lisa Marie replied, "I do."   **5.** "Yabba dabba doo!" Fred exclaimed. "This brontoburger looks great."

● Practice 34-3, page 585

Possible answers: **1.** "Revenge only engenders violence, not clarity and true peace," wrote Mexican-American author Sandra Cisneros. "I think liberation must come from within."   **3.** "Imagination is more important than knowledge," said physicist Albert Einstein.   **5.** "I hate admitting that my enemies have a point," wrote British novelist Salman Rushdie.

● Practice 34-4, page 586

Answers: **1.** Sui Sin Far's short story "The Wisdom of the New," from her book Mrs. Spring Fragrance, is about the clash between Chinese and American cultures in the early twentieth century.   **3.** Interesting information about fighting skin cancer can be found in the article "Putting Sunscreens to the Test," which appeared in the magazine Consumer Reports.
5. Ang Lee has directed several well-received films, including Crouching Tiger, Hidden Dragon and Brokeback Mountain.   **7.** The title of Lorraine

Hansberry's play A Raisin in the Sun comes from Langston Hughes's poem "Harlem."

● Practice 34-5, page 588

Answers: **1.** When fans of the television show *Lost* voted for their favorite episodes, "Through the Looking Glass," "The Shape of Things to Come," and "The Incident" were in the top ten.   **3.** Before being elected president, Barack Obama wrote and published two books: *Dreams from My Father* and *The Audacity of Hope.*   **5.** *Janis Joplin's Greatest Hits* includes songs written by other people, such as "Piece of My Heart," as well as songs she wrote herself, such as "Mercedes Benz."

● Practice 34-6, page 589

Answers: **1.** The ice-skating rink finally froze over.
3. The first-year students raised money for charity.
5. The hand-carved sculpture looked like a pair of doves.

● Practice 34-7, page 590

Answers: **1.** The doctor diagnosed a case of hypertension.   **3.** Derek registered for English literature and a psychology elective.   **5.** The clinic is only open Tuesday through Thursday and every other Saturday.

● Practice 34-8, page 591

Answers: **1.** Only two students in the eight o'clock lecture were late.   **3.** Chapter 6 begins on page 873.
5. Meet me at 65 Cadman Place.

Acknowledgments

Picture acknowledgments

2TL Bill Aron/PhotoEdit Inc.; **2TR** Chung Sung-Jun/Getty Images; **2BL** Tiffany Schoepp/Blend Images/Getty Images; **2BR** Rene Sheret/Getty Images; **28** Richard Ross/Photodisc/Getty Images; **50** Courtesy of Broward College. Used with permission; **60** Bill Aron/PhotoEdit Inc.; **62** Twentieth Century Fox/Photofest; **70** Jupiter Images; **72** Jacksonville Journal Courier/The Image Works; **80** Frank Siteman; **82** Juan Capistran, The Breaks, 2001; **92** C. Devan/Ivy/Corbis; **94** Henry Georgi/Aurora Photos; **104** Darren McCollester/Getty Images; **106** John Kraus/IPN Stock; **120T** Dennis MacDonald/Index Stock/Photolibrary New York; **120B** Richard Pasley; **122** Reed Saxon/AP Images; **130** G. Ferniz/San Antonio Express-News/Zuma Press; **132** The Visual Thesaurus (http://www.visualthesaurus.com). Copyright © 1998-2009 Thinkmap, Inc. All rights reserved.; **142TL** Alistair Berg/Photonica/Getty Images; **142TR** David Young-Wolff/PhotoEdit; **142BL** Ken Chernus/Photodisc/Getty Images; **142BR** Jeff Greenberg/PhotoEdit Inc.; **144** Robertstock; **157** Dan Gill/The New York Times/Redux; **160** Denis Sinyakov/Reuters; **194** Phil Schermeister Photography; **206** David Young-Wolff/PhotoEdit Inc.; **262** Kathy Willens/AP Images; **276** Stephen Ferry/Getty Images; **294** Eric Fowke/PhotoEdit Inc.; **308** Michael Ray/Senator John Heinz History Center; **326** Peter Essick/Aurora Photos; **334** Katja Heinemann/Aurora Photos; **354** Westend61/Getty Images; **370** Bill Aron/PhotoEdit Inc.; **394** *Daily News Strike* (1990), Ralph Fasanella. Oil on canvas. Courtesy ACA Galleries, New York; **410** Matthew Wakem/Aurora Photos; **420** Courtesy of Michèle Gentille from http://www.harriettstomato.com; **434** AP Images; **446** Paramount Classics/Everett Collection; **462** Jeff Christensen/Reuters; **488** Bridget Besaw/Aurora Photos; **500** *The Fourth of July, 1916*, Childe Hassam. Oil on canvas. Private collection/Photo copyright © Christie's Images/The Bridgeman Art Library International; **542** Justin Sullivan/Getty Images; **560** NASA; **570** Bonnie Jacobs; **578** Sony Pictures/Everett Collection; **596** Nancy P. Alexander/PhotoEdit Inc.; **622** Spencer Grant/PhotoEdit Inc.

Text acknowledgments

Brooks Barnes. "A Star Idolized and Haunted, Michael Jackson Dies at 50." From *The New York Times*, June 26, 2009. Copyright © 2009 by The New York Times Company. Reprinted by permission. All rights reserved.

Bobbi Buchanan. "Don't Hang Up, That's My Mom Calling." From *The New York Times*, December 8, 2003. Copyright © 2003 by The New York Times Company. Reprinted by permission. All rights reserved.

Rachel Carson. "A Fable for Tomorrow." From *Silent Spring* by Rachel Carson. Copyright © 1962 by Rachel L. Carson, renewed 1990 by Roger Christie. Reprinted by permission of Houghton Mifflin Harcourt Publishing Company. All rights reserved.

Judith Ortiz Cofer. "The Myth of the Latin Woman: I Just Met a Girl Named Maria." From *The Latin Deli: Prose and Poetry* by Judith Ortiz Cofer. Copyright © 1993 by The University of Georgia Press. Reprinted by permission.

Edwidge Danticat. "Impounded Fathers." From *The New York Times* (Editorial Section), June 17, 2007. Copyright © 2007 by The New York Times Company. Reprinted by permission. All rights reserved.

Alex Espinoza. "An American in Mexico." From *Newsweek* February 27, 2007. Copyright © 2007. Reprinted by permission.

Nicols Fox. "Volunteer Workers of the World, Unite." From *The New York Times* (Editorial Section), April 9, 2005. Copyright © 2005 by The New York Times Company. Reprinted by permission. All rights reserved.

Adam Goodheart. "Mummy Arts." By Adam Goodheart, originally published in *Civilization Magazine*. Copyright © 1995 by Adam Goodheart, reprinted with permission of The Wylie Agency, LLC.

John Hartmire. "At the Heart of a Historic Movement." Reprinted in *The New York Times* July 24, 2000 Copyright © 2000. Reprinted by permission of The New York Times Company. All rights reserved.

Paul Hoffman. "Do You Have Triskaidekaphobia?" Reprinted by permission of SLL/Sterling Lord Literistic, Inc. Copyright by Paul Hoffman.

Jhumpa Lahiri. "My Two Lives." From *Newsweek*, March 6, 2006. Copyright © 2006. Reprinted by permission.

Yiyun Li. "Eat, Memory: Orange Crush." By Yiyun Li, originally published in *The New York Times Magazine*. Copyright © 2006 used with permission of The Wylie Agency, LLC.

Amy Ma. "My Grandmother's Dumpling." From the *Wall Street Journal*, January 30, 2009. Copyright © 2009. Reprinted by permission of the Dow Jones Company in the format Text via Copyright Clearance Center.

David Matthews. "Pick One." From *Newsweek*, January 21, 2007. Copyright © 2007. Reprinted by permission.

Charles Murray, "For Most People, College Is a Waste of Time." From the *Wall Street Journal*, August 31, 2008. Copyright © 2008. Reprinted by permission of The Dow Jones Company in the format Text via Copyright Clearance Center.

John Schwartz. "NOTEBOOK: The Poncho Bearer." From *The New York Times* (Education Life Supplement Section), January 7, 2007. Copyright © 2007 by The New York Times Company. Reprinted by permission. All rights reserved.

Carolyn Foster Segal. "The Dog Ate My Disk, and Other Tales of Woe." Originally published in *The Chronicle of Higher Education*, August 11, 2000. Copyright © 2000 Carolyn Foster Segal. Reprinted with permission of the author.

Gayle Rosenwald Smith. "The Wife-Beater." Copyright © 2001. Reprinted by permission of the author.

Deborah Tannen's adaptation of text as submitted from *Talking from 9 to 5* by Deborah Tannen. Copyright © 1984 by Deborah Tannen. Reprinted by permission of HarperCollins Publishers. E-book rights reprinted by permission of the author.

Louisa Thomas. "Color My World Burnt Sienna." From *Newsweek*, June 15, 2009. Copyright © 2009. Reprinted by permission.

William Zinsser. "The Transaction." Copyright © 1976, 1980, 1985, 1988, 1990, 1994, 1998, 2001, 2006 by William K. Zinsser. Reprinted by permission of the author.

Index

Note: Page numbers in **bold** type indicate pages where terms are defined.

A

abbreviations, **589**, 589–90
academic courses, capitalizing title of, 581
accept/except, 605
acronyms, **590**
action verbs, **268**, 268–69
active reading, **623**, 721
active voice, **415**
    changing passive voice to, 415
addition
    coordinating conjunctions for, 278
    transitional words/phrases for, 284, 624
addresses, comma in, 552–53
addressing, **547**
adjectives, **489**
    adverbs formed from, 490
    comparatives and superlatives, 492–95
    demonstrative, 489
    good, use of, 491
    good/bad, 495
    identifying, 489
    order in sentence, 508, 523
    past participles as, 457
    in series, 318
adverbs, **311**, **490**
    beginning sentence with, 311–12
    comparatives and superlatives, 492–95
    identifying, 490
    -ly ending, 490, 493
    well, use of, 491
    well/badly, 495
affect/effect, 98, 234, 605
agree, **395**
agreement. *See* pronoun-antecedent agreement;
    subject-verb agreement
all ready/already, 605
alternatives
    coordinating conjunctions for, 278
    transitional words/phrases for, 285

"American in Mexico, An" (Espinoza), 650–53
a.m./p.m., 590
annotating, during reading, **628**, 628–30
announcement
    thesis statement as, 172
    in title of essay, 198
antecedent, **468**. *See also* pronoun-antecedent
    agreement
anthology, MLA works-cited list, 739
apostrophe, **561**
    in contractions, 561
    incorrect uses, 564–65
    in possessives, 563–64
appositives, **320**, **375**, **548**
    appositive fragments, 375–76
    comma with, 320, 548
    sentence variety with, 320
    words/expressions to introduce, 376
argument, **145**, **251**
argument essays, **251**, 251–58, **701**
    compound and complex sentences in, 256
    conclusion, 252–53
    inductive and deductive arguments, 252–53
    major and minor premises, 252–53
    model, 254–56
    paragraphs, organizing, 253
    by professional writers, examples, 701–11
    refutation of opposing arguments in, 254
    thesis statement, 252
    transitional words/phrases with, 254
    wording of assignment for, 252
    writing process, 251
argument paragraphs, **145**, 145–58
    compound/complex sentences, use of, 148
    evidence in, 145–46
    refuting argument in, 145
    revising/editing, 154
    structure of, 147–48
    TEST for effective paragraphs, 153

argument paragraphs *(continued)*
    transitional words/phrases, 148
    writing guidelines, 146
    writing process, 151–54
articles, 510–12
    definite, 510–11
    indefinite, 511
    no articles, 512
    with proper nouns, 512
    in titles of works, 198, 587
articles, journal, MLA works-cited list, 739–40
as, case of pronouns following, 480
assignment, **5**
    essays, 167–68
    questions about, 5
assignment, wording of
    argument essays, 252
    cause-and-effect essays, 230
    classification essays, 242
    comparison-and-contrast essays, 236
    definition essays, 247
    descriptive essays, 218
    exemplification essays, 208
    narrative essays, 213
    process essays, 224
associations, names of
    abbreviating, 590
    capitalizing, 580
"At the Heart of a Historic Movement" (Hartmire),
    670–74
audience, **5**
    for essays, 167
    questions about, 6
authors of works
    MLA parenthetical references, 736–39
    MLA works-cited list, 736–39

B

base form of verb, **435, 447**
    irregular verbs, 435–36
    past participles, forming, 447
    past tense, forming, 435
BC/AD, 590
be
    form of, correcting sentence fragments with, 380
    past tense, 439
    subject-verb agreement with, 399
being, incomplete-verb fragment with, 380

body, **735**
body paragraphs
    essays, 162
    research paper, 735
    thesis-and-support essay, 186–87
boldface, as visual signal, 624
books, MLA works-cited list, 738–39
brainstorming, **8, 170**
    collaborative, **8**
    comparison-and-contrast paragraphs, 113–14
    during essay exams, 723
    exemplification paragraphs, 55–56
    ideas for writing, 8–9
    for main idea, 170–71
brake/break, 605
brand names, capitalizing, 581
Buchanan, Bobbi, "Don't Hang Up, That's My Mom
    Calling," 702–4
buildings, capitalizing name, 580
bulleted lists, parallelism, 330
"But What Do You Mean?" (Tannen), 681–88
buy/by, 605

C

calendars
    activities, posting on, 717
    organizers, 716–18
can/could, past tense, 440–41
capitalization
    in direct quotations, 583
    proper nouns, 579–81
    titles of works, 587
Carson, Rachel, "Fable for Tomorrow, A," 653–56
case. *See* pronoun case
categories, considering. *See* classification essays;
    classification paragraphs
causal relationship, **100**. *See also* cause-and-effect;
    cause-and-effect essays; cause-and-effect
    paragraphs
cause, **95, 229**
cause-and-effect
    coordinating conjunctions for, 278
    subordinating conjunctions for, 298
    transitional words/phrases for, 284, 624
cause-and-effect essays, **229**, 229–35, **666**
    affect versus *effect* in, 234
    model, 232–33
    paragraphs, organizing, 231

by professional writers, examples, 666–74
thesis statement, 230
transitional words/phrases with, 231
wording of assignment for, 230
writing process, 230
cause-and-effect paragraphs, **95**, 95–105
affect versus *effect* in, 98
causal relationship, making, 100
revising/editing, 101
structure of, 96–97
TEST for effective paragraphs, 101
transitional words/phrases, 97
writing process, 100–101
chapter of book, MLA works-cited list, 739
cite, **738**
MLA style. *See* Modern Language Association
(MLA)
classification, **123**, **241**
classification essays, **241**, 241–46, **681**
list, colon with, 245
model, 243–45
paragraphs, organizing, 243
by professional writers, examples, 681–93
thesis statement, 242
transitional words/phrases with, 243
wording of assignment for, 242
writing process, 242
classification paragraphs, **123**, 123–31
list, colon with, 125
revising/editing, 128
structure of, 124–25
TEST for effective paragraphs, 128
transitional words/phrases, 125
writing process, 127–28
clauses
nonrestrictive, 550–51
restrictive, 550
See also dependent clause; independent clause
clichés, **341**
phrases to avoid, 341
clubs, capitalizing name, 580
clustering, **10**, 10–11
Cofer, Judith Ortiz, "Don't Call Me a Hot Tamale,"
636–39
coherence in writing, **40**
and transitional words/phrases, 40–42, 111
collaborative brainstorming, **8**
collective nouns, **474**
frequently used, listing of, 402, 474

pronoun-antecedent agreement with, 474
subject-verb agreement, 402
college success, strategies for, 712–14
academic honesty, 724
day-to-day strategies, 714–16
exam-taking strategies, 721–24
first-week strategies, 712–14
homework strategies, 720–21
note-taking, 718–20
orientation period, 712
time-management, 716–18
colon, **573**
with lists, 125, 245, 573
using, 573
"Color My World Burnt Sienna" (Thomas), 258
comma, **543**
in addresses, 552–53
with appositives, 320, 548
in complex sentences, 298
in compound sentences, 277–78, 543
with coordinating conjunctions, 277–78, 359, 544,
554–55
in dates, 552
with dependent clauses, 298, 543, 572
in direct address, 547
with direct quotation, 543, 583–84
with *-ed* and *-ing* modifiers, 315–16
with introductory phrases, 545–47
with nonrestrictive clauses, 550–51
with series of items, 329–30, 543–44, 554
with subordinating conjunctions, 298
with transitional words/phrases, 54, 211,
283, 546
unnecessary, 554–55
comma splice, **355**, 355–63
correcting, 358–63
commands, **84**
in instructions, 84–85
common knowledge, **731**
common nouns, **463**
comparatives, **492**
adjectives and adverbs, 492–95
special problems, 493–94
compare, **107**
compare-and-contrast, transitional words/phrases
for, 285, 624
comparison(s), **235**
case of pronouns in, 480
parallelism, 329

comparison(s) *(continued)*
  personification, 219
  similes and metaphors, 219, 343
comparison-and-contrast essays, **235**, 235–41, **674**
  model, 238–40
  paragraphs, organizing, 237
  parallelism in, 240
  point-by-point comparisons, 237
  by professional writers, examples, 674–81
  subject-by-subject comparisons, 237
  thesis statement, 236
  transitional words/phrases with, 237
  wording of assignment for, 236
  writing process, 236
comparison-and-contrast paragraphs, **107**,
    107–19
  parallelism in, 111
  point-by-point comparisons, 109–11
  revising/editing, 116
  subject-by-subject comparisons, 115
  TEST for effective paragraphs, 115–16
  transitional words/phrases, 111
  writing process, 113–15
complex sentences, **295**, 295–307
  in argument essay, 256
  in argument paragraph, 148
  by combining simple sentences, 315–21
  comma in, 298
  relative pronouns in, 301
  structure of, 295
  subordinating conjunctions in, 297–98
compound(s), **478**
  pronoun case, 478–79
compound antecedents, 469
compound nouns, plurals, forming, 465
compound predicate, comma, unnecessary, 554
compound sentences, **277**, 277–93
  in argument essay, 256
  in argument paragraph, 148
  by combining simple sentences, 315–21
  comma in, 277–78, 543
  coordinating conjunctions in, 277–78
  semicolon in, 282–83, 571
  transitional words/phrases in, 283–85
compound subject, **263**, **397**
  case of pronouns in, 478–79
  comma, unnecessary, 554–55
  subject-verb agreement with, 397–98
compound words, **589**
  hyphens in, 589

concise language, **337**, 337–38
  repetition, avoiding, 338
  wordy versus concise words and phrases, 338
concluding remarks, **162**
conclusion, **162**, **199**, 199–202, **735**
  argument essays, 252–53
  concluding remarks in, 162–63, **199**
  essays, 162, 199–201
  narrative paragraph for, 200
  phrases to avoid in, 201
  prediction in, 201
  quotation in, 200–201
  recommendation in, 200
  research paper, 735
  summary statement in, 199
  verbal signals for, 624
condition, subordinating conjunctions, 298
conjunctions. *See* coordinating conjunctions; subordinating conjunctions
conscience/conscious, 606
consequences, discussing. *See* cause-and-effect essays; cause-and-effect paragraphs
consonants
  doubling final, 603–4
  listing of, 599
contractions, **561**
  apostrophe in, 561
  confused with possessive pronouns, 565
  frequently used, listing of, 561
contradiction
  coordinating conjunctions for, 278
  transitional words/phrases for, 284, 624
contrast, **107**, **235**
  coordinating conjunctions for, 278
  semicolon, creating with, 360
  subordinating conjunctions for, 298
  transitional words/phrases for, 284
  See also compare-and-contrast; comparison-and-contrast essays; comparison-and-contrast paragraphs
contributing factors, listing. *See* cause-and-effect essays; cause-and-effect paragraphs
coordinating conjunctions, **277**
  comma with, 277–78, 359, 544, 554–55
  in compound sentences, 277–78
  listing of, 277, 329
  meanings conveyed by, 278
  parallelism with, 329
  run-ons, correcting, 359
  in titles of works, 198, 587

could/can, past tense, 440–41
count nouns, **505**
    articles with, 512
    determiners with, 507–8
    ESL writers, 505–6
    examples of, 505
    guidelines for use, 506
    indefinite articles with, 512
critical reading, **623**

D

-d
    past participles, forming, 447
    past tense, forming, 435
dangling modifiers, **222**, **421**
    correcting, 222, 421–22
Danticat, Edwidge, "Impounded Fathers,"
      708–11
dash, **574**
    using, 574
databases, library, **726**, **728**
dates, comma with, 552
days of week, capitalizing, 581
deductive argument, **252**
    argument essays, 252–53
definite articles, **510**
    using, 510–11
definition, **133**, **246**
    formal, 133
definition essays, **246**, 246–51, **693**
    is when/is where, avoiding in, 250
    model, 248–49
    paragraphs, organizing, 248
    patterns of development for, 247
    by professional writers, examples, 693–701
    thesis statement, 247
    transitional words/phrases with, 248
    wording of assignment for, 247
    writing process, 246–47
definition paragraphs, 133–43, **134**
    as introductory paragraph, 196–97
    narration/exemplification in, 134–35
    revising/editing, 139–40
    structure of, 134–35
    TEST for effective paragraphs, 139
    transitional words/phrases, 135
    writing process, 138–39
demonstrative adjectives, **489**
    listing of, 489

demonstrative pronouns, **467**
    as determiners, 508
    listing of, 467
dependent clause, **295**
    comma, unnecessary, 298, 555
    comma with, 298, 543, 572
    in complex sentence, 295
    dependent clause fragments, 384–86
    and relative pronouns, 301
    and subordinating conjunctions, 384–85
dependent words, **362**
    in dependent clause, 384
    frequently used, listing of, 363, 384
    relative pronouns as, 385–86
    run-ons, correcting with, 358, 362–63
    subordinating conjunctions as, 384–85
description, **73**, **217**
descriptive essays, **217**, 217–23, **650**
    dominant impression in, 218
    figures of speech in, 219
    model, 220–22
    modifiers, use in, 222
    objective and subjective description, 219
    paragraphs, organizing, 218
    by professional writers, examples,
      650–56
    transitional words/phrases with, 219
    wording of assignment for, 218
    writing process, 217
descriptive paragraphs, 73–81, **74**
    flat versus rich description, 73
    revising/editing, 78
    structure of, 74–75
    TEST for effective paragraphs, 78
    transitional words/phrases, 75
    writing process, 77–78
details
    in essays, 162–63
    as evidence, 4
determiners, **507**
    with count and noncount nouns, 507–8
    listing of, 508
    order in sentence, 508, 523
    with plural nouns, 508
dictionary
    college dictionary, necessity of, 714
    as spelling aid, 597
direct address, comma in, 547
directions, writing. *See* process essays; process
    paragraphs

direct object, **266**
    gerunds as, 522
    objective case, 477
    pronoun as, 266, 477
direct quotations, **582**
    colon to introduce, 573
    comma with, 543
    identifying tags, 583–84
    plagiarism, avoiding, 732
    punctuating, 583–84
    research paper guidelines, 730–32
distinct category, **123**
    in classification paragraph, 123
do, subject-verb agreement with, 399
documentation, **731**
documentation of sources, **731**, **736**
    what to document, 731
    See also Modern Language Association (MLA)
documents, historical, capitalizing name, 580
"Dog Ate My Disk, and Other Tales of Woe, The"
    (Segal), 689–93
dominant impression, **218**
    in descriptive essays, 218
"Don't Call Me a Hot Tamale" (Cofer), 636–39
"Don't Hang Up, That's My Mom Calling"
    (Buchanan), 702–4
drafting
    essay exams, 724
    first draft, 19–20
    thesis-and-support essay, 179–80
    writing process, 19–22

E

-ed
    modifiers, combining sentences with, 316
    past participles, forming, 447
    past tense, forming, 435
edited books, MLA works-cited list, 739
editing, **24**, **183**
    essay exams, 724
    process of, 24–25, 183
    thesis-and-support essay, 183–87
editorials, MLA works-cited list, 740
effect(s), **95**, **97**, **229**
    cause-and-effect, 229–35
    See also cause-and-effect
effect/affect, 98, 234, 605
ei and *ie* words, spelling, 599

electronic sources, MLA parenthetical references, 737
emphasis, verbal signals for, 624
encyclopedia, online, MLA works-cited list, 741
-es, plural nouns, forming, 463–64
e silent, ending, adding suffix, 601–2
ESL writers
    articles, 510–12
    count and noncount nouns, 505–6
    gerunds, 522
    modal auxiliaries, 520–21
    modifiers, order of, 523
    negative statements, 514
    phrasal verbs, 530–32
    plural nouns, 504
    prepositional phrases, 525
    prepositions, 525–30
    questions, 515
    stative verbs, 518
    subject of sentence, 501–2
    verb tense, 517
Espinoza, Alex, "American in Mexico, An," 650–53
essay(s), **161**, 161–70
    argument, 251–58
    classification, 241–46
    comparison-and-contrast, 235–41
    conclusion, 199–202
    definition, 246–51
    descriptive, 217–23
    exemplification, 207–12
    format, 187–89
    ideas for. *See* main idea, finding ideas
    introduction, 195–99
    narrative, 212–17
    compared to paragraphs, 162–63
    process, 224–29
    purpose for writing, 167
    structure of, 161–65
    thesis-and-support, 171–93
    titles of, 198
essay exams, 722–24
    key words in question, 723
    paragraphs, writing, 140
essay in anthology, MLA works-cited list, 739
ethnic groups, capitalizing, 579
evaluate, **726**
everyday/every day, 606–7
evidence, **4**, **17**, **35**, **145**, **161**
    in argument paragraph, 145–46
    in paragraphs, 4

paragraphs, 161
to support main idea, 4, 17, 35
types of, 146
examples, **51, 146**
in class notes, 719
colon before, 573
essay assignment. *See* exemplification essays
in essays, 162–63
as evidence, 4, 146
exemplification paragraphs, 51, 56–57
general versus specific, 52, 56–57
verbal signals for, 624
exam-taking, 721–24
essay exams, 722–24
key words in question, 723
missing exams, 716
strategies during exam, 722–24
studying, 714–15, 721–22
except/accept, 605
exclamation point, **571**
with direct quotation, 583
exclamations, sentences as, 309
exemplification, **51, 207**
in definition paragraph, 134–35
exemplification essays, **207**, 207–12, **635**
introductory phrases, comma with, 211
model, 209–10
paragraphs, organizing, 208
by professional writers, examples, 635–43
thesis statement, 208
transitional words/phrases, 209, 211
wording of assignment for, 208
writing process, 207
exemplification paragraphs, 51–61, **52**
revising/editing, 57
structure of, 52–53
TEST for effective paragraphs, 57
transitional words/phrases, 53
writing process, 55–57
explanation, of process. *See* process essays; process
paragraphs

F

"Fable for Tomorrow, A" (Carson), 653–56
facts, **146**
as evidence, 146
in thesis statement, 172
-f/-fe, plural nouns, forming, 464

figures of speech, **219**
in descriptive essays, 219
fine/find, 606–7
first draft. *See* drafting
focused freewriting, **7, 169**
formal definition, **133**
formal outline, **178, 630**
for thesis-and-support essay, 178
format, **187**
thesis-and-support essay, 187–89
"For Most People, College Is a Waste of Time"
(Murray), 704–8
Fox, Nicols, "Volunteer Workers of the World,
Unite," 640–43
freewriting, **7, 169**
essays, 169
focused, 169
narrative paragraphs, 67
fused sentences, **355**, 355–63
correcting, 358–63

G

general words, **335**
utility words, 336
geographic regions, capitalizing, 580
gerunds, **522**
identifying, 522
going, gone, 271
good/bad, 495
Goodheart, Adam, "Mummy Arts," 656–59
good/well, 491, 495
Google, 727
government agencies, capitalizing name of,
580–81
grammar checkers, 355

H

had, past perfect tense, 455–56
Hartmire, John, "At the Heart of a Historic
Movement," 670–74
has, present perfect tense, 453
have
past perfect tense, 455–56
present perfect tense, 453
subject-verb agreement with, 399
headings, as visual signal, 624
hear/here, 607

helping verbs, **270**, 270–71, **379**
   can/could and *will/would*, 440–41
   with *-ing* verbs, 379–80
   listing of, 270–71
   with participles, 271
highlighting, **626**
   during reading, 626–28
   symbols for, 626
his/her, indefinite pronouns with, 472–73
historical periods/events/documents, capitalizing,
   580
hits, Internet search, **727**
Hoffman, Paul, "Triskaidekaphobia," 696–701
holidays, capitalizing, 581
home page, MLA works-cited list, 741
homework strategies, 720–21
honesty, academic, forms of, 724
hyphens, using, 589

I

ideas for writing. *See* main idea, finding ideas
identifying tags, direct quotations, **582**
idiomatically, **526**
   prepositions in common expressions, 526–29
ie and *ei* words, spelling, 599
illogical shifts, **411**, 413, 415
illustrate, essay assignment. *See* exemplification
   essays
"Impounded Fathers" (Danticat), 708–11
indefinite articles, **510**
   with count nouns, 512
   using, 511
indefinite pronouns, **403**, **471**, 471–73
   with *his/her*, 472–73
   listing of, 404, 471
   with *of*, 472
   possessive forms, 563
   pronoun-antecedent agreement, 471–73
   singular and plural, 403–4, 471–73
   as subject of sentence, 404
   subject-verb agreement with, 403–4
indenting
   outlines, 631
   paragraphs, **4**
independent clause, **263**, **277**, **295**, **385**
   in complex sentence, 295
   in compound sentence, 277–78, 572
   fragments, correcting with, 385

and relative pronouns, 301
   semicolon to connect, 572
   in simple sentence, **263**, 277
indirect quotations, **583**
   punctuating, 583
inductive argument, **252**
   argument essays, 252–53
infinitives, **382**
   infinitive fragments, 382
informal outline, **177**, **630**
   for argument paragraphs, 152
   steps in, 630–31
   for thesis-and-support essay, 177
Infotrac, 728
-ing
   gerunds, 522
   modifiers, combining sentences with, 315
   spelling rules, 601, 603
   verbs, helping verbs with, 379–80
   verbs, sentence fragments with, 379–80
inseparable phrasal verbs, **530**, 531–32
instructions, **84**, **225**. *See also* process essays; process paragraphs
Internet research, 727–28
   evaluating material, 728
   MLA works-cited list, 740–41
   plagiarism, avoiding, 727
   search methods, 727–28
introduction, **162**, **195**, 195–99, **735**
   definition in, 196–97
   essays, 162
   narrative as, 196
   opening remarks in, 195
   phrases to avoid in, 198
   questions in, 196
   quotation in, 197
   research paper, 735
   thesis statement in, 195
   unexpected statement in, 197–98
introductory phrases, **545**
   comma with, 211, 545–47
irregular past participles, 448–51
   listing of, 449–51
irregular plural nouns
   plural, forming, 464–65
   possessive forms, 507
irregular verbs, **436**, 436–38
   base/past tense, listing of, 435–36
   be, 399, 439

do, 399
have, 399
subject-verb agreement, 399
is where/is when, 136, 250
italics
titles of works, 586
as visual signal, 624
items. *See* list of items; series of items
its/it's, 607

J

journal (periodical), **739**
MLA works-cited list, 739–40
journal for writing, **12**
ideas for writing, 13

K

key words, **723**
in exam questions, 723. *See also* assignment,
wording of
Internet search, **727**
in title of essay, 198
knew/new, 607–8
know/no, 607–8

L

Lahiri, Jhumpa, "My Two Lives," 674–77
languages, capitalizing, 579
lay/lie, 608
Li, Yiyun, "Orange Crush," 643–46
library research, 726–27
electronic information sources, 726, 728
evaluating material, 727
lie/lay, 608
linking verbs, **269, 457**
listing of, 269
past participle as adjective after, 457
list of items
colon with, 125, 245, 573
parallelism, 330, 573
as visual signal, 624
location, subordinating conjunctions, 298
logical order, **52, 95, 107, 123**
cause-and-effect paragraphs, 95
classification paragraphs, 123
comparison-and-contrast paragraphs, 107

exemplification paragraphs, 52
reason for use, 40, 52
transitional words/phrases for, 41, 53, 97, 111,
125, 209
logical shifts, **411**, 413
loose/lose, 608
-ly ending, adverbs, 439, 490

M

Ma, Amy, "My Grandmother's Dumpling," 659–66
magazine, **740**
articles, MLA works-cited list, 740, 741
main idea, **14**
essay exams, 723–24
essays, 161
evidence to support, 35
generating. *See* main idea, finding ideas
topic sentence as statement of, 14–15
main idea, finding ideas, 6–13
brainstorming, 8–9, 170–71
clustering, 10–11
freewriting, 7, 67, 169
journal writing, 12–13
main verb, of helping verb, **270**
major premise, **252**
argument essays, 252–53
mapping. *See* clustering
Matthews, David, "Pick One," 646–50
metaphors, **219, 343**
use in writing, 343
minor premise, **252**
argument essays, 252–53
misplaced modifiers, **75, 423**
correcting, 423–24
in descriptive paragraphs, 75
modal auxiliaries, **520**
identifying, 520–21
listing of, 521
Modern Language Association (MLA)
essay, example of, 743–47
parenthetical references, 736–37
works-cited list, 738–42
modifiers, **75, 222, 421**, 489–91
adjectives, 489
adverbs, 490
combining sentences with, 315–16
in descriptive essays, 222
-ed and *-ing* as, 315

modifiers *(continued)*
    errors related to. *See* dangling modifiers; mis-
        placed modifiers
    functions of, 489
    order of, 523
    past participles as, 457
modifies, **421, 489**
months of year, capitalizing, 581
"Mummy Arts" (Goodheart), 656–59
Murray, Charles, "For Most People, College Is a
    Waste of Time," 704–8
"My Grandmother's Dumpling" (Ma), 659–66
"My Two Lives" (Lahiri), 674–77

N

narration, **63, 212**
    in definition paragraph, 134–35
narrative essays, **212,** 212–17, **643**
    model, 214–15
    paragraphs, organizing, 213
    by professional writers, examples, 643–50
    run-on, avoiding in, 216
    thesis statement, 213
    transitional words/phrases, 214
    wording of assignment for, 213
    writing process, 212
narrative paragraphs, 62–71, **63**
    as conclusion, 200
    as introductory paragraph, 196
    revising/editing, 68
    structure of, 63–65
    TEST for effective paragraphs, 67–68
    transitional words/phrases, 64
    writing process, 66–68
negative statements, ESL writers, 514
new/knew, 607–8
newspaper articles, MLA works-cited list, 740, 741
no/know, 607–8
noncount nouns, **505**
    determiners with, 507–8
    ESL writers, 505–6
    examples of, 505
    guidelines for use, 506
nonrestrictive clauses, **550**
    comma with, 550–51
    introductory words, 551
note-taking, 718–20
    annotating during reading, 628–30
    before exams, review of notes, 721–22

    notebooks, 714
    for research paper, 728–30
    time for, 719–20
nouns, **263, 402, 463**
    and appositives, 320, 375, 548
    collective, 402, 474
    common, 463
    compound, 465
    count and noncount, 505–10
    gerunds acting as, 522
    in object of sentence, 266
    possessive, 508, 563
    proper, 463
    in series, 317
    in subject of sentence, **263**
    See also plural nouns; singular nouns; specific
        types of nouns
number, **469**
    pronoun-antecedent agreement, 469
    shifts in, 86
numbered lists, parallelism, 330
number(s)/numerals, **590**
    use in writing, 590–91

O

objective case, **477**
objective description, **219**
object of sentence, **266**
    objective case, 477
    See also direct object; object of the
        preposition
object of the preposition, 266, **525**
    gerunds as, 522
of, singular indefinite pronouns with, 472
online catalogs, **726, 728**
opening remarks, **162**
    in essay, 162
    in introduction, 195, **195**
opposing arguments, refutation of, 145, 254
"Orange Crush" (Li), 643–46
organizers, scheduling tasks, 716–18
organizing, writing process, 17–19
outline, **630,** 630–31
    formal, 178, 630
    informal, 152, 177, 630–31
    parallelism, 330
    for research paper, 734–35
    sentence, 734–35
    topic, 734

P

paired items, parallelism with, 329
paragraph(s)
   argument, 145–58
   cause-and-effect, 95–105
   classification, 123–31
   coherence, 40
   compared to essays, 162–63
   comparison-and-contrast, 107–19
   conclusion, 199–202
   definition, 133–43
   descriptive, 73–81
   details in, 4, 162–63
   effective. *See* TEST for effective paragraphs
   essay exams, writing for, 140
   evidence in, 4, 17, 35–38, 145–46
   examples in, 51, 56–57, 162–63
   exemplification, 51–61
   ideas for. *See* main idea, finding ideas
   indenting, 4
   narrative, 62–71
   process of writing. *See* writing process
   process paragraphs, 83–93
   response paragraph, 633
   summary statement, 4
   supporting points in, 17–18
   topic sentences, 4, 30–31
   transitions, 40–42
   unified, 30–31, 38–39
parallelism, **111**, **327**, 327–31
   comparison-and-contrast paragraphs, 111
   comparison-and-contrast essays, 240
   comparisons, 329
   and coordinating conjunctions, 329
   items in a series, 329–30
   items in list, 330, 573
   in outline, 330
   paired items, 329
   recognizing, 327
paraphrase, **728**
   writing, 728–29, 732–33
parentheses, **574**
   using, 574
parenthetical references, MLA guidelines, 736–37
participles, **271**
   going, gone, 271
   helping verbs with, 271
   See also past participles
passed/past, 608
passive voice, changing to active, 415

past participles, **447**, 447–58
   as adjectives, 457
   irregular, 448–51
   past perfect tense, 455–56
   present perfect tense, 453
   regular verbs, forming, 447
past perfect tense, **455**
   forming, 455–56
past progressive tense, **518**
   stative verbs, 518
past tense, **435**, 435–45
   be, 439
   can/could, 440–41
   irregular verbs, 436–38, 448–51
   regular verbs, 435
   will/would, 441
peace/piece, 608
period, **571**
   with direct quotation, 583–84
   run-ons, correcting with, 358
periodicals, MLA works-cited list, 739–40
person, **413**
   shifts in, 86, 413–14
personal pronouns, **476**. *See also* pronoun case
personification, **219**
phrasal verbs, **530**, 530–32
   inseparable, 530–31
   prepositions in, 530–32
phrase(s), **375**
   introductory, 545–47
   See also prepositional phrases; transitional words
      and phrases
phrase fragments, 375–79
   appositive, 375–79
   prepositional, 377
"Pick One" (Matthews), 646–50
piece/peace, 608
plagiarism, **724**, **727**, **731**
   avoiding, 724, 731–34
   and essay exams, 724
   and Internet research, 727
planning, writing process, 4–17
plural nouns, **463**, 463–65
   determiners with, 508
   ESL writers, 504
   hyphenated-compound nouns, 465
   irregular, 464–65
   possessive, 563, 564
   regular, forming, 463–65
   subject-verb agreement, 395

plural pronouns
  gender neutral, 345
  identifying, 467
  indefinite, 404, 472
  reflexive, 483
plural subject, **263**, 263–64
point-by-point comparisons, **109**, **237**
  comparison-and-contrast paragraphs,
    109–11
  comparison-and-contrast essays, 237
"Poncho Bearer, The" (Schwartz), 667–70
possessive case, **477**
possessive forms, **563**
  apostrophe in, 563–64
possessive nouns, as determiners, 508
possessive pronouns
  as determiners, 508
  listing of, 565
  sound-alike contractions, 565
predicate, **268**. *See also* verb(s)
prediction
  in conclusion, 201
  of outcome. *See* cause-and-effect essays; cause-
    and-effect paragraphs
prefixes, **600**, 600–601
premise, major and minor, **252**
  argument essays, 252–53
preposition(s), **266**, **525**
  in common expressions, 526–29
  ESL writers, 525
  listing of, 266–67
  object of preposition, 266, 525
  in phrasal verbs, 530–32
  in prepositional phrases, 266, 525
  in titles of works, 587
prepositional phrases, **266**, **312**, **377**, **525**
  beginning sentence with, 312
  ESL writers, 525
  parts of, 266
  prepositional phrase fragments, 377
  in simple sentences, 266–67
  subject of sentence, identifying with, 404
present perfect tense, **453**
  forming, 453
present progressive tense, **518**
  stative verbs, 518
preview, written assignment, **623**, 623–24
principal/principle, 609
process, **83**, **224**

process essays, **224**, 224–29, **656**
  instructions in, 225
  model, 226–27
  paragraphs, organizing, 225
  process explanations in, **225**
  by professional writers, examples, 656–66
  shifts, avoiding in, 228
  thesis statement, 224
  transitional words/phrases, 225–26
  wording of assignment for, 224
  writing process, 224
process paragraphs, **83**, 83–93
  instructions in, 84–85
  process explanations, 84
  revising/editing, 90
  structure of, 83
  TEST for effective paragraphs, 90
  transitional words/phrases, 85
  writing process, 88–90
pronoun(s), **263**, **467**
  and appositives, 320, 375, 548
  case. *See* pronoun case
  demonstrative, 467
  in gender neutral language, 345
  identifying, 467
  indefinite, 403–4, 471–73, 563
  in object of sentence, 266, 477
  personal, 476–79
  possessive, 565
  pronoun-antecedent agreement, 468–69
  relative, 301, 385–86
  in subject of sentence, **263**
  See also plural pronouns; singular pronouns
pronoun-antecedent agreement, 468–69
  with collective nouns, 474
  compound antecedents, 470
  identifying, 468–69
  indefinite pronouns, 471–73
  reflexive pronouns, 482–83
pronoun case, 476–79
  objective, 477
  possessive, 477
  for pronouns in comparisons, 480
  for pronouns in compounds, 478–79
  subjective, 476
  who/whom, 481
proofreading
  in editing process, 24
  for spelling errors, 597

proper nouns, **463**, **579**
    articles with, 512
    capitalizing, 579–81
purpose for reading, **623**
purpose for writing, **5**
    essays, 167
    questions about, 5

Q

question(s)
    forming, ESL writers, 515
    in introductory paragraph, 196
    sentences as, 309
question mark, **571**
    with direct quotation, 583
quiet/quite, 609
quotation(s)
    in conclusion, 200–201
    direct, 583–84
    indirect, 583
    in introductory paragraph, 197
    short versus long, MLA formatting, 737
    from sources, in research notes, 730
    in title of essay, 198
quotation marks
    with borrowed words, 732
    with direct quotation, 583–84, 730
    with titles of works, 586
quote, **730**

R

raise/rise, 609
reading, 623–33
    active reading, 623
    annotating during, 628–30
    highlighting, 626–28
    outlining, 630–31
    previewing material, 623–24
    purpose for reading, 623
    response paragraph to, 633
    summarizing, 632
    verbal signals during, 624
    visual signals during, 624
recommendations, in conclusion, 200
reflexive pronouns, **482**
    pronoun-antecedent agreement, 482–83
    singular and plural, 483

refute, **145**, **254**
    in argument essay, 254
    in argument paragraphs, 145
regular verbs, **435**
    past participles, 447
    past tense, forming, 435
relative pronouns, **301**, **385**
    in complex sentences, 301
    and dependent clause fragments, 385–86
    and independent clause, 301
    listing of, 301, 386
    who/whom, choosing in sentences, 481
religions, capitalizing, 579
repetition, of words, avoiding, **338**
research, **725**
research paper, 725–35
    documentation of sources, 736–47
    example essay (MLA style), 743–47
    Internet research, 727–28
    library research, 726–27
    note-taking, 728–30
    outline, 734–35
    parts of, 735
    plagiarism, avoiding, 731–34
    TEST for review of, 735
    thesis statement, 734
    topic, choosing, 725
response paragraph, **633**
restrictive clauses, **550**
    comma, unnecessary, 555
    introductory words, 551
revision, **22**, **182**
    essay exams, 724
    process of, 22–24, 182
    thesis-and-support essay, 182–87
    writing process, 22–24
run-on sentences, **65**, **355**, 355–66
    comma splice, 355–63
    correcting, 358–63
    fused sentences, 355–63
    in narrative essays, 216
    in narrative paragraphs, 65

S

-*s*, plural nouns, forming, 463–64
Schwartz, John, "Poncho Bearer, The,"
    667–70
search engine, **727**

Segal, Carolyn Foster, "Dog Ate My Disk, and Other Tales of Woe, The," 689–93
semicolon, **282**, **571**
  in compound sentences, 282–83, 571
  run-ons, correcting with, 358, 360–62
  with transitional words/phrases, 283–85, 361–62
  using, 571–72
sentence(s), **263**
  complex, 256, 295–307
  compound, 256, 277–93
  modifiers, 489–91
  object of, 266
  parallelism, 327–31
  participles, 271
  prepositional phrases, 266–67
  pronoun-antecedent agreement, 468–69
  series of, 318–19
  simple, 263–75, 277
  subject of, 263–65
  subject-verb agreement, 395–409
  variety in writing. *See* sentence variety
  verbs, 268–72
sentence errors
  dangling modifiers, 222, 421–22
  misplaced modifiers, 75, 423–24
  parallelism, faulty, 327
  run-ons, 216, 355–66
  sentence fragments, 282, 371–86
  shifts, 86, 411–19
sentence fragments, **371**, 371–86
  appositive fragments, 375–76
  dependent clause fragments, 384–86
  identifying, 371–72
  incomplete-verb fragments, 379–80
  infinitive fragments, 382
  joining with semicolon, misuse of, 282
  missing-subject fragments, 373–74
  prepositional phrase fragments, 377
sentence outline, **734**
sentence variety, 309–25
  appositives, use of, 320
  combining sentences, 315–21
  concise language for, 337–38
  exclamations, 309
  length of sentences, varying, 321–22
  openings, varying, 311–14
  questions, 309
  series of words for, 317–18

  statements, 309
  word use, 335–46
separable phrasal verbs, **530**, 530–31
series, **543**
series of items
  colon before, 573
  comma with, 329–30, 543–44, 554
  parallelism, 329–30
series of words, **317**
  forming from sentences, 317–18
sexist language, **344**, 344–45
  examples of, 345
  pronouns, neutral use, 345
shifts, **411**, 411–19
  avoiding in process essays, 228
  illogical, 411, 413, 415
  logical, 411
  in number, 86
  in person, 86, 413–14
  in process paragraphs, 86
  in tense, 86, 228, 411
  in voice, 86, 228, 415
similarities and differences. *See* comparison-and-contrast essays; comparison-and-contrast paragraphs
similes, **219**, **343**
  use in writing, 343
simple sentence, **263**, 263–75, **277**
  combining, 315–21
  series of words created from, 317–18
singular nouns, **463**
  collective, 402
  compound, 465
  possessive, 563–64
  subject-verb agreement, 395
singular pronouns
  identifying, 467
  indefinite, 404, 471–73
  reflexive, 483
singular subject, **263**
sit/set, 609–10
slang, **340**
Smith, Gayle Rosenwald, "Wife-Beater, The," 693–96
spatial order, **74**
  descriptive paragraphs, 74–75
  reason for use, 40, 74
  transitional words/phrases for, 41, 75, 219
specific words, **335**

spelling
    commonly misspelled words, 598
    ie and *ei* words, 599
    mastering, tips for, 597–98
    prefixes, 600–601
    spell checker, 24, 597
    suffixes, 601–4
statements, sentences as, 309
statistics, library resources for, 726
stative verbs, **518**
    listing of, 518
    present and past progressive tense, 518
student services, 715
studying for exams
    guidelines for, 721–22
    organizing time/place for, 714–15
    study groups, 721, 722
subject-by-subject comparisons, **108, 237**
    comparison-and-contrast essays, 237
    comparison-and-contrast paragraphs, 108–9, 115
subject complement, gerunds as, 522
subjective case, **476**
subjective description, **219**
subject of sentence, **263**, 263–65
    complete, 263
    compound, 263, 397–98
    ESL writers, 501–2
    gerunds as, 522
    indefinite pronoun as, 404
    missing-subject fragments, 373–74
    plural, 263–64
    singular, 263
subject search, Internet, 727–28
subject-verb agreement, 395–409
    with *be, have, do*, 399
    with collective noun subjects, 402
    with compound subjects, 397–98
    with indefinite pronoun subjects, 403–4
    prepositional phrases, omitting to finding subject, 404
    with regular verbs, 395
    and singular/plural nouns, 395
    with verbs before subjects, 405–6
    with words between subject and verb, 400–401
    words between subject and verb not affecting, 401
subordinating conjunctions, **297, 384**
    comma with, 298
    in complex sentences, 297–98

    and dependent clause, 384–85
    and dependent clause fragments, 384–85
    frequently used, listing of, 297
    listing of, 385
    relationships expressed by, 298
suffixes, **601**
    spelling rules, 601–4
summary, **632, 729**
    of sources' information, writing of, 729–30
    verbal signals for, 624
    writing, steps in, 632
summary statement, **4, 161, 162, 199**
    argument paragraphs, 146, 153
    conclusions, 199
    essays, 161–63
    paragraphs, 4, 161
    and unified paragraphs, 38–39
superlatives, **492**
    adjectives and adverbs, 492–95
    special problems, 493–94
supporting points, **17**, 176–78
    arranging order of, 18, 177
    choosing, 17–18
    thesis-and-support essay, 176–78
suppose/supposed, 610
syllables, hyphen in divided words, 589
syllabus, **713**
synonyms, familiar expressions as, 528–29

    T

Tannen, Deborah, "But What Do You Mean?" 681–88
tense. *See* verb tense
TEST for effective paragraphs, **21, 29**, 29–48
    argument paragraphs, 153
    cause-and-effect paragraphs, 101
    classification paragraphs, 128
    comparison-and-contrast paragraphs, 115–16
    definition paragraphs, 139
    descriptive paragraphs, 78
    evidence, 35–38
    exemplification paragraphs, 57
    narrative paragraphs, 67–68
    process paragraphs, 90
    purpose of, 21–22
    for research paper, 735
    summary statement, 38–39
    thesis-and-support essay, 181

TEST for effective paragraphs *(continued)*
  topic sentences, 30–31
  transitions, 40–42
than, case of pronouns following, 480
that
  in complex sentences, 301
  restrictive clause, introducing, 551
their/there/they're, 610
then/than, 611
there is/there are, subject-verb agreement with, 406
thesis statement, **162**, **171**, 171–73, **195**, **734**
  argument essays, 252
  cause-and-effect essays, 230
  classification essays, 242
  comparison-and-contrast essays, 236
  definition essays, 247
  effective, features of, 172–73
  essay exams, 724
  exemplification essays, 208
  with formal outline, 178
  in introduction, 195
  narrative essays, 213
  process essays, 224
  research paper, 734
  vague versus effective, 172–73
thesis-and-support essay, **162**, 171–93, **179**
  drafting, 179–80
  formal outline for, 178
  format, 187–89
  ideas for. *See* main idea, finding ideas
  informal outline for, 177
  revising/editing, 182–87
  structure of, 162–65
  supporting points, 176–78
  TEST for effective essay, 181
  thesis statement, 171–73
  typing guidelines, 188
  wording of assignment for, 722
Thomas, Louisa, "Color My World Burnt Sienna," 258
threw/through, 611
time-management
  essay exams, 723
  strategies, 716–18
time order, **83**
  narrative paragraphs, 63
  process paragraphs, 83
  reason for use, 40, 85
  subordinating conjunctions, 298

transitional words/phrases for, 41, 64, 85, 214, 226, 285
title of essay, **198**
  choosing, examples of, 198
  punctuating, 198
titles of persons
  abbreviating, 590
  capitalizing, 579
titles of works
  capitalizing words in, 587
  italicized, 586
  quotation marks, 586
to, with infinitives, 382
topic(s), **14**
topic outline, **734**
topic sentences, **4**, **14**, **161**
  effective, elements of, 14–15
  essay exams, 724
  essays, 162–63
  paragraphs, 4, 161
  supporting points in, 17–18
  to unify paragraphs, 30–31
to/too/two, 611
"Transaction, The" (Zinsser), 678–81
transition(s), **40**
transitional words and phrases, **4**, **40**, 40–42, **161**, **283**, **546**
  argument essays, 254
  argument paragraphs, 148
  cause-and-effect essays, 231
  cause-and-effect paragraphs, 97
  classification essays, 243
  comma with, 54, 211, 283, 546
  comparison-and-contrast essays, 237
  comparison-and-contrast paragraphs, 111
  in compound sentences, 283–85
  definition paragraphs, 135
  descriptive essays, 219, 248
  descriptive paragraphs, 75
  essays, 161–63
  exemplification essays, 209
  exemplification paragraphs, 53
  frequently used, listing of, 41, 284, 361
  logical order signals, 41, 53, 97, 111, 125
  meanings conveyed by, 40–42, 285–86
  narrative essays, 214
  narrative paragraphs, 64
  process essays, 225–26

process paragraphs, 85
run-ons, correcting with, 358, 361–62
semicolon with, 283–85, 361–62
spatial order signals, 41, 75, 219
time order signals, 41, 64, 85, 214, 226
as verbal signals, 627
translation, MLA works-cited list, 739
"Triskaidekaphobia" (Hoffman), 696–701
typing guidelines
essays, 188
title of essays, 198

U

unexpected statement, in introductory paragraph, 197–98
unified paragraphs, **30**
and summary statement, 38–39
and topic sentence, 30–31
URL (uniform resource locator), **727**
MLA works-cited list, 740–41
use/used, 611
utility words, **336**

V

verb(s), 268–72
action, 268–69
helping, 270–71
incomplete-verb fragments, 379–80
irregular, 436–38
linking, 269, 457
main, 270
past participles, 447–58
phrasal, 530–32
regular, 435
reversed order in sentences, 405–6
in series, 318
stative, 518
tense. *See* verb tense
verbal signals, **624**
and highlighting, 627
transitional words and phrases as, **627**
written text, 624
verb tense, **411**, **435**, **517**
ESL writers, 517

past, 435–45
past perfect, 455–56
past progressive, 518
present perfect, 453
present progressive, 518
shifts in, 86, 228, 411
visual signals, **623**
and highlighting, 627
written text, 623–24
voice, **415**
active voice, 415
passive voice, 415
shifts in, 86, 228, 415
"Volunteer Workers of the World, Unite" (Fox), 640–43
vowels, listing of, 599

W

weather/whether, 612
Web sites
MLA works-cited list, 741
URL of, 727
See also Internet research
well/badly, 495
well/good, 491
where/were/we're, 612
which
in complex sentences, 301
nonrestrictive clauses, introducing, 551
who, restrictive/nonrestrictive clauses, introducing, 551
whose/who's, 612
who/whom
case, 481
choosing in sentences, 481
in complex sentences, 301
"Wife-Beater, The" (Smith), 693–96
will/would, past tense, 441
word processing
grammar checkers, 355
spell checkers, 597
word use, 335–46
clichés, avoiding, 341
concise language, 337–38
general words, 335
sexist language, avoiding, 344–45

word use *(continued)*
    similes and metaphors, 343
    slang, avoiding, 340
    specific words, 335
Works-Cited
    format for, 741–42
    MLA guidelines, 738–42
would/will, past tense, 441
writing process, **3**, 4–26
    drafting, 19–22
    editing, 24–25
    organizing, 17–19
    planning in, 4–17
    revision, 22–24

Yahoo! 641
-y ending
    adding suffix to, 602–3
    plural nouns, forming, 464–65
you, as singular and plural, 467
your/you're, 612

Z

Zinsser, William, "Transaction, The," 678–81

Index of Rhetorical Patterns

Argument

Buchanan, Bobbi, 702–703
Danticat, Edwidge, 708–710
"Don't Hang Up, That's My Mom Calling"
    (Buchanan), 702–703
"For Most People, College Is a Waste of Time"
    (Murray), 704–707
Hale, Ashley (student), 147–148
"Impounded Fathers" (Danticat), 708–710
"In Support of a Guest-Worker Program" (Rathmill),
    149
Murray, Charles, 704–707
Rathmill, Scott (student), 149
"Taxing Soda" (Hale), 147–148
"Unfair Searching" (Zhu), 154
Zhu, Phillip (student), 154

Cause and Effect

"At the Heart of a Historic Movement" (Hartmire),
    670–672
Burrell, Sean (student), 98
Hartmire, John, 670–672
"Health Alert" (Toll), 96
Jin, Sean (student), 101
"The Poncho Bearer" (Schwartz), 667–669
Schwartz, John, 667–669
"Second Thoughts" (Tarr), 97
Tarr, Dan (student), 97
Toll, Jen (student), 96
"Wal-Mart Comes to Town" (Jin), 101

Classification

Burrell, Melissa (student), 124–125
"But What Do You Mean?" (Tannen), 681–687
"The Dog Ate My Disk, and Other Tales of Woe"
    (Segal), 689–691
"Giving Back" (Levin), 128
Levin, Corey (student), 128
Segal, Carolyn Foster, 689–691
Tannen, Deborah, 681–687

"Three Kinds of Shoppers" (Toomer), 125–126
Toomer, Kimberly (student), 125–126
"Types of Bosses" (Burrell), 124–125

Comparison and Contrast

Caracappa, Margaret (student), 110–111
Curen, Tad (student), 109
"Getting to Boston" (Curen), 109
Hernandez, William (student), 112
Lahiri, Jhumpa, 674–676
Love, Jermond (student), 116
"My Two Lives" (Lahiri), 674–676
"Saint Croix versus the United States" (Love), 116
"The Transaction" (Zinsser), 678–680
"Two Sisters" (Caracappa), 110–111
"Virtual and Traditional Classrooms" (Hernandez),
    112
Zinsser, William, 678–680

Definition

Eddy, Thaddeus (student), 136
Fernandez, Edward (student), 135
"Happiness" (Fernandez), 135
Hoffman, Paul, 696–700
Scipio, Lorraine (student), 139–140
Smith, Gayle Rosenwald, 693–695
"Triskaidekaphobia" (Hoffman), 696–700
"The Wife-Beater" (Smith), 693–695
"Writer's Block" (Eddy), 136

Description

"An American in Mexico" (Espinoza), 650–652
Carson, Rachel, 653–655
Espinoza, Alex, 650–652
"A Fable for Tomorrow" (Carson), 653–655
Lentz, Nicole (student), 74–75
"The Lincoln Memorial" (Lentz), 74–75
Lopez, Jared (student), 78
"My Uncle Manny" (Lopez), 78

"Red Rocks" (Yoonas), 76
Yoonas, Alyssa (student), 76

Exemplification

Broderick, Bill (student), 54
Cofer, Judith Ortiz, 636–638
"Don't Call Me a Hot Tamale" (Cofer), 636–638
Fox, Nicols, 640–641
Herman, Sarah (student), 57
"Jobs of the Future" (Broderick), 54
"My Worst Job" (Herman), 57
Smith, Jeffrey (student), 53
"Visiting Philadelphia" (Smith), 53
"Volunteer Workers of the World, Unite" (Fox),
    640–641

Narration

Clark, Christine (student), 64
Kinzer, Todd (student), 68
Li, Yiyun, 643–645

Matthews, David, 646–648
"Orange Crush" (Li), 643–645
"Overnight Success" (Clark), 64
"Pick One" (Matthews), 646–648
Smiley, Kevin (student), 65
"Thanksgiving Memories" (Kinzer), 68

Process

Bari, Manasvi (student), 90
Cooper, Adam (student), 85
Goodheart, Adam 656–658
"How a Fire Extinguisher Works" (Turner), 84
Ma, Amy, 659–665
"Man vs. Machine" (Cooper), 85
"Mummy Arts" (Goodheart), 656–658
"My Grandmother's Dumpling" (Ma), 659–665
"An Order of Fries" (Rodriguez), 86–87
Rodriguez, Cheri (student), 86–87
"Surviving Rush Hour" (Bari), 90
Turner, David (student), 84

Correction Symbols

This chart lists symbols that many instructors use to point out writing problems in student papers. Next to each problem is the chapter or section of *Focus on Writing* where you can find help with that problem. If your instructor uses different symbols from those shown here, write them in the space provided.

YOUR INSTRUCTOR'S SYMBOL	STANDARD SYMBOL	PROBLEM
_____	adj	problem with use of adjective 29A
_____	adv	problem with use of adverb 29A
_____	agr	agreement problem (subject-verb) 23
		agreement problem (pronoun-antecedent) 28D–E
_____	apos	apostrophe missing or used incorrectly 32
_____	awk	awkward sentence structure 24, 25
_____	cap	capital letter needed 34A
_____	case	problem with pronoun case 28F–G
_____	cliché	cliché 20D
_____	coh	lack of paragraph coherence 1I, 2D
_____	combine	combine sentences 16, 18C
_____	cs	comma splice 21
_____	d	diction (poor word choice) 20
_____	dev	lack of paragraph development 1B, 2B
_____	frag	sentence fragment 22
_____	fs	fused sentence 21
_____	ital	italics or underlining needed 34C
_____	lc	lower case; capital letter not needed 34A
_____	para or ¶	indent new paragraph 1A
_____	pass	overuse of passive voice 24C
_____	prep	nonstandard use of preposition 30L–N
_____	ref	pronoun reference not specific 28E
_____	ro	run-on 19
_____	shift	illogical shift 24
_____	sp	incorrect spelling 35
_____	tense	problem with verb tense 26, 27
_____	thesis	thesis unclear or not stated 12D
_____	trans	transition needed 2D
_____	unity	paragraph not unified 2A
_____	w	wordy, not concise 20B
_____	//	problem with parallelism 19
_____	⊙	problem with comma use 31
_____	⊙	problem with semicolon use 33A
_____	⟨" "⟩	problem with quotation marks 34B
_____	◠	close up space
_____	^	insert
_____	ℓ	delete
_____	∼	reversed letters or words
_____	x	obvious error
_____	✓	good point, well put